Also by John Updike

HUGGING THE SHORE

John Updike

HUGGING
THE SHORE

ESSAYS AND CRITICISM

THE ECCO PRESS

Published by The Ecco Press in 1994
100 West Broad Street
Hopewell, New Jersey 08525
Published simultaneously in Canada by
Penguin Books Canada Ltd., Ontario
Printed in the United States of America

Library of Congress Cataloging-in-Publication Data

Updike, John.
Hugging the shore : essays and criticism / John Updike.
p.   cm.
Includes index.
ISBN 0-88001-398-2
1. Character sketches.   2. Literature,
Modern—History and criticism.   I. Title.
PS3571.P4H8   1994
814'.54—de20
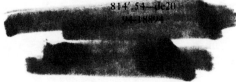

Acknowledgments

Grateful acknowledgment is made to the following magazines and publishers, who first printed the pieces specified, sometimes under different titles and in slightly different form:

THE NEW YORKER: "Venezuela for Visitors," "The Chaste Planet," "Invasion of the Book Envelopes," "Golf Dreams," "Out There," "A Mild 'Complaint,'" "Vale, VN," "Melville's Withdrawal," and ninety-two of the book reviews, including three published as "Briefly Noted."

THE NEW YORK REVIEW OF BOOKS: "Whitman's Egotheism," "An Introduction to Nabokov's Lectures," and "An Introduction to Three Novels by Henry Green." Also "Hawthorne's Creed," which first appeared in the PROCEEDINGS OF THE AMERICAN ACADEMY AND INSTITUTE OF ARTS AND LETTERS (Second Series, No. 30).

THE NEW YORK TIMES BOOK REVIEW: "Polish Metamorphoses" ("Bruno Schulz, Hidden Genius"), "Czech Angels" ("The Most Original Book"), "Owlish and Fishy" ("Fly by Night"), "Sissman's Poetry" ("Witness to His Dying"), "Stand Fast I Must" ("Gathering the Poets of the Faith"), "Magic Mirrors" ("Uses of Enchantment"). Copyright © 1976, 1978, 1980, 1982 by The New York Times Company. Reprinted by permission. And, in the appendix, the material on pages 839–40, 862–5, and 870–5.

THE ONTARIO REVIEW: "The Counsellor," "The Golf Course Owner," "The Child Bride," "The Mailman," "The Widow," and "The Undertaker."

THE TRANSATLANTIC REVIEW: "The Pal" and "One's Neighbor's Wife."

ESQUIRE: "The Running Mate," "The Bankrupt Man," and "The Tarbox Police."

GOLF: "Thirteen Ways of Looking at the Masters."

THE BOSTON GLOBE: "The First Kiss."

THE GLOBE PEQUOT PRESS: Introduction to Great New England Churches.

ANCHOR PRESS/DOUBLEDAY & CO.: "Going Barefoot."

HOUGHTON MIFFLIN COMPANY: "Common Land" from New England: The Four Seasons by Arthur Griffin. Copyright © 1980 by Arthur Griffin. Reprinted by permission of Houghton Mifflin Company.

THE NEW REPUBLIC: the bulk of "Edmund Wilson's Fiction: A Personal Account," later expanded for An Edmund Wilson Celebration (Phaidon).

PAN BOOKS, LTD.: Introduction to Loving/Living Party/Going, by Henry Green.

PENGUIN BOOKS, LTD.: Introduction to Sanitorium Under the Sign of the Hourglass, by Bruno Schulz. Copyright © 1979 by John Updike.

HARCOURT BRACE JOVANOVICH and WEIDENFELD & NICOLSON, LTD: Introduction to Lectures on Literature, by Vladimir Nabokov; copyright © 1980 by the Estate of Vladimir Nabokov, Editor's Foreword copyright © 1980 by Fredson Bowers, Introduction copyright © 1980 by John Updike. Reprinted by permission of Harcourt Brace Jovanovich, Inc. and Weidenfeld & Nicolson, Ltd.

VANGUARD PRESS, INC.: Introduction to Innocent Bystander, by L. E. Sissman. Reprinted by permission of the publisher, Vanguard Press, Inc. Copyright © 1975 by L. E. Sissman.

LORD JOHN PRESS: Introduction to Talk from the Fifties.

THE FRANKLIN LIBRARY: "A special message to the members of The First Edition Society" was written for the limited first edition of Marry Me by John Updike. Copyright © 1976 Franklin Mint Corporation. "A special message to subscribers from John Updike" was written for the signed, limited edition of Rabbit, Run and of Rabbit Redux by John Updike. Copyright © 1977, 1981 Franklin Mint Corporation. Reprinted by permission of The Franklin Library.

DOUBLEDAY & CO.: Translations of three poems, "Monologue of an American Poet," "Monologue of a Polar Fox on an Alaskan Fur Farm," and "Smog" translated by John Updike and Albert C. Todd. Copyright © 1968 by The Curtis Publishing Company. From Stolen Apples, by Yevgeny Yevtushenko. Reprinted by permission of Doubleday & Company, Inc.

for EDITH OLIVER
who proposes
and SUSAN MORITZ
who disposes

Contents

Other People's Books

Foreword

WRITING CRITICISM is to writing fiction and poetry as hugging the shore is to sailing in the open sea. At sea, we have that beautiful blankness all around, a cold bright wind, and the occasional thrill of a gleaming dolphin-back or the synchronized leap of silverfish; hugging the shore, one can always come about and draw even closer to the land with another nine-point quotation. This is a big book but perhaps a quarter of the words belongs to other people. A good review is, among other things, a little anthology; my own experience of authorship urges me to heed the author's exact expressions and to condemn him, if he must be condemned, out of his own mouth. One of the chief labors, strange to say, of this assembling has been to ascertain which paragraph indentations, in the excerpted passages, really are part of the text: *The New Yorker*, where most of these reviews appeared, mechanically indents every such excerpt in smaller type, so I had to look up all the originals again. Also, for reasons known only to the fabled ur-fathers of its style manual, all titles are set in quotes instead of—my orthodox preference—italics. But for such fine points, I have changed little, and have nothing to complain of in the handsome way this most scrupulous and considerate of magazines has sponsored my improvised sub-career as a book reviewer. Edith Oliver calls me up to suggest books or to approve my suggestions; Susan Moritz patiently escorts the untidy manuscript into smooth, error-free type. Under the wings of their recurrent kindness and acumen and coddling good humor the bulk of this book was produced, and it is gratefully dedicated to them.

As with this collection's predecessor volumes, *Assorted Prose* and *Picked-Up Pieces*, I have included a number of oddments—brief essays turned to oblige a friend, attempts at humor and fantasy, journalistic assignments. The oldest piece in the "Persons and Places" section is "A Mild 'Complaint,' " which was blithely composed in January of 1961, accepted promptly by *The New Yorker*, and then allowed to languish on the bank of unpublished "casuals" as the years and the decades lumbered by. I assumed that the piece, so fragile and literary in its joke, was thus informally killed; but when I suggested that I be allowed to give it decent burial in this omnibus the editors pronounced the little thing still vital despite its long coma and ran it in the issue of April 19, 1982—twenty-one years, three months, and a day after the date of its composition. The second-oldest piece is "The Tarbox Police," originally published in the March 1972 issue of *Esquire* and waiting since then for the kindred company of other "insufficiently famous Americans" to bring Cal, Hal, Sam, and Dan into hardcovers. The ten imaginary interviews were published separately as an elegant slim brown volume by the Lord John Press under the title *People One Knows*, a title I have omitted but echoed here in the last section, which immodestly marshals some "autobibliographical" prefaces and responses but at least has the good taste to exclude all of those spoken interviews pulled from a limp-witted and complaisant author, whirled onto cassette tape, and then elevated, with many a typist's flub, to the dignity of graven utterance. Let them perish in the pit of media-inspired ephemera! Every word in this book has been *written*.

I have tried to group the reviews into bundles handy for piece-meal reading. Since it is my habit, by way of giving good measure, to review several books together, some violence has been done to achieve these new groupings: for the sake of national cohesion, Muriel Spark had to be disentangled from both Ann Beattie and Raymond Queneau, and Queneau from D. M. Thomas. But in general, since the pairing of books often gives the review its coda, and yields chords that could not be struck otherwise, I have striven to keep the reviews as they originally were, at the cost of some disorder. Italo Calvino and Stanislaw Lem appear in two different sections, for instance, and my running appreciation of Anne Tyler is interrupted by considerations of Ursula K. Le Guin and John Cheever. The general trend of arrangement is chronological, patriotic (America first), and from fiction to non-fiction. Not counting the classics pondered in "Three Talks on American Masters," one hundred thirty-one of "other people's books"—34,869 pages, by my calculation—are specifically reviewed or introduced, all within the eight years since I wrapped up *Picked-Up Pieces* with the prayer "Let us hope, for the sakes of artistic purity and paper conservation, that ten years from now the pieces to be picked up will make a smaller heap."

The heap is not smaller, and the ten years are not even up. What is my excuse, and why do I feel obliged to offer one? How better would my eyes, wits, and fingertips have been employed than with those 34,869 pages? Would I really, instead, have read through the complete works of Dickens and Thackeray and taught myself Italian? Or would I have misspent the time in hardware stores, searching for the perfect doohickey to fit into my broken thingamabob? What is this shore I hug so repeatedly, with such a squint of guilt? Were not these exercises in appreciation and exposition composed, like anything else, by taking a deep breath, leaning out over the typewriter, and trying to dive a little deeper than the first words that come to mind? Of some I am proud enough, as work completed and self-education achieved. Of none am I ashamed, else I would not have admitted them to my summer-long clerical labor, my mustering of deteriorating tearsheets into the hefty form of this book. Another book. Another slain forest. Another pious claim on our besieged pocketbooks. Even in the age of Ecclesiastes (third century B.C., according to most scholars), the need for more books seemed doubtful. Whereas book *reviews* perform a clear and desired social service: they excuse us from reading the books themselves. They give us literary sensations in concentrated form. They are gossip of a higher sort. They are as intense as television commercials and as jolly as candy bars. I myself usually turn to the book reviews in a magazine or a newspaper just after the cartoons or the sports section, and I want them to be well done. That must be why I began to do them myself, in 1960.

The world craves book reviews far more heartily than it craves books: therein lies the beguilement and the nagging unease of the trade. Unlike the poet and the teller of tales, the reviewer writes by editorial invitation, in near-certainty of his product's being paid for and printed. He is safe, too, in his tone, which merely has to preserve the grammatical forms and a semblance of sagacity to win his audience to him, in satisfying collusion against the clumsiness, deludedness, and conceit of the book writer. Critical prose, like the prose of business letters, has its set locutions and inevitable rhythms, which begin to wear a drone into even the user's head. One misses, hugging the shore, the halting mimetic prose of fiction, which seeks to sink itself in the mind of a character or the texture of a moment. What we love about fiction writers is their willingness to dare this submergence, to give up, in behalf of brute reality, the voice of a wise and presentable man. The critic comes to us in suit and tie. He is a gentleman. He is *right*. A pox on him, as Goethe said.* Among the many pieces of paper I sifted to make this collection I came across the following note, evidently addressed, so sternly, to myself:

> An artist mediates between the world and minds; a critic merely between minds. An artist therefore must even at the price of uncouthness and alienation from the contemporary cultural scene maintain allegiance to the world and a fervent relation with it.

A fervent relation with the world: I suppose this is my critical touchstone, with its old-fashioned savor of reverence and Creation and the truth that shall make you free. I find myself, in these pieces, circling back to man's religious nature and the real loss to man and art alike when that nature has nowhere to plug itself in. The sheer difficulty, nowadays, of investing fiction with seriousness is a kin-

---

*Or something like it, in German. Feminists: if the preceding sentences trouble you, try this version: ". . . the voice of a wise and presentable woman. The critic comes to us in black dress and pearls. She is a lady. She is *right*. A pox on her, as Goethe said."

dred theme. Decline—in manners, craft, landscape, and communal vitality—is not, I hope, unduly harped upon. At all times, an old world is collapsing and a new world arising; we have better eyes for the collapse than the rise, for the old one is the world we know. The artist, in focusing on his own creation, finds, and offers, relief from the tension and sadness of being burdened not just with consciousness but with historical consciousness; this relief is afforded minimally by the critical role. To show, in a series of quotations, the author himself (dead or not) what he has indeed written: this does approach creativity, and some of the pieces included here ("A Feast of Reason," "Dark Smile, Devilish Saints") give me in retrospect the bliss (as Nabokov and Barthes would say) of having seen a knotty thing through and phrased a clear conclusion. On grayer days I have felt, as a reviewer, engaged in mere summary and obliged to smother under explicit opinionizing those intuitive sensations of delight or illumination or their absences that accompany a purely gratuitous, spontaneous reading of a book. In such a reading, there are no symptomatic sentences to underline, no private index scrawled on the endpapers for use in the judicial summing-up ahead; one scans the pages as one scans life, half asleep in the dream of sequentiality, now and then poked awake by a flash of beauty or the crackle of truth. The ideal reader's freely given, irresponsible attentiveness cannot be the reviewer's; and the reviewer, insofar as he foretells (as he must) what the book is about and what should be thought about it, destroys ideal readership for others. His role is as impure as his pronouns, which so insidiously slide from "I" to "one" to "we," surrounding the reader, who is suddenly enlisted in this small mob as "the reader," while "this reviewer" stands off to one side like an ironic clone.

Well, who said life, or a life, can be pure? Here, then, without further apology, is the fruit of eight years' purposeful reading, carried out, much of it, to secure me the pleasures and benefits of appearance in *The New Yorker*. Some of the best-researched and most happily undertaken reviews belong to my twenty months of living alone in Boston, with two great libraries—Harvard's Widener and the Boston Public—minutes away, and my foam-rubber reading chair three paces from my dining table and two paces from my bed. Solitude and small quarters are great inciters of literacy. Also, as it happened, in this land of fragmentation held together by legalities, the payment for a monthly review roughly balanced a monthly alimony payment that was mine to make. At the beginning of those eight years, I had left a big white house with a view of saltwater. An inland interim of reconsolidation followed, and now I live again in a big white house with a view of saltwater. I keep looking out the window. The clean horizon beckons. All sorts of silvery shadows streak the surface of the sea. Sailboats dot it, some far out. It looks like literature. What a beautiful sight!

J. U.
September 1982

Persons and Places

INTERVIEWS WITH
INSUFFICIENTLY FAMOUS AMERICANS

The Pal

THE PAL is pale, like water. He is everywhere, in different forms. On the golf course, he is present as a swing and a slice, then a swing and a hook. Or as the rattle of the ball into the cup, unexpectedly, from far away. He is a good putter, the pal.

At poker, he is inscrutable. He is a face above cards one cannot see. He raises the bet. What does this mean? Is he going high or low? If he loses, he will borrow money from one. If he wins, he will keep it. When he shows his cards, he has the cased King. Or he was bluffing and folds, scrambling his cards together in a quick exasperated little tent-shape, beside the tall golden cylinder of beer. He is most lovable then.

Look at that pal ski! Swish, swish, down the chute, over the moguls, away! He is not easy to keep up with, but one wants to. One wants to for the camaraderie of the ski lodge, his pale face ruddy above the steaming coffee mug. Or the camaraderie of the long drive home, in the chain of headlights, his eyes blinking, his head nodding, with sleepiness. A sleepy pal is a dear pal. Even were he to nod off and drive head-on into a trailer rig, it would be a good way to go, there would be no grudge.

At tennis is he less benign. He slashes, he wheels, he whaps an easy overhead into the net. *"Come up to the net,"* he insists. *Fuck you,* one thinks. Still, the parallel patter of sneakers on the clay is pretty, though the opponents lob over our heads, and we lose the set.

At parties, one never talks to the pal. In this he is like a mistress. He observes and he sulks. He dances only the slow dances, often with one's wife. That, too, is a mode of palship. That, and calling one's children "Butch," no matter what their names.

Interviewers find him elusive, almost rude.

Q: Could you in a word or two describe the gratifications of being—how shall we put it?—a pal?

A: Meagre. Few.

Q: Would you advise young men, freshly graduated from college and as yet undecided about their careers, to follow in your footsteps and become pals?

A: No.

Q: What has been the principal ingredient, in your experience, of palship?

A: Beer.

Q: And its sustaining teleology and ambient essence?

A: Death.

Q: Thank you very much, sir.

A: Forget it.

Then he is on the phone, trying to set up a paddle-tennis date, or a fishing trip, or a rendezvous in a duck blind at 4 A.M. Refused, he sounds hurt. He has no other fun. He is at the bottom of one's swimming pool in a snorkeling mask, picking up hairpins and pennies. He is silhouetted on one's roof, adjusting the television aerial. One returns from a trip, and the dregs of his dinner wine are on the table, his pajamas are underneath the bed. Ambushed, he is unembarrassed. "Butch here cut his knee while you were gone." What can one say? One says, "Have a beer."

The pal is a mist, he is a puddle. He fogs the rearview mirror, he is a gratefully gulped glass of water at the kitchen sink. As at sea, there is a horizon of melancholy, which recedes, and cannot be crossed, though one sails for days, in stubborn silence, the rigging creaking, the waves slapping the prow, a single gull weeping off the stern. His beauty is, he opens up this horizon within oneself. For if he is your pal, you are his. The male desert within us is coterminous. He is a mirage.

One's Neighbor's Wife

WHAT IS THERE about this wonderful woman? From next door she comes striding, down the lawn, beneath the clothesline, laden with cookies she has just baked, or with baby togs she no longer needs, and one's heart goes out. *Pops* out. The clothesline, the rusted swing set, the limbs of the dying elm, the lilacs past bloom are lit up like rods of neon by her casual washday energy and cheer, a cheer one has done nothing to infuse.

In certain party lights the mat slant of the plane of her cheek wears beneath the lamp the somber rose glow of earth seen from the window of a jet pouring west against the sunset; to fall would be death.

Her house is full of crannies, of cluttered drawers and dusty shelves, repositories of wedding gifts and high-school charm bracelets and snapshots of herself as a child. These are unimaginable treasures—bones of her flesh, relics her life has generated. One studies her husband wonderingly: how can he withstand such a daily pressure of bliss? His skull looks two inches thick, all around.

She touches her children, and they rotate in the oven of her love. Her dog, too, dumb sharer of her hours, is stroked and ruffled. Her hands, oval and firm, bear no trace (if one excepts the wedding ring) of awareness that they are sacred instruments—much like those Renaissance paintings wherein the halo of the Christ child, having dwindled from the Byzantine corolla of beaten gold to a translucent disc delicately painted in the perspective of a three-dimensional caplike appurtenance, disappears entirely, leaving us with an unexpectedly Italian-looking urchin.

Her conversation is inane, sublimely.

There is a scent to her, a scent to the sight of her in her clothes, that rustles free into the air when she moves, though her movements are brisk rather than voluptuous. Desire attaches, one notices, less to her person than to her surroundings, to the landscapes she walks through, the automobile she slides packages in and out of, the garden she tends, her crannied house, its curtains and rugs and towels—as though she were a sachet of lavender scent in a drawer of tumbled, cloudy fabrics.

Her person. She has freckles wherever one can see. A bikini reveals the demure little saddle of fat that pads the base of her spine. When she lifts her arms, shaved and powdered patches are revealed. What color would her pussy be?

A: My pussy is the color of earth, of fire, of air shuddering on the vein of a rock by the side of a stream, of fine metals spun to a curly tumult, of night as to the expanded eye of the prowler it yields its tints of russet and umber, subtle husks of daylight colors. Each hair is precious and individual, serving a distinct rôle in the array: blond to invisibility where the thigh and abdomen join, dark to opacity where the tender labia ask protection, hearty and ruddy as a forester's beard beneath the swell of belly, dark and sparse as the whiskers of a Machiavel where the perineum sneaks backward to the anus. My pussy alters by the time of day and according to the mesh of underpants. It has its satellites: the whimsical line of hairs that ascend to my navel and into my tan, the kisses of fur on the inside of my thighs, the lambent fuzz that ornaments the cleavage of my fundament. Amber, ebony, auburn, bay, chestnut, cinnamon, hazel, fawn, snuff, henna, bronze, platinum, peach, ash, flame, and field mouse: these are but a few of the colors my pussy is.

Q: How can you bear to be the constant carrier of such splendor?

A: I don't think about it most of the time. Just when I take a bath, and when Joe says something.

Q: That shmoe.

A: Think you could do better?

One's neighbor's wife's *life,* not her womb, is the theatre wherein covetousness raves. One wishes to curl up on her furniture, to awaken to the dawns that break upon her windows, to see the eleven o'clock news on her set. Would it be the same old news? Impossible.

The Running Mate

HER EYES are blue. Her breath comes easily, from her diaphragm and out through her nostrils, in time with her strides. She never tires. Though the seasons change, and day and night flicker like the wingbeats of a circling predator, she is always there, beside one, running.

She wears Adidas jogging shoes, and a dove-gray sweat suit with canary-yellow piping down the sleeves and legs. In winter, she adds a cable-knit Norwegian sweater; in summer, she strips down to crimson track shorts, with slits in the sides for greater freedom of motion, and a grape-colored tank top, stained to dark wine where she sweats. When it rains, she produces from somewhere a transparent polyethylene bandanna.

At corners, she shortens her stride, courtesy having long ago assigned her the inside position. On the straightaways, she may fall a bit behind, and one looks back with a heart-skip of hope, but she is still there, breathing easily, through her nose, above her smile, displaying in her upraised hand a chewing-gum wrapper she paused to pick up, or a wildflower, or a snowball.

The steady soft thump of her running becomes one's pulse.

Her blue-eyed face floats in the side of one's vision like a corneal scar, and though one lashes out, and occasionally strikes bone, so that she bobs and staggers, the effort of running leaves insufficient leverage for the crippling blow one would like to deliver.

At zero, her breath flies from her lips in sheets of frozen vapor; at ninety above, her hair pastes itself in tendrils to her temples and nape, and every square inch of her exposed skin shines. One is told that by the eighteenth mile of a marathon blood has begun to mix with a runner's urine, from the incessant concussion of heels on cement. There is no sign of that with the running mate. At every milepost she says, "Isn't this fun?," an utterance she varies only with the exclamation "What a glorious view!"

Some of the views *are* glorious. Velvet autumnal valleys where a ribbon of river glints. Cityscapes, like organ chords rising, of glass and steel. Sandy country lanes lined with cowbells and raspberries. Suburban tracts where each child has a tricycle, each sprinkler has a lawn. Summer estates muffled by snow, the verandas deep in drifts and the tennis courts scored by rabbit tracks. Glorious, if one could but have an intermission. Why can't we stop?

An interviewer capers alongside and asks her this very same question. Her answers flow evenly, in time with her strides.

A: We have not been given permission to stop.
Q: Who would give this permission?
A: The same impersonal force or personal Divinity Who set us thus to running together.
Q: Together—exactly. Why must you always run beside this man?
A: He and I are plighted. He cannot run without me. I cannot imagine running without him.
Q: Where are you running to?
A: Wherever he leads me. He leads. I follow. That is the pattern. It is mutually sustaining, a mutual spur and inspiration.

A tunnel mouth looms ahead. A traffic of trucks and buses makes the air of the tunnel cacophonous and foul. The tiled walls, set in the Depression, under FDR, have lost half their grouting, and leak dubious fluid. The catwalk for pedestrians is rickety and narrow. A single patrolman, doing penalty duty, stands guard above the hissing of air brakes, the squealing of tires, the shattering rush and rumble. Carbon monoxide asphyxiates the lights, and it is a matter of a moment in the murk to half-kneel and to trip the running mate. She flies over the pipe rail, and the crushing traffic never pauses. There is not a cry, not a stain, not a trace, save the trembling of guilt in one's knees as they pump toward the light.

Outside the tunnel, tenement houses the colors of mustard and olives top a man-made escarpment. The roadway lifts, grows level. A flattened squirrel marks the presence of nature. A homing pigeon circles toward an upper window of a tall granite prison. Some dingy children have uncapped a fire hydrant and are playing in the resultant lake. One of the children seems to be following behind one, with taunting soft footsteps.

But it is no child. It is the running mate. Her blue eyes. Her encouraging smile. One can look through her now, to curbstones and litter, as if through her polyethylene bandanna; but her pace is unchecked, her breathing easy and deep. A light rain begins, tingling. She offers like a flower a red truck reflector on a stem of bent wire.

The Counsellor

ONE FEELS REASSURED, in the presence of the counsellor. There are those humming brown elevators that lift you toward his firm, and that stunning receptionist whose face is as soaked in powder as a Turkish Delight used to be in sugar, before the candy manufacturers began to feel the pinch. And then, his view! All of the metropolis seems encapsulated in his windows, like a town in a spherical paperweight—the spires, the bridges, the penthouses, the traffic jams, the harbor, all there, twinkling. He rises in a cascade of pinstripes. His face is so clean and rosy it looks skinned. He is broad-shouldered, and not exactly four-dimensional, but making more of the three dimensions than the rest of us do: he *bulks*. "Fill me in," he says, "on the problem."

While being filled in, he leans back in his chair and presses his fingertips together. They must teach that in law school—a variant of prayer, with the eyes wide open. He does not take a note. For he has summoned in another lawyer, younger, less bulky, to take notes, on a yellow legal pad held on his gaunt young knee. One feels, of course, wretched, fetching one's clinging shreds of the organic world—life, that begins in the bursting of membranes and ends with a relaxation of the sphincter muscle—into such impeccable presences, such well-groomed offices. Since childhood, one has been told that there can be no squaring of the circle, but one hopes of the counsellor that he can cube an egg, and a scrambled egg at that. He leans forward, touches the desktop with his elbows, lets his slow silence bulk him larger, and at last offers, "There may be a way around that."

One could cry in gratitude.

With manicured hands he outlines in the air a program of counter-terror, writ responding to writ, tort (from *tortus*, crooked) nullifying tort. There may be depositions taken. The demeanor of the judge cannot be foreseen. You want to call a bluff, but you don't want to call it to the point where it *feels* called. In a situation involving X, Y, and Z, who is to say that Z will prove rational, and not do the self-destructive thing? This is still a free country, with great opportunities for self-destruction. There are variables. Variables cost money. Show me a free variable, I'll show you totalitarianism. In a nation of laws not men, brinkmanship prevails from sea to shining sea. *Et cetera, sub rosa, entre nous.*

A twinkling maze of imponderable possibilities has arisen above the counsellor's glass desktop. One feels driven outward, from one's petty fate to general considerations of an abstract and ramifying nature. One asks,

Q: What is justice?

A: Depends on the state. Justice in Delaware is mere mischief in South Dakota. Alabama, who knows? Had a client last week who was made to look pitiable in Alabama. This same fellow came up smelling like roses in Maryland. *Non serviam,* I say.

Q: Do you feel you are providing an essential service?

A: I service human foolishness. If foolishness were non-essential, it would have faded away aeons ago, with the hand-held flint chopper. *Requiescat in pace,* chopper.

Q: Let me put it another way. Do you feel that the noble intent of the law is always commensurately served by its minions?

A: Define me a minion. We build on air. All of us. We build on air. When the Pilgrims landed at that there rock, this was lawless forest. From here to Big Sur, lawless forest. Now we've got such a structure the average man can't go two hours without committing a misdemeanor. I don't say that's good. I don't say that's bad. I say that's a fact. Out of this fact some fortunate few of us have generated an industry. Out of some other fact our worthy colleagues at the bar have generated a contrary industry. It all comes out in the locker room, where they polish your shoes while you shower. Define me a minion, I'll give you a misdemeanor. *Sic semper tyrannis.* You follow me?

Q: I'm getting there. Can you estimate how much this lecture has cost me?

A: It would be ill-advised to comment at this time.

Q: Can you tell me if you think we have a case?

A: It would be premature to venture a comment this far down the road.

Q: In general, *sub specie aeternitatis,* what are my chances?

A: All I can say at this juncture is *Nihil ab nihilo, de profundis.* Best of luck to you and yours. I've really enjoyed our conversation. [*One stands to go.*] Here, let me show you these Polaroids of my wife and kids. Cute as buttons, huh? The house in the background, we bought it for seventy grand in 1967, it would go for two hundred big ones now, easy; and that leaves us an acre out back to retire on. Keep your nose clean, your powder dry, your chin up. Have a stick of Juicy Fruit, foul stuff but it saved my sanity when I gave up smoking ciggyboos. If that ain't your cup of tea, take a lick of the receptionist on your way out. Ha-ha-ha. Ha-ha-ha-*ha.*

At the hourly rate that his counselling commands, each "ha" has cost 12½ ¢.

The Golf Course Owner

HE SITS by the little clubhouse, in a golf cart, wearing black. He is Greek. Where, after all these years in America, does he buy black clothes? His hat is black. His shirt is black. His eyes, though a bit rheumy with age now, are black, as are his shoes and their laces. Small black points exist in his face, like scattered punctuation. His smile is wonderful, an enfolding of the world as his hand enfolds yours. Many little gray teeth, all his, they must be: something of the ancient marriage of tragedy and comedy in that smile.

How ancient is he? He has been sitting here since one learned golf twenty years ago. In those years, it was his son who manned the tractor with his gang of mowers, going up and down the fairways methodically as a lover's caresses. Now, it is his grandson. Once, in Homeric times, it must have been he, Harílaos, who manned the tractors. But times so epic are hard to imagine.

The first, second, third, and ninth holes can be seen from where he sits, and the fourth tee, where many a man has been tempted by the broad downhill leftward dog-leg to hook into the marsh. The ridge holds its writhing occupants in profile, a frieze against the sky, before they mourn their shots, pocket their tees, and drag their carts down into the underworld. The fifth, sixth, seventh, and eighth holes are entirely out of sight, but the men in their bright slacks eventually return, advancing down the ninth fairway like a thinned army pulling its own chariots. Their odyssey ends in a ritual exchange with the owner, who has that essential capacity mythic characters have for waiting, waiting decades if need be, for the foreordained moment in the adventure to arrive.

Q: How goes it, Harry, how goes it?
A: Not so good, John, not so good.
Q: Lovely day out there.
A: [*nods*]

Weather and health are discussed but never, oddly, golf. What does he know about golf? Among the mysteries that radiate as he in his black clothes soaks up the sun are:

Q: How did he come to acquire this frivolously utilized acreage?
Q: Does it turn a profit?
Q: What *is* this Greek genius for acquisition?

*

The questions go unanswered. The seasons turn from spring (raw winds, patchy greens, plugged drives) to summer (insect repellent, lost balls) to fall (morning dew, goose feathers, baked fairways, terrific roll); the tractor mows back and forth, back and forth, on the contours of the course. Harry is aging. He is shrinking in the golf cart, his handclasp grows feverish, his eyes misty; he disappears. Over the winter, one hears he has had a stroke. Speculation is rife. The course will be sold, a thousand ranch houses will spring up.

In the spring, the golfers return, in cleated rubbers, but he is not here. The golf cart sits empty, like Agamemnon's throne. The dandelions come, the greenhead flies, the August thunderstorms. Suddenly, he is there. His black clothes are faded to gray, and his face matches his clothes. He searches one's face almost blindly, through his feeble enfolding of the offered hand.

Q: How goes it, Harry, how goes it?
A: Τις δ' οἶδεν εἰ το ζῆν μεν ἐστι κατθανειν,
το κατθανειν δε ζῆν κατω νομιζεται.*
Q: We thought you were dead. What's your secret?
A: [*gestures toward golf course*]**

The Child Bride

AS ONE ENTERS THE PARTY, she is at the door, greeting. But how can this be the hostess? She is a child. A child in high heels, true; but baby fat presses with a delicate meniscus through the straps of these shoes and fills her red satin dress so it glows like a spanking new pillow. Her oval face is innocent of any wrinkle, though the pursed lips and focused brow indicate where wrinkles will come. Her hand, as one shakes it, has that slightly clammy bonelessness of an infant's.

---

*Translation: Who knows if life is death, and death is considered life in the world below? [Euripides]

**Translation: He will not die. He is land, and land does not die.

Throughout the party, she tends to the little things—seeing that the nuts are in their little bowls, and that the little bowls are distributed fairly among the available tabletops, and that the windows are open a crack but not more than a crack. As she performs these tasks, she dodges among her guests like a puppy seal amid hoary, craggy icebergs. These guests are her husband's friends, and like him they are enjoying late middle age, with its warts, its wens, its grizzled facial crevasses, its tufts of falling hair, its snaggle teeth, its arthritic hips, its bad backs, its wheezes, its sorry breath and boozy reminiscences.

The child bride shares none of this. She stands benignly at the side of some rambling uproarious elderly conversation waiting for her moment to duck down and adjust the dish of celery and olives, but she talks only, and then only briefly, to her stepdaughter, a lanky blasé blonde five years older than she. This aging stepdaughter is the product of one of her husband's earlier marriages. His first wife was a woman in her early twenties, and so the rest of them have been, all six or seven.

In this room of veteran partygoers, getting louder by the minute —the men barking and snuffling and staggering, though the glasses in their hands hold steady as gyroscopes; the women talking in voices parched to a whisper by decades of cigarettes and quarrelling with servants—the child bride should be a breath, a sprig, of spring. But in truth she has that heaviness of youth, that density of bones still supple and muscles still elastic and closely interwoven, of blood as yet undistilled into bitter wisdom. Among the resonating barrel chests floating upon skinny pained old legs, her succulence, her silence make her fascinating. One cannot help asking,

Q: How did you get into this?
A: The same way you did. By being born. I was born later, is the only difference.
Q: Do you miss your own generation?
A: I never had much to say to them. I don't have much to say to these people, either, but they don't notice. Or if they do, they don't blame me for it.
Q: Uh—but isn't there a rapture in marching through history

many abreast, arm in arm, singing the same songs, taking the same drugs, remembering the same wars and assassinations?

A: There is, but it doesn't compare to the rapture of being oneself. Have you ever read *Alone*, by Admiral Byrd?

Q: Your husband—how do you confront his flatulence and distemper, his sheer bad complexion, not to mention his houseful of closets, from which all his previous lives must keep tumbling?

A: I confront these things understandingly. I am his wife.

Q: But so young and smooth, and he so old and rough.

A: I'm not sure you understand women.

Q: Tell me.

A: One gives oneself to the abyss, and it becomes a cradle.

They stand side by side at the party's end, husband and wife; there is little disparity in their heights. He is effusive, drunk, funny, pocked, and aerated by the sinuous channels of experience. She is as sober and smooth and solid and sleek as when we entered. We say good-bye reverently to this wonder. When we come again, she may not be here. She has sacrificed herself, that one of us may live.

The Mailman

HE LOVES all weathers. In summer he wears short sleeves, in winter he wears a cotton turtleneck under his regulation cardboard-gray long-sleeved shirt; that is the only concession he makes to inclemency. When it rains, his booming smile turns even a downpour into a drizzle, from which his visage is impishly sheltered by the visor of his regulation cap. When it snows, that is the most fun; amid the wide secretive radiance his footsteps thump-thump up the steps as if enlarged by burlap wrappings, and the clack of the letter slot resounds through the house like a shot. His cheeks are red, his eyes maniacal with merriment as, shifting his lightened sack on his shoulders, he heads down the freshly plowed sidewalk to bring the next house its parcel of joy. He is Santa Claus without the beard, Uncle Sam without the top hat; he is police without the brutality, dailiness without ennui.

This blue thread who stitches together our weeks, who with the same benign aplomb delivers gold futures solicitations on clay-coated stock, and electric bills with their carbon copy and even their carbon paper cunningly inserted within an integral paper cocoon like butterfly wings, and creamy stiff invitations to weddings and wine tastings, and dusty-rose stationery dented and crinkled by the tears and furious quill of a mistress or lover, and common-sense proposals from businesslike men, and epistles that like St. Paul's need no immediate answer—this ebullient human shuttle of our continent-spanning social weave, one is moved one day to ask him,

Q: Do you ever feel blue?

A: Some days, but I kick it. Some days the old pouch weighs on me, but once I dump off the first couple *Vogue*s I feel good again.

Q: Dogs? Gloom of night?

A: The dogs, I don't know, you don't see real bitey dogs like you used to. I don't know what it is. Their teeth get soft, watching television. They have the bark but not the nip. Like I was saying to the man down the street, next war comes along, us old guys'll have to go fight it. Gloom of night—well, I conk out pretty early. Walk fifteen miles in black shoes every day, you would, too.

Q: Monotony?

A: No, most folks are real nice, I stop and have a word with the different ones. Some people still send registered, so there's the receipts to mess with. Always something a little novel, you know. Can't say I thought much of that Francis Perkins stamp, though. Too serious. A stamp ought to give you a little lift, when you hit it with your tongue.

Q: I've always been interested in what you might call the romance of the mails. It's really a wonderful thing, to put a letter in some clanging box out at the corner of Grant and Woodbine and have it pop up in Colorado Springs two days later. The slots, the dark sacks, and all the ins and outs of it—do you follow me? I mean [*blushing*] it's a *mystery*.

A [*puzzled*]: Well, not if you break it down step by step. They have these new computers now that you punch the zips into as the letters go by, I've heard it's the most unnatural job in the world. They have to take them off duty every twenty minutes or the guys go crazy.

Q: Junk mail? How do you feel about that? And for that matter isn't there a, how can I say, certain stench of the un*nec*essary about most of it?

A: Yeah, but we love it, don't we? It's life, and life is sweet. Like sun and rain, bright and gray, it all beats pushing up daisies. You know what they say, don't you? The dead have no zip.

Q [*having exposed oneself with a serious concern and obsession, and been short-changed with facile optimism*]: Huh. Hadn't heard it put that way.

A: Think it over. Have a nice rest of the day.

Q: O.K. You, too.

A: No need to worry about *me*.

He goes off whistling, loving the weather. Photons beat on his broad chest, neutrinos penetrate black leather and swamp his toenails. There is a secret to life, but he hasn't delivered it yet.

He is moved to another route. Routes change. Years pass. One day an unsigned postcard arrives, with pencilled block letters saying, NOTHING NECESSARY ABOUT CREATION FOR THAT MATTER.

The Widow

Q: NICE PLACE you have here.

A: I try to keep it up. But it's hard. It's hard.

Q: How many years has it been now?

A: Seven. Seven come September. He was sitting in that chair, right where you are now, and the next minute he was gone. Just a kind of long sigh, and he was gone.

Q: Sounds like a pretty good way to go. Since we all have to go sometime.

A: That's what everybody said. The minister, the undertaker. I suppose I should have been grateful, but if it had been less sudden, it might have been less of a shock. It was as if he *wanted* to go, the way he went so easy.

Q: Well. I doubt that. But it's you I'm interested in, you in the years since. You look wonderfully well.

A: Ever since I stopped taking the pills. These doctors nowadays, they prescribe the pills, I honestly believe, to kill you. I was having dizzy spells, one leg seemed to be larger than the other, my hands felt like they were full of prickers . . . it all stopped, once I stopped taking the pills.

Q: And your . . . mental state?

A: If you mean do I still have all my buttons, you'll have to judge that for yourself. Oh, I'm forgetful, but then I always was. I know if I stand in the middle of the room long enough it'll come to me. It's like the sleeping. At first I used to panic, but now if I wake up at three in the morning I just accept it as what my body wants. Trust your body, is the moral of it all, I suppose.

Q: By mental state I meant more grief, loneliness, sense of self, since . . . you became a widow.

A: Well, first, there's the space. No, first, there's the ghosts. Then there's the space.

Q: Ghosts?

A: Oh yes, right there. All the time. Talking to me, telling me to put one foot in front of the other, not to panic. Rattling the latches at night. As certain as you're sitting there. Many a time I've seen it rock by itself.

Q: Perhaps I should change chairs.

A: Oh no, sit right there. People do all the time.

Q: After the ghosts, space?

A: An amazing amount of it. Amazing. I never noticed the sky before. Seventy years on earth and I never looked at the sky. Just yesterday, there were clouds in it with little downward points, like a mountain range seen upside down, or a kind of wet handwriting, it looked ever so weird, I can't describe it properly. And the trees. The way the trees are so patient, so *themselves*, gathering their substance out of air—it sounds silly, in words.

Q: So you would say then that since your husband's passing your life has taken a turn toward the mystical?

A: Not mystical, *prac*tical. The income tax, for instance. I do it all myself, federal and state. I never knew I had it in me to enjoy numbers. And people. I have friends, of all ages. Too many at times, I take the phone off the hook. I think what I meant about the space before, it's space you can arrange yourself, there's nobody pushing at you with *his* space, nobody to tell you you're crazy when you're weeding the peas at four in the morning and start singing.

Q: You often sing to yourself?

A: I'm not sure.

Q: I don't mean to pry—

A: Then don't pry.

One must be prepared, in interviewing the elderly, for these sudden changes of mood, for abrupt closure of access. Human material rubbed so thin by longevity resembles a book whose pages in their tissue fineness admit phrases from the next page or, in their long proximity *en face,* have become scrambled inky mirrors one of the other. Paranoia is the natural state of a skidding organism. Volatility is the inevitable condition of angels. The widow's face, so uncannily tranquil and spacious before, has grown hard and narrow as a gem that is cutting the transparent interface of the interview. One must return to scratch:

Q: But, er, ma'am, prying wasn't—I mean, what we want to do here, your testimony is so positive, so unexpectedly so, that we want to bring to the widest possible audience . . . uh, its great value in this era of widows, to all those others who find themselves alone.

A: You are not alone. You are not. Not.

The Undertaker

THE MAN is so young, is what strikes one forcibly. As if only the dead should bury the dead, we are startled by his downy cheeks, his supple puppyish bulk, his handshake limp and damp and silken as the handshakes of the very young are. Inherited the kit and caboodle—six downstairs rooms wired for Musak and a basement full of coffins—from his father, probably. Or maybe the old man is stashed around the corner, coiled to cinch the deal.

But he never shows, it is the young man we must deal with. He wears the correct suit of lugubrious blue, and his voice is right, that strange *timbre* undertakers achieve, not quite deep enough to be ministerial nor high enough to be eunuchoid, but pitched in-between, and resistless as a mountain stream of salad oil, onflowing but tranquil; nothing will ripple it. What they must see, these childlike blue eyes gliding through these rooms whose wallpaper holds faint veins of silver. Joy-riders decapitated. The last twisted husks of alcoholic ruin. Plump churchwomen turned skeletal by cancer. Beaming former athletes dyed purple in the final fit of asphyxia. Nobody should have to see such things. Who can begrudge him his fleet of Cadillacs outside in the parking lot, and the lambskin-lined Maserati he keeps for his private use, on weekends?

He responds to questions sympathetically, perceiving the interviewer as a kind of mourner, to be handled with care.

Q: Do you enjoy your work?

A: I'm not sure "enjoy" is right. Work it is. I had wanted to be a florist. My father runs a greenhouse. My uncle took me on here instead.

Q [*the inevitable joke, delivered quickly*]: Well, you plant in both cases.

A [*unsmiling*]: It's human-relations work mostly. The craft angle of it anybody could learn in six months. It's the dealing with the relatives, the newspapers, even the old fogeys who control the cemetery lots, that is gratifying to me. That part of it you never get a hundred-percent grip on.

Q: Do you have a basic philosophy for dealing with the—the survivors?

A: Neutral.

Q: Neutral?

A: I try to maintain neutrality. I take the cue from them. If they want to crack jokes, I know a few. If they want to have hysterics, we got soundproofing in the walls. Open coffin, closed coffin, public viewing, private service, scatter the ashes—it doesn't faze us. We're at your service. Last winter we had an old lady who wanted to be hung in a tree as food for the birds, but the state doesn't allow it. Scattering the ashes isn't so popular in some localities, either. What people don't realize, there can be *bones*. Teeth, too. Do it at sea, sometimes the receptacle floats, and you should keep the tide charts in mind. That's the kind of problem that's gratifying to me, one that tests your general knowledge.

Q: Have you read any Jessica Mitford?

A: That's the lady said we worked short hours and overcharged.

Q: 'Fraid so.

A: With all due respect, I don't think the lady quite got a grip on the extent of the service we have to provide. Door to door, so to speak. Deathbed to grave. Once the deceased becomes the deceased, he's on our hands entirely. That's quite an—

Q: Undertaking?

A: You said it. Also there's the sociological aspect. We try to leave the fabric intact, with one thread snipped out. Who's there when that nasty bit of work needs to be done? Not Miss Mitford.

Q: Right. In conclusion, might we see your—receptacles?

They are beautiful. Big baby's cribs, lined with baby blue, pink, peach, lemon. A little sea of them down here, below ground level. Marine metaphors flock to the swimming consciousness. These caskets are boats, calked and mortised and varnished for a long row in black water. Of course they will be rowed, not wind-driven or motor-propelled. *Row, row, row your boat:* we began in first grade by singing that round, and went on to *Michael, row the boat ashore, Hallelujah.* Charon used to pole his skiff of stiffs across the Styx, but this is an age of self-service; you row your own. The undertaker, down here in his watery cave of treasure, amid the silent waves of curved mahogany and plumped-up satin, with frills or without, has grown even more boyish, broad, erect, and translucent; his blue eyes reflect an inner sky, and one remembers where one has seen him before. On the deep imagined sea. He is Billy Budd.

The Bankrupt Man

THE BANKRUPT MAN dances. Perhaps, on other occasions, he sings. Certainly he spends money in restaurants and tips generously. In what sense, then, is he bankrupt?

He has been declared so. He has declared himself so. He returns from the city agitated and pale, complaining of hours spent with the lawyers. Then he pours himself a drink. How does he pay for the liquor inside the drink, if he is bankrupt?

One is too shy to ask. Bankruptcy is a sacred state, a condition beyond conditions, as theologians might say, and attempts to investigate it are necessarily obscene, like spiritualism. One knows only that he has passed into it and lives beyond us, in a condition not ours.

He is dancing at the Chilblains Relief Association Fund Ball. His heels kick high. The mauve spotlight caresses his shoulders, then the gold. His wife's hair glistens like a beehive of tinsel above her bare shoulders and dulcet neck. Where does she get the money, to pay the hairdresser to tease and singe and set her so dazzlingly? We are afraid to ask but cannot tear our eyes from the dancing couple.

The bankrupt man buys himself a motorcycle. He is going to hotdog it all the way to Santa Barbara and back. He has a bankrupt sister in Santa Barbara. Also, there are business details to be cleared up along the way, in Pittsburgh, South Bend, Dodge City, Santa Fe, and Palm Springs. Being bankrupt is an expansionist process; it generates ever new horizons.

We all want to dance with the bankrupt man's wife. Sexual health swirls from her like meadow mist, she sparkles head to toe, her feet are shod in slippers of crystal with caracul liners. "How do you manage to keep up ap—?" We drown our presumptuous question murmurously in her corsage; her breasts billow, violet and gold, about our necktie.

The bankrupt man is elected to high civic office and declines, due to press of business. He can be seen on the streets, rushing everywhere, important-looking papers flying from his hands. He is being sued for astronomical amounts. He wears now only the trendiest clothes—unisex jumpsuits, detachable porcelain collars, coat sleeves that really unbutton. He goes to the same hairdresser as his wife. His children are all fat.

Why do we envy him, the bankrupt man? He has discovered something about America that we should have known all along. He has found the premise that has eluded us. At our interview, his answers are laconic, assured, delivered with a twinkle and well-spaced, conspiratorial, delicious lowerings of his fine baritone.

Q: When did you first know that you were bankrupt?

A: I think from birth I intuited I was headed that way. I didn't cry, like other infants.

Q: Do you see any possibility for yourself of ever being non-bankrupt?

A: The instant bankruptcy is declared, laws on the federal, state, and local levels work in harmony to erode the condition. Some assets are exempted, others are sheltered. In order to maintain bankruptcy, fresh investments must be undertaken, and opportunities seized as they arise. A sharp eye on economic indicators must be kept lest the whole package slip back into the black. Being bankrupt is not a lazy man's game.

Q: Have you any word of advice for those of us who are not bankrupt?

A [with that twinkle]: Eat your hearts out.

The interview is concluded. Other appointments press. He and his family must put in a splendid appearance at the Meter Readers' Benefit Picnic. They feed grapes to one another, laughing. The children tumble in the tall grass, in their private-school uniforms. The bankrupt man's wife is beginning to look fat, sunlight dappling her shoulders. Only he maintains a hard edge, a look of bronze. He wins the quoit toss and captains the winning tug-of-war team; the other side, all solvent small-business men in gray suits, falls into the ditch. Magnanimously, he holds down to them a huge helping hand. By acclamation, he is elected to the vestry of all the local Protestant churches and eats the first piece of the Meter Readers' Bicentennial Chocolate Layer Cake.

This galls us. We wish to destroy him, this clown of legerity, who bounces higher and higher off the net of laws that would enmesh us, who weightlessly spiders up the rigging to the dizzying spotlit tip of the tent-space and stands there in a glittering trapeze suit, all white, like the chalk-daubed clown who among the Australian aborigines moves in and out of the sacred ceremonial, mocking it. We spread ugly rumors, we mutter that he is not bankrupt at all, that he is as sound as the pound, as the dollar, that his bankruptcy is a sham. He hears of the rumor and in a note on one-hundred-percent-rag stationery, with embossed letterhead, he challenges us to meet him on West Main Street, by the corner of the Corn Exchange, under the iron statue of Cyrus Shenanigan, the great Civil War profiteer. We accept the challenge. We experience butterflies in the stomach. We go look at our face in the mirror. It is craven and shrivelled, embittered by ungenerous thoughts.

Comes the dawn. Without parked cars, West Main Street seems immensely wide. The bankrupt man's shoulders eclipse the sun. He takes his paces, turns, swiftly reaches down and pulls out the lining of both pants pockets. Verily, they are empty. We fumble at our own, and the rattle of silver is drowned in the triumphant roar of the witnessing mob. We would have been torn limb from limb had not the bankrupt man with characteristic magnanimity extended to us a protective embrace, redolent of cologne and smoking turf and wood violets.

In the locker room, we hear the bankrupt man singing. His baritone strips the tiles from the walls like cascading dominoes. He has just shot a minus sixty-seven, turning the old course record inside out.

He ascends because he transcends. He deals from the bottom of the deck. He builds castles in air. He makes America grow. His interests ramify. He is in close touch with Arabian oil. With Jamaican bauxite. With antarctic refrigeration. He creates employment for squads of lawyers. He gets on his motorcycle. He tugs a thousand creditors in his wake, taking them over horizons they had never dreamt of hitherto.

He proves there is an afterlife.

THE TARBOX POLICE

Cal.

Hal.

Sam.

Dan.

One has known them since they were boys in the high school. Good-natured boys, not usually among the troublemakers, going out for each sport as its season came along, though not usually among the stars.

Indeed, they are hard to tell apart, without a close look. Cal is an inch taller than Hal, and Dan has a slightly wistful set to his jaw that differentiates him from Sam, who until you see him smile looks mean. Downtown, they don't smile much; if they started, they would never stop, since almost everybody passing by they know. If you look them in the eye for a second they will nod, however. A bit bleakly, but nod. In the summer they wear sunglasses and their eyes are not there. In their short-sleeved shirts they would melt into the summer crowd of barefooted girls and bare-chested easy riders but for the knobby black armor of equipment, strapped and buckled to their bodies in even the hottest weather: the two-way radio in its perforated case, the billy club dangling overripe from their belts, the little buttoned-up satchel of Mace, and the implausible, impossible gun, its handle peeking from the holster like the metal-and-wood snout of an eyeless baby animal riding backward on its mother's forgetful hip.

They not only know everybody, they know everything. When

dear Maddy Frothingham, divorced since she was twenty-two and not her fault, upped and married the charmer she met on some fancy island down East, it was the Tarbox police who came around and told her her new husband was a forger wanted in four states, and took him away. When Janice Tugwell fell down the cellar stairs and miscarried, it was the police who knew what house down by the river Morris's car was parked in front of, and who were kind enough not to tell her where their knock brought him to the door, fumbling with his buttons. It is the police who lock up Squire Wentworth Saturday nights so he won't disgrace himself; it is the police, when there's another fatal accident on that bad stretch of 84, who put the blanket over the body, so nobody else will have to see. Chief Chad's face, when the do-good lawyers come out from Boston to get our delinquents off, is a study in surprise, that the court should be asked to doubt things everybody *knows.* We ask them, the police, to know too much. It hardens them. Young as they are, their faces get cold, cold and prim. When in summer they put on their sunglasses, little is hidden that showed before.

They want to be invisible.

In an ideal state, they would wither away.

My wife and I had an eerie experience a year ago. Our male pup hadn't come back for his supper, and the more my wife thought about it the less she could sleep, so around midnight she got up in her nightie and we put on raincoats and went out in the convertible to search. It was a weekday night, the town looked dead. It looked like a fossil of itself, pressed white into black stone. Except downtown—the blank shop fronts glazed under the blue arc lamps, the street wide as a prairie without parked cars—there was this cluster of shadows. I thought of a riot, except that it was quiet. I thought of witchcraft, except that it was 1971. Cal was there. His blue uniform looked purple under the lights. The rest were kids, the kids that hang around on the green, the long hair and the Levis making the girls hard to distinguish. Half in the street, half on the pavement, they were having a conversation, a party in the heart of our ghostly town.

My wife found her voice and asked Cal about the dog and he

answered promptly that one had been hit but not badly by a car up near around the shopping center around four that afternoon, without a collar or a license, and we apologized about the license and explained how our little girl keeps dressing the dog in her old baby clothes and taking his collar off, and, sure enough, found the animal in the dogcatcher's barn, shivering and limping and so relieved to see us he fainted in the driveway and didn't eat for two days; but the point is the strangeness of those kids and that policeman in the middle of nowhere, having what looked like a good time. What do they talk about? Does it happen every night? Is something brewing between them? Nobody can talk to these kids, except the police. Maybe, in the world that's in the making, they're the only real things to one another, kids and police, and the rest of us, me in my convertible and my wife in her nightie, are the shadows. As we pulled away, we heard laughter.

But they have lives too. The Sunday evening the man went crazy on Prudence Street, Hal arrived in a suit as if fresh from church, and Dan wore a checked shirt and bowling shoes that sported a big number 8 on their backs. Dainty feet. Chief Chad had to feather his siren to press the cruiser through the crowd that had collected—sunburned young mothers pushing babies in strollers, a lot of old people from the nursing home up the street. All through the crowd people were telling one another stories. The man had moved here three weeks ago from Detroit. He was crazy on three days of gin. He was an acidhead. He went crazy because his wife had left him. He was a queer. He was a Vietnam veteran. His first shot from the upstairs window had hit a fire hydrant—ka-*zing!*—and the second kicked up dust under the nose of the fat beagle that sleeps by the curb there.

The crazy man was in the second story of the old Cushing place, which the new owners had fixed up for rental with that aluminum siding that looks just like clapboards unless you study the corners. The Osborne house next door, without a front yard, juts out to the pavement, and most of the crowd stayed more or less behind that, though the old folks kept pushing closer to see, and the mothers kept running into the line of fire to fetch back their toddlers, and the dogs raced around wagging the way they do at festivities.

It was strange, coming up the street, to see the cloud of gun-smoke drifting toward the junior high school, just like on television, only in better color. The police crouched down behind the cruiser, trading shots. Chief Chad was huddled behind the corner of the Osbornes', shouting into his radio. The siege lasted an hour. The crazy man, a skinny fellow in a tie-dyed undershirt, was in plain sight in the window above the porch roof, making a speech you couldn't understand and alternately reloading the two rifles he had. One of the old folks hobbled out across the asphalt to the police car and screamed, "*Kill* him! I paid good taxes for fifty years. What's the problem, he's right up there, *kill* him!" Even the crazy man went quiet to hear the old man carry on: the old guy was trembling; his face shone with tears; he kept yelling the word "taxes." Dan shielded him with his body and hustled him back to the crowd, where a nurse from the home wrestled him quiet.

The plan, it turned out, wasn't to kill anybody. The police were aiming around the window, making a sieve of that new siding, until the state police arrived with the tear gas. While the crazy man was being entertained out front, Chief Chad and a state cop sneaked into the back yard and plunked the canisters into the kitchen. The shooting died. The police went in the front door wearing masks and brought out on a stretcher a man swaddled like a newborn baby. A thin sort of baby with a sleeping green face. Though they say that at the hospital when he got his crazy consciousness back he broke all the straps and it took five men to hold him down for the injection.

"Go home!" Chief Chad shouted, shaking his rifle at the crowd. "The show's over! Damn you all, go home!"

Most people forgave him, he was overwrought.

Bits of the crowd clung to the neighborhood way past dark, telling one another what they saw or knew or guessed, giving it all a rerun. Experience is so vicarious these days, only reminiscence makes it real. One theory was that the crazy man hadn't meant to hurt anybody, or he could have winged a dozen old folks. Yes, but on the corner of the Osbornes', you can still see where a bullet came through one side and out the other, right where Chief Chad's ear had been a second before. Out of all that unreality, the bullet holes remained to be mended. It took weeks before the aluminum man showed up.

And then this March, in town meeting, the moderator got rattled and ejected a citizen. He was the new sort of citizen who have moved into the Marshview development, a young husband with a big honey-colored beard; they appear to feel the world owes them an explanation. We were on the sewer articles. We've been passing these sewer articles for years and the river never smells any better, but you pass them because the town engineer is president of Rotary and doing the best he can. Anyway, young Honeybeard had raised four or five objections, and had the selectmen up and down at the microphone like jack-in-the-boxes, and Bud Perley, moderator ever since he came back from Japan with his medals, got weary of recognizing him, and overlooked his waving hand. The boy— taxpayer, just like the old cuss at the shoot-out—had smuggled in a balloon and enough helium to float it up toward the gym ceiling.

LOVE, the balloon said.

"Eject that man," Perley said.

Who'll ever forget it? Seven hundred of us there, and we'd seen a lot of foolishness on the town-meeting floor, but we'd never seen a man ejected. Hal was over by the water bubbler, leaning against the wall, and Sam was on the opposite side joking with a bunch of high-school students up on the tumbling horses observing for their civics class. The two policemen moved at once, together. They sauntered, almost, across the front of the hall toward the center aisle.

And you saw they had billy clubs, and you saw they had guns, and nobody else did.

Actually, young Honeybeard was a friend of Sam's—they had gone smelt-fishing together that winter—and both smiled sheepishly as they touched, and the boy went out making a big "V" with his arms and people laughed and cheered and no doubt will vote him in for selectman if he runs.

But still. The two policemen had moved in unison, carefully, crabwise-cautious under their load of equipment, and you saw they were real; blundering old Perley had called them into existence, and not a mouth in that hall held more than held breath. This was it. This was power, our power hopefully to be sure, but this was *it*.

VENEZUELA FOR VISITORS

ALL VENEZUELA, except for the negligible middle class, is divided between the Indians *(los indios)* and the rich *(los ricos)*. The Indians are mostly to be found in the south, amid the muddy tributaries of the Orinoco and the god-haunted *tepuys* (mesas) that rear their fearsome mile-high crowns above the surrounding jungle, whereas the rich tend to congregate in the north, along the sunny littoral, in the burgeoning metropolis of Caracas, and on the semi-circular shores of Lake Maracaibo, from which their sumptuous black wealth is drawn. The negligible middle class occupies a strip of arid savanna in the center of the nation and a few shunned enclaves on the suburban slopes of Monte Avila.

The Indians, who range in color from mocha to Dentyne, are generally under five feet tall. Their hair style runs to pageboys and severe bangs, with some tonsures in deference to lice. Neither sex is quite naked: the males wear around their waists a thong to which their foreskins are tied, pulling their penises taut upright; the females, once out of infancy, suffer such adornments as three pale sticks symmetrically thrust into their lower faces. The gazes of both sexes are melting, brown, alert, canny. The visitor, standing among them with his Nikon FE and L. L. Bean fannypack, is shy at first, but warms to their inquisitive touches, which patter and rub across his person with a soft, sandy insistence unlike both the fumblings of children and the caresses one Caucasian adult will give another. There is an infectious, wordless ecstasy in their touches, and a blank eagerness with yet some parameters of tact and irony. *These are human presences,* the visitor comes to realize.

The rich, who range in color from porcelain to mocha, are generally under six feet tall. Their hair style runs to chignons and blow-dried trims. Either sex is elegantly clad: the males favor dark suits of medium weight (nights in Caracas can be cool), their close English cut enhanced by a slight Latin flare, and shirts with striped bodies but stark-white collars and French cuffs held by agates and gold; the females appear in a variety of gowns and mock-military pants suits, Dior and de la Renta originals flown in from Paris and New York. The gazes of both sexes are melting, brown, alert, canny. The visitor, standing among them in his funky Brooks Brothers suit and rumpled blue button-down, is shy at first, but warms to their excellent English, acquired at colleges in London or "the States," and to their impeccable manners, which conceal, as their fine clothes conceal their skins, rippling depths of Spanish and those dark thoughts that the mind phrases to itself in its native language. They tell anecdotes culled from their rich international lives; they offer, as the evening deepens, confidences, feelers, troubles. These, too, are human presences.

The Indians live in *shabonos*—roughly circular lean-tos woven beautifully of palm thatch in clearings hacked and burned out of the circumambient rain forest. A *shabono* usually rots and is abandoned within three years. The interiors are smoky, from cooking fires, and eye diseases are common among the Indians. They sleep, rest, and die in hammocks *(cinchorros)* hung as close together as pea pods on a vine. Their technology, involving in its pure state neither iron nor the wheel, is yet highly sophisticated: the chemical intricacies of curare have never been completely plumbed, and with their blowpipes of up to sixteen feet in length the Indians can bring down prey at distances of over thirty meters. They fish without hooks, by employing nets and thrashing the water with poisonous lianas. All this sounds cheerier than it is. It is depressing to stand in the gloom of a *shabono,* the palm thatch overhead infested with giant insects, the Indians drooping in their hammocks, their eyes diseased, their bellies protuberant, their faces and limbs besmirched with the same gray-brown dirt that composes the floor, their possessions a few brown baskets and monkey skins. Their lives are not paradise but full of anxiety—their religion a matter of fear, their statecraft a matter of constant, nagging war. To themselves, they are "the people" *(Yanomami)*; to others, they are "the killers" *(Waikás)*.

The rich dwell in *haciendas*—airy long ranch houses whose roofs are of curved tile and, surprisingly, dried sugar-cane stalks. Some *haciendas* surviving in Caracas date from the sixteenth century, when the great valley was all but empty. The interiors are smoky, from candlelit dinners, and contact lenses are common among the rich. The furniture is solid, black, polished by generations of servants. Large paintings by Diebenkorn, Stella, Baziotes, and Botero adorn the white plaster walls, along with lurid religious pictures in the colonial Spanish style. The appliances are all modern and paid for; even if the oil in Lake Maracaibo were to give out, vast deposits of heavy crude have been discovered in the state of Bolívar. All this sounds cheerier than it is. The rich wish they were in Paris, London, New York. Many have condominiums in Miami. *Haute couture* and abstract painting may not prove bulwark enough. Constitutional democracy in Venezuela, though the last dictator fled in 1958, is not so assured as may appear. Turbulence and tyranny are traditional. Che Guevara is still idealized among students. To themselves, the rich are good, decent, amusing people; to others, they are *"reaccionarios."*

Missionaries, many of them United States citizens, move among the Indians. They claim that since Western civilization, with all its diseases and detritus, must come, it had best come through them. Nevertheless, Marxist anthropologists inveigh against them. Foreign experts, many of them United States citizens, move among the rich. They claim they are just helping out, and that anyway the oil industry was nationalized five years ago. Nevertheless, Marxist anthropologists are not mollified. The feet of the Indians are very broad in front, their toes spread wide for climbing avocado trees. The feet of the rich are very narrow in front, their toes compressed by pointed Italian shoes. The Indians seek relief from tension in the use of *ebene,* or *yopo,* a mind-altering drug distilled from the bark of the *ebene* tree and blown into the user's nose through a hollow cane by a colleague. The rich take cocaine through the nose, and frequent mind-altering discotheques, but more customarily imbibe cognac, *vino blanco,* and Scotch, in association with colleagues.

These and other contrasts and comparisons between the Indians and the rich can perhaps be made more meaningful by the following anecdote: A visitor, after some weeks in Venezuela, was invited to fly to the top of a *tepuy* in a helicopter, which crashed. As stated, the *tepuys* are supposed by the Indians to be the forbidden haunts of the gods; and, indeed, they present an exotic, attenuated vegetation and a craggy geology to the rare intruder. The crash was a minor one, breaking neither bones nor bottles (a lavish picnic, including *mucho vino blanco,* had been packed). The bottles were consumed, the exotic vegetation was photographed, and a rescue helicopter arrived. In the Cessna back to Caracas, the survivors couldn't get enough of discussing the incident and their survival, and the red-haired woman opposite the visitor said, "I *love* the way you pronounce '*tepuy.*'" She imitated him: *tupooey.* "Real zingy," she said. The visitor slowly realized that he was being flirted with, and that therefore *this woman was middle-class.* In Venezuela, only the negligible middle class flirts. The Indians kidnap or are raped; the rich commandeer, or languorously give themselves in imperious surrender.

The Indians tend to know only three words of Spanish: "*¿Como se llama?*" ("What is your name?"). In Indian belief, to give one's name is to place oneself in the other's power. And the rich, when one is introduced, narrow their eyes and file one's name away in their mysterious depths. Power among them flows along lines of kinship and intimacy. After an imperious surrender, a rich female gazes at her visitor with new interest out of her narrowed, brown, melting, kohl-ringed eyes. He has become someone to be reckoned with, if only as a potential source of financial embarrassment. "Again, what is your name?" she asks.

Los indios and *los ricos* rarely achieve contact. When they do, *mestizos* result, and the exploitation of natural resources. In such lies the future of Venezuela.

THE CHASTE PLANET

IN LATE 1999, space explorers discovered that within the warm, turbulent, semi-liquid immensity of Jupiter a perfectly pleasant little planet twirled, with argon skies and sparkling seas of molten beryllium. The Earthlings who first arrived on the shores of this new world were shocked by the unabashed nakedness of the inhabitants. Not only were the inhabitants naked—their bodies cylindrical, slightly curved, and longitudinally ridged, like pearl-gray pickles, with six toothpick-thin limbs stuck in for purposes of locomotion, and a kind of tasselled seventh concentrating the neural functions—but there appeared to be no sexual differentiation among them. Indeed, there was none. Reproduction took place by an absentee process known as "budding," and the inhabitants of Minerva (so the planet was dubbed, by a classics-minded official of the Sino-American Space Agency) thought nothing of it. Evidently, wherever a mathematical sufficiency of overlapping footsteps (or jabs, for their locomotion left marks rather like those of ski poles in crusty snow) impressed the porous soil of intermingled nickel and asbestos, a new pickleoid form slowly sprouted, or "budded." Devoid both of parentage and of progenitive desires, this new creature, when the three Minervan years* of its maturation period brought it to full size,** eagerly shook the nickel from its roots and assumed its place in the fruitful routines of agriculture, industry,

---

*Equivalent to five earthly weeks.
**Approximately eighteen of our inches.

trade, and government that on Minerva, as on Earth, superficially dominated life.

The erotic interests of the explorers and, as argon-breathing apparatus became perfected, of the ambassadors and investigators and mercantile colonists from our own planet occasioned amazement and misunderstanding among the Minervans. The early attempts at rape were scarcely more of a success than the later attempts, by some of the new world's economically marginal natives, to prostitute themselves. The lack of satisfactory contact, however, did not prevent the expatriate Earthlings from falling in love with the Minervans, producing the usual debris of sonnets, sleepless nights, exhaustive letters, jealous fits, and supercharged dreams. The little pickle-shaped people, though no Pocahontas or Fayaway emerged among them to assuage the aliens' wonderful heat, were fascinated: how could the brief, mechanical event described (not so unlike, the scientists among them observed, the accidental preparation of their own ground for "budding") generate such giant expenditures of neural energy? "We live for love," they were assured. "Our spaceships, our skyscrapers, our stock markets are but deflections of this basic drive. Our clothes, our meals, our arts, our modes of transportation, even our wars are made to serve the cause of love. An Earthling infant takes in love with his first suck, and his dying gasp is clouded by this passion. All else is sham, disguise, and make-work."

The human colonies came to include females. This subspecies was softer and more bulbous, its aggressions more intricate and its aura more complacent; the Minervans never overcame their distaste for women, who seemed boneless and odorous and parasitic after the splendid first impression made by the early space explorers carapaced in flashing sheets of aluminum foil. These females even more strongly paid homage to the power of love: "For one true moment of it, a life is well lost. Give us love, or give us death. Our dying is but a fleck within the continuous, overarching supremacy of Eros. Love moves the stars, which you cannot see. It moves the birds, which you do not have, to song." The Minervans were dumbfounded; they could imagine no force, no presence beneath their swirling, argon-bright skies, more absolute than death—for

which the word in their language was the same as for "silence."
Then the human females, disagreeably and characteristically,
would turn the tables of curiosity. "And you?" they would ask their
little naked auditors. "What is it that makes *you* tick? Tell us. There
must be something hidden, or else Freud was a local oracle. Tell
us, what do you dream of, when your six eyes shut?" And a blue-
green blush would steal over the warty, ridged, colorless epiderms
of the Minervans, and they would titter and rustle like a patch of
artichokes, and on their slender stiff limbs scamper away, and not
emerge from their elaborate burrows until the concealment of night
—night, to Earthling senses, as rapid and recurrent as the flicker-
ings of a defective lamp.

The first clue arose from the sonnets the lovelorn spacemen used
to recite to their pickleoid enamoratas. Though the words, however
translated, came out as nonsense, the recitation itself held the
Minervans' interest, and seemed to excite them with its rhythms.
Students of the pioneer journals also noted that, by more than one
account, before prostitution was abandoned as unfeasible the
would-be courtesans offered from out of the depths of themselves
a shy, strangulated crooning, a sort of pitch-speech analogous to
Chinese. Then robot televiewers were sufficiently miniaturized to
maneuver through the Minervans' elaborate burrows. Among the
dim, shaky images beamed back from underground (the static from
the nickel was terrific) were some of rods arranged roughly in
sequence of size, and of other rods, possibly hollow, flared at one
end or laterally punctured. The televiewer had stumbled, it turned
out, upon an unguarded brothel. The objects were, of course, crude
Minervan equivalents of xylophones, trumpets, and flutes. The
ultimate reaches of many private burrows contained similar objects,
discreetly tucked where the newly budded would not find them,
as well as proto-harps, quasi-violins, and certain constructions per-
cussive in purpose. When the crawling televiewers were fitted with
audio components, the domestic tunnels and even some chambers
of the commercial complexes were revealed as teeming with a
constant, furtive music—a concept for which the only Minervan
word seemed to be the same as their word for "life."

Concurrent with these discoveries, a team of SASA alienists had persuaded a number of Minervans to submit to psychoanalysis. The pattern of dream-work, with its loaded symbolization of ladders, valves, sine curves, and hollow, polished forms, as well as the subjects' tendency under drugs to deform their speech with melodious slippage, and the critical case of one Minervan (nicknamed by the psychiatric staff Dora) who suffered from the obsessive malady known as "humming," pointed to the same conclusion as the televiewers' visual evidence: the Minervans on their sexless, muffled planet lived for music, of which they had only the most primitive inkling.

In the exploitative rush that followed this insight, tons of nickel were traded for a song. Spies were enlisted in the Earth's service for the bribe of a plastic harmonica; entire cabinets and corporation boards were corrupted by the promise of a glimpse of a clarinet-fingering diagram, or by the playing of an old 78-rpm "Muskrat Ramble." At the first public broadcast of a symphony, Brahms's Fourth in E Minor, the audience of Minervans went into convulsions of ecstasy as the strings yielded the theme to the oboe, and would doubtless have perished *en masse* had not the sound engineer mercifully lifted the needle and switched to the Fred Waring arrangement of "American Patrol." Even so, many Minervans, in that epoch of violated innocence, died of musical overdose, and many more wrote confessional articles, formed liberational political parties, and engaged, with sometimes disappointing results, in group listening.

What music meant to the Minervans, it was beyond the ken of Earthlings to understand. That repetitive mix of thuds, squeaks, and tintinnabulation, an art so mechanical that Mozart could scribble off some of the best between billiard shots, seemed perhaps to them a vibration implying all vibrations, a resolution of the most inward, existential antagonisms, a synthesizing interface—it has been suggested—between the nonconductivity of their asbestos earth and the high conductivity of their argon sky. There remained about the Minervans' musicality, even after it had been thoroughly exploited and rapaciously enlarged, something fastidious, balanced, and wary. A confused ancient myth gave music the resonance of the forbidden. In their Heaven, music occurred without instruments, as it were inaudibly. An elderly Minervan, wishing to memorialize his life, would remember it almost exclusively in terms of music he had heard, or had made.

When the first Minervans were rocketed to Earth (an odyssey deserving its own epic: the outward flight through the thousands of miles of soupy hydrogen that constituted Jupiter's thick skull; the breakthrough into space and first sight of the stars, the black universe; the backward glance at the gaseous stripes and raging red spot dwindling behind them; the parabolic fall through the solar system, wherein the Minervans, dazzled by its brightness, mistook Venus for their destination, their invaders' home, instead of the watery brown sphere that expanded beneath them, and cushioned their fall), the visitors were shocked by the ubiquitous public presence of music. Leaking from restaurant walls, beamed into airplanes as they landed and automobiles as they crashed, chiming from steeples, thundering from parade grounds, tingling through apartment walls, carried through the streets in small boxes, violating even the peace of the desert and the forest, where drive-ins featured blue musical comedies, music at first overwhelmed, then delighted, then disgusted, and finally bored them. They removed the ear stopples that had initially guarded them from too keen a dose of pleasure; surfeit muffled them; they ceased to hear. The Minervans had discovered impotence.

1975

INVASION OF
THE BOOK ENVELOPES

SMALL PUDDLES of gray fluff had been appearing for years on office floors and in the vestibules of suburban homes, but no one paid attention. An occasional book reviewer or mail clerk showed up in city-hospital out-patient clinics bearing the tiny double marks of "staple stab" all over their thumbs, but it never made the newspapers. It was not until the iron-gray fluff was augmented by a ubiquitous snow of magnetized white plastic pellets and entire secretarial staffs were incapacitated with digital cuts and sprained wrists suffered while wrestling with thread-reinforced strapping tape that the full scope of the horror dawned upon the public—by which time the plague was far advanced. The book envelopes and their deadly, drifting spore were everywhere.

From what dying star had they been launched into space, and upon what deserted patch of our planet had they made their unwitnessed landing? Northern New Jersey seemed the best guess. No one could remember when they had not existed, when books had been simply wrapped in brown paper and string, like everything else. At first, the envelopes had parted with their contents easily, releasing what seemed a negligible spattering of dull-colored matter as innocuous as the woolly beige corymbs maple trees drop in the spring. Then their staples seemed to lengthen and to become baroquely tenacious in shape, so that only a prolonged struggle pried open the limp brown pods, with a proportionately lavish dissemination of the ominous fluff. People began to notice the book envelopes piling up in corners of their basements and garages, with no recollection of who had put them there. The post offices, in a move whose dire significance was grasped only in vain retrospect, began to sell the things—disarmingly named "mailers," after a civic-minded, prize-winning author of the era—over the counter, in every precinct and hamlet. The infiltration had spread to the top levels of government, and soon contaminated the entire globe.

Distracted by tension abroad and economic malaise at home, the nation did not concern itself with the strangely swelling bales being unloaded by "banana boats" in New Orleans and Galveston and "macadamia freighters" along the vulnerable, already fad-ridden West Coast. A mutant third species of book envelope entered from Japan, lined with a plastic bubble-paper that children in their innocence loved to pop, releasing odorless vapors into the atmosphere. Paid experts pooh-poohed any correlation between bubble-paper and acid rain. Canada, long regarded by the anti-envelopment underground as a refuge, ceased to be so when André Jiffy was elected Prime Minister and ordered the border stapled shut.

Within the tormented maze of the U.S. Postal Service regulations was born the rumor that strapping tape had become obligatory, rendering each envelope impervious to mechanical attack. All fourth-class mail, the lifeblood of an educated citizenry, now travelled back and forth unopenable. Drifts of fluff reached knee-high into the Rockies. The President and his joint security chiefs had themselves shipped to Bimini via UPS, and over the radio rustling, muffled spokesthings declared the country to be sixty percent recycled fibres and entirely under the rule of a tan, pre-stamped junta, in a variety of handy sizes.

Somewhere near the dotted Mason-Dixon Line, the last human voice expired, crying, "Pull here!"

1981

GOLF DREAMS

THEY STEAL upon the sleeping mind while winter steals upon the landscape, sealing the inviting cups beneath sheets of ice, cloaking the contours of the fairway in snow.

I am standing on a well-grassed tee with my customary summer foursome, whose visages yet have something shifting and elusive about them. I am getting set to drive; the fairway before me is a slight dog-leg right, very tightly lined with trees, mostly conifers. As I waggle and lift my head to survey once more the intended line of flight, further complications have been imposed: the air above the fairway has been interwoven with the vines and wooden cross-pieces of an arbor, presumably grape, and the land seems to drop away no longer with a natural slope but in nicely hedged terraces. Nevertheless, I accept the multiplying difficulties calmly, and try to allow for them in my swing, which is intently contemplated but never achieved, for I awake with the club at its apogee, waiting for my left side to pull it through and to send the ball toward that bluish speck of openness beyond the vines, between the all but merged forests.

It is a feature of dream golf that the shot never decreases in difficulty but instead from instant to instant melts, as it were, into deeper hardship. A ball, for instance, lying at what the dreaming golfer gauges to be a 7-iron distance from the green, has become, while he glanced away, cylindrical in shape—a roll of coins in a paper wrapper, or a plastic bottle of pills. Nevertheless, he swings, and as he swings he realizes that the club in his hands bears a rubber tip, a little red-rubber tab the color of a crutch tip, but limp. The rubber flips negligibly across the cylindrical "ball," which meanwhile appears to be sinking into a small trough having to do, no doubt, with the sprinkler system. Yet, most oddly, the dreamer surrenders not a particle of hope of making the shot. In this instance, indeed, I seem to recall making, on my second or third swing, crisp contact, and striding in the direction of the presumed flight with a springy, expectant sensation.

After all, are these nightmares any worse than the "real" drive that skips off the toe of the club, strikes the prism-shaped tee marker, and is swallowed by weeds some twenty yards *behind* the horrified driver? Or the magical impotence of an utter whiff? Or the bizarre physical comedy of a soaring slice that strikes the one telephone wire strung across three hundred acres? The golfer is so habituated to humiliation that his dreaming mind never offers any protest of implausibility. Whereas dream life, we are told, is a therapeutic caricature, seamy side out, of real life, dream golf is simply golf played on another course. We chip from glass tables onto moving stairways; we swing in a straitjacket, through masses of cobweb, and awake not with any sense of unjust hazard but only with a regret that the round can never be completed, and that one of our phantasmal companions has kept the scorecard in his pocket.

Even the fair companion sleeping beside us has had a golf dream, with a feminist slant. An ardent beginner, she says, "I was playing with these men, I don't know who they were, and they kept using woods when we were on the green, so of course the balls would fly miles away, and then they had to hit all the way back. I thought to myself, *They aren't using the right club,* and I took my putter out and, of course, I kept *beating* them!"

"Didn't they see what you were doing, and adjust their strokes accordingly?"

"No, they didn't seem to *get* it, and I wasn't going to tell them. I kept *win*ning, and it was *won*derful," she insists.

We gaze at each other across the white pillows, in the morning light filtered through icicles, and realize we were only dreaming. Our common green hunger begins to gnaw afresh, insatiable.

THIRTEEN WAYS OF
LOOKING AT THE MASTERS

1. As an Event in Augusta, Georgia

IN THE MIDDLE of downtown Broad Street a tall white monument
—like an immensely heightened wedding cake save that in place
of the bride and groom stands a dignified Confederate officer—
proffers the thought that

> No nation rose so white and fair;
> None fell so pure of crime.

Within a few steps of the monument, a movie theater, during
Masters Week in 1979, was showing *Hair,* full of cheerful mis-
cegenation and anti-military song and dance.

This is the Deep/Old/New South, with its sure-enough levees,
railroad tracks, unpainted dwellings out of illustrations to Joel
Chandler Harris, and stately homes ornamented by grillework and
verandas. As far up the Savannah River as boats could go, Augusta
has been a trading post since 1717 and was named in 1735 by James
Oglethorpe for the mother of George III. It changed hands several
times during the Revolutionary War, thrived on tobacco and cot-
ton, imported textile machinery from Philadelphia in 1828, and
during the Civil War housed the South's largest powder works.
Sherman passed through here, and didn't leave much in the way
of historical sites.

The Augusta National Golf Club is away from the business end of town, in a region of big brick houses embowered in magnolia and dogwood. A lot of people retire to Augusta, and one of the reasons that Bobby Jones wanted to build a golf course here, instead of near his native Atlanta, was the distinctly milder climate. The course, built in 1931–32 on the site of the Fruitlands Nursery property, after designs by Dr. Alister Mackenzie (architect of Cypress Point) and Jones himself, has the venerable Augusta Country Club at its back, and at its front, across Route 28, an extensive shopping-center outlay. At this point the New South becomes indistinguishable from New Jersey.

2. As an Event Not in Augusta, Georgia

How many Augusta citizens are members of the Augusta National Golf Club? The question, clearly in bad taste, brought raised eyebrows and a muttered "Very few" or, more spaciously, "Thirty-eight or forty." The initial membership fee is rumored to be $50,000, there is a waiting list five years long, and most of the members seem to be national Beautiful People, Golfing Subspecies, who jet in for an occasional round during the six months the course is open. When Ike, whose cottage was near the clubhouse, used to show up and play a twosome with Arnold Palmer, the course would be cleared by the Secret Service. Cliff Roberts, chairman of the tournament from its inception in 1934 until his death in 1977, was a Wall Street investment banker; his chosen successor, William H. Lane, is a business executive from faraway Houston.

A lot of Augusta's citizens get out of town during Masters Week, renting their houses. The lady in the drugstore near the house my wife and I were staying in told me she had once gone walking on the course. *Once:* the experience seemed unrepeatable. The course had looked deserted to her, but then a voice shouted "Fore" and a ball struck near her. The ghost of Lloyd Mangrum, perhaps. The only Augustans conspicuous during the tournament are the black caddies, who know the greens so well they can call a putt's break to the inch while standing on the fringe.

3. As a Study in Green

Green grass, green grandstands, green concession stalls, green paper cups, green folding chairs and visors for sale, green-and-white ropes, green-topped Georgia pines, a prevalence of green in the slacks and jerseys of the gallery, like the prevalence of red in the crowd in Moscow on May Day. The caddies' bright green caps and Sam Snead's bright green trousers. If justice were poetic, Hubert Green would win it every year.

4. As a Rite of Spring

"It's become a rite of spring," a man told me with a growl, "like the Derby." Like Fort Lauderdale. Like Opening Day at a dozen ballparks. Spring it was, especially for us Northerners who had left our gray skies, brown lawns, salt-strewn highways, and plucky little croci for this efflorescence of azaleas and barefoot *jeunes filles en fleurs*. Most of the gallery, like most of the golfers, had Southern accents. This Yankee felt a little as if he were coming in late on a round of equinoctial parties that had stretched from Virginia to Florida. A lot of young men were lying on the grass betranced by the memories of last night's libations, and a lot of matronly voices continued discussing Aunt Earlene's unfortunate second marriage, while the golf balls floated overhead. For many in attendance, the Masters is a ritual observance; some of the old-timers wore sun hats festooned with over twenty years' worth of admission badges.

Will success as a festival spoil the Masters as a sporting event? It hasn't yet, but the strain on the tournament's famous and exemplary organization can be felt. Ticket sales are limited, but the throng at the main scoreboard is hard to squeeze by. The acreage devoted to parking would make a golf course in itself. An army of over two thousand policemen, marshals, walkway guards, salespersons, trash-gleaners, and other attendants is needed to maintain order and facilitate the pursuit of happiness. To secure a place by any green it is necessary to arrive at least an hour before there is anything to watch.

When, on the last two days, the television equipment arrives, the crowd itself is watched. Dutifully, it takes its part as a mammoth unpaid extra in a national television spectacular. As part of it, patting out courteous applause at a good shot or groaning in chorus at a missed putt, one felt, slightly, *canned*.

5. As a Fashion Show

Female fashions, my wife pointed out, came in three strata. First, young women decked out as if going to a garden party—makeup, flowing dresses, sandals. Next, the trim, leathery generation of the mothers, dressed as if they themselves were playing golf—short skirts, sun visors, cleated two-tone shoes. Last, the generation of the grandmothers, in immaculately blued hair and amply filled pants suits in shades we might call electric pastel or Day-Glo azalea.

6. As a Display Case for Sam Snead and Arnold Palmer

Though they no longer are likely to win, you wouldn't know it from their charismas. Snead, with his rakishly tilted panama and slightly pushed-in face—a face that has known both battle and merriment—swaggers around the practice tee like the Sheriff of Golf County, testing a locked door here, hanging a parking ticket there. On the course, he remains a golfer one has to call beautiful, from the cushioned roll of his shoulders as he strokes the ball to the padding, panther-like tread with which he follows it down the center of the fairway, his chin tucked down while he thinks apparently rueful thoughts. He is one of the great inward golfers, those who wrap the dazzling difficulty of the game in an impassive, effortless flow of movement. When, on the green, he stands beside his ball, faces the hole, and performs the curious obeisance of his "side-winder" putting stroke, no one laughs.

And Palmer, he of the unsound swing, a hurried slash that ends as though he is snatching back something hot from a fire, remains the monumental outward golfer, who invites us into the game to share with him its heady turmoil, its call for constant courage.

Every inch an agonist, Palmer still hitches his pants as he mounts the green, still strides between the wings of his army like Hector on his way to yet more problematical heroism. Age has thickened him, made him look almost muscle-bound, and has grizzled his thin, untidy hair; but his deportment more than ever expresses vitality, a love of life and of the game that rebounds to him, from the multitudes, as fervent gratitude. Like us golfing commoners, he risks looking bad for the sake of some fun.

Of the younger players, only Lanny Wadkins communicates Palmer's reckless determination, and only Fuzzy Zoeller has the captivating blitheness of a Jimmy Demaret or a Lee Trevino. The Masters, with its clubby lifetime qualification for previous winners, serves as an annual exhibit of Old Masters, wherein one can see the difference between the reigning, college-bred pros, with their even teeth, on-camera poise, and abstemious air, and the older crowd, who came up from caddie sheds, drove themselves in cars along the dusty miles of the Tour, and hustled bets with the rich to make ends meet. Golf expresses the man, as every weekend foursome knows; amid the mannerly lads who dominate the money list, Palmer and Snead loom as men.

7. As an Exercise in Spectatorship

In no other sport must the spectator move. The builders and improvers of Augusta National built mounds and bleachers for the crowds to gain vantage from, and a gracefully written pamphlet by the founder, Robert Jones, is handed out as instruction in the art of "letting the Tournament come to us instead of chasing after it." Nevertheless, as the field narrows and the interest of the hordes focuses, the best way to see anything is to hang back in the woods and use binoculars. Seen from within the galleries, the players become tiny walking dolls, glimpsable, like stars on a night of scudding clouds, in the gaps between heads.

Examples of Southern courtesy in the galleries: (1) When my wife stood to watch an approach to the green, the man behind her mildly observed, "Ma'am, it was awful nice when you were sittin' down." (2) A gentleman standing next to me, not liking the smell of a cigar I was smoking, offered to buy it from me for a dollar.

Extraordinary event in the galleries: on the fourth hole a ball set in flight by Dow Finsterwald solidly struck the head of a young man sitting beside the green. The sound of a golf ball on a skull is remarkably like that of two blocks of wood knocked together. *Glock.* Flesh hurts; bone makes music.

Single instance of successful spectatorship by this reporter: I happened to be in the pines left of the seventh fairway on the first day of play, wondering whether to go for another of the refreshment committee's standardized but economical ham sandwiches, when Art Wall, Jr., hooked a ball near where I was standing. Only a dozen or so gathered to watch his recovery; for a moment, then, we could breathe with a player and experience with him—as he waggled, peered at obtruding branches, switched clubs, and peered at the branches again—that quintessential golfing sensation, the loneliness of the bad-ball hitter.

Sad truth, never before revealed: by sticking to a spot in the stands or next to the green, one can view the field coming through, hitting variants of the same shots and putts, and by listening to the massed cheers and grunts from the other greens, one can guess at dramas unseen; but the unified field, as Einstein discovered in a more general connection, is unapprehendable, and the best way to witness a golf tournament is at the receiving end of a television signal. Many a fine golf reporter, it was whispered to me, never leaves the set in the press tent.

The other sad truth about golf spectatorship is that for today's pros it all comes down to the putting, and that the difference between a putt that drops and one that rims the cup, though teleologically enormous, is intellectually negligible.

8. As a Study in Turf-Building

A suburban lawn-owner can hardly look up from admiring the weedless immensity of the Augusta National turf. One's impression, when first admitted to this natural Oz, is that a giant putting surface has been dropped over acres of rolling terrain, with a few apertures for ponds and trees to poke through. A philosophy of golf is expressed in Jones's pamphlet: "The Augusta National has much more fairway and green area than the average course. There is little punishing rough and very few bunkers. The course is not intended so much to punish severely the wayward shot as to reward adequately the stroke played with skill—and judgment."

It is an intentional paradox, then, that this championship course is rather kind to duffers. The ball sits up on Augusta's emerald carpet looking big as a baseball. It was not always such; in 1972, an invasion of *Poa annua,* a white-spiked vagabond grass, rendered conditions notoriously bumpy; in remedy a fescue called Pennlawn and a rye called Pennfine were implanted on the fairways and greens respectively and have flourished. Experimentation continues; to make the greens even harder and slicker, they are thinking of rebuilding them on a sand base—and have already done so on the adjacent par-three course.

From May to October, when the course is closed to play, everything goes to seed and becomes a hayfield, and entire fairways are plowed up: a harrowing thought. The caddies, I was solemnly assured, never replace a divot; they just sprinkle grass seed from a pouch they carry. Well, this is a myth, for I repeatedly saw caddies replace divots in the course of the tournament, with the care of tile-setters.

9. As Demography

One doesn't have to want to give the country back to the Indians to feel a nostalgic pang while looking at old photos of the pre–World War II tournaments, with their hatted, necktied galleries strolling up the fairways in the wake of the baggy-trousered players, and lining the tees and greens only one man deep.

The scores have grown crowded, too. The best then would be among the best now—Lloyd Mangrum's single-round 64 in 1940 has not been bettered, though for the last two years it has been equalled. But the population of the second-best has increased, producing virtually a new winner each week of the Tour, and stifling the emergence of stable constellations of superstars like Nelson-Hogan-Snead and Palmer-Player-Nicklaus. In the 1936 and 1938 Masters, only seven players made the thirty-six-hole score of 145 that cut the 1979 field to forty-five players. Not until 1939 did the winner break 280 and not again until 1948. The last total over 280 to win it came in 1973. In 1936, Craig Wood had a first-day round of 88 and finished in the top two dozen. In 1952, Sam Snead won the Masters in spite of a third-round 77. That margin for intermittent error has been squeezed from tournament golf. Johnny Miller chops down a few trees, develops the wrong muscles, and drops like a stone on the lists. Arnold Palmer, relatively young and still strong and keen, can no longer ram the putts in from twenty feet, and becomes a father figure. A cruel world, top-flight golf, that eats its young.

10. As Race Relations

A Martian skimming overhead in his saucer would have to conclude that white Earthlings hit the ball and black Earthlings fetch it, that white men swing the sticks and black men carry them. The black caddies of Augusta, in their white coveralls, are a tradition that needs a symbolic breaking, the converse of Lee Elder's playing in the tournament.

To be fair, these caddies are specialists of a high order, who take a cheerful pride in their expertise and who are, especially during Masters Week, well paid for it. Gary Player's caddie for his spectacular come-from-nowhere victory of 1978 was tipped $10,000—a sum that, this caddie assured an impudent interrogator, was still safe in the bank. In the New South, blacks work side by side with whites in the concession stands and at the fairway ropes, though I didn't see any in a green marshal's coat. I was unofficially informed that, at the very time when civil rightists were agitating for a black player to be invited to play even if one did not earn qualification—as Elder did in 1975—blacks were not being admitted to the tournament *as spectators*. I wonder about this. On pages 26–27 of the green souvenir album with a text by Cliff Roberts, one can see a photograph of Henry Picard hitting out of a bunker; behind him in the scattering of spectators are a number of ebony gentlemen not dressed as caddies. At any rate, though golf remains a white man's game, it presents in the Masters player and caddie an active white-black partnership in which the white man is taking the advice and doing the manual work. Caddies think of the partnership as "we," as in "We hit a drive down the center and a four-iron stiff to the pin, but then *he* missed the putt."

11. As Class Relations

Though the Augusta National aspires to be the American St. Andrews, there is a significant economic difference between a Scottish golf links thriftily pinked out on a wasteland—the sandy seaside hills that are "links"—and the American courses elaborately, expensively carved from farmland and woods. Though golf has plebeian Scottish roots, in this country its province is patrician. A course requires capital and flaunts that ancient aristocratic prerogative, land. In much of the world, this humbling game is an automatic symbol of capitalist-imperialist oppression; a progressive African novelist, to establish a character as a villain, has only to show him coming off a golf course. And in our own nation, for all the roadside driving ranges and four o'clock factory leagues, golf remains for millions something that happens at the end of a long driveway, beyond the MEMBERS ONLY sign.

Yet competitive golf in the United States came of age when, at The Country Club, in Brookline, Massachusetts, a twenty-year-old ex-caddie and workingman's son, Francis Ouimet, beat the British legends Vardon and Ray in a playoff for the U.S. Open. And ever since, the great competitors have tended to come from the blue-collar level of golf, the caddies and the offspring of club pros. Rare is the Bobby Jones who emerges from the gentry with the perfectionistic drive and killer instinct that make a champion in this game which permits no let-up or loss of concentration, yet which penalizes tightness also. Hagen acted like a swell and was called Sir

Walter, but he came up from a caddie's roost in Rochester. The lords of golf have been by and large gentlemen made and not born, while the clubs and the management of the Tour remain in the hands of the country-club crowd. When genteel Ed Sneed and Tom Watson fell into a three-way playoff for the 1979 Masters title, you knew in your bones it was going to be the third player, a barbarian called Fuzzy with a loopy all-out swing, who would stroll through the gates and carry off the loot.

12. As a Parade of Lovely Golfers, No Two Alike

Charles Coody, big-beaked bird. Billy Casper, once the king of touch, now sporting the bushy white sideburns of a turn-of-the-century railroad conductor, still able to pop them up from a sand-trap and sink the putt. Trevino, so broad across he looks like a reflection in a funhouse mirror, a model of delicacy around the greens and a model of affable temperament everywhere. Player, varying his normal black outfit with white slacks, his bearing so full of fight and muscle he seems to be restraining himself from breaking into a run. Nicklaus, Athlete of the Decade, still golden but almost gaunt and faintly grim, as he feels a crown evaporating from his head. Gay Brewer, heavy in the face and above the belt, nevertheless uncorking a string-straight mid-iron to within nine inches of the long seventh hole in the par-three tournament. Miller Barber, Truman Capote's double, punching and putting his way to last year's best round, a storm-split 64 in two installments. Bobby Clampett, looking too young and thin to be out there. Andy Bean, looking too big to be out there, and with his perennially puzzled expression seeming to be searching for a game more his size. Hubert Green, with a hunched flicky swing that would make a high-school golf coach scream. Tom Weiskopf, the handsome embodiment of pained near-perfection. Hale Irwin, the picture-book golfer with the face of a Ph.D. candidate. Johnny Miller, looking heavier than we remember him, patiently knocking them out on the practice tee, wondering where the lightning went. Ben Crenshaw, the smiling Huck Finn, and Tom Watson, the more pensive

Tom Sawyer, who, while the other boys were whitewashing fences, has become, politely but firmly, the best golfer in the world.

And many other redoubtable young men. Seeing them up close, in the dining room or on the clubhouse veranda, one is struck by how young and in many cases how slight they seem, with their pert and telegenic little wives—boys, really, anxious to be polite and to please even the bores and boors that collect in the interstices of all well-publicized events. Only when one sees them at a distance, as they walk alone or chatting in twos down the great green emptiness of the fairway, does one sense that each youth is the pinnacle of a buried pyramid of effort and investment, of prior competition from pre-teen level up, of immense and it must be at times burdensome accumulated hopes of parents, teachers, backers. And with none of the group hypnosis and exhilaration of team play to relieve them. And with the difference between success and failure so feather-fine.

13. As a Religious Experience

The four days of 1979's Masters fell on Maundy Thursday, Good Friday, Holy Saturday, and Easter Sunday. On Good Friday, fittingly, the skies darkened, tornadoes were predicted, and thousands of sinners ran for cover. My good wife, who had gone to divine services, was prevented from returning to the course by the flood of departing cars, and the clear moral is one propounded from many a pulpit: golf and churchgoing do not mix. Easter Sunday also happened to be the anniversary of the assassination of Abraham Lincoln and the sinking of the *Titanic,* and it wasn't such a good day for Ed Sneed either.

About ninety-nine percent of the gallery, my poll of local vibes indicated, was rooting for Sneed to hold off disaster and finish what he had begun. He had played splendidly for three days, and it didn't seem likely he'd come this close soon again. When he birdied the fifteenth and enlarged his once huge cushion back to three strokes, it seemed he would do it. But then, through no flagrant fault of his own, he began "leaking." We all knew how it felt, the slippery struggle to nurse a good round back to the clubhouse. On the seventeenth green, where I was standing, his approach looked no worse than his playing partner's; it just hit a foot too long, skipped onto the sloping back part of the green, and slithered into the fringe. His putt back caught the cup but twirled away. And his putt to save par, which looked to me like a gimme, lipped out, the same way my two-footers do when I lift my head to watch them drop, my sigh of relief all prepared. Zoeller, ten minutes before, had gently rolled in a birdie from much farther away. Sneed's fate seemed sealed then: the eighteenth hole, a famous bogey-maker, waited for him as ineluctably as Romeo's missed appointment with Juliet.

He hadn't hit bad shots, and he hadn't panicked; he just was screwed a half-turn too tight to get a par. The gallery of forty thousand felt for him, right to the pits of our golf-weary stomachs, when his last hope of winning it clean hung on the lip of the seventy-second hole. It so easily might have been otherwise. But then that's life, and that's golf.

NEW ENGLAND

The First Kiss

THE MANY-HEADED MONSTER called the Fenway Faithful yesterday resumed its romance with twenty-five youngish men in red socks who last year broke its monstrous big heart. Just showing up on so dank an Opening Day was an act of faith. But the wet sky dried to a mottled pewter, the tarpaulin was rolled off the infield and stuffed into a mailing tube, and we Faithful braced for the first kiss of another prolonged entanglement.

Who can forget the ups and downs of last year's fling? First, the Supersox; then, the unravelling. Our eyeballs grew calluses, watching Boomer swing from the heels and Hobson throw to the stars. Dismal nights watching the Royals play pinball with our heroes on that plastic prairie in Kansas City. Dreadful days losing count of Yankee singles in the four-game massacre. Fisk standing ever more erect and stoic at the plate, looking more and more like a Civil War memorial financed with Confederate dollars. The Noble Lost Cause.

In September, the mini-resurrection, Zimmer's last stand, the miraculous last week of no losses, waiting for the Yankees to drop one. Which they did. And then, the cruellest tease, the playoff game surrendered to a shoestring catch and a shortstop's cheap home run. Enough. You'll never get us to care again, Red Sox.

But monsters have short memories, elastic hearts, and very fool-

---

An account of the baseball season's Opening Day in Fenway Park, on April 5, 1979, for the Boston *Globe*.

able faculties, as many an epic attests. From natty-looking to nasty-looking, the fans turned out. "We Miss Louis and Bill," one large cardboard complained. "Windsor Locks Loves the Sox!" a bed-sheet benignly rhymed. Some fellow behind us exhaled a sweetish smell, but the dragon's breath was primarily flavored with malt.

Governor King was booed royally. Power may or may not cor-rupt, but it does not win friends. A lady from Dedham not only sang all the high notes in "The Star-Spangled Banner" but put in an extra one of her own, taking "free" up and out of the ballpark. We loved it. Monsters love high notes and hoards of gold.

The two teams squared off against each other in a state of statisti-cal virginity. Every man in both lineups was batting .000. On the other hand, both pitchers had earned-run averages of 0.00. And every fielder there had thus far played errorless ball.

Eckersley looked quick. A moment of sun made some of the windows of the Prudential Center sparkle. The new Red Sox uni-forms appeared tight as outfits for trapeze artists but otherwise struck the proper conservative note, for a team of millionaires: buttons on the shirt and a single red pinstripe. Eckersley yielded a double and then struck out two. The first nicks in statistical virginity had been taken. The season had begun.

Rick Wise didn't look so quick. Jim Rice began to earn his money immediately, singling. Next time up, he looked even more intense than usual and homered to center field, scoring Remy and Burleson ahead of him, and we were back in Sox heaven, where extra bases flow like milk and honey and whence the ghosts of Jimmy Foxx and Johnny Mize, Jackie Jensen and Theodore Wil-liams, Walt Dropo and Clyde Vollmer look smiling down. Before the gray day's long work was over, Lynn had launched a rocket high over right field, Evans had artfully found the corner of the left-field net, and Brohamer and Montgomery had offered speci-mens of that rarest of base hits, the triple. Seven runs scored while Eckersley, his long hair seeming to grow while we watched, al-lowed two hits. This first kiss tingled down to the toes.

The last inning seemed designed just to remind us that bad things can happen. A walk, an error, a wild pitch. Still, no harm done, and the monster went home happy.

It's a long season. Even an individual game seems long enough. By the sixth inning, that capillary action had begun in the stands that shows the crowd is leaving. What auguries did the Faithful take away, to mull in the gloomy bars of the Back Bay or contemplate among the burgeoning daffodils of suburbia?

Well, we learned that umpires recruited from Buzzards Bay, North Andover, and Hyannis can maintain law and order in the major leagues.*

We learned that Bob Montgomery and Jack Brohamer, filling in momentarily for the legendary Fisk and doughty Hobson, don't look like spare parts at all.

We saw that Freddy Lynn may this year remind us of his former super self. Stay well, Freddy.**

We saw that Jim Rice can strike out (twice) as well as get hits (two). Still, this is the heart of the club. Other players shine; Rice glitters, as if faceted. Only a Mercedes looks as nicely tooled.

We witnessed a little by-play at the beginning that may tell it all. After the Cleveland lineup had been called out, the Red Sox roll began with Zimmer. Out he trotted, last year's anti-hero, the manager who watched ninety-nine victories be not quite enough, with his lopsided cheeks and squint, like a Popeye who has let the spinach settle to his middle. The many-headed monster booed furiously, and Zimmer laughed, shaking hands with his opposite manager, Torborg.

That laugh said a strange thing. It said, *This is fun.* Baseball is meant to be fun, and not all the solemn money men in fur-collared greatcoats, not all the scruffy media cameramen and sour-faced reporters that crowd around the dugouts can quite smother the exhilarating spaciousness and grace of this impudently relaxed

---

*This was the spring of the major-league umpires' strike.

**He did, and enjoyed his best season—the league batting title at .333, and thirty-nine home runs, matching Rice. But the club finished eleven and a half games behind Baltimore, taking what satisfaction it could in nosing out the hated Yankees by two games. Zimmer was fired at season's end, and a year later Fisk, Lynn, Burleson, and Hobson were all traded away; thus was dismantled one more of those highly talented Red Sox teams that deserved better luck, or better pitching, than they got.

sport, a game of innumerable potential redemptions and curious disappointments. This is fun.

A hard lesson for a hungry monster to master, but he has six months to work on it. So let's play ball.

Out There

WENT UP to Newburyport, Massachusetts, to view the Ross's gull that has materialized between there and Salisbury. North American bird-watching event of the century. Ross's gull a denizen of Siberia —rare even there. Bird first sighted several months ago; report disregarded by the local Audubon Society. Sighted again, and now believers come from thousands of miles away—from Tennessee and California, from redwood forest and Gulf Stream waters. Newburyport sleepy little city of sixteen thousand. Flourished during China trade, rested on its oars since. Known best for Towle silver and J. P. Marquand hitherto. Day a Sunday, sunny, chill. Approached from the south, past dark seventeenth-century houses, white eighteenth-century houses, village green with hockey players on icy pond. Took turnoff to Plum Island, proceeded east along Water Street. Out-of-state cars in evidence; bird-watchers sighted. Markings: down parkas, woolly hats, sensible boots, roseate cheeks, eyes ringed by binoculars, eager intent expressions. Characteristic cry: "He's out there! He's out there somewhere!"

"Out there" referred to wide estuary where Merrimack River disposes of itself into the sea. Narrow line of bright houses on other side. In middle, steely blue water ebbing from high tide, with white gulls circling, hopping, feeding as mud flats emerged. Which gull Ross's? Lifted binoculars to eyes, poked an eye. Gulls still looked the same, through binoculars and tears. Nature less organized than zoo. Ross's gull, apparently under illusion it was just another gull, refused to come forward and take bow.

Proceeded by foot along Water Street, toward seawall where bird-watchers were flocking most hungrily. Binoculars, telescopes

Written for *The New Yorker*'s "Talk of the Town" section in March 1975.

—more glass than at a cocktail party in Lever House. Mature watchers distinguished from counterculture fledglings by length of apparatus, thickness of clothing. Happy staring elderly faces. Looked in general direction of stare—same mess of white spots. Tide running out and gulls settling down. Stir of excitement among watchers. Cry: "There he is! I got him, got him!" Answering call: "Where? Where?" Man with tripodded telescope, head cocked, eye asquint, went into song: "See the red triangle? See the church roof, just under the triangle? To the left of the church roof, see four gulls in a line? No, five. He's the one on the end. No, there he goes. He's the third from the end. No, the second. He's flying right. There he goes down. See him? You have to see him. Now I've lost him." Answering song: "There's two black ducks, just past that patch of, like, seaweed. He's just over the duck on the left, over and to the right. You can tell because he's smaller. He doesn't even fly like the others. There's more of a flip to his downbeat. God, it's him! It's beautiful!" Telescopes all trained in the same direction now. Bird-watchers in full cry: "Can you see the triangular tail? The roseate flush? Do you have the roseate breast flush? The wings, the dusky underside. Nobody ever said there was a dusky underside!" Cameras snapping, cars stopping, tripods scraping. Same old patch of jiggling white dots to us.

Looked through neighbor watcher's telescope. Saw quivering blur. Breeze making the telescope tremble. Thanked very much, tried own binoculars again. Way out—world of their own—gulls posing on shiny mud, above own reflections. Something dandyish about their white, their quickness. Like *promeneurs* at the races. Eying mud, one another, horizon, sky. Four in a row, behind black ducks. Second from end looked smaller, seemed to move in more flitting fashion. Oriental grace. May have imagined it. Saw no rosy breast, no red feet, as *Times* had promised. Triangular tail moot. Eyes went blurry again, hands hurting from cold. Excitement of fellow bird-watchers no longer warming influence. Wondered if Ross's gull (if Ross's gull) felt strange amid bigger, New England gulls. Bird we saw (if Ross's gull) seemed at home, jaunty, on top of strange situation. Could see us, no doubt, better than we saw it. Went home (us, not gull) with a song in our hearts.

Going Barefoot

WHEN I THINK of the Vineyard, my ankles feel good—bare, airy, lean. Full of bones. I go barefoot there in recollection, and the island as remembered becomes a medley of pedal sensations: the sandy rough planks of Dutcher Dock; the hot sidewalks of Oak Bluffs, followed by the wall-to-wall carpeting of the liquor store; the pokey feel of an accelerator on a naked sole; the hurtful little pebbles of Menemsha Beach and the also hurtful half-buried rocks of Squibnocket; the prickly weeds, virtual cacti, that grew in a certain lawn near Chilmark Pond; the soft path leading down from this lawn across giving, oozing boards to a bouncy little dock and rowboats that offered another yet friendly texture to the feet; the crystal bite of ocean water; the seethe and suck of a wave tumbling rocks across your toes in its surge back down the sand; sand, the clean wide private sand by Windy Gates and the print-pocked, overused public sand by the boat dock that one kicked around in while waiting for friends to be deferred; the cold steep clay of Gay Head and the flinty littered surface around those souvenir huts that continued to beguile the most jaded child; the startling dew on the grass when one stepped outside with the first cup of coffee to gauge the day's weather; the warmth of the day still lingering in the dunes underfoot as we walked back, Indian-file, through the dark from a beach party and its diminishing bonfire. Going to the post office in bare feet had an infra-legal, anti-totalitarian, comical, gentle feel to it, in the days before the Postal Service moved to the other side of Beetlebung Corner and established itself in a lake of razor-sharp spalls. (When Bill Seward ran the postal annex in his store, it was one of the few spots in the United States that would hand over mail on Sundays.) Shopping at Seward's, one would not so carefreely have shelled out "island prices" for such luxuries as macadamia nuts and candied snails had one been wearing shoes; their absence, like the cashless ease of a charge account, gave a pleasant illusion of unaccountability. The friend of mine who took these photographs

Written as a contribution to *On the Vineyard*, a collection of photographs by Peter Simon, with prose and poetry by many Vineyarders (Doubleday, 1980).

used to play golf at Mink Meadows barefoot. My children and I set up a miniature golf course on a turnaround covered with crushed clamshells; after we had been treading this surface for a while, it did not seem too great a transition, even for a middle-aged father of four, to climb a tree barefoot or go walking on a roof. The shingles felt pleasantly peppery, sunbaked.

These are summer memories, mostly August memories; for that's the kind of resident I was. Now it has been some summers since I was even that, and a danger exists of confusing the Vineyard with my children's childhood, which time has swallowed, or with Paradise, from which we have been debarred by well-known angels. Let's not forget the rainy days, the dull days, the cranky-making crowding, and the moldy smell summer furniture gives off when breezes don't blow through the screen door that one keeps meaning to fix, though it's really the landlord's responsibility. Beach pebbles notoriously dry to a disappointing gray on the mantel. The cozy roads and repeated recreations can begin to wear a rut. One wet summer we all, kids and cousins and friends of cousins, kept walking down through poison ivy, *not* barefoot, to look at a heap of large stones that was either a ninth-century Viking cromlech or a nineteenth-century doghouse, nobody was certain which. Still, there was under it all, fair days and foul, a kicky whiff of freedom, a hint, whispered from the phalanges to the metatarsals, from the calcaneus to the astragalus, that one was free from the mainland's paved oppressions.

Going barefoot is increasingly illegal and does have its dangers. One house we rented overlooked Menemsha Bight from a long porch whose spaced boards had the aligned nicety of harp strings or the lines of type in a book. One of my boys, performing some stunt on these boards, rammed splinters into the soles of his feet so deeply a doctor in Edgartown had to cut them out with a surgeon's knife. I wonder if even the most hardened hippies still pad along the tarry streets of Oak Bluffs barefoot as they used to. At Jungle Beach, I remember, nudity spread upward from toes to head and became doctrinaire. But then nudism, interwoven with socialism in the island's history, has always had a doctrinaire side. Being naked approaches being revolutionary; going barefoot is mere populism.

"Barefoot boy with cheek of tan" was a rote phrase of my own childhood, quaint even then. But that cliché had once lived and can be seen, not only in illustrations of Mark Twain but also in Winslow Homer's level-eyed etchings and oils of his contemporary America, a place of sandy lanes and soft meadows. There are few places left, even summer places, where one can go barefoot. Too many laws, too much broken glass. On Long Island, the cuffs of one's leisure suit will drag on the ground, and on the Cape, pine needles stick to the feet. Even on Nantucket, those cobblestones are not inviting. But the presiding spirits of Martha's Vineyard, willfully and not without considerable overhead, do preserve this lowly element of our Edenic heritage: treading the earth.

Common Land

WE SEEK, Americans, to inhale freedom, and the air is here, in these communities of houses built one by one, along roads whose curves were derived from the lay of the land. Predating the merciless grid that seized Manhattan and possessed the vast Midwest, New England towns have each at their center an irregular heart of open grass, vestige of the Puritan common, holding, perhaps, a village pump, a weathered monument, a surviving elm. In Rowley, there is a vacant triangle beside Route 1A that, as December narrows, becomes suddenly alive with whirling dervishes of Christmas lights. Ipswich has two hearts—the teardrop-shaped Meetinghouse Green at the old center, now overburdened by its sprawling modern meetinghouse, and the elongate, gracious South Green, since the 1830s made Arcadian by the backdrop of a Doric-columned church that in one cold recent night burned to its granite foundation. Away from the sea, the old greens merge with the wider lawns and what fields remain of New England's agriculture. This white house in West Newbury was once a farmhouse; once there would

---

Written to go with a winter photograph of the green in West Newbury, Massachusetts, in *Arthur Griffin's New England: The Four Seasons* (Houghton Mifflin, 1980).

have been determined paths beaten to the pump through this cold blue purity of snow.

In New Hampshire, the sheds of the houses reach backward to the barns, to afford the busy occupants roofed passage, and one deduces the intensity of winter from such actively sheltering shapes. Here, in regions becoming suburban to Boston, the land is allowed to sleep, and the clapboarded saltboxes remember summer as they accept the weak sun on their sides. Wires trace a secret traffic in heat and light, and no doubt feed that cool new hearthfire, the television set. The houses seem to enjoy no very intrinsic relation to the greens in their midst; they send out only an occasional band of children to inherit with casual play the spaces originally set aside for pasturage and militia drills. But the idea of land held in common, as (more than park or playground) part of a manifest, workaday covenant with the Bestower of a new continent, has permanently imprinted the maps of these towns, and lengthens the perspectives of those who live within them.

New England Churches

HENRY JAMES, writing of the young Hawthorne, imagined him gazing out upon a landscape of negatives: "No sovereign, no court... no country gentlemen, no palaces, no castles, nor manors, nor old country-houses, nor parsonages, nor thatched cottages, nor ivied ruins; no cathedrals, nor abbeys, nor little Norman churches . . ." By the time, in 1879, that James penned these words, rich Americans were aggressively supplying some of the lacks, including that of ivied ruins; but even in Hawthorne's youth ecclesiastical structures of considerable grandeur existed in New England, in positions of the utmost civic centrality. Perhaps the index of the degree of civilization which James found wanting in his native land lies less in the landscape's furniture than in the intensity of satisfac-

Written as a foreword for *Great New England Churches*, by Robert Mutrux (The Globe Pequot Press, 1982).

tion with which the living population regard their surrounding of visible heritage. With such books as this enthusiastic and knowledgeable guide by Robert Mutrux, an American can now conduct his own tour of cathedrals without crossing the Atlantic—indeed, by staying within the compass of a pleasant day's drive out of Boston.

The settlement of the Massachusetts Bay sprang from Old World church disputes, and the meetinghouse was the pivot of those first theocratic villages in the New World. To this day, the white Protestant spire identifies New England on calendars and postcards:

> On a thousand small town New England greens,
> the old white churches hold their air
> of sparse, sincere rebellion . . .

One of the marvels of Mr. Mutrux's selection of notable churches is that he has been able to discriminate among so many—so many white-spired Greek-columned structures lending charm and focus to greens and squares from the borders of Canada to the suburbs of New York City. The fullest use of this book would be as travel companion, its pages laid open like Sabbath church portals on the front seat while its precious subjects are approached mile after rolling mile and discovered within their often cluttered and incongruous settings.

As with the stone cathedrals of Western Europe, one may be struck, sadly, by their grand emptiness, an emptiness as yet little relieved, in America, by the shuffle of other tourists. The religious *raison d'être* of handsome churches sometimes persists as a furtive and feeble undercurrent to the architecture, an embarrassing human impurity—in Europe, the guttering votive candle and unshaven sacristan; in America, the tattered bulletin board and wistful pamphlet rack and garish decorations provided by the Sunday School. Many of the churches described within have slipped from one denomination to another; a number sit in neighborhoods that no longer form an adequate parish. Some—including one of the most recent, the Michael Pierce Chapel in Lenox—have passed into secular use. All that have not, it seems safe to say, present headaches to their building committees and cost far more to heat than formerly. Joy and aspiration have shaped these churches, but a certain melancholy may fill them. Puritanism faded into Unitarianism and thence into stoic agnosticism; these gallant old shells hold more memories than promises. Robert Lowell, who wrote the lines above, wrote as well:

> I see His vanishing
> emblems, His white spire and flag-
> pole sticking out above the fog,
> like old white china doorknobs, sad,
> slight, useless things to calm the mad.

Like Mr. Mutrux, I came late to New England. The first regional church of which I had experience was Harvard's Memorial Church, that splendid but slightly cold reproduction of the colonial manner, with its immaculate box pews and huge dark choir screen. Attending, I would sit back on the left-hand side near a small bronze plaque that seemed to me the epitome of New England fair-mindedness; opposite the great wall covered with the names of Harvard alumni killed fighting for the Allies, the plaque gave the names of four German graduates *"qui diversis sub signis pro patria spiritum reddiderunt."* Above their names appeared this transcendent assurance: *"Academia Harvardiana non oblita est filiorum suorum"*—Harvard has not forgotten her sons.

Returning some years later to live north of Boston, I would attend the Congregational church in Ipswich, a handsome, town-dominating example of "carpenter Gothic" tipped with wooden pinnacles and walled with boards and battens. The interior posed a delicate white-painted heaven of shapely roof trussing; the light came through tall pointed windows of old gray-glass lozenge panes. Some winter mornings, hardly a dozen of us showed up, while the minister shouted across the empty pews and the groaning furnace in the basement sent up odorous warmth through the cast-iron grates and the wind leaned on the crackling panes. I have never felt closer to the bare bones of Christianity than on those bleak and drafty Sunday mornings, with the ghosts of frock-coated worshippers and patient carpenters making up for our sparse attendance. That church is gone; a lightning stroke burned it down on a dark June day in 1965; one hundred nineteen years old, it had stood longer than any of its four predecessors on the site. Through its hushed and graceful spaces, so different from the colorful and stolid Lutheran interiors of my childhood, I entered into the spiritual life of my adopted region.

Can this life be distinguished, even minutely, from that of other regions? There are the Puritan beginnings and the stony soil, the four sharp seasons and the nautical outlook of the indented shore. To Calvinism, Irish Catholicism added its own austerities and wit. Is it too fanciful to imagine a certain stylistic humor that pervades even the great urban barns of Romishness and Anglicanism, the mock-ecclesiastical institutional buildings of Yale, and the perfect little Russian Orthodox church that Igor Sikorsky and some of his employees erected in Stratford, Connecticut, during the worst days of World War II—a living humor that licenses the creativity of the modern church architects so liberally represented herein? "Live free or die" runs the motto of one of our six states, and we do scent in our chilly, salty local air an extra tang of the free, of the voluntary. The New England spirit does not seek solutions in a crowd; raw light and solitariness are less dreaded than welcomed as enhancers of our essential selves. And our churches, classically, tend to seek through their forms, so restrainedly adorned, their essence as houses for the inner light.

A MILD 'COMPLAINT'

I DO NOT KNOW exactly 'what' it 'is,' but 'something' about a close
and reverent 'exposure' to the work of Henry James seems to lead
his commentators into a virtually 'manic' use of quotation marks.
I have just read—or, rather, 'read' until my eyelids became abraded
'beyond endurance' by incessant typographical 'pricking'—the in-
troduction, by Alma Louise Lowe, to 'the master's' *English Hours.*
The edition was 'printed in England,' so the intrusive 'marks' were
'single.' Some 'specimens':

> Because he listened 'with proper credulity' at Haddon Hall, he seemed
> to hear the 'ghostly footfalls' of Dorothy Vernon and Lord John Man-
> ners 'on the flags of the castle court.' On occasions he 'did see' ghosts
> 'as we see ghosts nowadays.' . . .
>
> The material he plucked while travelling accounts in a large measure
> for the 'air of reality' in James's fiction. . . .
>
> That James, the 'master,' the celebrity so devoted to the 'art' of
> writing . . .
>
> There were scores of other Americans who felt the 'pull' of Europe.
>
> He was reminded of 'the early pages of "Oliver Twist" ' as he watched.

Now, what is the 'point'? Are we to assume that 'commonplace
expressions' such as 'air of reality,' 'art,' 'pull,' and 'the early pages
of "Oliver Twist," ' by their presumed preappearance in the 'vast
body' of James's prose, have acquired a 'magic,' a 'special sense,'

which their 'unadorned' use would allow to 'slip through the net'? Or is it merely that the 'good' Miss Lowe wishes to demonstrate her 'fingertip mastery' of 'the material'? Thinking that it might be an 'eccentricity peculiar' to her, I turned to John L. Sweeney's introduction to *The Painter's Eye* and 'in an instant' encountered

His eye and memory were thus filled with images of a 'world' . . . long before discriminations had begun to 'bristle.' . . .

. . . what he expected of them in terms of 'subject' and why, for example, he 'detested' Winslow Homer's . . .

We have no conclusive evidence that James eventually 'embraced' the Impressionists. We have, however, some convincing hints that he learned to appreciate them and to utilize their 'suggestion.' . . .

And Morton Dauwen Zabel's introduction to *In the Cage and Other Tales* yielded, in American typographical style, a 'double harvest':

The "germ" that gave James his story . . . that the "spark" of his tale was kindled by the "wonderment" of his "speculation" . . .

And it was thus that his "young woman," the "caged telegraphist" . . .

Without denying that in some 'instances' an 'atom' of 'pertinency' may be glimpsed in this 'practice,' 'wonderment' is nevertheless aroused. It is not 'enough' to observe that here we have a 'contagion' originating in the 'punctuational excesses' of James's own 'later style.' The 'effect' is 'different.' In James himself, these footless exclamation marks serve as a 'kind of spice' to the 'lavish feast' whose most 'delicious' ingredient is the host's visible relish in the 'fare' he is 'setting forth.' Whereas with the scholars 'barnacled' to the underside of his 'stately gliding' reputation, the 'marks' are 'symptomatic of' a mere 'itch,' if for which an appropriate cure, or at least 'implement for scratching,' can be located, I will, indeed, 'be grateful.'

Other People's Books

THREE TALKS ON AMERICAN MASTERS

Undertaken to educate the speaker as much as the audience. The audience in each case had to be imagined beforehand, and to some extent set the tone of the talk. For the Hawthorne, I foresaw a drowsy post-prandial crew of American Academicians who were already learned and would be grateful for brevity and compression. For the Melville, I had in mind an attentive, benign, but non-academic upstate audience for whom Melville's later development should be limned in broad and lively terms. And for the Whitman, I envisioned a crowd of rather elegant bibliophiliac Manhattanites expecting to hear a capsule eulogy; the talk had been described to me as one in a series by contemporary American writers speaking upon American classics. Though all three of these essays were subsequently revised for journal publication, traces remain of the informal oral mode in which they were first cast. The theme of religious belief that connects them emerged like a gravestone rubbing.

Hawthorne's Creed

WHAT did Hawthorne believe? The author of our classic novel of religious conscience and religious suffering, and of works imbued throughout with religious concerns and religious language, boasted

Given as the Evangeline Wilbour Blashfield Address at the annual ceremonial of the American Academy and Institute of Arts and Letters, in New York City, on May 24, 1979.

: 73 :

of not being a churchgoer. His baptism, if it occurred, left no trace on the records. His mother, who became a widowed recluse when Nathaniel was only four, did take the boy and his sisters to services at the East Meeting House in Salem, where the Hathornes (the "w" was added by our subject, after college) had had a pew for one hundred seventy years—"the old wooden meetinghouse," Hawthorne was to write, "which used, on wintry Sabbaths, to be the frozen purgatory of my childhood." At Bowdoin College, he jested of "Sunday sickness" and was frequently fined for missing chapel. From there he wrote his mother, "The being a Minister is of course out of the question. I shall not think that even you could desire me to choose so dull a way of life." During his adoring courtship of Sophia Peabody, he rather resolutely declined to accompany her to hear her favorite preacher, the Methodist Edward Thompson Taylor, called Father Taylor and immortalized as Father Mapple in *Moby-Dick*. Not long after the idyll of their married life together had begun, Hawthorne confided to his notebooks: "My wife went to church in the forenoon, but not so her husband." As the United States consul in Liverpool, he did conduct family prayer services, in deference perhaps to his official position in Victorian England. But his son Julian, in his memoir of his father, admitted, "He never discussed religion in set terms either in his writings or in his talk. . . . Our mother upon occasions expressed her faith and reverence in speech; our father in caverns submarine and unsounded, yet somehow apparent." Melville, one of the few men ever to break through Hawthorne's reserve, held with him, in Lenox in 1850, late-night conversations that Hawthorne in his journal described as "about time and eternity, things of this world and the next, and books, and publishers, and all possible and impossible things"; but he did not record his own position on these deep matters. Six years later, when Melville showed up in Liverpool and the two of them went walking together on the links at Southport, Hawthorne noted: "Melville, as he always does, began to reason of Providence and futurity, and of everything that lies beyond human ken. . . . It is strange how he persists—and has persisted in wandering to-and-fro over the deserts, as dismal and monotonous as the sand hills amid which we were sitting. He can neither believe, nor be comfortable in his unbelief." In Concord, Hawthorne was skeptical about the Transcendental enthusiasms of Emerson and Channing; in Rome, he was attentive to, but in the end skeptical of, the manifold consolations of the Roman Catholic Church. Puritanically, he disdained dilutions. His short story "The Celestial Railroad" satirizes Unitarianism, and Church of England services he called "mummery, which seemed to me worse than papistry because it was a corruption of it." Yet this same skeptic could write that "religious faith is the most valuable and most sacred of human possessions" and say of the evangelist John Eliot, "There is no impiety in believing that, when his long life was over, the apostle of the Indians was welcomed to the celestial abodes by the prophets of ancient days and by those earliest apostles and evangelists who had drawn their inspirations from the immediate presence of the Saviour." True, the context of the first assertion is a campaign biography, and of the second a book of historical tales aimed at children; but in an essay on the very subject of his refusal to attend church, entitled "Sunday at Home," he assures the reader that "doubts may flit around me, or seem to close their evil wings, and settle down; but . . . never can my soul have lost the instinct of its faith. . . . though my form be absent, my inner man goes constantly to church."

Now, Protestantism by the beginning of the nineteenth century presented a wide grid of doctrinal emphases and shades of fervor. Hawthorne at one point was attracted by Shakerism, and then repulsed by it; at a later juncture he was interested, though at a characteristic distance, in the Swedenborgians. Religious belief is an elusive and volatile part of a man, and our inquiry here would be impudent, as well as impossible, were it focused upon the always "submarine," and by now profoundly sunk, question of what settled belief or unbelief Hawthorne held, that he could find curious the perpetual discomfort of Melville. Unlike Whitman, Hawthorne did not set himself up as a happy pagan; nor, like Emerson, as a post-Christian prophet. Hawthorne's vocabulary retained phrases of conventional piety while neither sermons nor rites enriched his personal life. In this he resembled many male citizens of the Christendom of his time. Yet the religious life within his writings does not fade but, if anything, intensifies, and the work itself invites us to search out the involuntary creed professed by his recurrent themes and artistic reflexes. A very vivid ghost of Christianity stares out at us from his prose, alarming and odd in not being evenly dead, but alive in some limbs and amputate in others, blurred in some aspects and otherwise basilisk-keen.

Hawthorne's creed perhaps begins with this: he feels himself as delicate, fragile, and threatened, and identifies the menace of the world with the Puritanism of his ancestors. His essay "Main-street" prays: "Let us thank God for having given us such ancestors; and let each successive generation thank him, not less fervently, for being one step further from them in the march of ages." "And what hast thou to do with all these iron men, and their opinions?" Hester Prynne cries out to Dimmesdale, in a world permeated by iron grayness. In *The Scarlet Letter* (1850), alone of Hawthorne's novels, we do not feel the social surround of the principal characters to be thin, for it is solidly composed of ancient Boston's communal righteousness. And Dimmesdale, insofar as he speaks for Puritanism, is not the hero but the villain, so that we rejoice in his fall; thus D. H. Lawrence read the novel as the triumphant story of a husband and wife, Mr. and Mrs. Chillingworth, conspiring to seduce and torment an insufferably flawed agent of an iron domination. In *The House of the Seven Gables* (1851), the blood of the Pyncheons descends as a curse; Hawthorne needs no Max Weber to connect Puritanism with the dark forces of material enterprise. By his fancy the dead, witch-hanging Colonel and the contemporary, greedy, pharisaical politician are twins; in a chapter of embarrassing venom the author gloats above the corpse of Judge Pyncheon as above the body of an enemy dispatched. With *The Blithedale Romance* (1852), the iron men have shrunk to a single blacksmith, the philanthropist Hollingsworth, whom Hawthorne again castigates in terms scarcely justified by the action of the novel. Another blacksmith figures in the short story "The Artist of the Beautiful"; the artist-hero protests of him, "His hard, brute force darkens and confuses the spiritual element within me."

From Christianity Hawthorne accepted the dualism, and made it more radical still. Orthodox doctrine bridges matter and spirit with a scandalous Incarnation, Jesus Christ. In Hawthorne, matter verges upon being evil; virtue, upon being insubstantial. His insistence on delicate, ethereal heroines goes against not only our modern grain but his own as well—for in *The Blithedale Romance* it seems clear that it is not the ectoplasmic Priscilla the narrator loves, as the last sentence proclaims in capitals, but the dark, sensual, and doomed Zenobia. Zenobia does not fit into his vision: "I know not well how to express, that the native glow of coloring in her cheeks, and even the flesh-warmth over her round arms, and what was visible of her full bust—in a word, her womanliness incarnated,—compelled me sometimes to close my eyes, as if it were not quite the privilege of modesty to gaze at her." *The Blithedale Romance*, long considered the least of his four mature romances, is yet the most actual, the most nervously alive, in its first-person voice and in its overwarm, perversely shunned heroine—"the nearest approach," Henry James thought, "that Hawthorne has made to the complete creation of a *person.*" The novel in its smallest details conveys Hawthorne's instinctive tenet that matter and spirit are inevitably at war. "The soul gets the better of the body after a wasting illness," Miles Coverdale tells us; when he has recovered sufficiently to engage in farm work, his mind is got the better of: "The clods of earth, which we so constantly belabored and turned over and over, were never etherealized into thought. Our thoughts, on the contrary, were fast becoming cloddish."

Where the two incompatible realms of Hawthorne's universe impinge, something leaks through; there is a *stain.* A sensation of blasphemous overlapping, of some vast substance chemically betraying itself, is central to the Gothic tradition of which Hawthorne's tales are lovely late blooms. The stain, this sinister spillage from another world, can take the form of poison, of a potion, of dreams and mirrors, of overinsistent symbols like the scarlet letter or Donatello's presumably pointed ears. Hawthorne's wish to saturate his imagery with the import of symbolism is itself a kind of staining, and his meditations on sculpture in *The Marble Faun* take an eerie tincture from his notion of the art as a potential invasion of the inanimate by the animate. Allegory, whose last earnest practitioner he was, is a kindred form of animation, in the realm of abstractions rather than of marble. An aura of supernatural puppet-ry, of imminent spontaneous generation, haunts his tales; we are not surprised, in "Feathertop," when a scarecrow takes on life.

The haunted is a degenerate form of the sacred. Two sacred ideas especially precious to Calvinism, Providence and guilt, haunt Haw-thorne's mind, but in curious form. Providence seems to be his sensation of inner delicacy projected outward upon the universe, where it is threatened by human monomania; the obsessed experi-menter and philanthropist recur as ill-fated disrupters of the univer-sal balance—men who, he writes in "The Hall of Fantasy," "had got possession of some crystal fragment of truth the brightness of which so dazzled them that they could see nothing else in the wide universe." Guilt, of which Hawthorne was such a connoisseur, pervades his work without any corroborating conviction of sin—for we do not feel that Dimmesdale and Hester, or Donatello and Miriam, are guilty of anything more than flashing out momentarily against, in their creator's phrase, "the moral gloom of the world." Yet they scrub and scrub at their stains, under a Providence too delicately balanced to offer absolution. In the masterly tale of "The Birthmark," the stain on the heroine's cheek is intrinsic to her life and beauty, and her husband kills her in removing it through alchemy. "Thus ever," the moral runs, "does the gross fatality of earth exult in its invariable triumph over the immortal essence which, in this dim sphere of half development, demands the com-pleteness of a higher state." Hawthorne, once described by an acquaintance as "a fine ghost in a case of iron," was severely faithful to his sense of our "dim sphere of half development" as one of necessarily incompatible essences; when his susceptible Sophie took up spiritualism in Rome, he was interested in the apparent evidence of séances and spirit writing, but concluded (in *English Notebooks*), "I cannot consent to let Heaven and Earth, this world and the next, be beaten up together like the white and yolk of an egg."

The axis of Earth-flesh-blood versus Heaven-mind-spirit with a little rotation becomes that of the world versus the self. In this opposition the self fights submergence. Hawthorne's first hero, the autobiographically reclusive Fanshawe, dies at the age of twenty of no certain disease, simply easing from "a world for which he was unfit," leaving "the ashes of a hard student and good scholar"—an epitaph whose real model concluded, "and a great Christian." Though not claiming that latter title, the delicate personae of Hawthorne's novels do gather strength as they evolve. Dimmesdale perishes only after a prolonged struggle, and flouts the world as he departs. *The House of the Seven Gables* has two delicate characters, Clifford and Phoebe, who survive Judge Pyncheon and inherit his wealth. Delicacy, shifted to femininity, takes on a new resilience. In *The Blithedale Romance,* the translucent Priscilla sees her rival into the grave and exerts a wifely mastery over the shattered Hollingsworth. The dark Puritan vein, here shrunk to one cowed man, becomes with the final romance, *The Marble Faun* of 1860, a mere pleasant Yankee mettle in the culminating embodiment of delicacy, Hilda—Hilda, who, with the pragmatic aid of a Catholic confessional to which she has no right, expunges the stain of having witnessed murder and accepts full-bodied happiness.

This submarine Pilgrim's Progress is paralleled by Hawthorne's own career; circumstances marvellously contrived to pull the fantasizing young hermit of the dozen Salem years, venturing forth only at sunset and publishing anonymously, slowly out, through public employment, respectable marriage, literary success, and political office, into a thorough international worldliness.

He returned from England to his own land at a time when it was, in a struggle within itself more ghastly than Dimmesdale's, expunging the stain of slavery; Hawthorne sickened and died, like one of his own blighted characters. The writer who profited most from his example, Henry James, yet said, "I feel that his principle was wrong. . . . Imagination is out of place; only the strictest realism can be right." Hawthorne himself coveted novels like those of Trollope—"as real as if some giant had hewn a great lump out of the earth and put it under a glass case." Yet what is reality? We do not feel material to ourselves, and matter itself is transient. "The Hall of Fantasy," Hawthorne wrote, "is likely to endure longer than the most substantial structure that ever cumbered the earth."

He believed, with his Puritan ancestors, that man's spirit matters; that the soul can be distorted, stained, and lost; that the impalpable exerts force against the material. Our dreams move us: this is a psychological rather than a religious truth, but in a land where, as Emerson said, "things are in the saddle," it gives the artist his vote.

Melville's Withdrawal

IN THE MYTHOLOGY of American letters, the popular and critical failure of *Moby-Dick*, and Melville's subsequent withdrawal into wounded silence, is a central image, ranking with Henry James's self-exile to England and Mark Twain's final phase as a white-suited pet of the rich, and with Fitzgerald's alcoholic crackup and early death and Hemingway's spendthrift exercises in celebrity. Something is wrong, these images tell us, with being a writer in America; one of Melville's biographers, Newton Arvin, calls his subject's treatment by the public "the heaviest count in our literary annals against the American mind."

Invited to speak by the friends of a library, I thought to make an excuse for repairing a gap in my own reading—the later Melville. I began with the assumptions that *Moby-Dick* is a masterpiece and that Melville in his endowment of ability and ambition is second to no American writer of fiction. Like many another, I had read *Moby-Dick*, with a pleasure and admiration not entirely free of dutifulness, and as well those two tales of the sea, *Typee* and *Billy Budd*, that constitute the alpha and omega of Melville's career; the first indeed inspired me with an enthusiasm that carried me forward through *Omoo* and *Redburn* if not through all of *Mardi*. *Pierre* and *Clarel* and *The Confidence-Man*, until my fateful summons to Rochester, were no more to me than titles, and of the biographical particulars framing Melville's famous silence I was equally ignorant. My ignorance recently patched, I come before you tonight to

---

Given as the third annual Harold Hacker Lecture, sponsored by the Friends of the Rochester, New York, Public Library, in Xerox Square Auditorium on October 23, 1981.

share a few surprises and thoughts. If any Melville specialists are present, I invite them to leave the auditorium.

The first surprise that greets us is how young Melville was when he wrote *Moby-Dick.* He was thirty when, on the first day of February 1850, he returned to New York from a four-month excursion to England whose ostensible purpose was to settle the details of the British publication of his fifth book, *White-Jacket.* He had been married not three years before, to Elizabeth Shaw; his first child, Malcolm, was not quite a year old. Shortly after Melville's return, we presume, he, who had written *White-Jacket* and *Redburn* together in a mere five months, settled to compose a sixth book based upon his seafaring days—his whaling experiences in this case. The most prolonged of his voyages had been his eighteen months on the whaling ship *Acushnet,* with briefer stints on the whalers *Lucy Ann* and *Charles & Henry;* but until 1850 whaling had been conspicuously absent from the running fictionalized account he had made of his adventures. The whaling ships in *Typee, Omoo,* and *Mardi* were all points of departure; their actual business was left undescribed, it would seem, until the writer felt worthy of the task. He worked in a room of a New York household that included his mother, four unmarried sisters, a married brother with his pregnant wife, and two children, plus domestic help. We first hear of his new book in a letter of May 1, 1850, to another literary sailor, Richard Henry Dana, Jr.:

> About the "whaling voyage"—I am half way in the work. . . . It will be a strange sort of a book, tho', I fear; blubber is blubber you know; tho' you may get oil out of it, the poetry runs as hard as sap from a frozen maple tree;—& to cook the thing up, one must needs throw in a little fancy, which from the nature of the thing, must be ungainly as the gambols of the whales themselves. Yet I mean to give the truth of the thing, spite of this.

In the midsummer of that year, while a friend, Evert Duyckinck, was informing his brother that "Melville has a new book mostly done—a romantic, fanciful & literal & most enjoyable presentment of the Whale Fishery—something quite new," Melville almost all at once visited his cousin Robert's farm in Pittsfield, Massachusetts, was given a copy of Hawthorne's *Mosses from an Old Manse,* decided to bring his wife and young son from New York to Pittsfield for a summer vacation, met Hawthorne at the famous picnic on Monument Mountain, wrote an enraptured anonymous appreciation of Hawthorne for the Duyckinck brothers' journal *The Literary World,* and decided to buy the farm, six miles from Hawthorne's new home near Lenox, that Melville called Arrowhead. He and his family were to live at Arrowhead for the next thirteen years. That first year he was stimulated and emboldened by the proximity of the older author, of whom he had written in his review, "I feel that this Hawthorne has dropped germinous seeds into my soul. He expands and deepens down, the more I contemplate him; and further, and further, shoots his strong New England roots into the hot soil of my Southern soul." Melville thoroughly revised the whaling story, making of it the elaborate, symbolic, rhapsodic, pessimistic volume of wonders it became. He finished the last chapters in New York, while the first chapters were already in the printer's press, and passed the last proof sheets in late July, a week or so before his thirty-second birthday.

A second surprise is that the reviews weren't all that bad. Not as bad, certainly, as those which had greeted *Mardi* two years before. In London, *The Athenæum,* whose review, on October 25, of the English edition (entitled *The Whale*) was the first and almost the strongest blast against the book, as "an ill-compounded mixture of romance and matter-of-fact," yet bestowed a back-handed compliment in its judgment that "our author must be henceforth numbered in the company of the incorrigibles who occasionally tantalize us with indications of genius, while they constantly summon us to endure monstrosities," and as one who "seems not so much unable to learn as disdainful of learning the craft of an artist." The magazine *John Bull* on the other hand, and on the same day, recognized that "Of all the extraordinary books from the pen of Herman Melville this is out and out the most extraordinary" and noted "the flashes of truth . . . which sparkle on the surface of the foaming sea of thought . . . The profound reflections uttered by the actors in the wild watery chase . . . and the graphic representations of human nature in the startling disguises under which it appears on the deck of the *Pequod.* " In New York three weeks later, *Moby-Dick; or, The Whale* was greeted warmly by the *Morning Courier and New-York Enquirer:* "No American writer is more sure, at every re-appearance, of a more cheerful welcome than the author of Typee. . . . This book has all the attractiveness of any of its predecessors; in truth, it possesses more of a witching interest . . . The author writes with the gusto of true genius, and it must be a torpid spirit indeed that is not enlivened with the raciness of his humor and the redolence of his imagination." *The Albion* thought *Moby-Dick* "not lacking much of being a great work," and offered criticism that even the most reverential modern Melvillian might admit to be sound: that the seamen don't talk like seamen, and that the central character of Captain Ahab has been "grievously spoiled, nay altogether ruined, by a vile overdaubing with a coat of book-learning and mysticism." *The Home Journal* reported that "the result is a very racy, spirited, curious and entertaining book, which affords quite an amount of information, while it enlists the curiosity, excites the sympathies, and often charms the fancy." *Harper's New Monthly Magazine* asserted that *Moby-Dick,* "in point of richness and variety of incident, originality of conception, and splendor of description, surpasses any of the former productions of this highly successful author." Enough, perhaps, has been quoted to show that even those with strong reservations about *Moby-Dick* spoke respectfully of the author's talent, and that a number of early enthusiasts for this willful and extravagant work were among the reviewers. It is true, Melville did not receive what might have been psychologically useful at this time—a fully generous public salute from a high-minded peer, such as he had given Hawthorne, or as Emerson was to give Whitman (in a private letter that became public) upon receipt of *Leaves of Grass.* The "joy-giving and exultation-breeding" letter that Hawthorne did write Melville about this work that borrowed so much courage from their neighborliness was destroyed, along with almost all of the letters that Melville received. In a letter to Evert Duyckinck, Hawthorne wrote, "What a book Melville has written! It gives me an idea of much greater power than his preceding ones." And Melville might have taken additional comfort by glancing over Longfellow's shoulder as he noted in his journal one November night, "sat to read all the evening in Melville's new book, 'Moby Dick or the Whale.' Very wild, strange, and interesting." Melville's critical and popular position after the publication of *Moby-Dick* was still high; he was commonly written of as a genius and, in a London New Year's survey of new presences in American literature, ranked with Hawthorne and the now forgotten Richard Burleigh Kimball and Sylvester Judd. There is nothing in his situation like the obscurity in which, at his age, Hawthorne and Whitman labored, or for that matter in which Joyce, Proust, and Kafka secreted their modern classics. Newly established in the Berkshires, his farm and his wealthy relatives ready to supplement his income from writing, Melville had every apparent motive and means to continue triumphantly within his literary vocation.

Moby-Dick stands, indeed, in the middle of his shelf of books; two novels, a collection of short stories, a novelization of another man's memoir, four books of poetry, and a novella followed it. Sometime during the fall when *Moby-Dick* was published and Melville's second son, Stanwix, was born, he began work on his next novel, *Pierre*. He worked with his usual fury. His Pittsfield neighbor, Sarah Morewood, wrote to Evert Duyckinck: "I hear that he is now engaged in a new work as frequently not to leave his room till quite dark in the evening—when he for the first time during the whole day partakes of solid food—he must therefore write under a state of morbid excitement which will soon injure his health—I laughed at him somewhat and told him that the recluse life he was leading made his city friends think that he was slightly insane—he replied that long ago he came to the same conclusion himself." Dr. Amos Nourse, the husband of Melville's favorite aunt, Lucy, and sometime physician to his wife, also worried, in a letter to Elizabeth's father: "Her husband I fear is devoting himself to writing with an assiduity that will cost him dear by & by." Melville expressed fond hopes for this new work; to Sophie Hawthorne he promised it to be "a rural bowl of milk," and to his English publisher, Richard Bentley, he described it as "very much more calculated for popularity than anything you have yet published of mine—being a regular romance, with a mysterious plot to it, & stirring passions at work, representing a new & elevated aspect of American life." In the event, *Pierre* proved to be—and this is our third surprise—grindingly, ludicrously bad. It is doubtful if elsewhere in the history of literature two books as good and bad as *Moby-Dick* and *Pierre* have been written back to back. The action is hysterical, the style is frenzied and volatile, the characters are jerked to and fro by some unexplained rage of the author's. These five hundred pages, as T. S. Eliot said of some plays by the Elizabethan John Marston, "give the effect of work done by a man who was so exasperated by having to write in a form which he despised that he deliberately wrote worse than he could have written, in order to relieve his feelings."

The plot is this: Pierre, a young country gentleman happily ensconced in rural wealth and in lyrical engagement to a suitable local gentlewoman called Lucy, upon discovering that his dead father in likelihood was also the father of an illegitimate daughter named Isabel, reacts by renouncing his fiancée, his wealth, and his mother's affection and by carrying his sister off in the semblance of a wife to the big city, where, the gentle fiancée with equal quixoticism following him, all three eventually perish. Whereas in *Moby-Dick* the figure of Ahab takes all the madness upon himself, here it belongs to the author; where the basic chase action of the earlier book carries us through all the elaborations, digressions, and explosions of authorial wit, in *Pierre* the white whale never surfaces, and slides as an unsighted horror beneath the clashing, improbable waves. When Pierre receives the news that he has a bastard sister, and reacts by swooning and vowing to love and protect her "through all," Melville wonders in print at so violent a reaction to "a piece of intelligence which, in the natural course of things, many amiable gentlemen, both young and old, have been known to receive with a momentary feeling of surprise, and then a little curiosity to know more, and at last an entire unconcern." Throughout the book we long for that amiable gentleman, that representative of orderly, elastic, mundane society. Instead, the book runs a constant fever, and seems especially unreal in the Arcadian setting of its first half, though Melville had his own aristocratic background and the surrounding hills of Berkshire to draw upon. Melville was, in truth, at sea on land. The domestic and social arrangements he imagines are as gothic and moldering as those in Poe, with few of the natural affectionate details of home life we might expect from a man who was simultaneously, under his roof at Arrowhead, father, son, brother, and husband. His first six books had all been first-person narratives derived from his sea-faring days. "The Paradise of Bachelors" is the title of one of his short pieces and seems to represent his ideal of the good life; men adrift or at ease in a company, eating and talking and struggling against fate together, constitute his recurrent and sufficient subject. The third of the world that is dry land and the half that is the female sex turned the compass of his imagination away. Never again, after *Pierre*, will he attempt to make significant characters of women, and hereafter the ground beneath his major fictions will be watery, if not the sea then the Mississippi of *The Confidence-Man* or the Palestinian desert of *Clarel* transformed by innumerable nautical metaphors into a ghost ocean. The masterpiece of his old age, *Billy Budd*, is of course a sea tale, as are "Benito Cereno" and "The Encantadas" in *The Piazza Tales*. Even the characters in *Pierre* at the end seek relief in a short ride on a ferryboat, the hero announcing, "I must get on some other element than earth. I have sat on earth's saddle till I am weary."

Where *Pierre* does burn through to reality is in the evocation, in the city part of the novel, of the menace of poverty and the ordeal of writing. Pierre, we are tardily told, is something of a writer; eloping to New York with not only Isabel but also another country waif, Delly Ulver, and then acquiring as one more dependent the wronged but faithful Lucy, much as Melville's Berkshire household was composed of a multiplication of women, Pierre hopes to support them all by writing a book. The description of his labors is horrendous and heartfelt:

> From eight o'clock in the morning till half-past four in the evening, Pierre sits there in his room;—eight hours and a half! . . .
> He will not be called to; he will not be stirred. Sometimes the intent ear of Isabel in the next room, overhears the alternate silence, and then

the long lonely scratch of his pen. It is as if she heard the busy claw of some midnight mole in the ground. Sometimes she hears a low cough, and sometimes the scrape of his crook-handled cane. . . . In the heart of such silence, surely something is at work. Is it creation, or destruction? Builds Pierre the noble world of a new book? or does the Pale Haggardness unbuild the lungs and the life in him?— Unutterable, that a man should be thus!

. . . He cannot eat but by force. He has assassinated the natural day; how then can he eat with an appetite? If he lays him down, he cannot sleep; he has waked the infinite wakefulness in him; then how can he slumber? Still, his book, like a vast lumbering planet, revolves in his aching head.

Here we have a book describing its own composition, and that of all the hurried and bulky books before, which yet have secured the writer no sure immortality, and no lasting income.

In *Pierre,* to judge by his comments in the letters just quoted, Melville imagined he was concocting "a regular romance," "calculated for popularity." When the book upon which poor Pierre so painfully labors is rejected by the publisher, it is with the note: "Sir: — You are a swindler. Upon the pretence of writing a popular novel for us, you have been receiving cash advances from us, while passing through our press the sheets of a blasphemous rhapsody, filched from the vile Atheists, Lucian and Voltaire." Among the reviews of *Pierre,* that in *The American Whig Review* spoke of "atrocious doctrines" and "glaring abominations," while that in the *Southern Literary Messenger* warned, "if one does not desire to look at virtue and religion with the eye of Mephistopheles . . . he had better leave 'Pierre or The Ambiguities' unbought on the shelves of the bookseller." Author and hero alike are unable to turn their pens to the necessary task, sinking instead into "blasphemous rhapsody." *Pierre* both in style and in action verges on parody, a quality that some recent critics have sought to make a virtue but that modern readers are as apt to find disorienting as did the novel's few contemporary reviewers. *Typee* and *Omoo* successfully took up the engaging manner of a purveyor of romance and adventure. With the enormous intellectual expansion and relative commercial failure of *Mardi,* Melville entered into a bitter relation with his pro-

spective readers. *Redburn* and *White-Jacket,* quickly written to re-
coup the disaster of *Mardi,* were, he wrote his father-in-law and the
chief underwriter of his household, the wealthy Massachusetts
judge Lemuel Shaw, "two *jobs,* which I have done for money—
being forced to it, as other men are to sawing wood. . . . So far as
I am individually concerned, & independent of my pocket, it is
my earnest desire to write those sort of books which are said to
'fail'—pardon this egotism."

Melville, like Norman Mailer and Lord Byron, began, in his
mid-twenties, with a success that ever after he had to live up to. On
both sides of the Atlantic *Typee* created a sensation that still rever-
berated when all else of Melville's production had been forgotten.
But what did best-sellerdom mean in mid-nineteenth-century
America? Two and a half years after *Typee*'s publication in 1846,
Melville's brother Allan drew up an account of the American edi-
tion, brought out by Wiley & Putnam. Of a total printing of
sixty-five hundred copies, 2,178 copies bound in muslin and costing
a dollar each had been sold, and 3,575 paperbound at 75¢ each,
bringing total receipts (somehow) to $3,235.94, less publishing
expenses of $1,663.01, making a profit of $1,572.93, of which Mel-
ville's half was $786.46. *Omoo* also did well, though less well. Its
edition, by Harper & Brothers, had by the first of August in 1847
sold about thirty-six hundred copies, giving Melville a profit of
$718.79, less his advance of $400. After *Mardi,* which sold a little
over two thousand copies, Harper's statements show Melville, as a
result of his unearned advances, in debt to them, even though
Redburn and *White-Jacket* enjoyed respectable sales. *White-Jacket,*
indeed, was his second most successful book. *Moby-Dick* eighteen
months after its publication had sold a not inconsiderable twenty-
three hundred copies, but *Pierre,* for which Melville had received
a $500 advance, eight months after publication had found custom-
ers for a miserable 283 copies of a hopeful edition of 2,310. In
Melville's entire lifetime, royalties on the "bowl of milk" amounted
to $157. Of course, English publication should not be left out of
account; it could win for a nineteenth-century American author
more prestige and no less profit than native publication, and was

usually arranged to fall earlier. By Allan's reckoning, Melville's British receipts from the first five books totalled $3,775.05, or slightly more than the American total of $3,591.21. These sums, plus a seven-hundred-dollar English advance on *Moby-Dick*, come to over eight thousand dollars: an average annual earning, over five years, of sixteen hundred dollars—making Melville one of the best-paid American authors of this era. Yet by 1851 he was deep into debt, owing Harper & Brothers hundreds and his father-in-law thousands. In England, the firm of Richard Bentley refused to pay any advance for *Pierre*, reporting losses from Melville's last four books of four hundred and fifty pounds.

Now, how do these figures translate into today's terms? The population of the United States of 1850 was about twenty-three million, so *Typee*'s sale here of nearly six thousand can be multiplied by ten to give us a modern equivalent; a sale of sixty thousand hardbound copies might get you a low rung on the *Times* best-seller list for a month or so. The same rough rule of ten might be applied to the dollar amounts, in a world where a clothbound book cost a dollar, an apple a penny, a first-class stamp three cents, a restaurant meal forty cents, a slave a thousand dollars, and a farm in Pittsfield sixty-five hundred. Even if we allow the 1850 dollar to be worth fifteen of ours, Melville would not have been rich, by, say, the standards of his brother-in-law Lemuel Shaw, Jr.—who left an estate of over three hundred thousand dollars—even had his sales continued at the rate of *Typee*'s. When at last, in late 1866, Melville secured a government post as a deputy inspector of Customs in the City of New York, his salary was four dollars a day, which came to around twelve hundred annually—a "pittance," in the word of his brother-in-law John Hoadley in 1873, but a sufficient living, with his wife's unearned income, and far more than he averaged in twenty years of authorship. The United States of his time would seem to have been like Third World countries today—able to breed a literary community of sorts but with a reading public insufficiently large to sustain a free-lance writer of books. The first significant professional American writers, Washington Irving and James Fenimore Cooper, were men of some wealth; it was Melville's additional irritation to have wealthy relatives whose doles merely underlined the pathos of his own struggle to support a family with an increasingly willful pen. "Dollars damn me," he wrote Hawthorne. "What I feel most moved to write, that is banned,—it will not pay. Yet, altogether, write the *other* way I cannot. So the product is a final hash, and all my books are botches."

There remained the burgeoning world of journals and magazines, which had employed and published Poe and had first led the young hermit of Salem, Hawthorne, out into the light of print. To this form of professionalism Melville turned, with surprisingly solid results. After *Pierre*, whose reception was almost as devastating to its author as its plot had been to its hero, Melville's family attempted to obtain for him a consular post such as Hawthorne had received from the new administration of Franklin Pierce; but no such sinecure forthcame. However, the editors of a new journal, *Putnam's Monthly Magazine*, sent Melville in October of 1852 a letter inviting him to become a contributor, and he evidently turned aside from several book-length projects he was working on —one a "Tortoise Hunting Adventure" for which Harper had advanced him $300, and the other an idea that he had tried to persuade Hawthorne to execute, the tale of a sailor's grass-widow named Agatha—to compose in 1853 his celebrated short story, "Bartleby, the Scrivener." In the following year he wrote five more stories and a long work called *Israel Potter*, which was serialized in *Putnam's* before publication in book form. In the two years after that, he wrote eight more tales as well as his farewell to the novelist's art, *The Confidence-Man*. As far as is known, *Putnam's* only ever rejected one submission, and that not for aesthetic reasons but for fear that it ("The Two Temples") would offend the sensibilities of parishioners of Manhattan's Grace Church. He was paid by the page, and for "Bartleby" received $85 from the magazine, for the Hawthornian tale "The Bell-Tower" $37.50, and for *Israel Potter* all of $421.50. These were good fees for the time, but the rewards of magazine publication did not induce Melville to continue long in that field. After the Civil War, *Putnam's Monthly*, having failed in 1857, was revived as *Putnam's Magazine;* its prospectus asked, "And where . . . is Herman Melville? Has that copious and imaginative author . . . let fall his pen just where its use might have been so remunerative to himself, and so satisfactory to the public?" Though Melville wrote the editors, "You may include me in the list of probable contributors," he never did contribute again. When, in 1856, he had collected his published tales and sketches in *The Piazza Tales*, he left over half of them out and was done with selling short pieces to magazines. His total earnings for these three years of piecework have been calculated as $750.*

The Piazza Tales are, with *Moby-Dick*, *Typee*, and *Billy Budd*, the most read of Melville's work, and I feel the need to say little of them here, beyond that they evinced a surprising competence, even mastery, which Melville chose not to exercise much. "I would prefer not to," Bartleby famously says, and there is in all these tales a certain reserve, a toning down into brown and somber colors the sunny colors and brilliant blacks of the earlier work, a desolation hauntingly figured forth by the eerie slave-seized ship of "Benito Cereno" and the cinder-like islands of "The Encantadas." The style, though a triumphant recovery from the hectic tropes of *Pierre*, is not quite the assured, playful, precociously fluent, and eagerly pitched voice of the sea-novels. It is a slightly *chastened* style, with something a bit abrasive and latently aggressive about it. However admirable, these tales are not exactly comfortable; their surfaces are not seductive and limpid, like those of Hawthorne's tales. How uncomfortable Melville was will burst forth in *The Confidence-Man*, which has the texture of gnashing teeth; but before we grapple with it I would like to linger a moment upon *Israel Potter*, the one book of Melville's quite out of print, and yet a charming one, and one indicating how entertainingly Melville could perform when bound to the constraints of a brisk professional intent.

Like "Benito Cereno" and *Billy Budd* and the aborted (and utterly perished) *Agatha*, *Israel Potter* is based upon a document— a pamphlet, printed in Providence in 1824, that Melville had picked up, "rescued by the merest chance from the rag-pickers." The cover describes the *Life and Remarkable Adventures of Israel R.*

---

*By William Charvat, in his very informative "Melville's Income" (*American Literature* XV [1944], pp. 251–61).

Potter, "who was a soldier in the American Revolution and took a distinguished part in the Battle of Bunker Hill . . . after which he was taken Prisoner by the British, conveyed to England, where for 30 years he obtained a livelihood for himself and family, by crying 'Old Chairs to Mend,' through the Streets of London— . . . he succeeded (in the 79th year of his age) in obtaining a passage to his native country, after an absence of 48 years." In the footsteps of this bizarre, not very consequential memoir Melville trots along amiably, elaborating, poeticizing, inventing portraits of such eminences as Ben Franklin, John Paul Jones, and Ethan Allen, and giving us a vivid notion of our country's patriotic pantheon while its deities were not many decades in the grave. Though caustic at places, the book has something of its hero's naïve patriotism, and that innocence of an Edenic America lost forever with the 1850s. *Israel Potter* is notable for containing the one sketch in all post-Polynesian Melville of a woman perceived as an inviting sexual object: our hero is the guest of Ambassador Franklin in Paris, and

in tripped a young French lass, bloom on her cheek, pink ribbons in her cap, liveliness in all her air, grace in the very tips of her elbows. The most bewitching little chambermaid in Paris. All art, but the picture of artlessness.

"Monsieur! pardon!"

"Oh, I pardong ye freely," said Israel. "Come to call on the Ambassador?"

"Monsieur, is de—de—" but, breaking down at the very threshold in her English, she poured out a long ribbon of sparkling French, the purpose of which was to convey a profusion of fine compliments to the stranger, with many tender inquiries as to whether he was comfortably roomed, and whether there might not be something, however trifling, wanting to his complete accommodation.

For the equivalent of those ribbons and graceful elbow tips one has to go back to Fayaway in *Typee. Israel Potter* also holds a number of matchless descriptions of battles at sea, Olympian in their mood and startling in their poetry:

The sun was now calmly setting over the green land of Ireland. The sky was serene, the sea smooth, the wind just sufficient to waft the two vessels steadily and gently. After the first firing and a little manœuvring, the two ships glided on freely, side by side; in that mild air exchanging their deadly broadsides, like two friendly horsemen walking their steeds along a plain, chatting as they go.

Metaphors abound: Melville transmutes the lowly fact that Potter labored for a time in a brickworks into a meditation on mankind; bricks become men, in the kiln of imagination, and Israel Potter as he slaps wet clay into the molds thinks, " 'What signifies who we be, or where we are, or what we do?' Slap-dash! 'Kings as clowns are codgers—who ain't a nobody?' Splash! 'All is vanity and clay.' "

No writer, not even Dickens, invents from whole cloth; but Melville was especially an embroiderer, who needed the ready-made fabric of either his own recalled adventures or an account of someone else's to get his needle flying. His sense of truth held him stubbornly close to the actual; he was, in a style we can recognize as modern, both bookish and autobiographical. Though such a writer can never run out of other men's books, he can run out of autobiography.

Now, many burdensome things happened to Melville in the years after *Moby-Dick*'s writing besides that novel's indifferent reception. Hawthorne and his family rather abruptly left the Berkshires for eastern Massachusetts, after a brief year and a half; though too much can be made, I believe, of Melville's love for Hawthorne, it undoubtedly existed, as his monody on the older man's death and the oddly inactive but intense figure of Vine in *Clarel* show. Melville, like Hollingsworth to Coverdale in *The Blithedale Romance* (which Hawthorne wrote in the year immediately after leaving the Berkshires), came on too strong with his wish to be called "brother," but it is unlikely this was what drove Hawthorne away; the friendship straggled on for years. Nearer to home, two daughters were added to Melville's responsibilities, and his health, the constant theme of worry in his wife's letters, decisively broke in 1855; rheumatism and sciatica sent him to bed for weeks. While convalescing, he wrote the sketch "I and My Chimney," which, though fondly quoted by the present civic caretakers of Arrowhead, is, in thin and facetious disguise, a harrowing revelation of Melville's domestic attitudes. The sketch is a fantasy that the narrator's wife and daughters are conspiring to tear down the massive central brick chimney that is his chief comfort and pride. The chimney seems a phallic symbol of male independence and also, with its many secret chambers, a symbol for his creative life.

"I must say a few words about this enterprising wife of mine," the narrator tells us. "Her maxim is, 'Whatever is, is wrong; and what is more, must be altered; and what is still more, must be altered right away.' Dreadful maxim for the wife of a dozy old dreamer like me." This ogress proposes "to take upon herself all the responsibilities of my affairs," and a certain Mr. Scribe is called in to attest to the chimney's soundness. The reference may be not only to Melville's sciatica but also to an earlier occasion, around the time of the publication of *Pierre*, when—according to a scholar, William Braswell, who based his information upon conversations with Melville's granddaughter Eleanor and with Raymond Weaver, Melville's first biographer—"he had worked himself into so frightful a nervous condition that his family had physicians examine him for insanity."* They pronounced Melville sane, as Scribe pronounces the chimney sound, but the reviewers of *Pierre* brutally impugned its author's sanity. The Boston *Post* speculated that "the craziest fiction extant . . . might be supposed to emanate from a lunatic hospital rather than from the quiet retreats of Berkshire" and *The Southern Quarterly Review* stated, "The sooner this author is put in ward the better." Though Melville left no record of his reaction, such insults surely pained a man who at the age of twelve had watched his own father die a raving maniac. The question of "soundness" hovered about Melville, and self-doubt must often have visited his bedside in these stressful mid-1850s. But more important than all oppressions and deprivations, real or imagined, was, perhaps, an event within the oeuvre: *Moby-Dick* used up the last major portion of Melville's artistic capital, his years at sea.

---

*Quoted in Willard Thorp, "Melville's 'I and My Chimney' " (*American Literature* XIII [1941], pp. 142–54), which also discusses the possibility that Oliver Wendell Holmes, the Melvilles' sometime Berkshire neighbor and of course a scribe as well as a doctor, is the story's officious Scribe.

Henceforth, he must draw upon the accounts of other seafarers or write about land. And little that he saw about him in Pittsfield interested him enough to write about or could be written about with frankness. "I and My Chimney" is a virtual assault upon the women in his life; Elizabeth Melville felt obliged to pen in self-defense, alongside the printed copy kept in a scrapbook of her husband's magazine contributions, "All this about his wife, applied to his mother, who was very vigorous and energetic about the farm, etc. The proposed removal of the chimney is purely mythical."

Melville's last attempt to rewin the public that had once existed for his novels took up a fashionable subject: the West and the riverboat swindler, the frontier sharper. Very likely Melville read in *Harper's New Monthly*, to which he contributed and subscribed, Thomas Bangs Thorpe's sketch "Remembrances of the Mississippi"; it appeared in the issue of December 1855, just before *The Confidence-Man* was begun. Melville himself had been to the Mississippi in 1840, on a visit to his charming, eccentric, unsuccessful Uncle Thomas. Whatever hopes he had for the excursion went unrealized, and by the year's end he had returned East and signed up for the fateful first whaling voyage. Memories of the Mississippi trip and of his unhappy family and dismal youth may have contributed to the dire pessimism of *The Confidence-Man*. This crabbed and inert work has attracted much learned comment and appreciation in recent decades, second in this respect only to *Moby-Dick*, and no doubt there is much to be said for it: it yields many evidences of ingenuity to academic analysis, and does anticipate an apocalyptic vein of American fiction, from the later Twain to Nathanael West to yesterday's black humorists. Black the book is, and humorous its intent; but appreciation should begin with the acknowledgment that it is suffocatingly difficult to read. As one commentator (R. W. B. Lewis) has wittily said, it is more rereadable than readable, and "seems rather to bulge and thicken than to progress." Where *Pierre* is at least a bad novel, *The Confidence-Man* is no novel at all; it is a series of farfetched but rather joyless conversations upon the theme of trust, or confidence. The Confidence-Man himself, implausibly tricked out in an early appearance as a "grotesque negro cripple . . . cut down to the stature of a

Newfoundland dog," assumes a series of less contorted disguises and deprives a few fellow-passengers on the riverboat *Fidèle* of a few dollars; but by mid-excursion Melville seems to forget his trickster theme and permits his shifty central figure to stay in one costume and to indulge in a parade of haranguing dialogues. A number of critics have noticed the dizzying, vertiginous effect of *The Confidence-Man;* there is the sensation of wheels whirling to no purpose. The objective of swindling has sunk within some murkier purpose satisfied, it seems, by sheer discourse. The novel, with hardly a female character though many women must have ridden the riverboats, strikes me as the most homosexual of Melville's works; as in many an off-Broadway play, men try to "get at" one another with a merciless, adhesive nagging. The action is all verbal and takes place in a sensory vacuum; almost no attempt is made to render the boat itself or the river and its banks real—how far a fall is here from the sea-sense the early books give us! Melville's style has dismissed the voluptuousness that excited and even scandalized his first readers, and ranges from sharp and dry to monstrous, as in this sentence:

> Analogically, he couples the slanting cut of the equivocator's coat-tails with the sinister cast in his eye; he weighs slyboot's sleek speech in the light imparted by the oblique import of the smooth slope of his worn boot-heels; the insinuator's undulating flunkyisms dovetail into those of the flunky beast that windeth his way on his belly.

However, the theme, of confidence, is a mighty one. Confidence is the lubricant of American enterprise, "the indispensable basis of all sorts of business transactions," the boosterism needed to fling a rickety economic frame across the still-ragged and sparsely populated nation; the theme is worth a satire or a tragedy, neither of which Melville was well equipped to write. One cannot help thinking of what Mark Twain would have done with this material; and at moments, interestingly, the Confidence-Man sounds like Whitman: "No man is a stranger. You accost anybody. Warm and confiding, you wait not for measured advances." But Melville, though born the same year and in the same area as Whitman, looked the other way—not forward toward the democratic apotheosis but backward to Calvinism and its dark negations. What fascinated and enraged him was confidence universalized as religious faith. The linkage of the business and religious senses of the concept was, and is, firmly established in the American success formula. The Confidence-Man, in his longest role as "the cosmopolitan," sweeps it all together, extolling the press as "defender of the faith in the final triumph of truth over error, metaphysics over superstition, theory over falsehood, machinery over nature, and the good man over the bad." Optimism, whether encountered in Emerson or Goethe or the American press, galled Melville; his ship of fools is called *Fidèle*—faithful. "A proper view of the universe," the Confidence-Man prates, "that view which is suited to breed a proper confidence, teaches . . . that . . . all things are justly presided over." Melville doubted this; but was dismayed to doubt it; and his dismay hobbled him.

Ishmael tries to tell us, in *Moby-Dick*'s famous chapter on whiteness (XLII), what the great whale is a symbol of:

> Is it that by its indefiniteness it shadows forth the heartless voids and immensities of the universe, and thus stabs us from behind with the thought of annihilation, when beholding the white depths of the milky way? Or is it, that as in essence whiteness is not so much a color as the visible absence of color, and at the same time the concrete of all colors; is it for these reasons that there is such a dumb blankness, full of meaning, in a wide landscape of snows—a colorless, all-color of atheism from which we shrink?

Melville shrank from atheism, and from all facile theisms. The great sperm whale's head is a "dead, blind wall, without a single organ or tender prominence of any sort whatsoever;" it is "one broad firmament of a forehead, plaited with riddles; dumbly lowering with the doom of boats, and ships, and men." "In that full front view, you feel the Deity and the dread powers more forcibly than in beholding any other object in living nature." At the book's climax, in a very curious phrase, when Moby-Dick smashes the ship of his pursuers with "the solid white buttress of his forehead," he is seen "vibrating his predestinating head." Predestinating: the awful absence of God, the Calvinist God, becomes, in a way, God. Moby-Dick represents the utter blank horror of the universe if Godless, a horror so awesome as to excite worship. Melville has been described as a mystic, but to me he has nothing of mysticism such as might be ascribed to Wordsworth or D. H. Lawrence. Melville is a rational man who wants God to exist. He wants Him to exist for the same reasons we all do: to be our rescuer and appreciator, to act as a confidant in our moments of crisis and to give us reassurance that, over the horizon of our deaths, we will survive. After completing *The Confidence-Man*, but without waiting for its publication, Melville took a restorative voyage to the Holy Land. Landing first in Great Britain, Melville met with Hawthorne, then the American consul in Liverpool, and told him, in a famous conversation noted in Hawthorne's journals, that he "had pretty much made up his mind to be annihilated." "But still," Hawthorne went on, "he does not seem to rest in that anticipation." One wonders if Melville knew at this time that the prodigious prose writer within him had already been laid to rest.

Upon his return from his travels through Europe and the Middle East, he made an announcement, according to his brother-in-law Lemuel Shaw, Jr.: "Herman says he is not going to write any more at present & wishes to get a place in the N.Y. Custom House." Not until 1866 was this ambition satisfied; for the remainder of the crucial decade of the Fifties Melville turned to lecturing, at never more than fifty dollars a lecture. On the circuit, talking about Roman statuary or Polynesian islands, he received mixed notices. In early December, the Boston *Daily Journal* reported,

> The lecture was quite interesting to those of artistic tastes, but we fancy the larger part of the audience would have preferred something more modern and personal.

The Cleveland *Daily Herald* opined a month later,

> Mr. Melville has a musical voice, and a very correct delivery, but a subdued tone and a general want of animation prevents his being a popular lecturer. . . . We repeat our axiom—good writers do not make good lecturers.

In Rockford, Illinois, the local newspapers were less philosophical: one protested, "It has rarely been our lot to witness a more painful infliction upon an audience," and the other concluded, "No man has a right to set himself up as a lecturer at $50 per night, who cannot for one minute take his eyes from his manuscript."

With such chastisements before me, I hasten to bring my account of Melville's withdrawal to a close, and to compress the last thirty years of his life into a few sentences. He gave his last lecture early in 1860, having earned by this method a total of $1,273.50, and in 1863 he and his family moved from Pittsfield, from a farm that had never been an idyll, to 104 East Twenty-sixth Street, New York City, where Melville stayed, working as a customs officer and collaborating in his own ever profounder obscurity. Toward the end of his life, there would be an occasional flurry of excitement in literary columns over the fact that he was still alive. Robert Buchanan, an English versifier and student of American letters, upon a visit to New York in 1885 was unable to find the man he termed "the one great imaginative writer fit to stand shoulder to shoulder with Whitman on that continent" and published a poem complaining that

> Melville, whose magic drew Typee,
> Radiant as Venus, from the sea,
> Sits all forgotten and ignored,
> While haberdashers are adored!

The enchantments of *Typee* and *Omoo* were never quite forgotten, however, and figure in the memoirs of younger writers such as Jack London and Robert Louis Stevenson. Strangely, in those late, silent years the statements Harper & Brothers sent Melville showed no longer a debit but some modest earnings on his royalties.* After he died, in the fall of 1891, a communication to the New York *Times* headed "The late Henry Melville" remembered how one pilgrim to his dwelling was solemnly told by the author that he owned no copies of his own books.

---

*And in 1892 U.S. Books brought out new editions of *Typee, Omoo, White-Jacket,* and *Moby-Dick*—Elizabeth Melville wrote that they had "very good sale."

Yet—our last surprise—Melville never really stopped writing; he never surrendered his pursuit of literary greatness, merely shifted the mode and slackened the pace. No sooner had he given up prose fiction than he began to study and write poetry, as a medium perhaps better suited to his pure aspirations and metaphysical bent. By May of 1860, he had prepared a volume of poems, which Charles Scribner declined to publish. Through the Civil War, he wrote poems based upon battle dispatches—one of the best deals with an event he witnessed at a distance, the New York draft riots of 1863—and these were collected in *Battle-Pieces*, which Harper published in 1866. After his retirement from the Customs Service in 1885, Melville privately published two small collections of poems in paperbound editions of just twenty-five copies each—*John Marr and Other Sailors* (1888) and *Timoleon* (1891). Melville's poetry has been among the last of his production restored to favor; but now it can be found in every anthology, and critics no less than Randall Jarrell and Robert Penn Warren rank him with Whitman and Emily Dickinson. We have, perhaps, more tolerance for the awkwardness and obliquity that damned his verse with contemporary reviewers; but even the most sympathetic reader now cannot but be struck by a feeling of deliberate and stubborn effort in the poems, an effect of *muttering* quite unlike the full-throated ease of the prose. Like another novelist turned poet out of disgust, Hardy, Melville moves us with his effort to thrust honesty and complex insight toward us through the resistant slats of metre and rhyme. Whereas Whitman and Dickinson turned their backs on the ornate variety of Victorian verse forms and created individual prosodies, Melville set himself to school with traditional metrics, wielding the stanzas of English balladry with frequent archaism of diction and striking a resolute music of iron and wood. *Battle-Pieces* was Melville's last bid for public attention, and his last commercially published volume. The publication of his magnum opus in poetry, *Clarel*, was privately financed with a benefice from his uncle Peter Gansevoort, in 1876. No more incongruous volume could have been issued in our centennial year, amid the coarse flourishings of the Gilded Age. A massive work of over eighteen thousand lines in rhyming tetrameter, it is an epic of doubt scored for a dozen male voices and set, as it were, amid the menacing wrinkles of Moby Dick's brow.

The Confidence-Man has an abrupt, Beckett-like ending, crammed by Melville with more cosmic meaning than it can hold. Below-decks, the Confidence-Man persuades a feeble-witted old man that a commode with its chamber-pot will serve as a life preserver, and with this reassurance leads him away into darkness. "Something further may follow of this Masquerade," the last sentence reads, and though many more learned in Melville than I have worried this hint to no conclusion, I will venture to assert, following a suggestion of Jay Leyda's,* that a sequel *is* promised, and that *Clarel* is that sequel. Immediately upon finishing *The Confidence-Man,* Melville embarked for the Holy Land with, my presumption is, the reasonable hope that this voyage would yield the material for another picaresque satire along the lines of confidence and deception. He kept a conscientious journal, and his reactions in Palestine were negative but forceful. Of Jerusalem he wrote, "The color of the whole city is grey & looks at you like a cold grey eye in a cold old man . . . in the emptiness of the lifeless antiquity of Jerusalem the emigrant Jews are like flies that have taken up their abode in a skull." Barrenness and decay assaulted his senses; of the site of Christ's Resurrection he noted, "It is like entering a lighted lanthorn. Wedged & half-dazzled, you stare for a moment on the ineloquence of the bedizened slab, and glad to come out, wipe your brow glad to escape as from the heat & jam of a show-box. All is glitter & nothing is gold. A sickening cheat. The countenance of the poorest & most ignorant pilgrims would seem tacitly to confess it as well as your own." Slowly, during the nearly twenty years after taking these notes, Melville, working in the mood and metre of Matthew Arnold's "Stanzas from the Grande Chartreuse," and drawing upon guidebooks and all the sore wisdom of his disillusioned life, built up a tangled, talky tale of pilgrims circling from Jerusalem to the Dead Sea to Bethlehem and back, over rocky

---

*On page 563 of *The Portable Melville,* which Leyda edited, he observes in a note, "No wonder he planned a sequel to his *Masquerade,* not realizing that he had written the last novel that he was to see published. . . . The characters he 'picked up' in Egypt, Asia Minor, and Europe were to remain as notes in his journal."

wasteland; one line near the end exclaims, "O blind, blind, barren universe!" The characters, as in *The Confidence-Man*, represent a cross-section, but are more leisurely and tolerantly drawn; Melville has put two versions of himself in the poem, the troubled young divinity student Clarel and the more robust middle-aged humanist Rolfe, as well as a version of Hawthorne called Vine, and a meliorist Anglican clergyman called Derwent, and an assortment of exiled European and American monomaniacs, and several Muslim escorts all of whom speak a very elegant English. The poetry can be comically awkward, with its rhyming inversions:

> Beneath the toppled ruins old
> In series from Moriah rolled
> Slips Kedron furtive?

And its innocent flatness:

> Roving along the winding verge
> Trying these problems as a lock,
> Clarel upon the further marge
> Caught sight of Vine. Upon a rock
> Low couchant there, and dumb as that,
> Bent on the wave Vine moveless sat.

But it can also be quite lively, its desert imagery compulsively shot through with memories of the sea:

> Towers twain crown Saba's mountain height;
> And one, with larger outlook bold,
> Monks frequent climb or day or night
> To peer for Arabs. In the breeze
> So the ship's lifted topmen hold
> Watch on the blue and silver seas,
> To guard against the slim Malay,
> The perilous imp whose slender proa
> Great hulls have rued—as in ill hour
> The whale the sword-fish's lank assay.

Compared with that of *Pierre* and *The Confidence-Man*, the air of *Clarel* breathes with relief; there is still pain in the topic, but less in the writing. Melville is here engaged in his favorite pastime—

woolgathering upon absolute matters in an atmosphere of male companionship. The characters are not quite rounded, but, like sets of facts, they are seen in different lights as the controlling mind restlessly moves. After quite convincing us of Palestine's and Christianity's desolation, Melville as fatherly author comes forward in a pentameter epilogue to reassure his fictional progeny Clarel:

> But through such strange illusions have they passed
> Who in life's pilgrimage have baffled striven—
> Even death may prove unreal at the last,
> And stoics be astounded into heaven.

> Then keep thy heart, though yet but ill-resigned—
> Clarel, thy heart, the issues there but mind;
> That like the crocus budding through the snow—
> That like a swimmer rising from the deep—
> That like a burning secret which doth go
> Even from the bosom that would hoard and keep;
> Emerge thou mayst from the last whelming sea,
> And prove that death but routs life into victory.

Thirty-three years after his own death, Melville emerged with one last evidence of greatness, the completed but unpublished *Billy Budd*, begun as a mere headnote to the poem that concludes it. The novella combines Melville's preoccupations in a beautifully calm, enigmatic fashion. Like Shakespeare's *Tempest*, it seems to sum up, and takes us beneath the troubled waves. Billy at the end lies full fathom five, and oozy weeds about him twist. The message of *Billy Budd* is no more consoling, really, than that of Father Mapple's sermon in *Moby-Dick;* that is, a counterfeit Christ legend is shown in the coining, and Billy goes to death blessing his condemner as credulous men everywhere go down to their doom praising God. But the story is enclosed in serenity, as, from what biographical evidence there is, Melville's later years of obscurity and silence were—years of faithfully observed official duty, of wide reading whose underlinings and marginalia are among the chief surviving clues to his thinking, and of opportune inheritances from both his own and his wife's family. The fate of his sons imposed a double sorrow in these years: Malcolm committed suicide at the age of eighteen, and Stanwix, a pathetic drifter, died of tuberculosis at thirty-five. Like some metamorphic outcropping, his sons' ruin hints of the fierce strains of the household in which they were children; not idly did Melville make his most tenderly conceived father figure, Captain "Starry" Vere in *Billy Budd*, the filial Billy's executioner.

Considerations of Melville's withdrawal, whether that withdrawal is dated from *The Confidence-Man* of 1856, or the move from Pittsfield in 1863, or *Battle-Pieces* of 1866, tend to center upon the neurasthenic symptoms reflected in family letters of the early Fifties, symptoms come to a head in his long siege of illness in 1855. His biographers all—Newton Arvin most sensitively, Edwin Haviland Miller most relentlessly—read his life and works for the pattern of a neurosis that, after *Moby-Dick*, cramped and truncated a career of infinite promise. The ineffectual father, early dead in a dreadful scene of madness; the domineering mother; the shaming poverty amid genteel pretensions; the latent (or, in his shipboard years, active) homosexuality—all these existed, as well as the pressing financial limitations of authorship and a general uncomprehension of the expressive experiments the mature Melville was determined to make. But the golden day, as Lewis Mumford has called it, of American literature was no feast of best-sellers; of its four masterpieces—*The Scarlet Letter* (1850), *Moby-Dick* (1851), *Walden* (1854), and *Leaves of Grass* (first edition, 1855)—only *The Scarlet Letter* was an immediate worldly success.* There are other sorts of success, and Melville's withdrawal—not so instant or so complete, we have seen, as the mythic image of it—can be viewed as itself a necessary and therefore successful artistic gesture.

The word "novel," at root, means "news," and no novelist, even though he explore no further than the closets and back stairs of his own home, can be without some news he wishes to bring. Melville, by a series of accidents of which not the least remarkable was the

---

*Two other books of this period that were popular, and whose merit can still be appreciated along with their value as indices to the taste of their time, are Harriet Beecher Stowe's *Uncle Tom's Cabin* (1852) and Longfellow's *Hiawatha* (1855).

luxuriant verbal gift he discovered in himself, brought the news from the South Seas—the first to bring it, and still among the best. The next piece of news that he had—that God was dead and life a cruel fraud—would have been less warmly received even if Melville had himself taken more joy in it. A writer with a democratic public for a patron must hope that he will in his work instinctively line up with enough people's notion of what is entertaining and informative to make that work pay. *Pierre* and *The Confidence-Man*, for all the huge talent ensnared in their designs, and for all their uncanny foreshadowing of aspects of modernism, were written with Melville's instincts in rebellion; they are protest novels cast in a would-be popular vein, and brim with tensions the author cannot express. *Israel Potter* and *Clarel*, though relatively unknown, are relatively relaxed, if curious, productions. History elicits a certain fatalism from its students, and this little self-imposed project has left me with a sense that Melville was right to withdraw, when he did, from a battle that had become a losing battle. His rapport had been broken with an audience that cared about him chiefly as the "man who had lived among the cannibals." He had taken the sea tales as deeply into cosmic significance as he could, and had spent the artistic capital laid up in his youth. He had come to writing, at the age of twenty-five, rather suddenly, with scant record of earlier literary ambition, and had no great love for the small change—the proofreading, the polite hustling and catering—of the authorial profession. By mid-life, though not yet forty, he had come to care only about greatness, in the sense that Shakespeare and Dante possessed it, and that Hawthorne—cool, slight Hawthorne—had once represented it to his fervent, impressionable prime. In that youthful prime he wrote to Hawthorne of his own rapid and furious development, "Until I was twenty-five, I had no development at all. From my twenty-fifth year I date my life. Three weeks have scarcely passed, at any time between then & now, that I have not unfolded within myself. But I feel that I am now come to the inmost leaf of the bulb, and that shortly the flower must fall to the mould." By bowing to that organic fall, and abstaining from a forced productivity, and turning to public silence and private poetry, Melville preserved his communion with greatness, and enhanced with the dignity of a measured abstention the communion we enjoy with him.

Whitman's Egotheism

"THE PROOF OF a poet is that his country absorbs him as affectionately as he has absorbed it": thus Walt Whitman's preface to *Leaves of Grass* concludes, and the twelve decades since this brave assertion was launched upon the air by an obscure Brooklyn journalist have given the proof. Whitman not only is the first name that comes to mind when we think of an American poet, but he has done what not even Shakespeare achieved in his nation's literature: he has appropriated to his own image the very idea of poetry. Poetry is truth, he claims; it is facts and candor; poetry is free and unbuttoned and inclusive and fearless; its matter is "the roughs and beards and space and ruggedness and nonchalance that the soul loves"; its manner is that of "performance disdaining the trivial." Whitman wrenched from American poetry forever the possibility of its being a mere craft, and thrust upon it the duty to be celebration and prophecy—to be, no less, a verbal appropriation of the universe. Further, he thrust upon America the idea that it was, this crass green nation, poetic. "The Americans of all nations at any time upon the earth have probably the fullest poetical nature. The United States are essentially the greatest poem."

Such ideas did not arise altogether suddenly with Whitman. Six years before the first publication of *Leaves of Grass* in 1855, Longfellow had a character in *Kavanagh* say, "We want a national literature altogether shaggy and unshorn, that shall shake the earth, like a herd of buffaloes thundering over the prairies." And eighteen years before, in addressing the Phi Beta Kappa Society of Cambridge, Emerson had sounded the American boast with a ringing recourse to the first person singular that might be Whitman's:

Given at the Pierpont Morgan Library in New York City, on October 4, 1977.

The world—the shadow of the soul, or *other me,* lies wide around. Its attractions are the keys which unlock my thoughts and make me acquainted with myself. I run eagerly into this resounding tumult. I grasp the hands of those next me, and take my place in the ring to suffer and to work, taught by an instinct that so shall the dumb abyss be vocal with speech. I pierce its order; I dissipate its fear; I dispose of it within the circuit of my expanding life. So much only of life as I know by experience, so much of the wilderness have I vanquished and planted, or so far have I extended my being, my dominion.

Toward the end of his peroration, Emerson throws out the challenge to the young scholars of his audience: "We have listened too long to the courtly muses of Europe . . . if the single man plant himself indomitably on his instincts, and there abide, the huge world will come round to him. . . . A nation of men will for the first time exist. . . ."

If the single man plant himself indomitably on his instincts, and there abide. The world in which Emerson, and the American artist, finds himself is not one subdued to human uses by previous generations but a "dumb abyss," a wilderness radically strange, in which has been planted the other radical strangeness of one's self. Emerson frames the problem in enduring terms: the hunt is for power, the means to power is authenticity, and authenticity begins with the brute self. When this prescription was filled, Emerson recognized the fact: he gave to an unsolicited copy of Whitman's self-published, self-peddled, self-reviewed, and otherwise unnoticed volume the most generous and prescient puff in American literary history:

Dear Sir,

I am not blind to the worth of the wonderful gift of "Leaves of Grass." I find it the most extraordinary piece of wit & wisdom that America has yet contributed. I am very happy in reading it, as great power makes us happy. It meets the demand I am always making of what seemed the sterile & stingy Nature . . . I give you joy of your free & brave thought. I have great joy in it. I find incomparable things said incomparably well, as they must be. I find the courage of treatment, which so delights us, & which large perception only can inspire. I greet you at the beginning of a great career, which yet must have had a long foreground somewhere, for such a start.

Yet the foreground of the career remains a mystery; critics agree that, until the publication of *Leaves of Grass* when he was thirty-six, Whitman showed little promise. Perhaps a long sojourn within banality had to precede his explosive celebration of the mundane. A believer, it would seem, in reincarnation, he invented a fresh incarnation for himself, a persona that gave him, in Emerson's repeated word, power. From this incarnation date a number of ideas with us still, to wit:

> The Poet as Bard
> The Writer as Egoist
> The Writer as Celebrity
> The Poem as Confession
> Poetry as Power, as Simple Reality Itself.

In his preface Whitman wrote, among many words, these: "The art of art, the glory of expression and the sunshine of the light of letters is simplicity. Nothing is better than simplicity . . . to speak in literature with the perfect rectitude and insouciance of the movements of animals and the unimpeachableness of the sentiment of trees in the woods and grass by the roadside is the flawless triumph of art. . . . Great genius and the people of these states must never be demeaned to romances. As soon as histories are properly told there is no more need of romances. The great poets are also to be known by the absence in them of tricks and by the justification of perfect personal candor." Whitman added candor to the list of poetic virtues, and because of his own endured calumny, loss of a civil-service job, and—that definitive evidence of high-minded authorship—a change of publishers. He furthermore, with long-range results even more mixed, placed ambitiousness in the canon of artistic virtues, enrolled his own art in the American expansionism that Thoreau had pointedly turned his back on, and has bewitched subsequent generations with an ideal of all-inclusiveness, with an intriguing, self-defeating image of "vast oceanic tides" of feeling and notation that will make the poet nothing less than "the age transfigured." The totem-image of the poet that Whitman prophesied and appeared to embody still lies at the core of American poetry, for any who attempt to unriddle it—a kind of Excalibur that none but the pure of heart can seize and wield.

*

The nameless long poem that is placed first in the first edition of *Leaves of Grass* announced Whitman's star with thunder, and has been called by Malcolm Cowley "Whitman's greatest work, perhaps his one completely realized work, and one of the great poems of modern times." Cowley persuasively prefers the first, unrevised text—quoted here—but I cannot share his dislike for the eventual title, "Song of Myself." Whitman did not call the poem this until the edition of 1881, after titling it in earlier editions "A Poem of Walt Whitman, an American" and then, quite baldly, "Walt Whitman." The final title has ample justification in the text, beginning with the famous first line, "I celebrate myself," and echoing such lines as

> The feeling of health . . . the full-noon trill . . . the song of me rising
>   from bed and meeting the sun

and

> And nothing, not God, is greater to one than one's-self is

and

> What is commonest and cheapest and nearest and easiest is Me.

The title proclaims, that is, the superb subject of the poem, the exultant egoism which only an American could have voiced. By mid-nineteenth century the creed of American individualism was ascendant: the communal conscience of the Puritan villages lay far behind, and the cruel personal diminishments of industrialism were yet to be sharply felt. Our political institutions and our still-vast unexploited territories permitted the enterprising individual an illusion of unlimited importance and sublime potential scarcely tasted since the Garden of Eden. Whitman developed a religious philosophy out of this geopolitical fact. He was no doubt inspired by personal experiences, sexual or mystical, belonging to the early 1850s. His own experiences, however, and the specific impressions gathered in the course of a Long Island childhood and Brooklyn manhood are not the message but the vocabulary, intelligible to most of his countrymen, in which he couches his message—that is, the majestic and multitudinous yet unified miracle of being oneself.

By "egoism" I mean not the egotist's overvaluation of his own attributes—though Whitman *was* absurdly vain about his own body—but a recognition of each man's immersion in a unique and unexchangeable ego which is, in a sense, all he's got, but something he indeed does, short of madness and the grave, have. This has been true for all men in all times; only an American, perhaps, could have proclaimed it as a discovery, as an astounding thing. Henry James, in his youthful yet of course not unintelligent review of *Drum-Taps*, accused Whitman of a "plan to adapt the scheme of the universe to your own limitations." He also called the volume "an offence against art," as if—the deficiencies of *Drum-Taps* aside—such a plan of adaptation was not in fact artful. The Whitmanesque pose is a thorough artifact, and, the duty of the artist being to make a virtue of necessity, Whitman is existentially artful at a depth far beyond the easy rhymers with whom James felt at home.

In 1855 Tennyson was writing, in his "Song of the Brook,"

> For men may come and men may go,
> But I go on forever.

Whitman inverted the terms of the old tired *memento mori* by announcing that brooks and all such insensate, recurrent phenomena are dependent for their existences upon the individual human consciousness:

> And I know I am solid and sound,
> To me the converging objects of the universe perpetually flow . . .
> Through me the afflatus surging and surging . . . through me the current and index.

The embrace of apprehension sanctifies all that the "soul" takes into itself:

> I and this mystery here we stand.
> Clear and sweet is my soul . . . and clear and sweet is all that is not my soul.
> Apart from the pulling and hauling stands what I am . . .
> I pass death with the dying, and birth with the new-washed babe . . . and am not contained between my hat and boots,

And peruse manifold objects, no two alike, and every one good,
The earth good, and the stars good, and their adjuncts all good.
I am the mate and companion of people, all just as immortal and
   fathomless as myself;
They do not know how immortal, but I know.

His egoism—the egoism of this persona not contained between his
hat and his boots—is companionable; he urges it upon others; the
"you" of his poem is as important, as vivacious, as the "I":

Who goes there! hankering, gross, mystical, nude?
How is it I extract strength from the beef I eat?

What is a man anyhow? What am I? and what are you?
All I mark as my own you shall offset it with your own,
Else it were time lost listening to me.

His egoism is suffused and tempered with a strenuous empathy.
Egoism is scarcely an adequate word for what obtains here: the
unabridged Webster's dictionary supplies, with the warning *Rare*,
the word "egotheism." The hero of "Song of Myself" is a god,
whose palms cover continents, but also a God, who enters into the
egos of the suffering: "I am the hounded slave . . . I wince at the
bite of the dogs . . . I am the mashed fireman with breastbone
broken . . . I am the man . . . I suffered . . . I was there." He is open
to stranger, more ecstatic sufferings: a soprano singing with an
orchestra forces him to cry:

I am exposed . . . cut by bitter and poisoned hail,
Steeped amid honeyed morphine . . . my windpipe squeezed in the fakes
   of death,
Let up again to feel the puzzle of puzzles,
And that we call Being.

The I-centered universe has a geometrical property which Whit-
man does not blink at: each phenomenon, as it moves into the ego's
sensational field, is absolute. There is no relativity, almost no form:

To be, in any form, what is that?
If nothing lay more developed the quahaug and its callous shell were
   enough.

Mine is no callous shell,

I have instant conductors all over me whether I pass or stop,
They seize every object and lead it harmlessly through me.

I merely stir, press, feel with my fingers, and am happy,
To touch my person to some one else's is about as much as I can stand.

In another poem, "There Was a Child Went Forth," he reaches the
rim of solipsism, the unprovability of the real existence of anything
but the perceiving ego:

The doubts of day-time and the doubts of night-time, the curious
whether and how,
Whether that which appears so is so, or is it all flashes and specks?
Men and women crowding fast in the streets, if they are not flashes and
specks what are they?

In "Crossing Brooklyn Ferry" he triumphantly, acceptingly apos-
trophizes:

Appearances, now or henceforth, indicate what you are.
You necessary film, continue to envelop the soul.

In this enveloping—this *merge,* as Whitman would say—the animal
health of the perceiver suffuses the witnessed universe with benevo-
lence and confidence; the obligatory optimism of American enter-
prise has found its theology, a panoramic egotheism. An ideal
equality is extended not only to persons but to things as well; in
the ecstasy of consciousness,

The insignificant is as big to me as any,
What is less or more than a touch?

The perfect democracy of stimuli—"Not an inch nor a particle of
an inch is vile"—gives Whitman's tireless catalogues at their best
a beautiful surprisingness of sequence, and an unexpected tender-
ness of exactitude as the admiration freely focuses now here, now
there:

I believe a leaf of grass is no less than the journeywork of the stars,
And the pismire is equally perfect, and a grain of sand, and the egg of
the wren,

And the tree-toad is a chef-d'oeuvre for the highest,
And the running blackberry would adorn the parlors of heaven,
And the narrowest hinge in my hand puts to scorn all machinery,
And the cow crunching with depressed head surpasses any statue,
And a mouse is miracle enough to stagger sextillions of infidels,
And I could come every afternoon of my life to look at the farmer's girl
   boiling her iron tea-kettle and baking shortcake.

And, do I, the "you" among millions of "you"s to whom Whitman addresses his giant hymn, find it, a long century later, as uplifting, liberating, and aesthetically pleasing as he intended it? My answer would be eighty-five percent affirmative. The attempt is broad and even inflationary, but the tools are new, the details are many and vivid, the transitions between sections are brilliantly swift and vital. An instinctive American realism, an almost mischievous alertness that is the opposite of complacency, balances Whitman's monistic, Hindu side. We are surprised by many of the things that found their way into "Song of Myself." The words "baseball" and "photograph" are in it, for instance, as of 1855, and four years before Darwin's *Origin of Species* a rather evolutionary passage:

My embryo has never been torpid . . . nothing could overlay it;
For it the nebula cohered to an orb . . . the long slow strata piled to rest
   it on . . . vast vegetables gave it sustenance,
Monstrous sauroids transported it in their mouths and deposited it with
   care.

We are surprised, too, to find the word "puff" used apparently in the modern sense:

The day getting ready for me when I shall do as much good as the best,
   and be as prodigious,
Guessing when I am it will not tickle me much to receive puffs out of
   pulpit or print . . .

And, in the preface, the phrase "well hung": "Will it help breed one good shaped and well hung man, and a woman to be his perfect and independent mate?"
   The wandering observer of the original "Song of Myself" is a

much less distinct and obtrusive personality than Walt Whitman later became; he is permeated with others, with human vignettes long and short, with cameo portraits as mysteriously specific as

> The snag-toothed hostler with red hair redeeming sins past and to come,
> Selling all he possesses and traveling on foot to fee lawyers for his brother and sit by him while he is tried for forgery . . .

His preface stated, of the poet, that "He sees health for himself in being one of the mass. . . . The attitude of great poets is to cheer up slaves and horrify despots." Blunter still, he should "stand up for the stupid and crazy." Whitman's own irregular and unfortunate family, which included an idiot brother with whom he shared a bed for years, no doubt figured in his empathetic compassion for the lowly and even the criminal. A short poem of 1860, entitled "To a Common Prostitute," contains the grand assurance, "Not till the sun excludes you, do I exclude you." The previous line, we might note, reads, "Be composed—be at ease with me—I am Walt Whitman, liberal and lusty as Nature"; and though his exact sexual activity was well hidden by secrecy and fantasy both, we might speculate that the androgynous nature and homosexual passions boasted of in the poems did expose him to strata of society where an uxorious family man would not have felt compelled to mingle. Even his celebrated nursing of wounded soldiers in Washington had a privately gratifying aspect; to his mother he wrote, "It is the most affecting thing you ever see, the lots of poor, sick, and wounded young men that depend so much, in one word or another, upon my petting or soothing or feeding. . . ." The dependency, one feels, flowed two ways. In a letter to two ex-patients he felt it of interest to confide:

> My health, strength, personal beauty, etc. are, I am happy to inform you, without diminution, but on the contrary quite the reverse. I weigh full 220 pounds avoirdupois, yet still retain my usual perfect shape—a regular model. My beard, neck, etc., are woolier, fleecier, whiteyer than ever.

Among the autograph documents in the Morgan Library exists an ostensibly disinterested introduction he himself penned to the English edition of *Leaves of Grass*, so shameless it was never used. The second paragraph reads,

> The Poet is now in his 49th [*x*ed out], 53rd [*x*ed out], 62nd years, & is pourtrayed by one who knows him intimately, as tall in stature, with shapely limbs, slow of movement, florid & clear face, bearded & gray, blue eyes, an expression of great equanimity, of decided presence & singular personal magnetism.

Then, there is to acknowledge along with his sometimes cloying vanity the relative unconvincingness and melodrama of the human tableaux and visitations in *Leaves of Grass;* for all his professed ardor for humanity, the verses of the retiring Emily Dickinson show more appetite for the grits and quiddities of human psychology than do Whitman's paeans. Too often, as he suffers with the slave, sweats with the midwife, marries with the trapper, lusts with the spinster, and so on, we are reminded of D. H. Lawrence's jibe,

> As soon as Walt *knew* a thing, he assumed a One identity with it. If he knew that an Eskimo sat in a kyak, immediately there was Walt being little and yellow and greasy, sitting in a kyak.

A paradox of democratic mobility seems to be that our imaginative access to other persons, force it though we will, is less sure than under a clearly demarcated class system. Free to make our own society, we make it of those that echo ourselves, and enjoy few of the enlightening contacts a more feudal and role-conscious society generates. Whitman is at heart rather shy, less a poet of souls than of landscapes. Having proposed that "a kelson of the creation is love," he instinctively turns his attention, in the precise, rather desolate, and very American lines that follow, to inhuman nature:

> And limitless are leaves stiff or drooping in the fields,
> And brown ants in the little wells beneath them,
> And mossy scabs of the wormfence, and heaped stones, and elder and
>   mullen and pokeweed.

But Whitman never ceased willing a Oneness with his fellow-man, and it redeems his solipsism from selfishness and smallness. "And nothing, not God, is greater to one than one's-self is"—but incessant creative recourse to one's self ends, as youthful illusions of infinite capacity fade, in an arid emptiness and a desperate lunge over the frontier of sanity. Such a doom, so frequent among poets after Whitman, was avoided by him, who in the next line warned, "And whoever walks a furlong without sympathy walks to his own funeral, dressed in a shroud."

Along with his magnanimity there went an elusive quality I can only call good humor—a kind of cloudlessness of atmosphere wherein what shadows exist serve to model palpable truths. This translucence, free of personal miasma, is possessed, I believe, by the noblest literature always, and is what leads us to turn to it out of the petty depressions and defeats of our lives. We feel it in the tone of words more than their content—in the simplicity of the assertion:

And I say it is as great to be a woman as to be a man,

in the comedy of the famous passage on animals:

I think I could turn and live awhile with the animals . . .
They do not sweat and whine about their condition,
They do not lie awake in the dark and weep for their sins,
They do not make me sick discussing their duty to God . . .

in the surreal beauty, Shakespearean in its casual compression, of his farewell:

I depart as air . . . I shake my white locks at the runaway sun,
I effuse my flesh in eddies and drift it in lacy jags.

I bequeath myself to the dirt to grow from the grass I love,
If you want me again look for me under your bootsoles.

The reflective and judicious "Backward Glance" that Whitman composed for the 1888 edition—the so-called Deathbed edition—of *Leaves of Grass* claims, "That I have not gain'd the acceptance of my own time, but have fallen back on fond dreams of the future . . . is all probably no more than I ought to have expected." This surprises us, for our impression is, ninety years later, of a triumphant acceptance, of a vocation unfalteringly pursued from total obscurity to popular adoration. Such hindsight leaves eclipsed Whitman's great courage. It appeared, at the midpoint of his life, a blithe courage, "as insouciant as the movements of animals," but surely was deliberate and longer meditated than most apparitions in the sparse skies of genius—the courage not merely of a novel and easy-to-ridicule style, or of his candor and scorn for the tame, but the courage it took to imagine an audience for himself—to assert that in this hurrying, culturally thin land there was a place for the poet, a vast place, and that he, Walt Whitman, would occupy it. Like many of his radiant literary generation, he borrowed courage from Emerson; but Whitman's brave advice bears no accent of the lectern, and small flavor of the stoic. At the center of the Whitmanesque storm of posture and exhortation lies a curious tranquillity, a reserve of reasonableness. The self he celebrated included a capacity for self-appraisal. His Backward Glance contains some very pragmatic sentences: "Behind all else that can be said, I consider *Leaves of Grass* and its theory experimental—as, in the deepest sense, I consider our American republic to be, with its theory."

I find that calm sentence thrilling, and also the following: "Whatever may have been the case in years gone by, the true use for the imaginative faculty of modern times is to give ultimate vivification to facts, to science, and to common lives, endowing them with glows and glories and final illustriousness which belong to every real thing, and to real things only." The mystery of Me proclaimed, what Emerson called the "other me"—the world itself —can be sung in its clean reality, and real things assigned the sacred status that in former times was granted to mysteries. If there is a distinctive "American realism," its metaphysics are Whitman's.

LETTERS

The Bear Who Hated Life

THE LETTERS OF GUSTAVE FLAUBERT 1830–1857, selected, edited, and translated by Francis Steegmuller. 250 pp. The Belknap Press, 1980.

Flaubert, that most fastidious and deliberate of great novelists, might blanch and scowl, as at one more vulgar bourgeois misapprehension, at the importance posterity has assigned to letters he scribbled off after midnight, at the end of a long day agonizing over a few phrases of fiction, in order to keep an importunate mistress at bay. The letters he wrote to Louise Colet during the five years' composition of *Madame Bovary*, together with some few to male friends during this same period, compose, as the French critic Albert Thibaudet has said, *"un bréviaire de l'honneur littéraire."* Wearied by a thousand textbooks and treatises, his statements still ringingly sound the call to artistic dedication and adamant integrity:

> An author in his book must be like God in the universe, present everywhere and visible nowhere. Art being a second Nature, the creator of that Nature must behave similarly. In all its atoms, in all its aspects, let there be sensed a hidden, infinite impassivity.

> The less you feel a thing, *the more capable you are of expressing it as it is* (as it *always* is, in itself, in its universality, freed from all ephemeral contingencies). But one must be able to *make oneself feel it*. This faculty

is, simply, genius: the ability to *see*, to have the model posing there before you.

Everything should be done coldly, with poise.

At the present moment I believe that a thinker (and what is an artist if not a triple thinker?) should have neither religion, country, nor even any social conviction.

I do not want my book to contain a *single* subjective reaction, nor a *single* reflection by the author.

There are no noble subjects or ignoble subjects; from the standpoint of pure Art one might almost establish the axiom that there is no such thing as subject—style in itself being an absolute manner of seeing things.

I envision a style: a style that would be beautiful, that someone will invent some day, ten years or ten centuries from now, one that would be rhythmic as verse, precise as the language of the sciences, undulant, deep-voiced as a cello, tipped with flame: a style that would pierce your idea like a dagger, and on which your thought would sail easily ahead over a smooth surface, like a skiff before a good tail wind. Prose was born yesterday: you have to keep that in mind. Verse is the form par excellence of ancient literatures. All possible prosodic variations have been discovered; but that is far from being the case with prose.

I like clear, sharp sentences, sentences which stand erect, erect while running—almost an impossibility. The ideal of prose has reached an unheard-of degree of difficulty: there must be no more archaisms, clichés; contemporary ideas must be expressed using the appropriate crude terms; everything must be as clear as Voltaire, as abrim with substance as Montaigne, as vigorous as La Bruyère, and always streaming with color.

May I die like a dog rather than hurry by a single second a sentence that isn't ripe!

It takes more genius to say, in proper style: "close the door," or "he wanted to sleep," than to give all the literature courses in the world.

When literature attains the precision of an exact science, that's something!

The artist must raise everything to a higher level: he is like a pump; he has inside him a great pipe that reaches down into the entrails of things, the deepest layers. He sucks up what was lying there below, dim and unnoticed, and brings it out in great jets to the sunlight.

Live like a bourgeois, and think like a demigod.

Between the crowd and ourselves, no bond exists. Alas for the crowd; alas for us, especially. But since there is a reason for everything, and since the fancy of one individual seems to me just as valid as the appetite of a million men, and can occupy an equal place in the world, we must (regardless of material things and of mankind, which disavows us) live for our vocation, climb up our ivory tower and there, like a bayadere with her perfumes, dwell alone with our dreams.

Mankind hates us: we serve none of its purposes; and we hate it, because it injures us. So let us love one another "in Art," as mystics love one another "in God."

There are two kinds of literature: one that I would call "national" (the better of the two); and the other, "individual"—works produced by gifted writers. For the first to be realized, there must be a fund of opinions shared by the mass of the people, a common bond such as does not now exist; and for the full development of the second, there must be *liberty*.

Flaubert's portrait of the artist in a materialist, fragmented society and his prescription for the artist's recourse set the tone for a modernism that, a century later, has perhaps been exhausted but not superseded. His vehemence became, in an apostle like Pound, something like fury; his purism, in a figure like Wilde (who wrote in 1888, "Flaubert is my master"), somewhat effete. Joyce took Flaubert's call for impassivity and the simile of the hidden God to extreme conclusions both stern and droll; and Proust undertook, it would seem, to write the book of which Flaubert dreamed, one "which would entail only the writing of sentences," a book "which would be held together by the internal strength of its style, just as the earth, suspended in the void, depends on nothing external for its support." Flaubert's demand that writers *see* found an echo in a famous preface by Conrad, and his call for prose to be purged of rhetoric and subjectivism has its homage in styles as diverse as those of Ernest Hemingway and Vladimir Nabokov. Strange to say, the very idea of "good writing," now gropingly inculcated in a wide world of writing courses, had no very distinct presence in prose until Flaubert; he himself frequently marvels at the artlessness of Rabelais and Cervantes. Flaubert's influence as a theoretician and father-figure is immense, and comes precariously close to outweighing the impression his works make. Postwar American writers have expressed restiveness under his sway. Saul Bellow couldn't write *The Adventures of Augie March,* he has told interviewers, until he cast off the Flaubertian principles he sought to embody in *The Victim,* and J. D. Salinger's fictional poet Seymour Glass once wrote to his story-writing brother Buddy:

> I'm positive tonight that all "good" literary advice is just Louis Bouilhet and Max Du Camp wishing Madame Bovary on Flaubert. All right, so between the two of them, with their exquisite taste, they got him to write a masterpiece. They killed his chances of ever writing his heart out. He died like a celebrity, which was the one thing he wasn't. His letters are unbearable to read. They're so much better than they should be. They read waste, waste, waste. They break my heart.

Another broken-hearted unenthusiastic reader of the letters was their principal recipient, Louise Colet. She wanted to hear about love and marriage, and all she got was Art. She wanted him to come to Paris and her bed, and he stubbornly stayed in his ivory tower near Rouen, with his mother and his mission. The tristful comedy of the mortal context of this immortal correspondence is nicely indicated in *The Letters of Gustave Flaubert 1830–1857,* selected, edited, and translated by Francis Steegmuller.

Mr. Steegmuller is, of course, an old Flaubert hand—the translator of *Madame Bovary* into its definitive English-language form and the author of a book-length study, *Flaubert and Madame Bovary.* As editor, he has been over the ground of Flaubert's correspondence twice before, once in 1953 as the editor of the Flaubert volume in the lamentably defunct Great Letters Series by Farrar, Straus & (then) Young, under the general editorship of Louis Kronenberger, and again in 1972 as the editor of *Flaubert in Egypt,* a colorful narrative of Flaubert's travels of 1849–51 as drawn from his letters and journals, with added perspective from the writings of his companion on the trip, Maxime DuCamp. The present volume announces itself to be the first of two that will be derived from the new French text of Flaubert's letters, edited by Jean Bruneau and still in preparation. Mr. Steegmuller has availed himself of some of M. Bruneau's notes, of a number of letters not heretofore available, and of our broadened freedom of printed expression, in order to render more precisely some of Flaubert's blunt language.* The scholarship, like its object, is fastidious and deliberate, and the editorial bridges between the letters carry their burden of clarification lightly and altogether give this selection commendable biographical coherence. However, the production, fine as it is, is not beyond cavil. For a volume of only two hundred and fifty pages, the page is exceptionally large, and the print meanly small and set in lines twenty-eight picas long, which, if not quite as ungainly as the lines in which the Magna Carta was inscribed, still challenge the eye not to lose its place. Flaubert's signature is not indicated at the end of the letters, and no typographical distinction is observed—neither a shift to italics nor a change in size—between the epistolary text and the editor's commentary: the result is a passing ambiguity, on several pages, as to who is speaking, Flaubert or Mr. Steegmuller. The footnotes are given at the end of each letter, which is a convenience for the printer but a trouble to the reader.

---

*For example, "I pitied the baseness of all the people who have attacked that poor woman because she spread her legs to admit a prick other than the one officially designated for the purpose," written to Alfred LePoittevin on April 2, 1845, of Mme. Louise Pradier, was translated in the 1953 selection simply as, "I pitied the baseness of all those people at the throat of the poor woman." The earlier edition translates the first but not the second of these sentences to Louis Bouilhet on November 14, 1850: "We are dancing not on a volcano, but on the rotten seat of a latrine. Before very long, society is going to drown in nineteen centuries of shit, and there'll be a lot of shouting." And it omits the many lascivious details with which Flaubert's letters from Egypt are crowded. By 1972, when *Flaubert in Egypt* was published, such suppressions were no longer thought necessary—indeed, without erotic adventures like the young traveller's night with the Esna courtesan Kuchuk Hanem, the book would have slender substance. A certain poetry can arise from Flaubert's emphatic crudities: on November 14, 1840, upon his return to Rouen from Corsica, he wrote to Ernest Chevalier, "I'm disgusted to be back in this damned country where you see the sun in the sky about as often as a diamond in a pig's ass-hole. I don't give a shit for Normandy and la belle France."

Professedly a translation from the French, this volume contains quite a sprinkling of French untranslated, from snatches of idiom like *"c'est la vie," "pauvre vieux," "à contrecœur,"* and *"je t'embrasse"* to more than a few lines of poetry; e.g., *"Il ira, joyeux oiseau, saluer dans les pins le soleil levant."* Undoubtedly, these words would lose something in an English rendering, but such loss is part of the contract of any translation, *ça va sans dire.* And though one rarely wishes any book longer than it is, one wonders in this instance why quite so many ellipses have been inserted, and why some letters included in the earlier, smaller selection (four, for instance, of the letters written to Louise Colet before their final break in 1855) have been excluded from this, which feels, all in all, patchier and less complete than it should.

No great matter: this edition with its apparatus provides access as direct as can now be had to an aloof and, in a number of ways, a repellent man. Repelling, indeed, was his forte; his maneuvers with Louise Colet—subverting a mistress into an absentee confidante of his aspirations, setting his superb tirades upon Art between him and the seductive neediness of an impoverished widow—constitute one of his many refusals to do what other people wanted him to do. His father, the formidable Dr. Achille-Cléophas Flaubert, judged his second son not to have the makings of a doctor and sent him to law school; Gustave managed to crystallize his disgust and boredom there into a case of epilepsy that secured his return home to the dreaming, reading, and writing that obsessed him. After his father died, his epilepsy eased off and his inherited income protected him from all incursions save that of a marriageable temptress. Early fascinated by St. Anthony, he was himself a great resister of temptations. Lust he recognized as a chink in his armor, and he used both prostitutes and chastity to seal it. He was charmed by whores and in these letters has much good to say of them. "Naples is a charming city thanks to its great numbers of pimps and whores." "Our century is a century of whores, and so far what is least prostituted is the prostitute." He noted that "my heart plays the very whore, gushingly receptive to anything and everything" and admired how "brothels provide condoms as protection against catching the pox from infected vaginas. Let us always have a vast condom within us to protect the health of our soul amid the filth into which it is plunged."

Flaubert, after a typical Continental sexual initiation by a female servant and a Marseilles hotel-keeper, voluntarily remained chaste for two years in his early twenties, and with much protestation allowed himself to be launched into an affair with Mme. Colet. He met her, a married poetess eleven years his senior, in the studio of a Paris sculptor shortly after the sudden deaths of his sister and his father. "You are the only woman," he wrote her soon afterward, "whom I have both loved and possessed. Until now I used women to satisfy desires aroused in me by other women. You made me untrue to my system, to my heart, perhaps to my nature." A letter later: "Don't you know that to love excessively brings bad luck to both? It's like over-fondled children: they die young. Life is not made for that. Happiness is a monstrosity; they who seek it are punished." The theme of children enters their correspondence as a dread undercurrent. As it becomes clear that his visits to Paris and her will be at best bimonthly, she waxes importunate, and he rebukes her by likening himself, gloriously, to a tree: "Its branches may be unruly, but they are thick and leafy, and they reach out in all directions to breathe the air and the sun. You want to tame that tree, to make it into a charming espalier that would be trained against a wall: true, it would then bear lovely fruit, which a child could pick without a ladder." The metaphorical child becomes actual in the next day's letter: "You desire a child—admit it. You are wishing for one, as yet another bond that would unite us . . . the very idea sends a shiver up my spine. And if to prevent its coming into the world I had to leave the world, the Seine is right here, and I'd jump in this very moment with a 36-pound cannon-ball attached to my feet."

To his mother Flaubert confided, "For me, marriage would be an apostasy: the very thought terrifies me. . . . I know very well that I shall never love another woman as I do you." Yet it is less his mother who looms in these letters as Louise's rival than his male friends. Toward four of them—Ernest Chevalier, Alfred LePoittevin, Maxime DuCamp, and Louis Bouilhet, who in that order occupied the center of his affections—he directs effusions that, even allowing for the diction of male friendship in that era, have homoerotic content. Before he lost his hair and put on weight, Flaubert was a handsome man as well as, in his surly way, a brilliant one; jealousies over his friendship existed between DuCamp and Le-Poittevin and then between Bouilhet and DuCamp. When Le-Poittevin married, it was regarded by Flaubert as a sad betrayal ("Too late! Let be what will be. I will always be here for you"), and when LePoittevin died, Flaubert was at his bedside for two nights, and in a letter to DuCamp described the vigil ("I wrapped him in his shroud, I gave him the farewell kiss, and saw him sealed in his coffin") as if LePoittevin's wife were not there. With Du-Camp, amid the homosexual enticements of Egypt, Flaubert addresses Bouilhet in such language as "Ah, you old bardash [catamite; kept boy]" and "The thought of you was like a constant vesicant, inflaming my mind and making its juices flow." In recounting one lubricious episode, Flaubert teases Bouilhet about the size of his penis and indulges in friendly misogyny: "Which in turn goes to show, dear Sir, that women are women everywhere: say what you will, upbringing and religion make no difference: they only cover up a little." Bouilhet, on his side, enlisted by Louise (whose husband had died while Flaubert was in the Orient) to further her case with her elusive lover, instead describes to Flaubert her natural wish to marry him as "monstrous" and in his fervor inadvertently pens an Alexandrine—"*Elle veut, elle croit devenir ton épouse!*" But Flaubert's male companionships, like his female contacts, took second place to his art; when DuCamp, a literary activist now best remembered for his historic photographs of Egypt and his not always trustworthy memoirs of Flaubert, became importunate in *his* way, pleading with Flaubert to come up to Paris and publish something speedily, Flaubert responded with a firm rebuff: "You and I are no longer following the same road; we are no longer sailing in the same skiff. May God lead each of us to where each of us wants to go! As for me, I am not seeking port, but the high seas." To Louise Colet he wrote of the exchange:

I have sent him another letter from the same barrel (of vinegar) as my first. I think he'll be reeling for some time from such a blow, and that he will now keep quiet. I am a very peaceable fellow up to a certain point—up to a certain frontier (that of my freedom), which no one is to pass. So, since he chose to trespass on my most personal territory, I knocked him back into his corner.

His abnegations and defenses turned him prematurely old. At the age of eighteen, he wrote to Ernest Chevalier, "I have nothing but immense, insatiable desires, frightful boredom and incessant yawns," and at the age of twenty-two he was "already suffering from old men's illnesses." A year later, he confided to LePoittevin, "I no longer feel the glowing enthusiasm of youth . . . I am ripe. . . . I try to pass the time in the least boring way possible, and I have found it. Do as I do. *Break with the outside world,* live like a bear." He frequently described himself as a bear, and came to resemble one. Before he was thirty, he was writing to Bouilhet, "I am getting fat and paunchy and repulsively common-looking. . . . Yes, I am growing old. I feel that I am no longer capable of coming up with anything good. I have a terror of everything to do with style." Writing to Louise Colet while in the first throes of *Madame Bovary,* the hibernating bear—perhaps dramatizing his own self-tortures to counterbalance her complaints—avowed more terror: "When I reflect that so much beauty has been entrusted to me—to me—I am so terrified that I am seized with cramps and long to rush off and hide, no matter where." A month later: "You speak of your discouragements: if you could see mine! [I] am sustained only by a kind of permanent frenzy, which sometimes makes me weep tears of impotence but never abates. I love my work with a love that is frantic and perverted, as an ascetic loves the hair shirt that scratches his belly."

His correspondence late and early brims with vows and allusions to his version of religion. "I am turning toward a kind of aesthetic mysticism (if those two words can go together), and I wish it were more intense," he wrote to Louise Colet, and this: "The true poet, for me, is a priest." Nor did he shirk the duty of the religious to hate the world; indeed, it came naturally to him. To Maxime Du-Camp he wrote at the age of twenty-four, "While still very young

I had a complete presentiment of life. It was like a nauseating smell of cooking escaping through a ventilator: you don't have to eat it to know it would make you vomit." And, five years later: "My youth . . . steeped me in an opiate of boredom, sufficient for the remainder of my days. I hate life. There: I have said it; I'll not take it back. Yes, life; and everything that reminds me that life must be borne." And he sees, in true Christian fashion, the great worth of suffering, inveighing against modern Socialists that "they have denied suffering; they have blasphemed three-quarters of modern poetry, the blood of Christ that stirs within us. Nothing will extirpate suffering, nothing will eliminate it. Our purpose is not to dry it up, but to create outlets for it." "The soul," he claims, "expands with suffering, thus enormously increasing its capacity; what formerly filled it to the point of bursting now barely covers the bottom." The doctor's son, who as a child witnessed many dissections, seems to join voices with the desert saint manqué: "The human heart can be enlarged only by being lacerated."

A curious cruelty in Flaubert led him to dote, in foppish fashion, upon the ancient tyrants and their sybaritic world of slavery and slaughter, the realm most congenial to his imagination, and the site of his more foppish novels. This attraction was present early; at the age of seventeen he wrote to Chevalier, "I love to see men . . . like Nero, like the marquis de Sade. When you read history, when you see the same old wheels always rolling along the same old roads in the midst of ruins, turning, turning in the dusty path of the human race, those figures loom up like Egyptian priapi . . . Those monsters explain history for me, they are its complement, its apogee, its moral, its dessert." For such an imagination, locked into perpetual protest against the impure and tedious world around him, to set a novel in that very world—circumambient and common, provincial and drab—was a tour de force so brutal he recoiled from repeating it. In thanking the great Sainte-Beuve for his favorable review of *Madame Bovary*, Flaubert wrote, "I regard this book as a work of pure art, the result of an inflexible resolve. Nothing more. It will be a long time before I write anything else of the kind. It was *physically* painful for me to write it. Now I want to live—or rather resume living—amid less nauseating scenes." He commenced

Salammbô, set in barbaric Carthage, where, amid the torture and butchery and child-devouring gods, he could indeed write his heart out.

It is difficult, reading *Madame Bovary* now, to sense much of the disgust with which Flaubert claimed he wrote it. Its rural Normandy, pre-electricity and pre-automobile, has become for us as exotic as the Oriental vistas Flaubert loved to dream about, and is rendered with a fidelity that passes, after a century's lapse, as affection. The heroine is beautifully felt, from within, by the author's feminine side, and vividly seen from without by his masculine self. The satire on poor M. Homais has lost its sting, and seems now merely comic and, in what we insist on reading as a love story, disproportionate. Flaubert himself, as he reported to Louise Colet his epic progress—moving along scene by scene, never advancing until he was satisfied with the previous pages, so that the book took form in one glacially slow draft—sometimes betrayed enthusiasm. Of the celebrated scene at the agricultural fair, he wrote her:

> If the effects of a symphony have ever been conveyed in a book, it will be in these pages. I want the reader to hear everything together, like one great roar—the bellowing of bulls, the sighing of lovers, the bombast of official oratory. The sun shines down on it all, and there are gusts of wind that threaten to blow off the women's big bonnets.

A scene from Tolstoy seems conjured up. Though *Madame Bovary* is often extolled as the first modern novel, its realism is no more limpid and telling than Stendhal's, or more strenuous and determined than Balzac's. At the outset of his five years' labor, Flaubert expressed wariness of "producing a kind of chateaubriandized Balzac," and at the end of it he confessed to Sainte-Beuve that he regarded himself not as a man of his own generation but as "a rabid old Romantic—or a fossilized one."

The other discerning critic of *Madame Bovary* to whom Flaubert addressed a letter was Charles Baudelaire, who in striking parallel was, in poetry, bringing something new and hard out of Romanticism's rabid decadence, and whose *Fleurs du mal* was prosecuted for obscenity the year after *Madame Bovary* was. Flaubert, no spendthrift of praise, praised *Les Fleurs du mal* in terms he might have applied to himself: "You resemble no one—the greatest of all virtues. The originality of your style springs from the conception; each phrase is crammed to bursting with its idea." Sentence after sentence in *Madame Bovary* is crammed to bursting with its idea. In the fair scene, the gravedigger Lestiboudois enriches himself by renting church seats to the crowd:

> The villagers were hot; they clamored for the straw-seated chairs that gave off a smell of incense, and they leaned back with a certain veneration against the heavy slats stained with candlewax.

The entire atmosphere of a church is transposed to the out-of-doors in these few apparently simple sensory images and lifted into comedy by the "certain veneration." Of the wind that Flaubert forecast to Louise Colet, we read:

> A gust of wind coming in the windows ruffled the cloth on the table; and down in the square all the tall headdresses of the peasant women rose up like fluttering white butterfly wings.

We are inside an upstairs room with Emma and Rodolphe, as her virtue is coaxed away; we are outside with the dutiful peasant women in traditional holiday costume. A gust of wind unites them, and we feel the space beneath Emma's gaze at this moment of falling, and the casual uncaring breath of Nature. *Madame Bovary* is like the railroad stations erected in its epoch: graceful, even floral, but cast of iron.

Simple-Minded Jim

SELECTED LETTERS OF JAMES JOYCE, edited by Richard Ellmann. 440 pp. Viking Press, 1975.

James Joyce did not write letters for fun. Those in the first half of his *Selected Letters* are mostly about his need for money, and those in the second are mostly about his work, its explication and promotion. Between these two kinds of begging there is a third

kind, the erotically importunate ("Write me a long long letter
. . . about yourself, darling. . . . Tell me the smallest things about
yourself so long as they are obscene and secret and filthy. Write
nothing else. Let every sentence be full of dirty immodest words
and sounds. They are all lovely to hear and to see on paper even
but the dirtiest are the most beautiful") letters that he addressed to
his wife, Nora, when they were apart for a few months in 1909.
These *are* fun, but in their way as utilitarian as the others; meant
to facilitate masturbation in the sender and recipient, they are
published in full for the first time in the four-hundred-page selec-
tion Mr. Ellmann has made from the approximately fourteen hun-
dred pages of Joyce's letters that have been previously collected in
three volumes—the first (1957) assembled by Joyce's friend Stuart
Gilbert, the next two (1966) edited by Mr. Ellmann and consisting
in large part of letters brought to light by him in the course of
researching his huge and beautiful biography *James Joyce* (1959).
Mr. Ellmann's saturation in Joyce's life and work is one of the
wonders of present American literary scholarship; how delightful
to find a wish expressed in an early letter ("we might take a small
cottage outside Dublin in the suburbs") mated, in a footnote, to its
echo nearly four decades later in *Finnegans Wake* ("a roseschelle
cottage by the sea for nothing for ever")! Joyce's letters could have
no more scrupulous, attentive shepherd into print. Mr. Ellmann has
seized the opportunity of this published selection to bridge hiatuses
not only in the scandalous letters to Nora Joyce but also in Joyce's
correspondence with his patroness Harriet Shaw Weaver, which
was willed to the British Museum under seal. Additionally, two
new letters to Lady Gregory have appeared, and Ellmann has
brought Gilbert's transcriptions and footnotes up to snuff and re-
stored all letters written in a language other than English to the
original—translation, no doubt impeccable, being provided in foot-
notes. Against the obvious advantages of having a handy, though
still bulky, volume of Joyce's epistolary essence, it must be said that,
given an inordinate interest in Joyce (and he asked no other kind),
the unabridged volumes, with their greater continuity and higher
proportion of letters *to* Joyce, offer more sense of the master's daily
life, and of the life of the times around him. Ellmann, having once

chronicled so thoroughly the external events of his hero's peripatetic, finagling earthly adventures, seems now to want to extract a testament, a record of the inner life. He says in his preface, "In making this selection I have chosen letters which seemed to me the most interesting, rather than those most conspicuous for information . . . [Readers] will recognize here Joyce's principal assertions of his character and of his literary aims."

Joyce began asserting his character and his literary aims early; not long after his nineteenth birthday he dispatched his famous letter to Ibsen, which he himself translated into Dano-Norwegian, saluting the lofty recipient's seventy-third birthday in a tone commensurately lofty:

> I have sounded your name defiantly through the college where it was either unknown or known faintly and darkly. I have claimed for you your rightful place in the history of the drama. I have shown what, as it seemed to me, was your highest excellence—your lofty impersonal power. . . . Your battles inspired me—not the obvious material battles but those that were fought and won behind your forehead, how your wilful resolution to wrest the secret from life gave me heart and how in your absolute indifference to public canons of art, friends and shibboleths you walked in the light of your inward heroism.

From this blueprint of high intent and absolute indifference Joyce, as artist, never significantly wavered. His first book, the pallid *Chamber Music,* was published without resistance, but *Dubliners* waited eight years, while evasive lawyers and irresolute publishers and censorial printers quarrelled, until its "nicely polished looking-glass" could be set before the public. *A Portrait of the Artist as a Young Man* and *Ulysses* were pushed to their final form through a harrowing obstacle course of serialization, attempted bowdlerization, and incomprehension; and, after *Ulysses* had made Joyce's "lofty impersonal power" a matter of international fame, many admirers and long-time friends turned in dismay from the elaborate, jocular obscurities of *Finnegans Wake.* His "wilful resolution" carried him from book to book, each one a genre in itself, each one a departure in style, and the battle behind his forehead to "wrest the secret from life" gave

Joyce heart enough to withstand a thousand distractions and humiliations.

His final accomplishment should be measured against his early situation as he described it to Lady Gregory (a nearer, though lesser, star than Ibsen) in 1902: "I have broken off my medical studies here. . . . I intend to study medicine at the University of Paris supporting myself there by teaching English. I am going alone and friendless. . . . I am not despondent however for I know that even if I fail to make my way such failure proves very little. I shall try myself against the powers of the world. All things are inconstant except the faith in the soul, which changes all things and fills their inconstancy with light. And though I seem to have been driven out of my country here as a misbeliever I have found no man yet with a faith like mine." And though a reader of his letters may weary of their tireless self-regard, and a patient biographer may blink, as Ellmann does, at their "absurdities," at Joyce's "power to read into his own inclinations the imperatives of cruel necessity," the heroism remains; Joyce is the wily Odysseus of modernism, the survivor who did everything he asked of himself. While undergoing the last and longest of his adventures, the composition of his "night-book" *Finnegans Wake,* he blames some of "the indignant hostility shown to my experiment" upon the "personal rancours of disappointed artists who have wasted their talents or perhaps even their genius while I with poorer gifts and a dreadful lot of physical and mental hardship have or seem to have done something." A few years earlier, writing to John Quinn about *Ulysses* (a valuable letter not included in this selection), Joyce ended simply, "The book has reduced me to a state of helplessness in the face of many material difficulties . . . but I am satisfied that I have done what I set out to do." The filmmaker Eisenstein, meeting Joyce in the 1930s, said to a friend, "This fellow really *does* what all of you *wanted* to do."

Mr. Ellmann, thriftily reusing the biographical interlarding prepared for his earlier editions of the letters, has cast the book in five sections; each has its geographical locus and its central correspondents. The first, "Dublin and Paris (1882–1904)," shows Joyce as a young Dubliner and divides between stately dispatches to the greats whom he expects to join and letters home, many of a hurried and desperate sort. His mother's illness ("Dear Mother Please write to me at once if you can and tell me what is wrong," a postcard reads in its entirety) brings him back from Paris, and in June of the next year he meets Nora Barnacle. Very soon he is writing her sentences like "It is strange from what muddy pools the angels call forth a spirit of beauty," confessing his "contemptuous, suspicious nature," and committing himself to his "dear simple-minded, excitable, deep-voiced, sleepy, impatient Nora." "How I hate God and death! How I like Nora!" he exclaims in one letter, and little more than a month later, in October of 1904, a flurry of notes to friends ("I have absolutely no boots / J A J") signals his departure for the Continent, his life's mate at his side and the material of his life's work locked inside his head.

His two chief confidants in the decade of "Pola, Rome, Trieste (1904–1915)" are his brother Stanislaus, left behind in Dublin, and, for an interval when Joyce is also in Dublin, his wife, Nora, left behind in Trieste. During this time, four of his books are written, and the fifth *(Ulysses)* is planned, yet the world remains ignorant of his genius. To Stanislaus he confides the domestic details of his survival, the travails of his Berlitz School teaching and the private English lessons he gives, the birth of his children, and the progress of his works. The highfalutin and frolicsome tone of the brilliant, arrogant student hardens to a steely diffidence: "The stories in *Dubliners* seem to be indisputably well done but, after all, perhaps many people could do them as well. I am not rewarded by any feeling of having overcome difficulties." And he reads; though hard to impress ("Without boasting I think I have little or nothing to learn from the English novelists"), he is capable of generous enthusiasms—"As for Tolstoy I disagree with you altogether. Tolstoy is a magnificent writer. He is never dull, never tired, never pedantic, never theatrical!" When the publisher Grant Richards begins the series of small balks that were to delay the publication of *Dubliners* for eight years, Joyce, only twenty-four, sounds the clarion note of his fully developed integrity:

> I cannot do any more than this. I cannot alter what I have written. All these objections of which the printer is now the mouthpiece arose in my mind when I was writing the book, both as to the themes of the stories and their manner of treatment. Had I listened to them I would not have written the book. I have come to the conclusion that I cannot write without offending people . . . I can see plainly that there are two sides to the matter but unfortunately I can occupy only one of them.

In the annals of the writer-publisher relationship there is no nobler passage than this.

The "dirty" letters to Nora have claimed much of the attention this book has received, and Ellmann devotes several pages of his general introduction to a consideration of Joyce's erotic attitudes. "The atmosphere is not one of Catholic guilt, but it is certainly not one of pagan insouciance either. He feels compelled to set images of purity against images of impurity." What Joyce saw in Nora, and why he stayed with her, puzzled his contemporaries; his early letters to Stanislaus give glimpses of a shared "simplicity." "She says I have a beautiful character. She calls me simple-minded Jim." In one letter Joyce mildly complains, "Nora, of course, doesn't care a rambling damn about art," and in the next defends her: "You are harsh with Nora because she has an untrained mind. . . . Her disposition, as I see it, is much nobler than my own, her love also is greater than mine for her. I admire her and I love her and I trust her—I cannot tell how much. I trust her. So enough." Six months later, he writes, "Cosgrave, too, said I would never make anything of her, but it seems to me that in many points in which Cosgrave and I are deficient she does not require any making at all." One of these points, evidently, was a healthy sexuality—remarkably healthy, perhaps, for a provincial girl reared in Irish Catholicism. His letters of 1909 record an instance in which she taught him a new position, and trace her—at first reluctant—collaboration in an exchange of pornographic letters. None of hers have survived, but Joyce admits of one letter that "Yes, it is worse [than his own] in one part or two." His own become quite frenzied. The amorousness of this "extraordinary lover," as he styles himself, had a powerful voyeuristic component, and a pronounced gravitation toward the "bum" and its functions. That she cheerfully indulged his anal, puerile, even masochistic sexual nature considerably explains her value as wife to this man who, in most non-sexual respects, was a resolute "minority of one." His letters, savagely and laughably obscene as parts of them are, in other parts—in the same breath, indeed—become supremely tender, and overall testify, touchingly and convincingly, to that gift Joyce found it so hard to bestow, of trust. In these dozen or so pages, a mere rumor up to now, and no doubt destined to be pirated by the porno presses, one finds the Joyces' marital bond embodied—flesh given the more lasting flesh of words.

In "Zurich, Trieste (1915–1920)," Joyce, war-locked with his family in Switzerland, emerges as a published writer at last, a celebrity, and, to the growing number of his patrons and friends, a cause. Grant Richards had finally brought out *Dubliners*, and Yeats's friend "Ezra Pound who is indeed a wonder worker" arranged for the serial publication in *The Egoist* of *A Portrait of the Artist as a Young Man*. Harriet Shaw Weaver, editor of *The Egoist*, became Joyce's benefactress, sending him, anonymously at first, gifts of money; his letters to her have a tone of genuine humble gratitude unique in Joyce's correspondence:

> You have given me most generous and timely help. I wish I could feel myself worthy of it either as a poet or as a human being. All I can do is thank you.

In 1916 he haughtily refers his newly acquired American publisher, B. W. Huebsch, to *Who's Who* for biographical information. His letters begin to be filled with mention of "the wretched book" that he is writing, "as Aristotle would say, by different means in different parts." He correctly predicts, "The elements needed will fuse only after a prolonged existence together." And in Zurich he makes the acquaintance of Frank Budgen, an expatriate English painter with whom he strikes up a comradely warmth absent from his letters since his relationship with Stanislaus cooled: "Need I tell you what a great privation it is to me to have not here within ear-shot your ever patient and friendly self?" Joyce's life was acquiring a proper equipment, of money, fame, and friends. Still, in 1920 as in 1904, he seemed to have no boots, writing to Ezra Pound,

"I wear my son's boots (which are two sizes too large) and his castoff suit which is too narrow in the shoulders . . . I spend the greater part of my time sprawled across two beds surrounded by mountains of notes."

"Paris (1920–1939)" holds the Joyce of literary legend, of *Ulysses* and Shakespeare and Company, of the mytho-comic encounters with Proust ("I've headaches every day. My eyes are terrible," Joyce is supposed to have said by one account, to which Proust replied, "My poor stomach. What am I to do?") and Hemingway ("The report is that he and all his family are starving," Hemingway wrote Sherwood Anderson in 1922, "but you can find the whole celtic crew of them every night in Michaud's where Binney and I can only afford to go once a week"). Joyce's letters from this time are rather dull. The epic event comes and goes early in the decade. In 1920, he writes Harriet Weaver, "The book contains (unfortunately) one episode more than you suppose in your last letter. I am very tired of it and so is everybody else." To Frank Budgen he writes of "Circe which by the way is a dreadful performance." To an Italian friend he writes of the "libraccio" (horrible book). To his Aunt Josephine, in Dublin, he writes three weeks before the projected publication date for information about Molly Bloom's prototype and her relatives: "Get an ordinary sheet of foolscap and a pencil and scribble any God damn drivel you may remember about these people." Then the book is out (on Joyce's fortieth birthday, thanks to the heroics of the Dijon printers), and the reader and the writer of these letters are left with the afterwash of a great achievement; celebrity does not bring ease, nor recognition wealth. "My position is a farce," Joyce wrote in 1927. "Picasso has not a higher name than I have, I suppose, and he can get 20,000 or 30,000 francs for a few hours work. I am not worth a penny a line . . ." For the twelve years to come, he is occupied with his daughter Lucia's growing madness and his son Giorgio's bad marriage and his own gathering blindness, and, above all, with the composition of *Finnegans Wake*. We tend to picture the Joycean oeuvre as a single peak with foothills (where the shallow stream of *Chamber Music* twinkles and the perfect gray village of *Dubliners* basks in its own "scrupulous meanness") that slope up through the confessional scree of *A*

Portrait and *Exiles* to the mountain of *Ulysses,* beyond whose grand crags there is a kind of giddy Irish mist none save graduate students of philology dare venture into. But from the perspective of Joyce's own life, as graphed by these selected letters, the creation of *Finnegans Wake* was the fondest and longest and bravest labor of all. By 1923, he was sending Miss Weaver fragments of the strange "Omniboss" he was building in his head; in March of 1924 he wrote,

> I have finished the Anna Livia piece. Here it is. After it I have hardly energy enough to hold the pen and as a result of work, worry, bad light, general circumstances and the rest. A few words to explain.

He kept explaining *Finnegans Wake* to her, hoping she would like it; several of the newly published letters are word-by-word breakdowns of individual passages as they appeared in the Paris review *transition.* "One great part of every human existence is passed in a state which cannot be rendered sensible by the use of wideawake language, cutandry grammar and goahead plot." She wrote, "It seems to me you are wasting your genius," and cited Ezra Pound in support. Joyce said, "It is possible Pound is right but I cannot go back," and, amid a hail of familial and medical problems, he went slowly forward, shedding old supporters and gaining a few new ones, accumulating the compacted puns of the most esoteric book ever written, a verbal Book of Kells that must be read letter by letter. Looking into *Finnegans Wake* naïvely, without benefit of the analyses that can now be found in every paperback bookstore, one receives, unexpectedly, an impression of joy, of exclamation (has any book ever had so many exclamation points?), of ceaseless Irish talk. Though the meaning is in most places obscure, the accent is everywhere unmistakable. Through his long exile, Joyce attempted to re-create the sound of the voices that had surrounded him in Dublin's homes and streets and pubs; of *Ulysses* he told Djuna Barnes, "They are all there, the great talkers, they and the things they forgot"—the remark is even truer of *Finnegans Wake.* "A high old tide for the barheated publics and the whole day as gratiis!" Perhaps one should not even resist the impression of drunken mumbling, of children's mispronunciation. The book brims with games, with childish manipulations, with shouting, and there is something on every page to make us laugh out loud. The last chapters of *Ulysses* and all of *Finnegans Wake* are remarkably cheerful. Through the polymathic richness of allusion—the "enigmas and puzzles that . . . will keep the professors busy for centuries arguing over what I meant"—we gaze into a strange simplicity, the simple-mindedness that Nora Barnacle had felt in her young lover and that Joyce had confessed to Frank Budgen, saying, "With me, the thought is always simple." At the outset, Joyce had credited Ibsen with wresting "the secret from life"; *Finnegans Wake,* that illiterate-looking climax of literacy, that babble of "barheated" voices, offers Joyce's secret. Its paradox of simplicity and complexity descends from the father of whom Joyce writes to Harriet Weaver in 1932, upon his death, "He was the silliest man I ever knew and yet cruelly shrewd . . . Hundreds of pages and scores of characters in my books came from him." That same year, he confides to Alfred Bergan, "No man could be worthy of such intense love as my father had for me." His secret, then, and the secret of his demonic powers of celebration and defiance, may be this simple: he felt loved by a father he loved.

"Saint-Gérand-le-Puy, Zurich (1939–1941)" sees Joyce into the grave. The coming of war chased him from Paris, as he had been chased from Trieste in 1915. He writes most of his letters now in other languages—in French, Italian, and German. He does not, though idle, begin a new book. His last one seems to have fallen into silence. *"Vous me parlez d'un certain 'roman' que j'ai écrit,"* he writes from the village, near Vichy, of Saint-Gérand. *"Ici personne n'a soufflé mot de son existence."* Not a word of its existence. Not a word, either, of a new beginning; he rereads *Finnegans Wake,* "adding commas." An old friend and amanuensis, Paul Léon, shows up in the village, fleeing the Germans. He and Joyce together methodically compile the list of nine hundred misprints in *Finnegans Wake* that is Joyce's last literary labor. In 1906, he wrote his brother, "I have written quite enough and before I do any more in that line I must see some reason why—I am not a literary Jesus Christ." In 1941, he writes his brother, in Italian, a list of people who might help Stanislaus survive in Hitler's Europe, and within the month is dead, of a duodenal ulcer he had been harboring. His desk was clean.

Advancing Over Water

LETTERS TO FRIENDS, FAMILY, AND EDITORS, by Franz Kafka, translated from the German by Richard and Clara Winston. 509 pp. Schocken Books, 1977.

Letter writing meant a good deal to Kafka. The short story that was his own favorite, "The Judgment"—written in a single long night in September of 1912, a night when, his diaries tell us, "I heaved my own weight on my back," a night of "complete opening out of the body and the soul"—concerns the sending of a letter and was composed soon after Kafka inaugurated his voluminous, hectic correspondence with Felice Bauer. His only published book review was of an epistolary novel, whose form he extolled:

> The epistolary form permits sudden change to be depicted as in the midst of a permanent situation, yet without depriving the sudden change of its suddenness: it permits a permanent situation to be made known by an outcry, and its permanency, moreover, continues to prevail.

To a man torn between an unmanageable "reality" and an impossibly ideal "literature," a letter might seem a bridge, an emissary from one cruelly demanding realm to another. To a man whose increasing physical frailty compelled retreat from social excitements, the mails remained a mode of confrontation—perhaps the favored mode. Kafka conducted two strenuous love affairs by letter, bound into books titled in English *Letters to Felice* and *Letters to Milena.* Erich Heller likens the letters to the songs of a medieval minnesinger: "She to whom they are addressed is not 'really' being courted." The diary entry of February 12, 1922, which must have been written with Milena in mind, seems to concur, in language that might be borrowed from de Rougemont's *Love in the Western World:*

> The gesture of rejection with which I was forever met did not mean: "I do not love you," but: "You cannot love me, much as you would like; you are unhappily in love with your love for me, but your love for me is not in love with you."

A letter from Kafka's mother to Felice's mother in 1914 throws a cool maternal ray of light into the superheated mysteries of Kafka's emotional maneuvers: "I know that Franz, in his way, is very devoted to Felice. But he has never had the gift of demonstrating his affection like other people. I am firmly convinced that he loves me most tenderly, and yet he has never shown either me, his father, or his sisters any particular affection." When the explosive moment came, in 1919, to address his father with passionate frankness, it took the form of forty-five typewritten pages—the superb, lacerating "Letter to His Father," which his mother, no doubt wisely, declined to hand to the intended recipient. "Writing letters," Kafka wrote to Milena, "means to denude oneself before the ghosts, something for which they greedily wait." Over fifty years after his death, we greedy ghosts of posterity know Kafka in large part through his salvaged and published letters. Their wordage now exceeds that of his surviving fiction, with the publication of five hundred pages of *Letters to Friends, Family, and Editors.*

A few criticisms might be offered of this volume of treasure. The "Family" of the title signifies a few letters to his sisters and one to his parents; they might have been more fittingly placed in a volume of family letters such as exists in German, as *Briefe an Ottla und die Familie* (1974).* In the present volume, the footnotes are cumbersomely lumped at the back, but are far from so ample that they couldn't have been put at the bottom of the page. The dexterous and docile reader who rummages in the rear for enlightenment of "She loves me and it does not occur to her to ask whom I was with in Stechowitz[13]" is not told who "she" was or whom he was with

---

*Translated in 1982 and briefly reviewed on pp. 149–50.

but merely that Štěchovice is a "village on the Moldau, 19 miles south of Prague, with steamboat service from the city." Fabled German scholarship seems to have drawn a blank on a lot of Kafka's allusions to periodical articles. And the print seems small and the price big; soaking the captive audience of the college libraries also dampens those few devotees who wish to come privately to the Kafka chapel. Still, such demurs are mere semiquavers within the gratitude we must feel for so generous a sheaf of testimony from one of the most acute and original of sensibilities ever to commit itself to print.

These letters illuminate especially Kafka's literary side. From the first pages, his preternatural sensitivity and wry, twisted searchingness are present, along with intimations of his having been called to an impossible verbal task. "Words are clumsy mountaineers and clumsy miners," he inscribes in a girl's album at the age of seventeen. At the age of eighteen, he writes his first intensely held friend, Oskar Pollak, "When we talk together, the words are hard; we tread over them as if they were rough pavement. The most delicate things acquire awkward feet and we can't help it." In the autumn of 1902, at nineteen, he sees "fields which now lie brown and mournful with abandoned plows but which all the same glisten silvery when in spite of everything the late-afternoon sun comes out and casts my long shadow (yes, my long shadow, maybe by means of it I'll still reach the kingdom of heaven) on the furrows." At twenty, he is working on his first novel, *The Child and the City*, which is lost but which must have contained the peculiar somber reverence, the benign hopelessness, and the furtive vitality behind such an epigram as this, from another letter to Pollak: "We human beings ought to stand before one another as reverently, as reflectively, as lovingly, as we would before the entrance to hell." By the age of twenty-one, he is frequently writing to Max Brod, and has begun that enduring friendship, marked on Brod's side by a staunch fidelity to what he quickly recognized as genius and on Kafka's by a certain wonderment at his champion's uncomplicated energy, by a considerable tact and wisdom as Brod's later romantic turmoil impinged on his own sheltered debility, and above all by a comradely directness of outpour pleasanter to follow than the tortuous *Winkelzüge* of Kafka's correspondence with women. His youthful letters to Brod overflow into Kafka stories:

> On a walk my dog came upon a mole that was trying to cross the road. The dog repeatedly jumped at it and then let it go again, for he is still young and timid. At first I was amused, and enjoyed watching the mole's agitation; it kept desperately and vainly looking for a hole in the hard ground. But suddenly when the dog again struck it a blow with its paw, it cried out. *Ks, ks,* it cried. And then I felt—no, I didn't feel anything. I merely thought I did, because that day my head started to droop so badly that in the evening I noticed with astonishment that my chin had grown into my chest. But next day I was holding my head nice and high again. Next day a girl put on a white dress and fell in love with me.

Girls did fall in love with Kafka. The chronology at the back of this volume lists under July-August 1905, "Vacation in Zuckmantel. First love affair." Two summers later, he became involved with Hedwig W., whom he describes to Brod as "very near-sighted, and not only for the sake of the pretty gesture with which she places her pince-nez on her nose—whose tip is really beautifully composed of tiny planes; last night I dreamed of her plump little legs." His flirtatious, fond letters to her, from whose tone a physical relationship seems not too much to conjecture, end with the return of hers, and a reversion of "*Du*" to "*Sie.*" Even so, he cannot quite leave her alone, and follows his letter of parting with one reassuring her that "lonesomeness looks bleak when viewed from outside . . . but inside the walls, so to speak, it has its comforts." Then there is Felice, and, the chronology tells us, a flirtation with Margarethe Kirchner, a relationship with "G. W., 'the Swiss girl,'" and a year-long engagement to Julie Wohryzek. Further, there is reason to believe (Brod but not Erich Heller believed it) that Grete Bloch, a friend of Felice, became pregnant by Kafka, and bore him a son, who died at the age of seven, without Kafka's ever knowing it. In 1919, he met Milena Jesenská-Pollak, and broke with her in 1923. By this time, he was clearly a dying man, and yet he captivated Dora Dymant and, more surprisingly still after a lifetime of eluded nubility, lived with her in Berlin until he was hospitalized for the last time. An amateur graphologist once analyzed his handwriting as that of someone "extremely sensual." He vehemently denied this, but his letters to Brod show a constant eye for feminine charm. A letter of 1921 confesses, "The fact was that the body of every other girl tempted me, but the body of the girl in whom I placed my hopes (for that reason?) not at all." This ambivalent regard of bodies takes on Swiftian overtones in a letter a year later:

> Four days in the city in summertime are to be sure a great deal: for instance, one could scarcely put up a longer resistance against the half-naked women. Not until summer does one really see their curious kind of flesh in quantities. It is soft flesh, retentive of a great deal of water, slightly puffy, and keeps its freshness only a few days. Actually, of course, it stands up pretty well, but that is only proof of the brevity of human life.

In his relations with publishers, as in his relations with women, Kafka contrived to be courted. His person and his prose were magnetic. Far from neglected, he was, in the "small world of German-Jewish writing," esteemed without any avowed effort of his own. In early 1907, before Kafka had published a word, Brod, that tireless litterateur, had praised him in a Berlin magazine for his style, along with three established writers. It was Brod who showed bits of Kafka's work to the fledgling firm of Rowohlt Verlag; their combined solicitations finally, in 1912, dragged from the twenty-nine-year-old perfectionist the manuscript of brief prose pieces called *Meditation (Betrachtung)*. Its submission was accompanied by one of the most deprecatory notes ever written in this circumstance, warning the prospective publishers, "Ultimately, even with the greatest experience and the greatest keenness, the flaws in these pieces do not reveal themselves at first glance." He signed his letters to them "Dr. Franz Kafka," on the strength of his law degree, and, in contrast to almost all the other letters in this volume, those to his publishers manifest a laconic briskness. When they promptly accepted his first manuscript and asked for his conditions and wishes, he responded, "Conditions that limit your risk as far as possible will also be those I prefer. . . . I would only ask for the largest possible typeface consistent with your plans for the book."

They obliged him with sixteen-point, a display size, which he found "altogether beautiful." For their next publication, Kafka fiddled with different groupings of the few stories that met his own exalted standards. One grouping of three was to be called *The Sons* and another *Punishments;* the two suggested titles nicely bracket his early obsessions. As it turned out, Kurt Wolff Verlag (Wolff, a partner, had split off from Rowohlt to found his own firm) published "The Judgment," "The Metamorphosis," "The Stoker," and "In the Penal Colony" in separate slim volumes, with little more hope of profit than slim volumes offer now. A surviving letter from Wolff to Kafka does ask for a longer work, but in the most deferential terms:

> You must not consider the outward results achieved by your books as a measure of the work we put into selling them. You and we know that it is generally just the best and most valuable things that do not find their echo immediately. . . . The stir which a longer prose work would make would at least enable us to achieve incomparably greater sales than we have so far done.

Apropos of "The Metamorphosis," Kafka in 1915 wrote to Wolff of his fear that the illustrator "might want to draw the insect itself. Not that, please not that! I do not want to restrict him, but only to make this plea out of my deeper knowledge of the story. The insect itself cannot be depicted. It cannot even be shown from a distance." His suggestion, of an open door giving on darkness, was followed. And there is also a letter, written evidently to none other than Robert Musil, rejecting the *Neue Rundschau*'s suggestion that he shorten "The Metamorphosis" by a third. Kafka is most courteous but firm, and it was published instead in another journal, the *Weissen Blätter*. His firmness in the one instance where he needed to resist an editorial suggestion should be set against such protests of diffidence, bordering on shame, as the diary entry of January 19, 1914: "Great antipathy to 'Metamorphosis.' Unreadable ending. Imperfect almost to its very marrow." His friendly and enterprising correspondence with his publishers should be set against such disclaimers as those reported by Gustav Janouch in *Conversations with Kafka:* "All my friends . . . take me by surprise with a completed contract with the publisher. I do not want to cause them any unpleasantness, and so it all ends in the publication of things which are entirely personal notes or diversions."

His literary exertions were never purely personal; his letters to Brod show a healthy interest in his reviews and an appetite for literary gossip. He was a friend of Martin Buber, Franz Werfel, and many forgotten figures of the Middle European intelligentsia. As early as 1916, Rilke had enlisted himself among Kafka's admirers. In 1923, Carl Seelig, of Vienna, editor of a series of de-luxe editions whose contributors included Maeterlinck, Hermann Hesse, and Romain Rolland, wrote asking for an unpublished work from Kafka, for the sum of a thousand Swiss francs, a fortune at that time of German inflation. Though Kafka had recently virtually com-pleted the wonderful "Investigations of a Dog," and had on hand hundreds of pages of *The Castle,* he declined. Yet in these same failing, bedridden months he did accede to the solicitations of the newly established publishing house Die Schmiede, to which Brod had introduced him, with a collection of four stories, *A Hunger Artist.* He was reading its proofs on his deathbed. Among the "conversation slips" that Kafka, his larynx so deteriorated he could not talk, used in order to communicate with Dora Dymant and Robert Klopstock, and that the two friends piously saved, is one that betrays a dream of literary eminence:

> Tremendous amount of sputum, easily, and still pain in the morning. In my daze it went through my head that for such quantities and the ease somehow the Nobel Prize

The incidental literary criticism within his letters to his friends gently implies standards of excellence that are both adamant and visceral. When Hedwig W. submits a poem written by another male friend, he tells her, "I have read the poem and since you give me leave to judge it I can say that there is much pride in it, but unfortunately pride that walks very much alone. On the whole it seems to me a childlike and therefore endearing expression of admi-ration for admirable contemporaries." After reading a play by Wer-fel that he detests, Kafka still admires him, "although in this case only for his having the strength to wade through these three acts of mud." His fastidious aesthetic reactions frequently seek dietary analogies. In an article of Max Brod's, "a good many things seemed to me to have been cooked too hot, some passages actually burnt," and an essay by Thomas Mann "is a wonderful broth, but because of the quantity of [neo-Romantic] hairs floating around in the soup, one is more inclined to admire than to eat." His own writing, too, is not unpolluted. Of "In the Penal Colony," he tells Kurt Wolff, "Two or three of the final pages are botched, and their presence points to some deeper flaw; there is a worm somewhere which hollows out the story, dense as it is." The German language itself feels alloyed and clouded to him. He writes Brod, "In German only the dialects are really alive, and except for them, only the most individual High German, while all the rest, the linguistic middle ground, is nothing but embers which can only be brought to a semblance of life when excessively lively Jewish hands rummage through them." His own lively Jewishness is racked, in practice, by a need to be perfect, to be complete, to be, indeed, tranced. Of the night that produced "The Judgment," he wrote, "only *in this way* can writing be done, only with such coherence, with such a complete opening out of the body and the soul." Such a pure state takes its toll: "The fearful strain and joy, how the story developed before me, as if I were advancing over water." And there must be silence, absolute monastic silence. In 1913, he writes to Felice, "I have often thought that the best mode of life for me would be to sit in the innermost room of a spacious locked cellar with my writing things and a lamp. . . . And how I would write! From what depths would I drag it up! Without effort! For extreme concentration knows no effort." His letters abound with complaints about noise, which cannot be muffled even by earplugs: "You hear exactly as much as you did before, but after a while a mild stupefaction of the brain ensues and a faint sense of being protected." (He concludes one letter with an unsolicited testimonial: "I could not get along without Ohropax either by day or by night.") He tells Robert Klopstock, "The amount of quiet I need is not to be found on the face of this earth." When we write, Kafka tells Brod, "we have moved to the moon with everything we have."

This search for absolute quiet may help explain the blissful equanimity with which Kafka seemed to greet the diagnosis of his tuberculosis in 1917. His letters to Brod and Felix Weltsch following the ominous hemorrhage on the night of August 9 are playful, dulcet, serene: "In any case my attitude toward the tuberculosis today resembles that of a child clinging to the pleats of its mother's skirts. . . . [I] feel the disease in its initial stages more like a guardian angel than a devil. . . . I find living with it far too easy. . . . All that is certain is that there is nothing to which I would surrender with more complete trustfulness than death." Life for this most sensitive of men was scarcely endurable—a torture of headaches, sleeplessness, breathlessness, and anxiety. His three attempts at engagement, at marrying into the world, were, the "Letter to His Father" admits, self-defeated:

> Why, then, did I not marry? There were certainly obstacles, as there always are, but then life consists in taking such obstacles. The essential obstacle, however . . . is that obviously I am mentally incapable of marrying. This manifests itself in the fact that from the moment I make up my mind to marry I can no longer sleep, my head burns day and night, life can no longer be called life, I stagger about in despair.

His initial view of his fatal disease was of rescue: "Sometimes it seems to me that my brain and lungs came to an agreement without my knowledge. 'Things can't go on this way,' said the brain, and after five years the lungs said they were ready to help."

But as the years went on, and Kafka's weakness increased, a less original and serene sensation begins to be confessed in his letters to his friends—fear. To Oskar Baum, of a visit he does not pay: "Moreover, not only is the journey there terrible but the departure from there will also be. In the last or in the next-to-the-last analysis, it is of course nothing but a fear of death." To Max Brod: "What I have playacted is really going to happen. I have not bought myself off by my writing. I died my whole life long and now I will really die." Among the conversation slips that Robert Klopstock and Dora Dymant saved are "Fear again and again," and "Put your hand on my forehead for a moment to give me courage."

I do not mean to deny the consistency of Kafka's intuitions of alienation and hopelessness when I suggest that sometime around

1920 he became more human: neurotic anxiety edged toward "the commonest sort of funk, the fear of death," as he wrote to Brod in 1921, and a new breadth and benevolence descended upon his writing. After three years of severe sickness and of distractions that included his third broken engagement, his possibly cathartic letter to his father, and his last serious spate of work at the Workers Accident Insurance Institute for the Kingdom of Bohemia, he began to write again, and the fiction he produced between 1921 and his death—*The Castle,* "Investigations of a Dog," "The Burrow," and the four stories of *A Hunger Artist*—lifts Kafka into the empyrean of the epic artists. The strange struggles and nightmarish details—the infested wound of "A Country Doctor," the rotting apple in the back of the metamorphosed Gregor Samsa, the penal colony's scintillating torture machine—of the early fiction yield to a cosmic comedy, to fables of anthropomorphic animals and elusive, inscrutable authorities.

His letters, too, grow less tortured and arch, plainer and more genial. With Robert Klopstock he has the most relaxed of his male friendships, the least defensively needy, just as with Dora Dymant he falls at last into a complete liaison. He resumes his lessons in Hebrew and ponders Jewishness afresh. Becoming a bookbinder in Palestine had been one of Kafka's joking dreams. Among the playing children of the vacation camp maintained by the Berlin Jewish People's Home at Muritz, he writes a correspondent in Palestine, he is "not happy . . . but on the threshold of happiness." A late letter to Brod admits, "Being closed is my eyes' natural state, but playing with books and magazines makes me happy." His absolute demands on writing itself perhaps relaxed, too—at least enough for him to publish again. His ferocious, often quoted letter to Brod of July 5, 1922, may be read as an attempt to desecrate, to desacralize, the act that he had once described in terms of a miracle, and which he now confronts as a diabolical activity:

> In the night it became clear to me, as clear as a child's lesson book, that it is the reward for serving the devil. This descent to the dark powers, this unshackling of spirits bound by nature, these dubious embraces and whatever else may take place in the nether parts which the higher parts no longer know, when one writes one's stories in the sunshine. . . . And

the diabolic element in it seems very clear to me. It is vanity and sensuality which continually buzz about one's own or even another's form—and feast on him. The movement multiplies itself—it is a regular solar system of vanity.

Such a libel of the old idol is a form of renunciation, parallel to the renunciation Kafka's body was forcing upon him, and similarly—we might conjecture—fertile. Kafka was granted new life, for a few years, and relative peace. One speculates timidly about the movements within so great a spirit. The temptation should be resisted, I think—though Kafka inspired piety even in his lifetime, and Janouch's *Conversations* is frankly hagiographical—to enlist among the sages and saints this epitome of modesty and precision, whose fictions partake of the austerities and absolutes of the old religions while refusing their satisfactions. Brod's own religious disposition has colored the portrait he made of his friend: "The category of sacredness (and not really that of literature) is the only right category under which Kafka's life and work can be viewed. . . . He had an unusual aura of power about him . . . he never spoke a meaningless word. . . . If the angels made jokes in heaven it would have to be in Franz Kafka's language. . . . Here is truth, and nothing but the truth." But these letters contain along with their truth a scarcely tolerable amount of pain. If Kafka was a saint, it was of a new, forever unsettled, never utterly eased sort; his last written words were—concerning a doctor who had left the room—"So the help goes away again without helping."

Nothing Is Easy

LETTERS TO OTTLA AND THE FAMILY, by Franz Kafka, translated by Richard and Clara Winston and edited by N. N. Glatzer. 130 pp. Schocken, 1982.

Ottla was the youngest of Kafka's three sisters, and his favorite, a peaceful presence in his tormented landscape: "If everything in the world were to disturb me—and it has almost reached that point

—not you." Intelligent and gentle, she shared her brother's vegetarianism and something of his saintliness; twenty years after Kafka's death, Ottla divorced her Christian husband for the sake of his safety and that of their daughters, and volunteered to accompany a transport of children to the death camp at Auschwitz, where she ultimately met her own death. While Franz was alive, she served him as confidante and as go-between as he negotiated, from a succession of mountain sanatoriums, with his family and his employer. The letters become more copious as his disease worsens, and reflect the grim comedy, also portrayed in Mann's *The Magic Mountain,* of pre-antibiotic lung therapy—a touching concoction of fresh air, hearty food, and vain hope. Kafka's attitude toward his own wasting was fatalistic, and even welcoming: "It would be quite wrong for you . . . to see this development as having only the saddest consequences for me. It would much more be the other way. As things are and as they seem to be going, it is for the best and enters my life at the right point." His illness held out the hope of peace with "the enemy inside my head," the curious tumult of his hypersensitivity. "Yes, nothing is easy," he tells Ottla, "and even happiness, even true happiness—flash of lightning, beam of light, command from on high—is a terrible burden." Many of the communications are on postcards, which the book reproduces, including one showing the Friedland Schloss, in Bohemia—the original of his unattainable Castle.

An Armful of Field Flowers

LETTERS FROM COLETTE, selected and translated from the French by Robert Phelps. 214 pp. Farrar, Straus & Giroux, 1980.

In a time of biographical blockbusters and elephantine assemblages of the letters of the dead, *Letters from Colette* is an attractively airy, relatively skimpy production. Robert Phelps, previously the compiler of the ingenious *Earthly Paradise,* a portrait of Colette's life as drawn from her writings, and of the charming

Belles Saisons, a scrapbook, with full captions, of photographs from that colorful life, has here, in a veritable mist of the triple dots of ellipsis, distilled a mere two hundred twelve pages of English from the five volumes of Colette's letters already published by Flammarion in France, plus a number printed by her third husband, Maurice Goudeket, in his memoirs and a few that have appeared in periodicals and catalogues. This mass of material does not include the major correspondences that Colette energetically conducted with such important figures in her life as her three husbands and "Missy"—the Marquise de Belbeuf, her lesbian consort from 1906 to 1911. Approximately two thousand letters that Colette wrote to her mother, the beloved Sido, were destroyed by her brother Achille when Sido died, in 1912; but Colette's abundant epistles to her daughter, her editors and publishers, and a number of close friends survive and await publication. Her French editors, on principles of priority no doubt well considered, have issued, as of 1980, in separate volumes, Colette's letters to the actress Marguerite Moreno, her "greatest friend," according to Maurice Goudeket; to Hélène Picard, a poet and at one time Colette's secretary on *Le Matin*, "after which she lived in aloof retirement in an apartment decorated in blue, tending her parakeets and writing poems"; and to Renée Hamon, a traveller and journalist whom Colette nicknamed "*le petit corsaire.*" These three female friends, and most of the assorted correspondents lumped in the two additional French volumes, *Lettres de la vagabonde* and *Lettres à ses pairs*, are more witnesses to Colette's life than actresses or actors in it, and are addressed with candor but not with passion, in blithe accents, so that our and Mr. Phelps's disposition to perceive Colette's checkered and sometimes tumultuous career as a kind of idyll meets little that will contradict it. Not only were the letters themselves, the "Editor's Note" tells us, "all spontaneous, abundant, dashed-off, like nothing so much as an armful of field flowers, fresh, fragrant, still sparkling with dew, which Ceres, let's say, brought in from her morning walk" but an idyllic carefreeness characterized the editor's labors "all through the summer by the sea that I worked on this translation," in a place he specifies as "Gayhead, Mass."—a more tripping version of the spondaic "Gay Head" one finds on maps of Martha's Vineyard. Mr. Phelps, his sunburn still rosy, explains:

> I have followed my own taste, trimming freely and trying simply to show Colette in her daily zest, meeting her deadlines, paying her bills, at play with her family and friends, at work in the theatre, on the lecture platform, in her short-lived beauty salon, and at her lifelong writing desk. Letters and memoirs to come will certainly deepen the image this book makes, but it is unlikely that they will radically alter it.

The image this freely trimmed book makes will perhaps most enchant those who come to it already loving Colette. I am not sure one could begin to love her from these letters, though they are, like her fiction, swift, frank, tender, balanced, witty, and vivid, yet with something severe just beneath their deceptively accessible and limpid surfaces. The art of pantomime—which she practiced as a trouping professional in her six-year period as a "vagabond" between leaving her first husband, the deplorable "Willy" (Henri Gauthier-Villars), in 1906, and marrying her second, the eventually deplorable Henry de Jouvenel, of *Le Matin*, in 1912—lent her literary art something of its silence, its effective minimalism. The critic Edmond Jaloux spoke aptly of "the feline and sometimes aggressive grace with which she writes." The reader is aggressively tweaked by such a simile as "My bulldogs are adorable, with faces like toads that have been sat on." Her beautiful passion for nature does not balk at handling a shark: "I caught a little 75-centimeter shark yesterday—in my two hands. What a mug, and what teeth, and above all, what strength! No viscosity. A skin like a moist leather slipper." Somehow, though all the letters Mr. Phelps has chosen are friendly and many are loving, one never quite forgets that in the prize ring of life few of us would have lasted ten rounds with Colette.

The first letter in this selection was written in 1902, when she was twenty-eight and already trained in the ways of the world. Writing to the critic Lucien Muhlfeld, she said of the play *Claudine à Paris*, which was about to open, "It has nothing to do with literature or art, of course. It's idiotic, and you should say so. But please also say that it will be a 'box-office hit.' It has to be, because

we need the money." She had been married to Willy for nine years
at this point, and two years had passed since her first Claudine
novel was published, under his name. This strange man, a walking
pseudonym, a conspicuous dandy, a sleepless manipulator and
compulsive seducer, operated a kind of word factory in an age
when reading had no electronic rivals and books were items of the
crassest consumption. Many hands labored to produce the books he
signed, but the genius among his slaves turned out to be his little
country bride. Without Willy, there would have been no Colette;
it was via her unhappy marriage with him that she made the great-
est transition of her versatile career, from a clever village girl to an
ornament of the Belle Époque and, enduringly, a writer. There
is a great deal about writing in these letters, and a fair amount
about money. Before Colette, it has been pointed out, the female
writers of France had been aristocrats, from Mme. de Lafayette
to Anna de Noailles; there were no Jane Austens or Brontë sisters,
perhaps because there were virtually no clergymen's daughters.
Colette, the daughter of a tax collector (albeit an improvident one),
brought to her pioneering role the traditional bourgeois zest for
hard bargaining:

> If the Alhambra cannot pay me as much as the Gaîté-Rochechouart, so
> much for the Alhambra. It's an outfit which should be able to pay, at
> the least, *reasonably*. And then, too, when I have a name with proved
> box-office value, why should I contract myself never to get more than
> five louis? . . . If business is poor, so much for business.

> I've had a strange letter from Robert de Flers, the editor of *Figaro*, in
> which he speaks of unavoidable "retrenchments," the high cost of liv-
> ing, etc., and asks me to limit myself to two columns per month.
> . . . So I replied with a note overflowing with affection, tearfully
> regretting that in that case I would have to cut off my contributions
> altogether, since the same high cost of living obliged me, as well, not
> to disperse my copy in too many places.

To the Comtesse Anna de Noailles, she confided, "I have a com-
puter soul." As a performer on the stage, she exulted in her "proved
box-office value"; as a literary performer for half a century, she was
undoubtedly canny at keeping her name before the public, through

scandal and skillful self-promotion as well as intrinsic excellence. She was a popular writer not by accident. At the outset of her career, asking Francis Jammes to write the introduction to the first book—*Dialogues de bêtes*—to which she was free to sign her own name, she wrote simply, "It is neither nice nor gay to earn money with what one loves, but we live almost entirely that way."

She worked hard, with increasing perfectionism. "Am I working? Yes, if working means tearing up what I wrote last week and beginning over." "This *Fin de Chéri* will be my own, it torments me so. But I'm working terribly." "I've finished—or think I've finished—*Le Seuil*. But not without torment! The last page, precisely, cost me my entire first day here—and I defy you, when you read it, to suspect this. Alas, that a mere twenty lines, without fancy effects or embossing of any kind, should make such demands. It's the *proportions* that give me the greatest trouble. And I have such a horror of grandiloquent finales. . . ." "Scratching paper is such a somber battle. There are no witnesses, no one else in your corner, no passion. And all the while, waiting outside, there are your blue spring, the cries of your peacocks, and the fragrance of the air. It's very sad." She accepted and executed many drudging assignments. She scribbled off the Claudine novels for Willy, which he muddled with touches of lubricity and malice; she edited the literary page of *Le Matin* while she was de Jouvenel's wife; for five years she served as drama critic for *Le Journal*. In 1932, "to make a bit of money, I've agreed to write the French subtitles for a German film, 'Mädchen in Uniform.' " With her third husband, after a trip to America in 1935, she translated a Broadway play by George Kaufman and Edna Ferber, *The Royal Family*. Yet amid all this facility the artist's necessary curse of self-doubt never deserted her: "All the same, it's terrible to think, as I do every time I begin a book, that I no longer have any talent, that in fact I never had any." She disliked discussing *"la littérature,"* and the exact shape of her strict inner standards must be guessed at, from such clues as the word "rhythmical" in a confession from *The Vagabond*—"I have a writer's need to express my thoughts in rhythmical language"— and her exhortations to Marguerite Moreno, who had composed some reminiscences:

Do you realize that in all that not one *word makes me see and hear* what you're talking about? If you were telling me this in person, you would paint old Madame A. and her husband, Papa Anatole France, and the whole company in fifteen lines. You would transform your "untethered mischiefmaking" into a single line of *dialogue,* of heard conversation, and it would all come alive. No mere narration, for God's sake! Concrete details and colors! And no need of summing up!

The gods had given her a splendidly vital nature. The youngest of four coddled and imaginative children, in adulthood she appeared younger than she was, as if a certain postponement had entered her life during those caged years as Willy's wife. Throughout her thirties, once free of him, she performed semi-nude on the stage; the photograph of her "in an Egyptian costume," in Michèle Sarde's biography *Colette* and in Phelps's *Belles Saisons,* might be of a solid girl of eighteen, though it is 1912 and Colette is thirty-nine. Not until the age of forty did she become a mother. At the age of fifty-one, she took up skiing, with a fearless exuberance:

> I had my first ski lesson at once and since then I have been skating and tobogganing as well. I don't miss a chance to fall! They find me on the neighboring slopes, on my back like a scarab, waving my rear paws tangled in the skis. Passersby stop, pick me up, and I go again.

The next year, she took as lover the thirty-five-year-old man who was to become her third husband; she describes him to Marguerite Moreno in a purring tone that usurps the old male prerogative of sexual connoisseurship:

> That boy is exquisite. I prefer to add nothing more. But what masculine grace there is in a certain softness, and how touching it is to watch the inner warmth thaw the outer envelope. There are very few males who, without changing their tone or raising their voice, can say . . . what needs to be said.

At the age of fifty-five, she adopted water-dowsing ("As you approach water, the forked stick becomes live, imperious, and twists like a snake in your hands. Véra tried, but she has less 'witching' power than I. . . . So I have finally found a means of earning a living"), and at the age of sixty-eight, already feeling the arthritis that was to cripple her, she bought a bicycle. Over seventy, in occupied, besieged Paris, she wrote, "This morning the sky was a ceiling of airplanes. How strange it all is, and how eager I am not to die before I have seen it all!" Bedridden and in constant pain, laden with more honors than the French republic had ever before bestowed upon a woman, she died at the age of eighty-one. One of her letters speaks of "that elasticity which is the miraculous resort of the female creature, and about which I know something." Her own had enabled her to survive poverty, scandal, and the repeated heartbreak that an adventurous woman must suffer. From provincial maiden to Paris bohemian, from marriage to lesbianism and back again, from the demi-monde to the Académie Goncourt —Colette managed these transformations without sacrificing to her necessary elasticity a central firmness and clarity of vantage marvellous in man or woman. Throughout a life of celebrity, she kept her distinct Burgundian accent and a self-esteem rooted in her native village of Saint-Sauveur.

Freud's assertion that a mother's favorite keeps for life "that confidence of success which often induces real success" was put forward with boys in mind but, of course, can apply to girls; and the youngest child as well as the oldest—especially if her sibling rivals were two "savage" brothers and a reclusive older sister fathered by a detested former husband—might attract that heaping measure of maternal love which makes for an infrangible soundness of spirit. Colette and her mother enjoyed a reciprocity of affection which, whether rare or common in families, is rarely commemorated as it has been in *My Mother's House* and *Sido*. Sido gave a blessing to her daughter's body that enabled Colette to feel her instincts and emotions as an aspect of nature and its eternal innocence. Compared to Proust's disquisitions upon homosexuality, those by Colette in *The Pure and the Impure*—written with Proust in mind—are quite insubstantial; for her there is nothing impure, nothing worth moralizing or romanticizing about, not even her friend Renée Vivien's suicidal alcoholism. Colette is like Proust, however, in that her single volumes compose one great book of life, an autobiography transformed by the needs of art and a mysterious obligation to give the world back its glory. An instructive contrast to her career is that of Jean Rhys, another pretty vaudevillian with an irregular love life and a scrupulous prose style. Though Rhys had her admirers and her rewards, her work is elliptical and brittle and suffused with bitterness, and her life the opposite of a triumph, except in its haggard, lonely length. Where Sido's unstated presence fills Colette's world to the brim with permission to be joyful, the painful absence of Rhys's own bemused, indifferent, possibly mad mother drains reality and leaves it sere and cryptic.

Colette, already, seems old-fashioned in a way not true of Rhys —too genial, too ample, too well turned, too much part of *"la littérature"* she distrusted. We are so secure in the lap of her velvety and resilient natural paradise that, knowing nothing very bad can happen, we sometimes doze. When her fiction drifts into essay, as in *Break of Day*, a kind of grand complacency throws a shadow of the orotund—a tone almost priestly, as of a maternal Chateaubriand. But Colette remains, even now, the century's best translator of feminine vigor into words, the woman who brought to her vocation of writing the most generous measure of experience and health. *The Vagabond* still reads as a remarkably just and debonair study of a female consciousness waking to the possibility of independence—a feminist novel to shame, in its subtlety, the feminists. It is not easy, to be another Colette. Her verve and discipline, her exhibitionism and classicism do not combine every day. Her younger sisters in self-revelation seem, often, merely bawdy, or caustic, or beyond or above it all, whereas she placed herself at the center of the wide and living world:

> You cannot imagine the pure—and purgative—joy of eating black cherries which the sun has ripened on the tree. It rains, it shines, I get up at six and am in bed by nine. I am turning the color of a pigskin valise.

> It's raining gently, and feels very good on the face and in the eyes. The entire park is starred with the white behinds of rabbits!

> I am the friend of humidity and a west wind.

The book of life she was always composing gains, in this breezy selection of letters, another chapter.

Hem Battles the Pack; Wins, Loses

SELECTED LETTERS, 1917–1961, by Ernest Hemingway, edited by Carlos Baker. 948 pp. Charles Scribner's Sons, 1981.

Hemingway signed his early letters Ernest, Ernie, EH, Hemingstein, Hemmy, Stein, Hem, Wemedge, Steen, Love Pups, Oin, Yogi Liveright, and Herbert J. Messkit. Such a wealth of inventive and jocular monickers suggests a powerful wish to be somebody, whatever it takes. A few days before his nineteenth birthday, he became, he wrote his family back in Oak Park, "the first American wounded in Italy." While recovering from this, the most important wound in his life of many wounds, he was the youngest patient at the Milan Red Cross Hospital, and while still there received a promotion that made him, he proudly told his father, "the youngest 1st Lieut. in the Army." Returning home, he began a campaign against—he wrote his fellow-veteran James Gamble—"the Sat. Eve. Post. I sent them the first story Monday last. And havent heard any thing yet of course. Tomorrow another one starts toward them. I'm going to send 'em so many and such good ones, no, I haven't really got the big head, that they're going to have to buy them in self defence." He did not sign himself Papa until 1927, in a letter to Archibald MacLeish. Indeed, he employed this most famous of his sobriquets rather more sparingly than one might expect—largely in relation to younger writers for whom he adopted a paternal fondness (Lillian Ross, George Plimpton), to a few favored females who appeared to him in a daughterly aspect (Marlene Dietrich, Adriana Ivancich), and to his own three sons. A letter to Harvey Breit in 1954 he signed Papa and then thought better of it, crossing it out and writing Ernest instead. (After the publication of *The Old Man and the Sea* in *Life*, he complained to Wallace Meyer, "Then some perfectly innocent character thinks he bought the right to call you 'Papa' by paying 20 cents for the copy of LIFE and you say, 'I may be your father but you look like a son of a bitch to me,' and the next thing you have hurt somebody's feelings and you have to cool him to put him out of his misery.") To his first wife, Hadley,

Hemingway was Tatie or Edward Everett Waxen, and to Mary Welsh, who became his fourth and last wife, he was Bear Mountain or Old Mountain Man or Your Big Kitten. Three letters to Lillian Ross, who brought out in him a maximum of playfulness, are signed Mister Papa, Mr. Pappa, and H. von H., which is short for Huck von Hemingstein, a self-designation merging his ideal concepts of himself as an Old World gallant and an incarnation of the American literary genius epitomized by *Huckleberry Finn.* "All modern American literature comes from one book by Mark Twain called Huckleberry Finn. . . . It's the best book we've had. All American writing comes from that. There was nothing before. There has been nothing as good since." So he claimed in *Green Hills of Africa;* the other quotations above come from Hemingway's *Selected Letters 1917–1961.*

Hemingway did not want his letters published. In 1958, he wrote his executors, "It is my wish that none of the letters written by me during my lifetime shall be published. Accordingly, I hereby request and direct you not to publish or consent to the publication by others, of any such letters." He did not regard himself as a good letter writer, and frequently ends a letter with an apology for it: "This letter is stupid"; "Please forgive such a stupid letter"; "Please forgive me for writing dull and stupid letters." Of his missives to Charles Scribner, Sr., many of which are printed in this volume, he wrote to Wallace Meyer:

> I think you or the family should take great care that nobody gets hold of them nor that they are ever "consulted" by any of the personal approach critics; or any critics or biographers. The personal letters are often libellous, always indiscreet, often obscene and many of them could make great trouble.

During his lifetime, especially after the cost of being somebody had grown exorbitant, he bitterly resented and resisted invasions of his privacy by scholars. To Charles A. Fenton, the author of *The Apprenticeship of Ernest Hemingway: The Early Years* (1954), he declared, "The writing published in books is what I stand on and I would like people to leave my private life the hell alone. What right has anyone to go into it? I say no right at all." When Fenton proposed to publish some of Hemingway's early, unsigned journalism, he was told, "Writing that I do not wish to publish, you have no right to publish. I would no more do a thing like that to you than I would cheat a man at cards or rifle his desk or wastebasket or read his personal letters." And to Arthur Mizener, the biographer of Scott Fitzgerald, Hemingway once wrote, "I figure to have all my papers and uncompleted Mss. burned when I am buried. I don't want that sort of shit to go on." Yet here, just twenty years after the great man's death, we have a towering excremental heap —nearly six hundred letters and over nine hundred pages published through the connivance of Mary Hemingway, her attorney Alfred Rice, Charles Scribner, Jr., and Carlos Baker. By one of those disservices of which only reverence is capable, the letters are all reproduced uncut (Hemingway was not naturally laconic, it turns out) and with their "endearing" misspellings carefully preserved. One reaction seems certain: Hemingway, who so heroically strove to keep anything inferior from his pen out of hard covers, and who even at his most flamboyant retained strict notions of propriety and dignity vis-à-vis his reading public, would have hated this overlong, sludgy, and frequently humiliating book.

Well, what's done is done. As a piece of manufacture and editorial work, the volume warrants an A–, perhaps a B+. Mr. Baker knows his Hemingway, but the apparatus of footnotes is minimal, with frequent references, in lieu of helpful explication, to *Ernest Hemingway: A Life Story,* by the same Carlos Baker (1969), which in turn derives much of its content from summary of these same letters. The biography alludes to a number of interesting letters (for example, a letter of August 18, 1938, to Mrs. Paul Pfeiffer, his mother-in-law at the time, describing his break with Catholicism and prayer because of the conduct of the Spanish Church during the Civil War; a letter of August 27, 1940, to Arnold Gingrich, of *Esquire,* "computing what *For Whom the Bell Tolls* had cost him"; and a number of his last, sad, wild communications to Mary Hemingway) that are not present in this selection. Without knowing the full correspondence, as only God and Carlos Baker do, one cannot judge the selecting. One *can* wonder why, if the object is a scholarly monument to a native giant whose every word is precious, a complete, multi-volume edition of letters such as the French are giving Colette and the English have given Virginia Woolf has not been launched; and why, if the intended audience is the general reader, a somewhat less cumbersome and expensive selection was not made. The proceeds, we are piously told, "are to be devoted to the Ernest Hemingway Foundation, which [makes] annual awards in the field of American fiction under the aegis of the P.E.N. Club." Ten dollars off the sales price would have been a well-deserved award to the heroic American book-buyer. Yet there is something exiguous about the volume anyway. One letter after another slogs past without a single chapter break or interval of biographical essentials. There is no chronology of Hemingway's life, no bibliography of his works, no glossary of his major correspondents, and no typographical distinction in the index between simple references to a person and letters written to that person. This user found the index erratic. For instance, no reference exists under "Hemingway, Grace Hall" to this definitive blast, in a letter to Charles Scribner, Sr.:

> My mother is very old, her memory is more than spotty and she is addicted to fantastic statements. Lately, because she is so old, I have played the role of a devoted son in case it pleased her. But I hate her guts and she hates mine. She forced my father to suicide . . .

The index also ignores this interesting verdict upon the Spanish philosopher Miguel de Unamuno:

> Do you remember what a dull and conceited man Unamuno was? But often he was right. I used to sit around by the hour listening and waiting for him to be right.

It cannot be said that these letters add anything substantial to the picture of Hemingway's life already provided by his own fiction and journalism, by the heavy publicity he received while alive, by the personal accounts of A. E. Hotchner and Mary Hemingway and others, and by Mr. Baker's own biography. No skeletons such as have been recently found in several Presidential closets come to light. Nor do the letters enhance or soften with newly glimpsed humanity the writer's image, as do the letters of Scott Fitzgerald and John O'Hara. Hemingway in fact is seen in these missives, in their cruel dismissals and constant boasting, as even more of a bully and braggart than we had suspected. Nor are they, like the letters of Kafka and Keats, literature; written usually at the end of a long day of work and play, sometimes with the aid of inhibition-loosening spirits, they are more often than not garrulous, repetitious, and coarse. There are some exceptions: the letters of condolence to Gerald and Sara Murphy and to Mrs. Charles Scribner are quite beautiful, as are the first and last letters in the book—the first a letter to his grandfather from an eighteen-year-old boy who has spent the summer in upper Michigan working on a farm and who is worried about the potato crop and proud of three large rainbow trout he has caught, and the last from a sixty-one-year-old man with a Nobel Prize and a bad case of hypertension writing to console a nine-year-old boy hospitalized with viral heart disease. Himself hospitalized in Minnesota, Hemingway wrote young Frederick Saviers, "Saw some good bass jump in the river. I never knew anything about the upper Mississippi before and it is really a very beautiful country and there are plenty of pheasants and ducks in the fall."

From first to last, his letters do homage to whatever beautiful country the writer is in—part bragging and part simple praise of the world. In a letter to Maxwell Perkins, he described himself as "having a great deal of fondness and admiration for the earth and not a hell of a lot for my generation." His correspondence pulses with the subliminal message "Having wonderful time" that Harry Levin, in his unsurpassed essay upon Hemingway's style (reprinted in last year's *Memories of the Moderns*), saw as the essential burden of those generalized pet adjectives "fine" and "nice" and "good" and "lovely":

> The races at Auteuil with everybody crowded around the big charcoal brazier and a November bright blue sky and the turf hard and the fields good and we watching each race from the top of the stands . . . and we went up in the mountains at a Swiss old brown chalet and skied and had a bob sled and drank hot punch in the evenings and the days were cold and clear and there was lots of snow.

*

Pamplona is a swell town of about 30,000, on a plateau in the middle of the Mountains of Navarre. Greatest country you ever saw and right on the edge of the only trout fishing that hasn't been ruined by motor cars or railroads . . . Spain is the real old stuff.

The grub is excellent and there is good red and white wine and 30 kinds of beer. . . . It [Shruns, Austria] is a swell place. Wonderful town and the people very God fearing and good drinkers.

We bring our drinking water and ice and fresh vegetables on the pilot boat that comes once a week from Miami. There is no kind of sickness on the Island [Bimini] and the average age of people in the cemetery is 85.

The blunt yet somehow urgent and luminous style was there from the start, and can be detected even in the letters written at the age of nine which Mr. Baker quotes in his introduction:

I looked in a clam that I had brought to school from the river. Had shut down on one of our big Japanese fantail gold fishes tales. On Saturday Mama and I went across the ford at the river.

Words for Hemingway were elemental and chaste, spurning any secondary life of wordplay. In the over four hundred thousand words of these letters, there is rarely a simile—so rarely that this extended metaphor, concerning the sudden death, eleven years after their divorce, of his second wife, Pauline, comes with grotesque effect, as of a pained contortion:

The wave of remembering has finally risen so that it has broken over the jetty that I built to protect the open roadstead of my heart and I have the full sorrow of Pauline's death with all the harbour scum of what caused it.

Occasionally but not often in the correspondence, a word picture leaps up as sharp as the italicized paragraphs between the stories of *In Our Time.* To Harvey Breit, concerning the burial of the Spanish novelist Pio Baroja, in 1956:

The day was misty with the sun breaking through and burning off over the bare hills and on the way out to the un-consecrated ground cemetery the side of the streets were jammed solid with flowers, the flower sellers stands for Nov 2—All Souls day, and we rode out to the cemetery through the country he wrote about in Hierba Mala, La Busca, and Aurora Roja. There were not too many of us. He was buried in a plain pine coffin, newly painted black so that the paint came off on the faces and hands of the pall bearers and on their coats.

Certain traits, not especially attractive, of Hemingway's psyche surface through these letters. He reflexively saw wives as the ruin of their husbands. In 1924, he wrote his Chicago friend William B. Smith, Jr., from Paris, "The number of genuwind all Caucasian white guys in the world is limited. . . . There'd probably be a number more if they didn't marry foecal matter in various forms. There's a guy named Lewis Galantiere over here was a priceless guy and he has been hooked and married by the most absolute copper plated bitch in the world and he aint a good guy any more." Smith's older brother Y. K. and Maxwell Perkins ("Max was Max with five daughters and an idiot wife") and Scott Fitzgerald were among the other priceless guys that Hemingway viewed as unworthily wed. Even Gertrude Stein he saw as maliciously dominated by her companion, Alice Toklas. "Alice had the ambition of the devil and was very jealous of Gertrude's men and women friends. . . . Alice was her evil angel as well as her great friend." When Fitzgerald's "evil angel," Zelda, fell ill, Hemingway's heart did not soften. He wrote Maxwell Perkins:

A woman ruined Scott. It wasn't just Scott ruining himself. But why couldn't he have told her to go to hell? Because she was sick. It's being sick makes them act so bloody awful usually and it's because they're sick you can't treat them as you should. The first great gift for a man is to be healthy and the second, maybe greater, is to fall with healthy women. You can always trade one healthy woman in on another. But start with a sick woman and see where you get.

About his own ex-wives he could wax sentimental, but only the divorce from Hadley seems to have given him real pain. He was an unabashedly unfaithful husband and, of course, antagonistic to his mother, whom he blamed for her lack of loyalty to his early published work, for his father's suicide, and for an obscure oppression upon himself; he wrote to Maxwell Perkins that he could not "write anything true [about Scott Fitzgerald] as long as Zelda is alive anymore than I can write with my bitch of a mother still able to read." Yet, at the same time, he was a ladies' man, virile and courtly, and even something of a mama's boy. A curious juvenile tone runs through his letters like a plaintive uninvited music. To Pauline Pfeiffer, in the period immediately after he left Hadley for her, he whimpered, "And all the time when you won't get letters and me instead of us being so happy and having all the world just being made into the figure representing sin and I get the horrors . . ." Years later, in the midst of leaving Pauline for Martha Gellhorn, he turned back to Hadley as to an ideal mother and confided, "I'm in the wrong of course. But I never do what I shouldn't just to do it; nor from carelessness. Only sort of when you have to." With the same ingenuous trustingness, like a little boy bravely reporting from camp, he assured Mary Hemingway in the last year of his life, "Plenty others [problems] but we will work them out and I'll get healthy and write fine."

In his last months, he was haunted by the fear that he was being trailed by the IRS and the FBI, and there is no more touching, or brave, document in this volume than the letter written in the Mayo Clinic "To Whom It May Concern" absolving Mary Hemingway of complicity in his phantasmal crimes:

> She knew nothing of my misdeeds nor illegal acts and had only the sketchiest outline of my finances and only helped me in preparing my returns on material I furnished her. The bags that I carried had her labels on them but she always believed from the time I met her in New York that the only reason I traveled as I did was to avoid the press a practice I had followed for years. She was never an accomplice nor in any sense a fugitive and only followed the advice of a doctor friend that she trusted.

The letters of previous years back to 1940, when *For Whom the Bell Tolls* gave him his first big income, show an exceptional concern with scrupulous payment of his taxes. When the matter of obscene words in his early novels arose he several times expressed a slightly off-key fear of going to jail, of "trouble." "I do not want trouble," he wrote Perkins. "—But want everything that can be had without trouble." Also to Perkins, he wrote, "You see my whole life and head and everything had a hell of a time . . . (and you must never let anyone know even that you were away or let the pack know you were wounded.)" This vague, menacing pack seems to have included critics, legal authorities, predatory and jealous women, and even (in an anecdote related by Edmund Wilson)* the fictional characters of William Faulkner; it helps account for his quickness to turn and make enemies out of friends, and for the shocking viciousness with which he phrases repudiation. "It is dangerous when you have an enemy to do anything but kill him," he wrote Maxwell Perkins. For whatever irretrievable reason, he was a man on the defensive, on the run.

In the Army, amid buddies and declared enemies, he felt safe from authority, and relished the share of it that fell to him as soldier and officer. In the Second World War, he was threatened with the loss of his press credentials for taking upon himself a degree of military command and martial ardor improper to a middle-aged war correspondent; before going to the European theatre, in 1944, he had concocted a maverick naval command for himself in the Caribbean; and during his last trip to Africa he relished his official role as honorary game warden. Repeatedly he stated that his months with the American armies in France and Germany in 1944 and 1945 were the happiest days of his life—the most wonderful time of all. "You will be very proud of what the Division has done and I have never been happier nor had a more useful life ever," he

---

*". . . Hemingway told me of a recent trip through the South that he had made in a car with his young son. He had at one point suddenly become aware that he had entered the state of Mississippi: 'I realized that we were in the Faulkner country.' At the country hotel where they spent the night, he had had the boy go to bed, then had sat up all night himself, with his 'gun' on the table in front of him. Two ideas, I believe, were revealed by this story, which he told me with the utmost seriousness: the assumption that Mississippi was inhabited by Faulkner characters and the assumption that Faulkner was a dangerous rival, who would take the same view of Hemingway that Hemingway did of him and, now that he had invaded Faulkner's territory, might well send some of these characters to do him violence. I thought this was rather queer, but no queerer, perhaps, than some other things that came out in drinking conversations." From "That Summer in Paris," published in 1963 and reprinted in *The Bit Between My Teeth* (Farrar, Straus & Giroux, 1965).

wrote his son Patrick from the battlefield. To the Russian writer Konstantin Simonov, he explained, "The time with the R.A.F. was wonderful but useless. With the 4th Infantry Division and with the 22nd regiment of Infantry I tried to be useful through knowing French and the country and being able to work ahead with the Maquis. This was a good life and you would have enjoyed it." After the war, to prolong his joy and usefulness, he wrote long letters to his former superiors, the Generals R. O. Barton, Charles T. Lanham, and J. Lawton Collins. To Collins, in 1949, he wrote, "I would like to say that I will be happy to serve under you in any capacity (preferably in one which involves writing) at any time, any where, and against any enemies of our country." Hemingway's wish to sign up under somebody motivates much, I think, of his fulsome correspondence with men, and produced in his last lonely decade pathetic effusions to Bernard Berenson, one of which winds up:

> But B.B. (my brother and father) if you ever wanted to father a really bad repeat bad (Give no quarter—Take no quarter) boy then you have this worthless object who will make the small pilgrimage but I promise will not embarrass you. Specially with Miss Mary who is under the impression that she (SHE) keeps the discipline in the column.
> Please forgive me for continuing writing. It is only because I am lonely. You with your lovely achieved age are, in a way, or without any stupid compliments my HERO.

One need not be a psychoanalyst to hear in such abject ramblings the inner voice of the small, mysteriously "bad" boy who found refuge from the pack led by his redoubtable mother at the side of his father—doctor and hunter, healer and killer.

The letters make more vivid than even his previously published descriptions of blood sports and war how sincerely Hemingway liked to kill. "I like to shoot a rifle and I like to kill and Africa is where you do that." His detailing of animal death is remorseless:

> Charles [Thompson] shot a bull elk, we shot one together, and I killed one alone. . . . Bull went down in gulch. We started over, Charles watching to see if he got up. ½ way there bull got up and Charles opened on him. I ran back under his fire, got a rest against tree and hit

him. He slumped forward and spraddled but still going. Charles shot his hind leg clean off (really) at knee joint and he went down. He was hit five times and when we opened him up found the top of his heart shot off—both lungs—Charles first shot was through and through but in his mouth just above back bone.

I killed a 7 point huge bull at 11,000 about one shot, running, (he and I both running!) bullet went in ribs above kidneys took top off lungs. He bled internally—ran 50 yards down hill without a drop of blood and was stone dead.

Even more gruesome is his tale, to Charles Scribner, of his murder of a German prisoner of war:

One time I killed a very snotty SS kraut who, when I told him I would kill him unless he revealed what his escape route signs were said: You will not kill me, the kraut stated. Because you are afraid to and because you are a race of mongrel degenerates. Besides it is against the Geneva Convention.

What a mistake you made, brother, I told him and shot him three times in the belly fast and then, when he went down on his knees, shot him on the topside so his brains came out of his mouth or I guess it was his nose.

Whether or not this is fantasy, his proposed treatment of Max Eastman, who had criticized his "literary style . . . of wearing false hair on the chest," certainly is:

I've got one ambition. Not an obsession. Just an ambition to nail that son of a bitch max eastman to the top of a fence post with a twenty penny spike through the base of his you know what and then push him backwards slowly. After that I'd start working on him.

Cheerfully he machine-gunned sharks, yearned "to take the tommy gun and open up at 21 or the N[ew] R[epublic] offices," boasted of killing in war 122 "sures" ("armeds not counting possible or necessary shootings"), and complained to General Barton that "writing is dull as hell after what we used to do. I haven't killed a son of a bitch for over four years now." His last quarry he brought down by setting the butt of a double-barrelled shotgun on the floor of his house in Ketchum, Idaho, resting his forehead on the business end of the gun, and—an enthusiast's nicety—tripping the trigger on both barrels.

Any lifetime's worth of letters read straight through will trace a grim organic curve from obscure and hopeful youth through success of some sort (else why would we be reading the letters?) into decay, decline, disappointment, and death. The aroma of death is present in *Selected Letters* almost from the start; on page 13 we have a drawing, done by the artist on his nineteenth birthday, of the young hero lying on his back with his legs wrapped in bandages lettered "227 wounds"—always a great tabulator, Hemingway—and the words "gimme a drink!" floating in a balloon out of his mouth. Ten years later, the now mature artist was to transcribe that formative trauma into these sentences of *A Farewell to Arms*:

> I ate the end of my piece of cheese and took a swallow of wine. Through the other noise I heard a cough, then came the chuh-chuh-chuh-chuh—then there was a flash, as when a blast-furnace door is swung open, and a roar that started white and went red and on and on in a rushing wind. I tried to breathe but my breath would not come and I felt myself rush bodily out of myself and out and out and out and all the time bodily in the wind. I went out swiftly, all of myself, and I knew I was dead and that it had all been a mistake to think you just died. Then I floated, and instead of going on I felt myself slide back. I breathed and I was back.

Back from that supernatural experience, Hemingway enjoyed ever after an ambiguous, exhilarating intimacy with the idea of dying, with religion, with pain and danger. Authentically cool and stoical, he was accident-prone to a grotesque degree, and survived more injuries than normally befall a dozen men: skylights dropped on his head, drunks (including, once, Wallace Stevens) challenged him to fistfights, cars he was in ran off the road into ditches or steel water tanks. To Maxwell Perkins in 1932 he wrote, "Since I started this book have had compound fracture of index finger—bad general smash up in that bear hunt—14 stitches in face inside and out—hole in leg—then that right arm—muscular spiral paralysis—3 fingers in right hand broken—16 stitches in left wrist and hand." In 1945, he figured that he "had 5 concussions in a little over two years." In January of 1954, in Uganda, he and Mary were involved in two crashes of small planes on successive days, and while recuperating from his very serious injuries (concussion; ruptured liver, spleen, and kidney; a crushed vertebra; temporary loss of vision in the left eye and of hearing in the left ear; and paralysis of the sphincter), Hemingway insisted on helping put out a brushfire and fell into the flames, acquiring second- and third-degree burns. Just before this last episode, he had dictated a fifteen-thousand-word account of his misadventures for *Look,* a masterpiece of droll understatement ending with a confession of his new "vice," the reading of his own obituaries. These had appeared, prematurely, worldwide. "I intend to read them at least once a year in order to keep my morale up to par when the critics have recovered their aplomb and return to the assault."

But his battered head and body never recovered completely, and he published no more books in his lifetime and toward the end looked much older than his years. The letters hold a number of curious, flirtatious thoughts about dying. From his hospital bed in Milan, he wrote his family, "Dying is a very simple thing. I've looked at death and really I know. If I should have died it would have been very easy for me. Quite the easiest thing I ever did. But the people at home do not realize that. They suffer a thousand times more." This was so much what the people at home wanted to hear that the letter was published in the local newspaper, the *Oak Parker.* To the terminally ill Ernest Walsh, he offered from Paris, "Altho the more I think of it the more I think that any form of dying can be made pretty swell. One of the things that I really look forward to is dying—but want to be at least 85 when it happens." After his tour of the Spanish Civil War, he wrote Pauline's mother, "This last spell of war completely eliminated all fear of death or anything else. It seemed as though the world were in such a bad way and certain things so necessary to do that to think about any personal future was simply very egoistic." Hemingway's disillusion with the rightist Church during the Civil War eliminated, as well, the last vestiges of his professed Catholicism. His involvement with the Catholic Church also could be described as curious and flirtatious. Confirmed as a Congregationalist, and in his youthful letters given to reassuring his mother of his Christianity ("Just because I'm a *cheerful* Christian ought not to bother you"), Hemingway by 1920 was writing to Grace Quinlan of how, in Boyne City, he and his friend Kate Smith "went to the catholic church and burnt a candle and I prayed for all the things I want and won't ever get and we came out in a very fine mood." Amid the cathedrals of Europe, he kept some kind of look-in. Jake Barnes, hero of *The Sun Also Rises*, is a professing Catholic, and Lieutenant Henry, in *A Farewell to Arms*, when asked "Are you *Croyant?*" answers, "At night." Hemingway married Pauline Pfeiffer in a Catholic service at the Paris Church of Passy in 1927, claiming to have been baptized into the faith in an Italian dressing station nine years earlier. In a letter quoted in Baker's biography but not published in *Selected Letters*, he assured an inquiring Dominican father that he possessed "so much faith" that he "hated to examine into it." A letter of 1929 mentions attending Mass in Paris with Pauline and Allen Tate, and his pre-1940 fiction not infrequently alludes to Christian symbols and prayers. A wry, Unamunoesque sort of faith compels shadowy blasphemies like the "our nada who art in nada" parody in "A Clean, Well-Lighted Place" and the interior soliloquy of Robert Jordan in *For Whom the Bell Tolls* that runs in part, "Now and forever now. Come now, now, for there is no now but now." By 1953, all mystical light has been filtered from the stoic stricture he presents to Bernard Berenson: "About dying: We must do it but there is no reason we should give it importance." However, years before, he had written a private reserve clause into his contract with death: upon receiving the volume of his collected short stories in 1938, he wrote Maxwell Perkins, "When I got the book and saw all those stories I knew I was all right as a sort of lasting business if I kicked off tomorrow."

For this rough, rude, appetitive, and even murderous man had bent his thoughts more intently toward literary immortality and perfection of prose than any American fiction writer since Henry James. His writing competed with his life—at first, with the need to make a dollar and the wish to have a good time; later, with celebrity, ill health, and the wish to have a good time.

> In going where you have to go, and doing what you have to do, and seeing what you have to see, you dull and blunt the instrument you write with. But I would rather have it bent and dulled and know I had to put it on the grindstone again and hammer it into shape and put a whetstone to it, and know that I had something to write about, than to have it bright and shining and nothing to say, or smooth and well-oiled in the closet, but unused.

Thus he introduced the book of stories that certified him, he felt, as "a sort of lasting business." In all conditions of convalescence and hangover, in hotel rooms and at his homes in Paris and Key West, Cuba and Sun Valley, he wrote, rising early and lovingly noting the number of words achieved each morning—a habit left over from his days of counting words for foreign dispatch. Through those last addled years, though the words kept sliding and bloating and not coming right, he battled on, piling up manuscript. In February of 1961, invited to contribute a sentence for a presentation volume to be given John Kennedy, he wrote all day, covering sheets of paper, and could get nothing to satisfy himself; Baker's biography reports that "tears went coursing down his cheeks." A few months later, he killed himself. He had never believed writing should be easy. In a letter of 1927 to Waldo Peirce, he says disapprovingly of Henry James, "He had obviously developed a fine very easy way for himself to write and great knowledge of drawing rooms." Hemingway began with difficult, outdoorsy theories. "I'm trying to do the country like Cezanne and having a hell of a time and sometimes getting it a little bit," he wrote Gertrude Stein in 1924, of the short story "Big Two-Hearted River," which represented to him a breakthrough. "It is much better than anything I've done," he told Edward J. O'Brien, one of his first appreciators. "What I've been doing is trying to do country so you don't remember the words after you read it but actually have the Country. It is hard because to do it you have to see the country all complete all the time you write and not just have a romantic feeling about it. It is swell fun." The young modernist of the Paris years, eagerly consorting with Pound and Joyce and Stein, living above a sawmill with his pretty Hadley and little Bumby and tapping out his elliptical tales of a boy's Michigan and a soldier's Europe in a language as clean as dawn air, scarcely needs the idyll of *A Moveable Feast* to strike us as Hemingway's best self. In obscurity and poverty, alloying the direct voice of his journalism with the exalted resolves of the Mandarin expatriates, he stubbornly forged a style that became, for a generation and more of stoic, hedonistic, "lost" men, a life style.

The style seemed to some (but not to Pound, or Fitzgerald, or Wilson) naïve; there were always New York critics who found Hemingway simply stupid. Yet the letters show a remarkable range of reading, classics and contemporaries both ("Thank God for books," he wrote Berenson fervently), and, though professors and translators find errors in the foreign phrases with which he garnished his fiction and his letters, he did make his way, through sheer quickness of ear, in French, Italian, Spanish, and German. As Malcolm Cowley has attested, "he learned almost anything with amazing speed." On the subjects of writing and being an author, he is always interesting, shrewd, and sound, if sometimes ill-tempered. He cared about every facet of his craft, however small. He wrote of typos, "There is nothing to spoil a persons appreciation of good stuff like typographical errors," and cannily saw that too many blurbs on a book jacket "simply put the reader on the defensive." Slang, he thought, should be used sparingly, because it "goes sour in a short time." He never had an agent, didn't like advances (though he came to depend on "loans" from Scribner's), and said that critics "have ruined every writer that reads them." "When they do not understand it you get angry; if they do understand it you only read what you already know and it is no good for you." Even fan mail, when, after *A Farewell to Arms*, it began to arrive in quantity, he found disturbing: "People write swell letters about it and I am so sick of it that a fan letter only makes you embarrassed and uneasy and vaguely sick. It's hard enough to write—and writing prose is a full time job and all the best of it is done in your subconscious and when that is full of business, reviews, opinions, etc., you don't get a damned thing." In his faith in the sub-conscious, he is almost a Surrealist. A lot in his life that seemed like wasteful fun—the drinking, the marlin fishing—was an attempt to keep the vessel of his mind clean for next dawn's distillation of words. He had keen senses of smell and taste, and purity was his dominant ideal. "When you tell so much of the truth you can't afford to have anything not true because it spoils the taste." He thought Scott Fitzgerald ruined *Tender Is the Night* by putting in too much that was not true of the Murphys and himself and Zelda. Concerning the residue of actuality in his own fictions, Heming-way testified variously: "I believe when you are writing stories about actual people, not the best thing to do, you should make them those people in everything except telephone addresses," he told Ernest Walsh in 1926; a few years later he confessed to Perkins, of *In Our Time*, "The reason most of the book seems so true is because most of it is true and I had no skill then, nor have much now, at changing names and circumstances. Regret this very much." His short stories were more *à clef* than his novels; he assured Perkins, "I invented every word and every incident of A Farewell to Arms except possibly 3 or 4 incidents. All the best part is invented. 95 per cent of The Sun Also was pure imagination. I took real people in that one and I controlled what they did. I made it all up." Joyce, the one contemporary writer he always respected, made up Bloom, and Bloom was the character, in Hemingway's opinion, who saved *Ulysses* from the dully autobiographical Stephen Dedalus. The defin-itive pronouncement on this uncomfortable matter is perhaps given in a letter in 1951 to Thomas Bledsoe: "Every writer is in much of his work. But it is not as simple as all that."

Readers of *A Moveable Feast* startled by the acid sketches Hem-ingway provides of his former friends and fellow-writers would not have been surprised had they read these letters first. They abound in harsh and even rabid put-downs. "Tom Wolfe was a one book boy and a glandular giant with the brains and the guts of three mice." "Scott [Fitzgerald] was a rummy and a liar and dishonest about money with the in-bred talent of a dishonest and easily

frightened angel." "Sherwood Anderson was a slob." And so on.*
He said that Scott Fitzgerald was "generous without being kind,"
but the remark seems truer of Hemingway himself. Though self-
forewarned, he did not entirely avoid following Gertrude Stein's
bad example when "she started taking herself seriously rather than
her work seriously." In all the personal anecdotes related in these
letters, there is hardly a one in which Hemingway lets himself look
bad, or in need of the kindness and expertise of others. He several
times relates scornfully that Fitzgerald advised him to bring in the
United States Marines at the end of *A Farewell to Arms*, but slurs
over (and, in *A Moveable Feast*, coldly disowns) the crucial good
advice Fitzgerald gave him on *The Sun Also Rises*, which began
with a mean-spirited and mock-suave essay on the chief characters
that Fitzgerald found "careless and ineffectual" and that Heming-
way accordingly cut, assuring Perkins, "I think it will move much
faster from the start that way. Scott agrees with me." As Fitz-
gerald's letter and the discarded opening chapters, both printed in
the Spring 1979 *Antæus*, demonstrate, it was Hemingway who
agreed with Fitzgerald, just as Eliot agreed with Pound's brilliant
suggested cuts in "The Waste Land." No doubt there are other
sides to many of the boasts that pass unchecked in the letters.

A man less committed to dominating every room he was in

---

*"[Faulkner] has the most talent of anybody and he just needs a sort of con-
science that isn't there. Certainly if no nation can exist half free and half slave no
man can write half whore and half straight." (10/17/45)

"[Dos Passos] I always liked and respected and thought was a 2nd rate writer
on acct. no ear. 2nd rate boxer has no left hand, same as ear to writer, and so gets
his brains knocked out and this happened to Dos with every book." (7/23/47)

"All [Ring Lardner] has is a good false ear and has been around. The poor guy
really hates everything but Purity." (4/3/33)

T. S. Eliot: "A damned good poet and a fair critic; but he can kiss my ass as a
man and he never hit a ball out of the infield in his life and he would not have
existed except for dear old Ezra, the lovely poet and stupid traitor." (7/9/50)

". . . Gertrude Stein who since she has taken up not making sense some eighteen
years ago has never known a moments unhappiness with her work." (10/9/28)

"E. Wilson is a serious and honest bird who discovered life late. Naturally he
is shocked and would like to do something about it." (7/6/32) "I know no one who
works so hard at being honest and [has] less true inner honesty within himself. His
criticism is like reading second rate gospels by some one who is out on parole.
. . . He is the great false-honest, false-craftsman, falsegreat-critic of our exceedingly
sorry times. . . ." (2/25/44)

might have developed more as a writer. He knew the problem: "Publicity, admiration, adulation, or simply being fashionable are all worthless and are extremely harmful if one is susceptible to them." His projection and protection of himself as Superpapa swallowed the authentically bookish, sensitive man and contaminated his alter egos; the heroes of his seven novels—Jake Barnes, Frederic Henry, Harry Morgan, Robert Jordan, Richard Cantwell, Santiago, and Thomas Hudson—are progressively sentimentalized. It is a pity, too, and a mystery, that after the four egocentric but compelling tales of the Spanish Civil War published in 1938 and 1939, when Hemingway was not yet forty, his large and lively gift for the short story sank from sight—swamped, it would seem, by the nightmare of violence always lurking beneath the pellucid tense sentences. Still, much unsinkable work was done. A reader of *Selected Letters* should keep nearby, as did this reader, some volumes of the oeuvre to turn to when overwhelmed by the braggadocio, brutality, and bathos that Hemingway inflicted upon his correspondents and now, without his willing it, upon posterity. The valuable—the fine and good and true and lovely—Hemingway is to be found in the writing he published in books, just where he said it would be.

The Doctor's Son

Selected Letters of John O'Hara, edited by Matthew J. Bruccoli. 538 pp. Random House, 1978.

This volume should sweeten the reputation of a notoriously irascible and hypersensitive author. As a correspondent, O'Hara was frank, fond, full of gossip (some of which gives Mr. Bruccoli fits of dashitis; e.g., "—— took her away from —— ——, with whom she had been in love for five years, and then he married — —— —— instead of Louie"), lively, and even wise. Not that his prickly temper is nowhere in evidence. He wrote to F. Scott Fitzgerald in 1934, "My message to the world is Fuck it!" He advised a fellow-journalist who was still in Pottsville, "If you're going to get out of that God awful town, for God's sake write something that will *make* you get out of it. Write something that automatically will sever your connection with the town, that will help you get rid of the bitterness you must have stored up against all those patronizing cheap bastards." Writing, at least in his earlier years, automatically presented itself to him as an act of aggression; to Hemingway in 1935 he volunteered, "I am writing a novel, or what is called sticking my chin out, leading with my puss." Some of his social ventures were equally truculent: "Hoefel dropped in a couple of weeks ago, and I got tight and finally let him have it. Not with my fist, but with words of abuse. I told him all the things, or at least quite a few of the things, that I have been wanting to tell him for a couple of years. I scored his social climbing, his attitude toward his old playmates, etc., etc. When he left I refused to shake hands." The years did not drastically mellow him. When an old Pottsville acquaintance died in 1962, he wrote, "I'm sure my sister shed a tear for him, and I feel frustrated because I never gave him a crack in the mouth." He reminisced fondly about his father's violence: "My father was pretty good with his hands, whether he was operating on a man's skull to relieve the pressure on the brain, or breaking a Kluxer's jaw for calling him a Molly Maguire." This echoes an incident in that most autobiographical of O'Hara's short stories, "The Doctor's Son":

My father . . . was a good, savage amateur boxer, with no scruples against punching anyone smaller than himself. Less than a year before all this took place my father had been stopped by a traffic policeman while he was hurrying to an "OBS." The policeman knew my father's car, and could have guessed why he was in a hurry, but he stopped him. My father got out of the car, walked to the front of it, and in the middle of a fairly busy intersection he took a crack at the policeman and broke his jaw. Then he got back and drove around the unconscious policeman and on to the confinement case.

From his father he learned to work hard at his trade and to hit out at interference. From the clan O'Hara, "one of the seven or eight ancient Irish names," he had a more mystical inheritance: "Whenever I am in the company of the Irish (and this has been true all my life) I instantly get a feeling of being a little superior to the other ones—and they in turn look at me as though whatever I had to say was going to be important."

Brash as a young man, he became with success a slightly desperate braggart. To Bennett Cerf in 1961 he wrote, "I was infuriated by that piece by Nichols last Sunday about fiction not selling, including the quote from that jerk at Knopf's. . . . At the moment I am probably the country's most formidable competition to television, and should remain so for at least three years, but there is no gratitude among the booksy folk, only envy." No amount of riches or fame could appease his ire at booksy folk. He was sore at Cerf for not advertising his books enough, sore at Yale for not giving him an honorary degree, sore at the National Institute of Arts and Letters for not electing him to membership sooner. When they omitted to nominate him for a Gold Medal, he resigned. He lectured two generations of *New Yorker* editors on how to run their magazine. In 1949, shortly after writing to Katharine White, "It does seem to me that for the past year and a half the magazine has gone out of its way to antagonize me," he broke for eleven years his connection with the journal that was his first and favorite forum. He hankered noisily after the Nobel Prize. In some of these letters he covers himself with the praise that should have come from others: "There isn't anyone else today—and I don't know when there has been anyone else—who takes this whole country and all social strata to work with. . . . At 57-less-one-month there is no time for spurious modesty, and I think I am the best."

Yet these combative traits, however difficult they may have made O'Hara to deal with personally, in this large and entertaining collection of letters fall into place as relatively harmless by-products of his energy and pride, and as defenses erected by a genuinely artistic sensibility. It is not clear from his correspondence and the outpourings of his career that he quite knew how artistic he was; but he had a fair gift, in moods free of grievance, for self-appraisal, and was certainly less self-deluding than Hemingway and less self-destructive than Fitzgerald, about both of whom he has penetrating things to say. Though O'Hara had placed Hemingway beside Shakespeare in his half-cocked but gallant touting of the much-panned *Across the River and into the Trees*, he was distressed by the bullfight articles that appeared in *Life* in 1960. He wrote to William Maxwell:

> There was always great art in Hemingway, often when he was at his mumbling worst. But in the *Life* pieces we see our ranking artist concerned with a disgusting spectacle, adopting a son-hero and wishing him dead in conflict with a former son-hero, Dominguin, whom he also wishes dead. He wants to see them die, to be there when they die, and I got the feeling that he particularly wanted Dominguin to die because Dominguin had not been as easy to adopt as Ordonez. Hemingway is *afraid* to lose Dominguin in life, and rather than lose him in life he wishes him dead.

Hemingway's idealization of violence, which acquired psychotic overtones, was alien to O'Hara's worldly sanity. There is cruelty in his fiction, but it is never confused with beauty. There are few heroics—not even the heroics of stoicism. The impact of many of his stories springs from his extreme sensitivity, which felt annihilation in a snub and found in common social discriminations the violence that Hemingway sought out in war and blood sports. With Fitzgerald O'Hara enjoyed a friendship in the early Thirties; they were fellow-Irishmen in a literary emergence comparable to the Jewish emergence a generation later. "You helped me finish my novel," he wrote the slightly older writer after completing *Appointment in Samarra*, in 1934. "The best parts of my novel are facile pupils of The Beautiful and Damned and The Great Gatsby." But he could remember, of this literary hero, an incident more discreditable than any in Hemingway's sardonic *Moveable Feast:*

> It was one Sunday afternoon in Towson, in 1934, that I had Scott and Zelda in my car and I wanted to kill him. Kill. We were taking her back to her Institution, and he kept making passes at her that could not possibly be consummated. We stopped at a drug store to get him some gin. The druggist would not give it to him. I had to persuade the druggist to relent, and he got the gin. But I wanted to kill him for what he was doing to that crazy woman, who kept telling me she had to be locked up before the moon came up.

Fitzgerald remained a touchstone for him; he likens their careers ("Off to a good start with a first novel, then a pasting for the second novel") and marvels at his own relative durability ("In spite of the abuse I have given my body, I was always stronger than Scott"). And yet: "Fragile Fitzgerald had some inner resources that I haven't got, one of which is arrogance."

Arrogance of the sort that ignored slights O'Hara did lack. He never grew the thick skin of genius, which he admired in Faulkner: "The only one who really escaped [the critics] was Faulkner, but he was made invulnerable by his genius. You cannot hurt a genius, even with a silver bullet." O'Hara's early estimates of his own talent, between bursts of jejune ebullience, sound touchingly, vulnerably modest. To Kyle Crichton, then an editor at *Scribner's Magazine,* he wrote, "I know so much better than anyone else that I have an inferior talent. The reason I think I have an inferior talent is that when I write I can't sustain an emotion. . . . I'm not important, and I never will be. The next best thing is to be facile and clever." He regretted not going to college, and doubted his own intelligence. Of a woman he knew in the late Twenties, he wrote an old Pottsville friend, "She has a much better education than mine, both from college and what she has taught herself, and she has, I'll concede, a better brain except for versatility of information and an interest in trifles." To his brother Thomas, who also had literary aspirations, he confided, "My wife read your pieces and her conclusion was that you today have a better mind than I have. I bopped her on the snout and let it go at that." His rage at adverse criticism, his almost shameful hunger for recognition, his clumsy and dogged self-promotion all testify to a gap of self-doubt that never healed over. Compelled by his father's sudden death to forgo college and make his own way in the world, he supported himself by writing, and by the end of the Depression had a comfortable income and a national reputation; but, looking back upon these accomplishments, he saw only a string of prizes he didn't get. "When I was young, right up to prep school graduation, at which I was valedictorian and class poet (!) and top man in Spanish—I got used to getting badges and ribbons and prayerbooks and certificates . . . without trying very hard for them. I was brighter than most of my classmates, and I had a kind of Xerox memory. But from 1924 to 1952, I got nothing, and it took a revival of PAL JOEY to break that long string of defeats." On the two occasions when he did receive a considerable prize—the National Book Award for Fiction, in 1956, and the Award of Merit bestowed by the American Academy of Arts and Letters, in 1964*—he broke down and cried in the middle of his acceptance speeches. Of the second occasion, he wrote to John Hersey, "I thought I was getting by, and then my eyes lit on two words—obsolescent, and love. Then I felt the effect of those thousands of nights-till-dawn, and I had no control."

Such naked neediness, in a giant, is endearing. These letters, even when they scold and complain, turn outward, toward the social surround. Though he strikes an egotistical pose, it is hard to think of another significant twentieth-century fiction writer who was less of an egoist—less of an autobiographical self-celebrator. His interest in other people and their lives is so unfeignedly keen that anything about them, any window-glimpse into their psychologies and social predicaments, will serve him for a story. The action in his stories is often surprisingly slight; he considerately refuses to manipulate characters beyond what their systems will naturally stand. A doctor's son, he was proud to hear that "a Dr. Nathan Brandon . . . reads everything I write and has said that I never make a mistake about the psychological treatment of my characters." O'Hara's strange nocturnal working hours echoed, perhaps, his father's night calls, and his irritation with booksy folk stemmed from a disappointment that he wasn't accorded, in the literary community, the respect and gratitude that Dr. Patrick O'Hara had received in Pottsville. His father's death thrust him early and raw into a man's role. Had he remained secure in the upper middle class and gone to Yale, he might have become a true snob, instead of the conscious parody of a "rich and stylish country squire" he became. At an age when many writers leave their native milieu for good, he was compelled

---

*Given to a non-member of the Academy/Institute; O'Hara had resigned shortly before, thus inadvertently qualifying himself.

to stay in town and with mature perceptions and experiences to regrasp the realities he had grown up among. A small city is an excellent microcosm of a society—big enough to contain some of everything, yet all of it accessible to a venturesome witness. The sloping streets of his Pennsylvania coal town set O'Hara an unforgettable lesson in class distinctions. As Pottsville journalist and playboy, he became expert in the grimy anatomy of human transactions; the back rooms of bars and the upstairs of mansions held few secrets from him. Beneath the epidermis of social nuance, the same tough, broad muscles of money, sex, and group loyalty operated. By the time, at the age of twenty-three, O'Hara graduated from Pottsville and went to New York City, he had a diagnostic framework for any American situation, a framework in which he placed his ambitious novels and which decades of prosperity and cosmopolitan living could not dim: Gibbsville for him was no less than the human condition.

His postgraduate struggles, his benders and affairs and firings, his not very profitable sojourns in Hollywood ("I regret to report that since returning to California I have been living at the bottom of a bottle") are reflected in his early letters, along with two polar themes: his obsession with clubs, and his skill at eliciting rejection. The very first letters published here, to his boyhood friend Robert Simonds, drip with frat talk. " 'When I get to college' I want to rate a good national social, a drinking club, a minor varsity letter, varsity play, and 'The Lit.' I would also like to be a political boss." Shut off from this world, he invents a name for himself: "The ΨY Type," which a letter to Joseph Bryan III twenty years later echoes as Phi Upsilon, whose phonemes stand for his favorite phrase of defiance and whose pin shows "clasped hands, only in this case both hands will be mine." In his youth, he made up clubs for himself and a few others to belong to; in his maturity, he kept trying to turn professional associations—with his editors, his critics, his Hollywood employers—into fraternities, and winding up with more hurt feelings to nurse. He who leads with his puss gets slapped; shame and exclusion lurk at the edge of every O'Hara page. He was an overcompensatory joiner. To Edgar Scott in 1956 he wrote:

The favor: do you still belong to the Philadelphia Racquet Club? If you do, would you consider putting me up for non-resident membership? I now belong to The Century, The Leash, the Coffee House, the Nassau Club, the Quogue Field Club, the Shinnecock Yacht Club, the National Press Club and The Beach Club of Santa Monica, which makes me the William Rhinelander Stewart of Pottsville, Pa.

A month later he is writing Scott, "If the word seeps back to you that I am not going to make it at the Philadelphia R.C., I am going to ask you another favor of more or less the same kind. Do you think you could get me in the Klein Klub?" Six years later, he has Scott put him up for the Brook:

> The two reasons I wanted to join it are, first, it is a prestigious club; and, second, I am disheartened by the number of creeps who have been creeping into the Century. . . . They will not get in The Brook, and maybe I won't either, but I had to make the try.

As it turned out, he did get into the Philadelphia R.C. but not into the Racquet & Tennis Club of New York or the Brook; nor did he succeed in getting a commission in the Army or the Navy, win a writing fellowship at the University of Minnesota, win the Pulitzer Prize, get the honorary degrees he wanted, or have a single one of his many plays produced on Broadway—though he did write the book of *Pal Joey*. He was regularly fired from jobs he held, and countless in these pages are the projects he proposed that came to nothing. Long after he needed the money, he was attempting to engineer futile movie deals, including, according to a footnote by Mr. Bruccoli, "an original screenplay for Ingrid Bergman about the 'fascinating life of the ore and wheat boats on the Great Lakes.'" Writing to John Steinbeck, he proposes himself for yet another club: "Writing. You and Ernest and Faulkner only. Me, of course. But room for all of us." It speaks well for both men that from this forward, chummy, and perhaps boozy overture of 1949 a friendship developed. In 1963, Steinbeck was operated on for a detached retina, and O'Hara offered to read to him in the hospital. This offer was accepted.

Certain acceptance and security he found, finally, in the little club of his immediate family. The parents of his first love, Margaretta Archbald, and of his first wife, Helen Ritchie Petit, had not thought him quite acceptable socially, and "Pet" had divorced him after two years. But his second marriage, to Belle Wylie, who died at only forty-one, and his third, to Katharine Barnes Bryan, were happy. "I just go on, in these lucky years of contentment, trying to avoid the slings and arrows by ducking behind my work, loving my wife and child and a few friends, hoping that some day I'll win the Nobel." This was written to John Hayward in 1960, seven years after O'Hara gave up drinking for good, five years after his third marriage, and not long after he had rediscovered "the ease with which I write and sell short stories." In 1959, his only child, a daughter, Wylie, went off to boarding school in Maryland, and O'Hara's handsomely paternal letters to her form the supreme document of these "lucky years" and of his affectionate, honorable nature. "Responsibility, and responsibilities, can be a pleasure. The greatest pleasure I have in life is the responsibility of being your father. It is a greater pleasure than my work, which is saying a lot because I love my work. . . . You and I are really very close, I think. I think we understand each other because we are both sensitive people. . . . When I was a young man (and not too young, too) I learned that girls liked two things about me: one, I was a good dancer; two, I made them laugh. . . . In the past week or so I have called you 'Kid' but subconsciously I have been doing that because your kid days are over, or just about. I suspect that you are going through the experience of first love, and no matter what else happens, after that experience you are never a kid again. . . . But you gain more than you lose. You gain in understanding, in appreciation of people, in understanding and appreciation of yourself. You begin to see the wisdom in that quotation I have so often repeated to you: to thine own self be true."

This man who so freely and seriously entrusts his wisdom to his daughter had decades ago written his younger brother Thomas:

> Here is the only piece of straight advice: never forget that your girl or your wife is every damn bit as much a person as you are. . . . She thinks the world revolves around her just as you do around yourself, just as anyone does. She has a vote in life as well as in politics, she eats and

sleeps and suffers and loves and thinks (regardless of how badly you or I may think she thinks) like you and me. She was born, she lives, she's got to die; and for you to attempt to dominate her, to pinch her personality, is some kind of sin.

Rare advice for one man to be giving another in 1934. O'Hara's ability and willingness to portray women has not been often enough complimented. He became, in such late stories as "The Women of Madison Avenue" and "Sunday Morning," virtually a feminist writer. Throughout his fiction, women occupy the same merciless space his men do, with an equal toughness. "*I* hate *them*," concludes one of the unfaithful wives of "Mary and Norma" to the other; "It isn't only them hating us." The disadvantaged position of women and the strength of the strategies with which they seek advantages are comprehended without doctrine, and without a loss of heterosexual warmth. To perceive the atrocity in Scott Fitzgerald's flirting with his insane wife took moral imagination and courteous instincts; this sensitivity, one suspects, set O'Hara a little apart from the boys even during his roistering days.

Humanity in all its divisions was present to him; his gifts of curiosity and empathy were so strong that one must ask what, if anything, his art lacked. Love of language might be an answer— language as a semi-opaque medium whose colors and connotations can be worked into a supernatural, supermimetic bliss. He wrote rapidly, and rarely rewrote; his books were set from first-draft typescripts. Tuned to less than highest pitch, his prose and dialogue just run on. "One of my troubles may be that I *like* to write dialog; I like to hear my people talk." From the length of these letters— reading through them is like eating through a bushel of jumbo salted peanuts—one guesses he liked to hear himself talk, too. His prose was not unconsidered, as his responses to editorial queries among these letters show; he defended every particularity. To Albert Erskine, his editor at Random House, he snapped, "And don't cite dictionaries to me, on dialog or the vernacular. Dictionary people consult me, not I them." But the interest of the human life in his mind's eye was so self-evident he saw no need to *make* it interesting. A thing was itself, and rarely reminded him of another. Language seldom led him with its own music deeper into the matter at hand. Hemingway's flatness had about it a willed point, a philosophical denial of depth; O'Hara's was serenely post-philosophical. His best short stories have a terrific delicacy, and the calm compositional weirdness of a Degas or an Oriental print. He wanted to be a Jules Romains or a Balzac but more suggests Hokusai, the prolific Japanese printmaker who would sometimes sign himself Old-Man-Crazy-About-Drawing. O'Hara was crazy about writing, and his writing has the innocence of enthusiasm. He continued to claim Booth Tarkington as an influence long after Tarkington had ceased to be fashionable. "Much as I admired Hemingway and Fitzgerald's work, my considered opinion is that I was more strongly influenced by Tarkington, Galsworthy, and Lewis than by the younger men." What innovations his art contains— including his once scandalous sexual frankness—were forced upon him, one feels, by his reverence before the facts of life. O'Hara's inward delicacy and chaste impressionability consorted uncomfortably with his burly body, his frank appetites, his uneven education, his blockbuster aspirations. His "thousands of nights-till-dawn" became, he recognized in a letter to Wylie, a way of "not participating in life," taking dictation from his characters ("I *hear* the dialog before I put it down on paper") in the still, pre-dawn hours of Quogue and Princeton. "Dorothy Parker told me I would never be happy because I am a genius": this is recorded in a letter to Tom in 1932. A letter of 1964, to Bennett Cerf, describes an earlier diagnosis:

> I will be 60 next month and have lived twice as long as my father said I would. I am trying to achieve peace of mind. I went in to see my father on his deathbed and my mother said to him, "John has a sore knee." My old man said (and they were his last words to me), "Poor John."

The Shining Note

LETTERS OF E. B. WHITE, edited by Dorothy Lobrano Guth. 686 pp. Harper & Row, 1976.

A rare thing it is for the living to collect and publish their letters; as E. B. White says, with his unfailing crispness, in a prefatory note to *Letters of E. B. White*, "ideally, a book of letters should be published posthumously. The advantages are obvious: the editor enjoys a free hand, and the author enjoys a perfect hiding place—the grave, where he is impervious to embarrassments and beyond the reach of libel." The advantages of pre-posthumous publication are obvious also: the living epistolist can supply his editor, in this case Dorothy Lobrano Guth, with leads and clarifications; he can write, as White has done, delightful introductory and interstitial paragraphs; he can help shape the collection of letters toward its ideal condition, of involuntary autobiography. White's refining touch is felt throughout this well-designed, considerately annotated volume —six hundred and sixty-two pages' and sixty-eight years' worth of prose treasure strewn along the wayside by a diffident-appearing but at heart highly determined literary pilgrim.

Mrs. Guth's introduction states that when a collection of his letters was suggested to White by one of his editors at Harper & Row, he "wrote back that he didn't really consider himself much of a letter writer." In a letter to his brother Stanley in 1968, White said, "I avoid writing letters—it resembles too closely writing itself, and gives me a headache." Yet, once settled to the typewriter, he is a generous communicant—devoting, for example, nearly a thousand exquisitely chosen words to a librarian who petulantly mailed back a letter White had written to a little girl explaining how overwhelmed by mail he was and suggesting that the child form a movement called "Don't write to E. B. White until he produces another book." White's mail, indeed, swollen by all those adults and children who feel that in his work he has addressed them personally, must be as voluminous as a movie star's, and only an extravagantly decent man would answer as much as he seems to.

In this collection one can find, recovered from their recipients by heaven knows what miracles of retrieval, perfect examples of the types of letter an author is called upon to write: to the term-paper writer ("Dear Mr. Cole: I don't know how to 'reveal any aspect' of myself deliberately. Everything a person does or says is, of course, revealing. But *you're* going to write that term paper, not me"); to the random inquirer ("Dear Miss Gravely: I don't know where to begin. I am five feet eight inches tall—but that's an odd place to begin. I am fifty years old—but that's a dreadful place to begin. I ate too much for lunch—but nobody would want to begin *there*. As for my work, the only thing I can tell you about it is that a lot of it has been published, all of it was hard, and some of it was fun"); to the proposer of a deal ("Dear Miss Strauss: . . . Your proposal is certainly challenging enough for anybody. It had never occurred to me that the life of Christ could be a subject for a comic book—probably because it doesn't seem funny. Now that I have adjusted to the idea, I still don't want to undertake it, as it is primarily a labor of adaptation, rather than of creation, and I'm not a very adaptable man"). White's letter of January 14, 1948, to E. J. McDonald is a consummate specimen of the Apology to a Friend Who May Have Been Offended by a Story (here the ungratefully received narrative was a masterpiece, "Death of a Pig"), and his communication of June 6, 1950, to James Thurber a model of the Letter to a Friend Who Has Sent His Book (*The Thirteen Clocks*, and White manages to disguise as pleasantries a number of shrewd criticisms). Refusals to lecture, to comment on galleys, to name three favorite books of the year—there is no piece of professional fending so mechanical that White begrudges its phrasing a pinch of grace and fun. His responses to children who are baffled by the ending of *Stuart Little* or the meaning of *Charlotte's Web* are marvels of affectionate patience. At guileless length he defends himself against the charge, by "some students of children's literature," that there was too much money and violence in *The Trumpet of the Swan*. His gingerly relationships, fond yet sometimes fiercely firm, with publishers and editors weave a pretty pattern as White steers one book after another around his own doubts and the helpful interferences of others. His correspondence, in 1971 and 1972,

with the makers of the unfortunate film of *Charlotte's Web* consti-
tutes a heartbreaking outpour of justified anxieties and ignored
advice. His letter to Katharine White, his wife, in June of 1948
describes drolly and harrowingly another authorial peril, the hon-
orary degree—even the hood proves a menace: "I guess it must
have been when I reached over to pick the program off the chair
that my hood got hung up on Ben Ames Williams. Anyway, when
I got seated the thing was up over my face, as in falconry." His
letter to William Maxwell of November 16 that same year, worry-
ing about the foreign translations of *Stuart Little*—"I'm not
enough of a linguist to know whether a Dutch Stuart Little should
be called Stuart Little or Tom Trikkelbout. But it is beginning to
dawn on me that I damn well better find out"—stands as a rebuke
to those authors who imagine that their responsibilities are confined
to the language they write in. White has taken his citizenship in the
community of letters seriously; whenever he has felt freedom of
expression threatened, whether by McCarthyism in the Fifties or
by the Xerox Corporation's sponsorship of an *Esquire* article in
1976, he has spoken up, and his public letters, written gratuitously
to newspapers, are among the more impressive extensions of his
vocation. Even in indignation he twinkles: "I can only assume that
your editorial writer, in a hurry to get home for Thanksgiving,
tripped over the First Amendment and thought it was the office
cat."

A trio of letters from December of 1936 shows White's ethical
sense, and his generous epistolary nature, thrice activated by the
same affront: Alexander Woollcott had lent himself to a Christmas
promotion of Seagram's whiskey. Woollcott's bulk-mailed solicita-
tion for Seagram's as a Christmas present was reprinted in *The New
Yorker*'s Open-Letters Department, with a mordant response,
signed "Eustace Tilley" but composed by White, which con-
cluded, ". . . this Christmas of 1936, thanks to your thoughtful note,
has been given an unforgettable flavor, has become a season per-
vaded with the faint, exquisite perfume of well-rotted holly ber-
ries." In a personal Christmas card to Woollcott, White continues
in the same saucy style, referring quite uncontritely to his pub-
lished jape at "your open affair with La Seagram. After all, a man's

personal excesses are his own business. Privately, I may wish you joy of the lady, but publicly I must give so lewd an alliance a jab, mustn't I?" The third letter, at great length, and with a courtesy as total as its frankness, carefully explains the abuse of trust that White sees in the older writer's commercial involvement:

> My other reason is the one that everything really hangs on: the importance of a writer's maintaining his amateur standing. . . . I still cling (by my teeth these days) to the notion that writing is a trust. . . . The next time I come across you, in the mail, in print, I feel I must be on my guard, must see what the catch is, may have to read half way through before I can determine whether this is an affiliated utterance or an unaffiliated utterance.

White's own determination to remain amateur and unaffiliated is reflected in his affectionate, respectful, yet edgy correspondence with Harold Ross. White's value to the young *New Yorker* was estimated by James Thurber for *The Saturday Review* in 1938: "Harold Ross and Katharine Angell, his literary editor, were not slow to perceive that here were the perfect eye and ear, the authentic voice and accent for their struggling magazine . . . His contributions to the Talk of the Town, particularly his Notes and Comment on the first page, struck the shining note that Ross had dreamed of striking." Yet the shining-note producer's early notes to the persistent dreamer are gruff and wary and often mailed from afar, like this one from Ontario in 1929:

> On account of the fact that *The New Yorker* has a tendency to make me morose and surly, the farther I stay away the better. I appreciate very much your extraordinary capacity to endure, and in fact cope with, my somewhat vengeful attitude about *The New Yorker* and my crafty habit of slipping away for long intervals . . . Next to yourself and maybe one or two others, I probably have as tender a feeling for your magazine as anybody. For me it isn't a complete life, though.

The search for the complete life took him out of New York City entirely from 1938 to 1942 and from 1957 to the present, and to Maine every summer from 1930 on: "I would really rather feel bad in Maine than good anywhere else." While remaining a supremely prized contributor, visible and invisible, to *The New Yorker*, and identified in the public mind with what is best and blithest about it, White has often asserted his unaffiliated talent elsewhere; his fame in large part rests upon his three best-selling novels for children, the essays of the "One Man's Meat" column he wrote for five years in *Harper's,* his surprising revival and revision of his old Cornell professor's handbook of English grammar and usage (*The Elements of Style,* by William Strunk, Jr.), and an essay done at *Holiday*'s behest, "Here Is New York." "If I had no responsibilities or obligations of a domestic sort, I would most certainly arrange my life so that I was not obliged to write anything at any specified time for anybody," White wrote Ross in 1939, after he had taken on the *Harper's* commitment; though he has felt editorial pressure and constraints (and quit "One Man's Meat" when its writing seemed only "to fulfill a promise, or continuing obligation") he has not passed this feeling on to his readers. His readers, instead, feel flattered by the directness of his prose and caught up in its playfulness as his apparently unconstrained utterances gracefully poke toward the light. His quintessentially American style aspires to the very texture of freedom, the unfussy smoothness of something growing. "Many of the things he writes seem to me as lovely as a tree," Thurber wrote in 1938. This quality, of arboreal self-shaping, was not unearned; White struggled to keep it, to keep his distance from whatever would claim him and crowd him, even his beloved and hard-working wife, to whom he wrote in 1937, in explanation of a year's holiday he proposed to take from magazine work,

> A person afflicted with poetic longings of one sort or another searches for a kind of intellectual and spiritual privacy in which to indulge his strange excesses. To achieve this sort of privacy—this aerial suspension of the lyrical spirit—he does not necessarily have to wrench himself away, physically, from everybody and everything in his life . . . but he *does* have to forswear certain easy rituals, such as earning a living and running the world's errands.

Most of these letters scarcely touch on literary matters. He mentions reading Santayana and Thoreau, and writes John Kieran a fan letter for his *Natural History of New York City.* He several times casts a skeptical sibling eye in the direction of Hemingway, a fellow-lover of the outdoors and clean prose, and with easier fraternity confides some of his professional acumen and ambition to Thurber, Frank Sullivan, and Howard Cushman. Cushman, a Cornell friend who drove with White across the country in 1922, lived to act as his Philadelphia legman in the research for *The Trumpet of the Swan,* and never quite dropped from correspondence in between. "Sweet Hum," White addresses him, and signs himself "Ho." Thurber, in those years before (in White's obituary phrase) "blindness hit him, before fame hit him," offered himself as a partner to White's sensibility, and received letters unique, among these many, in their tone of frank, urbane, wised-up ennui:

> Sunday afternoons are about the same as when you left, people walking their dog out, and the dog not doing anything, the sky grey and terrible, and the L making the noise that you hear when you are under ether. . . . Even when an artist has the ability and the strength to assemble something of the beauty and the consternation which he feels, he is usually so jealous of other artists that he has no time for pure expression. Today with the radio yammering at you and the movies turning all human emotions into cup custard, the going is tough. Or I find it tough.

This letter also holds one of the few glimpses through White's eyes of the New York literary scene: "Joe Sayre is back from the Vineyard with third act trouble. . . . Walter Lippmann and Mrs. Lippmann are getting a divorce." White deliberately snubbed the cosmopolitan he could have become, and his later letters tend to confirm his diagnosis of himself as "not a bookish fellow."

But what a busy fellow! The launching ground of these missives is crammed with poultry and livestock, with goslings White has helped to hatch ("as green as grass, and they immediately begin playing their flutes, an enchanting sound") and with trout he is helping to spawn, with hurricanes and early risings, sailing and shingling, orphaned robins and willful dogs, and chores, chores, chores. Any impression that his retreat to rural life had an evasive or ironical side should be dispelled by these letters. White is a doer, a maker.

Practically the most satisfying thing on earth (specially after fifteen years of trying to put English sentences together against time) is to be able to square off a board of dry white pine, saw to the line (allowing for the thickness of the pencil point) and have the thing fit perfectly.

In 1943, he "produced 14 lambs, 5 pigs, and 272 chicks and 5 goslings in spite of the weather" and expressed willingness to take on Louis Bromfield in a farming duel, "he to choose the weapons —anything from dung forks to post-hole diggers or 2-ounce syringes for worming sheep." Nor is this willingness to tackle anything a late offshoot; in his trip West with Cushman, White repaired their Model T, sold pocket calculators, picked pears, sandpapered a dance floor in Cody, Wyoming, played the piano in Hardin, Montana, and, in Louisville, Kentucky, wrote a sonnet on a race horse and sold it on the spot. White is so handy, so faithfully amused by his transactions with the material world, that his writing comes to us as largesse. The fine words have been trickled through a sieve of natural busyness. Another screen on the sieve has been his physical frailty, an unsteadiness in the head and a queasiness in the stomach that seem always there, or around the corner of the next ominous hour (though, airily, he shows no nervousness in high places; at Cornell he tried to walk across the Fall Creek gorge on the handrail of a bridge, and as a Talk of the Town reporter he ascended the unfinished Chrysler Building by ladder and scaffold). In 1936, he wrote Christopher Morley, "My health is always whimsical, and I turn out shockingly little work in the course of a week."

His attitude toward his own writing is volatile. Against the discouragement he expressed to Thurber may be set the happiness of his statement to Stanley White in 1929 that "to write a piece and sell it to a magazine is as near a simple life as shining up a pushcart full of apples and vending them to passersby." To Ross, who found in White's shined apples the shining note he was looking for, White wrote in 1945, "I am not as sure of myself as I used to be, and write rather timidly, staring at each word as it comes out, and wondering what is wrong with *it.*" To a college student he wrote in 1963, "I was a writing fool when I was eleven years old and have been tapering off ever since." For all his protests of fragile gifts progressively enfeebled, the sustained energy and charm of these letters, dashed off from odd corners of crowded days, confirm our impression of a writing fool still, irrepressibly felicitous and fluent. As early as his Western trip of 1922 he could with impish lyricism say that a small town "consists mainly of four stores and an excellent view of the mountains."

His letters to his brother Stanley, who taught him to read before first grade, trace the longest curve in the book, and make the most deliberate accounting. Stanley, a landscape architect, lived in Illinois and has retired to Colorado, and White's periodic letters record the writer's life with the caringness of a family album, and a sepia touch of "the literary":

> The lake hangs clear and still at dawn, and the sound of a cowbell comes softly from a faraway woodlot. In the shallows along shore the pebbles and driftwood show clear and smooth on bottom, and black water bugs dart, spreading a wake and a shadow. A fish rises quickly in the lily pads with a little plop, and a broad ring widens to eternity.

In praise of a cane, White writes, "It gives dignity, direction, restraint, and a general sense of owning whatever you set the point of the cane down on," and, in memory of Robert Coates, "Bob shining like a great red lantern over everybody and everything, with his mind darting about like a swallow in air."

Well, one expects to find gems in Tiffany's. This collection, addressed to many people, will speak to many more. The index is excellent, and the photographs, of snowy, grassy yesteryears, are haunting. White was born in a Mount Vernon castle and works in a Maine boathouse, and both are shown. Young or old, he has parted his hair next to the middle. This is his biggest book—the only one, indeed, hard to hold with one hand—and, as he says, his most naked. "A man who publishes his letters becomes a nudist—nothing shields him from the world's gaze except his bare skin." In 1964, he described an essayist as one "who must take his trousers off without showing his genitals. (I got my training in the upper berths of Pullman cars long ago.)" His drawers here are not altogether off, as we can see by the polka dots of ellipsis that intervene sometimes; nevertheless White has allowed some tart thoughts to slip into print: "The firm of Harper, I have discovered over a period of years which might roughly be described as too long, is feeble-minded, but it is the sort of feeble-mindedness which holds a man in thrall." We laugh, and even his publisher must be disarmed by the aptness of expression. White's style, in the manner of the eighteenth-century journalist-philosophers and of Thoreau, strikes a colloquial pose but seeks the finality of aphorism:

A writer is like a beanplant—he has his little day, and then gets stringy.

There is some slight advantage in living as a recluse, in that one makes one's own crises, instead of getting them out of the newspaper.

I don't know which is more discouraging, literature or chickens.

Medals should be edible, so you could get it over with and have a moment of enjoyment.

It is always sobering to encounter the intellectual idealists at work, for they seem to live in a realm of their own, making their plans for the world in much the same way that any common tyrant does.

When I get sick of what men do, I have only to walk a few steps in another direction to see what spiders do.

I always write a thing first and think about it afterwards, which is not a bad procedure, because the easiest way to have consecutive thoughts is to start putting them down.

WILSON AND NABOKOV

Edmund Wilson's Fiction: A Personal Account

Memoirs of Hecate County came out in 1946; I read a copy borrowed from the Reading (Pa.) public library, where it sat placidly on the open shelves while the book was being banned in New York State. Mere reading must have seemed a mild sin in the Reading of those years; it was a notoriously permissive town, famous for its rackets, its whores, and its acquittal-minded juries. The head librarian was a sweet Miss Ruth, who had been in Wallace Stevens's high-school class, she told me years later. In 1946 I was fourteen. What that slightly sinister volume, a milky green in the original Doubleday edition, with the epigraph in Russian and a three-faced Hecate opposite the title page, meant to me, I can reconstruct imperfectly. Certainly I skipped the pages of French that the curious Mr. Blackburn spouts toward the end, and probably I skimmed the inside-the-book-business ax-grinding of "The Milhollands and Their Damned Soul." But the long, central story, "The Princess with the Golden Hair," the heart and scandal of this collection of six "memoirs," I read, as they say, *avidly,* my first and to this day most vivid glimpse of sex through the window of fiction.

First written, in 1975, as one of *The New Republic*'s series of "Reconsiderations," about *Memoirs of Hecate County.* Expanded to include the other fiction for *An Edmund Wilson Celebration,* edited by John Wain (Phaidon, 1978). Then trimmed back and thriftily reused as an afterword for Nonpareil Books' paperback reissue of *Hecate County* in 1980. This version is the wrap-up, full of footnotes.

All of my life I have remembered how Anna, "as a gesture of affection and respect," held the hero's penis in her hand as they drifted off to sleep; and how Imogen in coitus halted her lover and "did something special and gentle" that caused her to have her climax first; and how one of the women (I had forgotten which) gazes at the narrator, and through him at the amazed young reader, over the curve of her naked hip. This last image, redolent of the casual intimacy and exposure that adults presumably enjoyed, affected me so powerfully I was surprised, rereading, to discover how brief it is:

> . . . once, when I came back into the room, I found her curled up on the bed and was pleased by her eyes, very cunning and round—at once agate like marbles and soft like burrs—looking at me over her hips.

It is Anna, of course, and the emphasis—typical of Wilson's erotic art—is all on her eyes. The mechanically and psychologically complicated business of Imogen's back brace touched me less memorably, but like the images above it smelled of the real, it showed sex as a human transaction that did honestly take place, not in the elastic wonderland of comic-book pornography but on actual worn furniture, in moods of doubt and hangover, in a muddle of disillusion and balked comfort: the hero does not omit to let us know that he found Anna's fond trick of penis-holding "in the long run . . . uncomfortable." There was something dogged and humorless and pungent about Wilson's rendition of physical love: the adjective "meaty" recurs, spoiling pleasant contexts, and the simile everyone remembers from *I Thought of Daisy* tells of the heroine's held feet, "in pale stockings . . . like two little moist cream cheeses encased in covers of cloth." Pungent, and savage: I was blinded by the journal entry, in "Princess," that begins "——ing in the afternoon, with the shades down and all her clothes on—different from anything else—rank satisfactory smell like the salt marine tides we come out of . . ." And a very naked moment comes in the last story, at the Blackburns' party, when the hero throws Jo, the third of his willing fornicatrices, onto the bed full of guests' wraps:

She put one arm up over her eyes; her legs dangled, like a child's, from her knee—the dignity of her hostess's gown all going for nothing now. "Move forward," I said, and put her legs up. Her white thighs and her lower buttocks were brutally now laid bare; her feet, in silver openwork sandals, were pointing in opposite directions.

Of course I could have got this sort of thing, in 1946, from Erskine Caldwell or John O'Hara, indeed *did* get it from the southern-California detective fiction of James Cain and Raymond Chandler; but the sex in these writers was not fortified by Wilson's conscious intention of bringing European sexual realism into American fiction at last. The publication of Wilson's notebooks, *The Twenties*, from which the Anna sections of *Hecate County* are taken almost verbatim, show his sexual scorecards mingled as if naïvely with landscape descriptions and intellectual ruminations and the anecdotes of his rather silly upper-class friends. The original jacket of *Hecate County* describes it as "the adventures of an egoist among the bedeviled." America seemed incorrigibly alien to Wilson, though fascinating, and intrinsic to his destiny. Like Dante, he is a tourist *engagé*. The lonely bookish child stares with a frown from the shadows of the Red Bank mansion, where the mother was deaf and the father nervously fragile; the America he perceives seems grim and claustrophobic, though hectic. There is a true whiff of hell in Hecate County, less in the specific touches of supernatural diabolism with which this utter rationalist forcibly adorned his tales, but in the low ceilings and cheap underwear of the sex idyll, the clothes and neuroses of the copulators. America has always tolerated sex as a joke, as a night's prank in the burlesque theatre or fairground tent; but not as a solemn item in life's working inventory. It was Wilson's deadly earnest, his unwinking naturalistic refusal to release us into farce, that made *Hecate County* in all its dignity and high intent the target of a (successful!) prosecution for obscenity. Earnest, but not Ernest Hemingway, who never in his fictional personae shows himself compromised, as this sweating, fumbling hero of Wilson's so often is; Hemingway's heroes make love without baring their bottoms, and the women as well as the men are falsified by a romantic severity, an exemption from the odors and awkwardness that Wilson, with the dogged selfless honesty of a bookworm, presses his own nose, and ours, into with such solemn satisfaction.

Rereading, now, in this liberated age, and in the light of the notebooks, one expects to find the sex tame. And so, in a sense, it is. "——ing" turns out to be, in the unexpurgated journals, merely "Fucking," rather than the more exotic activity I tried to imagine, and the tender journal accounts of cunnilingus and fellatio* and of Anna's "monthlies" did not find their way into even the revised edition of 1959.

In the fiction, Wilson sets down no sexual detail in simple celebration, to please and excite himself, but always to illuminate the social or psychological condition of the two women. The Anna of "Princess," compared with the confusing love-object of the journals, is admirably coherent, as the product of certain cultural and economic conditions in Brooklyn; how telling, for instance, is her reluctance to be seen naked, as if nudity—to the upper classes an aesthetic proclamation, a refutation of shame—evokes inhibitions having nothing to do with sexual acts, which she performs freely. And how plausibly, if ploddingly, are the clothes of the two women described and made to symbolize their social presences. Such details—seized, we sometimes feel, by a sensibility that doubts its own grasp on the "real"—lend the factual sexual descriptions a weight, a heat, far from tame.

It is Imogen (her original may be waiting exposure in the unpublished journals of the Thirties; married for sixteen years, she seems too old for the narrator at the age he assigns himself, "on the verge of thirty") who occasions Wilson's subtlest, harshest instances of sexual realism. After two years of yearning, the hero greets their tryst in a mood of nervous lassitude. The very perfection of her body distances her—"I found that I was expressing admiration of

---

*". . . the cool moisture of her lips when she has bent lower for fellatio, so delightful, so curiously different from the warm and mucilaginous moisture of ordinary intercourse—the incredible-feeling caress, gently up and down, until the delightful brimming swelling of pleasure seems to make it flow really in waves which fill her darling woman's mouth." The passage, so lyrical, goes on, however, to observe "the man a little embarrassed, feels a little bit differently about her mouth, but affectionately kisses her."

her points as if she were some kind of museum piece"—and her
eager lubricity, "making things easy for the entrant with a honey-
sweet sleek profusion," dulls his triumph: "She became, in fact, so
smooth and open that after a moment I could hardly feel her.
. . . I went on and had a certain disappointment, for, with the
brimming of female fluid, I felt even less sensation; but—gently
enough—I came, too." Gently enough, the failure of an overpre-
pared, ideal love to connect is masterfully anatomized, and mov-
ingly contrasted with his tawdry, harried affair with Anna, which
involves him with criminal types and gives him gonorrhea. One's
breath is snatched to see, in the journals, the patrician, pontifical
Wilson led by sex to the edge of the abyss of poverty, its diseases,
its tangled familial furies, its hopeless anonymity. He did not fall
in. The last story of *Hecate County*, surreal and troubled, prefigures
the hero's marriage to Jo Gates, a well-off, cheerful "Western girl"
like Margaret Canby, whom Wilson married in 1930, closing out
the decade, and clamping down on a suspicion "that, fond though
I was of Margaret and well though we got along, we did not have
enough in common."

The journals make clear more abundantly than the novella how
much Wilson had loved Anna, how fully she satisfied him and gave
him his deferred manhood. "The Princess with the Golden Hair"
is a love-poem to her and one of the best of his writing generation's
obligatory love-poems to the lower classes.

> Yet for them the depression was always going on like a flood that swept
> away their houses . . . and the attitudes, I knew, that I assumed to myself
> and in my conversations with others meant nothing in that bare room
> in Brooklyn where Anna and her garment-worker cousin were so sober
> and anxious and pale.

Like Thornton Wilder's *Heaven's My Destination*, "Princess" is a
generous aberration, a visit to the underworld by a member of the
last predominantly Wasp generation of writers, the last that con-
ceived of itself as an aristocracy. Wilson's portrait of this one slum-
child lives by her light, the "something so strong and instinctive
that it could outlive the hurts and infections, the defilements,
among which we live." The fiction she inhabits, as its true princess,

overtops the flanking gothic vignettes (though "Ellen Terhune" has its authenticity, and the last story a wrenched pain) and makes plausible Wilson's insistence that *Memoirs of Hecate County* was his favorite among his many books. His fiction, generally cluttered, savoring of the worked-up, of collected details moved by *force majeure* of the writer's mind, here finds a theme that moves *him*. Sex was his one way *in*, into the America to which his response, however much he wished it otherwise, was to reach for anesthesia, whether found in books or bottles. Imogen, in this respect, is a better metaphor for America than Anna; her flamboyant costumes and greedy orgasms serve the same narcissism, reflect the same blank passion to succeed; in her richly, ironically particularized and overfurnished setting, she ends as a comic vision, empty but not unlovable, a gaudy suburban witch, in a land where, after 1946, Hecate Counties would spread and multiply and set the new cultural tone. Freud more than Marx would bias our lives; the suburban home would replace the city street as the theatre of hopes; private fulfillment and not public justice would set the pace of the pursuit of happiness. Until the mid-Sixties this remained true, and Wilson, writing out of notebooks kept in the Twenties, foretold it, casting his fiction in the coming mode of sexual candor, sardonic fantasy, and confessional fragment. No longer shocking, and never meant to be, *Hecate County* remains, I think, a work of exemplary merit, still the most intelligent attempt by an American male to dramatize sexual behavior as a function of, rather than a suspension of, personality.

I read *I Thought of Daisy* years later, and there is some inverse progression in this, for it is the more rounded novel, more thoroughly intended and unified than the six disparate "memoirs," though in the earlier book, too, Wilson has composed his narrative in a series of—in this case, five—discrete panels. Here, too, is the first-person narrator given to essayistic asides and hopeful of unriddling America through the person of a female native less intellectual and well born than himself. Again, the book is liveliest in its landscapes and erotic scenes, and relatively leaden in its sociological disquisitions; the presentation, for instance, of Hugo Bamman as the type of Twenties radical seems "blocked in" with large shadows and thick lines, and lifts free into specificity only in the mad moment when Hugo apparently embarks on a boat to Afghanistan straight from a taxi containing the hero and Daisy. The hero tells us that he is under Hugo's sway, but in fact seems, as narrator-analyst, on top of him from the start. In his introduction to the revised edition of 1953 Wilson confesses how "schematic" *Daisy* is, and claims to be "rather appalled by the rigor with which I sacrificed to my plan of five symphonic movements what would normally have been the line of the story." The character of Rita, based upon that of Edna St. Vincent Millay, especially resisted his scheme, dominating sections where she was meant to be subordinate, and yet remaining more mysterious, in her involvement with the narrator, than she should have been.

Yet for all Wilson's strictures upon himself the book has much that is lovely about it, beginning with the title. The phrase "I thought of Daisy" occurs in each section but the last, and here, oddly, in the excursion to Coney Island that is closely derived from an account in the journals of such a trip with "Florence," Wilson fails to transcribe a note of what may be the original inspiration:

postcards: American flag with silver tinsel inscription—"I thought of you at Coney Island."

The Twenties journals throw considerable light upon the genesis of this novel. Wilson began it in 1926 or '27, and rewrote it drastically in a beach house in California, near the home of Margaret Canby, late in 1928. He confided to Maxwell Perkins that *Axel's Castle,* which he was carrying forward simultaneously, "being literary criticism, is easier to do, and in the nature of a relief, from *Daisy.*" To John Peale Bishop he wrote that "it was to be a pattern of ideas and all to take place, as to a great extent it does, on the plane of intelligence—and when I came to write the actual story, this had the effect of involving me in a certain amount of falsified psychology." He got the book off to Perkins early in 1929, and in the midst of his near-breakdown later that winter, within the sanatorium at Clifton Springs, New York, he went over the page proofs. The period of crisis in which he completed this novel is also the time of his romance with Anna, and in his journals he was writing, without knowing it, his one other extended fiction. After 1929 a certain abdication and consolidation took place; he got a divorce and remarried, forsook Anna, and settled on criticism as his métier. As a critic, he has said all that need be said against his own first novel. What needs to be added is how good, if ungainly, *Daisy* is, how charmingly and intelligently she tells of the speakeasy days of a Greenwich Village as red and cozy as a valentine, of lamplit islands where love and ambition and drunkenness* bloomed all at once. The fiction writer in Wilson was real, and his displacement a real loss.

In 1953 he stated that *Daisy* was "written much under the influence of Proust and Joyce." Though the novel constitutes a kind of portrait of the artist as a young man, and gives New York a little of the street-guide specificity Joyce gave Dublin, the influence of Proust is far more conspicuous. The *longueurs,* the central notion of changing perspectives and "intermittences of the heart," the importance of party scenes, the contraction of some intervals of time (e.g., the hero's European trip) into mere summary while other moments are expansively and repeatedly treated, the search for "laws" of behavior and perception, the mock-scientific rigor with which aesthetic and subjective impressions are examined, the musical, wide-ranging speculativeness—all this is Proustian. Wilson, indeed, was one of the few Americans intellectually energetic enough to put Proust's example to work. This example fused surface and thought, commonplace reality and a "symphonic" prose of inexhaustible refinement. Wilson had Proust's love for whatever could be assimilated to his mind. Daisy, with her cream-cheese feet and her way of saying "um" for "them," is not as floral an appari-

---

*There is quite a lot of drunkenness in Wilson's scant fiction. The third chapter of *Daisy* and the last of *Hecate County* both show the gradual derangement of the narrator within "That enchanted country of drink that was the world one had been young in, in the twenties!" The funniest and most harrowing bibulous episode occupies the 1934 sketch, "What to Do Till the Doctor Comes (From the Diary of a Drinker-Out)," reprinted in *The American Earthquake,* with three other pieces of reportorial "fiction."

tion as Odette, nor do Wilson's glimpses of our hard seaboard resonate like the steeples at Martinville; but there is that same rapt reception of the glimpse as a symbol:

> Then suddenly I had almost caught my breath—I had been curiously moved by the sight of a single, solitary street lamp on the Staten Island shore. It had merely shed a loose and whitish radiance over a few feet of the baldish road of some dark, thinly settled suburb. Above it, there had loomed an abundant and disorderly tree. But there was America, I had felt with emotion—there under that lonely suburban street lamp, there in that raw and livid light!

The young hero, coming out onto Professor Grosbeake's glassed-in porch at Princeton after an evening spent in intoxicating conversation, feels the winter chill mix with his mentor's abstract theology:

> . . . and as I took leave of Grosbeake—gazing out through the glass at the pavement lightly dappled with leaves and the dark grass glittering with wet—my mind bemused with a vision of God as a vast crystal fixing its symmetry from a liquefied universe—I felt a delicious delicacy of iciness, glossy fall-leaf slivers and black rain-glinting glass.

Such interpenetration of mind and matter is surely a great theme, and few Americans were better qualified to dramatize it than Wilson, with his polymathic curiosity and his pungent earthiness, his autocratic intellect and initially quite benign and humble willingness to sniff out the grubbiest lessons that mysterious America could set for him.

In its final printing in his uniform edition, *Daisy* is bound with a short story, "Galahad," composed by Wilson in the early Twenties. Its adolescent hero, Hart Foster, about to assume leadership of his prep-school Young Men's Christian Association, is nearly seduced by the sister of a friend, who takes off her clothes and gets into bed with him.

> As she bent over him for a moment, Hart had a glimpse of her firm round breasts; he was surprised to find them so big: he had always supposed that girls' breasts were little low dotted things.

The ingenuously confessed surprise is Wilsonian, as is the genuine ethical struggle of the boy upon his return to the school. He does not lightly dismiss the puritan morality, or the opposed morality that follows the revelation that "this was the real Barbara, this solid living body!—not merely the face at the top of a dress that one knew in ordinary life." He plays truant from the school to visit her, and faced with her again becomes "a helpless child" before "the terrible prestige of her sexual experience." She advises him to return, and he does. The story commands considerable suspense, as it presents in open conflict, near the outset of their long-conjoined career, the polarities of Wilson's self-education: the conscientious humanist and the anarchic concupiscent. Especially vivid for me, in "Galahad," was the train ride down from New England toward New York, a ride I often took in my own student days, gazing like Hart Foster through the gliding windows "with a kind of morbid relish for every dry winter meadow mottled with melting snow, for every long flat factory building, for every black ice-glazed stream, for every hard square-angled town with its hollow-looking boxlike houses . . ." Wilson is peculiarly a poet of this wintry, skeletal, Northeastern landscape, and his journals of the Twenties end with a glorious display of Connecticut snowbound as the Thirties begin.

Why did the author of "Galahad" produce so little else in the way of short fiction? Why did the author of *Daisy* not go on to become the American Proust? Why, for that matter, did the best-selling memoirist of *Hecate County* not follow this most favorite of his books with something similar?

One answer, no doubt, is drably practical: no one much encouraged him to write fiction—not those who praised him as a critic and employed him as a journalist, and not the *New Yorker* editors, who never accepted a story of his though they took readily to those of Mary McCarthy, Wilson's third wife, and of Vladimir Nabokov, whom Wilson had urged upon the magazine.*Another answer may

*In 1947 he wrote Katharine White, then the head fiction editor, rather plaintively: "I have felt that there were stories in both my last two books that might perfectly well have appeared in *The New Yorker* and that the only thing that kept them out was that they were done from a sharp point of view, that they were not pale and empty and silly enough."

lie in the nature of his great intelligence: he could extrapolate from facts but not easily budge them. An immensely mobile gatherer of information, he wrote no fiction without a solidly planted autobiographical base, and his fantasy, when it intervenes, as in the sidepieces of *Hecate County,* seems clumsy and harsh. He drew on journal notations as if he didn't trust his memory, that great sifter of significance; forgetfulness, the subconscious shaper of many a fiction, had no place in his equipment. And a third answer, of course, is that the fiction writer went underground and greatly enriched the reporter, lent the critic his bracing directness and energy, co-authored the plays and vivacious self-interviews of Wilson's antic moods, and lay behind the flamboyance of those feats of reading and startling acquisitions of expertise that kept lengthening the shelf of his squat, handy volumes. He worked up subjects like the Dead Sea scrolls and the Iroquois Indians somewhat as popular novelists like Irving Stone and James Michener appropriated Hawaii or Michelangelo, to turn them into books. The comparison is well meant: Wilson wrote in the marketplace; he aimed to become a writer in a professional sense unimaginable to most aspiring young intellectuals now. If fiction turned out to be not his métier, he wrote with the industry of a Balzac and the range of a Joyce in forms that were.

An Earlier Day

THE THIRTIES: *From Notebooks and Diaries of the Period,* by Edmund Wilson, edited with an introduction by Leon Edel. 753 pp. Farrar, Straus & Giroux, 1980.

Alas, a certain testiness has been noticeable in the reviews of *The Thirties.* Morris Dickstein, in the *Times Book Review,* found the writing bland and gray and the sexual episodes depressing. Gore Vidal, in *The New York Review of Books,* complained of Wilson's foot fetishism, boring landscape descriptions, and nervous if not derisive attitude toward male homosexuals. And Harry Levin, whose every review nicely approaches the definitive, concluded in the *Saturday Review* that the volume "adds a little—not very much —to the record, and nothing at all to his stature as man and writer." Even the suave and conscientious editor of these papers, accustomed to dealing with the elegant leavings of Henry James, allows in his introduction that Wilson's "candor may seem at times gratuitous" and asks the question "Why do authors keep journals?" Why, to be specific, has this author already heavy on the shelf inflicted upon us from beyond the grave yet one more portly volume: over seven hundred pages of quasichaotic journalistic jottings and personal notes upon erotic conquests, psychologically fraught dreams, sociologically limp conversations, dreadful parties, melancholy inklings, landscapes seen, and meals eaten? The answer, perhaps, is on the dust jacket, where the visage of Wilson in early middle age —one eyebrow lifted, both collar wings impeccably stiff—gazes sideways with a humorless and ungainsayable arrogance. Because he wanted to.

There is something here to offend everyone. The gratuitous candor to offend puritans (if any still exist) and living survivors of Wilson's companionship. The frequent references to "fairies" to offend Mr. Vidal. A schoolboyish satyrism to offend women, and an unchivalric post-coital eye—his wife Margaret in bed gives him the impression of "little arms and legs, turtle paws, sticking out on each corner," and after toying with a mistress, Wilson confides, "I kept thinking when I got my hand near my face, that we had been eating fish." A host of casually condescending ethnic and racial epithets and speculations figure in these pages, along with an instinctive coupling of the words "Anglo-Saxon" and "civilization," as in "her high and nobly modeled brow and temples were no longer merely Anglo-Saxon, but showed the modeling of a high civilization" and "their fine clear complexions, blond hair, thin and pale, fine civilized Anglo-Saxon types." "Nigger" seems to be Wilson's natural way of referring to black people (even "coon" occurs), though as the decade wears on, and he has visited the shacks of Kentucky and the slums of Chicago, the more respectful term "Negro" gradually takes over. Wilson rarely fails to omit mention of Jewishness, however often he encounters it in literary and Communist circles, and includes in his journals considerable callow theorizing, his and other people's, along the lines of "Jewish men thought themselves ugly, so had to keep proving to themselves what they could do in the way of getting Gentile girls" and "[Jews] tend naturally perhaps to exclude non-Jews—love excluding people, asserting moral superiority (Communism, psychoanalysis)." Of course, overt anti-Semitism flourished among the upper-class friends he retained from Princeton, and even in his own family circle at Red Bank: his Uncle Win thought there were too many Jewish comedians on the radio and too many Jewish advisers in Roosevelt's Washington and, when admonished by his nephew that Hitler's persecution of Jews (as of Christmas 1933) was a terrible thing, answered, "Of course it is, but—" Edmund Wilson came a long way from the prejudices he was born to, and the assumptions and tensions they reflect are part of what *The Thirties* in sum is: a haphazard but relentless exposing of the great gray underbelly of this gray decade and the psyche of one of its more sensitive denizens.

At the beginning of the Thirties, Wilson married Margaret Canby and published his first major critical work, *Axel's Castle* (1931). A versatile, rather rakish journalist, editor, and poet five years older than the century, he travelled around the country, to Southern mining towns and strike-bound New England mills and his wife's native California, to report at first hand on the worsening Depression. Along with taking notes to be worked into articles for *The New Republic* and then collected in *The American Jitters* (1932), he scribbled down snatches of conversation and descriptions of landscape in the faith that he would eventually create "a work of fiction made out of the materials that I had been compiling in these notebooks." But the decade was to produce no fiction, and what Wilson did manage of creative writing, in the form of plays and poetry, was rather sour and skewed. In September of 1932, while he and his wife were on opposite coasts, Margaret tripped at the top of a flight of stone stairs while leaving a party in Santa Barbara, fractured her skull, and died within hours. For the next six years, Wilson led a morose, sometimes sordid, but productive bachelor life, dividing his time among New York City, Provincetown, and

Stamford, Connecticut. In 1935, on a Guggenheim fellowship, he spent five months in the Soviet Union, promptly publishing his impressions in *Travels in Two Democracies* (1936). Two more collections—one of plays, the other of critical essays—followed, and in 1940 Wilson published the magnum opus, *To the Finland Station*, that had preoccupied him since the early Thirties, when it first occurred to him that "nobody had ever presented in intelligible human terms the development of Marxism and the other phases of the modern idea of history." In 1938, he had married, after a swift courtship, the twenty-five-year-old Mary McCarthy. The last pages of these journals record a touch of rheumatism and a pressing awareness

> of death, of a person who never again can reach one, that one never again can reach—you cannot hear her voice because it is no longer there —she is not somewhere far away now, even sitting alone, writing you a letter—she is no part of this house, of these houses, of any houses of people—she cannot make, cannot hear, a sound—all around there is nothing and I lie alone with silence sloping on every side, slipping (sliding) away to nothing, and I, as it were, content.

"You're a cold fishy leprous person, Bunny Wilson," Margaret once told him. Yet the long delirium of writing in which he recalls this—an outpouring of description and reminiscence and self-recrimination that he began to set down immediately after boarding a plane in Newark to go view her body in California—contains piercing evidences of deep and complex feeling. "But then when I would bring her back in imagination, the sadistic impulses would come back—at other times I would begin to cry with grief, my face would contract in a grimace of grief, how sweet and pretty and darling she had been, all soft and cunning, so affectionate and gentle, how we had slept together, she always turning with me, no matter when or how many times I had wanted to turn. . . ." For the rest of the decade, he will dream of her—dreams that tell him she is not dead. In 1940, he makes this entry:

> *Margaret.* For years, I have been like a spring, uncoiled with difficulty and kept straight with effort, that snaps back into its twisted state as soon as sleep begins to relax the effort: the images that disguise

reversion to the past, the convulsive twitching that wakes me up and represents the reassertion of the effort that keeps me straight by day.

In 1929, Wilson had had a mental breakdown that sent him to a sanatorium for three weeks. Morbidity accompanied him through his long and vigorous life. Like many of the great Victorians whose tireless careers his own recalls, he was a bedevilled man, prone to despair—"How I'd wake up in the night, strained, suicidal, couldn't see any end to it"—and hallucinations of a sort:

> When I first came back to New York from Provincetown after having been driving all day, first in the chill rain, then in the sweltering sun, arriving in a daze, the people in the streets looked like sinister specters—I was almost afraid of them, looked askance at them uneasily as if they might be going to bite or slug me.

Darwinism was no mere theory to him. Getting out of an elevator, he glimpsed a workman who "looked, not like an ape, but like some kind of primitive man" and whose face proved that "humanity was still an animal, still glaring out of its dark caves, not yet having mastered the world, not even comprehending what he saw. I was frightened—at him, at us all. *The horrible look of the human race.*" On another occasion, he suddenly saw his hand on the page of a book as "an animal's paw with the fingers lengthened to claws and become prehensile for climbing around." The lurking malevolence of the primitive beneath the façade of civilization haunted him; in one of the last pieces he saw through the press, the epilogue to *Upstate* (1971), he wrote, "I look at the creatures on the street and think, well, we have begun to walk upright and our toes, now more or less impractical, are shrinking like the toes of elephants' feet."

A streak of the macabre and surreal runs through his reporting. In *The American Jitters*, Los Angeles is dissolved in Joycean word-play:

> For a theme song you can buy a Moorish sinagogue, a dream of dreams, a regular pitti-pitti palace, with many bathrooms done in onyx Napole-onics and pornographic Pompeian red, mauve and emerald sateen coverlimps on all the die-away divans for didoes and a private slipping

pool filled with green fountain-pen ink—a little bit blushful perhaps at selling itself to the pictures for $20,000 a year but happy as a real bribe and with all its prollems slobbed!

His notes for this article in *The Thirties* begin, "Los Angeles (the goozly-floofy beach, flou, floozy, goosy, goozley, goofy, floozent, flooey, floozid, foozled, the flooffy goosey beach)." And of course the fiction he did eventually produce, out of some of the material in his notebooks, was *Memoirs of Hecate County*, where men turn into turtles and the Devil spouts pages of French at a drunken suburban party. Social realist though he strove to be, and admirer though he was of the sparkling atmospherics of Hemingway and Fitzgerald, he had a sardonic, stringent imagination akin to that of an Ambrose Bierce. There is scarcely a sunlit scene in his fiction, though he loved the summer life of Provincetown, and its great wide light.

Not cold, but dark, and drawn to piscine and claustrophobic imagery, and leprous in a sense. "You don't like people" was another of Margaret's accusations, and though many people pass through these journals, the rare note of happiness is struck in settings of solitude:

> The kick I got out of my room at the back corner of the sordid rooming house kept by a blowzy yellow-haired woman . . . to be away in the little back room of a house in a provincial Southern city when spring has just definitely come on!—away from family, politics, engagements, even love affairs, where I could lie in bed in the morning and think about pleasantly but coolly at my leisure. . . . Clearness, simplification, and peace.

And in Provincetown, after the season:

> On damp days, when the brown of the trees was almost gone and the sea and the sky were gray, all colors neutralized, Provincetown was like being on a boat—for me, living alone, writing during the day and reading at night, the external world was almost obliterated.

His visits to old friends sound stifling, and the parties he attends barbarous:

Ann, in her blond phase, while acting up over Cummings's escapades, at a party at the Rogerses', in the bathroom with Margaret and Katy, seized the fancy guest towels, such as no one would even think of using, soiled them in the toilet, and threw them across the room. Katy's eyes grew round as saucers.

. . . Bill kept directing guests who wanted to go to the can to take the wrong turning when they got to the floor below so that men kept trooping into the room of an unknown girl, fumbling at their flies.

Dawn Powell's knock-down-and-drag-out party. George Hartmann . . . (his hair now grizzled) found in the kitchen snuffing up the gas out of the range.

Waughs' party for Bubs Hackett . . . Barbara Jones, at the end of the evening, discovered that her finger was bleeding and had an idea that Bill L'Engle, with whom she had been talking, had bitten her. . . . They all, more or less, ended up at Ticino's, and as the Waughs were coming back, Coulton knocked Bubs down in the snow.

Some fun. During Prohibition, Wilson drank a great deal of illegal and poisonous liquor, and after Repeal (which he describes under the melancholy head *"Ghostliness, dreariness, of night of Repeal"*) consumed legal poison at the same rate, not impairing his marvellous critical cogency but contributing, we may surmise, to his after-hours sense of foreboding and phantasmagoria. On more than one occasion recorded here, liquor rendered him impotent.

And what *of* his notorious sexual adventuring, set down in his journals with such fishy, clinical candor? The episodes provide, tedious though they seemed to fastidious reviewers, the only narrative suspense in these jumbled pages, and the nearest approach to three-dimensional character studies. Seven distinct women can be counted among Wilson's paramours of the period. Margaret Canby Wilson is not just one of the erotic partners but, persisting in memory and dream, the romantic heroine of *The Thirties.* The proletarian dance-hall girl Anna, who figured so prominently in the notebooks of *The Twenties,* continues into these. The elderly Wilson, annotating the journals forty years after the event, troubles to tell us that even while he and Margaret were married, earlier in the fatal summer of their separation, he entertained Anna at their New

York apartment: "Eventually I looked up Anna and had her come to see me. I would not let her go into the bedroom, but made love to her on the couch." Time, too, has been less than kind to Anna: "—Anna has gotten so 'skinny,' there were depressions on her hips at the side, and I could feel her little pubic bone—the Oxfords I bought her began to bag—hands always cold—hair turned dull, lost most of its red tinge, got dandruff and began to come out—when her ovaries were bad, she wanted to die." And the other heroine of the central tale of *Hecate County*—"The Princess with the Golden Hair"—the princess herself, called there Imogen Loomis, makes her début in the journals under the initial "D.," as a flirtatious and skittish married woman with "round eyes and nose" and an "Isoldesque, Guineveresque beauty." The climactic—anticlimactic, from the hero's point of view—sexual scene of the novel actually occurred, it turns out, in the Colonial Inn in Concord, Massachusetts, four years after Wilson was first smitten by the lady. But the details, including her disconcerting perfection of form and "honey-sweet sleek profusion" (in the journals, "honey-sweetly-smooth profusion"), are all here, along with her piquant mix of narcissism, distraction, and efficiency. Wilson's hottest times in this era, however, occurred with one "K.," a Chicago belle who liked being spanked with a hairbrush and whose interest in "funny ways" proved even Wilson to be satiable. There is also "O.," with whom he enjoyed a fiasco, for all of her "delicacy and beauty," and Maria Michelaevna, a hat-check girl in a Lexington Avenue restaurant who his black maid in Stamford thought would have been a good person for him to marry. Instead he married Mary McCarthy, who, with the son born to them on Christmas Day 1938, figures in these journals hardly at all. The marriage, which Mr. Edel speculates was too "strained and . . . stormy" to write about, and of which Wilson in a retrospective note said, "Our life—though we had also a great deal of fun—was sometimes absolutely nightmarish," lasted eight years, and contributed, possibly, some shadowy forms to "The Weeds" and *A Charmed Life* in Miss McCarthy's own oeuvre.

By the time of this marriage, Wilson was writing in his journals relatively little. Over six hundred pages of *The Thirties* take us up to the end of 1935, and the remaining half of the decade passes in little more than a hundred. To his critical and reportorial chores for *The New Republic* he had added a teaching stint at the University of Chicago and the vast reading—in English, French, German, and Russian—necessary for *To the Finland Station*. Also, the anecdotal and descriptive wealth of the pre-1935 journals feels tilted toward the eventual objective of an ambitious novel, perhaps on the scale of Dos Passos's *U.S.A.*, which Wilson much admired; and this ambition faded. The true and habitual creator of fiction, it could be asserted, does not work from journals but trusts to memory and imagination, which are forms one of the other. The welding together of descriptions written down on the spot is a technique of journalism. The eye of fiction does not see the multifarious thing itself; it would lose momentum and the subliminal music if it did. A passage of observation like

> An earlier day, when, as we set out to Provincetown, a strange autumnal pink light of sunset made the sand dunes toward the Coast Guard station pink-beige in front of the equally amazing laid-on blue, somewhat unharmonious, of the water, and brought out in the roots of the beach grass, where the gash of the path to the house laid them bare, gray in ordinary light, a ruddy color almost like that of willow roots in a brook

makes a fine watercolor, suitable for framing, but would clog any narrative where it was inset. Nor was Wilson's tropism, in his notetaking, toward the strikingly idiomatic, the especially illustrative, a good sign; for fiction proceeds in the faith that it can animate the mundane and breed significance out of its own accumulating context. So the publication of these journals is justified if only in that they contain much beautiful writing and many telling vignettes that could have found their niche in print nowhere else. Their poignance, over all, stems from the transformation, by the mute years, of an immediate presentness for the writer to an irrevocable pastness for us, the readers.

Edmund Wilson died before he could elucidate and expand upon the journals of *The Thirties* as he did those of *Prelude* and *Upstate* and even—partially—*The Twenties*. Many entries remain mysterious, some deliciously so:

The wood she had been buying in sealed envelopes—you could more easily boil it than burn it—when you put it on the fire, great quantities of water came gushing out from both ends of the log.—They climbed mountains and had photographs of the peaks.

Albany. Using O.'s name and signing it to checks; my collapse; new little Ford roadster. I stopped off at Pittsfield.

When one turns from the notes he took on his travels to the finished articles he based upon them, one is grateful for the coherence and whole new amounts of material he has injected, but the surface seems relatively hard, flashy, and repellent. The verbal scaffolding within the journals has a dreamlike delicacy, by comparison. Though disoriented, we enter in. Wilson wanted these journals with all their embarrassments published, and they do have a questing, tentative, vulnerable quality he rarely manifested elsewhere, where the breadth and firmness of his opinions occlude any sense of a mind in the process of education.

Criticism and historiography, which so snugly engaged the thrust of Wilson's mind, make surprisingly small inroads into the matter of the journals. In all the pages of *The Thirties,* only a handful hold notes on his reading—of Dos Passos and Tolstoy, and these near the end—and we learn little about the literary lights whom Wilson knew. Cummings tells a dirty joke, Dos Passos's wife is a delightful cook, Fitzgerald has "expressionless birdlike eyes," and Auden, we hear from a young man at a dinner party, "was animated wholly by hatred—envied everybody, imitated *Beowulf* because he envied *Beowulf.*" In the realm of politics, the Marxists and fellow-travellers with whom Wilson mingles at rallies and strikes seem no less frivolous and prone to extravagance than the personnel of the dinner parties he attends in Connecticut or than the artistic crowd in Provincetown. Though he was engaged with Marxism throughout this decade, the advocate subsiding into the analyst, our principal political impression is his refusal to be favorably impressed by Roosevelt—"the popular enthusiasm for him had more warmth and force than he." As the Second World War swept into irrelevance so many of the Thirties' debating points, Wilson came to a determined (and offensive) denial of moral content not only to that conflict but also to the American Civil War; just as the street crowds loomed to him as cavemen, so all wars illustrated merely "the irresistible instinct of power to expand itself, of well-organized human aggregations to absorb or impose themselves on other groups." He was himself, after the Thirties, to hole up in Wellfleet and Talcottville, and to relinquish commentary on the present American scene; he lost touch with contemporary realities so completely that he ignored his income taxes and ran afoul of the federal authorities. In the early Forties, he did compose an extended work of fiction, but one most alive in its personal confessions, and far narrower and more saturnine than the one he seems to have envisioned. There is much that is magnificent about the second half of Wilson's career, and the journals he continued to keep surely hold their rewards and revelations. He did succeed in not being absorbed by the aggregations of spectral primitives outside his study walls, as he went from one self-assignment to another, his mind grinding away at Indian lawsuits and French-Canadian novels, at languages as far afield as Hebrew and Hungarian. He remained an immense digester, a bringer of news from afar. But in the journals of *The Thirties* a hope is said good-bye to, the hope of a civilized intelligence to identify itself with America, to absorb it all, and to proclaim, as Melville said, "the truth of the thing."

The Cuckoo and the Rooster

THE NABOKOV-WILSON LETTERS: *Correspondence Between Vladimir Nabokov and Edmund Wilson, 1940–1971*, edited by Simon Karlinsky. 346 pp. Harper & Row, 1979.

Edmund Wilson and Vladimir Nabokov both valued literature above all else, and friendship between them flourished and then foundered on the basis of this shared trait. "Our conversations have been among the few consolations of my literary life through these last years," Wilson wrote Nabokov in 1945. "I simply must see you both," Nabokov wrote in 1943 to Wilson and his then wife, Mary, "I miss you a lot." The warmth of these averrals was not unusual in the first decade of their correspondence. Wilson died in 1972 and Nabokov in 1977; their widows, Elena Wilson and Véra Nabokov, have helped Simon Karlinsky assemble and elucidate the letters, more than half of which date from before 1950. After 1957, the excited, entertaining exchanges between the two men fell away as if in anticipation of their public battle over Nabokov's translation of *Eugene Onegin* (1964) and the final, bitter break occasioned by a few pages of reminiscence in Wilson's *Upstate* (1971) and sealed by Nabokov's letter to the *Times Book Review* icily characterizing Wilson as his "former friend": "I am aware that my former friend is in poor health but in the struggle between the dictates of compassion and those of personal honor the latter wins." So it is good to have, even in a dust jacket that looks like butcher's paper, this ample record of a former friendship between two polymathic, intensely committed minds and drolly stubborn, cagey personalities. If the letters of writers are to be published at all (and it seems there is no stopping it, as our zeal for "people" and our impatience with intellectual and artistic constructs conspire to unmask all who during their lifetimes presumed to the title of fabricator), then an epistolary dialogue such as this is an energetic and coherent way to package them. And this package is blessed in its editor, a professor of Slavic able to footnote with authority and a fine thoroughness the copious quibbling between the two men as one sought to educate the other in Russian and its versification while the other provided like services in English, amid much mutual one-upping in French. Dr. Karlinsky, for instance, has troubled to discover that the later editions of Nabokov's *Bend Sinister* and *Pnin* failed to adjust a number of solecisms that Wilson had kindly listed, and that Wilson reprinted unaltered a translation and interpretation of Pushkin that Nabokov had laboriously, eloquently corrected. Both the correspondents, tireless devotees of linguistic fine points, would have relished their editor's scrupulous rigor, if not always agreed with his adjudications.

The first letter in the correspondence was composed by Nabokov in 1940, a few months after he had landed in this country, and simply stated that his cousin Nicolas had suggested he get in touch with Wilson. Wilson at that time was literary editor at *The New Republic*, and within a few more months was accepting material the Russian émigré had composed in English, giving him a few lessons in editorial usage, and sending him small checks. Before the year was out, Nabokov wrote in gratitude, "It is really wonderful to be living at last in a country where there is a market for such things." Wilson, with only a shadowy idea of the brilliant body of work Nabokov had created in Russian, was in truth immensely helpful and encouraging to the immigrant. He recommended Nabokov's work to Edward Weeks of *The Atlantic Monthly* and James Laughlin of New Directions, both of whom liked and accepted it, and he guided Nabokov into *Partisan Review*, *Decision*, the New York *Sun*, and *The New Yorker*. "You *are* a magician," Nabokov wrote Wilson in gratitude, and, again, "The magic of your approbation always works." Wilson liked *The Real Life of Sebastian Knight* ("It's absolutely enchanting. It's amazing that you should write such fine English prose and not sound like any other English writer") better, it turned out, than any of Nabokov's subsequent novels in English, and on the other side Nabokov found much to praise in Wilson's fledgling efforts to read and write about Russian literature, in Wilson's Cyrillic handwriting ("Your hand in Russian is absolutely Russian—I almost am inclined to doubt that you wrote out those lines yourself"), and in Wilson's constant production ("I liked both your verse and your prose enormously"). Nabokov assures his American chum that "this is not a case of 'кукушка хвалитъ пѣтуха'," referring to the Ivan Krylov fable "The Cuckoo and the Rooster," which ends:

> Why then, without fear of blame
> Does the cuckoo praise the rooster?
> Because he praises the cuckoo.

Each man had something to offer the other. Wilson knew his way around the American literary scene, and Nabokov knew the Russian language and its literature. Two scarcely precedented experiments were being simultaneously carried out in those early

Forties—a distinguished American critic was attempting to master the language of Tolstoy and Chekhov, and a virtuoso Russian stylist was attempting to become a writer in the land of Hemingway and Faulkner. As Dr. Karlinsky's introduction points out, Wilson and Nabokov had a great deal in common: "Both were at home in French literature and language. Both had a skeptical, albeit divergent, view of religion and mysticism. Both were sons of jurists who [had been] involved in politics." Both were the children of wealthy homes, and both had fallen on hard times financially; it is surprising and, by today's inflationary lights, touching to read of the grudging advances and slippery lectureships the two men schemed to obtain. When Nabokov complains, "I am underpaid here in a ridiculous and insulting manner," Wilson responds with "You can't be any more broke than I am—I have never been so badly in debt in my life." Both were pedants but not academics, instructors above all of themselves; both were mavericks and non-joiners, combative and uncompromising in their critical estimations. Both men took pride in being frank about what mattered, and nearly from the start the friendliness of their letters has to surmount such abrasive opening lines as "I am going to steal an hour from Gogol and thrash out this matter of Russian versification, because you are as wrong as can be" (Nabokov) and "I was rather disappointed in *Bend Sinister,* about which I had had some doubts when I was reading the parts you showed me, and I will give you my opinion, for what it is worth" (Wilson). Their disagreements about versification seem derived from a serene and mutual deafness. Their disagreements about politics stem from Wilson's willingness to peer with some sympathy into Russian historical events that for Nabokov are absolutely damnable: "Any changes that took place between November 1919 and now have been changes in the decor which more or less screens an unchanging black abyss of oppression and terror." Their disagreements about literary reputations are, as Wilson remembered them in *Upstate,* "really intellectual romps, sometimes accompanied by mauling"; Wilson seems more amused than surprised when Nabokov indignantly routs a Wilsonian favorite like Malraux ("quite a third-rate writer"), Faulkner ("quite impossible biblical rumblings"), or Henry James ("that pale porpoise and his plush vulgarities"), and he falls rather silent when a nominee like Jane Austen or Dickens is accepted into Nabokov's select little pantheon. As long as an educational process was going on, the correspondence survived its quarrels and lapses—with Nabokov, my unexpected impression was, the more eager and open student of the two. It was Nabokov who initiated the relationship, and it was Nabokov who, in 1971, long after the *Eugene Onegin* furor, attempted to patch it up, writing from Montreux, "A few days ago I had the occasion to reread the whole batch . . . of our correspondence. It was such a pleasure to feel again the warmth of your many kindnesses, the various thrills of our friendship, that constant excitement of art and intellectual discovery."

Without minimizing the kindnesses and excitements that Wilson contributes, this reviewer found Nabokov's letters the more alive and giving, certainly the more poetic and dense. Librarians in a quandary are hereby advised to shelve this book under "N"; Edmund Wilson's shelf of opinion, autobiography, and belles-lettres is already loaded to overflowing, and in reading his letters to Nabokov we are frequently conscious of how much else awaited attention on his desk. He quotes a letter to him from a certain Polly Boyden as saying, "I read Nabokov's *Gogol* by accident and liked it so much I bought the *Sebastian Knight*. I think Nabokov is more inescapably the artist than anyone I have ever met personally and it chilled my blood. . . ." This is the sort of unstinting recognition that Wilson never quite accords his faithful correspondent, praising Nabokov's early English prose, the memoirs of *Speak, Memory,* and the sad comedy of *Pnin* yet resisting the charm of much else and, shockingly, reporting of *Lolita* that "I like it less than anything else of yours I have read. . . . Nasty subjects may make fine books; but I don't feel you have got away with this." After *Lolita,* the relationship ceases to be comfortable. The letters grow less frequent, with shorter paragraphs. The men write hastily of get-togethers that rarely come off. By the Fifties, Nabokov is established as a *New Yorker* contributor and a Cornell professor, and moving ahead on his own. It did not escape his notice that America's foremost critic, while cordial and generous in private, never gave him the public approbation that would have been useful. In his rebuttal of Wilson's adverse review of *Onegin* (which Nabokov had once proposed they translate together!), the Russian with suave irony remembers:

> When I first came to America a quarter of a century ago, he wrote to me, and called on me, and was most kind to me in various matters, not necessarily pertaining to his profession. I have always been grateful to him for the tact he showed in not reviewing any of my novels while constantly saying flattering things about me in the so-called literary circles where I seldom revolve.

Wilson's often-promised "étude un peu approfondie which I hope to *consacrer à votre œuvre*" never materialized—which, in view of the incidental remarks he did let drop in print, was perhaps fortunate. He had a good eye for what was defective or lopsided in Nabokov, but something of a tin ear for the unique music this "inescapably" artistic man could strike from anything. Even that first, stiff letter of self-introduction has a Nabokovian touch, a flirt of natural observation: "I am staying with friends in Vermont (goldenrod and wind, mostly), but shall be back in New York in the second week of September." In the letters that follow, Nabokov apologizes for his "imitation English" and laments that "I am too old to change conradically"—itself a jest of genius. By the time he has completed his first native book (*Sebastian Knight* was composed in Europe), his American prose is bumptious: "My Gogol book is out, and I have asked good old Jay to mail you a copy. Its brilliancy is due to a dewy multitude of charming little solecisms," and his final verdict on his Conradical accomplishment is "Conrad knew how to handle *readymade* English better than I; but I know better the other kind. He never sinks to the depths of my solecisms, but neither does he scale my verbal peaks." Nabokov's cheerful arrogance was a form of exhilaration, and his letters, like his art, display a flying factuality that creates a sensation of multiple overlay which is dizzying. Here is a Colorado peak he tossed up, or laid down, for Wilson in 1951, when *Lolita* was brewing in him:

I went to Telluride (*awful* roads, but then—endless charm, an old-fashioned, absolutely touristless mining town full of most helpful, charming people—and when you hike from there, which is 9000', to 10000', with the town and its tin roofs and self-conscious poplars lying toylike at the flat bottom of a *cul-de-sac* valley running into giant granite mountains, all you hear are the voices of children playing in the streets —delightful!) for the sole purpose, which my heroic wife who drove me through the floods and storms of Kansas did not oppose, of obtaining more specimens of a butterfly I had described from eight males, and of discovering its female. I was wholly successful in that quest, finding all I wanted on a steep slope high above Telluride—quite an enchanted slope, in fact, with hummingbirds and humming moths visiting the tall green gentians that grew among the clumps of a blue lupine, *Lupinus parviflorus,* which proved to be the food plant of my butterfly.

A friendship that lived by language died by language. It was not politics that created lasting animosity, it was not even their differing opinions of Mann and Gorky; it was Russian words like *netu, vse, zloy,* and *pochuya,* English words like "curvate," "habitude," "dit," "gloam," "scrab," and "mollitude," all of which figure in the great *Onegin* debate. In *Upstate,* readied for publication in the shadow of his death, Wilson recalls with rancor that Nabokov doubted his information "that *fastidieux* in French meant *tiresome* and not *fastidious,* and . . . declared with emphasis—contrary to the authority of Dahl, the great Russian lexicographer—that *samodur* had anything in common with the root of *durak.* He tried to tell me . . . that *nihilist* in English was pronounced *neehilist.*" From recounting these indignities Wilson went on to say that "the element in his work that I find repellent is his addiction to *Schadenfreude* [malicious joy]." Nabokov had the last tweaked word by agreeing, in a final letter to the *Times,* with a suggestion that "*Schadenfreude,* as used by Mr. Wilson, really means 'hatred of Freud.'"

An Introduction to Nabokov's Lectures

Upon Mansfield Park, *by Jane Austen;* Bleak House, *by Charles Dickens;* Madame Bovary, *by Gustave Flaubert;* "The Strange Case of Dr. Jekyll and Mr. Hyde," *by Robert Louis Stevenson;* The Walk by Swann's Place [sic], *by Marcel Proust;* "The Metamorphosis," *by Franz Kafka; and* Ulysses, *by James Joyce*

VLADIMIR VLADIMIROVICH NABOKOV was born on Shakespeare's birthday in 1899, in St. Petersburg (now Leningrad), into a family both aristocratic and wealthy. The family name, indeed, may stem from the same Arabic root as the word *nabob,* having been brought into Russia by the fourteenth-century Tatar prince Nabok Murza. Since the eighteenth century the Nabokovs had enjoyed distinguished military and governmental careers. Our author's grandfather, Dmitri Nikolaevich, was State Minister of Justice for the tsars Alexander II and Alexander III; his son, Vladimir Dmitrievich, forsook a certain future in court circles in order to join, as politician and journalist, the doomed fight for constitutional democracy in Russia. A courageous, combative liberal who was sent to prison for three months in 1908, he nevertheless without misgiving maintained himself and his immediate family in what one biographer has called "a splendid and luxurious Russian version of Edwardian timelessness,"* divided between the large townhouse built by his father in the fashionable Admiralteiskaya region of St. Petersburg, and the country estate, Vyra, brought by his wife—of the immensely rich Rukavishnikov family—to the marriage as part of her *dot.* Their first surviving child, Vladimir, received, in the testimony of his siblings, a uniquely generous portion of parental love

---

*Andrew Field, *Nabokov: His Life in Part* (Viking Press, 1977). Disapproved of by its proud subject, and far from error-free, this biography yet constitutes a creditable, if overanimated and indexless, replication of Nabokovian high spirits: astute, searching, amusing, and, for the time being, indispensable. The other principal biographical source is, of course, Nabokov's grand memoir, *Speak, Memory.* See also his *Strong Opinions* (McGraw-Hill, 1973), his various introductions to the English translations of his Russian works, and the Winter 1970 issue of *Triquarterly,* No. 17, a special issue devoted to Nabokov on his seventieth birthday.

and attention. He was precocious, spirited, at first sickly and then robust. A friend of the household remembered the young "Volodya" as "the slender, well-proportioned boy with the expressive, lively face and intelligent probing eyes which glittered with sparks of mockery."

V. D. Nabokov was something of an Anglophile, and his children were tutored in English as well as French. His son, in *Speak, Memory*, claims, "I learned to read English before I could read Russian," and remembers an early "sequence of English nurses and governesses," as well as a procession of comfortable Anglo-Saxon artifacts: "All sorts of snug, mellow things came in a steady procession from the English Shop on Nevski Avenue: fruitcakes, smelling salts, playing cards, picture puzzles, striped blazers, talcum-white tennis balls." Of the authors discussed in this volume,* Dickens was probably the first the young Vladimir encountered. "My father was an expert on Dickens, and at one time read to us, children, aloud, chunks of Dickens, in English, of course," Nabokov wrote to Edmund Wilson forty years after the event. "Perhaps his reading to us aloud, on rainy evenings in the country, *Great Expectations* . . . when I was a boy of twelve or thirteen, prevented me mentally from re-reading Dickens later on." It was Wilson who directed his attention to *Bleak House* in 1950. Of his boyhood reading, Nabokov recalled to a *Playboy* interviewer, "Between the ages of ten and fifteen in St. Petersburg, I must have read more fiction and poetry —English, Russian, and French—than in any other five-year period of my life. I relished especially the works of Wells, Poe, Browning, Keats, Flaubert, Verlaine, Rimbaud, Chekhov, Tolstoy, and Alexander Blok. On another level, my heroes were the Scarlet Pimpernel, Phileas Fogg, and Sherlock Holmes." This last level of reading may help to account for Nabokov's surprising, though engaging, inclusion of such a piece of late-Victorian fog-swaddled Gothic as Stevenson's tale of Jekyll and Hyde within the course on European classics he gave at Cornell in the 1950s.

A French governess, the stout, well-memorialized Mademoiselle,

---

Lectures on Literature, by Vladimir Nabokov, edited by Fredson Bowers (Harcourt Brace Jovanovich, 1980).

took up abode in the Nabokov household when young Vladimir was six, and though *Madame Bovary* is absent from the list of French novels which she so trippingly ("Her slender voice sped on and on, never weakening, without the slightest hitch or hesitation") read aloud to her charges—"We got it all: *Les Malheurs de Sophie, Le Tour du Monde en Quatre Vingts Jours, Le Petit Chose, Les Misérables, Le Comte de Monte Cristo,* many others"—the book undoubtedly existed in the family library. After V. D. Nabokov's senseless murder on a Berlin stage in 1922, "a fellow student of his, with whom he had gone for a bicycle trip in the Black Forest, sent my widowed mother the *Madame Bovary* volume which my father had had with him at the time and on the flyleaf of which he had written 'The unsurpassed pearl of French literature'—a judgment that still holds." Elsewhere in *Speak, Memory,* Nabokov writes of his rapturous reading of the work of Mayne Reid, an Irish author of American Westerns, and states of a lorgnette held by one of Reid's beleaguered heroines, "That lorgnette I found afterward in the hands of Madame Bovary, and later Anna Karenin had it, and then it passed into the possession of Chekhov's Lady with the Lapdog and was lost by her on the pier at Yalta." As to the age at which Nabokov first perused Flaubert's classic study of adultery, we can safely guess it was a precious one; he read *War and Peace* for the first time when he was eleven, "in Berlin, on a Turkish sofa, in our somberly rococo Privatstrasse flat giving on a dark, damp back garden with larches and gnomes that have remained in that book, like an old postcard, forever."

At this same age of eleven, Vladimir, having been tutored entirely at home, was enrolled in St. Petersburg's relatively progressive Tenishev School, where he was accused by teachers "of not conforming to my surroundings; of 'showing off' (mainly by peppering my Russian papers with English and French terms, which came naturally to me); of refusing to touch the filthy wet towels in the washroom; of fighting with my knuckles instead of using the slaplike swing with the underside of the fist adopted by Russian scrappers." Another alumnus of the Tenishev School, Osip Mandelstam, called the students there "little ascetics, monks in their own puerile monastery." The study of Russian literature emphasized medieval Rus—the Byzantine influence, the ancient chronicles—and proceeded through study of Pushkin in depth to the works of Gogol, Lermontov, Fet, and Turgenev. Tolstoy and Dostoevski were not in the syllabus. At least one teacher, Vladimir Gippius, "a first-rate though somewhat esoteric poet whom I greatly admired," impressed himself forcibly on the young student; Nabokov at the age of sixteen published a collection of his own poems and Gippius "brought a copy with him to class and provoked the delirious hilarity of the majority of my classmates by applying his fiery sarcasm (he was a fierce man with red hair) to my most romantic lines." Andrew Field proposes that "from Gippius . . . Nabokov learned a manner, a literary posture, which to a certain extent he has never abandoned. . . . It does not take a very gifted ear or imagination to hear the soft echoes of Gippius's proprietorial devotion to literature and easy viciousness of judgment in much of what Nabokov has said and written about books and their authors."

Nabokov's secondary education ended as his world was collapsing. In 1919, his family became émigrés. "It was arranged that my brother and I would go up to Cambridge, on a scholarship awarded more in atonement for political tribulations than in acknowledgment of intellectual merit." He studied Russian and French literature, much as at the Tenishev School, and played soccer, wrote poetry, romanced a number of young ladies, and *never once* visited the University Library. Among his desultory memories of his college years there is one of "P. M. storming into my room with a copy of *Ulysses* freshly smuggled from Paris." In a *Paris Review* interview Nabokov names the classmate, Peter Mrosovsky, and admits that he did not read the book through until fifteen years later, when he "liked it enormously." In Paris in the mid-Thirties he and Joyce met a few times. Once Joyce attended a reading Nabokov gave. The Russian was pinch-hitting for a suddenly indisposed Hungarian novelist before a sparse and motley crowd: "A source of unforgettable consolation was the sight of Joyce sitting, arms folded and glasses glinting, in the midst of the Hungarian football team." On another inauspicious occasion, in 1938, they dined together with their mutual friends Paul and Lucie Léon; of their conversation Nabokov remembered nothing and his wife, Véra, recalled that "Joyce asked about the exact ingredients of *myod,* the Russian 'mead,' and everybody gave him a different answer." Nabokov distrusted such social conjunctions of writers and in an earlier letter to Véra recounted a version of the legendary single, fruitless encounter between Joyce and Proust.

When did Nabokov first read Proust? The English novelist Henry Green in his memoir *Pack My Bag* wrote of Oxford in the early Twenties that "anyone who pretended to care about good writing and who knew French knew his Proust." Cambridge was likely no different, though as a student there Nabokov was intent upon his own Russianness to an obsessive degree—"my fear of losing or corrupting, through alien influence, the only thing I had salvaged from Russia—her language—became positively morbid." At any rate, by the time he granted his first published interview, in 1932, to a correspondent for a Riga newspaper, he could say, rejecting the suggestion of any German influence on his work during the Berlin years, "One might more properly speak about a French influence: I love Flaubert and Proust."

Although Nabokov lived for over fifteen years in Berlin, he never learned—by his own high linguistic standards—German. "I speak and read German poorly," he told the Riga interviewer. Thirty years later, talking in a filmed interview for the Bayerischer Rundfunk, he expanded upon the question: "Upon moving to Berlin I was beset by a panicky fear of somehow flawing my precious layer of Russian by learning to speak German fluently. The task of linguistic occlusion was made easier by the fact that I lived in a closed émigré circle of Russian friends and read exclusively Russian newspapers, magazines, and books. My only forays into the local language were the civilities exchanged with my successive landlords or landladies and the routine necessities of shopping: *Ich möchte etwas Schinken.* I now regret that I did so poorly; I regret it from a cultural point of view." Yet in his 1944 book on Gogol, he speaks of "the other [than Russian] three European languages I happen to know"—English, French, and what else but German? He had been acquainted with German entomological works since boyhood, and his first literary success was a translation, in the Crimea, of some Heine songs for a Russian concert singer. With his wife's help he checked translations of his own works into German and ventured to improve, in his lectures on "The Metamorphosis," upon the English version by Willa and Edwin Muir. There is no reason to doubt the claim he makes, in his introduction to the translation of his rather Kafkaesque novel *Invitation to a Beheading,* that at the time of its writing he had read no Kafka. In 1969 he told a BBC interviewer, "I do not know German and so could not read Kafka before the 1930s when his *La métamorphose* appeared in *La nouvelle revue française*"; two years later he told Bavarian Broadcasting, "I read Goethe and Kafka *en regard* as I also did Homer and Horace." Whether it occurred in French or in ponied German, Nabokov's first encounter with Kafka must postdate 1935, when *Invitation to a Beheading* was composed, "in one fortnight of wonderful excitement and sustained inspiration."

On April 17, 1950, Nabokov wrote to Edmund Wilson from Cornell, where he had recently taken academic employment: "Next year I am teaching a course called 'European Fiction' (XIX and XX c.). What English writers (novels or short stories) would you suggest? I must have at least two." Wilson promptly responded, "About the English novelists: in my opinion the two incomparably greatest (leaving Joyce out of account as an Irishman) are Dickens and Jane Austen. Try rereading, if you haven't done so, the later Dickens of *Bleak House* and *Little Dorrit.* Jane Austen is worth reading all through—even her fragments are remarkable." On May 5, Nabokov wrote back, "Thanks for the suggestion concerning my fiction course. I dislike Jane, and am prejudiced, in fact, against all women writers. They are in another class. Could never see anything in *Pride and Prejudice.* . . . I shall take Stevenson instead of Jane A." Wilson countered, "You are mistaken about Jane Austen. I think you ought to read *Mansfield Park.* . . . She is, in my opinion, one of the half dozen greatest English writers (the others being Shakespeare, Milton, Swift, Keats and Dickens). Stevenson is second-rate. I don't know why you admire him so much—though he *has* done some rather fine short stories." And, uncharacteristically, Nabokov capitulated, writing on May 15, "I am in the middle of *Bleak House*—going slowly because of

the many notes I must make for class-discussion. Great stuff. . . .
I have obtained *Mansfield Park* and I think I shall use it too in my
course. Thanks for these most useful suggestions." Six months
later, he wrote Wilson with some glee:

> I want to make my mid-term report on the two books you suggested I
> should discuss with my students. In connection with *Mansfield Park* I
> had them read the works mentioned by the characters in the novel—
> the two first cantos of the "Lay of the Last Minstrel," Cowper's "The
> Task," passages from *King Henry the Eighth*, Crabbe's tale "The Parting
> Hour," bits of Johnson's *The Idler*, Browne's address to "A Pipe of
> Tobacco" (Imitation of Pope), Sterne's *Sentimental Journey* (the whole
> "gate-and-no-key" passage comes from there—and the starling) and of
> course *Lovers' Vows* in Mrs. Inchbald's inimitable translation (a scream).
> . . . I think I had more fun than my class.

Nabokov in his early Berlin years supported himself by giving
lessons in an unlikely quintet of subjects: English, French, boxing,
tennis, and prosody. In the latter years of exile, public readings in
Berlin and in such other centers of émigré population as Prague,
Paris, and Brussels earned more money than the sales of his works
in Russian. So, but for his lack of an advanced degree, he was not
unprepared, arriving in America in 1940, for the lecturer's role that
was to provide, until the publication of *Lolita*, his main source of
income. His *Strong Opinions* tells us: "In 1940, before launching
on my academic career in America, I fortunately took the trouble
of writing one hundred lectures—about 2,000 pages—on Russian
literature, and later another hundred lectures on great novelists
from Jane Austen to James Joyce. This kept me happy at Wellesley
and Cornell for twenty academic years." At Wellesley for the first
time, in 1941, he delivered an assortment of lectures with intriguing
titles—"Hard Facts About Readers," "A Century of Exile," "The
Strange Fate of Russian Literature," "The Art of Literature and
Commonsense." Until 1948 he lived with his family in Cambridge
(at 8 Craigie Circle, his longest-maintained address until the Palace
Hotel in Montreux received him for keeps in 1961) and divided his
time between two academic appointments: that of resident lecturer
at Wellesley College, and as research fellow in entomology at

Harvard's Museum of Comparative Zoology. He worked tremendously hard in those years, and was twice hospitalized. Besides instilling the elements of Russian grammar into the heads of young women and pondering the minute structures of butterfly genitalia, he was creating himself as an American writer, publishing two novels, a book on Gogol, and stories and reminiscences in *The Atlantic Monthly* and *The New Yorker.*

Among the growing body of admirers for his English writings was Morris Bishop, light-verse virtuoso and head of the Romance Languages Department at Cornell; Bishop mounted a successful campaign to hire Nabokov away from Wellesley, where his resident lectureship was neither remunerative nor secure. According to Bishop's reminiscence "Nabokov at Cornell" in *Triquarterly,* Nabokov was designated Associate Professor of Slavic and at first gave "an intermediate reading course in Russian Literature and an advanced course on a special subject, usually Pushkin, or the Modernist Movement in Russian Literature. . . . As his Russian classes were inevitably small, even invisible, he was assigned a course in English on Masters of European Fiction." According to Nabokov, the nickname by which his course was known, "Dirty Lit," "was an inherited joke: it had been applied to the lectures of my immediate predecessor, a sad, gentle, hard-drinking fellow who was more interested in the sex life of the authors than in their books." According to Robert M. Adams, a colleague of Nabokov's at Cornell, "Dirty Lit," of whom the instructor had been Charles Weir, continued under a new number, Literature 309–310, and a new instructor, Victor Lange of the German Department. Titled "Development of the European Novel," it offered "special attention to the history of ideas and the related evolution of the forms of fiction," whereas Nabokov's course promised that, in the words of the catalogue, "Special attention will be paid to individual genius and questions of structure." The two courses met at the same hour (Monday, Wednesday, and Friday at noon) to prevent a student from taking both. Literature 311–312 met in Goldwin Smith "C," a hall containing two hundred seats, and the registration was around one hundred fifty.

One student from the course, Ross Wetzsteon, contributed to the

Triquarterly special issue a fond remembrance of the many altera-
tions in translation Nabokov insisted upon, of Véra Nabokov's
regal white-haired presence at every lecture, of the antic diagrams
Nabokov scribbled on the blackboard with a mock plea that the
students "copy this exactly as I draw it." His accent caused half the
class to write "epidramatic" where Nabokov had said "epigram-
matic." " 'Caress the details,' Nabokov would utter, rolling the r,
his voice the rough caress of a cat's tongue, 'the divine details!' "
Wetzsteon concludes, "Nabokov was a great teacher not because
he taught the subject well but because he exemplified, and stimu-
lated in his students, a profound and loving attitude toward it."
Another survivor of Literature 311–312, quoted by Field, recalled
how Nabokov would begin the term with the stern words, "The
seats are numbered. I would like you to choose your seat and stick
to it. This is because I would like to link up your faces with your
names. All satisfied with their seats? O.K. No talking, no smoking,
no knitting, no newspaper reading, no sleeping, and for God's sake
take notes." Before an exam, he would say, "One clear head, one
blue book, ink, think, abbreviate obvious names, for example, Ma-
dame Bovary. Do not pad ignorance with eloquence. Unless medi-
cal evidence is produced nobody will be permitted to retire to the
W.C."

A third former student, who sat in the last classes Nabokov
taught before, suddenly enriched by the American publication*
and *succès de scandale* of *Lolita*, he took a leave of absence that never
ended, does not remember the course's being referred to as "Dirty
Lit"; on campus it was called, simply, "Nabokov." Nor does my
informant (who happens to be my wife) remember any talk of
numbered seats. Though the course was popular, many students
preferred not to entrust themselves to Nabokov's notoriously
tough grading standards, and simply audited the entertaining lec-
tures. As a lecturer he was enthusiastic, electric, evangelical. She,
my connubial informant, was so deeply under his spell that she
attended one lecture with a fever high enough to send her to the

---

*By G. P. Putnam's Sons (New York) in 1958, and not to be confused with its
first publication in English by the Olympia Press, in Paris, three years earlier.

infirmary immediately afterward. "I felt he could teach me how to read. I believed he could give me something that would last all my life—and it has." She cannot to this day take Thomas Mann seriously, and has not surrendered a jot of the central dogma she culled from "Nabokov": "Style and structure are the essence of a book; great ideas are hogwash."

Yet even his rare ideal student might fall prey to Nabokov's mischief. When our Miss Ruggles, a tender twenty, went up at the end of one class to retrieve her blue book from the mess of graded "prelims" strewn there, she could not find it, and at last had to approach the professor. Nabokov stood tall and apparently abstracted on the platform above her, fussing with his papers. She begged his pardon and said that her exam didn't seem to be here. He bent low, eyebrows raised. "And what is your name?" She told him, and with prestidigitational suddenness he produced her blue book from behind his back. It was marked 97. "I wanted to see," he told her, "what a genius looked like." And coolly he looked her up and down, while she blushed; that was the extent of their exchange.

Seven years after his retirement, Nabokov in *The Paris Review* remembered the course with mixed feelings:

> My method of teaching precluded genuine contact with the students. At best, they regurgitated a few bits of my brain during examinations. . . . Vainly I tried to replace my appearances at the lectern by taped records to be played over the college radio. On the other hand, I deeply enjoyed the chuckle of appreciation in this or that warm spot of the lecture hall at this or that point of my lecture. My best reward comes from those former students of mine who ten or fifteen years later write to me to say that they now understand what I wanted of them when I taught them to visualize Emma Bovary's mistranslated hairdo or the arrangement of rooms in the Samsa household. . . .

In more than one interview handed down, on 3×5 cards, from the Montreux-Palace, the publication of a book based upon his Cornell lectures was promised, but (with such other rumored works in progress as the continuation of his autobiography, entitled *Speak On, Memory,* and his illustrated treatise on *Butterflies in Art,* and the novel *Original of Laura*) the project still hovered in the air at the time of the great man's death in the summer of 1977.

Now here, wonderfully, the lectures are. And still redolent of the classroom odors that an authorial revision might have scoured away. Nothing one has heard or read about them has quite foretold their striking, enveloping quality of pedagogic warmth. The youth and, somehow, femininity of the audience have been gathered into the urgent, ardent instructor's voice. "The work with this group has been a particularly pleasant association between the fountain of my voice and a garden of ears—some open, others closed, many very receptive, a few merely ornamental, but all of them human and divine." For longish stretches we are being read to, as young Vladimir Vladimirovich was read aloud to by his father, his mother, and Mademoiselle. During these stretches of quotation we must imagine the accent, the infectious rumbling pleasure, the theatrical power of this lecturer who, now portly and balding, was once an athlete and a participant in the Russian tradition of flamboyant oral presentation. Elsewhere, the intonation, the twinkle, the sneer, the excited pounce are present in the prose, a liquid speaking prose effortlessly bright and prone to purl into metaphor and pun: a dazzling demonstration, for those lucky Cornell students in the remote, clean-cut Fifties, of the irresistibly artistic sensibility. Nabokov's reputation as a literary critic, heretofore circumscribed, in English, by his laborious monument to Pushkin and his haughty dismissals of Freud and Faulkner and Mann, benefits from the evidence of these generous and patient appreciations, as they range from his delineation of Jane Austen's "dimpled" style and his hearty identification with Dickens's gusto to his reverent explication of Flaubert's counterpoint and his charmingly awed—like a boy dismantling his first watch—laying bare of Joyce's busily ticking synchronizations. His diagrams and insistences show him to be the most passionate of pedants. His pedantry, which piles up so much tangential erudition in the *Onegin* commentaries and in this volume brusquely mutilates so many of Scott-Moncrieff's graceful translations of Proust, must be understood as a religious devotion, a way of paying back to Nature the bliss he has received in the witness of her precisions. Nabokov took early and lasting delight in the exact sciences, and his entranced hours spent within the luminous hush of microscopic examination carry over into his tracing of the horse theme in *Madame Bovary* or the twinned dreams of Bloom and Dedalus; lepidopterology placed him in a world beyond common sense, where "when a butterfly has to look like a leaf, not only are all the details of a leaf beautifully rendered but markings mimicking grub-bored holes are generously thrown in," and where on a butterfly's hindwing "a large eyespot imitates a drop of liquid with such uncanny perfection that a line which crosses the wing is slightly displaced at the exact stretch where it passes through." One of the first poems he attempted in English, "The Poem" in 1944, sums up poetic creation thus:

> in the tangle of sounds, the leopards of words,
> the leaflike insects, the eye-spotted birds
> fuse and form a silent, intense,
> mimetic pattern of perfect sense.

He asked, then, of his own art and the art of others a something extra—a flourish of mimetic magic or deceptive doubleness—that was supernatural and surreal in the root sense of these degraded words.* Where there was not this shimmer of the gratuitous, of the superhuman and non-utilitarian, he turned harshly impatient, in terms that imply a lack of feature, a blankness peculiar to the inanimate: "Many accepted authors simply do not exist for me. Their names are engraved on empty graves, their books are dummies. . . . Brecht, Faulkner, Camus, many others, mean absolutely nothing to me. . . ." Where he did find this shimmer, producing

---

*Of course, natural explanation exists; indeed, the precisions of protective mimicry are a favorite illustrative theme of Darwinism. Caterpillars imitate twigs to avoid being eaten by birds; the less twiglike are removed from the genetic rolls. Fish underwater imitate rocks to let their prey swim closer; the less rocklike go hungry. Natural ingenuity approaches the fiendish: Certain species of firefly imitate the mating signal of other species and then consume the amorous male who answers the call. Some butterflies, non-noxious, evolve markings twin to those of butterflies that do taste nasty. Some flowers imitate the sexual smell of female wasps and get themselves fucked to achieve pollination. All grim and logical enough, understood amid Nature's heartless teeming; but Nabokov took a resolutely non-Marxian view of reality's intricate formations.

its tingle in the spine, his enthusiasm went far beyond the academic, and he became an inspired, and surely inspiring, teacher.

The Fifties, with their emphasis upon private space, their disdainful regard for public concerns, their sense of hermetic, disengaged artistry, and their New Criticism faith that all essential information is contained within the work itself, were a more congenial theatre for Nabokov's ideas than the following decades might have been. But in any decade Nabokov's approach would have seemed radical in the degree of severance between reality and art that it supposes. "The truth is that great novels are great fairy tales—and the novels in this series are supreme fairy tales. . . . Literature was born on the day when a boy came crying wolf wolf and there was no wolf behind him."

Another priest of the imagination, Wallace Stevens, could allow that "if we desire to formulate an accurate theory of poetry, we find it necessary to examine the structure of reality, because reality is a central reference for poetry." Whereas for Nabokov, reality has less a structure than a pattern, a habit, of deception: "Every great writer is a great deceiver, but so is that arch-cheat Nature. Nature always deceives." In his aesthetic, small heed is paid to the lowly delight of recognition and the blunt virtue of verity. For Nabokov, the world—art's raw material—is itself an artistic creation, so insubstantial and illusionistic that he seems to imply a masterpiece can be spun from thin air, by pure act of the artist's imperial will. But works like *Madame Bovary* and *Ulysses* glow with the heat of resistance that the will to manipulate meets in banal, heavily actual subjects. Acquaintance, abhorrence, and the helpless love we give our own bodies join in these transmuted scenes of Dublin and Rouen; away from them, in works like *Salammbô* and *Finnegans Wake*, Flaubert and Joyce yield to their dreaming, dandyish selves and are swallowed by their hobbies. In his passionate reading of "The Metamorphosis," Nabokov deprecates as "mediocrity surrounding genius" Gregor Samsa's philistine and bourgeois family without acknowledging, at the very heart of Kafka's poignance, how much Gregor needs and adores these possibly crass, but also vital and definite, inhabitants of the mundane. The ambivalence omnipresent in Kafka's rich tragi-comedy has no place in Nabokov's credo, though in artistic practice a work like *Lolita* brims with it, and with a formidable density of observed detail—"sense data selected, permeated, and grouped," in his own formula.

The Cornell years were productive ones for Nabokov. After arriving there he completed *Speak, Memory*. It was in an Ithaca back yard that his wife prevented him from burning the difficult beginnings of *Lolita*, which he completed in 1953. The good-humored stories of *Pnin* were written entirely at Cornell, the heroic researches attending his translation of *Eugene Onegin* were largely carried out in her libraries, and Cornell is reflected fondly in the college milieu of *Pale Fire*. One might imagine that his move two hundred miles inland from the East Coast, with his frequent summer excursions to the Far West, gave him a franker purchase on America than precious, Anglophile Cambridge had afforded. Nabokov was nearly fifty when he came to Ithaca, and had ample reason for artistic exhaustion. He had been exiled twice, driven from Russia by Bolshevism and from Europe by Hitler, and had created a brilliant body of work in what amounted to a dying language, for an émigré public that was inexorably disappearing. Yet in this his second American decade he managed to bring an entirely new audacity and panache to American literature, to help revive the native vein of fantasy, and to bestow upon himself riches and an international reputation. It is pleasant to suspect that the rereading compelled by the preparation of his college lectures at the outset of the decade, and the admonitions and intoxications rehearsed with each year's delivery, contributed to the splendid redefining of Nabokov's creative powers; and to detect, in his fiction of those years, something of Austen's nicety, Dicken's *brio*, and Stevenson's "delightful winey taste," added to and spicing up the Continental stock of Nabokov's own inimitable brew. His favorite American authors were, he once allowed, Melville and Hawthorne, and we may regret that he never lectured upon them. But let us be grateful for the lectures that *were* called into being and that are here given permanent form. Tinted windows overlooking seven masterpieces, they are as enhancing as "the harlequin pattern of colored panes" through which Nabokov as a child, while he was being read to on the porch of his summer home, would gaze out at his family's garden.

The Fancy-Forger Takes the Lectern

LECTURES ON RUSSIAN LITERATURE, by Vladimir Nabokov, edited and with an introduction by Fredson Bowers. 342 pp. Harcourt Brace Jovanovich, 1981.

By the end of his life, fame and long exile had so internationalized Vladimir Nabokov that it was easy to ignore the technically unforgettable fact that he had been born and raised Russian. The posthumous publication of his *Lectures on Russian Literature* comes as a bracing reminder of his original and deepest cultural allegiance; these talks on Gogol, Turgenev, Dostoevski, Tolstoy, Chekhov, and Gorky show a more confident intimacy, a more fraternal warmth than his lectures upon European and English masters. Only a fellow-Russian could say of Chekhov's "everyday" prose style:

> Chekhov managed to convey an impression of artistic beauty far surpassing that of many writers who thought they knew what rich beautiful prose was. He did it by keeping all his words in the same dim light and of the same exact tint of gray, a tint between the color of an old fence and that of a low cloud. The variety of his moods, the flicker of his charming wit, the deeply artistic economy of characterization, the vivid detail, and the fade-out of human life—all the peculiar Chekhovian features—are enhanced by being suffused and surrounded by a faintly iridescent verbal haziness.

Where Nabokov is enthusiastic, as he is for Chekhov, Tolstoy, and Gogol, he is exhilarating, and effortlessly reaches into that dimension of cultural and historical surround decisively absent from last year's *Lectures on Literature.* Gogol's rambling metaphors, with the superfluous "little people" they engender and animate in passing, delight him, and lead him to generalize upon "the remarkable creative faculty of Russians, so beautifully disclosed by Gogol's own inspiration, of working in a void. Fancy is fertile only when it is futile." Consideration of Tolstoy leads Nabokov to the following resounding summation:

Essential truth, *istina,* is one of the few words in the Russian language that cannot be rhymed. It has no verbal mate, no verbal associations, it stands alone and aloof. . . . Most Russian writers have been tremendously interested in Truth's exact whereabouts and essential properties. To Pushkin it was of marble under a noble sun; Dostoevski, a much inferior artist, saw it as a thing of blood and tears and hysterical and topical politics and sweat; and Chekhov kept a quizzical eye upon it, while seemingly engrossed in the hazy scenery all around. Tolstoy marched straight at it, head bent and fists clenched, and found the place where the cross had once stood, or found—the image of his own self.

The curious meditations upon the nature of Time in *Ada* can now be linked with the author's earlier attempt to analyze a perceived excellence in Tolstoy: "He discovered a method of picturing life which most pleasingly and exactly corresponds to our idea of time. . . . Tolstoy's prose keeps pace with our pulses, his characters seem to move with the same swing as the people passing under our window while we sit reading his book." These subtle considerations of perspective yield up a beautiful aphorism: "Readers call Tolstoy a giant not because other writers are dwarfs but because he remains always of exactly our own stature, exactly keeping pace with us instead of passing by in the distance, as other authors do."

Where Nabokov is less than enthusiastic, as with Turgenev, Dostoevski, and Gorky, he is not quite worthless as a critic but certainly impatient. Least so with Turgenev, to whom he grants status as a contriver of "purple patches," of "mellow colored little paintings—rather watercolors than the Flemish glory of Gogol's art gallery—inserted here and there into his prose." But Turgenev's style as a whole suffers, producing "a queer effect of patchiness, just because certain passages, the artist's favorites, have been pampered much more than the others." He was, however, "the first Russian writer to notice the effect of broken sunlight or the special combination of shade and light upon the appearance of people." Though Nabokov praises *Fathers and Sons* as "one of the most brilliant novels of the nineteenth century," what sticks in the mind, as he leads the auditors of his lecture through its story, are his dry asides:

One will observe a queer feature of Turgenev's structure. He takes tremendous trouble to introduce his characters properly, endowing them with pedigrees and recognizable traits, but when he has finally assembled them all, lo and behold the tale is finished and the curtain has gone down whilst a ponderous epilogue takes care of whatever is supposed to happen to his invented creatures beyond the horizon of his novel.

For Gorky, beyond the drama of his life, he has little use. "Twenty-six Men and a Girl" has "not a single live word in it, not a single sentence that is not ready-made; it is all pink candy with just that amount of soot clinging to it to make it attractive. From here on there is but one step to so-called Soviet literature." And we all know what that is, or do we? "That a country exists where . . . literature has been limited to illustrating the advertisements of a firm of slave-traders is hardly credible to people for whom writing and reading books is synonymous with having and voicing individual opinions." In an address, "Russian Writers, Censors, and Readers," given at Cornell in 1958, Nabokov manages to work up a certain wry empathy with the artistic maneuvers of the proletarian novelists "faced with the dreadful task of having to weave an interesting plot when the outcome is in advance officially known to the reader."

His treatment of Dostoevski is most debatable, though not as obdurate as some of his later "strong opinions." He at least admits him to his curriculum, granting to his students that "some of you may like it [*Notes from Underground*, its title drolly improved to *Memoirs from a Mousehole*] more than I do," and that "there are many critics who would not agree with [his own, adverse] view." His indictment is in part stylistic ("the intonation of obsession, the hundred percent banality of every word, the vulgar soapbox eloquence") and in part moral ("I do not like this trick his characters have of 'sinning their way to Jesus' "). The plot of *The Idiot* is a "crazy hash" wherein the characters "never say anything without either paling, or flushing, or staggering on their feet." The first part of *The Possessed* is "tedious, being unreal," but the climax at Varvara Petrovna's becomes "grand booming nonsense with flashes of genius illuminating the whole gloomy and mad farce." As to the revered *Brothers Karamazov,* it is "a riotous whodunit—in slow motion." Dostoevski's pen, we are told, comes alive when dealing with Dmitri, but when he takes up his saint Alyosha, "we are immersed in a different, entirely lifeless element. Dusky paths lead the reader away into a murky world of cold reasoning abandoned by the spirit of art."

Though Nabokov's discourse upon Dostoevski contains a number of perfunctory and unsubstantiated slurs, he has some thoughtful points as well. Landscape, weather, dress, and physical appearance scarcely exist in Dostoevski's fiction, which has the texture of "a straggling play, with just that amount of furniture and other implements needed for the various actors: a round table with the wet, round trace of a glass, a window painted yellow to make it look as if there were sunlight outside, or a shrub hastily brought in and plumped down by a stagehand." His characters never change in the course of a book but, like the characters in a detective novel, or "like chessmen in a complicated chess problem," remain the same "to the bitter end." Pan-Slav though he became, Dostoevski remained a disciple of the gothic sentimentalism of Richardson, Ann Radcliffe, Dickens, and Eugène Sue; he "was the most European of Russian writers," with "something second-rate French in the structure of his plots." For all his interest in the irrational and abnormal, he is "much too rational in his crude methods, and though his facts are but spiritual facts and his characters mere ideas in the likeness of people, their interplay and development are actuated by the mechanical methods of the earthbound and conventional novels of the late eighteenth and early nineteenth centuries." All of which is not so far from the more sympathetic and measured judgments of D. S. Mirsky, who in his classic *History of Russian Literature* (1927) wrote that Dostoevski "dealt in spiritual essences, in emanations of his own infinitely fertile spiritual experience." What Nabokov's appraisal of Dostoevski lacks is any sympathy with that spiritual experience, any interest in abasement, humiliation, and perversity as paths to wisdom and revealers of our human nature. Against the central idea of *Crime and Punishment*—that without God all things are possible, including gratuitous acts of murder—Nabokov raises the hypothetical figure of a "sturdy young man" whose "healthy human nature would inevitably balk before the perpetration of deliberate murder. For it is no accident that all the criminal heroes of Dostoevski . . . are not quite sane." In Nabokov's view, sanity equals kindness; for him, as for Socrates, to know the good is to do it. So the superb and desperate message of *Notes from Underground*, to the effect that we will assert our own free will even against our own self-interest, and prefer obnoxious misery to nonentity, is quite lost on him, and is airily waved away: "Philosophically this is all bunkum since harmony, happiness, presupposes and includes also the presence of whim." So stout a refusal to descend into the Dostoevskian underground comes surprisingly from the creator of Humbert Humbert; it stems, I think, from an unwillingness to concede that the disappearance of God is much of a blow to our essential humanity, and from, furthermore, a distaste for the idea of any underground, including Freud's, beyond the luminous ken of the conscious mind.

These lectures, written in the main shortly after Nabokov arrived in this country, in 1940, in a careful handwriting still bearing some Cyrillic curls and with an English vocabulary that was the mere packed bud of its eventual luxuriant bloom, show him to have been not only sturdy and sane but of a rather sunny disposition. The comic, descriptive, and harmonic elements of the works are emphasized rather than the tragic and gloomy aspects that usually strike an initiate into Russian liturature, and sheer spontaneous admiration prompts him to phrases like, of Tolstoy's art, "so powerful, so tiger bright." The lecturer seems eager to share with his audience of New World students "a literature which in artistic worth, in wide-spread influence, in everything except bulk, equals the glorious output of England or France." He proposes to make of each of his auditors an "admirable reader" who "enjoys what the author meant to be enjoyed, beams inwardly and all over, is thrilled by the magic imageries of the master-forger, the fancy-forger, the conjuror, the artist." Of artistry, he optimistically asserts, "Whenever talented people approach art with the sole idea of serving it sincerely to the utmost measure of their ability, the result is always gratifying." And of the literary art, conventionally assumed these days to be non-progressive, if not, in our era, actually regressing, he offers a tonic evolutionary theory:

> ... the whole history of literary fiction as an evolutionary process may be said to be a gradual probing of deeper and deeper layers of life. It is quite impossible to imagine either Homer in the ninth century B.C. or Cervantes in the seventeenth century of our era—it is quite impossible to imagine them describing in such wonderful detail childbirth [as Tolstoy does in *Anna Karenina*]. The question is not whether certain events or emotions are or are not suitable ethically or esthetically. The point I want to make is that the artist, like the scientist, in the process of evolution of art and science, is always casting around, understanding a little more than his predecessor, penetrating further with a keener and more brilliant eye. . . .

We are startled and heartened by a meliorism so blunt, by an apprehension of art's benefice so firm and brisk; just so, his college audiences, even in those days before it became mandatory to mock and spurn the American "way of life," must have tittered to hear this august visitant with his unexpungeable accent remind them stoutly of "freedom . . . that spiritual open where you were born and bred" and urge them to "realize with new purity and pride the value of real books written by free men for free men to read." The French Enlightenment migrated to the Russia of Pushkin and still kept its force in liberals like Nabokov. The gifts of light were manifest to him, and the triumphs of obscurantism and oppression that he witnessed first in his native land and twenty-five years later in his adopted Germany appeared mere shadows, illusory and comic beneath their savage actuality. His pure mental energy, expended in spite of political ugliness and the general darkness that the twentieth century, with its sense of exhaustion and the wild cosmological verities of its science, inflicts upon each soul, now shines out from his departed example, where once it dazzled. Nabokov, his memoirs confide, could scarcely sleep, his brain was so excited. What other major imaginer of our time exercised his mind in so many fields apart from his art—in the study of lepidoptera, in the concoction of chess problems, in scholarship of a fanatically exhaustive and original sort? In the innocence of his cerebral self-delight he could be, like any innocent, cruel, and cruel to his own characters at that. But his was also the cruelty of those who believe in devils, and the curtness of his dismissals (of Freud, of "Falkner-mann," of "Upton Lewis") and the malignancy of some of his creations (Paduk, Axel Rex, Clare Quilty) show the nether side of a fervent faith. Art, he tells us in these lectures, is a "divine game," and pleasure in art consists in reliving the moves of the game with the artist. A strange creed, it kept him robust and undiscouraged; it enabled him to be unrepentantly productive in two or three languages, three or four genres, and four or five distinct milieux, and to communicate through the pages of every book his own playful, "divine" bliss.

Proud Happiness

DETAILS OF A SUNSET AND OTHER STORIES, by Vladimir Nabokov, translated from the Russian by Dmitri Nabokov in collaboration with the author. 179 pp. McGraw-Hill, 1976.

With this collection of thirteen short stories written between 1924 and 1935, Nabokov completes the translation and publication of all his short fiction in the Russian language "meriting to be Englished." Read in the order of their composition (which is not the order of their arrangement here), the stories trace the evolution of the artist from an almost deliriously happy young impressionist to a somewhat somber, albeit quizzically alert, manipulator of humanoid designs. The earliest stories are saturated in the tang and the scent, the trolley cars and the rain showers, the sunsets and the dawns of the Berlin in which the youthful émigré found lodging and food for his senses. In an ecstasy of notation, he observes "the damp Berlin asphalt whose surface resembles a film of black grease with puddles nestling in its wrinkles." He declares, writing to a Russia he has lost, that he is "ideally happy. . . . As I wander along the streets and the squares and the paths by the canal, absently sensing the lips of dampness through my worn soles, I carry proudly my ineffable happiness." His happiness forces him to the invention of a supernatural—Godless but brimming with golden cornices and heavenly chariots. A little later, in stories like "Christmas" and "The Return of Chorb," he begins to develop, around characters who are not alter egos, the theme of grief, of abrupt, nonsensical loss. Autobiography returns after 1930, enhanced by an almost contemptuous verbal cunning and a kind of resigned, formalized nostalgia. The latest stories in this volume, "The Reunion" and "A Slice of Life," show a master fictionist moving his imagination at will through the population of disheartened eccentrics that make up the Russian community of Berlin. A certain Weimar sourness has entered his vision; we miss the exquisite freshness of the enraptured poet who began to write in the city eleven years before. As always, in his best phrases ("the light buzz of silence," "human consciousness, that ominous and ludicrous luxury") Nabokov is an incomparable distiller of the ineffable.

Vale, VN

July 1977

THE LAST NOVEL by Vladimir Nabokov, on one of its last pages, invites us, "Imagine me, an old gentleman, a distinguished author, gliding rapidly on my back, in the wake of my outstretched dead feet, first through that gap in the granite, then over a pinewood, then along misty water meadows, and then simply between marges of mist, on and on, imagine that sight!" This man had imagined death so often, from Luzhin the chessmaster's fall into a chasm of "dark and pale squares . . . at the instant when icy air gushed into his mouth" to Cincinnatus C.'s false beheading ("A spinning wind was picking up and whirling: dust, rags, chips of painted wood, bits of gilded plaster, pasteboard bricks, posters; an arid gloom fleeted") and to the reported demise of Mrs. Richard F. Schiller, née Dolores Haze, yclept Lolita, while "giving birth to a still-born girl, on

Christmas Day 1952, in Gray Star," and on to the death by gunshot of the poet John Shade and by "time-and-pain" of Van Veen—Nabokov had imagined death so often, so colorfully and variously and searchingly, that we felt him to be exempt, having already passed through, into that Switzerland he inhabited as a chocolate-box province of immortality, the last and most playful of his exiles. His death, at the ripe age of seventy-eight, comes too soon, too coarsely—an ugly footnote to a shimmering text, reality's thumb-print on the rainbow.

Posterity's judgment can sort out the best: in English, *Lolita*, perhaps, and, in Russian, *The Gift* ("Дар"). What matters now is that the least of his writings offered a bygone sort of delight: a sorcerer's scintillant dignity made of every sentence a potentially magic occasion. He wanted the reader to share his extraordinary intimations; this generosity gave even his scholarly dissertations and diatribes a certain spaciousness, a giddying other dimension. He lived in the world, and more peripatetically and traumatically than many of us, yet in his art declined to submit to the world; rather, he asked that the world submit to the curious, spotty evidence of its own mimetics, its streaks of insane tenderness, its infinitely ingenious markings. Few minds so scientific have deigned to serve the gods of fancy; with his passion for precision and for the complex design, he mounted for display the crudest, most futile lurchings of the human heart—lust, terror, nostalgia. The violence and violent comedy of his novels strike us, in the main, as merely descriptive, the way the violences of geology are. He saw from a higher altitude, from the top of the continents he had had to put behind him.

Though some of his asides sounded arrogant, and even peevish, his life in its actions demonstrated immense resilience and a robust optimism. Few men who have lost so much have complained so little. He brought to America the body of a forty-one-year-old man of genius in a language left behind, but offered no excuse of exhaustion; the same active mind that entertained his insomnia with the invention of chess puzzles now turned to inventing himself anew, as an American writer. That he succeeded, and taught us new ways to use our language and to experience our milieu, is perhaps less remarkable than his willingness to try, when a hundred college Slavic Languages departments held shelter against the raging of the strange democratic culture whose uncodified quirks swarmed about him. On page 53 of *Lolita,* as Humbert Humbert's love-fever comes to a boil, there is a sudden list of forty names, beginning

> Angel, Grace
> Austin, Floyd
> Beale, Jack

and ending

> Williams, Ralph
> Windmuller, Louise.

It is, the author explains, "a poem, a poem, forsooth!" It is one of Lolita's class lists; it is, with the odd chiming of its relentless alphabetization of fuzzy, budding souls, the class list all Americans have been part of. We have sat in those classes, Nabokov had not; yet it was he who put one into literature, along with so many other comic, correct details of his adopted "lovely, trustful, dreamy, enormous country." His patriotism won him few friends in our literary establishment, but it gave his American novels the fervor of the explicit. His most gracious compliment to the United States was to merge it, in *Ada,* with the Russia of his memory to make one paradisal Antiterra.

His prose was festive, though his characters were doomed. Now he has joined them, in that state he so often imagined—sometimes as the blackest of blacknesses and at other times as a transformation as harmless and amusing as that from chrysalis to butterfly. In his youthful novella *The Eye,* the hero shoots himself and reports, "Some time later, if one can speak here of time at all, it became clear that after death human thought lives on by momentum." Nabokov's momentum originated at the beginning of the century and should continue to its end and beyond. Gentleman, aesthete, metaphysician, wit: the words to describe him have an old-fashioned ring. The power of the imagination is not apt soon to find another champion of such vigor. He takes with him the secret of an ebullient creativity, he leaves behind a resplendent oeuvre.

BELLOW, VONNEGUT, TYLER,
LE GUIN, CHEEVER

Draping Radiance with a Worn Veil

HUMBOLDT'S GIFT, by Saul Bellow. 487 pp. Viking Press, 1975.

Charlie Citrine, the narrator and hero of Saul Bellow's new novel, takes a lot of abuse from the other characters. His brother Julius tells him, "Ah, you poor nut, you overeducated book . . . I can't read the crap you write. Two sentences and I'm yawning. Pa should have slapped you around the way he did me. It would have woken you up." His ex-wife, Denise, tells him, "When you get solemn you're a riot, Charlie. And now you're going in for mysticism, as well as keeping that fat broad, as well as becoming an athlete, as well as dressing like a dude—all symptoms of mental and physical decline. I'm so sorry, really. Not just because I'm the mother of your children, but because you once had brains and talent." Renata, his mistress, tells him, "Your sentiments and deep feelings may do you credit, but you're like a mandolin-player. You tickle every note ten times. It's cute, but a little goes a long way." Naomi, his childhood sweetheart, says, "I wonder what it is with you—a big important clever man going around so eager from woman to woman. Haven't you got anything more important to do?" Von Humboldt Fleisher, the spectacularly failed poet whose "gray stout sick dusty" ghost is the Minotaur of Charlie's mazelike narrative, tells him, "You're not a real American . . . You're a Yiddisher mouse in these great Christian houses. At the same time, you're too snooty to look at anyone," and, in a madder mood, "You're a crook. You're a traitor, a liar, a phony and a Judas," and, in a valedictory letter, "For you are, at one and the same time, no good at all and also a darling man." The character called Rinaldo Cantabile, a dapper Chicago punk who leeches onto Charlie in an inscrutable relationship of furious mutual fascination, is the most abusive of all: he compels Charlie to accompany him into the stall of a men's room and onto the catwalk of an uncompleted sky-scraper, cheats him at cards, smashes up his Mercedes, nearly gets him arrested as a hired gun, and entertains him with dialogue like

> "You don't think I know what I'm doing, Mr. Cantabile?"
> "No, you don't. You couldn't find your ass with both hands."

It is to Cantabile that we owe the book's most vivid physical charac-terization of its hero:

> "Now he's a faded beauty," said Cantabile. "I know it's killing him. He's losing the clean jawline. Notice the dewlaps and the neck wrin-kles. His nostrils are getting big and hungry-like, and they have white hair. It's a sign with beagles and horses too, turning white around the muzzle. Oh, he's unusual all right. A rare animal . . . And a sexy little bastard. He's slept with everything under the sun. Awfully vain, too. Charlie and his pal George jog and train like a couple of adolescent jocks. They stand on their heads, take vitamin E, and play racquet ball. Though they tell me you're a dog on the courts, Charlie."

As if putting down his racquet ball isn't enough, Cantabile goes on to dismiss Charlie's intellectual exertions: "All you have to do is ask him a question and he turns on. Can you see this as an act in a nightclub?" (Not a bad question: the end result of Citrine's friend-ship with Humboldt—the "gift" descending from their obsessions with poetry, history, nobility, great thought, and beauty—is a suc-cessful comic film plagiarized from an old piece of foolery they worked up to relieve their boredom at Princeton.) Nor does Charlie spare himself abuse; he is, by his own account, "a goofy old chaser" and "a dumb old silly." By the time he has reached the page (434) upon which this last characterization appears, the reader, worn out with the mental effort of defending Charlie against his accusers, is terribly tempted just to nod.

The concepts of goofiness, of silliness, of "shenanigans" keep recurring. Human activity, often frenzied and feverish in Bellow's fiction, is more than ever felt as a distraction to thought, an obstacle to some truth: "One thought, How sad, about all this human nonsense which keeps us from the large truth." Though the book begins as if it will be a wonderfully animated meditation upon the sociological question of the intellectual's place in America, the questions that really fascinate Charlie Citrine are more transcendental and mystical —questions of death, of immortality, of "light-in-the-being": "I mean a kind of light-in-the-being, a thing difficult to be precise about, especially in an account like this, where so many cantankerous erroneous silly and delusive objects actions and phenomena are in the foreground." Small wonder, then, that the events of the novel pull away from the issues, and effusion replaces conversation, with everybody, including the supposedly unintellectual Renata, sounding like Charlie. The many brilliant episodes become too many—a static of human busyness that prevents Charlie from tuning in and that leads the reader to tune out. Rinaldo Cantabile, for instance, is at first a compelling apparition, a figure of frantic menace and insecurity, a "nervous invention" that simultaneously illustrates Charlie Citrine's "weakness for the sensational" and demonstrates Saul Bellow's marvellous susceptibility to the eccentric particulars of American life in motion. When, toward the end of the book, amid a welter of exploded schemes and fresh entanglements, Cantabile reappears, he seems a mere annoyance, a bothersome shrill squawking over the telephone, a demented *deus* lowered from a needless *machina,* a thoroughly excessive device introduced to get the hero to go to a movie that is sweeping the world and would have come to his attention anyway; Cantabile is dismissed, by a suddenly unfascinated Citrine, like a messenger in Shakespeare. Cantabile has become a bore because the possibility of development is permitted no character but the omnipresent, amorphous, relentlessly self-regarding narrator.

Piecemeal faults might be found with *Humboldt's Gift.* When, a little more than halfway through, the novel leaves Chicago, it abandons a regional portrait of considerable accumulating richness. The Madrid section is relatively tenuous; the "shenanigans" are especially abstract and hurried. The novel has more characters than it can use; some, like Cantabile's girlfriend Polly and the crooked financier Stronson, exist as if only to occasion their descriptions, and none, save Humboldt and his wife, Kathleen, occupy more than one corner of the territory that the story's time span stakes out. Bellow's style, breezy and tough and not always grammatical, feels fallen away from a former angelic height. Contrast the opening sentences,

> The book of ballads published by Von Humboldt Fleisher in the Thirties was an immediate hit. Humboldt was just what everyone had been waiting for. Out in the Midwest I had certainly been waiting eagerly, I can tell you that. An avant-garde writer, the first of a new generation, he was handsome, fair, large, serious, witty, he was learned. The guy had it all. . . .

with the also idiomatic but far more electric and cadenced opening of *The Adventures of Augie March:*

> I am an American, Chicago born—Chicago, that somber city—and go at things as I have taught myself, free-style, and will make the record in my own way: first to knock, first admitted; sometimes an innocent knock, sometimes a not so innocent. But a man's character is his fate, says Heraclitus, and in the end there isn't any way to disguise the nature of the knocks by acoustical work on the door or gloving the knuckles.

And the stylistic recourse, new since *Mr. Sammler's Planet,* to commaless series, running to such lengths as "black bread raw onion bourbon whisky herring sausage cards billiards race horses and women," seems a rather too determined exercise in relaxation.

But Bellow's great gifts deserve great indulgence, and the only real trouble with *Humboldt's Gift* is that the problems that engage the author do not engage the gears of his story. Death, power, America—Charlie Citrine has much to say about these cherished topics, but his remarks are incongruously juxtaposed and interwoven with the "capers," the "daily monkeyshines," that compose his mystic's impression of natural human events. Tellingly, Charlie confesses, "I could read a little in the great mysterious book of urban America. I was too fastidious and skittish to study it closely —I had used the conditions of life to test my powers of immunity; the sovereign consciousness trained itself to avoid the phenomena and to be immune to their effects." Perception, for the supremely perceptive Citrine, has become a tic, a trick to exploit. Himself immune, he scoops up impressions, pours out descriptions. From high in the Plaza, he invites Renata to admire the view of Fifth Avenue at Christmastime:

> I was very good myself at putting other people on to views for the purpose of absenting myself. . . . I was like a deft girl, scooping all the jacks before the ball bounced back. It was as it had been with Renata last spring when we took the train to Chartres, "Isn't that beautiful out there!" she had said. I looked and yes, indeed it was beautiful. No more than a glance was necessary.

That glance was earlier described:

> I looked out, and she was right. Beautiful was indeed there. But I had seen Beautiful many times, and so I closed my eyes. I rejected the plastered idols of the Appearances. . . . I even thought, The painted veil isn't what it used to be. The damn thing is wearing out. Like a roller-towel in a Mexican men's room.

The vividness of the metaphor rather retracts the disclaimer, but the weary tone sounds honest. The veil of maya isn't what it used to be for Bellow, though he is not yet mystic enough—unlike I. B. Singer—to look at daily monkeyshines for glimmers of supernatural light. Nor, unlike the former celebrant of Chicago, Theodore Dreiser, can he accept the natural world as the only world, portentous by its own final weight. So he gives us a world as craziness, as "goofy . . . a solid mass of improbabilities," a world kept spinning by whimsical impulses and savage egos, an earth that is "literally a mirror of thoughts" to the central, immune viewer, who devotes his attention more and more to the world beyond death, to the anthroposophy of Rudolf Steiner, to the consoling curious possibilities that "our bones are crystallized out of the cosmos itself" and the universe is "the living garment of God" and "we occupy a point within a great hierarchy that goes far far beyond ourselves." These supernatural preoccupations of Bellow's are not in themselves unworthy—it takes a courageous humanism to perceive that life is infinitely cramped by the loss of an expectation of an afterlife —but they do make the veil of his fictional phenomena thin. We know, reading, that there will be many surprises but no revelations, that no turn of event will dreadfully deepen the theme, that the essentially cerebral and comic spirit of the creator will contrive to preserve his hero from essential harm. And so it is: Charlie Citrine loses Renata but takes comfort in one of those dazed, ignominious retreats so dear to Bellow heroes; he loses his money but more falls to him; he leaves his city and his children but in the spirit of a holiday; the sleep of his soul, as he thinks of it, is disturbed but not shattered. He rolls over, amid the rumpled sheets and untied threads of the plot.

And yet. Of course there are passages that no one but Bellow could have perpetrated—scenes that are, in the flow of their wit and felt detail, simply delicious. The giddying ascent with Cantabile up through the unfinished skyscraper ("the hollow interior filled with thousands of electric points resembling champagne bubbles") to a windy height from which the indignant hood sails airplanes folded from fifty-dollar bills; the visit to Humboldt's book-stuffed house in a rural slum of New Jersey (a "scant" terrain "good for nothing but chicken farms" and looking "like the still frame of an old movie on sepia film"); the opulent carnal landscape of Renata, her throat "ever so slightly ringed or rippled by some enriching feminine deposit"; the scenes of Chicago justice as manipulated by woolly, cannibalistic lawyers and urbane Slavic judges (hilarious scenes, as devastating to the legal profession as anything in *Bleak House*); the barbed caricatures of Manhattan intelligentsia; the unfailingly tender sketches of old Chicago neighborhoods—with such evocations, enlivened by love and alarm, Bellow fragmentarily makes good the book's implicit promise to illumine the "overwhelming phenomenon" of America, in its "abominable American innocence." The very thinness of the veil, for Bellow, enables him to exaggerate and poeticize. Mind permeates Bellow's renderings; permeability is the essence of his fluid, nervous, colorful mimetic art. The most transitory moment gets its infusion of magic. For instance: Briefly, Citrine remembers visiting Humboldt's widow on a ranch in Nevada. She has remarried; her new husband, a cowboy called Tigler, is particularized by "the bold bronze face with ginger tufted brows, the bent horse-disfigured legs." When, fishing on a lake with Charlie, Tigler falls into the water and has to be rescued, the bronze returns as more than a color—as his fatal substance—and metaphor elevates the incident into fable:

> . . . I could see the late Tigler's Western figure as if it were cast in bronze, turning over and over in the electrical icy water, and then I saw myself, who had learned swimming in a small chlorinated tank in Chicago, pursuing him like an otter.

The touch of fantasy is Bellow's obedient imp; he is as fertile in arresting incongruities as "this strange place, the earth" itself. Humboldt is prevented from committing street violence not by any faceless passersby but by a "group of lesbians gotten up as longshoremen"; Humboldt passingly mentions a hospital suicide who "took a fork and hammered it into his heart with the heel of his shoe"; and a pack of Humboldt's cats is made hyper-real by Charlie's recalling one "with a Hitler mustache." Bellow is not only the best portraitist writing American fiction, he is one of our better nature poets. What could be more palpable, more tastable and visible, than this glimpse of Princeton?—

> I stood under a brownstone arch, on foot-hollowed stone, while panhandling squirrels came at me from all directions across the smooth quadrangles, the lovely walks. It was chilly and misty, the blond dim November sun binding the twigs in circles of light.

Charlie ventures a number of epitaphs for Von Humboldt Fleisher, but the best one comes early: "Humboldt wanted to drape the world in radiance, but he didn't have enough material." The judgment seems self-reflective; the wonder about Bellow is how much radiant material he can provide, to drape a world he scarcely wants to touch.

This seventh (not counting *Seize the Day*) novel shares many qualities with Bellow's first, *Dangling Man*, written more than thirty years ago. The same Chicago, the same ruminativeness, the same moral passion oddly mixed with passivity and spurts of farce and quarrel. The early novel even runs the same calendar course, from December to April, an entombed time of the year whose vernal resurrection means much to Bellow, though "a city boy." From the outset, his fiction gravitated toward heroes suspended in, as *Dangling Man*'s Joseph puts it, "sheer dishevelment of mind." And out of Joseph's dishevelment emerge a number of principles that Charlie Citrine, in his slacker, racier tone, might still propound:

> I would rather be a victim than a beneficiary.

> Trouble, like physical pain, makes us actively aware that we are living, and when there is little in the life we lead to hold and draw and stir us, we seek and cherish it, preferring embarrassment or pain to indifference.

> . . . we are too ignorant and spiritually poor to know that we fall on the "enemy" from confused motives of love and loneliness.

> . . . there was an element of treason to common sense in the very objects of common sense.

Joseph is young, his novel is a scattered journal, he resolves "to begin schooling [himself] in shrewdness." Charlie Citrine has certainly acquired a worldly shrewdness, as well as (like Saul Bellow) the riband of an honorary Chevalier. But after making one's way through the worldly mass of *Humboldt's Gift*, so rich in information and speculation, one wonders if, for Bellow's kind of dangling, rather than doing, man, the shorter length and implicative texture of the youthful book weren't better. We marvel from a safe distance at Charlie's predatory relationships with his bitchy ex-wife and his mistress, whereas we entered into Joseph's gentle, mundane, unspokenly doomed marriage to Iva. *Dangling Man*, though in snippets, merged earth and air, whereas *Humboldt's Gift*, washed up on our drear cultural shore like some large, magnificently glistening but beached creature from another element, dramatizes, in its agitated sluggishness, the body/mind split that is its deepest theme.

Toppling Towers Seen by a Whirling Soul

THE DEAN'S DECEMBER, by Saul Bellow. 312 pp. Harper & Row, 1982.

The good thing about *The Dean's December*: it is by Saul Bellow, and therefore possesses wit, vividness, tenderness, brave thought, earthy mysticism, and a most generous, searching, humorous humanity. The bad thing about it, or at least not so good: it is *about* Saul Bellow, in an uncomfortable, indirect, but unignorable way. The dean of the title, Albert Corde, a "Huguenot-Irish-Midwesterner and whatnot else," a man in his middle fifties, "not quite elderly but getting there," doesn't feel like a dean: he is too eccentric, too catered to, too absorbed in his writing and in his ingenious but pointedly non-professional theorizing. In Bucharest, the American Ambassador sends a limousine for him; in Chicago, his celebrity status goes sour when articles he published in *Harper's* malign the local power structure. He is a man of charisma, of wide and wealthy acquaintance, of many sexual conquests, though happily married now, to an eminent Rumanian-born astronomer. A certain tweed-free glamour attaches to him: "His nonchalant way of looking at you, the extruded brown eyes, that drowned-in-dreams look, was probably the source of his reputation as a swinger, a chaser." His persona, with "swelled eyes, yoked goggles, whitening brow hairs, pale dish face and long, uncomplaisant (only complaisant-looking) mouth," is redescribed every few pages, as if the author were checking to make sure the mask was still in place. The author, indeed, has a rather anxious relation to his character, not only buzzing like a gnat in front of his pale, "dish" face at the cost of a steady point of view (for we have no other vantage in this book than Corde's mind; why and how do we keep seeing him from the outside?) but slipping him little reassuring compliments now and then: "Corde's speed in making connections never failed to please [his wife]." "What a man he was for noticing! Continually attentive to his surroundings. As if he had been sent down to *mind* the outer world, on a mission of observation and notation." This Huguenot-Irish academic, whose university is never named or rendered very palpable, is a "stand-in":

He was not exactly deanlike in appearance. He wore a three-piece suit; the vest wasn't buttoned right somehow (no up-to-date official courting favor with undergraduates would dress in this style). He was something of a stand-in, a journalist passing for a dean.

So? Why shouldn't Bellow and Corde enjoyably share Chicago, rakish pasts, excitable social consciences, scientific Rumanian wives? (Bellow's present wife is an eminent mathematician.) Should a novelist be penalized because his excellence has generated prizes and fame and made the broad facts of his life public knowledge? Bellow in truth minds his own business more than most, and deliberately left New York, we know from interviews, to achieve a more private life and a more authentic American witness. The personae of Moses Herzog and Charlie Citrine, however patently they, too, at moments appeared to be stand-ins, did not give us the uncomfortable sensations Albert Corde does. They seemed self-projections as reckless and free and viable as the hulking Connecticut Wasp Eugene Henderson and the elderly Manhattan savant Artur Sammler. We felt good about them; they were, as the phrase goes, up front. "I celebrate myself," Whitman said. "And what I assume you shall assume,/For every atom belonging to me as good belongs to you." Literature can do with any amount of egoism; but the merest pinch of narcissism spoils the broth. And there is more than a pinch in the emphasis here upon the articles about Chicago that Dean Corde has supposedly published, articles we overhear conversation and ruminations about for the first half of the book, intermittently, teasingly, and then in the second half are permitted to read sections of, articles we cannot but suppose to be fragments of the "nonfiction book about Chicago" that Bellow recently told Michiko Kakutani in the *Times Book Review* he had planned to write, accumulating "hundreds of pages of notes," before "he decided to abandon that approach and write a novel," a novel that we now hold in our hands. This book has swallowed the earlier one but has transparent sides, so that we can see the non-fiction book inside the novel and can observe how incomplete the digestion process has been. Into scenes of life in Bucharest, as Corde and his wife, Minna, wait for her mother, Valeria, to die, and into the potentially absorbing trial in Chicago of two blacks for the murder of a graduate student at Corde's university, the articles—quoted, alluded to, clucked over—intrude their alien, papery reality. We are asked to accept as part of Dean Corde's equipment "super-expressive" powers; we are invited to imagine "the spin he gave words"; we are expected to care whether or not he embarks upon another piece of exposition, this time propounding the theory of a scientist called Beech that excess lead in the environment is the root of all our social and psychological woes; we are made to read pages of commentary upon the articles and Corde's fascinating personality by one Dewey Spangler, an old high-school pal of Corde's and fellow-aspirant to literary glory, who delivers his remarks first in two boozy conversations in Bucharest and then in an impossibly long and wordy (for its supposed newspaper use) syndicated column. It is too much; it is not fact or fiction. Let a journalist pass for a dean; but can journalism pass for a novel?

Corde is too closely tied to his creator to be free, to fall, to be judged in the round, to have anything much happen to him. No stark Greek fate is going to flatten this coddled agonist, we can be sure. What does he do, other than brood? He helps press a legal prosecution in Chicago. He buys cartons of Kents at the international *valuta* shop to grease the wheels of his mother-in-law's Rumanian funeral. He tends cyclamens and drinks plum brandy and sleeps to pass his idle days in Bucharest. He opens his mail when the plot needs a nudge. He loves his wife. We miss, I suppose, the great scenes of male-female pursuit and combat that the old Bellow produced; but all conflict in *The Dean's December* is frittered away, consigned to retrospect, allowed to pass, resolved offstage. An amazing number of characters exist altogether offstage: Corde's cousin and archenemy Max Detillion; the black criminals Lucas Ebry, Riggie Hines, and Spofford Mitchell; the touching young widow Lydia Lester; the distinguished but perhaps slightly crazy geophysicist Beech. They figure large in Corde's meditations, but we never directly meet them in a scene. A number of others—Corde's sister, Elfrida, and his nephew, the odious young radical Mason Zaehner, Jr.; his provost at the university, Alec Witt; some members of his club and the interview subjects for his famous articles—are seen briefly and are particularized with Bellow's incomparable flair but remain vivid bundles of characteristics stuck fast in the central tar-baby of Corde's ruminations. They are all, even Minna, not so much encountered by Corde as interviewed by him.

As journalism, as writing, as *seeing*, much of *The Dean's December* is lovely. The Bucharest vistas, relatively untainted by the literary politics of the fictional factual Chicago articles, come through clear and drab, from the "strong dreary cars they drive in the satellite countries" to "the shops and the produce, the gloomy queues—brown, gray, black, mud colors, and an atmosphere of compulsory exercise in the prison yard." Never enchanted with Communism, Corde/Bellow observes without disenchantment the petty tyrannies and dishonesties of the "crypto-emotional life" led "in the shadow of the Party and the State"—a shadow that only vegetation does not feel:

> Three o'clock and dusk already, tragic boredom coming with it. The forms of winter trees, the beauty of winter colors, were excepted from this. The trees made their tree gestures, but human beings were faced by the organized prevention of everything that came natural.

The cremation of Valeria, a doctor once prominent in the Party and then fallen from favor, is splendid reporting. The funeral observance takes place in a cold dome of which the floor is warmed by the crematory fires underneath; the rites are attended by a large crowd of elderly friends who "came out with a sort of underfed dignity in what was left of their pre-socialist wardrobe, to affirm that there was a sort of life—and perhaps, as Communists or even Iron Guardists (it was conceivable), they had sinned against it—the old European life which at its most disgraced was infinitely better than this present one." Corde is required to descend to the floor below to provide official identification of the corpse. The observer becomes an actor, reporting becomes experience:

> Corde felt cut in half by the extremes of heat and cold. [His] breast, as narrow as a ladder, was crowded with emotions—fire, death, suffocation, put into an icy hole or, instead, crackling in a furnace. Your last option. They still appeared equally terrible. How to choose between them!

Later, safely away, he imagines the actual cremation:

> At this very instant Valeria might be going into the fire, the roaring
> furnace which took off her hair, the silk scarf, grabbed away the green
> suit, melted the chased silver buttons, consumed the skin, flashed away
> the fat, blew up the organs, reached the bones, bore down on the skull
> —that refining fire, a ball of raging gold, a tiny sun, a star.

This is the kind of serial evocation, breathless and hasty-seeming
but in every phrase ("grabbed away," "raging gold") vitally sharp
and right, with which *The Adventures of Augie March* abounds.
Compared to that inspired style of nearly thirty years ago, Bellow's
now is more studied, a little knotted and choppy, verging on the
abrupt:

> You poured from one of the buckets into the bowl. Corde himself now
> took charge and filled them when the water was running. The buckets
> were far too heavy for Gigi with her cardiac condition. The bathtub
> might have been a reservoir if the stopper had worked. All this was like
> the old times in the States, before the age of full convenience. It took
> you back.

Exclamations—"Give it to them!," "Have a look!," "Please, do!,"
"Christ, not me!"—pull the prose up short, and it all feels a bit
heavily worked, with a patient circling, so that details are repeated,
drilled in.

Bellow's imitation of spontaneity—his world gathering before
our eyes with the miraculous silent swiftness of stop-action films
of flowers blooming—is one of his special effects, and no doubt
harder-won than it looks. Some of his images in this book have a
beauty quite surreal, so unexpected is their tossed-off precision:

> Here in Eastern Europe, the morning's rain had turned to snow.
> The flakes were large—their shapes made Corde think of contact
> lenses—but as soon as they touched the pavements it was all over
> for them.

> Gigi also wore an imitation fur. To Corde these coats were odd—the
> lusterless needles mingled brown and purple, they felt soft enough, they
> had a heavy look but no actual weight; it was up to the wearer to put
> life into them.

When Ioanna, crouching by the coffin, lifted her eyes to Corde, the blue eyes burnt as if her tears were alcohol.

And what Bellow does with human bodies! Visually seizing upon humps of fat and hollows of bone and ridges of gristle no one has ever put into words before, he makes of each body a kind of physical myth, a flesh-and-blood ideogram. Mason Zaehner, Corde's agitator nephew, is tall, "skinny, lanky, ambling, with pointed elbows"; when he sits down, he is "about as graceful as a driller's rig—a long frame, a remote head." That is what is wrong with him: "His quiddity was overstretched." A few pages on, the image of attenuation undergoes some further diagnostic twists as Corde ponders his disagreeable nephew, who now looks "two-dimensional, like a drawing of a driller's rig. You had to study Mason to find the humanity in him. It was as hard to see as the thin line of mercury in some thermometers." Elfrida, Mason's mother and Corde's beloved sister, is "curiously put together—very slender at the top, with a smooth dark head, and wide in the hips"; as Corde studies her, she—who, by the default of severe, pale, abstracted, starlit, grieving Minna, takes to herself the novel's modest quota of female warmth—becomes a river goddess: "Yes, she was heavy in the thighs, big in the hips. There was a perennially strange ultra-familiar contrast between the elongated upper body, the upstream, and the broad estuary of the lower half, the lower flow of womanli-ness." Lest we think this an idle metaphor, Corde in far-off Bucha-rest, a hundred seventy-five pages later, remembers "the narrow dark head, the estuary hips." Elfrida's marrying a man of whom her brother disapproves—Judge Sorokin, "a Chicago type"—is, amid the displacements of this overpopulated, underplotted novel, the book's erotic climax, and Corde's muttered blessing ("She pressed her long cheek to his circular one. 'You did right, Elfrida,' he said") its one effectively understated moment, when we are shown more than we are told. For we are told much and shown little in the course of the narrative, and if Bellow's eye is still magical his ear seems dulled, allowing the voice of exposition to overwhelm the voices of character.

Since Corde's researches into Chicago form the novel's scattered centerpiece, something should be said about them. He sees Chicago as a tough place, and virtually all its citizens save himself as tough. His deceased brother-in-law, "Mason senior, a high-powered Loop lawyer with connections in the Daley machine, had been tough, arrogant, a bulldozing type. Brutal people, those Chicago insiders, a special breed." In the halls of academe, too, brute strength prevails: "One of the shrewdest operators that ever lived, the Provost was also very strong—the perfect, up-to-date American strongman. You felt his muscle the instant you engaged him." The good guys, the friends of the poor, also are full of muscle: Rufus Ridpath, a courageous prison reformer, "was a man of hillocky build, short in the neck, with a powerful intelligent Negro head. His brief arms were widely separated by his cylinder chest. . . ." Toby Winthrop, who runs an admirable detoxification center, is a "powerful man": "His trunk was enormous, his thighs were huge, his fingers thick." Of Sam Varennes, a public defender, Corde writes, "Mr. Varennes is a muscular man. Even his throat has muscles, a pillar throat. I think he pumps iron." The black underclass of Chicago, contemplating the misery, criminality, disconnectedness, and prospective doom of which has turned Corde into "a whirling soul," is, of course, tough, too; Riggie Hines, "as tough as they come, and all whore," had "the build of a boxer and a boxer's compact tough head. Even the way she tucked back the mannish shirt to show the tops of her breasts was pugilistic." Corde's passionate concern with the plight of black Chicago—its vast population, as he sees it, being "written off," and entire cities like Chicago and Detroit being written off, and as many as fifteen million people having "already accepted to be stoned out of their minds," and civilization itself collapsing along with the cities, "nobody teaching the young language, human usages or religion"—finds little response among the wised-up pugilistic types around him, and a mixed response in the heart of this reader. Insofar as black slum-dwellers are made vivid, and their context of urban squalor dramatic, well and good. If the several murders touched upon here were brought closer to us, as Zola and Dreiser dramatized newspaper murders, even better; but this does not quite happen. Corde descends into his interviews about contemporary urban reality from on high, and is distrusted therefore. His language is high-flown, extreme: "I was losing Mr. Varennes. Anguish beyond the bounds of human tolerance was not a subject a nice man like Mr. Varennes was ready for on an ordinary day." Corde cannot think of urban deterioration without bringing in metaphysics and epistemology, Marx and Aristotle, Idi Amin and Jonestown, "the breaking of nations" and "how the soul is worked on." Not that the situation does not deserve an apocalyptic exposition; as Corde says, "if there are mysterious forces around, only exaggeration can help us to see them." But one wonders if to, say, Henry James the ethnic neighborhoods of Chicago so engagingly particularized by Bellow in *Augie March* might not have seemed as much a hopeless wasteland as black Chicago appears to Albert Corde. A certain fastidiousness is speaking; a strange persistent theme of excrement lies in *The Dean's December* at the pole opposite Minna's stars and Corde's cyclamens. A cab taken to O'Hare Airport smells so that Corde jokes, "People have even stopped wiping themselves," and one of his articles makes much of a Chicago sewer project, a "Cloaca Maxima" possibly weakening the foundations of the skyscrapers. The impudent Dewey Spangler rhapsodizes in parody, "All those tons of excrement, stunning to the imagination. It won't be the face of Helen that topples those great towers, it'll be you-know-what." Corde, of course, lives in those towers, ivory or not. His happiest Chicago scene shows a party given by his new brother-in-law's rich brother, on the fortieth floor of a Lake Shore Drive high rise. The festivity, a birthday party for a pet dog, peaks when the guests release from the balconies balloons "the shade of green poured into the Chicago River on Saint Patrick's Day," which are "snatched straight up"; and the novel itself ends with Corde's almost literal ascent, at Mount Palomar Observatory, to the stars, into the clean heavenly cold.

Bellow believes in the soul; this is one of his links with the ancients, with the great books. At the same time, like those great books, he feels and conveys the authentic heaviness in which our spirits are entangled; he has displayed for thirty years an unsurpassedly active awareness of the corporeal, of the mortal, of human creatureliness in all its sexual and assertive variety. He is not just a very good writer, he is one of the rare writers who when we read them feel to be taking mimesis a layer or two deeper than it has gone before. His lavish, rippling notations of persons, furniture, habiliments, and vistas awaken us to what is truly there. Such a gift for the actual is not unnaturally bound in with a yen toward the theoretical; for how do we see but by setting ourselves to see? From *Augie March* on, a sense of intellectual quest moves Bellow's heroes and is expected to move his readers. The quest in *The Dean's December* is narrow enough to meet concentrated resistance. It was indeed courageous of Bellow, as he told his *Times* interviewer, to devise a fiction about "the problems of demoralized cities." I, for one, take his ideas about civilization seriously enough to wish he had gone ahead and completed his non-fiction book on Chicago, and made a separate novel, or novella, of his glimpses of Bucharest. The switching back and forth between the two cities, both demoralized but in such different ways, is as wearying as the effort of holding in the mind's eye an image of Albert Corde different from the image on the back of the jacket. Bellow has it in him, great poet and fearless mental venturer that he is, to write one of those unclassifiable American masterpieces like *Walden*. But such a book must ramify from a firm, simple center, and this *The Dean's December* does not possess.

All's Well in Skyscraper National Park

SLAPSTICK, OR LONESOME NO MORE! by Kurt Vonnegut. 243 pp. Delacorte Press, 1976.

Kurt Vonnegut abjures the appellation "Junior" in signing his new novel, and, indeed, after his furious performance in the preceding work, *Breakfast of Champions*, does seem relatively at peace with himself, his times, and the fact of his writing a novel at all. He introduces this one with the customary noises of exasperation over his "disagreeable profession" ("He asked me politely how my work was going. . . . I said that I was sick of it, but that I had always been sick of it"), but, once launched, the tale floats along without interruption, and is something of an idyll. A hundred-year-old man, Dr. Wilbur Daffodil-11 Swain, who has been President of the United States ("the final President, the tallest President, and the only one ever to have been divorced while occupying the White House"), lives with his granddaughter, Melody Oriole-2 von Peterswald, and her lover, Isadore Raspberry-19 Cohen, in the otherwise empty Empire State Building, on the almost deserted island of Manhattan, which has been decimated by plague and is variously known as "The Island of Death" and "Skyscraper National Park." The awkward middle names of the inhabitants, we might as well explain now, have been assigned them in the last and only reform of the Swain Presidency, a measure to combat "American loneliness" (the root of all our evil: "all the damaging excesses of Americans in the past were motivated by loneliness rather than a fondness for sin") through the division of the population into huge (ten thousand siblings, one hundred ninety thousand cousins) artificial families by means of computer-bestowed middle names, "the name of a flower or fruit or nut or vegetable or legume, or a bird or a reptile or a fish, or a mollusk, or a gem or a mineral or a chemical element." This scheme, the basis of President Swain's successful campaign (slogan: "Lonesome No More!") for the highest office in the land, was concocted years before, when Wilbur and his twin sister, Eliza, like himself a monstrous "neanderthaloid" two meters high, enjoyed in a secluded Vermont mansion an emotional and intellectual symbiosis that amounted to sheer genius, though separately the two were dullards named Bobby and Betty Brown.

Lost already? *Slapstick*, whose sole present action consists of the narrator's hundred-and-first birthday party, which kills him, is a reminiscence about the future, a future braided of a half-dozen or so scientific and sociological fancies. The lonesome-no-more-thanks-to-new-middle-names notion is about the silliest of them, the least charming and provocative, however dear to the author's heart. The others, roughly in descending order of charm and provocativeness, are:

1. That gravity on Earth has become variable, like the weather. "Well—the gravity . . . is light again today," Wilbur writes in his memoir. On days of light gravity, all males have erections, and lovers build a pyramid of large rubble at the intersection of Broadway and Forty-second Street. When the gravity is heavy, men crawl about on all fours, and the insides of horses fall out. Heavy gravity first struck when Wilbur Swain was fifty, and had just learned that his sister had died in an avalanche on Mars:

> An extraordinary feeling came over me, which I first thought to be psychological in origin, the first rush of grief. I seemed to have taken root on the porch. I could not pick up my feet. My features, moreover, were being dragged downward like melting wax.
>
> The truth was that the force of gravity had increased tremendously.
>
> There was a great crash in the church. The steeple had dropped its bell.
>
> Then I went right through the porch, and was slammed to the earth beneath it.
>
> . . .
>
> In other parts of the world, of course, elevator cables were snapping, airplanes were crashing, ships were sinking, motor vehicles were breaking their axles, bridges were collapsing, and on and on.
>
> It was terrible.

In this superbly simple fancy (and why not? what do we know about gravity, except that it is always there, and has not yet broken its own "law"?) Vonnegut gives enormous body to his own moodiness, and springs a giddy menace upon the city he inhabits.

2. That the Chinese, on the other side of the world from the lonely, destructive Americans, have succeeded in miniaturizing themselves, to the size first of dwarfs, then of dolls and elves, and finally of germs; the plague, called the Green Death, it turns out "was caused by microscopic Chinese, who were peace-loving and meant no one any harm. They were nonetheless invariably fatal to normal-sized human beings when inhaled or ingested." This last *reductio* is a bit much, but a radical divergence of the Chinese from our own brand of *Homo sapiens* sounds right; we laugh in recognition when the Chinese Ambassador, sixty centimeters tall, severs diplomatic relations "simply because there was no longer anything

going on in the United States which was of any interest to the Chinese at all." China is another planet, Vonnegut has discovered.

3. That a brother and a sister might "give birth to a single genius, which died as quickly as we were parted, which was reborn the moment we got together again." In childhood, Wilbur, who does the reading and writing, and Eliza, who makes the intuitive leaps and juxtapositions, concoct theories and manuscripts that a half-century later are of interest even to the Chinese. In adulthood, after a long separation, the siblings reunite in a kind of psycho-sexual explosion that produces, besides a houseful of wreckage, a manual on child-rearing which becomes the third most popular book of all time.

Vonnegut in his prologue claims this novel to be "the closest I will ever come to writing an autobiography" and movingly writes of the Indianapolis Vonneguts and of his sister Alice—her importance to him as "an audience of one," her death at the age of forty-one of cancer, her final days in the hospital, her hunched posture, her description of her own death as "slapstick." In *Slapstick* these memories become:

> She was so bent over that her face was on level with Mushari's—and Mushari was about the size of Napoleon Bonaparte. She was chain smoking. She was coughing her head off. . . .
>
> "Oh, Wilbur, Wilbur, Wilbur—" said my mother as we watched, "is that really your sister?"
>
> I made a bitter joke—without smiling. "Either your only daughter, Mother, or the sort of anteater known as an *aardvark*," I said.

The image shocks us, offends us, twists us inside, and successfully asks to be recognized as somber and tender. It is a moment peculiarly Vonnegutian, tapping the undercurrents of pure melancholy which nurture the aggressively casual surface growths of his style. These moments arise unexpectedly, and seem to take the author unawares as well—the pathetic valedictory conversation, for instance, between Salo and Rumfoord near the end of *The Sirens of Titan* (1959), or the odd interlude, amid the "impolite" "junk" of *Breakfast of Champions* (1973), wherein the homeless, jobless black ex-convict Wayne Hoobler, hanging out in a used-car lot, in his extreme of lonesomeness begins to talk to the high-way traffic:

> He established a sort of relationship with the traffic on the Interstate, too, appreciating its changing moods. "Everybody goin' home," he said during the rush hour jam. "Everybody home now," he said later on, when the traffic thinned out. Now the sun was going down.
> "Sun goin' down," said Wayne Hoobler.

It will vary, where Vonnegut's abashed and constant sorrow breaks through to touch the reader; here, though, in this fantasy, as it pays tribute not to the extended family he hopes for but to the nuclear family he has known, he places his rather mistrustful art in frank proximity to the incubator of his passion for—to quote his prologue —"common decency."

4. That the United States, as the world's energy resources have dried up, has pleasantly settled back into a rural society, powered by slaves and horses as before; that the old Inca capital of Machu Picchu, in Peru, has become "a haven for rich people and their parasites, people fleeing social reforms and economic declines"; and that when the White House, containing President Wilbur Swain, who is stoned on tribenzo-Deportamil, quite ceases to rule, the nation falls into a feudal anarchy dominated by such guerrilla chieftains as the King of Michigan and the Duke of Oklahoma.

5. That a religion has arisen called the Church of Jesus Christ the Kidnapped, which holds that Jesus has come again but has been kidnapped by the Forces of Evil and is being held captive somewhere. The members of this cult, the most popular ever in America, distinguish themselves by an incessant jerking of the head, as if to discover the Kidnapped Jesus peering out "from behind a potted palm tree or an easy chair."

6. That a scientist named Dr. Felix Bauxite-13 von Peterswald has discovered a way to talk to the dead, who irritably and disconsolately inhabit a dreary hereafter known as the Turkey Farm. The late Eliza reports to her living brother, "We are being bored stiff."

This saucy spaghetti of ideas, strange to report, seems in the consumption as clear as consommé, and goes down like ice cream. *Slapstick* has more science fiction in it than any other novel by

Vonnegut since *The Sirens of Titan* and lays to rest, in an atmosphere of comic exhaustion and serene self-parody, the obsessive Prospero figure who first came to life there. The Prospero in *Sirens* is Winston Niles Rumfoord, a Rhode Island aristocrat who acquires superhuman powers by steering his spaceship straight into a "chrono-synclastic infundibulum" and who thenceforth arranges an interplanetary war so that its guilt-engendered slaughters may form the basis for a new religion, the worship of God the Utterly Indifferent. With a demonic elaborateness that argues a certain demon of overplotting in the author, Rumfoord furthermore manipulates Malachi Constant (one of Vonnegut's long line of boob heroes) and his little family through a ramshackle series of space flights and changes of identity toward an ultimate goal that turns out to be the delivery, in Constant's son's pocket, of a replacement part for a spaceship from the planet Tralfamadore. The unseen Tralfamadorians are manipulating not just Rumfoord but much of the planet Earth; Stonehenge, the Great Wall of China, and other terrestrial wonders of human enterprise are in truth messages ("Replacement part being rushed with all possible speed"; "Be patient. We haven't forgotten about you") in the Tralfamadorian language to the messenger Salo, who in the course of delivering from "One Rim of the Universe to the Other" a message consisting of a single dot ("Greetings" in Tralfamadorian) has become stranded on Saturn's biggest moon, Titan, for hundreds of thousands of years. Well, it's some book, full of laughs yet operatically flaunting Vonnegut's concern with the fundamental issues of pain, purpose, and Providence. Though raised in a family of atheists, Vonnegut quarrels with God like a parochial-school dropout. In *Mother Night* (1961), Prospero has shrunk to the dimensions of a Second World War master-spy: Colonel Frank Wirtanen, the Blue Fairy Godmother, controls the hero's life by appearing to him only three times, and his final act of magical intervention is rejected.

In *Cat's Cradle* (1963), the idea of a religion devoted to an indifferent God is codified as Bokononism, and Prospero retreats to still lower visibility; Bokonon, the black founder of the cult, emerges from the underbrush of the Caribbean island of San Lorenzo only at the novel's end, to direct the hero (called John, and rather less of a boob) to commit suicide, while thumbing his nose skyward, at You Know Who. But Bokonon, who like Rumfoord has the gifts of foresight and cynicism, oversees the events on this island of survivors—a most *Tempest*-like setting. There is even a Miranda, called Mona.

In *God Bless You, Mr. Rosewater* (1965), Prospero and the boob have merged; the very prosperous Eliot Rosewater, after exercising the powers of the rich rather inchoately in the isolation of Rosewater County, Indiana, stands to full stature when threatened by a usurper, whom he smites down with a surprising disposition, both regal and cunning, of his fortune. In *Slaughterhouse-Five* (1969), Billy Pilgrim, like Winston Rumfoord, communicates with the Tralfamadorians and sees future and past as parts of a single panorama—"All moments, past, present, and future, always have existed, always will exist." But his prescience is impotent to change the sad course of Earthly events; planes crash, bombs fall, though he knows they will. His access to Tralfamadore merely gives him the wonderful accessory bubble of the second life he lives there, more Ferdinand than Prospero, mated with the gorgeous Montana Wildhack in a transparent dome in a Tralfamadorian zoo. *Breakfast of Champions* reveals the author himself as Prospero, "on a par with the Creator of the Universe," sitting in the cocktail lounge of a Holiday Inn wearing mirroring sunglasses, surrounded by characters of his own creation, whom he frees in the end: "I am going to set at liberty all the literary characters who have served me so loyally during my writing career." (Nevertheless, *Slapstick* revives the obnoxious lawyer Norman Mushari from *God Bless You, Mr. Rosewater;* Vonnegut's ongoing puppet show is irrepressibly self-cherishing.)

> Now my charms are all o'erthrown,
> And what strength I have's mine own,
> Which is most faint. . . .

Slapstick gives us the Prospero of Shakespeare's epilogue, his powers surrendered, his island Manhattan, his Miranda his granddaughter Melody. Vonnegut dreamed the book, he tells us, while flying to a funeral. "It is about desolated cities and spiritual canni-balism and incest and loneliness and lovelessness and death, and so on." It is about what happens after the end of the world. The end of the world is not an idea to Vonnegut, it is a reality he ex-perienced, in Dresden, as a prisoner of war, during the holocaustal air raid of February 13, 1945. He has described this repeatedly, most directly in the introduction to *Mother Night* added in 1966:

> We didn't get to see the fire storm. We were in a cool meat-locker under a slaughterhouse with our six guards and ranks and ranks of dressed cadavers of cattle, pigs, horses and sheep. We heard the bombs walking around up there. Now and then there would be a gentle shower of calcimine. If we had gone above to take a look, we would have been turned into artifacts characteristic of fire storms: seeming pieces of charred firewood two or three feet long—ridiculously small human beings, or jumbo fried grasshoppers, if you will.

Vonnegut's come-as-you-are prose always dons a terrible beauty when he pictures vast destruction.

> Eliot, rising from his seat in the bus, beheld the fire storm of In-dianapolis. He was awed by the majesty of the column of fire, which was at least eight miles in diameter and fifty miles high. The boundaries of the column seemed absolutely sharp and unwavering, as though made of glass. Within the boundaries, helixes of dull red embers turned in stately harmony about an inner core of white. The white seemed holy.

The end of the world can be by fire, as in the quotation above, from *God Bless You, Mr. Rosewater,* or by ice, as in *Cat's Cradle:*

> There was a sound like that of the gentle closing of a portal as big as the sky, the great door of heaven being closed softly. It was a grand AH-WHOOM.
> I opened my eyes—and all the sea was *ice-nine.*
> The moist green earth was a blue-white pearl.

The New York of *Slapstick* has been destroyed several times over. Gravity has pulled down its elevators and its bridges, plague has devoured its population. An ailanthus forest has grown up, and a rooster crowing in Turtle Bay can be heard on West Thirty-fourth Street. Amid collapse, the barbarous fabulous is reborn. Wilbur Swain's nearest neighbor, Vera Chipmunk-5 Zappa, arrives at his hundred-and-first birthday party encrusted with diamonds, in a sedan chair. "She had a collection of precious stones which would have been worth millions of dollars in olden times. People gave her all the jewels they found, just as they gave me all the candlesticks." Swain has become the King of Candlesticks, the possessor of a thousand. For a birthday present Vera Zappa gives him a thousand candles she and her slaves have made from a colonial mold. They set them about on the floor of the Empire State Building lobby and light them. Swain's last written words are "Standing among all those tiny, wavering lights, I felt as though I were God, up to my knees in the Milky Way." He dies, happy, but the narrative carries on, relating how Melody arrives in New York, fleeing the seraglio of the King of Michigan, helped along the way by her fellow-Orioles.

> One would give her a raincoat. . . .
> Another would give her a needle and thread, and a gold thimble, too.
> Another would row her across the Harlem River to the Island of Death, at the risk of his own life.

The novel ends *"Das Ende,"* reminding us of German fairy tales and of Vonnegut's pride in his German ancestry; in *Mother Night* he even dared to be a poet in the German language. In *Slapstick* he transmutes science fiction into something like medieval myth, and suggests the halo of process, of metamorphosis and recycling, that to an extent redeems the destructiveness in human history to which he is so sensitive. The end of the world is just a Dark Age. Through a succession of diminishingly potent Prosperos, the malevolent complexities of *The Sirens of Titan* have yielded to a more amiable conclusion.

Slapstick enjoys a first printing of a cool one hundred thousand copies, and Vonnegut's popularity, which has grown even as his literary manner becomes more truculent and whimsical, has attracted comment from many reviewers, who usually find it discreditable to author and audience alike. But there need be no scandal in Vonnegut's wide appeal, based, as I believe it is, on the generosity of his imagination and the honesty of his pain. Who of his writing contemporaries strikes us as an imaginer, as distinguished from a reporter or a self-dramatizer? There is in Vonnegut a fine disdain of the merely personal. His prologue to *Slapstick* says, "I find it natural to discuss life without ever mentioning love," and his fiction, stoic in an epicurean time, does have a pre-sexual, pre-social freshness; he worries about the sort of things—the future, injustice, science, destiny—that twelve-year-old boys worry about, and if most boys move on, it is not necessarily into more significant worries. Vonnegut began as a published writer with the so-called slick magazines—the credits for the stories in *Welcome to the Monkey House* feature *Colliers, The Saturday Evening Post,* and the *Ladies' Home Journal.* Rereading such exercises as "D.P.," "Deer in the Works," and "The Kid Nobody Could Handle" is a lesson in what slickness, Fifties vintage, was: it was a verbal mechanism that raised the spectre of pain and then too easily delivered us from it. Yet the pain in Vonnegut was always real. Through the transpositions of science fiction, he found a way, instead of turning pain aside, to vaporize it, to scatter it on the planes of the cosmic and the comic. His terse flat sentences, jumpy chapters, interleaved placards, collages of stray texts and messages, and nervous grim refrains like "So it goes" and (in *Slapstick*) "Hi ho" are a new way of stacking pain, as his fictional ice-nine is a new way of stacking the molecules of water. Such an invention looks easy only in retrospect.

If any slickness lingers, it is as a certain intellectual haste. Introducing his collected non-fiction, Vonnegut says he is impressed by the "insights which shower down on me when my job is to imagine, as contrasted with the woodenly familiar ideas which clutter my desk when my job is to tell the truth." His fiction itches to seize the human truth by its large handles—by its wars, its religions, its fortunes, its kings and prophets. Ordinary people in Vonnegut's novels live hapless in Rosewater County or its equivalents; a middle-class Midwestern car salesman like Dwayne Hoover goes insane from sheer mediocrity, it would seem. So, too, the little circumstantial nuances of history are rather condescended to; Thomas Jefferson, for instance, rates an automatic sneer for being "a slave owner who was also one of the world's great theoreticians on the subject of human liberty"—as if Jefferson were hypocritical in helping advance those concepts by whose light slavery, an institution deemed respectable and even humane for millennia, would eventually be condemned. And a patient reading of Vonnegut's pronouncements leaves me uncertain as to whether he thinks the United States was evil, foolish, or right in waging war against Nazi Germany. Of course, no need to decide is laid upon the fiction writer; indeed, the interestingness and fertility of the puzzle derives from its unsolvability: our pain deserves dramatization only where it is paradoxical. I, too, prefer his ideas as they come twisted into his imaginings, and *Slapstick* abounds in those. War is being waged in *Slapstick,* and slavery has reconstituted itself, and "the history of nations," President Wilbur Daffodil-11 Swain concludes, "seemed to consist of nothing but powerless old poops like myself, heavily medicated and vaguely beloved in the long ago, coming to kiss the boots of young psychopaths." Such is the world, Vonnegut seems to be saying, but it is the one we have, and beats the Turkey Farm, if not Tralfamadore.

Family Ways

SEARCHING FOR CALEB, by Anne Tyler. 309 pp. Knopf, 1976.

Out of her fascination with families—with brotherly men and auntly women, with weak sisters and mama's boys, with stay-at-homes and runaways—Anne Tyler has fashioned, in *Searching for Caleb,* a dandy novel, funny and lyric and true-seeming, exquisite in its details and ambitious in its design. She here construes the family as a vessel of Time. The Pecks, who live (as her families tend to) in Baltimore, are known for longevity. Great-Grandma Laura, the second wife of the clan's founder, Justin Montague Peck, lived to be ninety-seven, and at the age of ninety-three Daniel Peck, Justin's first son, is lively enough to be riding trains and buses in search of his half-brother, Caleb, who disappeared from Baltimore back in 1912. It is 1973, and Daniel is living with two of his grandchildren, Justine and Duncan, who, though first cousins, have married. The minister who officiated at the wedding remembers "the bride's and groom's joint family" occupying the front pews: "There was something dreamlike in the fact that almost everyone in the front section had the same fair, rather expressionless face—over and over again, exactly the same face, distinguished only a little by age or sex." The intensely blue Peck eyes—"those clear, level eyes that tended to squint a little as if dazzled by their own blueness"—run through the layers of this saga like a trickle of icy-pure spring water; the motif is distilled in the marriage of Justine and Duncan, "their blue eyes opening simultaneously to stare at each other across the pillow." In Miss Tyler's vision, heredity looms as destiny, and with the force of a miracle people persist in being themselves:

> But Duncan, who had changed her whole life and taken her past away from her, slept on as cool as ever, and on the crown of his head was the same little sprig of a cowlick he had had when he was four.

The family's conservatism and longevity defy time while embodying it; a nonagenarian father sits next to his elderly son on a couch, and "they might have been brothers. . . . In the end, the quarter-century that divided their generations amounted to nothing and was swept away. . . . Everything was leveled, there were no extremes of joy or sorrow any more but only habit, routine, ancient family names and rites and customs, slow careful old people moving cautiously around furniture that had sat in the same positions for fifty years."

Yet not all the Pecks hold fast to the household established by the first Justin in northern Baltimore after the Great Fire of 1904. Caleb, his second son, whose "tilted brown eyes must have snuck in from the Baum side of the family," literally gives his father apoplexy with his love of music—the old man's left side is paralyzed by the young man's defiance, and his mother tells Caleb, in one of this book's many astounding sentences, "You have killed your half of your father." Caleb repentantly works for a decade in the family shipping business, then vanishes, leaving the fortune and the dynasty to his brother, Daniel. There are other runaways. Daniel's wife, Margaret Rose, bears him six children, one a year, and in the seventh year leaves him and flees to her parents in Washington. The six children do what is expected of them, as the family business becomes law instead of trade, but of *their* children (and there are oddly few) Duncan, the oldest's son, runs away at the age of eighteen, and a little later Justine, the youngest's daughter, defies her parents and marries him, joining him in a life of job-to-job vagabondage in the small towns of Maryland and Virginia. Their daughter, Meg, defies them in turn and also marries to escape. And even old Daniel, the patriarch of Peckishness, allows himself in retirement to drift away in search of Caleb, and takes up residence with the shabby, fortune-telling, forty-year-old Justine, the one other member of the family willing to spend time "chasing rainbows on the Greyhound bus line."

Searching for Caleb is, among other things, a detective novel, with an eccentric detective, Eli Everjohn (he looks like Abraham Lincoln, "even to the narrow border of beard along his jawline"), and an ingenious unravelling; readers should be permitted unhampered enjoyment of the plot's well-spaced turns. Suffice it to say that, with the quest for Caleb as her searchlight, Miss Tyler warmly illumines the American past in its domestic aspect. Old Justine's turn-of-the-century illness evokes this:

> Therefore he undertook his own cure. He had all the panes in his windows replaced with amethyst glass, which was believed to promote healing. He drank his water from a quassia cup and ordered Laura to send away for various nostrums advertised in the newspaper—celery tonic, pectoral syrup, a revitalizing electric battery worn on a chain around the neck. His only meat was squirrel, easiest on the digestive tract.

Miss Tyler, who was twenty-three when her first novel was published and is now only in her mid-thirties, seems omniscient about the details of old Baltimore. When Laura finally dies, Daniel reflects that she was the one person who with him could remember "the rough warm Belgian blocks that used to pave the streets downtown." We are told that the 1908 Ford had "a left-hand steering wheel and splashless flower vases," and that in the 1900s women wore Pompeiian Bloom rouge, and little Caleb leaned out a window to hear an Irish tenor sing "Just a Lock of Hair for Mother." Such tender erudition never feels forced. Contemplation of the vanished induces in Miss Tyler a totally non-academic ecstasy:

> Whenever you heard distant music somewhere in the town, maybe so faint you thought you imagined it, so thin you blamed the whistling of the streetcar wires, then you would track the sound down and find Caleb straddling his little velocipede, speechless with joy, his appleseed eyes dancing.

The whistling of the streetcar wires is another motif that recurs, and the search for Caleb feels to become a search for the lyrical, mystical, irrational underside of American practicality. Duncan spouts facts but he rarely applies them, and Justine is, matter-of-factly, a fortune-teller. Her fortune-telling, along with Caleb's invisible presence, keeps this scrupulously exact novel of furniture and manners spooky and suspenseful. The career of fortune-telling —the methods and habitats of its practitioners—occasions another fine display of curious information, and of Miss Tyler's subtle psychologizing. Madame Olita, offspring of a gypsy and a high-school civics teacher, instructs Justine:

> "... you must think of these cards as tags. ... Tags with strings attached, like those surprise boxes at parties. The strings lead into your mind. These cards will pull out what you already know, but have failed to admit or recognize."

So, too, Miss Tyler's details pull from our minds recognition of our lives. These Pecks, polite and snide and tame and maddening and resonant, are *our* aunts and uncles; Justine and Duncan's honeymoon, when they are "isolated, motionless, barely breathing, cut loose from everyone else," is everybody's escape from a suffocating plurality of kin into a primitive two-ness; the America they truck their fraying marriage through is our land, observed with a tolerance and precision unexcelled among contemporary writers. Paragraph after paragraph, details kindle together, making heat and light. For, along with the power to see and guess and know, Anne

Tyler has the rare gift of coherence—of tipping observations in a direction, and of keeping track of what she has set down. Reading letters from Baltimore as a newlywed, Justine notes that "each envelope let out a little gust of Ivory soap, the smell of home." A generation later, when her daughter, Meg—who in rebellion against her mother's rebellion has become a super-Peck, prim and conventional—leaves home, Justine in the girl's abandoned room takes "a deep breath of Meg's clean smell: Ivory soap and fresh-ironed fabric." Dozens of such strands of continuity glint amid the cross-woven threads of this rich novel of nostalgia and divination, genes and keepsakes, recurrences and reunions.

Miss Tyler does not always avoid the pawky. Her ease of invention sometimes leads her to overdo. The secret of Caleb's departure, she would have us believe, was harbored for sixty years by a family servant whom no one ever thought to ask and who therefore, with the heroic stubbornness of a Faulkner character, declined to tell. Such moonbeams of Southern Gothic, without a sustained sense of regional delirium, shine a bit stagily. In a note following the text, the author's biography sounds cosmopolitan (born in Minneapolis, married to an Iranian psychiatrist, herself once a graduate student of Russian), but she says she "considers herself a Southerner"; and she does apparently accept the belief, extinct save in the South, that families are absolutely, intrinsically interesting. Are they? Her Pecks contain not only their milieu's history but every emotion from a mother's need "to be the feeder" to an old man's perception that "once you're alive, there's no way out but dying." Does Miss Tyler share Daniel Peck's preference when he says, "I would prefer to find that heaven was a small town with a bandstand in the park and a great many trees, and I would know everybody in it and none of them would ever die or move away or age or alter"? No other kind of goodness is suggested in this book, except Justine's hopeful forward motion. Miss Tyler gives us a border South busy commercializing its own legends, a New South where the traditional slave-boy iron hitching post has had its face (but not its hands) painted white and where faith healers live in hideously slick decors of sculptured carpets and glass knicknacks. The America she sees is today's, but, like the artist-hero of her previous novel, *Celes-*

tial Navigation, she seems to see much of it through windows. There is an elusive sense of removal, an uncontaminated, clinical benevolence not present in the comparable talent of, say, the young Eudora Welty, whose provincial characters were captured with a certain malicious pounce. Powerhouse and Old Mr. Marblehead and the narrator of "Why I Live at the P.O." have an outrageous oddity they would disown if they could decipher the fiction. Whereas we can picture Anne Tyler's characters reading through her novels comfortably, like Aunt Lucy in "her wing chair in which she could sit encircled, almost, with the wings working like mule's blinders. . . . The upholstery was embroidered in satin-stitch, which she loved to stroke absently as she read." Sit up, Aunt Lucy. This writer is not merely good, she is *wickedly* good.

Loosened Roots

Earthly Possessions, by Anne Tyler. 200 pp. Knopf, 1977.

Anne Tyler in her seventh novel continues to demonstrate a remarkable talent and, for a writer of her acuity, an unusual temperament. She is soft, if not bullish, on America: its fluorescent-lit banks and gas stations, its high schools and low life, its motels and billboards and boring backwaters and stifling homes and staggering churches and scant, innocent depravities and deprivations are all to her the stuff of a tender magic, a moonlit scenery where poetry and adventure form as easily as dew. Small towns and pinched minds hold room enough for her; she is at peace in the semi-countrified, semi-plasticized, northern-Southern America where she and her characters live. Out of this peace flow her unmistakable strengths —her serene, firm tone; her smoothly spun plots; her apparently inexhaustible access to the personalities of her imagining; her infectious delight in "the smell of beautiful, everyday life"; her lack of any trace of intellectual or political condescension—and her one possible weakness: a tendency to leave the reader just where she found him. Acceptance, in her fiction, is the sum of the marvellous

—or, as *Earthly Possessions* would have it, the end of travelling is to return. This is not untrue. Nothing Anne Tyler sets down is untrue. But the impending moral encloses the excitements of her story in a circle of safety that gives them the coziness of entertainment. It may be that in this Protestant land, with its reverence for sweat and constipation, we distrust artificers, peaceable cultivators of the imaginary. Miss Tyler tends her human flora for each book's season of bloom and then latches the garden gate with a smile. So, one could say, did Shakespeare; but in the tragedies, at least, the enclosure of final order is drawn around a group of chastened survivors, while Miss Tyler here gathers in to safety the very characters she has convincingly shown us to be sunk in "a rich, black, underground world . . . where everyone was in some deep and dramatic trouble." The depths that her lucid vision perceives through the weave of the mundane are banished, as it were, by a mere movement of the author's eyes. *Earthly Possessions* contains, for instance, a chilling portrait of a habitual criminal, Jake Simms, Jr., who blames every destructive and chaotic act of his own on someone else. He kidnaps our heroine, the surpassingly amiable Charlotte Emory, because while he was robbing a bank a bystander happened to produce a gun. "I could be clean free," he tells his victim, "and you safe home with your kids by now if it wasn't for him. Guy like that ought to be locked up." As the chase continues, and the kidnapping lengthens into a kind of marriage, he persuades himself, "It ain't *me* keeping you, it's them. If they would quit hounding me then we could go our separate ways. . . ." This is perfect loser psychology, the mental technology for digging a bottomless pit; but Anne Tyler would have us believe that Jake is saved from falling in by the doll-like apparition of a wee seventeen-year-old girl he has impregnated, Mindy Callender:

> She really was a tiny girl. The biggest thing about her was that stomach, which Jake carefully wasn't looking at. . . . She raised a thin, knobby wrist, with a bracelet dangling heart-shaped charms in all different colors and sizes. The pink stone in her ring was heart-shaped too, and so was the print of her dress. "Hearts are my *sign*," Mindy said. "What's yours?"

With such a figure, the Shakespearean ambience of dark comedy turns Spenserian; we are travelling in an allegory, and Love (Mindy) on page 193 points to the Grail with one of those bursts of articulate insight that overtake even the dimwitted in Anne Tyler's animated world.

The excitements of *Earthly Possessions* include both headlong suspense and surprises of retrospective revelation. Charlotte, the narrator and heroine, tells in her wry, patient voice two stories: she describes, hour by hour, the few days of her southward flight with Jake Simms and, synopsized in alternating chapters, the thirty-five years of her life. The two accounts flow parallel, to the same estuary of acceptance. As in the author's previous novels, a fundamental American tension is felt between stasis and movement, between home and escape. Home is what we are mired in; Miss Tyler in her darker mode celebrates domestic claustrophobia and private stagnation. Charlotte is the late and only fruit of a very fat first-grade teacher and a faded, fussy "travelling photographer named Murray Ames." Ames stops travelling, and sets up a studio in his wife's "dead father's house," where a child is born with grotesque inadvertence: the mother's obesity and innocence have hidden the pregnancy. "One night she woke up with abdominal spasms. . . . All around her the bed was hot and wet. She woke her husband, who stumbled into his trousers and drove her to the hospital. Half an hour later, she gave birth to a six-pound baby girl." The little girl grows up lonely. The common American escape from home into the "whole new world" of public school is feelingly evoked:

I hadn't had any idea that people could be so light-hearted. I stood on the edge of the playground watching how the girls would gather in clumps, how they giggled over nothing at all and told colorful stories of family life: visits to circuses, fights with brothers. They didn't like me. They said I smelled. I knew they were right because now when I walked into my house I could smell the smell too: stale, dark, ancient air, in which nothing had moved for a very long time. I began to see how strange my mother was. I noticed that her dresses were like enormous flowered undershirts. I wondered why she didn't go out more; then once, from a distance, I watched her slow progress toward the corner grocery store and I wished she wouldn't go out at all.

From embarrassing parents Charlotte moves to an embarrassing husband. Saul Emory, a boy who had lived next door, returns from the Army, courts her, weds her, and abruptly announces that he has been called to preach, in the local fundamentalist Holy Basis Church. Charlotte is a non-believer; while her husband preaches she sits deafly in church scheming how to get him into bed. "He was against making love on a Sunday. I was in favor of it. Sometimes I won, sometimes he won. I wouldn't have missed Sunday for the world." They live in what has become *her* dead father's house; she diffidently runs the studio that she has inherited, and the house fills up with charity cases and Saul's brothers. Charlotte says, "I felt like something dragged on a string behind a forgetful child. . . . I gave up hope. Then in order not to mind too much I loosened my roots, floated a few feet off, and grew to look at things with a faint, pleasant humorousness that spiced my nose like the beginnings of a sneeze." Childhood fantasies of flight recur; she keeps giving away the furniture; she finally decides to leave, goes to the bank "to get cash for the trip," and is seized by Jake Simms. Her adventure begins.

Writing a self-description for the Washington *Post*, Anne Tyler said, "Mostly it's lies, writing novels. You set out to tell an untrue story and you try to make it believable, even to yourself. Which calls for details; any good lie does." Her details are superb, tucked in with quick little loops of metaphor:

> When she was angry, her face bunched in now as if gathered at the center by a drawstring.

> When he lifted me up in his arms I felt I had left all my troubles on the floor beneath me like gigantic concrete shoes.

Without pushing at it, she establishes her characters in authentic occupations. Murray Ames's photography and his daughter's continuation of it become very real, and a paradigm for art:

> "Move that lamp off somewhat," he would tell me from his bed. "You don't want such a glare. Now get yourself more of an angle. I never did like a head-on photograph."
>
> What he liked was a sideways look—eyes lowered, face slanted

downward. The bay window displaying my father's portraits resembled a field full of flowers, all being blown by the same strong breeze.

The author's attention to American incidentals is so unblinking that we are rather relieved when she seems to nod, as when Charlotte observes the "snuff adds" ("ads," surely) in Georgia or a "pair of giant fur dominoes" (dice, more likely) hung from a rearview mirror. Every bit of junk food the fugitives nibble as they drive their stolen car south is affectionately noted, and the subtle changes in scenery and climate are continental in their cumulative effect. When, having at last arrived in Florida, Charlotte says, "It was one of those lukewarm, breezy evenings that make you feel you're expecting something," we have arrived, too, and feel exactly what she means.

What else do we feel, after our two hundred pages with Charlotte Emory? She belongs to what is becoming a familiar class of Anne Tyler heroines: women admirably active in the details of living yet alarmingly passive in the large curve of their lives—riders on male-generated events, who nevertheless give those events a certain blessing, a certain feasibility. Jake comes to need his victim: "Charlotte, it ain't so bad if you're *with* us, you see. You act like you take it all in stride, like this is the way life really does tend to turn out. You mostly wear this little smile." Amos, a brother of Emory's who turns amorous, exclaims in admiration, "Now I see everyone grabbing for pieces of you, and still you're never diminished. . . . You sail through this house like a moon, you're strong enough for all of them." These intelligent, bustling, maternal, helpless moon-women trouble us with the something complacent in their little smiles, their "faint, pleasant humorousness." Their detachment has been achieved through a delicate inner abdication, a multiplication and devaluation of realities. Anne Tyler stated in the *Post,* "I write because I want more than one life." Charlotte Emory as a photographer poses her subjects in odd bits of costume, "absent-mindedly" holding feathers and toys, antique words and pistols; she has come to believe that such elaborations "may tell more truths than they hide." In the crisis of her mother's dying, Charlotte says, "My life grew to be all dreams; there was no reality whatsoever." Her life, from lonely childhood to lonely marriage, spent in an old house between two gas stations, photographing workaday people with dream baubles, has a terror and a sorrow of which the outlines are acknowledged but not the mass, the terrible heft. She seems less a character than a creator, who among the many lives that her fantasizing, empathizing mind arrays before her almost casually chooses to live her own.

Imagining Things

THE BEGINNING PLACE, by Ursula K. Le Guin. 183 pp. Harper & Row, 1980.

MORGAN'S PASSING, by Anne Tyler. 311 pp. Knopf, 1980.

The rather spacey name of Ursula K. Le Guin has for fifteen years been familiar to devotees of science fiction, but only recently has her reputation, passing through the same cultural space-warp utilized by Ray Bradbury and Kurt Vonnegut, entered what is hailed from the other side as "mainstream fiction." Her writing, even when under the exclusive aegis of Ace Books and *Amazing Stories*, had a mainstream tact, color, and intelligence, combined with the requisite sci-fi expertise and appetite for coining new worlds and languages. She has lived for years in Portland, Oregon. Her academic connections are multiple: born in Berkeley in 1929, daughter of the anthropologist Alfred L. Kroeber and the writer Theodora Kroeber, she received degrees from Radcliffe and Columbia, and during a Fulbright year in Paris met and married the historian Charles Le Guin. The social sciences inform her fantasies with far more earth-substance than the usual imaginary space flight, and her hypothetical futures have a strong flavor of familiar history. She herself, in an introduction to her prize-winning novel of 1969, *The Left Hand of Darkness*—a heartwarming tale of emerging statehood and evolved androgyny on a wintry planet sixty light-years from Earth—has argued that science fiction is not predictive but descriptive of the here and now, a "thought-experiment" in which "the moral complexity proper to the modern novel need not be sacrificed." Her new novel, *The Beginning Place*, describes with plenty of moral and psychological complexity the mating of two modern young people; its fantastic terrain, the twilight realm of Tembreabrezi, which the hero and the heroine enter through a miraculous gate in some scruffy woods within sight of a paint factory, belongs not to any conjecturable future but to that vast, vaguely medieval never-never land whose place in our shared nostalgia was sealed by Malory's telling of the Arthurian legends, revived by Tennyson and William Morris, and given phenomenal modern currency by Tolkien's saga of Middle-earth. Professor Tolkien's patient exercise in self-amusement, which so surprisingly came to amuse millions of others, has spawned a veritable galaxy of mock-archaic trilogic otherworlds, from Frank Herbert's dry Dune to Mrs. Le Guin's wet Earthsea, as well as giving new circulation to C. S. Lewis's theological fables of Narnia and Perelandra and even to James Branch Cabell's musty Poictesme series. Peter Beagle, introducing the paperback *Lord of the Rings,* asserts, in the furious vocabulary of the old counterculture, "The Sixties were no fouler a decade than the Fifties . . . but they were the years when millions of people grew aware that the industrial society had become paradoxically unlivable, incalculably immoral, and ultimately deadly. In terms of passwords, the Sixties were the time when the word *progress* lost its ancient holiness, and *escape* stopped being comically obscene. [Middle-earth offers] a green alternative to each day's madness here in a poisoned world."

Certainly the contemporary world presented in *The Beginning Place* is poisoned. Hugh Rogers, the hero, works as a checker in Sam's Thrift-E-Mart, in a well-evoked piece of littered suburban sprawl outside an unnamed city. He has seen fields from the highway but cannot find the way to walk to them: "Rubbish of paper and metal and plastic underfoot, the air lashed and staggering with suction winds and the ground shuddering as each truck approached and passed, eardrums battered by noise and nothing to breathe but burnt rubber and diesel fumes. He gave it up after half an hour and tried to get off the freeway, but the suburban streets were divided from the freeway embankment by chainlink fence. . . . The defeat left him shaky and angry, as if he had been assaulted." His home environment, too, in a dreary flat spread of streets called Kensington Heights, is poisoned; his father has deserted, and his mother is an aggrieved nagger whom dutiful Hugh, an only child, helplessly offends—"He knew that it was his deep voice, his size, his big feet and thick fingers, his heavy, sexual body that she couldn't stand, that drove her to the edge." He is twenty, has no friends his age, and his modest dreams are to go to library school and to own a car.

One day, he runs from his house in a panic and blunders upon his green alternative, a section of woods where it is strangely quiet and always twilight and a sweet cold little river runs. "This is a good place, Hugh thought. And I got here. I finally got somewhere. I made it." Time passes more slowly here than in the real world: a day equals an hour. Without being missed, he spends more and more time in the "wild, secret place": "It was there, and he could come back to it, the silence that gave words meaning, the center that gave the world a shape." Hugh is lugging camping equipment in, to prolong his stays, when, astoundingly, he finds he is not alone: someone has posted a NO TRESPASSING sign, and he encounters a girl. Irene Pannis also comes from a poisoned environment: a run-down farm where her dead father has been replaced by a sexually threatening stepfather. She has been visiting the twilit wood, which she thinks of as "the beginning place," or "the ain country," longer than Hugh—since she was thirteen—and knows the language. For the land has inhabitants; a town can be reached by walking the south road, across three rivers, up a steepening way through forests. There, in Tembreabrezi, "the fire was burning in the big hearth of the inn. An excellent perfume of onion, cabbage, and spices pervaded the rooms. Everything was as it had been, as it ought to be, with a couple of improvements to be admired: the floors were covered with a reddish straw matting, instead of sand scattered on the bare wood." The steep streets are stepped and cobbled, and white geese "vague and as if luminous" gabble in a pen by the Mayor's house, which has a dozen gables and dormers and whose "windows, bay and bow, many-paned, lay no two on one level."

The adventure that Irene and Hugh come to share in this storybook village is excitingly told, and boldly composed of the ancient motifs of curse and quest. Read as a metaphor of sexuality emerging from masturbatory solitude into the perilous challenge and exchange of heterosexual encounter, *The Beginning Place* is full of just and subtle touches. Both Irene and Hugh first fall in love with images of themselves: Irene is dark, and Hugh is fair, and the objects of their infatuation in Tembreabrezi—the saturnine Master, the fair Allia—exaggerate these aspects. The dragon they must slay —white and wrinkled and blind, hideous and piteous, loud with pain and craving, heavy with viscera—would appear to be our sorry carnality incarnate, with a runny touch of the subconscious chaos, the foul disorder of bad dreams, that threatens to melt Portland in *The Lathe of Heaven* (1971). Mrs. Le Guin is a magisterial imaginer, whose invented realities outrun any rigidly allegorical interpretation. The exact meaning of the paradox that Hugh can always get *into* the enchanted realm but gets lost within it and that Irene has trouble getting in but always knows the way and can get *out* eludes me but feels right. The terror that only Hugh fails to experience and the singing that only Irene can produce in this twilight devoid of birdsong are details that command belief without an equation, gathering their own weight within a fairyland that never seems too remote from actual states of mind. Daydream, trance, faith, and passion all exist on the borders of waking thought. Of his mother's interest in occultism, Hugh reflects, "It was screwy, but no screwier than most things people got interested in: baseball scores, aluminum futures, antique medicine bottles, nuclear proliferation, Jesus, politics, health foods, playing the violin." As deftly as she makes the muddled patchwork landscape around Kensington Heights yield a supernatural dell, the author manipulates the four personae her two characters yield: Hugh and Irene in their real, "poisoned" lives, and these same two in Tembreabrezi, where they bear the slightly altered names of Hiuradjas and Irena. In another feat of shading, she turns the "ain country" sinister and malevolent—as solitary sexual dreaming will become—and the polluted real world, returned to at night, in the rain, beautiful: the true beginning place.

This elegant parable of late adolescence fails of credibility only when it presses its moral too earnestly and starts to sound like a marriage manual, forcing Hugh to mumble slogans like "Two people are always sort of responsible for each other." Their first physical union comes on with far too many trumpets: "As he entered her, as she was entered, they came to climax together, and then lay together, mixed and melded, breast against breast and their breath mingled, until he rose in her again and she closed on him, the long pulse of joy enacting them." While not noted for her sexual realism, Flannery O'Connor renders devirgination more fairly in *Wise Blood*: "Since the night before was the first time he had slept with any woman, he had not been very successful with Mrs. Watts." The Catholic fabulist sees no need to thump the pulpit here, where Mrs. Le Guin does. *The Beginning Place* delivers its humane message well enough, before its make-believe is coarsened by good intentions.

Speaking of Flannery O'Connor, Anne Tyler is now nearing the age of thirty-nine, at which O'Connor died. After the eight inventive, polished novels of American life that the younger woman has produced since 1964, the only question remaining about her talent is: will it ever, in its scintillating display of plenitude, make a dent as deep in our national self-awareness and literature as that left by the work of O'Connor, and Carson McCullers, and Eudora Welty? For Anne Tyler, in her gifts both of dreaming and of realizing, evokes comparison with these writers, and in her tone and subject matter seems deliberately to seek association with the Southern ambience that, in less cosmopolitan times, they naturally and inevitably breathed. Even their aura of regional isolation is imitated by Miss Tyler as she holds fast, in her imagination and in her person, to a Baltimore with only Southern exits; her characters, when they flee, never flee North. Yet she is of our time. The brand names, the fads, the bastardized vistas of our great homogenized nation glint out at us from her fiction with a cheerful authority; nor is there anything narrow about her emotional anthropology—daughterhood, motherhood, sorority, and espousal all find vivid embodiment among her characters, where men are as confidently presented as women, and the range of particularized types is as broad as any in contemporary fiction. Still, her books, their dazzlements subsided, leave an unsettling impression of having been writ in water, with a cool laser of moonlight. Her latest novel, *Morgan's Passing*, compounds the faults of her quicksilver virtues, for it has as its heroine a fabricator of puppets, and as hero a man whose life is a succession of poses, struck in a thick beard and an array of funny hats and costumes. If we suspected we were being toyed with before, we know it now.

Halfway through the book, however, with the grudging paragraph above already assembling in the reviewer's head, there came a scene, of a messed-up family plowing through a summer weekend at a tacky beach house on the Delaware shore, that a reader would have to be heartless not to love and admire. The impulsively invited guests, the young puppeteers Emily and Leon, arrive, and the host, the middle-aged, costume-wearing hardware-store manager and father of seven daughters, Morgan, leads them in:

> He led them up the front steps and into the living room. The house's smell—mildew and kerosene—struck him for the first time as unfriendly. He noticed that the cushions in the rattan chairs were flat as pancakes, soggy-looking, and the rattan itself was coming loose in spirals from the arms. Emily and Leon stared around uncertainly. Gina slouched near the door and peeled a thumbnail. . . . Then Emily said, "I brought a camera."
> "Eh?" said Morgan. "Oh, a camera!"
> "Just a Kodak."
> "But that's wonderful!" he said. . . . He saw that things would be fine after all. (Life was full of these damp little moments of gloom that came and went; they meant nothing.)

It is by means of the snapshots Emily takes on this soggy, confused weekend, and later sends him, that Morgan confronts at last his love for her. It is by means of faithfully, modestly rendering life's minute ups and downs, its damp and sunny patches, and its trailing wisps of meaninglessness that Anne Tyler expresses her sense of reality. *Morgan's Passing* is a novel without a crisis. Like Mrs. Le Guin's *The Beginning Place*, it concerns the union of a man and a woman achieved in an unpropitious world, out of unlikely beginnings; but when Emily and Morgan confront their particular dragon—the married state they are both already in—the dragon does not so much fall as melt away, as their spouses obligingly accede and a shifted cast of characters resumes life much as it was before: fitful, zany, wistful, tender, and somehow hollow.

Puppetry, as announced by Brookie Maxwell's charming dust jacket, is the dominant metaphor. The descriptions of Emily's fond puppet-making remind us of Jeremy Pauling's papery sculpture in *Celestial Navigation,* not to mention Miss Tyler's own light-fingered artistry. Much of the action in this novel of jumpy behavior has the abruptness of a Punch-and-Judy show: a rejected husband walks fully clothed into the sea; a three-wheeled mail truck runs over a man's leg as he is stretched beneath his car; a senile mother mistakes her middle-aged son for a burglar. Emily has begun her married life with Leon among a troupe of young actors to whom "everything was a skit." Morgan's daily life, in which he goes about impersonating a doctor, a priest, a shoemaker, or a postman, is a succession of skits. His improvising, good-natured wife, Bonny, uses Magic Markers to color bare spots in their rugs and furniture, so that he feels "he was living in one of those crayoned paper houses that the twins used to make." Emily keeps her baby in a cardboard box. Morgan advises his daughter to organize her belongings in a cardboard box. He feels that in his household there are "always threads and tangles trailing," and notes that his wife's clothes are held together with safety pins and Scotch Tape. Both Morgan and Emily are puppeteers: she literally and he in his way of casting himself and people he meets in swiftly imagined roles. "We're not who you imagine," Emily protests to him. But she, too, lives in a fabricated world. When she visits her kinfolk in the South, she sees them sitting on the sofa "abandoned, sagging, like large cloth dolls." When her cousin's husband, Claude, reaches up to pat her on the shoulder, "the rest of him stayed sunk in the cushions; his arm seemed disproportionately long and distant from his body"—a puppet's gesture, that. The first time she sees Morgan, wearing a pointy red ski cap, he "really could have been someone from a fairytale. . . the troll, the goblin." As she gets to know him and his guises better, she thinks "he could have stepped into a puppet show and not been out of place." And when he looks at her, "she looked beautifully remote to him, so distinct from everyone else that she seemed smaller even than the children." Held in his arms, "her body was so thin and pliant that it always seemed he was missing something, leaving a part of it behind." When she runs, her legs "flew out like sticks," and another character complains to her, "You always act so *wooden.*" In bed, she feels like a puppet to herself: "At night in bed, she never lost her surprise at finding herself alongside this bearded man, this completely other person. She felt drawn to him by something far outside herself—by strings that pulled her, by ropes."

The passage continues, with an erotic expressiveness unusual for Miss Tyler, "Waking in the dark, she rolled toward him with a kind of stunned sensation. She was conscious of their two surfaces meeting noticeably: oil and water." (How fine that "noticeably" is!) The peculiar otherness that is one of love's preconditions, emphasized in *The Beginning Place,* figures here also; the puppets are opaque to each other. Morgan "couldn't imagine what it felt like to be Emily," and she listens solemnly, "unsmiling, trying to figure him out," to some jokey noises he has left on a tape recorder. She is later told, "He only feels he's real when he's in other people's eyes." He is sometimes left feeling "emptied" and insists of his life, "It's come to nothing. It's come to nothing." He complains, "Somehow it's as if this were all a story, just something that happened to somebody else. It's as if I'm watching from outside, mildly curious, thinking, So this is what kind of life it is, eh?" There is a certain melancholy in *Morgan's Passing*—the puppetmaster's ennui. Emily announces more than once, "I'm tired of puppets." The lovers collapse together as if in rebellious weary recoil from so much strenuous "imagining things." And it is tempting to ascribe some of this fatigue to Miss Tyler herself, in a work so forcedly buoyant, so scattered and manic in its episodes, so enigmatic and—dare we say?—fey in its central character. Though we are admitted to Morgan's head now and then, we never hear him talking to himself in the level, calculating voice that would make his "act" plausible, as the strategy of a sane masculine person.

Though many amusing episodes, Baltimore blocks, and shrewd home truths are winningly mustered, the scenes dance before our eyes; we rarely feel *in* them, as we do for those pages of seaside awkwardness, or during a Quaker meeting that Emily attends in her home town, or whenever a young child appears on the page.

Miss Tyler's first novel, *If Morning Ever Comes,* like *Morgan's Passing* shows an unlikely mating dance, and a houseful of women —six daughters instead of Morgan's seven—which the man of the house abandons, with eerily slight consequences. Both books concern home and running away from home, travelling light and enduring clutter—the two comic alternatives in Miss Tyler's America. The first novel, written when the author was only twenty-two, is prodigiously skillful, and calm in its skills; nothing of the virtuoso manipulator disturbs its steady and finally moving delineation of a marital commitment as it grows within a young man who, like Morgan (and like Hugh), doesn't quite know who he is. We feel—in the phrase of Warner Berthoff*—"that the writer's own most intimate apprehension of life stands directly behind everything presented." The most intimate apprehension behind *Morgan's Passing* seems to be a jauntily oblique unease about puppetry, fiction, and the like.

Still, what a magical puppeteer this writer remains! She snaps her minor characters onto the stage with a verve that makes us laugh:

> She was a small, hunched old lady with hair that was still jet black; it was held flat with tortoise-shell combs from which it crinkled and bucked like something powerful.

> His name was Jim. He had the flat, beige face of a department-store mannequin, and he seemed overly fond of crew-necked sweaters.

> The salesgirl, awkward on her platform sandals as some frail, hoofed animal, hung in the background, clutching one elbow.

This is O'Connor cartooning without the cruelty, without the pinpoint tunnel to Jesus at the end of all perspectives. With no obvious faith and no apparent paranoia to give her vision impetus,

---

*In his thoughtful and rather disappointed study of postwar American writing, *A Literature Without Qualities* (University of California Press, 1979).

Anne Tyler continues to look close, and to fabricate, out of the cardboard and Magic Markers available to the festive imagination, images of the illusory lives we lead. More than that it would be unkind to ask, did we not imagine, from the scope of the gift displayed, that something of that gift is still being withheld.

On Such a Beautiful Green Little Planet

OH WHAT A PARADISE IT SEEMS, by John Cheever. 100 pp. Knopf, 1982.

DINNER AT THE HOMESICK RESTAURANT, by Anne Tyler. 303 pp. Knopf, 1982.

Water as well as light has figured in John Cheever's work as an essence palpable, as a manifestation of the natural good that bubbles and pours and glints around us. The earliest short story that he saw fit to include in his collected *Stories*, "Goodbye, My Brother," dissolves its murderous fraternal tensions in the beatific vision of two women walking naked out of the "iridescent and dark" sea, and one of the most recent tells of "Artemis, the Honest Well Digger": water is Artemis's "livelihood as well as his passion," and he reflects, "Man was largely water. Water was man. Water was love." In between, "The Swimmer" traverses eight miles of swimming pools while his life ebbs away, and poor Nerissa Peranger is turned *into* a swimming pool, and many a man and woman lie awake with the seductive sound of rain in their ears. Cheever has called his latest book, *Oh What a Paradise It Seems*, an "ecological romance"; the main action traces the rapid (and what in Cheever's fiction is not rapid?) alteration of a body of water called Beasley's Pond, "shaped like a bent arm," from a splendid skating spot and piece of untroubled nature into a landfill zone—"a heap of rubbish, topped by a dead dog"—and, thanks to some swift and obscure political and technological heroics, back again to its former paradisiacal condition. "Air delivered by blowers at 4.4 cfm 30 psi continuously mix and turn over upward of three hundred million gallons of water. We have two auxiliary blower units in case of mechanical trouble. Fish kill has been cut by two-thirds and last month we ran tests at four water levels. These showed water temperatures of eighty-four degrees and dissolved oxygen of seven to nine mgl at all levels. A year ago the water was poison. Now it is quite potable."

The enunciator of these marvels of aquatic rebirth, and the hero of *Oh What a Paradise It Seems,* is Lemuel Sears, an "Old man but not yet infirm," with a smooth skater's stroke and a young man's erotic susceptibility. His battle in behalf of Beasley's Pond runs parallel with the ups and downs of his romance with one Renée Herndon, a younger if not girlish woman encountered in a line at a bank teller's window. When she, wanton nymph that she is, halts the gush of her favors, Sears turns for consolation, so fluid is his own sexual nature, to a homosexual fling with her elevator operator. These events take place in New York City and the not far-off but old-fashioned hamlet of Janice. In Janice, we witness some crisp suburban comedy involving the Salazzos and the Logans, neighbors on Hitching Post Lane with differing opinions upon not only land use but wind chimes and proper deportment in supermarket checkout lines. In addition to these characters, vivid and lovable as mayflies as they twirl for their moment in the sunshine, there is an unusually strong narrator's voice that promises us at the outset "a story to be read in bed in an old house on a rainy night" and presents us throughout with friendly *discursi* on matters as unexpected as Balkan villages, the archeology of fortresses and marketplaces, the evolution of the ice skate, the democratization of Freudian parlance, the antiquity and ubiquity of fried food, the possibility of a world wherein even the tenderest intentions will be communicated by means of signal lights on automobiles, and the decline of queues and caste sense—all of which, briskly interposed, enhance without hindering the flow of this tumbling, plashing little narrative, which chance or ingenious design has caused to be printed upon exactly one hundred pages.

The book is too darting, too gaudy in its deployment of artifice and aside, too disarmingly personal in its voice, to be saddled with the label of novel or novella; it is a parable and a tall tale—both sub-genres squarely within the Judeo-Christian tradition, North American branch. Cheever has lately taken the mantle of that tradition ever more comfortably upon his shoulders, and now unabashedly assumes the accents of a seer. Indeed, Sears, his hero, meets a seeress, in one of the most tangential episodes of this brief but wide-ranging narrative. It happened years ago, in Eastern Europe. The prophetess occupied a cave beneath an extinct volcano. Sears's official interpreter was terrified of encountering this fabled person, but Sears was "either too tired or too drunk or too solaced by the beauty of the farmland" to feel anxious. And, when they did meet, the seeress, who was prosaically middle-aged and wore nothing more esoteric than a clean cotton dress, felt his wallet (she was blind) and began to smile, began to laugh, and announced, *"La grande poésie de la vie."* Then Sears laughed, and they embraced, and parted still laughing. Ever more boldly the celebrant of the grand poetry of life, Cheever, once a taut and mordant chronicler of urban and suburban disappointments, now speaks in the cranky, granular, impulsive, confessional style of our native wise men and exhorters since Emerson. The pitch of his final page is positively Transcendental:

> The thought of stars contributed to the power of his feeling. What moved him was a sense of those worlds around us, our knowledge however imperfect of their nature, our sense of their possessing some grain of our past and of our lives to come. It was that most powerful sense of how singular, in the vastness of creation, is the richness of our opportunity. The sense of that hour was of an exquisite privilege, the great benefice of living here and renewing ourselves with love. What a paradise it seemed!

If such root affirmations ring, in this late age of median strips and polluted ponds, with a certain deliberate and wry gallantry, that, too, is accommodated in the tale—in the burlesque of its consumerism, the ogreish farce of its politics, the chemical pranks of its natural resurrection. The smooth phraseology of praise and idyll are suddenly roughened by a heartfelt qualification: Sears, remembering the "utter delight of loving" his lost Nereid, Renée, then admits that this utter delight "seemed, in his case, to involve some clumsiness, as if he carried a heavy trunk up a staircase with a turning." Cheever's instinctive belief in the purity and glory of Creation brings with it an inevitable sensitivity to corruption; like Hawthorne, he is a poet of the poisoned. His American landscape is dotted with tiny atrocities—back-yard charcoal braziers and "stand-up" swimming pools and domestic architecture that "was all happy ending" and in whose sad living rooms people pass one another "a box of crackers that the label promised would stimulate conversation." The tinge of snobbishness in his dismay is redeemed by the generosity with which Cheever feels, like an American of a century and a half ago, the wonder of this land of promises.

He loves nature—light, water, human love. Again and again, the elements are remembered by his paltry suburbanites. "You think I can turn off the wind?" Maria Salazzo asks when a neighbor complains about the night noise of her wind chimes. A gangster who daily picks up the loot from the landfill deal is described as "one of those small, old Italians who always wear their hats tipped forward over their brows as if they were, even in the rain, enduring the glare of an equinoctial sun. These same old men walk with their knees quite high in the air as if they were forever climbing those hills the summits of which so much of Italy stands." Nature stamps Man at every moment, and litters our lives with clues to the supernatural:

> When [Sears] was young, brooks had seemed to speak to him in the tongues of men and angels. Now that he was an old man who spoke five or six languages—all of them poorly—the sound of water seemed to be the language of his nativity, some tongue he had spoken before his birth. Soft and loud, high and low, the sound of water reminded him of eavesdropping in some other room than where the party was.

The party, for now, is here, in this shadow of paradise. Were Cheever less a New Englander than he is, with the breath of Thoreau and Emily Dickinson in his own lovely quick light phrasing, he might fail to convince us that a real glory shines through his transparent inventions. The gap in *Falconer* between the circumstantial prison and the spiritual adventure that it allegorized certainly took a reader's indulgence to bridge. But in *Oh What a*

Paradise It Seems there are no more gaps than between the blades of a spinning pinwheel. All is fabulous from the start; all is fancy, praise, and rue, seamlessly. Janice, that oddly named village, receives postcards from all the territories that Cheever's imagination has been happy in—Italy, Eastern Europe, the St. Botolph's of the Wapshot chronicles, and the Shady Hill and Bullet Park where America's dream of space and plenty and domestic bliss has come to so fragmentary a realization. The paradisiacal elixir has a chalky taste but in this testament survives its contaminants and is served up sparkling.

Anne Tyler, too, has sought brightness in the ordinary, and her art has needed only the darkening that would give her beautifully sketched shapes solidity. So evenly has her imagination moved across the details of the mundane that the novels, each admirable, sink in the mind without leaving an impression of essential, compulsive subject matter—the phobia portrayed in *Celestial Navigation* being something of an exception. Now, in her ninth novel, she has arrived, I think, at a new level of power, and gives us a lucid and delightful yet complex and somber improvisation on her favorite theme, family life. *Searching for Caleb* is the earlier book it most resembles, in its large cast and historical reach, and even in the perky monosyllabic name assigned the central family: Peck in the first case, Tull in this. Both novels play with the topic (a mighty one, and not often approached in fiction) of heredity—the patterns of eye color and temperamental tic as they speckle the generations. But genetic comedy, in *Dinner at the Homesick Restaurant*, deepens into the tragedy of closeness, of familial limitations that work upon us like Greek fates and condemn us to lives of surrender and secret fury.

The book opens in the mind of Pearl Tull, dying at the age of eighty-five, in 1979. The principal facts of her life emerge in the course of her circling reverie. Born in Raleigh of good family, small and intelligent and fair, she was still unmarried at the age of thirty when Beck Tull, a tall blue-eyed man of just twenty-four, with wavy dark hair and a salesman's position with a farm-and-gardening-equipment concern called the Tanner Corporation, courted and wed her. For six years, on the move as he was repeatedly transferred, they had no children; in 1930 they had a son, Cody, then, after an attack of croup nearly carried this only offspring away, two more children, Ezra and Jenny. In 1944, while they were living in Baltimore, Beck abruptly announced that he was leaving Pearl and his family; at first believing that he would return, and indeed never explicitly announcing to the children that their father had left, she took a job as cashier in a local grocery store, and there, in that job and in that Baltimore house, she stayed, raising her children, and eventually seeing two of the three through college.

By 1979—to anticipate the later chapters—Cody is married, with one son, Luke, and works as an efficiency consultant to various industries; like his father, he is a travelling man. Jenny has been twice divorced, has one child, Becky, and lives with a chap called Joe, who was recently abandoned by his wife and was left with their six children; Jenny, after being left by her second husband (she left the first one), finished her degree at medical school and enjoys a busy practice as a pediatrician. Ezra Tull did not go to college or marry; he lives with his now aged mother in the city and owns and runs a nearby restaurant, which he has called the Home-sick Restaurant. The Tulls, in short, present a not untypical American family history, marred by abandonment and scattering but redeemed by a certain persisting loyalty and, after early privation, respectable success. And the telling of the Tull saga is soaked through, you may be sure, with all the deft geographical, topical, professional, and cultural specifics required to make it stick, from 1903 to 1979, to the landscape of the upper South and to the curve of national life as glimpsed in its wars and fads and fashions. This type of authenticity Anne Tyler has provided consistently; what she has not shown before, so searchingly and grimly, are the violences, ironies, and estrangements within a household, as the easy wounds given dependent flesh refuse to heal and instead grow into lifelong purposes. A bitter *narrowness* of life is disclosed through all the richness of detail as the decades accumulate, to claustro-phobic and sad effect.

The novel leaves Pearl Tull's mind, and chapter by chapter gives us Cody's, Jenny's, Ezra's, and even young Luke's view of the

branching consequences of the primal event—Beck Tull's aban-
donment, as abrupt and mysterious as his courtship, of his wife. In
her own mind a doting and heroic mother, Pearl is seen by Cody
as a "witch," a terrible-tempered mother who "slammed us against
the wall and called us scum and vipers, said she wished us dead,
shook us till our teeth rattled, screamed in our faces." Cody's own
violences to his placid and harmless younger brother follow suit.
Jenny, too, has seen how her mother's "pale hair could crackle
electrically from its bun and her eyes could get small as hatpins,"
has felt her stinging slaps, has dreamed that her mother is raising
her to eat her. Even on her deathbed, Pearl calls her children
"duckers and dodgers." A perfectionist, a fanatic laundress and
housekeeper, she strives to keep her bare clean house free of con-
tamination. She disapproves of her children's friends and has few
friends herself; the isolation of this embattled family, in its Balti-
more row house, is dreadfully well felt. Of course, all children are
somewhat embarrassed by their parents and their homes; Pearl is
a witch but also our authentic heroine, and the novel ends with
Cody's adolescent vision of her beauty, "his mother's upright form
along the grasses, her hair lit gold, her small hands smoothing her
bouquet." The paradoxes of the family, *Dinner at the Homesick
Restaurant* suggests, include love that must for survival flee its
object, and daily communication that masks silence—that deep
resentful silence of those who live together. Ezra, the most loving
of Pearl's children, yet turns cold-hearted when she falls sick, be-
cause, it is explained, "he had trusted his mother to be everything
for him. When she cut a finger with a paring knife, he had felt
defeated by her incompetence. How could he depend on such a
person?" When Luke runs away from home, he is given rides by
three persons who all have a horror story of family life uppermost
in their minds—infants who die, daughters who are ingrates, wives
who leave. The family, that institution meant to shelter our frailty,
in fact serves as a theatre for intimate cruelties, and brims with the
cruellest of invisible presences, time. As Pearl's memories accumu-
late in the course of the novel, we become dizzied by the downward
perspective into a well of personal history wherein hereditary traits
reverberate and snapshots and frozen memories gleam amid the

blackness of loss. Pearl, blind in her last years, directs Ezra to describe old photos and read aloud her girlhood diaries. At last, near the bottom of the well, she finds what she has been looking for, the diary entry:

> Early this morning I went out behind the house to weed. Was kneeling in the dirt by the stable with my pinafore a mess and the perspiration rolling down my back, wiped my face on my sleeve, reached for the trowel, and all at once thought, Why I believe that at just this moment I am absolutely happy. The Bedloe girl's piano scales were floating out her window, and I saw that I was kneeling on such a beautiful green little planet. I don't care what else might come about, I have had this moment. It belongs to me.

The plot holds a number of such epiphanies and moves its extensive cast agilely along, with flashback and side glance, through ten chapters that are each rounded like a short story. Miss Tyler, whose humane and populous domestic novels have attracted (if my antennae are tuned right) less approval in the literary ether than the sparer offerings of Ann Beattie and Joan Didion, is sometimes charged with the basic literary sin of implausibility. To me, her characters seem persuasive outgrowths of landscapes and states of mind that are familiar and American. The principal characters in *Dinner at the Homesick Restaurant* have their tics but also real psychologies, which make their next moves excitingly unpredictable. It is true, no writer would undertake to fill a canvas so broad without some confidence that she can invent her way across any space, and some of Miss Tyler's swoops, and the delayed illuminations that prick out her tableaux, have not quite the savor of reality's cautious grind. But any reader who picks up a work of fiction enters into a contract whereby he purchases with credulity satisfactions of adventure and resolution that his lived life denies him. This novel does not abuse the terms of that contract; its entertainments become our recognitions.

SOME BRITISH

Jake and Lolly Opt Out

JAKE'S THING, by Kingsley Amis. 276 pp. Viking, 1978.

LOLLY WILLOWES, by Sylvia Townsend Warner. 247 pp. The Women's Press, 1978. Also in an edition of 252 pp. by Cassandra Editions of Academy Chicago Limited, 1978.

If the postwar English novel figures on the international stage as winsomely trivial, Kingsley Amis must bear part of the blame. Though he himself is a poet good enough to be generously represented in *The New Oxford Book of English Light Verse* (which Mr. Amis edited), it is a rare sentence of his prose that surrenders to the demons of language, that abdicates a seat of fussy social judgment, that is there for its own sake, out of simple awe, gratitude, or dismay in the face of creation. His universe is claustrophobically human, and his ambition and reputation alike remain in thrall to the weary concept of the "comic novel." There was something unabashedly sophomoric about *Lucky Jim* (1953) which bespoke an eternal schoolboy; adult experience appears unremittingly oppressive to James Dixon save for the chemical holiday, the physiological crime and punishment, of drunkenness and hangover. On this one Janus-faced topic Mr. Amis could and can write with inspiration; but as farce and satire *Lucky Jim* lay uneasily between the romantic good humor of Wodehouse and the sublime hard-heartedness of Waugh. Compared with a contemporaneous American study of reluctant pubescence, Salinger's *Catcher in the Rye,* it lacked not only private psychological intensity but, oddly enough, true comic edge. For there is no need to write "funny novels," when life's actual juxtapositions and convolutions, set down attentively, are comedy enough.

Amis's newest novel, *Jake's Thing,* is in fact a more ample and less artificial grab at life than *Lucky Jim,* though little in the book's reception would imply that. On the back of the jacket, the *Daily Mail* is quoted as chortling, "The funniest thing he has done since *Lucky Jim* . . . The book takes an unerring smack at our times." Well, the hilarious central subject of *Jake's Thing* is impotence and, beyond that, acedia, the deathlike condition of not caring; and the unerring smack is not at our times but at Mr. Amis's pained and isolated hero. Jake Richardson, an Oxford don who lives in London (apparently a not unusual arrangement), in an attempt to revive his libido subjects his fastidious sensibility and fifty-nine-year-old body to a series of humiliating psychiatric conferences, sex gadgets, and exhibitionistic workshops. Jake has once been a great womanizer, with over a hundred scores to his credit. He is married to his third wife, the overweight and wide-eyed Brenda. He wants, he thinks, to save his marriage. The muffled engine of the plot, the underplayed *primum mobile,* is the depth of anguish and affective embarrassment which glues this conservative, elderly man to psychologists and fellow-patients whom he despises; against the background of this poignance, nothing looms as very funny. Mr. Amis attempts to milk for a few mechanical laughs the juxtaposition of a snoopy cleaning lady with Jake's medically prescribed pornography-reading and the introduction into his home of a device called "the nocturnal mensurator." No doubt some of the therapeutic language ("inceptive regrouping," "genital sensate focusing") is meant to be droll. But the centerpiece of the satire, if satire it is—the lengthy workshop Jake and Brenda endure with the dwarfish psychologist Rosenberg, the workshop "facilitator" Ed (an American, always a bad sign), and eight sufferers from kleptomania, paranoia, inferiority complex, and assorted phobias—comes over as more horrifying than biting, more pathetic than amusing. It is by no means clear that Rosenberg and Ed are charlatans, though Jake comes to believe so, and the English reader might be disposed to expect so. To an

American, conditioned to tolerate all sorts of craziness on behalf of the soul, the extravagant exercises of group therapy seem at least a fresh attack upon virtually intractable forms of human loneliness and mental impasse. Brenda, who enters this strange world in the wake of Jake's impotence, comes to argue, "Now Ed has too good an opinion of himself I quite agree, but he does help people, or lets them help themselves which is just as good. I'm sure there are good reasons for saying he couldn't or he shouldn't or he doesn't really, but he does." The author in this debate stands a bit off to the side, giving Jake lots of space but Brenda some very good lines—better lines than her supposedly ill-educated, insecure character would warrant—and Mr. Amis's bemusement deepens as his hero, in an increasingly violent succession of verbal explosions, proceeds from wounded impotence to triumphant misogyny.

Jake, once the novel escorts him back to the predominantly male environment of Oxford, takes on some of Lucky Jim's manic recklessness, and through a drunken seduction he narrows in on the heart of his problem, which is the hatefulness of all things female. As long as he is in London, docilely bussing back and forth between his sex therapist and his wife, his inklings are no more malign than the private observation, of a female anatomical part featured in a magazine called *Mezzanine,* that "in itself it had an exotic appearance, like the inside of a giraffe's ear or a tropical fruit not much prized even by the locals." But back in the university precincts, where the female minority hoots at Jake as a "wanker" and sends him a plastic phallus in the post, he is led to perceive that "they [women] don't use language for discourse but for extending their personality." The indictment immensely widens, to include "their concern with the surface of things, with objects and appearances, with their surroundings and how they looked and sounded in them, with seeming to be better and to be right while getting everything wrong, their automatic assumption of the role of injured party in any clash of wills," etc., etc., all of which can be subsumed under the lament, in *My Fair Lady,* of Professor Henry Higgins: "Oh, why can't a woman be like us?" The ending of *Jake's Thing* is too good—too startling and too inevitable—to give away; but let it be hinted that it echoes with uncanny fidelity the notorious conclusion of Mickey Spillane's *I, the Jury.*

The novel's innocent air of not having wanted to come out this way is one of its charms. Much sorrow and some wit flourish in the chinks of the shambles as marital saga, reactionary diatribe, and pilgrim's progress vainly compete to set a consistent tone. The book is made up of twenty-eight jollily titled chapters that feel like consecutive essays. As a continuously developing stream of event and revelation, *Jake's Thing* suffers from contrived jokiness and unsteady perspective; the author seems now immersed in Jake, now on the verge of disowning him, and there are curious patches where the action is summarized rather than related, as though the writer had to avert his eyes. As a portrait of a man, however, and the times that enclose and infuriate him, the novel is satisfyingly ambiguous, relentless, and full. Jake has more complaints than the similarly indisposed Alexander Portnoy: he can't get used to seeing Asians and blacks in the streets of London; he can't help noticing that men in dirty overalls seem to have more money to spend than he; he conducts inwardly a running criticism of the architecture, dress, manners, and cuisine he daily confronts; he suffers from moments of seeing "the world in its true light, as a place where nothing had ever been any good and nothing of significance done." He is in a rage. Yet he is also dutiful, loyal in his fashion, and beset; we accept him as a good fellow, an honest godless citizen of the late twentieth century, trying hard to cope with the heretical possibility that sex isn't everything.

This possibility must have occurred earlier in life to Sylvia Townsend Warner than to Kingsley Amis. *Lolly Willowes; or, The Loving Huntsman,* her first novel, originally published in 1926 and now reissued in paperback by two different feminist presses, is the witty, eerie, tender but firm life history of a middle-class English-woman who politely declines to make the expected connection with the opposite sex and becomes a witch instead. The late Miss Warner, whose more than half a century of brilliantly varied and self-possessed literary production never quite won her the flaming place in the heavens of reputation that she deserved, began as a poet, like Mr. Amis, but, unlike him, did retain magic and music in her prose. Her last book was a sequence of vivacious, matter-of-fact short stories about elves, collected a year before her death as *Kingdoms of Elfin* (1977). Her first novel finds her already moving with somber confidence into the realm of the supernatural. Her prose, in its simple, abrupt evocations, has something preternatural about it. We meet Laura Willowes in 1902, when, upon the death of her father in the Somerset village where she has grown up, she moves to London to live with her elder brother and his family. The father's funeral is evoked:

> The bees droned in the motionless lime trees. A hot ginny churchyard smell detached itself in a leisurely way from the evergreens when the mourners brushed by them. The sun, but an hour or so declined, shone with an ardent and steadfast interest upon the little group. "In the midst of life we are in death," said Mr. Warbury, his voice sounding rather shameless taken out of church and displayed upon the basking echoless air. "In the midst of death we are in life," Laura thought, would be a more accurate expression of the moment.

In London, in her brother's prosperous and well-served house, Laura ages into Aunt Lolly. While a number of efforts are made to marry her off, "Laura would make no efforts at all." A certain stammering Mr. Arbuthnot, who "felt that being thirty-five he owed himself a wife," strikes a dim spark, until Laura suddenly tells him, "If you were a werewolf, and very likely you may be, for lots of people are without knowing, February, of all months, is the month when you are most likely to go out on a dark windy night and worry sheep." Though her kin then resign themselves to having Aunt Lolly with them forever, she experiences increasing disquiet, especially in the autumn months. In 1921, as she approaches fifty, she undergoes a definitive mystical experience, in a humble greengrocer's shop:

> Laura looked at the bottled fruits, the sliced pears in syrup, the glistening red plums, the greengages. She thought of the woman who had filled those jars and fastened on the bladders. Perhaps the greengrocer's mother lived in the country. A solitary old woman picking fruit in a darkening orchard, rubbing her rough fingertips over the smooth-

skinned plums, a lean wiry old woman, standing with upstretched arms among her fruit trees as though she were a tree herself, growing out of the long grass, with arms stretched up like branches. It grew darker and darker; still she worked on, methodically stripping the quivering taut boughs one after the other.

As Laura stood waiting she felt a great longing. It weighed upon her like the load of ripened fruit upon a tree. She forgot the shop, the other customers, her own errand. She forgot the winter air outside, the people going by on the wet pavements. She forgot that she was in London, she forgot the whole of her London life. She seemed to be standing alone in a darkening orchard, her feet in the grass, her arms stretched up to the pattern of leaves and fruit, her fingers seeking the rounded ovals of the fruit among the pointed ovals of the leaves. The air about her was cool and moist. There was no sound, for the birds had left off singing and the owls had not yet begun to hoot. No sound, except sometimes the soft thud of a ripe plum falling into the grass, to lie there a compact shadow among shadows. The back of her neck ached a little with the strain of holding up her arms. Her fingers searched among the leaves.

These two lapidary paragraphs embody what Michelet and other theorists on witchcraft merely propose: an identification of the witch with Nature.* Sylvia Townsend Warner was a great friend of Nature; she was one of the last bardic intimates of rural England and a witty, erudite explicator of those myths and sensations in which the agricultural underlay of civilization still makes itself felt. Having received her revelation, Lolly Willowes abandons family life in London for single life in the remote, agreeably sinister Buckinghamshire village of Great Mop, where with pleasant ease, feeling her way, she makes a pact with Satan, acquires a "familiar," attends a sabbat, joins a coven, and holds lengthy discourse with the

---

*Professor Margaret Murray's momentous *Witch-Cult in Western Europe,* asserting that witches after all had been real practitioners of ancient fertility rites and devoted worshippers of the "horned god," came out in 1921, the year of Laura's vision. Miss Townsend Warner sent the formidable Miss Murray a copy of *Lolly Willowes* and, according to her letter to David Garnett of February 20, 1926, "She liked my witch though she was doubtful about my devil, and wrote to me a very pleasant letter to say so. Now I have just come back from lunching with her. She is most fit and right; short and majestic, a Queen Victoria with the profile of Louis Quatorze and small fierce fat white hands. I wish I were in her coven, perhaps I shall be. Round her neck she wears a broad black velvet band probably for a good reason. She said things that would make the hairs of your head stand bolt upright."

Devil, who appears in the guise of a gardener. The subject they discourse upon is, of course, witchiness. "Is it true that you can poke the fire with a stick of dynamite in perfect safety?" Lolly asks. "I used to take my nieces to scientific lectures, and I believe I heard it then. Anyhow, even if it isn't true of dynamite, it's true of women. But they know they are dynamite, and long for the concussion that may justify them. Some may get religion, then they're all right, I expect. But for the others, for so many, what can there be but witchcraft? . . . That's why we become witches: to show our scorn of pretending life's a safe business, to satisfy our passion for adventure."

This concluding dialogue (to which the Prince of Darkness contributes mostly a docilely held tongue) is, I suppose, what made so delicate and puckish a novel a candidate for reissue by the Women's Press.* Its colophon, a vigorously hatched steam iron emitting the slogan "Steaming Ahead," is certainly too melioristic for our darkly fanciful authoress; and, indeed, when I recommended *Lolly Willowes* to a feminist friend she scowled and said, "Of course, that's what men like to tell us. Either marry one of them or become a witch." Let us respectfully construe the word "witch" as "free woman." Freedom, in daily things, is what Lolly Willowes likes about her condition. At the novel's end, the heroine misses a bus and exults in the realization that it does not much matter if she fails to return home that night. Her landlady, Mrs. Leak, herself a witch, will not mind, nobody will mind: "Lovely to be with people who prefer their thoughts to yours, lovely to live at your own sweet will, lovely to sleep out all night!" From the claustral comforts of domestic lovingness she has escaped to an indifferent lover, Satan, and falls asleep in the liberty of "his undesiring and unjudging gaze, his satisfied but profoundly indifferent ownership." Human love—

---

*The Academy Chicago "Cassandra" edition, issued in a different format and with an evidently fortuitous simultaneity, speaks for itself, in the lively introduction by Anita Miller, which concludes: "With a chilling immediacy this book speaks today, as it did in 1925, for women. Not only women like Laura who are incapable of loving men, but for all those who have been 'subdued' into ladyhood, or dwindled into wives. Women were strongly concerned with their status during the first forty years of this century. Now, after a sleep of twenty years, they, like Lolly Willowes, are awake again, seeking for lives of their own."

unnatural, undiabolical love—demands service in return for its ministrations, and not only Lolly in her village solitude but also Jake in his rough dons' chambers renounces this service. Dons and witches alike live consecrated lives apart from that middle terrain, overpopulated by lovers and kin, between private and abstract satisfactions. Both these thoroughly British novels advance—*Jake's Thing* more clumsily and apologetically—the case for asceticism in a world without religion. In the thick of a cultural consensus whose propaganda urges amorous conjunction, they argue for detachment and celibacy, not as an ordeal en route to a good afterlife but as a method (can it be?) of living well now.

Indestructible Elena

THE FLUTE-PLAYER, by D. M. Thomas. 192 pp. Dutton, 1979.

For most American readers, D. M. Thomas came out of nowhere with his astonishing novel *The White Hotel*—an elegantly experimental yet quite warm work whose unhyped best-seller status during much of 1981 represented an authentic triumph of reader discrimination and word of mouth. Now E. P. Dutton has thriftily put a sticker ("The author of THE WHITE HOTEL") on some of its unsold copies of Thomas's previous and largely ignored novel* and with a few ads has launched the book again. *The Flute-Player*, which had its admirers on the first go-round (Doris Grumbach, Iris Murdoch), deserves praise but at this retrospective juncture is of interest chiefly for the light it throws on the later, superior work. The two share a number of features: a female protagonist as patient and giving as Mother Earth, a forthright sensuality mixed with a fine historical feeling for the nightmare moments of modern history, a dreamlike fluidity and quickness in the telling reinforced by frequent description of characters' dreams, and an unusual and exalting concern with paradises and with healing. These last two preoc-

---

*His first. Thomas's second novel, *Birthstone*, has never been published in the United States. *The White Hotel* was his third.

cupations were combined in the final section of *The White Hotel*, which so daringly presented the postwar Palestine of the British Mandate as a heavenly hospital for the dreadful wounds of the Holocaust. The action of *The Flute-Player* also contains glimpses of paradise and many instances of healing, as freedom and oppression rhythmically alternate within an inscrutable and unnamed but on the whole distinctly Soviet state.

Elena, our heroine, is first found, "waiting for the meaning of her life to unroll," as a sculptor's model, with a "flawless, rather enigmatic face" and "equally perfect and unflawed" breasts. The sculptor is carving "her eyes in an expressionless, unpupilled gaze; the nose straight; the mouth firm and unsmiling"—the kind of icon, in short, that, whether met in American coinage or on Russian posters, is meant to provide an ideal image of the state. Elena, like Lara in *Doctor Zhivago*, symbolizes the motherland in her vicissitudes, and she does pose for posters and public statues in the course of her adventures. Her private life, however, surrounds her with neurotics. The man who becomes her first husband is first met a week after his wife has bitten off his foreskin in a rage; Elena takes him into her apartment and gradually reintroduces him to healthy sex. Later, he becomes a religious fanatic of a Dostoevskian sort and demands that she prostitute herself in order to bring him potential converts. Private violence, official torture, unofficial criminality, and war—now distant, now near—hurry the plot from one episode to the next, while intermittences of peace and the characters' prodigious resilience afford glimpses of what might be in a better world:

> The poet could feel, welling up inside him, an astonishing joy. The meaningless moment seemed alone meaningful. The chipped jug containing the sour wine held secrets unknown to Socrates. See, he was tipping the chipped jug and pouring the wine into Elena's chipped cup and some of it was splashing on to her lap! It was wonderful! A moment of utter clarity in which he saw God.

Just so, Lisa, the bedevilled and doomed heroine of *The White Hotel*, has by the Black Sea a moment of "unbearable joy," perceiving in the scent of a pine tree which resurrects her childhood "an endless extent, like an avenue, in which she was still herself, Lisa . . . and when she looked in the opposite direction, towards the unknown future, death, the endless extent beyond death, she was there still."

The Flute-Player is dedicated to the memory of Anna Akhmatova, Osip Mandelstam, Boris Pasternak, and Marina Tsvetaeva; Thomas, a translator of Akhmatova, intends a tribute to that artistic bohemia which, never utterly crushed and always ready to spring into flower, has more than any other segment of Soviet society kept human gaiety and hope of freedom alive. The book wears its allegorical intentions a bit too plainly on its sleeve. Though the poet and the painter are given names (Michael, Peter), they are figures more than personalities; in one especially cloying passage Peter recapitulates what seems to be Sir Kenneth Clark's history *The Nude*, painting by painting, using Elena as the model for Botticelli's Venus and figures from his *Primavera*, as Titian's Venus and Danae, as Coreggio's Antiope, as the nude in Manet's *Déjeuner sur l'herbe*, etc. The opaque, leaden clouds of government overhead are rendered as a palpable pressure, but too much history has been crowded into the range of allusions; there are counterparts of the siege of Leningrad, the Nazi Holocaust, the Berlin Wall, and the postwar West, with its "blankness of freedom . . . this not having anything to push against." Further, the novel suffers from a certain monotony as one change after another in the Kremlinesque halls of power sends the artists in and out of their apartments, to exile and back. In the ups and downs of the indestructible Elena, there is nothing like the propulsive telescopic action of *The White Hotel*, where the epistolary prologue yields to the heroine's erotic poem, the poem to its prose retelling, the retelling to Freud's psychoanalysis of the young lady, this analysis to her later history, her history to the historical horror of Babi Yar, and Babi Yar to a miraculous Palestine—at every shift new perspectives opening thrillingly and a superb suspense maintained. Since Elena, unlike Lisa, is early established as fundamentally a symbol and (like most symbols) a survivor, the main cause for suspense in *The Flute-Player* has to do with its title; Thomas saves his secret for the last page. Elena plays the flute—a hitherto undisclosed skill—and seems to be an acquaintance of a hitherto undeclared "I," the author.

D[onald] M[ichael] Thomas was born in Cornwall in 1935, his

dust jackets tell us, and he was busy lecturing, translating, and writing poetry before becoming a novelist. It is a happy move: he writes with a poet's care, an academic's knowledgeability, and the originality of a thorough unprofessional. The popular success of *The White Hotel*, though deserved, could not have been aimed at. Of his four books of poetry, I have been able to locate only one,* a ten-year-old, and never before checked-out, library copy of *Logan Stone*. These poems show a powerful, even brutal, combinative thrust, intersplicing textures and texts and achieving a jagged effect not smoothed by the inclusion of a number of barely relevant photographs. The wish, realized by the novels, to superimpose the tragically historical upon the intimately personal is shown here by a long erotic sequence involving images of Vietnam and modern war.

> A full moon rising over Finland
> set the radar screens flickering holocaust.
> Your crossed legs' nylon threads'
> rising moonlit field of forces
> unleashes a warhead.

The prototypical superwoman of his fiction is prefigured in "Gretchen":

> Lightning-conductor of tragedy,
> you absorb all suffering, all
> forked energy,
> and remain
> untouched.

Other poems mingle the runic stones of Cornwall and lines of Methodist hymns with glimpses of autobiography; the marked, not unorthodox religious streak in his imagination seems to date from a strong dose of chapel, among men who "would be lost without the cross." These disparate elements fuse better in the novels than in these poems, where the personal glimpses retain an enigmatic, abruptly egoistical intensity and the topical references seem mere

---

*In 1983 Viking published Mr. Thomas's *Selected Poems*, a number of them rather neo-Russian, and others of them homage to Freud.

baubles. Mr. Thomas brings to the art of fiction a plenitude of feeling and ambition, and an ardent, generalizing approach—rubbed off, perhaps, from his Russian studies—like little else in contemporary England or America.

An Introduction to Three Novels by Henry Green
(Living, Party Going, Loving)

IF I SAY that Henry Green taught me how to write it implies that I learned, and it is not a business one learns—unlearns, rather, the premature certainties and used ecstasies unravelling as one goes, with each day new blank paper to confront. Including this blank paper, where reverence gives me pause. For Green, to me, is so good a writer, such a revealer of what English prose fiction can do in this century, that I can launch myself upon this piece of homage and introduction only by falling into some sort of imitation of that liberatingly ingenuous voice, that voice so full of other voices, its own interpolations amid the matchless dialogue twisted and tremulous with a precision that kept the softness of groping, of sensation, of living.

Living is the title of the first novel he chose to keep in print and appraisal of his work must revert to this mysterious word. Elizabeth Bowen, one of the not many who while Green was practicing could see through his conspicuous mannerisms to his rare value, said that his novels "reproduce, as few English novels do, the actual sensations of living." And one of Green's few statements about his own intentions gives us not the gerund but noun, verb, and adjective: "to create 'life' which does not eat, procreate or drink, but which can live in people who are alive." Again, in 1950, as his creative life was coming to its sadly early end, he spoke of fiction "as diffuse and variously interpretable as life itself," and it is this surrender of self, this submersion of opinions and personality in the intensity of witnessing "life itself" with its weave of misapprehension, petty confusions, fitful and skewed communications, and passing but authentic revelations, that strikes us as momentous in Green's example, as heroic even, in the way that great dogmatics are. He is a saint of the mundane, embracing it with all his being. In his last novel, *Doting,* in the course of a trivial conversation (but Green's events are consistently trivial, and therein resides their great, level beauty), two young women have this exchange:

> ". . . D'you sometimes believe that nothing in the whole wide world matters?"
>
> "Oh Ann, but surely simply everything has supreme importance, if it happens."

From recognition of this supreme importance flow Green's infinite subtlety and untiring tenderness. Unlike Waugh, whose set he shared, he never asks us to side with him against a character, and unlike Céline, for whom he surprisingly expressed "tremendous admiration," he never dramatizes his own prodigious acceptance of human incorrigibility. His observations of the world appear as devoid of prejudice and preconception as a child's, and it is as a child—an ideally attentive and unnoticed child—that we seem to be present during the below-stairs exchanges of *Loving* and the factory scenes of *Living.* These maidservants and workmen are seen with more than egalitarian generosity; they loom as figures of a luminous, simplifying grandeur:

> She folded the shutters back into the wall. And Edith looked out on the morning, the soft bright morning that struck her dazzled dazzling eyes.

> He walked over nearer to where Craigan worked. This man scooped gently at great shape cut down in black sand in great iron box. He was grimed with the black sand.

Of the child Green was we learn a great deal in his cunningly relaxed "interim autobiography," *Pack My Bag,* written in 1938–39, under the shadow of the coming war, in which he expected to be killed. "That is my excuse, that we who may not have time to write anything else must do what we now can. If we have no time to chew another book over we must turn to what comes first to mind and that must be how one changed from boy to man, how one lived, things and people and one's attitude." His first sentence tells us he "was born a mouthbreather with a silver spoon in 1905." He does not in this memoir give his true name, Henry Vincent Yorke. Kinsmen of the earls of Hardwick, the Yorkes owned a Birmingham company, H. Pontifex & Sons, which manufactured distillery equipment. The family home was within hearing of the bells of Tewkesbury Abbey, "in soft lands and climate influenced by the Severn." Henry, the third son, grew up among servants, whom he describes much more vividly than he does his parents. "We were well brought up and saw our parents twice a day, that is to say my father worked in London through the week and we only saw him at weekends." He was sent away to school before he was seven; in an interview with the New York *Herald Tribune* he put it, "Children in my circumstances are sent away to boarding school. I went at six and three quarters and did not stop until I was twenty-two, by which time I was at Oxford, but the holidays were all fishing. And then there was billiards." His account of his school-days is as harrowing as anything in Orwell: "Home seemed a heaven and that we were cast out. . . ." "A private school is a fascist state and so are public schools. Their corporate doctrines teach one ugly sides and it is when one has forgotten to be as they taught that the experience begins to be worthwhile." Green as a boy was fat, "so fat my parents had had the doctor in and the headmaster did the same as soon as he saw me. I became an advertisement for their cooking and would be beckoned up to be examined by inspecting parents, to be thumped and fingered like fat stock at a show." And precocious, though not so satisfactorily so as his brother: "But they had great hopes and took me to see my brother's name in large gold letters on the scholarship board. Everything was lovely until they found I was not even up to the standard of these days, and then the old tyrant the headmaster did not speak to me for seven months as though I had stolen from him."

During World War I his family took wounded officers into their manor house, and young Green took this opportunity "to learn the half-tones of class," to feel at his feet "those narrow, deep and echoing gulfs which must be bridged." All the propaganda and paradox of that era's social reality are dismissed in a few sentences, too calm to be cruel:

In the war people in our walk of life entertained all sorts and conditions of men with a view to self-preservation, to keep the privileges we set such store by, and which are illusory, after those to whom we were kind had won the war for us. That is not to say the privileged did not fight, we did, but there were too few of us to win.

The second sentence, so equably and comically giving the privileged minority its due, is more remarkable, and more characteristic, than the first thought, which any passably enlightened social conscience could have framed if not phrased with such odd melody— the pietistic "and which are illusory" leaping in like another voice. Green in his childhood had imbibed the pugnacious piety of the public schools but by the time of his older brother Philip's death, still during the war, he could observe that the burial service was "the best the Church can do, the Church which seeks to share in all those few moments when we stand alone, at birth, in marriage, and at death."

One looks in vain for very much in *Pack My Bag* to explain how Green early became such an intensely original writer. In his last year at Eton he and some friends were allowed to form a Society of Arts. "This point is a watershed, after this there is no turning back. I determined to be a writer, the diary I began to keep with this in view was full of loud shouts about it, and a *nom de plume* was chosen, of all names Henry Michaelis." He cites three examples of youthful prose: he admits that the "second shows command of words in the way these are quite successfully repeated" (like Hemingway, Green had no fear of repeated words and indeed was an addict of their music), but condemns the first and third as "yells about self" and goes on to observe, "Any account of adolescence is necessarily a study of the fatuous." Of the Society of Arts: "All I know is it gave me confidence even if there was nothing in it so that, like everyone else, I began to write a novel." Unlike almost everyone else, he finished his while still at Oxford and had it accepted, by Dent. This first novel, *Blindness*, is just now being reprinted a half-century after its appearance in 1926. Green does not name it in his memoir, or describe it, or describe the gratification of having it published. He does, acridly, describe the mode of life in which the novel was pushed through to completion:

> I was usually put to bed about two in the morning to be called at mid-day with an orange and a brandy and soda. . . . I felt extremely ill and every day went alone to a cinema after which I tried to write. The novel was almost finished and it became the last foothold to write just one more page a day, the last line of defence because I was miserable in fits and starts and felt insane.

With that same dogged dedication he was to compose the rest of his novels, while fully employed in the factory of which he was to become managing director. "Going home it would be dark again and I would be tired. But after no more than thirty minutes in a chair I was ready for hard work again." He tells us, "I write books but I am not proud of this any more than anyone is of their nails growing." Literature is an "over-blown trumpet" and the literary influences upon him are scarcely mentioned. Before Oxford he was sent to France for a summer to perfect his French, and the only major writer he describes himself reading is Proust:

> the last volumes of *A la Recherche du Temps Perdu* were coming out and anyone who knew French knew his Proust. Though I am not a Jew a don compared me to Swann. This gave me great pleasure. . . .

Green's father had been an amateur connoisseur of country dialect, and it is the spoken words of the Birmingham factory workers that excite Green to quotation. Common speech, "unadulterated by literature as it is," "simple words so well chosen and arranged, so direct a communication they made one silly with laughing," became the aesthetic standard for this Swann turned foundryman: "I had been an idler who had at last found something to occupy his mind and hands." Here, amid working men and women, the memoirist, "changed from boy to man," found the mighty subject of *Living.*

Living was published in 1929, when Green was only twenty-four. It is of his books the most redolent of ambition. Its canvas is wide, its cast large, its design intricate, its tone epic and celebrative.

The author's love for his proletarian characters brims in these pages and might cloy but for the tart comedy of their talk, heard with the startling fidelity that mistakenly is considered a mere passive accomplishment—for to write how people talk one must know how they think, and a definite psychology and sociology inform Green's articulations on behalf of others.

In this novel his mature style is invented and employed with a vengeance. Never again will there be so many dropped articles and nounless sentences. His attempt is the customary avant-garde one, to "make it new," in Pound's phrase, to redeem language from the unfelt smoothness of usage. John Russell, in his fine book *Henry Green: Nine Novels and an Unpacked Bag* (1960), speaks of "the almost cumbersome effect of forcing things, already concrete, onto the page more concretely." This is good but does not prepare us for the flowing, effortless effect of Green's individual syntax, once we are attuned. His style's source, strange to say, or at least the source of its innovative courage, is Arabic, as transmuted to English by Charles M. Doughty in his *Travels in Arabia Deserta* (1888). Doughty's style originated, he wrote to his biographer, in "my dislike of the Victorian English; and I wished to show, and I thought I might be able to show, that there was something else." Arabic, as it was absorbed by Doughty on his travels, was a language of the ear, spoken by illiterates, and it is the alogical linkages of spoken language, with its constantly refreshed concreteness, that inform such sentences from *Arabia Deserta* as:

> Never combed by her rude master, but all shining beautiful and gentle of herself, she seemed a darling life upon that savage soil not worthy of her gracious pasterns.

> No sweet chittering of birds greets the coming of the desert light, besides man there is no voice in this waste drought.

Similar sentences by Green, their bold phrases roped together by a slack and flexible grammar, can be found everywhere in his work. Of course, many writers of the generation preceding Green's, Joyce and Virginia Woolf foremost, also loosened grammar to tighten subjective connections; but the popular formula "stream of consciousness" does not fit Green's style, with its mix of perception and reflection, and its increasingly minor component of interior monologue. Amid his human scenes he hovers more than dives, yet conveys quite well a sense of depth and spaces, and dares bursts of poetic exclaiming that, far from quaint, deliver us exactly into the rub of things. His style in *Living* well suits, and has been adjusted to, his craggy, sullen, yet lyrical industrial milieu. His terrain here is close to D. H. Lawrence's, with the difference that whereas Lawrence escaped from the working class, Green escaped into it, finding there a purpose and gaiety hitherto lacking from his life. His feat of equilibrium in *Living* was to show lives whose impoverishment he fully recognized as nevertheless sites of comedy, excitement, complex feeling, and beauty.

Party Going, though it takes place in less time—four hours—than any other novel, took him the longest time to write, from 1931 to 1938. It in a sense reverses the social proportions of *Living:* the well-to-do move into the foreground, and the working people become a choral mass, a background crowd in the fog. Yet the same human grasping after illusions and love is drawn, with the same tolerant omniscience. Perhaps because of its extended period of composition, the style changes, beginning with the dropped articles and enigmatic blunt motions of *Living* and becoming, after the entrance at midpoint of Amabel, rather luxuriant, even Faulknerian in some hymning moods. The neurotic anxieties and erotic maneuvering of a few conspicuously spoiled, silly young rich waiting for a train to take them away would not seem a momentous topic, or an urgent one, but Green, so long meditating these tiny events, magnifies and patterns them into a paradigm of life, life surrounded by a fog of death and threatened Departures. In the inflamed scale of those transitory hotel rooms a woman's taking a bath becomes a divine event, which we, unlike Actaeon, may witness without being torn to pieces.

  As she went over herself with her towel it was plain that she loved her own shape and skin. When she dried her breasts she wiped them with as much care as she would puppies after she had given them their bath, smiling all the time. But her stomach she wiped unsmiling upwards to make it thin. When she came to dry her legs she hissed like grooms do. And as she got herself dry that steam began to go off the mirror walls so that as she got white again more and more of herself began to be reflected.

A year after *Party Going*, Green published *Pack My Bag*. During World War II he joined the Auxiliary Fire Service, as it were descending into that struggling crowd the partygoers see from their hotel windows. This, his second immersion in the proletariat, immediately produced the, for me, least enchanting of his novels, *Caught*, written between 1940 and 1942. But *Caught* was followed, in 1945, by Green's best-known and possibly best novel, *Loving*. This master of the implied here implies the vast reality of war a small ocean away; the scene of *Loving* is an Irish castle staffed by mostly British servants who, in echo of the rumored conflict raging in Europe, conduct their own raids upon one another's provinces of authority, and in the absence of the castle's owners, the Tennants, create a cozy anarchy of pilfering, gossip, giddiness, and love. The novel is opulent in its display of accents, imagery, and emotions; the resplendent peacock has replaced as dominant symbol the dingy sparrows of *Living* and the fogbound pigeons of *Party Going*. *Loving* shares with these two others not only a gerundive title and an ambiguous ending but a distinctly double stage: upper-class and lower-class characters perform separately, though, in this anachronistic bastion in sullen neutral Ireland, below-stairs overflows and fills the castle from library to ballroom.

In Green's next two novels, *Back* and *Concluding*, the social gap has been lost sight of, and in his last two, *Nothing* and *Doting*, the author remains entirely on one side of it, with the *Party Going* class of people, now grown middle-aged. Yet the wit and poetry, the comedy and truth of these final two novels show so little slackening of powers (though perhaps a more restricted channeling of them) that Green's abrupt and lasting silence comes as a puzzle: he published nothing after 1952, though he lived until 1973, to the age of sixty-eight.* These twenty-two mute years mark perhaps a consummate artist's demand of perfection or nothing from himself, or could signify a more personal withdrawal into the despair that always fringed his pellucid world. A vision so clear can be withering; it takes great natural health to sustain a life without illusions. In any case, his precocious career is framed by this refusal or inability so that his nine novels seem a given light, like the poems of Rilke, that flooded through a momentarily open lens.

I have seen a reader of *Loving* cry at the end, not understanding why, for the book had been so funny that she had kept reading parts of it aloud. She fulfilled thereby the contract that Green elsewhere** draws up between author and reader: "Prose should be a long intimacy between strangers with no direct appeal to what both may have known. It should slowly appeal to feelings unexpressed, it should in the end draw tears out of the stone. . . ." This intimacy is my one connection with Green. He was famously shy of public-

---

*In his 1958 *Paris Review* interview, Green mentioned to Terry Southern "a very funny 3-act play" and a work of non-fiction, *London and Fire, 1940*, in progress. In 1963, when Green was in his late fifties, a young American admirer called Peter Guralnick wrote him a fan letter and was invited to visit the author in his handsome Belgravia home. According to an account Guralnick published in The Boston *Phoenix* in 1978, Green told him, "I'm ill, that's why I can't write (though I do still but don't print it)." He claimed, however, to be dictating a sequel to *Pack My Bag,* whose title he could not remember though he could quote the first sentence. He assured his young auditor that he had entirely forgotten all of his books, and abruptly boasted, "It's marvelous not to publish. I never made any money out of it anyway; it's so funny to confound the buggers." Who the buggers were is not quite clear; the most mysterious of his utterances upon his non-productivity that day was: "As you get older, you think increasingly of your readers. Pornography would be the simplest, because everyone's interested in that. But you get in trouble." In Guralnick's eyes, Green was a courteous but damaged apparition: "The bristle of his neck and chin was white, his neutral smile gap-toothed, and while he maintained a proudly aquiline profile, he had about him the ruined air of a man who shuffles when he walks and always has to 'pee,' as he frequently complained that he did." Yet he spoke of winning the Nobel Prize, and to Guralnick "his drinking, his chain-smoking, his aura of physical weariness only heightened the romantic, self-destructive image I constructed for him." To this twenty-year-old, Green appeared "simply a great man, a bit down on his creative luck." See also page 327. Green's decay as seen by Anthony Powell.

**In *Pack My Bag,* page 88.

ity, and was known by few outside his "set" and his factory. He was a successful businessman who wrote, and in this he resembled Wallace Stevens; they did no business on Grub Street, and whatever sellouts they found necessary were outside the realm of art. They wrote from the purest of motives: to make something. In equability of temperament and what Elizabeth Bowen called "straight, humanistic touch," Green suggests Defoe, Queneau, and the John O'Hara of the short stories. W. H. Auden once called him the finest living English novelist. But no need exists to set up a competition; his writing generation—but for Graham Greene and V. S. Pritchett—has passed on, and his novels are sufficiently unlike any others, sufficiently assured in their perilous, luminous fullness, to warrant the epithet "incomparable." And they have become, with time, photographs of a vanished England. Their substantive content, in what can be seen and heard by a man alive in a place and time, is as rich as their formal design is intricate, rounded, and pleasing. They are among the most *contemplated* novels of an age, not long ago, when novel-writing came easy, because "simply everything has supreme importance, if it happens."

Green's human qualities—his love of work and laughter; his absolute empathy; his sense of splendor amid loss, of vitality within weakness—make him a precious witness to any age. No stranger to the macabre and the vicious, he glorifies the petty virtues bred of human interdependence. With upper-class obliquity he champions the demotic in language and in everything. His novels, as Horace prescribed, give pleasure and instruct; moreover, they give that impression, of an irreducible density and a self-possessed rhythm, that belongs to reality and its most ardent imitations in art. They live, in short, and like all living feed on air, on the invisible; the spaces between the words are warm, and the strangeness is mysteriously exact, the strangeness of the vital.

Green Green

BLINDNESS, by Henry Green. 207 pp. Viking, 1978.

Henry Green began his first novel while a schoolboy of seventeen at Eton. Anthony Powell, who had long known Green as Henry Yorke, recalls in his memoir *Infants of the Spring*, "He had begun writing a novel at Eton, its nature unrevealed, though the fact admitted; an undertaking not regarded over seriously by relations and friends." However lightly regarded by his relations and friends, and however much slowed by Green's addiction, as confessed in his own memoir, *Pack My Bag*, to both alcohol and the cinema, the project was carried through to completion at Oxford and to publication, by Dent, in 1926. As even the diffident Powell, who tends to view his old friend's literary accomplishments with a skeptical politeness, has to admit, "a published novel could not altogether be laughed off." *Blindness*, as the book was called, came out in a small edition and was reprinted in 1932 but not thereafter. Why not? Green left Oxford without a degree—"I had taken English as my school and that meant learning Anglo-Saxon. This I found I could not do and for the rest discovered that literature is not a subject to write essays about"—and went to work in his father's factory in Birmingham. In 1929, he published *Living*. Possibly Green felt that this second novel began his mature work and rendered the first effort an embarrassment; *Pack My Bag* cites a passage from *Blindness* as an example of bad writing.* Also, his publisher had become Leonard and Virginia Woolf's Hogarth Press, and small incentive presumably existed for arranging with Dent for a new edition of *Blindness* as long as Green was producing, every other year or so, the novels that make him one of the most piquant and original English writers

---

*"The air began to get rid of the heaviness, and so became fresher as the dew soaked the grass. A blackbird thought aloud of bed, and was followed by another and yet another. The sun was flooding the sky in waves of colour while he grew redder and redder in the west, the trees were a red gold too where he caught them. The sky was enjoying herself after the boredom of being blue all day. She was putting on and rejecting yellow for gold, gold for red, then red for deeper reds, while the blue that lay overhead was green."

not only of his generation but of the century. Green-lovers (Chlorophiles, one might say) enamored of these works have had to search out *Blindness* in such archives as the British Museum or else content themselves with descriptions of the novel in scholarly treatises. In 1952, Green, a mere forty-seven, published what turned out to be his last novel, *Doting*. In the following two decades, when his unexpected silence (like Salinger's) afforded his reputation a space for further growing and retrospective enhancement, his long-buried first novel would have been welcome. But not until now, five years after Green's death, is *Blindness* again available, published in this country by Viking in a presentable if not entirely elegant edition. (The English edition published by Hogarth a year ago is distinctly prettier, and Viking has coped with some exigency by setting a number of lines of the text in a disturbingly different typeface. Book production, as the electronic gnomes move in, gets curiouser and curiouser.)

An anonymous reviewer of the original edition of *Blindness* summed up its plot succinctly: "An English schoolboy of seventeen, on the verge of living, is totally blinded in a railway accident." But, while the young author was himself on the verge of living—leaving Oxford, joining the working class, and writing *Living*—this first novel is real Green: proto- rather than pre-Green. Though relatively clumsy and uneven, and not as assertively mannered as the subsequent books, it contains abundant quantities not only of Green's characteristic poetry but, more remarkably, of his piercing empathy and effortless social range. Precocity, common to musicians and mathematicians, and not unknown to painters and poets, is rare in that art most dependent upon human experience, fiction. One of the fascinations of *Blindness* is to observe the schoolboy author move outward from innocent autobiography into a virtuose plurality of points of view. The book begins with a schoolboy's diary, no doubt much like the one that in *Pack My Bag* Green admits to having kept: "I determined to be a writer, the diary I began to keep with this in view was full of loud shouts about it." The hero of *Blindness*, John Haye, writes:

If only I could write! But I think I improve. Those terrible, involved sentences of mine are my undoing.

Fox was pleased at my admiring Carlyle.

Anthony Powell remembers of his friend Yorke that "he had a passion for Carlyle (an author tolerable to myself only in small doses), and (a taste I have never acquired) Doughty's *Arabia Deserta;* both indicating a congenial leaning towards obscure diction." John Haye is secretary to the Noat Art Society, as Yorke was of the Eton Society of Arts. He likes Carlyle. He thinks that "the most beautiful letter ever written is undoubtedly that of Charlotte Brontë's on her sister Emily's death." His diary, however, holds as well as literary opinions a great deal of unwittingly self-incriminatory schoolboy behavior—pranks on disliked classmates, mocking forays into the plebeian town nearby, an affected bit of costume meant to make himself conspicuous:

> Have bought the most gorgeous sun hat for a horse in straw for sixpence, and have painted it in concentric rings. . . . The hat is a masterpiece, and being so has, of course, started a violent controversy. Those who consider it merely bounderism, and those who think it amusing, talk very seriously together and stop when I approach, while the faithful come in occasionally to tell me what the others have said.

Just before his diary is broken off, John Haye turns his admiration to Dostoevski's *Crime and Punishment:* "What a force books are! This is like dynamite."

As he is sitting in the train going home from school, John Haye is blinded and disfigured. The incident, like many in the book, comes to us secondhand, in a letter from one school friend to another: "The train was somewhere between Stroud and Gloucester, and was just going to enter a cutting. A small boy was sitting on the fence by the line and threw a big stone at the train. John must have been looking through the window at the time, for the broken glass caught him full, cut great furrows in his face, and both his eyes are blind for good. Isn't it dreadful?" Having just admired, in his alter ego's diary, a novel that "cuts one open, tragedy after tragedy, like a chariot with knives on the wheels," the young author gashes his young hero's face at its most vulnerable part—the eyes, symbols of sensitivity and sexuality—and plunges him into nightmare. And makes it credible. The book successfully meets the primary challenge it sets itself: to convey the sensations of blindness. At first it is mixed with pain, "so that he was like a blind worm in a fire, squirming, squirming to get out." Worse than blind, he is eyeless, and is told so with a harrowing briskness:

> He felt with his hand, but the bandages were too tight. He remembered that men with amputated legs could still waggle the toes which by that time were in the dustbin. He squinted, and was sure that his eyes were there.
> "Nurse, have I any eyes?"
> "How do you mean? No, I am afraid they were both taken out, they had to be."

As his convalescence progresses, and "it was now so ordinary to be blind," he learns to listen: "Every wind was different, and as he listened to their coming and to their going, there was rhythm in their play. In the fields, beyond where the trees could be, a man cracked his whip, and a cow lowed. The long grass copied the trees with a tiny dry rustling." And as he attempts to participate in the world again and help a female servant move a heavy lily pot, a world of sensuous touches impinges maddeningly:

> Then, as he was groping forward again, the lily poked gently into his face, trying to tickle him, and shuddering, he pushed the thing away. He leant forward further to where he felt her presence and the stand. Her breath burned in his face for a moment and bathing in her nearness he leant further forward still, in the hopes of finding her, but she dropped his hand and it fell on the slick edges of the pot in which the lily grew. Despair was coming over him again, it was too awkward, this pursuit of her under a lily, when all at once her arm mysteriously came up over his mouth, glowing and cool at the same time, and the scent was immediately stronger, tangible almost, so that he wanted to bite it.

But we are not immersed in John Haye's blindness, as we were in his diary. The visual world around him—whose presiding deity, the sun, is evoked on nearly every page—persists, described in a kind of exultation by an author who now manifests powers and a range far beyond those of his hero. John Haye's blindness is seen from the outside, as not only a private but a social event, affecting the lives of those close to him—foremost, that of his guardian and stepmother, Emily Haye. The master novelist emerges from the fledgling writer in the early scene wherein this woman, "red with forty years reckless exposure to the sun," an avid gardener and a meddler in village affairs from her eminence as hostess of the estate called Barwood, talks to John and introduces another stream of consciousness into the book. To his agonized, fitful comprehension of his blindness is added her own anxious concern: "Her feelings had betrayed her. The great thing was to keep his mind off. One must go on talking, and it was so hard not to harp on it. A silence would be so terrible. There was always her [John's true mother, who died when he was born] between them." Difficult servants, a senile dog, the local Nursing Association, poor village-church attendance, the flourishing garden, the happier past, the need to answer the sympathy letters she has received, the parson's wife's need to borrow fifty teacups—all these worries mingle with her fretful worry for the boy ("They must find some occupation for the boy, he could not be left there rankling. Making fancy baskets, or pen-wipers, all those things blinded soldiers did, something to do"). Having accomplished and decided nothing, she finally sinks gratefully into one of Green's favorite conditions, the awareness of nothing. "She rubbed her face slowly in her hands, when she stopped it was redder still. Then she sat for some time looking at nothing at all, thinking of nothing at all. The specks kept on rising in the sunlight." Harassed and disarmed by tragedy though she is, and without any feeling for her stepson stronger than responsibility for him, Emily Haye stirs herself and in the course of the novel does the necessary selfless thing—she sells her beloved Barwood and moves the blind would-be writer to London, as he requests. Her thoughts orbit absurdly, yet she homes in on the right course; in her distracted decency, she is the first Henry Green character. She is a stepmother, perhaps because Green at that tender age could gaze at maternity only through some squint of untruth, or because the budding artist in him insisted on being inventive. In *Pack My Bag*, he disarmingly tells how he acquired "the sense to bring others in when I wrote about myself in order to blame as much as possible on others."

Green brings in others, in *Blindness*, besides the curiously distanced mother-figure: a servant population anticipatory of *Loving*, a grim yet somehow sexual nurse, and, most elaborately, the defrocked Reverend Entwhistle and his daughter Joan, whom the enamored John insists on calling June. (This sort of punning name-play, which in *Concluding* gives all the girls names beginning with "M" and in *Caught* calls two London Fire Brigade volunteers Pye and Roe, is not Green's most winning trick.) In a long section called, too archly, "Picture Postcardism," Green overwrites with a Lawrentian vengeance, and enshrines in a lush wealth of nature imagery a monstrously shabby situation: a teen-aged girl is taking care of her alcoholic, almost lunatic father, a defrocked minister. Mrs. Entwhistle has died, having confessed on her deathbed to an affair with the postman. Joan has been scarred by a piece of bottle thrown by her father, in mild echo of the scars—"His face, that awful face," she thinks—John incurred in the railway accident. The attempt of these two maimed young people to surmount the intellectual and class differences between them makes an uncomfortable idyll, shot through with moments of beauty and fumbling tenderness. Joan is vivid in her sly masochism; during a summer storm, her thoughts run, "Daylight, the sky fought. Darkness and rain. Sheet lightning never hurt anything, but how wonderful to be as afraid as this." Can it be that this same psychology is meant to be filtering onto the page such outrageously naïve examples of the pathetic fallacy as "The sun, who was getting very red, played at painting long shadows in the grass" and "The sky was enjoying herself after the boredom of being blue all day"? If so, the attempt seems labored. Green was always a poet of nature, especially of our airy companions on earth, the birds; they play flitting, cooing chorus to book after book. But here the tapestry of birds, flowers, and small animals is offered as a substitute for the necessary portrait of a girl. John Haye's venture at heterosexual conquest takes place in the constrained atmosphere conjured up by Anthony Powell when he remembers, of a famous Oxford tutor, "So far as sex was concerned, when I first knew him, [Maurice]

Bowra always talked as if homosexuality was the natural condition of an intelligent man . . . [He] would tease friends like Yorke and me for being 'heterosexual.' " Intuitive and loving as he is, the probably virgin author of *Blindness* seems less at ease with Joan/ June than in the whining company of her father, who genuinely believes that he is a genius, that he has cancer, and that gin does him good.

> She locks up the bottle in the cupboard, slips the key inside her dress, and begins to open the sardines. He is almost in tears, "insulted, by a girl, my daughter. When it was for the good of my health, as I was ill."

Sadly, this sounds rather like Henry Yorke when Powell last saw him, in the late 1950s:

> He began to speak excitedly. He was not in very good shape. . . . In the end he was almost in tears of emotion. "I'm not well," he said. "People say it's drink. It's not that. I'm not well. I think I'm going to die."

The acute, clairvoyant sensibility of Henry Green also had something eerie, morbid, and macabre about it—as many anecdotes about him testify. Disease is present in his works not only in the specific manifestations that rather comically carry off characters but also in the underlying weakness and, as it were, incurability of the human condition. He saw us, all tenderly, in a desperate Pascalian light. *Blindness,* an astoundingly sophisticated and compassionate work for an undergraduate to have produced, is yet less cunning than the later books, and bares some preoccupations that his fully developed, highly oblique art was to conceal:

First, a catastrophe occupies the center of *Blindness* rather than haunts the edges. Although he once told an interviewer (Harvey Breit, in 1950) that "the true life has nothing to do with sudden death and great tragedy," he was himself catastrophe-minded—for instance, he wrote *Pack My Bag* in confidence that he would be killed in the coming war: "Surely it would be asking much to pretend one had a chance to live." His specific sensitivity to life itself, to the local (cosmically speaking) phenomena of living, carried with it an acute awareness of that which is not life, and which threatens it. In *Blindness*, a rabbit is observed "feeding quietly, trembling at being alive," and John Haye, touching his own scars, finds them "smooth varnished things unlike the clinging life of his skin." The nervous skin of sensation just this side of darkness is where Green's writing lives.

Second, this youthful novel, in its schematic subdivisions (the three main sections are titled "Caterpillar," "Chrysalis," and "Butterfly") and its overt virtuosity, declares a formal ambitiousness, and an allegiance to the modernistic tradition of which Joyce is the epitome. The influence of Virginia Woolf can be felt in the dramatically varied interior monologues, and that of Proust— whom Green admired but little resembled—in the mixture of nature lyricism and wry psychology. But from the start Green was aiming, under cover of a limpid realism, at a static perfection that could be dissected and charted, as indeed it has been by a number of critics, mostly American; in this formalism Green, who was something of a Francophile and whose father was half-Dutch, is rather un-English.

Third, a religious vein almost invisible in the subsequent novels here exists, though thinly, on the surface. John Haye notes in his diary, "Mamma tonight on religion. What effect it had, and how far it went, at Noat? They are effectively stifling mine." It is not so stifled, however, that he does not respond, a few pages later in his diary, to Dostoevski: "What an amazing man he was, with his epileptic fits which were much the same as visions really." In the course of the book, the natural world, and especially that old divinity the sun, is felt with a pantheistic intensity, and the religious musings of both Mrs. Haye and Reverend Entwhistle are taken serious note of. Most surprisingly, and perhaps not very convincingly, John Haye himself, at the end of the novel, when their move to the city has only revealed his blindness as even more of a handicap than it was in rural isolation, experiences a Dostoevskian fit:

> He was rising through the mist, blown on a gust of love, lifting up, straining at a white light that he would bathe in. He half rose.
> "John!" [His stepmother is calling.]

And when he bathed there he would know all, why he was blind, why life had been so to him. He was nearer. To rise on this love, how wonderful to rise on this love. He was near now.

"John!!"

A ladder, bring a ladder. In his ears his own voice cried loudly, and a deeper blindness closed in upon him.

The Greek word for "ladder," John Russell points out, is "*klimax.*" After this climax—prefiguring all the milder, more secular ecstasies with which Green is to end his other novels—we are to believe that John Haye is ready to become a writer. Though this seems doubtful, we do believe that in the course of this first novel we have seen a real writer stretch his wings.

Through the Mid-Life Crisis with James Boswell, Esq.

BOSWELL, LAIRD OF AUCHINLECK, 1778–1782, edited by Joseph W. Reed and Frederick A. Pottle. 570 pp. McGraw-Hill, 1977.

The tenth volume of the so-called reading edition of the Boswell journals presents, all five hundred seventy pages and forty-one ounces of it, a façade of estimable solidity that yet eludes our gaze like the "visage incompos'd" of Milton's personified Chaos. We have here a piece of publishing and a piece of scholarship, a writing experience and a reading experience, the levels sliding one behind the other as our admiration fluctuates and our attention strains.

The writing experience occurred, as stated in the title, between 1778 and 1782 and belonged to James Boswell, Scots lawyer, husband, drunkard, libertine, celebrity-chaser, father, first son to the Laird of Auchinleck and prospective inheritor of the large Ayrshire estate of that name, but as of now, approaching and achieving the age of forty, discontented, "making no considerable figure in any way," living beyond his means, desultorily practicing law in Edinburgh with indifferent success, sending down to the *London Magazine* every month an essay in a series called "The Hypochondriack" but otherwise little advancing the literary career begun a decade earlier with his celebrated account of Corsica and its rebel chieftain Pasquale di Paoli. Boswell's classic chronicles of Dr. Samuel Johnson (*Journal of a Tour to the Hebrides,* 1785; *The Life of Samuel Johnson L.L.D.,* 1791) are hidden in his murky future as he gloomily, erratically passes his days dictating law, attending the Edinburgh Court of Session, staying home to nurse his many physical complaints, reading sermons to assuage his melancholy terrors, ineffectually seeking political patronage and prestige, drearily hobnobbing with the other local gentry, paying dutiful court to his ailing and surly father, hearing his children say their divine lessons, making love to his wife (an event noted with the Greek letter π, for "pleasure"), and betraying her with a succession of obliquely noted and often inked-out doxies and "Madames," one of whom earns the footnote "Unidentified. Probably no better than she should have been." He rehearses his son Alexander in "the history of the lairds of Auchinleck, that he may hold the family in some degree sacred." He entertains his brothers—John, who is "disturb'd with dreary fits / Of sullen madness," and David, who has an "inanimate appearance . . . I suppose from long habits of living in restraint among the Spaniards." James vows to drink moderately, drinks immoderately, spends the next day in bed, and keeps his journal. Why did Boswell keep, with a faithfulness that rarely flags, this running inventory of so many days when there was, as he says, "nothing particular to mark"? The London journal that inaugurated his ephemeristic habit in 1762, and the accounts of his travels in Holland, Germany, Switzerland, Italy, Corsica, and France which follow, were records of adventures, forays by a young Scot determined to make an impression on the world. There was a practical side to this endless self-memorializing: the Corsican journals had already served, as Boswell's notes on his tour of the Hebrides in 1773 with Dr. Johnson would serve, to make a book. And a thousand London jottings would feed into the great biography that constitutes Boswell's immortality. More generally, he used the journals as writing exercise. The first volume of them to be published in this century, the best-selling *London Journal,* happened to be the most studied, with the most thoroughly worked-out vignettes and dialogues; it was found "written throughout neatly and almost as legibly as a printed book" and—unlike *Laird of Auchinleck,* where clumps of pages were torn out by Boswell or his nervous heirs—wholly unmutilated. This first journal, which Boswell in his northern boredom sometimes takes out and rereads, was intended by the youthful writer to be a polished work of literary merit. His method of journal-keeping is to make immediate notes and then at some days' remove develop a batch of them into a sequence with some qualities of narrative suspense and liveliness. Relatively few episodes in this four-year installment receive rounded Boswellian treatment: his brief conversations with King George III in May of 1781 are set down in royal style, and the return of his brother David from Spain in the late spring of 1780 dramatically lights up the stagnant provincial scene. But many of his jottings, especially during his hectic visits to his beloved London, remain unorganized, and many a day in Scotland ("A wet dull day. No company came") gets little more notice than its number on the calendar. Sometimes the very haste of notation creates a Joycean density:

> WEDNESDAY 27 MARCH. George Preston with us morning. Maclaurin called. Had him to dine. Spoke of being Under-Secretary. His infidelity disagreeable. Went to Baron Gordon's, whist. Lost, was uneasy. Spoke of joy on wife's recovery. He laughed *incredulus.* Disliked him. Felt myself very young.

But such modernity of effect is inadvertent; when Boswell sits down to pen his monthly "Hypochondriack," his prose turns pompous and ornate.

"Why keep a journal of so 'weary a life'?" he asks, having forgotten his boast of a year and a half earlier that "I have certainly much more of *myself* thus preserved than most people have." The rock-bottom motive of his journal-keeping seems religious: to preserve himself, to stave off the dismal, though complacent, nihilism of old Lord Covington, who "said when one looked back on life, it was just a chaos of nothing." Not mere self-memorializing—self-scrutiny, too. Boswell in his fashion is a pious man, a Calvinist introvert who in his youth briefly converted to Roman Catholicism and who regrets he is "not Church of England." Position and breeding bind him to the Church of Scotland, with its "irreverent form" and grindingly long sermons: "I regretted living in a Presbyterian country." But the dour "dreariness of Presbyterianism" penetrates his bones, and the Protestant habit of introspection, rooted in the Calvinist anxiety concerning divine election, forms a main fibre of these pages. With the lucid dispassion of a recording angel he watches his own rise and fall, his vows and lapses, his drunkenness and lasciviousness; he constantly takes his own spiritual temperature. "My mind was sound enough, and though I had no high felicity, I was not at all unhappy. But I had nothing elevated about me either of my present or future state, as I have had in warmer and younger days." As inevitably as his gonorrhea recurs, gloom surges through the level marshes of his life. "I was so sunk today that I had scarcely any thought." "Got up in sad hypochondria. . . . Was quite in despair. Could not see any good purpose in human life." Reading in Lord Monboddo's *Ancient Metaphysics* of "an universal Necessity" that makes mock of our "delusive feeling of Liberty," Boswell is stunned: "I was shocked by such a notion and sunk into dreadful melancholy, so that I went out to the wood and groaned." In the second half of *Laird of Auchinleck*, his life begins to pick up: he becomes politically engaged, he begins to rework his journal on the tour of the Hebrides, he stops drinking, he becomes "very different from the dreary metaphysical wretch that I had been!" Yet happiness so closely watched is cramped from rising very high. "I was insipid but not unhappy." "Took the Sacrament, but without fervour." "Was happy, though not exquisitely." "An easy, cheerful day. But I had no high relish of life." Boswell comes across another journal, kept by a man, John Bogle, whose path to ruin was straight and smooth:

> He had absolutely died of intemperance and dissolute conduct of every kind. Yet he had for some time kept a regular diary of his life and account of his expenses; and in that diary his acts of profligacy were recorded in plain terms, and his folly and vanity set down, while at the same time there were several reflections on his own insignificancy and on the unhappiness of life, which I excerpted. Reading this journal made me uneasy to think of my own. It is preserving evidence against oneself. . . .

The momentary conclusion Boswell draws is that henceforth, for the sake of his children, he "must not be so plain"; but plain honesty was in his religious nature, and is the ethical genius of his journalism. "I do not recollect having had any other valuable principle impressed upon me by my father except a strict regard to truth, which he impressed upon my mind by a hearty beating at an early age. . . ." Often in these journals when he cannot remember the exact expression used in a reported conversation he leaves it blank. A feature of his published books puzzling to his own time but congenial to ours is that he was not afraid to make himself appear, in contrast to Johnson, foolish. To the unseen reader of these private journals, he is not afraid to confess himself contemptible.

These eighteenth-century journals are inextricably confused now with twentieth-century scholarship. Scarcely a page lacks footnotes, and one page bears thirty-nine lines of footnote to seven of text. The superb index runs to sixty-eight pages of double columns; the six pages of "Boswell, James" gather the diffuse material into telling condensations, such as "drinks heavily" (thirty-one references), "ill after drinking" (thirty-three), "follows, dallies with, visits prostitutes" (thirteen), and "fears, catches, is cured of venereal disease" (sixteen). Footnotes identify the immense cast of mentioned contemporaries, offer illuminating collations with other nooks of Boswelliana, and provide recipes for such obsolete beverages as plotty, bishop, and whiskey shrub punch. We are told that "raisin" was pronounced "reez'n" in 1781, and why, amid the modernization of spelling, the form "contemptous" has been kept. Much editorial ingenuity and tact are exercised in bridging gaps in the journals with letters, sections of the *Life*, and, at one point, an enthusiastic and hitherto unpublished account by Fanny Burney's younger sister Charlotte Ann of Boswell as he appeared at a London dinner party in 1781:

> I admire and like him beyond measure. He is a fine, lively, sensible, unaffected, honest, manly, good-humoured character. . . . He idolizes Dr. Johnson, and struts about, and puts himself into such ridiculous postures that he is as good as a comedy.

Equally complimentary and fond is the assiduous labor the editors of these journals bring to Boswell. Behind this latest beautifully tooled product of the "Boswell Factory" at Yale—the Yale Editions of the Private Papers of James Boswell—extends the portentous history of the papers' discovery and acquisition, dating back to 1920, when an anonymous note ("Try Malahide Castle") directed Professor Chauncey B. Tinker to chests, sacks, bundles, and bags of letters and journals tucked in closets with the other family skeletons. This massive collection passed from the hands of Colonel Ralph Isham, who had acquired it from Boswell's great-great-grandson, into the possession of Yale in 1949, at a cost of half a million dollars. Money continues to din in the saga of the papers: The Boswell Factory nearly ceased operations for the lack of it, until the National Endowment for the Humanities granted $143,-657, which, according to a recent newsletter from the Yale Editions, "will support the Project for one and a half years." Between 1949 and 1975, the Project got by on a great deal of free scholarly and secretarial services and financial gifts totalling above a quarter of a million dollars. The application to the National Endowment for the Humanities allows that "by any realistic forecast, the research series [that is, a full printing of the papers for scholarly use, with original spelling and fuller scholarship than the "reading," or trade, edition] will require twenty years more for its completion and will call for approximately $900,000 in funding, exclusive of sums collected by Yale University for indirect costs." The unspoken question is, of course, Is Boswell worth it? Dollars aside, the expenditure of human time and intelligence has been on the scale of Talmudic commentary. Three academic workers—Professor Frederick A. Pottle; his wife, Marion; and Miss Harriet A. Chidester—have for over twenty years devoted the major portion of their professional lives to the deciphering, cataloguing, editing, and publishing of these papers. One holds *Laird of Auchinleck* in hand aware of this gallant dimension of tenacity, of a bulky project scrupulously sustained. Many dozens more have toiled along the way; the energy expended exceeds by an unguessable factor that used by Boswell in scribbling the stuff down. Except for never having met him face to face, Pottle knows Boswell better than

Boswell knew Johnson. But saintly devotion does not prove a deity. One cannot help wondering whether the minions of the Boswell Factory ever feel barnacled upon a literary figure who, whatever his aesthetic charms and historical value, might be termed, relative to a host of nobler creative spirits in English letters, a second-rater. A second-rater, furthermore, whose sole previous claim to fame was his purposeful playing of second fiddle. The Boswell papers are a scholarly Happening, but this does not mean they are Art. The academic literature mill, having ground all the grain it can find, will grind chaff rather than shut down.

As a piece of publishing, the papers are a study in enlightened inertia. McGraw-Hill advanced $166,666 of the half-million needed to purchase the papers in 1949, and probably made this advance back on the sale of the initial volume, the *London Journal,* whose uncensored "plain truths" concerning Boswell's rakish sexual life seemed very bold material to the innocent book-buyers of 1950. Since then, public interest has waned, and McGraw-Hill, though it pays a mere three-percent royalty and has the Boswell Factory bear much of the copyediting and proofreading expense, has lost money on the more recent of these handsome, portly volumes. This is the first in seven years; with the new infusion of federal money, the three remaining volumes, taking Boswell into the grave in 1795, seem sure to be issued. A publishing monument of sorts will have been erected, to be viewed on the shelves of university libraries.*

The reading experience, in full, cannot belong to many people, for the erratic, racing entries coupled with the meticulous footnotes and textual niceties splay the concentration as a prism splays a sunbeam. The use of various brackets to protect the integrity of ragged texts a bit dulls the humor in a passage such as:

> I told Burke of contest between Johnson and Beauclerk. Said he, "Between Fury and Malevolence." I. "The < bear and > —what is a small animal < that stands ground?" > BURKE. "A polecat." BOSWELL.

---

*And on those of amateur Boswellians, more than one of whom wrote me in vigorous disagreement with my characterization of the man as a second-rater.

"Is < that spirit > ed enough?" "O yes," said Burke. BOSWELL. "Palmer[3]
wondered how I could help Johnson's < fury a > long." BURKE. "He'd[4]
rather see < your e > xecut[ion] than none." "But," < said I, "he > re-
covers me." "Yes," said < Burke, "he ta > kes you to [the] Humane
Society [afterwards.] He has it[5] in his breast."

Day after day, Boswell treads water. His flurries of zeal at court
come to little, and his trips to London seem often as fragmented
as the paragraph quoted above—surprisingly, these four years pro-
vided enough material to fill over a tenth of his life of Johnson.
Boswell is mostly in Edinburgh, and I, rather lost in the petty social
swirl there, found no character as continuously engaging as the
hero's big toe, with its ingrown toenail; this pathetic digit, already
familiar to readers of the Continental journals, makes its reappear-
ance on April 24, 1779 ("My sore foot was troublesome"), and
inflames and remisses, is maltreated and suffered and dreamed
about ("I dreamt that I saw the cause of my toe being so painful"),
and at last, to our great relief, before dinner on January 27, 1780,
is decisively cut into by the shilly-shallying surgeon ("I felt myself
resolved to bear the pain, so he cut a good deal of the nail of my
great toe out of the flesh. The operation hurt me much. But as soon
as it was over I perceived that I was much relieved for I felt only
the pain of a green wound instead of the pain of my toe irritated
by the nail in it"), and henceforth slowly heals, to fade finally from
notice on the 6th of May ("My toe is never well yet, but pretty
easy"). There is indeed something medical about the journal-read-
ing experience. Like doctor and patient, reader and writer grope
together through a puzzling mass of symptoms and uncathartic
crises that unfold with a maddening organic slowness toward the
ambiguous optimum of further survival. The writer of a novel or
a history holds over his reader the tyranny of a plan, of withheld
secrets and staged revelations. The writer of a journal is at sea in
his tides of detail, and after enough immersion with him we develop
a kind of infantile, pre-conscious sensibility, which knows at least
where the warm spots and the cold spots are.

Boswell's wife, Margaret, is one of the warm spots. She closed
out his day, if not with a pert "π," with consolation. The day of

his toenail dream concludes, "My wife was again exceedingly good to me tonight." When guests unexpectedly arrive, "my wife had a neat supper with her usual cleverness, and the evening went on easily." When his infidelities are discovered, she readily forgives: "I was now safe. Estrangement had discovered my deviation. I was sorry for it. She was very good. π." Some of his behavior even he perceives as difficult to bear: "I came home after this strange debauch and eat [*sic*] eggs and drank negus alone; and then, after having gone to bed with my dear wife, I started up in shocking gloomy intoxication and raved in solemn rage about my being miserable. It was a horrid night." She, too, has her rages:

> . . . I left this my journal lying open in the dining-room while I went downstairs to look for some book or paper, and my dear wife having taken it up, read the account of my life on Monday the 18, with which she was shocked, and declared that all connection between her and me was now at an end, and that she would continue to live with me only for decency and the sake of her children.

But less than two weeks later, "π" connubially concludes another day. Her suggestions to him, as his mental condition and professional commitments veer and slew, must have masked considerable exasperation. He notes, "Awaked in terrible distress. Thought I would lie all day. But upon my wife's suggesting that being frequently out of the House would hurt my practice, I resolved to show myself in court if it were but for a few minutes." Drawing up a solemn account of her defects and virtues, Boswell commends "her excellent sense, her penetration, her knowledge of real life, her activity, her genuine affection . . . and her total disinterestedness and freedom from every species of selfishness during all the time she has been my wife." He blames her only for having "nothing of that warmth of imagination which produces the pleasures of vanity and many others, and which is even a considerable cause of religious fervour." Her lack of such enthusiasm, which she extends to Fielding's novels and Auchinleck genealogy, at times makes him think that he has been "unlucky in uniting myself with one who, instead of cherishing my genius, is perpetually checking it." This oddly formal, valedictory-sounding appraisal is penned, on July 5,

1782, in the lengthening shadow of her ill health; she had tuberculosis, and Boswell had begun a separate journal of her illness. The chilling thought arises that, had not Margaret Boswell delayed dying for seven more years, her loving husband, whose journals of significant progresses in his life were sometimes refined and published, might have built a book upon the curve of her demise, and the carefully phrased sentences above would have found their way into its print. Death was nearer to hand in the eighteenth century, and was expected to occasion moralism. With healthy selfishness, Boswell reflects upon "the deplorable situation I and my children would be in if she should die, which a pretty severe cough which she now had made me fear." When he dreams of losing her, though, sexual jealousy dominates the oneiric presentation:

> Had dreamt that my dear wife was married to somebody else; yet I had a confused notion that she had been my wife. She looked smart and engaging as Miss Peggie Montgomerie. Resolved when awake to pay her all possible attention. I was quite vexed in my sleep at the thought of having lost her.

Her warmth can be felt not only reflected in his ("If a man lay with my wife, I would cut his throat") but also in passingly allowed glimpses of her own inner being: "She has always a dreary terror for death. . . . She said yesterday it was desirable to live long for one reason: because old people come to be as little afraid of death as children are."

A cold spot in the universe of the middle-aged James Boswell is certainly his father. The words "cold" and "dull" accompany the old Laird's appearance in these pages like footmen: "He was in a dull, cold humour and seemed quite indifferent about me." "He was still loaded with the cold, and he was dull and without any kindliness." "Visited Mrs. Dundas, then father, who was cold and dull." Lord Auchinleck—who married, for a second time, on the same day as James's wedding—is reported as icy to his daughter-in-law, indifferent to his grandchildren, and unmoved by his own brother's death. When invited to pity his pathologically morose son John, he snorts, "If my sons are idiots, can I help it?" To his prodigal son James, he seems cruelly ungenerous: "He declared upon his honour that if I ever again exceeded my income, he would give me no more." Among many practical grievances, one peculiar denial stands out as especially hurtful: the Laird refused to talk about religion. "But most certain it is, I have never been able to get him to talk with any frankness on religion. . . ." "During this stay at Auchinleck I several times tried to lead on my father to speak seriously of death. But he never said much, never spoke with any frankness." "Heard Dr. Blair in the forenoon. Dined at my father's between sermons. Observed that he avoided speaking on religion. Sir John Pringle indeed told me the other day that he had tried two or three times to bring him upon that subject. 'But he always escaped me,' said Sir John." Even on his deathbed, the attending physician observed, Lord Auchinleck "showed no more signs of religion than a stock or a stone."

In the twentieth century, the father's reticence seems in less need of explanation than the son's determined curiosity. But Boswell was not a man to come to a conclusion and button up; he craved sociable reassurance on all scores, and his faith, clung to in the Scotland of David Hume and Adam Smith, amid such mockers as his friend John Maclaurin and the Reverend Norton Nicholls, is an unsteady, doubting sort: "I was calmly religious, yet had shadows of doubt occasionally." It is commonplace to say of Boswell that he was searching for a surrogate father and found him in Dr. Johnson; here can be traced a specific way in which Johnson filled a void Lord Auchinleck had left, for he shared with Boswell a gloomy, anxious, ruminative Christianity, yet was far more firm and witty in upholding it.

> I said, "Has any man the same conviction of the truth of religion that he has in the common affairs of life?" He said, "No, Sir . . . We must, as the Apostle says, live by faith, not by sight."

When Boswell by letter confides the anguish over Liberty and Necessity awakened in him by Lord Monboddo's *Ancient Metaphysics*, Johnson replies with a bracing paternal cuffing:

> I hoped you had got rid of all this hypocrisy of misery. What have you to do with Liberty and Necessity? Or what more than to hold your

tongue about it? Do not doubt but I shall be most heartily glad to see you here again, for I love every part about you but your affectation of distress.

Do not doubt . . . I love every part about you . . . Later that same year of 1781, Boswell travels to London, and at first Johnson brushes aside his request for reassurance: "He and I were left alone. I tried in vain to bring him upon Liberty and Necessity. He shunned it, with a general averment for Liberty." But in June, as Boswell leaves for Edinburgh, Johnson amiably accompanies him for some days of the return journey. They attend church together in Southill, and in the security of Dr. Johnson's room afterward the predestinarian demons of Presbyterianism are set to rout: "He said, 'No man believes himself impelled irresistibly. We know that he who says he believes it, lies.' " This stout assertion, a gusty attempt to blow away dread by one who was himself no stranger to dread, is transcribed faithfully into the *Life* (for the day of June 3rd), as are the words, strikingly childlike in tone, with which Boswell had opened the conversation: "I said, 'I'd fain be good, and I am very good just now. I fear God and honour the King; wish to do no ill, and to do good to all mankind.' " The *Life* follows this with "He looked at me with a benignant indulgence; but took occasion to give me wise and salutary caution."

Benignant indulgence was what his own father withheld to the end. Boswell, denied access to the Laird's deathbed by the attendant's harsh "Don't torture him in his last moments," stood nearby and, his journal recorded, "wept; for, alas! there was not affection between us." He took possession of his father's estate on Johnson's birthday, and wrote him, "I hovered here in fluttering anxiety to be with you. . . . I felt myself drawn irresistibly." Only a letter from Johnson himself dissuaded the fatherless Laird from deserting his new station and his alarmingly ill wife. Even in its stretches of tedium, this installment of the journals embodies the need that led Boswell, amid the muddle of his dank and anxious mid-life, to fix his heart upon distant London, and the responsive old man there whose broad back he would ride into posterity.

SPARK, MURDOCH, TREVOR, DRABBLE

Topnotch Witcheries

THE ABBESS OF CREWE, by Muriel Spark. 116 pp. Viking, 1974.

THE SACRED AND PROFANE LOVE MACHINE, by Iris Murdoch. 374 pp. Viking, 1974.

Since the ambitious *Mandelbaum Gate*, Muriel Spark's novels have been short, brusque, bleak, harsh, and queer. They linger in the mind as brilliant shards, decisive as a smashed glass is decisive, evidences of unmistakable power rather casually applied. Beginning with her very first novel, *The Comforters*—utterly accomplished, perfectly her own—this author has exemplified the suitable virtue of *authority*. Under orders from first sentence to last, her books march unflinchingly to their dooms and always, to paraphrase Humpty Dumpty, mean what they choose to mean. Exactly what that is, however, has become something of a mystery, as is the event or idea that, during the years Mrs. Spark has been residing in Rome, has given an extra, tyrannical twist to her command over words and characters. Three of her four recent novels have as their basic situation an odd encompassment, or annexation, of death by life: in *The Public Image* (1968), Annabel Christopher's husband commits suicide in order to embarrass her publicly; in *The Driver's Seat* (1970), Lise with cool madness courts her own murder; in *Not to Disturb* (1972), a household of servants plan how to capitalize on the scandal while upstairs the master, the mistress, and their lover inexorably go through the fated motions of double murder and suicide. In *The Hothouse by the East River* (1973), most weirdly, an uncomfortable group of modern Manhattanites turn out to be ghosts, killed in London by a buzz bomb in 1944. Now, these books all had their scintillations of wit and slashes of dread, but, like letters from a daredevil friend abroad, they also had an unsettling air of concealing more than they told, and of having been posted in haste. Their most reassuring aspect was the photograph, like an enclosed snapshot, of the well-coiffed writer on the jacket. She was still alive.

Not only alive but evidently reading the newspapers, for Mrs. Spark has been roused out of her mood of arch spookiness by, of all things, Watergate. *The Abbess of Crewe: A Modern Morality Tale* is at the least a burlesque of Nixon's Presidency. The Abbey is bugged, even to the poplars outside; the Abbess, the conservative Alexandra, has just been elected (a "landslide victory") over a McGovern-style liberal called Felicity; in power, she rules through intrigues with Mildred and Walburga, "two of the finest nuns I have ever had the privilege to know"; and her perfidious regime founders upon the "third-rate burglary" of a thimble from Felicity's sewing basket. There is even a Kissinger-figure, the missionary nun Gertrude, who flies about the world creating détentes among pagans and avoiding incrimination at the highly electronic Abbey. The Abbess, of course, seeks self-justification in Gertrude's exploits, writing to Rome:

> By river, by helicopter, by jet and by camel, Sister Gertrude covers the crust of the earth, followed as she is by photographers and reporters. Paradoxically it was our enclosed community who sent her out.

As satire of Nixon's bizarre maneuvers, the book produces some droll jabs: the Abbess tells her henchnuns, "I must remain in the region of unknowing," and, when asked by the dull-witted Winifrede what a scenario is, replies:

> "They are an art-form . . . based on facts. A good scenario is a garble. A bad one is a bungle. They need not be plausible, only hypnotic, like all good art."

But as gloss on public reality the book runs down into a rather lame echo of a plot that in real life never wearied of thickening. *The Abbess of Crewe* was obviously completed pre-resignation, pre-phlebitis; the climax of Nixon's psychodrama was still to come.

Yet this matters little, for though travesty may have been Mrs. Spark's starting point, the Nixon scandals served her as inspiration for the creation of a lively, independent, highly characteristic world. Groups of females have always been a congenial subject for her, and the nuns, costumed to manifest outwardly the shadows that lurk beneath Mrs. Spark's apprehensions, excite her prose to a pristine piquance. "The black bodies lean over her, the white coifs meet above the pages of the letter." The first page announces an environment of pleasing rigor—stylized, sinister, and soothing:

> The poplars cast their shadows in the autumn afternoon's end, and the shadows lie in regular still file across the pathway like a congregation of prostrate nuns of the Old Order. The Abbess of Crewe, soaring in her slender height, a very Lombardy poplar herself, moving by Sister Winifrede's side, turns her pale eyes to the gravel walk where their four black shoes tread, tread and tread, two at a time, till they come to the end of this corridor of meditation lined by the secret police of poplars.

In such corridors, people can plausibly speak to the strict rhythms that in Mrs. Spark's less cloistered fiction sound mannered and rude:

> "Who could have leaked it?" says Walburga, her hands folded on her lap, immovable.
> "Her lax and leaky Jesuit, I dare say," the Abbess says, the skin of her face gleaming like a pearl, and her fresh, white robes falling about her to the floor. "That Thomas," says the Abbess, "who tumbles Felicity."

Felicity, the little liberal, who is having an affair with a Jesuit, personifies the revolutionary forces at work, in the name of love, within the Church and without. "Small as a schoolgirl, not at all like what one would have imagined from all the talk about her," she sews "in the tiniest and neatest possible satin-stitch," and has made the embroidery room "a hotbed of sedition." For her rival,

"lofty Alexandra," her sewing and her doctrines of love and free-
dom are distastefully bourgeois: "Felicity is a lascivious puritan,"
she says. Since, though defeated and driven from the nunnery,
Felicity triumphs in the end, by exposing the Abbess's machina-
tions and embezzlements, one might suppose that Mrs. Spark, ideo-
logically, is on her side, as she was on little Sandy Stranger's side
in her exposure of the autocratic Miss Brodie. But, confusingly,
though the author cannot approve of the Abbess Alexandra, she
does love her, love her as she hasn't loved a character in a decade.
She gives her all the spoken wit there is in the book, and dotes on
her grand aplomb with a parade of similes. The Abbess is a poplar,
a steeple, a "tower of ivory," a white swan, a lighthouse, a "mast-
head of an ancient ship," and, at the end, sailing to meet her
judgment in Rome, "straight as a white ship's funnel." We feel Mrs.
Spark's own thought and faith in the Abbess's criticism of Felicity:
"She wants a stamped receipt from Almighty God for every word
she spends, every action. . . . Felicity will never see the point of faith
unless it visibly benefits mankind." We sense a heartfelt asceticism
when the Abbess professes:

> "An aristocratic soul feels no anxiety nor, I think, do the famine-
> stricken of the world as they endure the impotent extremities of starva-
> tion. I don't know why it is, but I ponder on starvation and the starving.
> Sisters, let me tell you a secret. I would rather sink fleshless to my death
> into the dry soil of some African or Indian plain, dead of hunger with
> the rest of the dying skeletons than go, as I hear Felicity is now doing,
> to a psychiatrist for an anxiety-cure."

In her sublimely composed hauteur, the Abbess, of course, is the
very opposite of Nixon, a print from his negative. We cannot
believe it when her machinations go out of control. We scarcely
believe in her crimes (the nuns are fed catfood while their dowries
enrich a bejewelled statue); she has none of the dreadful insecurity
that led Nixon to turn a government's secret arm against the oppo-
sition party and to build himself palaces of privacy with public
funds. The Abbess is beautiful and charismatic, a "complete success
while she lasted on the [television] screen," whereas Nixon, as the
film clips assembled in *Millhouse* made plain, was the least charis-

matic, most painfully self-conscious politician since the invention
of newsreels. His television appearances were the pitiable ordeals
of a man at war with himself; the expletives deleted from the tapes
ring with false fellowship, a sadly toadying attempt to make human
contact even in his inner circle. What the Abbess of Crewe deletes
from *her* tapes, lest Rome find them heretical, are the stanzas of
English metrical verse (Yeats, de la Mare, Marvell, Auden) that she
recites while the other nuns chant the Mass. As a joke, this is clumsy
and unlikely; the poems chosen vibrate with the dry, exacting,
forlorn sensibility of Muriel Spark. To put in the mouth of your
villainess poems of your own cherishing—such paradoxes make
indifferent satire. In its last third, *The Abbess of Crewe* is dragged
to anticlimax by the pull of topical actualities; if the novel could
have been freed to follow out its original impudent inspiration, to
be less an aping of Watergate than a transfiguration of it, we would
have one of the purest, if the lightest, of this gaudy moralist's
mock-worlds. As is, it is good to have Mrs. Spark, amused by our
curious national occasion of self-betrayal and inscrutable justice, so
near the top of her form.

When she is last seen, the Abbess of Crewe is serenely sailing
toward Rome; at the end of Iris Murdoch's sixteenth novel, *The
Sacred and Profane Love Machine,* the character left on the scene
gets into his car and heads toward Oxford. These two venerable
centers of wisdom are apparently offered as points of moral refer-
ence in a, for Mrs. Spark, fallen and, for Miss Murdoch, falling,
rising, and churning world. Murdoch and Spark—how weary
they must be of being bracketed and reviewed together! Yet they
constitute a class by themselves—both so intelligent and fluent, so
quizzical and knowing, both such resourceful mixes of feminine
clairvoyance and masculine generalship, both such *makers.* Miss
Murdoch, true, is copious and explanatory where Mrs. Spark is
curt and oblique; she can hardly turn around in fewer than a
hundred thousand words where the other can't bring herself to
exceed novella length; she is wistfully theistic rather than flatly
so, and concerned with goodness instead of with faith. The two
of them together reappropriate for their generation Shakespeare's

legacy of dark comedy, of deceptions and enchantments, of shuddering contrivance, of deep personal forces held trembling in a skein of sociable truces.

Of the Murdochs this reviewer has read, *The Sacred and Profane Love Machine* seems the best since *A Severed Head,* the novel that discovered and presented her great theme with the solidity, economy, and vivacity of a classic. Her theme is, as the present book states it, that "erotic love is never still." In some of her novels the shifts of allegiance and attraction wrought by the inexhaustible, tempestuous force of erotic love approach the mechanical and unintentionally comic; a kind of square dance links every character to every other. And, as in a mystery novel the murderer can be spotted because he is the least likely candidate, so the Murdochian hero or heroine can be counted upon to love, at last, and *truly,* the most repulsive figure of the opposite sex—e.g., Honor Klein in *A Severed Head,* or the bloated, dying Bruno of *Bruno's Dream.* In the new novel, the turmoil generated by Miss Murdoch's obsession with affective volatility is moderated; the flippant title aside, she seems determined to grasp her reality more firmly and to present her argument, like the philosopher she is, with unarguable closeness. Her sensitive, declarative prose seems less impulsive and rushed than usual. Though the novel is long, it is rather sparsely populated, by no more than ten significant characters; the triangulations are few, the fringe eccentrics severely rationed, the copulations rare, until the end. Always circumstantial, with her phenomenal gift for image-spinning, Miss Murdoch devotes more than customary attention to the physical, earth world, detailing the flora and atmospheric nuances of her suburban acreage on the Buckinghamshire edge of London, giving abundantly of the furniture and history of the two adjacent houses that concern her, distinguishably characterizing (an especially tender tour de force) each dog of a pack of seven, touching the canvas of her vision everywhere with sharp, bright dabs of the recognizably actual. The endless vapors of emotion and conversation that steam and blow from her characters take drama from the contrasting silhouetted treetops and chimney pots of a mundane, midsummer London:

The great cloud fields had faded behind the bumpy tops of the orchard trees, whose silhouette was so familiar to Harriet that she seemed to be thinking it rather than seeing it, and the sky had dulled to a sort of dark lightless white netted over with grey, a colour which it would retain all night. It was midsummer. . . . Wilder Buckinghamshire was a little away, and the houses went on continuously among the trees in the direction of London, whose pink glare illuminated the night sky in winter. A light had just come on in Blaise's study. How pretty, how foursquare, how quite ridiculously *housey* Hood House looked with its shallow slate roof and its pretty flint and stone patterning and its tall early Victorian windows . . .

What an incorrigible, irresistible conjurer-up this woman is! With what an eager, effortless multiplication of adjectives does she throw a character onto the page:

After a second of shock he had recognized Edgar Demarnay. They had not met for several years. An Edgar grown fatter and grosser and older, but Edgar still, with his big pink boy's face and his fat lips and his copious short fluffy hair now pale grey instead of pale gold.

Let it be asked now: what other living novelist in the language is the peer of Iris Murdoch at inventing characters and moving them *fascinatingly,* at least as long as the book is in our hands? Whatever reservations or puzzles it leaves us with, *The Sacred and Profane Love Machine* reads like a breeze, a whirlwind of deepening surprise, a provocation to the intellect and an invitation to the heart, with its exacerbating dialogues, its compelling interior monologues, its pirouette points of aphorism, its expansive landscape, its insatiable exploration of what used to be called people's "souls," its revelation of the exalting, degrading, terrifying adventures love makes possible within our middle-class domestic world of work and nurturing.

Blaise Gavender, a successful if amateurish psychotherapist, doubles as the contented husband of Harriet Gavender and the enthralled lover of Emily McHugh. By both wife and mistress he has fathered a son; his illegitimate one, eight-year-old Luca, becomes the means whereby his two worlds, which he has successfully kept apart for nine years, meet and clash. A subplot concerns the Gavenders' neighbor Montague Small, the famous mystery writer,[*] who is paralyzed with grief over the recent death (cancer, we are told) of his wife. A visitor to this out-of-joint world of the two houses is the Edgar Demarnay already evoked, an alcoholic classics professor just named Master of an Oxford college. The Gavenders' son, David, is on the fastidious verge of sexual awakening, and Emily McHugh has a pushy friend, Constance Pinn. Monty Small has a possessive mother offstage, Blaise has a fictitious patient, Magnus Bowles, and there is a bright and sexy schoolgirl, Kiki St. Loy, whom we know Miss Murdoch will use, for she reminds us of her existence every hundred pages or so. That about sums it up; the caverns of feeling the groping, swerving characters find in one another are the author's province, where summary oversimplifies. Blaise, psychologist though he pretends to be, quite helplessly and cravenly clings to ambivalence, trying to keep both his sacred and profane loves; Harriet's reserves of generosity and strength are slowly depleted; Emily, with only two threadbare cards to play—the existence of Luca and a rather sordid (unspeakable "gadgets" are mentioned) sexual rapport with her middle-aged lover—finds her hand not so weak after all. The triangle's resolution has been criticized as abrupt and arbitrary, breaking into the hothouse situation from the outside like a rock thrown by a vandal: Harriet is murdered by terrorists in a German airport. But this event is conjured with a nice coolness, a brief waking nightmare to go with all the dreams the narrative contains, and just before it arrives the victim has annihilated herself in her own mind:

> There is no great calm space elsewhere, thought Harriet, where a tree stands between two saints and raises its pure significant head into a golden sky. What had seemed to be an intuition of freedom and virtue was for her simply a trivial enigma, an occasion for little meaningless emotions. She was caught in her own mind and condemned by her own being.

---

[*]One always looks to fictional fiction writers for tips from their creators. Here we read: "Monty wrote fluently and fast, hoping somehow that each novel would excuse and rescue its predecessor."

A juster criticism might be that the plot's resolution leaves us with no characters we like much—an austerity usually truer of Mrs. Spark's dispensations than of Miss Murdoch's. And it is disturbing that few of the book's incidents, so vivid and impressive as they passed into at least this reader's consciousness, linger in the mind a week afterward. Though she has endowed them with all the substance her remarkable powers of imagination and introspection could fabricate, their motions are not weighted by the persuasive inertia of nineteenth-century characters. They are, like atoms, discontinuous; we remember flares of their energy—Blaise's discovering, with Emily, that "the dark cupboard [of his sexual quirks] . . . was not dark, it was blazing with light and as large as the universe"; Harriet's activation as a woman ("her eyes were all dazed and glowing") by the shattering of her marriage; Emily's sensation of bliss ("her blood had turned into some heavenly golden liquor which lightly scorched all her flesh") when the tables turn again. Yet the heat, the light did not last, in the characters' lives or in the reader's. Miss Murdoch is less Shakespeare than Prospero, holding us enchanted as long as we stay on her island; then the insubstantial pageant fades, leaving embers and an impression, not of life's surging power but of the evanescence of its heat in the vacuum that even a passionate creatrix cannot fill. Montague Small, an author who has ceased to write, entertains in this book the thought "that there was no deep sense in things, that nothing and no one had real dignity and real deserving, that 'the world' was just a jumble and a rubble and a dream." Without "deep sense in things," the world of fictional imitation will be dreamlike, fantastic; and so Miss Murdoch's is. Though her title evokes a machine, a machine's grinding causality is just what her plots lack. The sociopsychological engines of Balzac and Flaubert might well, the reader feels, grab and destroy him as well as Père Goriot and Madame Bovary; but the midsummer-night's dreams of *The Sacred and Profane Love Machine* glimmer and are gone. The author so effortlessly invents interior monologues that we do not doubt she could illuminate and justify behavior totally other than what appears on the page. She bores so deep she goes right through bedrock. And however ravaged her characters are, we remain comfortable, reminded of our solid armchair by helpful literary flourishes from these same characters. Emily, tartish and desperate, announces to Blaise, to end a chapter, "You've killed me and sent me to hell, and you must descend to the underworld to find me and make me live again." When Harriet complains that Blaise lives in a dream world, Monty replies, with something like complacence, "We all live in dream worlds."

Unlike Monty and Prospero, Miss Murdoch has not broken her conjurer's wand and buried her "book." She continues to write, with unstinting energy; it is an act of faith as well as of magic. Her books abound in gestures toward faith, and the aborted versions of it. In this novel, Monty practices meditation, Harriet is an Anglican, David is haunted by Jesus, Emily is a militant atheist, Blaise is so wimbly-wimbly he cannot be said to believe or disbelieve anything. The author, one gathers, believes in sex and Oxford. But it takes a culture, not an individual literary will, to banish the dreamlike inconsequence of the world; we can choose to place credence in Oxford or Rome, but as long as the choice is felt *as* a choice it can be unmade, and remains precariously ours.

Worlds and Worlds

NUNS AND SOLDIERS, by Iris Murdoch. 505 pp. Viking, 1981.

OTHER PEOPLE'S WORLDS, by William Trevor. 237 pp. Viking, 1981.

There comes a point in many an Iris Murdoch novel when the enchantment sours, or cloys, and the hitherto rapt reader succumbs to the suspicion that some justice lies in the customary criticisms with which her faithfully produced fictions are faithfully belabored; e.g., that her prose can be as careless as it is abundant, and that her worthy preoccupation with the metamorphoses worked by ubiquitous, tireless Eros leads her to overillustrate her thesis and to produce a mechanical, farcical effect. On page 296 of her most recent and in many ways marvellous novel, *Nuns and Soldiers,* we are told, having persuasively experienced one heroine's typically Murdochian massaging by an unlikely but ineluctable passion, that another heroine is promptly in line for the same strenuous treatment. "Something terrible had happened to ———. It had happened some time ago and it was going on happening. She had fallen terribly terribly in love with ———. Of course she had told no one of this dreadful love." Names have been deleted, lest the novel be cheated of suspense. Adjectives and adverbs cannot be concealed— a "dreadful," a "terrible," and a double-barrelled "terribly terribly" in so short a compass. Deeper down the page, we are assured, "True love gallops, it flies, it is the swiftest of all modes of thought, swifter even than hate and fear. ——— grasped, like someone at last grasping a vast theorem, ———'s absolute charm. She worshipped him in her thought from head to foot, she embraced him in the soft beating of her passionate wings." From this point on, we cannot help noticing what seems to be the flailing of the author's own passionate wings: we read of a "terrible terrible rejection," of thought becoming "darker and more agonizingly and tightly knotted and more deeply and awfully frightening," of "a fierce wild almost cruel joy," of "all the loathsome irresistible machinery of jealousy," of "awful cancerous jealousy and envy and a dull anger," of "deep awful pain," of a heart "full of an incoherent tender joy," and of the "wonderful wonderful" act of breathing. The language is desperate, perhaps, because one of Miss Murdoch's central couples has been so firmly linked and married by the amorous alchemics of the novel that the case should have been rested, and the other couple, for all the verbal heat she breathes on the two unhappy souls, remains a pair of sticks—a nun and a soldier, too priggish and still and solitary to mate. By the final page (505) of the book, we have lost patience with *all* the characters, who if not stiff and sterile seem to be spoiled and selfish, and the connection at the plot's heart, the female friendship between Gertrude Openshaw and Anne Cavidge, no longer holds current and breaks off without a spark.

Hysterical love undoubtedly exists—indeed, it presidingly exists —and if what Miss Murdoch terms "the vast starry cosmos of the emotions" is to be accurately mapped, language cannot hang back timidly; perhaps it must dare to be loose and wild, though nothing like Miss Murdoch's adjectival torrents mars one's memory of such portraits of distraught love as *Wuthering Heights* and *Albertine disparue*. There is too much telling in *Nuns and Soldiers:* with an omniscient circumstantiality, we are told the history of Poland as well as that of each major character, we are treated to panoramas of landscape as well as of interior upheaval, we are repeatedly informed that what we are witnessing is portentous. Miss Murdoch has taken it upon herself to revive the cozy, bossy voice of the intervening author: "What Manfred was thinking will be revealed later"; "As has been explained, Tim's work rushed blindly on"; "The Count, as it turned out, had ample chances later to display his qualities"; "What Tim did not know was that Jimmy Roland..." We are not trusted to decipher the code of events ourselves and to lend it our own emotions. The plinth of descriptive preparation outweighs and dwarfs the inert statues upheld. There is much dramatizing but little dramatic action: one man dies, everybody else falls in love, and nobody can help anything. With her repeated images of near-drowning (Anne in heavy ocean waves, Tim in a swift-running canal), the author emphasizes her sense of universal helplessness, of Eros and Thanatos tossing individuals about like flecks of foam. What is important, Miss Murdoch seems to imply in her intense descriptions of water and rocks, is inhuman. She is not alone, of course, in finding under the hood of the modern novel a kind of anti-engine, a disbelief in human decisiveness and free will. Tolstoy, too, declared human beings, even Napoleon, helpless on vast tides; but his own vigor and authority appeared, in artistic practice, not to be impaired. Miss Murdoch in the course of her copious and fluent dreaming seems to get carried away; *Nuns and Soldiers* gave this reader, at least, an impression of having drifted rather far from its initial intentions and indicated promises.

The novel begins with a leisurely and dense evocation of the deathwatch maintained by the cancer-stricken Guy Openshaw's social circle, nicknamed *"les cousins et les tantes."* Guy, only in his mid-forties, is a rich, polymathic section head in the Home Office, and a dominant figure among the Openshaws, a Jewish family that has intermarried with Gentiles and left its Jewishness pretty much behind. Guy's wife, Gertrude, a "handsome woman" in her late thirties, "a little inclined to plumpness, with fine radiantly clear brown eyes," is half Scottish and half English. She is loved, not so secretly, by one of the circle's adopted strays, the Polish-born Wojciech Szczepanski, nicknamed the Count and sometimes called Peter. Another stray is Tim Reede, "a weedy young man . . . said to be a painter or something." But most of *les cousins et les tantes* are related by blood or marriage to the Openshaws—Manfred North, Stanley and Janet Openshaw, Veronica Mount, Sylvia Wicks, and Dr. Victor Schultz. The lineages, professions, and— oddly, in agnostic old England—religious opinions of all are briskly given, and, as Guy dies and his widow embarks upon her mourning, we expect to see something of a group study. The mad thought even crossed the mind of this reader, noting that *les cousins et les tantes* number about twelve and that Guy's favorite among them is called Peter and the group's shadowy Jewishness mingles with an untoward number of religious allusions and with certain hints as to the departed Guy's uncanny rectitude and authority (he made notes toward a study of justice and punishment, which might figure as a sacred testament)—the mad thought, I say, crossed my mind that this all might develop into an allegory of the first bereft, confused Christian community in the wake of the Master's death. But nothing, or very little, along these lines happens, though some skeletal remains of the clan aspect of the plot surface late in the book, like fossils. What does happen is that Anne Cavidge, a racy former school friend of Gertrude's who turned to religion and has spent fifteen years in a nunnery, calls up unexpectedly, having left the cloister, and is given shelter under Gertrude's roof. Then, in France, Tim Reede leaps out of insignificance to become Gertrude's lover. Tim's other life, which he shares with a stringy, slangy demi-artiste named Daisy Barrett, is thoroughly told about, as is the Count's melancholy, lovelorn, solitary existence, spent reading Carlyle and Proust while listening to the BBC. The Count, Gertrude, Anne, Tim, and Daisy utterly dominate the stage with their erotic and spiritual ups and downs; *les cousins et les tantes* remain little more than names, though toward the end a hasty and brittle interview between Manfred North and Veronica Mount, like Holmes clearing up matters with Watson, does reveal that they, too, offstage, have not been exempt from the seethe of infatuation, that Manfred thinks they should have said Kaddish for Guy, and that the author may have intended more for the Openshaws than she found room for.

What she intended to do with Anne Cavidge's religious crisis is moot. Religion figures persistently in Miss Murdoch's projection of the human comedy, but as a kind of anxious messing around rather than as a point of vantage or a central topic. Though she has described herself as an "ex-Christian," she worries at Christianity far more overtly than professed believers like Muriel Spark and Evelyn Waugh. In those two Catholics, faith serves as a crystalline index, an unseen whetstone sharpening the satiric knife, a settled judgment upon a world of vanity and folly. Miss Murdoch, more tender toward the world, looks for immanence, and finds muffled numinous gleams in her vivid and eerie landscapes and in the immaterial sphere of our furious and outreaching emotions. "Who can tell where his life ends?" Anne asks the Count. "Our being spreads out far beyond us and mingles with the being of others. We live in other people's thoughts, in their plans, in their dreams. This is as if there were God. We have an infinite responsibility." And Anne tells herself, "Happiness sought anywhere but in God tends to corruption." She shies, however, from what is absolutely transcendent and intellectually scandalous in Christian faith, denying belief in an afterlife and in a "personal God." (Both ideas are characterized as "anti-religious.") Yet Christ appears to her in a vision of astonishing particularity:

> Jesus was leaning with one hand upon the table and gazing down at her. He had a strangely elongated head and a strange pallor, the pallor of something which had been long deprived of light, a shadowed leaf, a deep sea fish, a grub inside a fruit. He was beardless, with wispy blond hair, not very long, and he was thin and of medium height, dressed in shapeless yellowish-white trousers and a shirt of similar colour, open at the neck, with rolled-up sleeves. He wore plimsolls upon his feet with no socks. Though the shape of the head seemed almost grotesque, the face was beautiful. It did not resemble any painting which Anne had ever seen. The mouth was thoughtful and tender and the eyes large and remarkably luminous.

She and the vision converse—rather whimsically, considering—
and when she reaches out to touch him her hand is burned with
a wound that will not heal. That is, medically, actually, it does not
heal, as several other characters in the novel, including a doctor,
observe. This miracle does not, however, restore Anne's faith, nor
does Christ's manifestation appreciably affect the course of her
earthly infatuation and spiritual quandary; she finally does not so
much reëmbrace nunnishness as shrink back into a diluted form of
it. Now, psychosomatic prodigies like mind-induced burns do
exist, and most likely we are intended to take Anne's word as
certain evidence of no more than the feverish hunger for God that
atheists as well as believers can acknowledge to be a frequent psy-
chological fact. Yet, somehow, in the context of the novel's discur-
sive questing, we feel that Anne's experience should amount to
more than this and we fear that we have been, as often before with
Miss Murdoch's sly and glossy spookiness, merely teased:

> [Christ] put both hands behind his back and stared at Anne with his
> dark brilliant eyes, his mouth whimsical as if he was teasing her.
> "So there is salvation?" said Anne.
> "Oh yes," but he said it almost carelessly.

The scene, it should be said, is an exciting one, comic and poi-
gnant, and feels right at the time. And it should be urged, amid this
catalogue of cavils, that many scenes and moments in *Nuns and
Soldiers* are splendid, full to the point of explosiveness with the
characters' capacities for ardor, deception, and self-contradiction.
Tim and Gertrude's dance of love when they are suddenly placed
together in the Openshaws' vacation house in southern France; the
abrasive yet exploratory encounter between Anne and Daisy, two
styles of nun from different worlds; the onrushing scene, every
pell-mell word exactly right, in which Tim and Gertrude dissolve
their marriage: in such conjurations of our strange human life Iris
Murdoch shows herself second to no living novelist. In peripheral
incidents, too, her gifts as a realist flash out. Gertrude, it is men-
tioned in passing, sometimes teaches English to Asian women, and
with no advance to the plot this sideline abruptly becomes vivid:

She took her pupils singly, and confronting those dark handsome thoughtful anxious women, dressed in the most beautiful clothes in the world, she sometimes felt that she herself was being transported far away. Sometimes, speechless, she reached across the table for a frail brown hand, and pupil and teacher communicated, almost with strange pleasant tears or else with helpless laughter. She tried to describe all this to Tim, but without meeting the women he could not understand.

The will to describe, the willingness to be transported by details of the humble actual, is a novelist's requisite, and Miss Murdoch is so willing that one puzzles over the nagging sense of thinness, of some hollowing discrepancy, her fiction too frequently arouses. Her adeptness as a trained philosopher leads her, it may be, toward large issues from which her comedic sense of life instinctively retreats. "What can morality, what can philosophy achieve, against the volatile faithlessness of the human mind?" asks the Count, one of several characters who seem to be inviting judgment upon their own novel. Philosophy and theology can be vexed but not conclusively discussed in fiction; cosmic conclusions depend upon evidence no novel—no mere emblem of the world—can contain. Through all the romantic and religious flurry of *Nuns and Soldiers*, one familiar hard truth emerges: the ancient truth, dear to the Greeks, of irrevocability. "There are eternal partings, all things end and end forever and nothing could be more important than that," Anne thinks. "We are not as we were," Gertrude tells Tim, echoing the immense, laconic exchange with which Henry James concludes *The Wings of the Dove*. Our actions, our decisions, our vows do matter; what can fiction tell us more important than that?

Other People's Worlds, by William Trevor, is a shorter, more efficient novel than *Nuns and Soldiers*, but bears some resemblances. It, too, has for a heroine a widow who marries a young man financially beneath her, and it, too, demonstrates that such a union, however rashly contracted, cannot be lightly undone. Julia Ferndale, like Gertrude Openshaw, is plump but still handsome; like Anne Cavidge, she undergoes a struggle with religious doubt. Catholicism haunts both books, and both are at their best showing different social worlds impinging, with painful and revelatory effect. Characters in both novels read novels, and we are told what they are reading—in *Nuns and Soldiers, Little Dorrit, The Heart of Midlothian, Mansfield Park, Sense and Sensibility,* and *War and Peace;* in *Other People's Worlds, Martin Chuzzlewit* and *Bleak House.* Like Miss Murdoch, Mr. Trevor was born in Ireland, and he brings to the anthropology of their adopted England an affectionate and attentive outsider's eye. Both writers began publishing novels in the Fifties; while he is not the international star she is, Mr. Trevor has a solid reputation in Great Britain and a growing one here. *Other People's Worlds* should help its growth; the novel is a dense and constantly surprising work, grimly humorous, total in its empathy, and pungent with the scent of evil and corruption. While Iris Murdoch's world has something incorrigibly sunny and donnish about it, and even her meanest characters have intellectual positions to articulate, Mr. Trevor's contains true depths, hells whose inhabitants do not know where they are.

Unlike Miss Murdoch, Mr. Trevor is a short-story writer as well as a novelist, and he has the habit of economy. His situations and characters are blocked in as quickly as a bricklayer lays a walk, and widely different milieux unfold almost dizzyingly. Julia Ferndale lives with her mother, Mrs. Anstey, in the Gloucestershire village of Stone St. Martin; the flora and local fauna—Mrs. Spanners, the gossipy cleaning lady; Diane, the girl who works in the Crowning Glory beauty salon; her unsuitable swain, Nevil Clapp; the village priests—are smartly sketched. Julia, who has two grown daughters leading trendy lives in London, has met and is going to marry a possibly unsuitable but disarmingly presentable actor, Francis Tyte, whose image, as a pipe-smoking figure in tobacco commercials, flits across telly screens all over the U.K. Well, one knows, this being a novel, after all, that things are going to go somewhat badly, but how very badly would be hard to foretell. Via her marriage, Julia (who has the "look of a Filippo Lippi madonna") and the reader are put in contact with the worlds of commercial television, of male prostitution, of old-people's homes, of squalid and chaotic London state schools, of advanced alcoholism and human ruin. How sheltered Julia responds to this exposure provides the adventure and moral message of the novel; the reader's response is to be appalled that the human condition contains so many hopeless pockets and to marvel at Mr. Trevor's imaginative ease within them. His portrait of Francis's twisted psyche is sinisterly fine, but the centerpiece of the novel is his characterization of Doris Smith, the mother of Francis's casually conceived child—a girl, Joy, who is now twelve. Francis has never lived with Doris, and rarely visits her; she sells shoes in a London department store, at night makes paper placemats for extra income, and protests that she's not really a drinker. She and, in her guarded fashion, Joy still love Francis, as a little band of faithful might love a cruelly absent God. Even while Doris slips deeper and deeper into alcoholism, she continues to espouse his cause, to plead his case, and in her agitated and incoherent way to seek justice for him. Her drunken and plaintive familiarities epitomize the misery that spills over, that will not remain out of sight, that refuses, under the delusion that it still has something to offer, to remain mute.

> "Put it this way, Julia, when Frankie and me sat in the Spread Eagle that day in '66 I've never known another human person to be as interested. I've never known another human person wanting to hear every single detail. Dad and myself and then Dad getting married again, and all about the shoes and the girls and what the fashions were, the time Gloria couldn't get the boot off her customer's leg, the time Mavis Soper hit her customer in the stomach. Put it this way, Julia, I was an eyeful in those days. I know I'm not now. I'm a bit of a weirdo myself, if you get what I mean. Oh, I'm definitely aware of that, dear."

Mr. Trevor has a keen and compassionate ear. The misaimed verbal thrusts of senility, the grimy prattle of a slum child, the pidgin-English advances of an Italian masher—all are here, ringing true. When Doris descends into the ultimate London depths, the society of "meths drinkers," these derelicts, "like bundles of rags," yet rumble with a curious courtesy and pertinence. The author does what Joyce never quite does in his underworld scenes—he gives these murky presences a mythic dignity:

> "This woman wants a drink, Con."
> "Ah, don't ye all want drinks? Isn't it drinks the entire long time with ye?" . . .

"Have you got it, Con? Have you a bottle on you?"

"Have ye two notes?"

"Two," the man with the limp said to Doris.

"That's very cheap, missus," his companion threw in, attempting to wag his head. "That's good value all round."

"You can rest yourself here, missus," the man with the limp said. "We'll keep an eye on you."

"I'm not an alcoholic," Doris said, finding the money in the bag that hung from her shoulder. "It's just that a friend's gone."

"It's shocking, that," agreed the man with the limp.

Mr. Trevor knows, and dramatizes, two principal truths about low life: it never utterly lies down, but persists in asserting claims and values of its own derivation; and it cannot be fenced off and disowned by the fortunate. There is indeed "infinite responsibility." As we watch Francis Tyte's derangement spread to Doris and Joy and thence to Julia Ferndale and her mother and the picture-book village of Stone St. Martin, Julia herself begins to seem crazy. Looking at herself naked in the mirror, she wants to be desired; she recalls the moment in Pisa when Francis disillusioned her and even so "she wanted to caress away the pain she knew was there, to rescue him at last from his awful world." This "awful" the author has earned.

Mr. Trevor has worked his text closely, to the compression, often, of poetry. Strange chimings, perhaps unintended, play across the surface: Francis Tyte's daughter attends the Tite Street Comprehensive School; one minor character is called Susanna Music and another Ned Tone; a Miss Upuku and a Mrs. Uprichard are named within a few pages of each other; and there is a curious free-floating "elephant" theme, which has Joy take a drug that is a tranquillizer for elephants, on the next page places an elephant's-foot umbrella stand in the old-people's home where the elder Tytes reside, and later brings us the news that "in the London Zoo an elephant was ill." The strangest chime of all is struck with the other novel under review. The first pages of *Nuns and Soldiers* display Guy Openshaw in semi-delirium. His verbal wanderings revolve around three mysterious allusions: to a white swan, to "the upper side of the cube," and to a ring that someone "shouldn't have sold."

Hundreds of pages later, "the upper side of the cube" is identified as a phrase from tennis instruction ("When you serve, imagine that the ball is a cube of which you are going to hit the upper side"), and the ring allusion is traced to Jessica's actions in *The Merchant of Venice;* but the swan image, though there is some mention of Leda and the swan, is never nailed down. Miraculously, it appears on the last page of *Other People's Worlds,* as a symbol of the "niceness" that partially redeems our travails and our shame: "All she completely knew was that the niceness of her world was not entirely without purpose, the white swan in its niche above the hall door, the roses and japonica of the garden, a plain house made the most of." Novels are worlds also: intercommunicating ones.

Drabbling in the Mud

THE REALMS OF GOLD, by Margaret Drabble. 354 pp. Alfred A. Knopf, 1975.

"Omniscience has its limits," Margaret Drabble tells the reader in her seventh novel, *The Realms of Gold.* Having taken upon herself the voice and manner of an omniscient Victorian novelist, she seems rather frequently to be appealing to the reader to help her out, to write the novel with her. Her particularizations suggest multiple-choice problems: "Something in her finally rebelled— pride, conscience, something like that"; "she ached, with either sympathy or envy for them: she was not sure which." A disarmed, if not disarming, vagueness afflicts her, especially in the vicinity of male characters: "The truth is that David was intended to play a much larger role in this narrative, but the more I looked at him, the more incomprehensible he became, and I simply have not had the nerve to present what I saw in him in the detail I had intended"; "as for Sir Frank Ollerenshaw and Harold Barnard, who knows what they were thinking?" Like a housewife quite overcome by the complexity of her household tasks, yet confident in her feminine charm, the author in amiable dishevelment apologizes for the thinness of some scenes and the fullness of others:

> And that is enough, for the moment, of Janet Bird. More than enough, you might reasonably think, for her life is slow, even slower than its description, and her dinner party seemed to go on too long to her, as it did to you.

Miss Drabble in some ways bears comparison with Iris Murdoch and Muriel Spark; she is as intellectually serious as they, though not as witty, and warmer than either. But, in sharp contrast to these two plotmakers, she does not *encompass* her material; rather, she seems half lost within it—mystified by her characters, ruminative where she should be expository, expository where she should be dramatic, shamelessly dependent upon coincidence, lackadaisical about locating her theme, and capable for long stretches of blocking in episodes devoid of dynamic relevance to what one takes to be the action. The plot of *The Realms of Gold* appears to be this: a pair of perfectly suited middle-aged lovers part, and are slow to reunite because a postcard is held up by a mail strike in Europe. As the postcard (declaring, "I miss you. I love you") languishes at the bottom of a letterbox, the book happens; that is, a number of familial and professional gatherings are described, while the heroine's heart is distinctly elsewhere, and the reader's attention threatens to wander also. The unseen mailman who finally moves the missive is the novel's active agonist; the other characters conduct a three-hundred-page holding action. When at last the lovers do reunite, they are relieved and, simply, pleased; their circumstances, through no doing of their own, are enough improved for them to marry, and they do. "Invent a more suitable ending if you can," the author writes, in a last plea for the reader's collaboration, or indulgence.

Since neither lover significantly wavers, in the months of separation, from fidelity, the book generates little suspense and depends on its essayistic interest, which luckily is high. The heroine, Frances Wingate, is a divorced archeologist enjoying the aftermath of celebrity that has followed her discovery and excavation of the ancient Saharan trading city of Tizouk. The amount of archeological detail and theory Miss Drabble has worked up attractively adorns her portrait of this mistress and mother, drinker and lecturer. Archeology brings a wealth of metaphors and incidental illuminations to the book, and in a sense informs its structure; we have less a plot than a lode of prose and description, through which, as he reads, the reader digs down toward some underlying message about kinship, ancestry, vitality, and life's meaning. An ingenious interlocking of academic disciplines broadens and unifies the terrain of significance. Frances's lover, Karel Schmidt, is a historian specializing in "the history of agriculture in the eighteenth century," and at the end Frances is awakened by happenstance to a vivid sense of her own ancestry among the rural laborers of the Midlands. She is by birth an Ollerenshaw, and the book's creaking machinations bring her into contact with two other Ollerenshaws. One of them, her cousin David, is a geologist, and geology is the discipline on the further side (history being the near side) of her archeology. Her other discovered cousin, Janet Bird, lives as a kind of human artifact in Tockley, the Ollerenshaw home country; buried amid the plastic gimcrackery of modern England, including a plastics chemist for a husband, she is unearthed—brought into the light both of Frances's attention and of television interviews—by the death of a mad old great-aunt, Connie Ollerenshaw, who lived alone in a primitive cottage and has occasioned a momentary scandal by dying of starvation there. Her death brings accusations of hard-hearted neglect upon her nearest relative, Sir Frank Ollerenshaw, Frances's father; he has risen from the mud of rural anonymity "to the golden world above" by the study of zoology—specifically, the biochemistry of newts, which abound in the ditches of Tockley. A second death, more scandalous than old Connie's, overtakes young Stephen Ollerenshaw, who, burdened by an infant daughter and a wife hospitalized with anorexia nervosa, commits suicide because of a revelation that "came to him like a light from heaven. It was better to be dead than alive. . . . Being alive was sordid, degrading, sickly, unimaginable . . ." His last conversation with Frances, the epitome of innate vitality and resilience, concerns Freud's *Beyond the Pleasure Principle*, with its assertion that "all living things strove for death." Psychology, zoology, geology, history—all frame our heroine's energetic unearthing of the dead, whose custom of child sacrifice bothers her, as she sacrifices her own children to her career, herself the child of multitudinous Ollerenshaws. In this web of reference, the central reunion is not with her lover but with the ghost of her dead great-aunt, whose cottage she visits in the book's most interestingly described moment:

> A terrible purity marked the scene, and Frances approached it without fear. Even a corpse would not have alarmed her. She was used to corpses; human bones were her familiars. She walked up to the front door, through the long swaths of grass, her feet wet with mud and dew: Oh, so different, so beautifully different from the parched red mud of Adra, from the glaring altitudes of rocky, weathered Tizouk. England. A bird sang in a tree. Frances paused at the door, feeling in her pocket for the key. She bowed her head in respect to Constance Ollerenshaw, who had lived here alone for so long, whose death had been so solitary, so unremarked, who had let the creepers and brambles and roses grow in through her windows.

Even the prosaic Janet Bird, walking to this same cottage earlier, is moved by solitude: "Loneliness possessed her sweetly, like a reassuring desolation. The grass was company, the birds were company."

The moments in *The Realms of Gold* that feel important tend to be those showing women alone: in hotel rooms, in suburban living rooms, in isolated cottages, wherever they are removed from the clutter of men and mating and freed to concentrate upon the silent solemn tasks—cooking and child-rearing, withstanding pain and depression—that seem to be their essence. In her dead great-aunt's cottage, Frances lights a fire; at the novel's culmination, its untidily numerous characters bury two of their number. These primitive human acts loom, jutting from Miss Drabble's ground of passion. English critics have already remarked, with raised eyebrows, her fiction's concern with motherhood; she has here broadened her family to include all the earth, described geologically, topologically, archeologically, botanically (her background of vegetation is luxuriant and precise). Her love scenes take place in the mud; Karel and

Frances gravitate to ditches, and in the end fall into one. Along with this earth-sense goes a naturalistic pessimism—"there never was a golden world, there was never anything but toil and subsistence, cruelty and dullness"—and something inchoate and defiantly, jauntily casual about the organization of at least this novel. The conversations, the dinner parties, the conferences (all trendy, flirtatious, and desultory) feel superficial, perhaps because they appear so to the author—a crust over the earthy realities. Before falling asleep one night, Frances contemplates a recently unearthed terra-cotta figurine with "a witchy, androgynous, yet friendly look, almost a comic look, as one who appreciates the twists of fate." The novel digs toward some such emblem of the feminine. In friendly mud Miss Drabble finds her strengths, and her paragraphs, though they come at one jumbled, at their best have the closeness, the intimate solemnity, of something personally discovered and held in the hand:

> Hundreds and hundreds of frogs were sitting down that pipe, and they were all honking, all of them, not in unison but constantly, their little throats going, their mouths open, their eyes staring up with curiosity at Karel and Frances and their large human shadows. . . . Oh, I love them, said Frances. They looked as though they had been bred from the clay, as in some medieval natural history. A natural product of the landscape, they were. And every time she thought of them, in later years, she felt such pleasure and amusement deep within her, a deep source of it, much deeper than that pipe.

Deeper than its scattered, diffident surface as a novel of manners, *The Realms of Gold* celebrates the human as a department of the natural.

Of Heresy and Loot

THE TAKEOVER, by Muriel Spark. 266 pp. Viking, 1976.

Muriel Spark's new novel is the longest of her last six, and there are signs that she has taken exceptional pains. Her language, always apt to spring up from its surface of prosy bluntness with a skewed adjective or a rapt little simile, seems especially alert. Her subject, the world of the rich as they lead their *dolci* lives in an increasingly chaotic Italy, stirs her, much as an Italian lawyer in her novel is stirred by the presence of her plutocratic American heroine, Maggie Radcliffe:

> As it happened, this lawyer, having sentimental sympathies towards the political left wing . . . loathed what he conceived Maggie to stand for at the same time as he was put into an ambivalent state of excitement by her glowing and wealthy presence.

Maggie indeed does loom excitingly:

> She had overdressed very tastefully, with a mainly-white patterned dress brilliant against her shiny sun-tan. Her hair was silver-tipped, her eyes large and bright. She had a flood-lit look up to the teeth.

Such an ambience transforms even the air to a servant:

> The spring evening air from the terrace stood around them like another ubiquitous servant, tendering occasional wafts of a musky creeper's scent.

Mrs. Spark has lived in Rome long enough to move with familiarity not only through the landscape but through the minds and hearts and family gatherings of Italian people. In the character of the lawyer, who double-crosses his client while yearning to have lunch with her, corruption and deceit are understood as modes of concrete loyalty, to self and family, in a society where for millennia power has flowed across legal channels, along more personal lines. "The primary unit in Roman politics is the family," Gary Wills wrote years ago, when he was a classics scholar. A funny, and thematically pregnant, scene in *The Takeover* shows Lauro, the dark young servant who sleeps with the rich—male and female, native and émigré, indiscriminately—being depressed by the Italian family he is about to marry into. They are "a good-looking, long-legged set, modern and, with the exception of his fiancée, slender." Yet these chic people as enthusiastically as peasant farmers plan aloud the details of the wedding feast: "It was a big food-babble, rising louder and louder and dinning around Lauro's ears, he being only half able to isolate the source of his unhappiness since certainly the family looked very good and up-to-date and prosperous and distinguished." He has been inwardly corrupted by his parasitical life amid the super-prosperous, where "nobody talked of the food at all; they took the good food for granted and if the men discussed wines or the women certain dishes, it was all like a subject that you study in a university like art history or wildlife." Mrs. Spark moves with ease from the ethereal tables kept by the Marchese di Tullio-Friole to the noisy luncheons of the bourgeoisie and on downward into the streets—into the conversation of servants whose "only tone for all occasions was one of lament" and into the operations of the calm and efficient criminals who give the new Italy its flavor of terror. The Italian characters in this novel stimulate the author to more verbal felicities (including a stunning paean to the splendors of eternal life, thrust in lordly overvoice upon the gossip of two servingmaids out shopping)* and fuller, more affectionate portraits than the rather skimped and querulous Anglo-American portions of her plot.

This plot, in brief, tells of how one Hubert Mallindaine, a homosexual Englishman who believes himself descended of a mating between the goddess Diana and the Emperor Caligula, occupies and refuses to leave a house built on the shores of Lake Nemi by his onetime patroness and confidante, Maggie Radcliffe, an American millionairess recently married to an Italian marchese. Lake Nemi, of course, was the site of the cult of Diana described in the opening paragraphs of J. G. Frazer's *Golden Bough,* paragraphs Mrs. Spark considerately quotes at length, as she elsewhere quotes

---

*". . . while the whole of eternal life carried on regardless, invisible and implacable, this being what no skinny craving cat with its gleaming eyes by night had ever pounced upon, no tender mole of the earth in the hills above had ever discovered down there under the damp soil, no lucky spider had caught, nor the white flocks of little clouds could reveal when they separated continually, eternal life untraceable and persistent, that not even the excavators, long-dead, who had dug up the fields of Diana's sanctuary had found; they had taken away the statues and the effigies, the votive offerings to the goddess of fertility, terracotta replicas of private parts and public parts, but eternal life had never been shipped off with the loot; and even the lizard on the cliff-rocks in its jerky fits had never been startled by the shadow or motion of that eternal life which remained, past all accounting, while Clara and Agata chattered on . . ."

Lord Byron's superb stanza on the lake in *Childe Harold* and St. Paul's imprecations, in Holy Writ, against the cult of Diana among the Ephesians. There are a number of subplots, mainly erotic, some so thinly sketched as to seem erasures, and the moral of it all is that there was, for the wealthy, as of the last quarter of 1973, "the beginning of something new in their world; a change in the meaning of property and money . . . a complete mutation not merely to be defined as a collapse of the capitalist system, or a global recession, but such a sea-change in the nature of reality as could not have been envisaged by Karl Marx or Sigmund Freud." This mutation, by its date, must be the boost in Arab petroleum prices; but what plagues the economy of the rich in this novel is not imported oil but domestic fraud.

The rich as Mrs. Spark describes them are victimized by their own lawyers and hangers-on even more than by technician-thieves who come from the outside. The sense of loss—stolen jewelry and paintings, embezzlement and chicanery—is sickening, and pitiable. One pities the rich, by one of those strange refractions of sympathy frequent in Mrs. Spark's novels; in *The Abbess of Crewe*, for instance, one's heart went out to the character closely based upon Richard Nixon and was repelled by the ascetic, sexual, Christian woman who recurs in Mrs. Spark's novels so often as to suggest, if not an alter ego, a spokesperson. In *The Takeover* this type is represented by Nancy Cowan, a severe, "well-informed, rather thin" Englishwoman who, in the classic double position of governess to the children and mistress to the master, has brought to Italy her "Englishness, her pale summer dresses, her sense of fair play, and many other foreign things." But she fades away as a character until the end, when without benefit of ordination she emerges as St. Paul's advocate and a furious disrober of false prophets at a riot in Hubert Mallindaine's temple of Diana. This riot, for this reader, fizzled; the political, religious, and sociological fuses threaded through the novel's crowded matter all meet here but fail to ignite powder. Instead, an acrid scent of heretic-burning hovers in the grove.

The author senses, in the dire economic "sea-change," a new world arising, "avid for immaterialism"; that is a fine apt phrase, but she seems unduly fearful that this avidity will seize upon footling neo-pagans like Hubert. No danger of that, as long as she gives him the stature of a petty crook and the psychology of a menopausal beauty. Hubert, having robbed his borrowed house of all its furnishings, agrees to vacate, and meets his former patroness, Maggie, costumed as a crone—a goddess in disguise—in the shade of the sacred grove; there she reveals that the rich are not so pitiable after all. Using the newest weaponry of kidnapping and ransom, she has reclaimed much of her fortune from the king of her defrauders, the scarcely glimpsed Coco de Renault. We are pleased, because she has occupied the center of the novel, and the rich have been shown as more entertaining and human than the criminals who feed off them. But is this the reaction toward which Mrs. Spark's many inventions and somber asides have tended? Her disclosures generate more mysteries than they resolve. A theme of fakery centering upon Hubert seems forfeited in the end; he really *is* the priest of Nemi. Amid this welter of frauds monetary and emotional, which is the takeover of the title? Hubert's of Maggie's house? Coco's of Maggie's financial empire? Rich Americans' of Italian estates? The Arabs' of industrialism's lifeblood? All we know for certain is that we have been ushered into the cave of an enchantress, and have there been dazzled, distracted, and peremptorily, as is befitting, dismissed.

Coming into Her Own

LOITERING WITH INTENT, by Muriel Spark. 217 pp. Coward, McCann & Geoghegan, 1981.

Loitering with Intent is autobiographical in tone; its narrator and heroine, Fleur Talbot, a successful and esteemed writer now "having entered the fullness of [her] years," reflects on the beginnings of her career, when, amid considerable sinister confusion in the London of 1949–50, she was composing her first novel, a well-received tale of violence and deception entitled *Warrender Chase*.

Mrs. Spark's own first novel, *The Comforters*, was not published until 1957, but in 1951 one of her uncanny short stories won first prize in an *Observer* competition, and since the war she had been an active if peripheral figure on the London literary scene, with considerable editing, a book of poems *(The Fanfarlo)*, and biographical studies of Mary Shelley, Emily Brontë, and John Masefield to her credit. *Loitering with Intent* looks back to the days of her rather leisurely maturation as an artist, when, in the words of one of her poems,

> Lying on the roof of everything I listen
> To the breath of ambition in her sleep. . . .
> Honour yawns, vanity foams in her coma, charity stretches
> A sham, luxurious limb.
> Until I gather you again when I come into my own,
> Lie low, my sleepy fortunes.

Though the characteristically tricky plot of *Loitering with Intent* concerns the parallel between its incidents and those of the heroine's novel-in-progress, *Warrender Chase*, it shares its ambience and a number of details with *The Comforters:* the heroines, Fleur Talbot and Caroline Rose, have a floral twist to their names; both are living semi-employed on the edge of bohemian circles; and both go dancing at a night spot (called the Pylon in the older novel, Quaglino's in the new) whose walls are decorated with empty picture frames. In *The Comforters*, the heroine finds herself living within a novel whose sentences she hears chanted by a chorus of voices accompanied by the sound of a typewriter; in *Loitering with Intent* she is working on a novel whose imaginary events predict and threaten to expose a real conspiracy afoot. Both Caroline Rose and Fleur Talbot are accused of being mad; both are truly in a state of considerable nervous distraction; and the same shadowy set of prototypes seems to lurk behind their sets of acquaintances—a sympathetic and mischievous old lady (Louisa Jepp, Edwina Oliver), a fleshy embodiment of a smarmy and idolatrous Catholicism (Georgina Hogg, Dottie Carpenter), a bohemian male pal good for all-night conversation (Willi Stock, Solly Mendelsohn), a more sexually involving but still dispensable boyfriend (Laurence Manders, Leslie

Carpenter, Wally McConnachie). These pleasant men are kept in their place. Fleur Talbot tells us:

> Wally was a love, and I wanted to keep him for the fun that we had and might have together. It involved keeping him in that compartment of life in which it had pleased God to place him, set apart from my present most mysterious, slightly hallucinatory concerns.

In both books, the heroine opts for creativity, Catholicism, and essential solitude: Caroline goes off on "a holiday of obligation" to write the novel she has been hearing in her head, while Fleur, her first book acclaimed, goes off to Paris to continue the career upon which she eventually reflects with measured satisfaction: "*All Souls' Day* gave as much pleasure as *Warrender Chase,* and after that, *The English Rose* and the others, some more, some less."

Thus encouraged to reflect upon Muriel Spark's own career (which took her to Roman exile, and not Parisian), and to reread her startlingly accomplished and individual first novel of some twenty-five years and fifteen novels ago, one is torn between admiration for her brilliantly sustained poise and regret that, somehow, since *The Prime of Miss Jean Brodie* (1961), she has held her prominent place without enlarging upon it. Occupying the same grid of concerns as *The Comforters,* deriving from the same area of experience, *Loitering with Intent* is, comparatively, arid and offhand. Beneath its smoothly interlocking farce and cryptic spookiness, *The Comforters* (whose very title suggests a predicament as severe as Job's) conveyed an authentic dilemma and a message of some militance. Though saluted by her fellow-converts Graham Greene and Evelyn Waugh, and showing a surface kinship with the work of these male masters of dark entertainment, the novel had a definite feminine, if not feminist, slant. It spoke to at least one female I know, then young and by no means Catholic, as a veritable revelation. Where else, in the fiction of the Fifties, do we find a heroine whose heterosexuality is so calmly brought forward and assigned a secondary priority, whose determination to value her own intelligence and spirituality is so levelly announced, whose own so-called neuroticism is so cheerfully embraced? Caroline talks to her priest:

"Do you think I'm mad?"

"No. But you're ill."

"That's true. D'you think I'm a neurotic?"

"Of course. That goes without saying."

Caroline laughed too. There was a time when she could call herself a neurotic without a sense of premonition; a time when it was merely the badge of her tribe.

"If I'm not mad," she said, "I soon will be, if this goes on much longer."

"Neurotics never go mad," he said.

The fiction that Mrs. Spark poured out so lavishly, once her novelistic gifts were released, turns variations upon her central contrast between the essentially sane individual neurotic, often wed to the mysterious comforts of the Church, and the essential madness of the heretical, male-dominated or male-mimicking "sect"—the heterodox circle that takes such various forms as the set of literary oldsters in *Memento Mori* (1959), Patrick Seton's spiritualist followers in *The Bachelors* (1960), Miss Brodie's nest of favorite students, the nuns gathered about *The Abbess of Crewe* (1974), and Hubert Mallindaine's band of "faithful" in *The Takeover* (1976). In some of the later, brutally curt novels, such as *Not to Disturb* (1972) and *Territorial Rights* (1979), devilish evil, with its weave of spying and blackmail, crowds even the most modest checkpoint of virtue off the canvas, dismayingly. In *Loitering with Intent* the prototype of wicked circles, Sir Quentin Oliver's Autobiographical Association, is sketched:

> Although in reality I wasn't yet rid of Sir Quentin and his little sect, they were morally outside of myself, they were objectified. I would write about them one day. In fact, under one form or another, whether I have liked it or not, I have written about them ever since, the straws from which I have made my bricks.

But the sketch, perhaps because the model has sat so often before, seems thin and hasty; the exact perverse use to which Sir Quentin is putting the autobiographical attempts of his little association of weak-minded and snobbish loners never comes clear, and the two-headed monster he and the fictional Warrender Chase form never menaces the reader, however much it menaces the heroine.

What does loom full-bodied, with a *dame de lettres* frankness we have never had from Mrs. Spark before, is Fleur Talbot's pride of profession and craft. Though she is not, no more than Nabokov's "MacNab" in *Look at the Harlequins!*, to be indiscriminately confused with the author, what Fleur divulges of her practice and theory of writing has an honest confessional ring. She tells us that as a young woman she was "aware of a *daemon* inside [her] that rejoiced in seeing people as they were, and not only that, but more than ever as they were, and more, and more." Her "swinish" landlord Mr. Alexander strikes her as "quite excellent as such, surpassingly hand-picked," and his aloof wife is also a cherishable type: "I fairly drank her in with my mind while smiling politely back." Fleur has "always been on the listen-in" for revealing phrases people use in conversation. Her secrets in the creating of characters seem simple enough: "To make a character ring true it needs must be in some way contradictory, somewhere a paradox." Fictional characters are, after all, only marks on paper—"some hundreds of words, some punctuation, sentences, pragraphs"—and one needs surprisingly little to be convincing: "I've come to learn for myself how little one needs, in the art of writing, to convey the lot, and how a lot of words, on the other hand, can convey so little." As for motives: "I didn't go in for motives, I never have." On style: "I like to be lucid." An enviable directness and certainty pervade her working methods. We see Fleur type up the entire manuscript of her first novel in a single arduous stretch of scarcely more than a day ("I had very few corrections to make, it was simple slog work"), her hands constantly blackened from handling carbon paper; when the novel comes back to her in proofs, she can't bring herself to read it through for typographical errors and farms the task out to friends. She is not so much a perfectionist as a happy fatalist: "I could see its defects as a novel but they weren't the sort of defects that could be removed without removing the entire essence. It's often like that with a novel or a story. One sees a fault or a blemish . . . but cosmetic treatment won't serve; change the setting of a scene and the balance of the whole work is adversely affected."

The novel's concluding image is of the middle-aged novelist casually kicking a soccer ball back at some small boys: "I kicked it with a chance grace, which, if I had studied the affair and tried hard, I never could have done." (And, it is true, *The Mandelbaum Gate*, the one novel by Mrs. Spark in which she strikes one as having tried hard, is the hardest to read.) This "chance grace" is allied to poetry and myth: "Without a mythology, a novel is nothing. The true novelist, one who understands the work as a continuous poem, is a myth-maker . . . and the methods are mythological by nature." Proceeding by these supernal lights, the novelist is surefooted; when confronted by a publisher's helpful offer of guidance, Fleur snaps, "I don't need your guidance." Her sense of herself as an artist predates any artistic accomplishment and is absolute:

> That I was a woman and living in the twentieth century were plain facts. That I was an artist was a conviction so strong that I never thought of doubting it then or since; and so, as I stood on the pathway in Hyde Park in that September of 1949, there were as good as three facts converging quite miraculously upon myself and I went on my way rejoicing.

This note of rejoicing, frequently sounded in *Loitering with Intent*, may presage a new verve and expansiveness in Mrs. Spark's fiction. The corrosive sense of evil which ate some of her previous novels to such spindly and enigmatic shape has been diluted; although this present novel still does not invite us very deep into the emotional states its complications of plot outline in air, the possibility of such an invitation lies within its benevolent and reminiscent mood. The ticklish relationship between publisher and writer has rarely been burlesqued to droller effect than here; and the ticklish relationship between men and women is given considerable space. Sex, as a kind of electric pouncing, has long been one of the predatory animals that roam Sparkland; but sexual embarrassment and botch, with its halo of fumbled tenderness, is a new creature:

> We walked home by the river and so to bed. It was simply no good. Anxious not to be abstracted and "not there" with Wally, my mind was now only too deliberately concentrated on the actuality of the occasion. I found myself vigilant of every detail in Wally's love-making, I was

noticing, I was *counting*. I was single-mindedly conscious. In despera-
tion I tried thinking of General de Gaulle, which made matters worse,
far, far, worse.

Such homely windows into human soliloquy can only enrich the
grave fun and lucid strangeness of Muriel Spark's constructions.
On the back of the jacket, the glamorized photos adorning some of
her stern fables from Rome have been supplanted by a friendlier
image, of the author gazing at us over her reading glasses with trim
amusement, still drinking us in.

SOME IRISH

Small Cheer from the Old Sod

MERCIER AND CAMIER, by Samuel Beckett, translated from the French by the author. 123 pp. Grove Press, 1974.

THE POOR MOUTH, by Flann O'Brien, translated from the Gaelic by Patrick C. Power. 128 pp. Viking Press, 1974.

There, in the dead center of the wall of books beyond the iron spiral staircase of my friend the Bennington professor's perfectly furnished home, they were: the slim, sans-serif spines of Grove Press's paperback editions of Samuel Beckett, complete. The books looked bought at one blow and, if not pristine, used delicately. So enshrined, they composed a canon: Beckett's work is a single holy book, an absolute of purity and negation by whose light all else in contemporary literature appears somewhat superfluous and unclean. A touchstone not often touched, for who except Hugh Kenner and his fellow-postulants in the bleak disciplines of modernism has really pushed his eyes through all the chop-logic of *Watt* and all the hopeless droning of *The Unnamable?* But then who has time to read anyway? Blankness and minimalism are balms poured upon our overused optical nerves and overcrowded brain cells. That Beckett has worked in isolation and obscurity, in a drastic privacy highlighted rather than relieved by the international success of *Waiting for Godot* and the Nobel Prize in 1969; that he has published parsimoniously; that his works get smaller and smaller ("the expression that there is nothing to express," as he put it in one of his rare interviews)—all this better consorts with our sense of what a writer should be than any Victorian exuberance and heedless pride of creatorship. Beckett's books feel honorably eked out on the edge of agony and silence; their pain is their integrity and their music.

Now a new work is slipped into the canon: *Mercier and Camier*, a short novel written in French in 1946, published in French in 1970, and, as translated by the author into English, offered to Americans by Grove Press. Like Nabokov, Beckett seems to be cleaning up his desk; as his imagination drives him ever closer to the terminal minimum (the fourteen-hundred-word opus *Lessness*, the thirty-five-second play *Breath*), he releases some relatively youthful and expansive works. *Mercier and Camier*, though in itself frivolous, brittle, and less than cathartic, occupies a pivotal place in the canon: it is the first of Beckett's prose works to be originally written in French. Indeed, it seems to be the first motion of that remarkable postwar exertion whereby Beckett, casting off his native tongue and perhaps thereby moving out from under the shadow of his mentor Joyce, transformed himself, in a five-year siege of writing in his Paris apartment, from a slothful dilettante into a master; by 1950 he had composed the three novels of his trilogy *(Molloy, Malone Dies,* and *The Unnamable),* a number of short stories, one play *(Eleutheria)* never published and one *(Waiting for Godot)* that is as surely a masterpiece as any work of the modern theatre. His shift from English to French coincided with the liberation of Europe from the oppression of war. Beckett, who chose to abandon the safety of Ireland in 1939 ("I preferred France in war to Ireland in peace," he told Hugh Kenner), ran genuine risks during the Occupation, as a member of the Resistance. Narrowly escaping the Gestapo in Paris, he survived in Vichy France by passing himself off as a peasant and laboring as one. During this period, in the evenings, he wrote his second, and last, English-language novel, *Watt. Mercier and Camier* is evidently the first creative fruit of his return to Paris. Though steeped in Beckettian futility and gloom, the book does have a holiday air; a sense of lifted nightmare hangs over its ambiguously located city, and its heroes, in their aimless wandering, seem to be hesitantly exploring a new freedom, as the author is exploring a new language.

To move from the prose of *Watt* to that of *Mercier and Camier* is to step into a relatively sparkling atmosphere. Too easily, in *Watt*, Beckett spins catalogues and inconsequential distinctions out of his lifelong preoccupations with arithmetic and scholastic logic. (His father was a quantity surveyor for construction projects, an estimator of bricks and man-hours, and, though Beckett's family was Protestant, no Irish writer is more obsessed with the quantitative aspect of Catholicism, its scholastic inventories and purgatorial durations.) In *Mercier and Camier,* the alien tongue encourages terseness in him; the stichomythic exchanges of the novel anticipate *Waiting for Godot:*

> You kept me waiting, said Mercier.
> On the contrary, said Camier.
> I arrived at nine five, said Mercier.
> And I at nine fifteen, said Camier.
> You see, said Mercier.
> Waiting, said Camier, and keeping waiting can only be with reference to a pre-arranged terminus.

Nothing is easy for them; having arranged to meet to begin a journey, they come and go alternately, just missing. At last met, at nine-fifty, they are confounded by a rain that begins to fall "with quite oriental abruptness." While keeping dry in a pavilion, they are diverted by two fornicating dogs and accosted by "the first of a long line of maleficent beings"—a uniformed "ranger," whose ferocious impersonation of authority ends by foisting off on them a bicycle that is not theirs. By now it is late afternoon. "The day of toil is ended, said Camier, a kind of ink rises in the east and floods the sky." Their destination as uncertain as their setting-out is tardy, they pedal off. And so it goes. They enter pubs. They encounter loquacious strangers. They visit a prostitute called Helen. They curse God. They lose their umbrella. They kill a policeman. They find their umbrella. They part on the edge of the city. They reunite, meeting Watt, from the previous novel. They part, finally. "Dark at its full" are the novel's last words. We have learned that

Mercier is bearded and tall, with a great, bony red nose and some-
where a wife, and even children, whom he abuses frightfully when
he chances upon them, and that Camier, "mirror of magnanimity
and ingenuity," has stout little bandy legs, four chins, beady eyes,
and a card identifying him as

> F. X. Camier
> Private Investigator
> Soul of Discretion;

but where their pilgrimage was meant to go, or why it was under-
taken, is never any clearer than the purpose of human life.

In the telling, the cruel and puerile incidents are relieved by rays
of descriptive beauty, sentences so finely balanced and quietly
phrased as to suffuse entire scenes with their melancholy tender-
ness. At Helen's:

> Before the blazing fire, in the twofold light of lamp and leaden day, they
> squirmed gently on the carpet, their naked bodies mingled, fingering
> and fondling with the languorous tact of hands arranging flowers, while
> the rain beat on the panes.

On the moors outside the city:

> . . . a moor unbroken save for a single track, where no shade ever falls,
> winding out of sight its gentle alternate curves. Not a breath stirs the
> pale grey air. In the far distance here and there the seam of earth and
> sky exudes a sun-flooded beyond. . . . It is here one would lie down,
> in a hollow bedded with dry heather, and fall asleep, for the last time,
> on an afternoon, in the sun, head down among the minute life of stems
> and bells, and fast fall asleep, fast farewell to charming things.

Beckett, of course, is bemused rather than persuaded by the "charm-
ing things" of "this hospitable chaos"; he greets dawn by saying,
"It's the foul old sun yet again, punctual as a hangman." Joy comes
in "saltspoonfuls . . . a bonny little agony homeopathically distilled,
what more can you ask?" His poetry is a motion of the dust:

> But there is still day, day after day, afterlife all life long, the dust of all
> that is dead and buried rising, eddying, settling, burying again. So let

him wake, Mercier, Camier, no matter, Camier, Camier wakes, it's night, still night, he doesn't know the time, no matter, he gets up and moves away, in the dark, lies down again a little further on, still in the ruins, they are extensive.

Why Beckett initially refused to publish—why he "jettisoned," as he described it—a work that secretes so much humor and beauty in its little wasteland invites speculation. The work (set distinctly in Ireland, though some of the references and the names of the heroes give a Gallic tint) is a kind of hybrid, holding within it the two divergent trends of the author's future production. Until the late, diagrammatic stories, of which the ninety-five-hundred-word "The Lost Ones" is the longest, Beckett would not again write fiction in the third person. His novels became first-person monologues. Dialogue and objectivity he relocated on the stage, and, indeed, *Mercier and Camier* has the feel of a play, even to the "curtains" that come every two chapters, in the form of placard-like summations of the previous action. Had this been published, *Waiting for Godot* might have seemed less of a revelation, and even redundant.

In his novels, beginning with *Molloy,* the mind alone, revolving in solipsism, sinking in upon its doubts, relishing the precisions of its imprecisions, became Beckett's home and his voice. Thus he released himself from the "chloroformed world" of Balzacian fiction, as he had diagnosed it in 1931: "[Balzac] can write the end of his book before he has finished the first paragraph, because he has turned all his creatures into clockwork cabbages and can rely on their staying put . . . The whole thing, from beginning to end, takes place in a spellbound backwash." How curiously well this description fits the fictional world Beckett evolved on opposed principles! The reality of the individual, he wrote, "is an incoherent reality and must be expressed incoherently." From 1946 on, his heroes find their coherence in confessed incoherence, and the calculating, sniping, intrusive author of the first three novels falls away, his Sisyphean writing difficulties absorbed by his personae. All of Beckett's French-language fiction after *Mercier and Camier* seems predicted in the final two lines of the last, and best, poem he composed in English, in this pivotal year of 1946:

> Vire will wind in other shadows
> unborn through the bright ways tremble
> and the old mind ghost-forsaken
> sink into its havoc

Brian O'Nolan, who wrote under the pen names of Flann O'Brien and Myles na Gopaleen, was five years younger than Beckett, sounded his genius earlier, husbanded it less thriftily, and died young, at the age of fifty-four. As with Scott Fitzgerald, there is a brilliant ease in his prose, a poignant grace glimmering off every page; and, like Fitzgerald, he had books to say about his student days, though less romantically. Ireland-bound from birth to death, he wrote of a "hard life" and a confined world where, as in Beckett's, threadbare monsters menace a slothful hero and "morning would come slowly, decaying to twilight in the early afternoon." His great book, *At Swim-Two-Birds,* was published in 1939. It savors of precocity, concerning, at bottom, the indolent, frivolous, but inspired attempt of a college student to write a book—a fantastic, parodistic stew of drunken banter, journalese, pulp fiction, and Celtic myth. Like Beckett, O'Brien (to give him his best-known name) has the gift of the perfect sentence, the art, which they both learned from Joyce, of tuning plain language to a lyric pitch. In O'Brien's case, the pedantic undertone is encouraged to surface as comedy:

> It was in the New Year, in February, I think, that I discovered that my person was verminous. A growing irritation in various parts of my body led me to examine my bedclothes and the discovery of lice in large numbers was the result of my researches. I was surprised and experienced also a sense of shame. I resolved at the time to make an end of my dissolute habits and composed mentally a regime of physical regeneration which included bending exercises.

Unlike Beckett and Joyce, O'Brien never internationalized himself; his subject matter remained provincial, without the enhancement of a willed imaginative return from exile, and his tone partakes, a bit tipsily, of local lilt and whimsy. The lousy narrator of *At Swim-Two-Birds* is upstaged by the Good Fairy:

> I recognize that that is good eating, said the Good Fairy, though myself I have no body that I could feed. As a feat of eating it is first-rate.

> When I spoke last, said the Good Fairy, I was kneeling in the cup of your navel but it is bad country and I am there no longer.

> There is little doubt but that you are overfond of the old talk, said the Good Fairy.

Two years after *At Swim-Two-Birds*, O'Brien published a short book truly in the "old talk," a satiric narrative in Gaelic: *An Béal Bocht*, now translated as *The Poor Mouth: A Bad Story About the Hard Life*, with appropriately dismal drawings by Ralph Steadman. Steadman's cartoons, in an especially smudgy charcoal, are an unusual modern instance of successful book illustration: they capture not only the foolery of O'Brien's tale but its harshness, its indignant anger. A marvellous literary mimic, O'Brien is here parodying a class of books unknown to all but a few Americans—the twentieth-century novels written in Gaelic by authors like Tomás Ó Criomhthainn and Máire (Séamus Ó Grianna). Helped by the translator's footnotes, we can see through this travesty into the originals: stories extolling, with phrases like "a child among the ashes" and "grey-wool breeches" and "their likes will not be there again," the simple life of the peasantry of "the little green country." O'Brien's "bad story" literally adheres to the literary clichés:

> It has always been the destiny of the true Gaels (if books be credible) to live in a small, lime-white house in the corner of the glen as you go eastwards along the road.

Before discoursing on the "old times," old Gaels always shove "two hooves" into the ashes and "redden" their pipes; once, because " 'tis said in the good books that describe the affairs of the Gaelic paupers that it's in the middle of the night that two men come visiting if they have a five-noggin bottle," two characters, arriving prematurely in midafternoon, sit for hours in the rain before knocking.

Yet more than the artifices of a romantic revival are pilloried; Irish poverty is placed beyond sentimentalizing by a series of comic exaggerations that are merciless. The narrator, a youth named Bonaparte O'Coonassa, lives in a "small, lime-white, unhealthy house" with his mother, his grandfather—the Old-Grey-Fellow, or Old-Fellow— and a number of livestock, including a pig called Ambrose, who is both huge and sick: "The pig was doubtlessly ill and vapour arose from him reminiscent of a corpse unburied for a month." Ambrose, furthermore, is too fat to be evicted from the cottage through the door. Bonaparte's mother is about to die of the odor when the Old-Fellow drags her outside into the perpetual rain and has the house sealed so that the pig, within, dies of its own stench. When Bonaparte goes to school, his skull is split by the master, a maniac who screams at all his students that their name is James O'Donnell. An especially poor native of this County Corkadoragha, Sitric O'Sanassa, lives in a hole in the ground and, discovering an underwater cave where he can chew the tasteless meat of dead seals, refuses to leave: "It did not appear that he would desert such a well-built comfortable abode after all he had experienced of the misery of Corkadoragha." Our hero, himself starving, discovers some gold, and when he dares buy a pair of boots with it is sentenced to twenty-nine years' imprisonment at a trial of which he doesn't understand a word. The connection between Gaelic and impoverishment is often made: "In one way or another, life was passing us by and we were suffering misery, sometimes having a potato and at other times having nothing in our mouths but sweet words of Gaelic." Though the Revolution is long by, the authorities speak English and have the insane ferocity of the policemen in Beckett. In two savage episodes, a visiting folklorist records and rewards a pig under the impression that its grunts are Gaelic, and the orators of a Gaelic *feis* extol the language while in the audience "many Gaels collapsed from hunger and from strain of listening."

As much as being defeated or exploited, people hate being condescended to, and the nationalist cherishing of Gaelic, O'Brien suggests, was a galling form of condescension. His little book, with its heaping "saltspoonfuls" of bitterness, was received as an outrage in Ireland and was not reprinted until 1964. Then the author, a few years before his death, noted in his foreword that people of the areas where "the sweet Gaelic dialect . . . is oftener in their mouths than a scrap of food" are thinning out; "the young folk are setting their faces towards Siberia in the hope of better weather." The emigration is apt. Irish and Russian literature both give us the impression of a race whose rich human nature has never been matched by its institutions or its climate.

Patrick C. Power has performed sorcery in translating a work so specific in its allusions and exotic in its language. Again and again, so consistently that we come to take it for granted, Mr. Power re-creates Gaelic music in English:

> The stars lighted me, the ground beneath my feet was level and the cold condiment of the nocturnal wind sharpened my appetite for potatoes.

> There was no sweet sound there and any hand which was raised did not accomplish a good deed.

> The darkness had now become rotten with its breath, causing my health to forsake me at full speed . . . Within me arose a storm of blood, a well of sweat and excessive fuss of mind.

This is more than translation; it is invention.

Flann Again

STORIES AND PLAYS, by Flann O'Brien. 208 pp. Viking, 1976.

Since Flann O'Brien, whose *Stories and Plays* has just been published, wrote a melodious fanciful prose that would charm even the stoniest reviewer into something like a song, complaints about the book had best be registered immediately. First, why is it called, on the title page, "A Richard Seaver Book"? Mr. Seaver's personal contributions to the volume are nowhere specified, so his name presents itself as a purely territorial assertion, and an illustration of the tendency, as publishing houses swallow one another and editors emerge from the general indigestion as semi-self-sufficient entrepreneurs, to load books with as many credits as an Academy Award acceptance speech. Second, why has Claud Cockburn given us such a pawky, sly, mannered, and uninformative introduction, when what we need is an outline of O'Brien's creative life and the location within it of the so various contents of this volume: an unfinished farcical novel; two short stories better called sketches; a playlet and a full-length play; and a scatterbrained though brilliantly phrased essay on Joyce, which once did service, we are left to deduce, as an introduction to a special issue of the magazine *Envoy?* The play, *Faustus Kelly,* was produced at the Abbey Theatre in 1943; the copyright credits for the other material run from 1941 to 1951; the incomplete novel, "Slattery's Sago Saga," contains references to President Kennedy's assassination, in 1963; and O'Brien died in 1966: such is the chronological information gleanable from this posthumous collection. If O'Brien is to be treated as a modern classic whose scraps and false starts merit preservation in hard covers, then let a few scholarly dignities be accorded. Viking Press, or Richard Seaver, could learn the proper style from a writer older than O'Brien who, thanks to the happy accident of his longevity, looks after the resurrection of his early works himself; Vladimir Nabokov's notes, in the volumes published by McGraw-Hill, on the stories and novels of his émigré period are models of factuality and orderly salvage. If old wine is good, let it be brought forth in new bottles decently labelled.

Although O'Brien is not to blame for the manner of this book's production, he must be held responsible for the not always enchanting oddity of its contents. "Slattery's Sago Saga, or From Under the Ground to the Top of the Trees" seems conceived for the lark of its title. Not only is the saga unfinished, it scarcely gets started. Each chapter makes a fresh grab at the greased pig of a plot, which was no doubt meant to concern the hilarious complications that ensue when Crawford MacPherson, the Scots wife of an emigrant Irishman called Ned Hoolihan, arrives in Ireland to put into effect her plan to replace the potato with the surpassingly starchy sago as the staple of the Irish diet. She proposes this scheme to Hoolihan's adopted son Tim Hartigan, who, while Hoolihan has become "absolutely stinking and crawling with money" in the oil fields of Texas, has remained peaceably behind in Poguemahone* Hall, reading *Jude the*

---

*Which, an informant wrote me from Kalamazoo, means "kiss my arse" in Erse.

Obscure. The entrance into his life of his adoptive stepmother occurs in a burst of O'Brien's descriptive bravado:

> The door was noisily flung inward and framed in the entrance was an elderly woman clad in shapeless, hairy tweeds, small red-rimmed eyes glistening in a brownish lumpy face that looked to Tim like the crust of an apple-pie. The voice that came was harsh, and bedaubed with that rumbling colour which comes from Scotland only.

Gustily she presents her headlong plan to purchase all the arable land in Ireland and lease it back to the natives on the provision they plant and, in fifteen years, harvest sago palms: "You are a young man, Hartigan. You will probably live to see your native land covered with pathless sago forests, a glorious sight and itself a guarantee of American health, liberty and social cleanliness." She is determined to prevent a recurrence of the potato famine of the 1840s, which caused a million starving Irishmen to migrate to America and nearly ruin it: "They bred and multiplied and infested the whole continent, saturating it with crime, drunkenness, illegal corn liquor, bank robbery, murder, prostitution, syphilis, mob rule, crooked politics and Roman Catholic Popery." To protect the United States from the Irish menace, she will invest the gushing wealth of Texas and oust that root of evil, the potato. Tim thinks, "What a strange spectre of a woman this was, to be sure! Where would her equal be found in the broad wideness of the world?" But most of the plan's fun lies in its exposition; though the characters dither and multiply for seven chapters, and the reader is treated to an O'Brienesque display of curious truths about the sago palm, idle and frantic conversations are all the action there is; the book's prankish premises prove barren, and O'Brien, unable to duplicate the miracle of *At Swim-Two-Birds* and spin a genuine novel out of schoolboy extravagance, understandably stopped writing "Slattery's Sago Saga."* The last chapter, a letter from Hoolihan to

---

*Another fan of Flann wrote me from Selinsgrove, Pennsylvania, to point out that while working on the novel O'Brien suffered from a second coronary attack, uremia, a broken right leg, sycosis, pleurisy, an abscess of the middle ear, anemia, and liver cancer. He listed these ailments himself in an article, "Can a Saint Strike Back?", that attributes them all to the revenge of St. Augustine, whom he had maligned in *The Dalkey Review.* He was repeatedly hospitalized during the writing of "Slattery's Sago Saga"; the cancer kept spreading, and killed him.

Hartigan, has a dark power irrelevant to Irish follies; like Kafka's *Amerika*, it is an evocation of the United States by a writer of genius who has never been here.

> You might think I'm now long enough in the U.S.A. to have a few friends here and there but honestly, Tim, I'm lonely as hell and have to keep fighting like a trojan to keep away from the licker. Some of my buddies, as they call themselves, may be all right under the skin but I just don't have the mental machinery to tell which of them are bums or hoods. They have all a profound, sincere, undisguised interest in money—MY money, I'd say—and I needn't tell you they mostly want it to prop up poor prostitutes in homes, teach the alphabet to blind cripples, found new Orders of nigger and octaroon nuns and make absolutely certain that the Democrats will never lose this State.

Amid foolery, a nerve is touched, a real voice speaks, close to paranoia, fighting "the licker." The manuscript stops as if appalled.

The other item of considerable length in the collection is the play, *Faustus Kelly*. A town politician, Kelly, sells his soul to the Devil to secure his election to the Irish Parliament. By the time three acts of confusion and oration are past, the Devil vows, "I want nothing more of Irish public life." The play is Shavian in form, but where Shaw would have filled the stage with luminous debate there is instead a compounded obfuscation of voices being carried away with themselves. The accents are lovingly done:

> Ah, Paddy Hourigan, may God be good to him, for a finer, neater, better-made, dacenter Irishman never wore a hat.

> I do, I do, sure I could go down there any day on me bicycle, I could meet you in Biddie Brannigan's and have a glass of good Irish whiskey with you, what grander, finer thing could we do?

O'Brien, a civil servant for most of his life, knew his town councils, and he certainly knew how men talk to one another—he creates an Irish roarer, named Reilly, to outdo the Cyclops of Joyce's *Ulysses*. But the action and the accuracies turn inward, to a local reality of private jokes; the crucial event of the plot, for instance, is the Devil's not being "sanctioned" as rate collector by "the Department." Not being sanctioned is apparently the ultimate misfortune in Ireland:

> You can be up for murder and welcome. You can take a hatchet and cut your wife into two pieces. People will say you're . . . an odd class of a man. But this business of not being sanctioned—oh, begob, that's a different pair of sleeves.

The Devil's discomfiture is amusing to behold, but an uneasy sense persists that we are outsiders at a party, and our laughter keeps coming a second late. Unlike Beckett and Joyce, Yeats and Shaw and even Synge, O'Brien seems obsessed by Irishness itself; his Irishmen never shed their racial and nationalist accoutrements and emerge simply as men.

The two short stories, and the anecdote in play form called *Thirst,* are thin things to come from the tradition that produced *Dubliners* and the stories of Frank O'Connor, Mary Lavin, Sean O'Faolain, Benedict Kiely, and the multitudes of others who have made Irish mores and manners a familiar garb of humanity. *Thirst* shows some men caught in a pub after hours teasing the constable into having a drink with them. "John Duffy's Brother" tells of a man who wakes with the mad idea that he is a train. The tales are monochromatic, though unerringly limned; they more suggest Kafka (in their bleak air of unhealth) and Pirandello (in their circling about the notions of delusion and fabrication) than the masters of Irish realism. They are sternly unsensual, except for the effortless music and lucidity of the prose. O'Brien can shock us with the crystalline quickness of his mind. His essay on Joyce, "A Bash in the Tunnel," begins, "James Joyce was an artist. He has said so himself. His was a case of Ars gratia Artist." Later, another pun captures in a word Joyce's peculiar voracious fusion of schemata and data:

> What was really abnormal about Joyce? At Clongowes he had his dose of Jesuit casuistry. Why did he substitute his home-made chaosistry?

But O'Brien's central image of the Irish artist as resembling a man who would lock himself into the lavatory of an uncoupled railway car to enjoy a "bash" of solitary whiskey-drinking reflects upon the something closeted and inebriated about his own talent. A sour trickle of alcohol runs through these inventions. "He was tired," we are told of Tim Hartigan, "and intestinally a bit irked by spent whiskey." *Stories and Plays* contains no felt glimpse of parentage, of love, of the private, animal, domestic life that meant so much to, say, Joyce. The most emotional moment occurs when the Devil is roused to the fear of social exclusion; the coziest times are passed in public houses. It was no mistake of fate that cast O'Nolan, under his other pen name of Myles na Gopaleen, as a newspaper columnist. His busy imagination seems that of a man who, richly endowed with the gifts one must develop in solitude, didn't want to be alone. "Humour, the handmaid of sorrow and fear" remained his muse, and writing became, under his magical pen, a sort of fooling away.

An Old-Fashioned Novel

THE PORNOGRAPHER, by John McGahern. 252 pp. Harper & Row, 1979.

Surely one of the novel's habitual aims is to articulate morality, to sharpen the reader's sense of vice and virtue. Yet, in a time of triumphant relativism, speckled with surreal outbursts of violence on both the public and the private level, light and shadow are so bafflingly intermixed that fiction exerts its old spell best in pockets of underdevelopment where the divisive ghosts of religious orthodoxy still linger. Out of a contemporary Ireland where the production of pornography is still a matter of, if not prosecution, self-reproach, and where a woman can still be concerned for her virginity and a man for his honor, and where the notion can persist in intelligent heads that "things were run on lines of good and bad, according to some vague law or other," and where erotic adventure is still enough freighted with guilt and pain to seem a mode of inner pilgrimage, John McGahern has produced his vivid and involving novel. His hero, a thirty-year-old unwed male citizen of Dublin, makes a tidy living by penning pornographic chronicles for an old friend, a frustrated littérateur called Maloney, who has resolved his frustrations by becoming a "rich and fairly powerful" publisher of smut in successful defiance of the land's "obsolete censorship laws." For our presumably high-minded delectation, the pornographer narrates the story of a season in his life when death and birth, exhaustion and renewal momentously conjoin.

While carrying on with the lubricious exploits of his fictitious Mavis Carmichael and Colonel Grimshaw, our youngish man is also dutifully carrying brandy and cheer to his dying aunt in a Dublin hospital, and dealing politely with his other kin and his inherited farm some hours' drive from Dublin. And at the same time, and not so incongruously as he appears to think, he seeks liquid solace in pubs and fleshly consolation in dance halls, which seem still to fulfill a respectable social role in Ireland. At least, our hero finds in one a very respectable pickup, a thirty-eight-year-old semi-virgin (the concept, a new one to me, might also be phrased as demi-deflowered) who with great speed and ease allows him to seduce and—less to his liking—to impregnate her. The pregnancy is mostly at her insistence, for she brushes aside his attempt at contraception with "It's unnatural. It turns the whole thing into a kind of farce." She also finds his pornography a bit much. But her enthusiasm for sex and maternity and marriage, though late aroused, is limited by naught save our hero's surliness; from initial attraction to her "clean, strong features" and lust for her body "lean and strong against my hand," he moves through irritation and alarm to loathing, the more intense the more intensely she persists in loving him. At the end, we are told, "The last I remember was striking out at her as she came towards me with outstretched hands." With some surliness of his own, Mr. McGahern shows great reluctance to divulge the names of his major characters, but that of the *demi-vierge* is given passingly as Josephine, and that of the narrator's aunt as Mary. Between the two desperately needy women, then, between Josephine's pregnancy and Mary's cancer, our weary pornographer shuttles for the nine and more months that make up his sorry, lyrical tale.

Such a tale of dance-hall seduction, undesired pregnancy, unre-quited passion, sickbed visitation, and self-righteously self-imposed solitude, with vistas of slate-roofed rural peace to lend darkening contrast to the moiling urban foreground, might almost be illustrated by Victorian steel engravings. Though located somewhere in our fast-departing decade, it wears a musty timelessness that might strike even an Irishman as quaint. But for the absence of parading British soldiery and horsedrawn streetcars, its milieu could be the well-detailed Dublin of June 16, 1904, with its reek of pubs and rasp of caustic and elaborate jesting among Jesuit-educated idlers. Nor is Joyce's soft-limbed swooningness, in loving echo of the sentimental songs and pious imagery of his upbringing, entirely absent from Mr. McGahern's prose:

> Within her there was this instant of rest, the glory and the awe, that one was as close as ever man could be to the presence of the mystery, and live, the encaged bird in its moment of pure rest before it was about to be loosed into the blinding light . . .

His flights of religious-seeming rhetoric fall short of the final clarity they promise:

> This body was the shelter of the self. Like all walls and shelters it would age and break and let the enemy in. But holding it now was like holding glory, and having held it once was to hold it—no matter how broken and conquered—in glory still, and with the more terrible tenderness.

And the stylist has an overindulged mannerism of running quotes into the next sentence with only a comma:

> "It was great to see you," he shook hands.

> "I wish I had taken you back to the room that evening," I stirred with desire.

> "Eleven would be fine. Say, at the gates of the priests' factory," it was one of his few jokes.

But let it be admitted—nay, proclaimed—that by and large Mr. McGahern writes entrancingly, with a lively pace and constant melody. Each sentence is tuned to a certain singing tension, the local lilt exploited subtly. "Way had to be pushed through the men crowded in the entrance at the top of the short steps." No American could have composed that sentence, or the echoing sentence that closes the paragraph: "On the irreversible way, many who loved and married met in this cattle light." Visiting his aunt, the narrator begins, "I caught her sleeping lightly, some late sun on the pillows from the high windows facing home." The pornography he writes, and gives us samples of, is rendered chaste by this same dainty magic of phrasing: "She came with a cry that seemed to catch at something passing through the air." Often a single cunning word lifts a description well up from the ordinary: a girl is seen as "young and healthy and strong, the face open and uncomplicated beneath its crown of shining black hair, a young woman rooted in her only life," and a man is "plainly Irish, from a line of men who had been performing feats of strength to the amazement of an infantile countryside for the past hundred years." Without straining, the happy compression of aphorism is attained; of his writing the narrator says, "Nothing ever holds together unless it is mixed with some of one's own blood." Mr. McGahern writes well, and for the usual reasons: he observes well, hears faithfully, and feels keenly.

He is a shrewd psychologist. The distances between people—the jagged rift between the lovers, the gradually widening space the aunt in dying sets around her—are beautifully sketched, in pages of laconic dialogue that are sometimes comic. His portrait, indeed, of the spurned Josephine is so telling that we wind up liking her more than the hero does, and losing sympathy with him; while in some novels this might be a feat of dramatic irony, in this it seems a flaw. The narrator's vacuous response toward her touching eagerness to be married, and then toward the brave act of her moving to London to bear their illegitimate child, never feels justified, though it is often explained. He has earlier suffered a romantic rejection that has left him numbed. He states near the outset of the book, as if in warning, that "energy is everything, for without energy there can be no anything, no love and no quality of love." As the little society around him registers its disapproval ("It won't do at all," his cynical friend Maloney surprisingly insists. "You've got this woman into a frightful mess. In your conceit you refuse to marry her though she is a beauty, a far cry from your own appearance. . . . Your behavior has dropped the moral averages to zero overnight"), and as his own remorseless inventory of ignoble acts and emotions mounts, our hero comes to suggest *l'étranger* in tweeds, droning like some Hibernian Camus to the effect that "we have to go inland, in the solitude that is both pain and joy, and there make our own truth, and even if that proves nothing too, we have still that hard joy of having gone the hard and only way there is to go, we have not backed away or staggered to one side, but gone on and on and on even when there was nothing . . ." As Maloney says, it won't do, even though the narrator pleads guilty to "shameful shallowness" and finally proclaims that "there comes a time when you either run amok completely or try to make a go of it. I'm going to try to make a go of it"—i.e., marry the next girl he seduces, a twenty-three-year-old nurse who, like Josephine, is apprehended as a "strong" and "healthy" female animal. What stuck to this reader's ribs was the hero's deadly coldness, and Josephine's credible, vital, naïve humanity. Perhaps an American reader is less pained than would be an Irish bachelor by her "touch of an American accent," her way of saying "O boy," and her hopeful air of "forget-me-nots":

> She walked quickly towards me, chin raised, smiling so hard that her dimples seemed to rise and fall. Her strong body was perfectly formed, the features clear and handsome. She would have been beautiful, I thought, except for this flurry of blue forget-me-nots she seemed to send quivering out with every step.

We remember her raised chin and her smile well after our hero forgets them, while he chases after his own flickering "instinct for the true" and after the fey young nurse in her strangely moony and impalpable hospital setting.

Of course, the author has created the character the narrator fails to love, and Mr. McGahern's other works amply include among their aims a wish to display human ugliness. In the short story "Hearts of Oak and Bellies of Brass," the ugliness exists as an end in itself, dreadful to contemplate; in "Lavin," it clashes with a sense of lost beauty in such a way as to become, itself, a kind of beauty. The personal ugliness in the long story "Peaches"—one of Mr. McGahern's few portraits of marriage, and a discouraging one—

pales beside the political ugliness of the brilliant denouement. These stories all achieve what they grimly set out to do, but *The Pornographer* goes somehow awry. We feel impatience with the hero and a frustrated suspicion that the real story occurred elsewhere.

It is not unusual in fiction for a character to overrespond to a writer's demands and to throw out of balance the moral intended. The rebel Satan makes Milton's God look bad, and Don Quixote's foolishness becomes heroism. Here chin-up, pregnant Josephine makes our narrator look bad, with a badness that taints his narrative. Why is he telling us all this? The question bothers every piece of first-person fiction to a degree, and lays upon it a responsibility to come back with witnessed marvels *(Moby-Dick)* or a clear confessional urgency *(Notes from Underground)*. Otherwise, we seem to have bragging without much to brag about—"conceit," to quote Maloney. We would probably judge Mr. McGahern's hero less sternly if we encountered him and his problems in life rather than in a novel. Novel readers are ruthlessly sentimental. We want characters to marry, out of our own need to be done with them, to have them off our consciences.

JARRY, QUENEAU, CÉLINE, PINGET

Human Capacities

THE SUPERMALE, by Alfred Jarry, translated from the French by Ralph Gladstone and Barbara Wright. 81 pp. New Directions, 1977.

THE SUNDAY OF LIFE, by Raymond Queneau, translated from the French by Barbara Wright. 180 pp. New Directions, 1977.

In the case of a living author, at least until senility is medically certified, the possibility exists that his new book will be better than his last. In the case of a writer whose works in another language are brought into English many years after their composition, the odds are that the best were translated first and a kind of dutiful rounding-out is in progress. New Directions has played the dutiful hand-maiden to modernism for forty years, and continues to do so by bringing us more Alfred Jarry and more Raymond Queneau. The Jarry is a rather frantic eighty-page trifle, the Queneau is unevenly entertaining; yet both volumes have their unexpected beauties, slightly alter our impression of the creative spirits behind them, and offer some hours' relief to American readers groggy with the hustle and clamor of their own literary marketplace. Both books have black-and-white jackets, which is soothing, and neither boasts a seven-figure paperback-rights resale, which comes as a cool breeze in these overheated days of the print-media industry. We are reminded of innocent times when publishing houses owned themselves and au-thors' ambitions were bound, as it were, between hard covers.

Not that Jarry was not megalomaniacal; he was, and aspired always to revolutionize nothing less than human limitations. "Human capacities have no limits," he has the "Supermale" say, and in this fervid faith Jarry is a bizarre, terminal spokesman of nineteenth-century optimism. An undersized dynamo who had burned himself out by the age of thirty-four on a diet of absinthe, ether, and hypercerebration, he won notoriety in 1896 with the play *Ubu Roi*, a frenzied farce whose note of nihilistic violence still resounds on the contemporary stage. His personality made a vivid impression upon a smaller audience of fellow-littérateurs: André Gide remembered him as a "plaster-faced Kobold, gotten up like a circus clown and acting a fantastic, strenuously contrived role which showed no human characteristic." Fantastic, strenuously contrived, and inhuman also was his prose; during the eleven years of his life remaining after the celebrated performance of *Ubu Roi*, Jarry, who had been a brilliant and industrious student at the *lycées* of Laval and Rennes, produced a succession of erudite, whimsical, cruel, science-obsessed, provocative, and tiresome short works already, one would think, made sufficiently available to Americans in the *Selected Works of Alfred Jarry* (edited by Roger Shattuck and Simon Watson Taylor; Grove, 1965).

The Supermale (Le Surmâle) was published in 1902 and is set in the futuristic time of 1920. It is a novel, of the special sort associated with the Marquis de Sade; that is, there is a lavishly equipped château (the Château de Lurance), a distinguished group of guests ("the celebrated American chemist William Elson, a widower, with his daughter Ellen; the millionaire engineer, electrical expert, and manufacturer of automobiles and aircraft, Arthur Gough, with his wife; General Sider; Senator de Saint-Jurieu with his baroness, Pusice-Euprépie de Saint-Jurieu; Cardinal Romuald; the actress Henriette Cyne, and Doctor Bathybius"), and a philosophical debate that ends, by way of settlement, in an orgy.

An orgy, however, of narrow scope. The hero and host, André Marcueil, proposes in *The Supermale*'s first sentence that the act of love can be performed indefinitely. Marcueil, an unprepossessing man of thirty with tinted lenses in his pince-nez, a face as pale as his starched shirtfront, and ankles that resemble his wrists in dark frailty, makes his assertion that "human capacities have no limits" and, since his creator shares this demented conviction, has no trouble in demonstrating its truth. Indeed, Jarry, postponing the looked-for love feast to the last quarter of the book, stages an extensive and grotesque sporting event in additional evidence of human illimitability: five men strapped on a bicycle, their "ten legs joined on either side by aluminum rods," and chewing for nutrition only "small, colorless, crumbly, and bitter-tasting cubes of Perpetual Motion Food" based on the "superfood" of pure alcohol, outrace a locomotive over no less a distance than ten thousand miles, along a track specially laid across Siberia for the event. This gargantuan ordeal, described by one of the five American racers, Ted Oxborrow, is a notably macabre permutation of Jarry's obsessional fantasy: Man as Machine. When one of the racers, Jewey Jacobs, dies in the saddle, the odor of decomposition arises rapidly ("due to the secretion of an extraordinary abundance of muscular toxins") but the mechanical inconvenience passes. The putrefying corpse is taught to pedal better than ever:

> Soon Jewey Jacobs began to pedal, with a bad grace at first, and we couldn't see whether he was making any grimaces, as his face was still in his mask. We encouraged him with friendly insults. . . . Little by little he entered into the swing of it, his legs caught up with ours, the ankle-play returned, and finally he started pedaling madly.
> "He's acting as a flywheel," said the corporal. . . .
> Indeed, not only did he catch up with us, he increased his speed beyond ours, and Jacobs' death-sprint was a sprint the like of which the living cannot conceive.

There is a rich mix of unpleasantnesses here, but a pathos, too, for it is not hard to read into Jewey Jacobs's propulsive triumph over death, and the bicycle team's invincibility, Jarry's own mad hope, as he drank himself to death, that by sufficient acceleration he could elude mortal consequences. As Miss Wright well says in her introduction, "his megalomania was a mask for a great deal of misery." By an odd twist, the very fuel that drives the human organisms to transcend possibility quenches the locomotive; as Elson prepares to pour alcohol into the engine, the engineer shouts, "You're not going to give it to the locomotive to drink? It would hurt it! It's not a human creature!"

An unexpected tenderness also characterizes the erotic passages of *The Supermale.* These are less ribald and explicit than almost any contemporary writer, given the theme, would have made them. Though Marcueil procures seven whores for his demonstration, they are not utilized, and instead the American chemist's gracile daughter Ellen offers herself to be the Supermale's partner—"a little slip of a girl," "round-faced with a slightly snub nose, thin-lipped, with immense eyelashes and practically no eyebrows, so that, seen in profile, her brown lashes seem to detach themselves from her face . . ." Naked, Ellen is "seemingly transparent in the lamplight," and, having fainted from her exertions, she is examined with the sequential care of a naturalist:

> Her teeth were minute and well-kept toys. . . .
> Her ears, there was no doubt, had been "hemmed" by some lace-maker.
> The tips of her breasts were curious, pink things, which looked like each other, and like nothing else.
> Her genitals seemed like a small, eminently stupid animal, as stupid as a shellfish—really, there was quite a resemblance—but not less pink.

We care, amid the monstrous mechanisms of this tale, about this loving couple, and feel at their final parting the same cheated exasperation we do at the narrowly missed appointment of Romeo and Juliet. Jarry, who talked like a nutcracker and lived in a room where a normal-sized man could not stand up, nevertheless had a space of experience in his life that enabled him to write not about lovemaking but about love:

> And he began to sink softly down beside his companion, who was asleep in the absolute, just as the first man had awoken near Eve and thought that she had come out of his side because she was beside him, in his quite natural surprise at finding the first woman, whom love had made to blossom, in the place where some still anthropoid female had slept before.

The Absolute, the cruel companion of Jarry's fantasies, momentarily relented, permitting waking thoughts. In the passage above, a female becomes a woman; in another, the ferocious visions of men wedded to hyperbolic bicycles yield their secret origin, in what Pascal called the heart: Ellen Elson explains to her lover, "The Absolute Lover must exist, since woman can conceive of him, just as there is but one proof of the immortality of the soul, which is that man, through fear of nothingness, aspires to it!"

Serenity, which Jarry so flagrantly lacked, Raymond Queneau exemplifies. His books have a double calm: that of a satisfactorily finished design and that of a pleased acceptance of reality. "The Sunday of life"—a phrase even more lyrical in the French, *"le dimanche de la vie"*—comes, the epigraph tells us, from Hegel, who, in meditating the world of Dutch painting, spoke of "the Sunday of life, which levels everything, and rejects everything bad." There is much bad that the characters of this novel must reject or ignore: death strikes often, greed manifests itself, an ineluctable dissatisfaction and restlessness permeate their moods. A stroke paralyzes the heroine, Julia, and the coming of war threatens the hero, Private Valentin Brû. The years are 1936–40, and in France conversation "always came back to Hitler's innermost thoughts." As in *The Magic Mountain,* a war earlier, the characters' romances, hobbies, and self-aggrandizements are X-rayed to their foolish bones by the blast of black light from the future. Published in 1952, *The Sunday of Life,* employing the same cavalier touch with which Queneau in *The Flight of Icarus* etched the 1890s, portrays those gray pre-war years when *vin blanc gommé* could still be ordered in cafés and President Fallières (1906–13) could still be remembered. It is a France of small shops and returned colonial soldiers. Through the window of her notions shop in Bordeaux, Mlle. Julia Segovia, whose age is "something like forty-five," sees the young Private Brû pass, "joyfully clad in khaki," and determines to marry him. Since he is twenty years younger and they have never met, her desire might seem susceptible to many frustrations; "it was all plain sailing, however." Three months and thirty-five pages later, they are married; he takes a honeymoon trip by himself, to Bruges. Her mother dies, and they inherit her framer's shop in Paris. Meanwhile, Julia's sister Chantal and her husband, Paul—a nonentity so slippery the author gives his surname in over fifty different forms —have become rich by manufacturing rifle butts. Valentin's framing enterprise fails, Julia has a stroke, and he takes over her *sub rosa* business as a fortune-teller, assuring his customers that war will not come, until war does come. Recalled to the service, he is last seen boosting three girls, "inexplicably dressed as mountaineers," by their behinds into a window of a crowded train. His beloved, half-paralyzed, impoverished wife, witnessing this, laughs.

The plot is scarcely worth retelling. Some of the incidents, especially the needling, coarse, slangy conversations among the sisters and the brothers-in-law, seem scarcely worth reading, their banality is so thorough. And the translator's attempts to render Queneau's cunningly "demotic" French with contractions like "Zthe" (for "It's the") and "Tsava" ("Let's have a") and Krazy Kat distortions like "eggzactly" and "wisecraps" are valiant but wear a grimace of false gusto. Queneau's famous de-Academizing of the French language by means of phonetic spellings like *"Pololicacru"* for *"Paul aussi l'a cru"* and *"Doukipudonktan"* for *"D'où qu'ils puent donc tant"* defies translation totally, as the introduction admits. The nuances of slang, like the nuances of poetry, must be taken on faith. But even to a French reader, one suspects, *The Sunday of Life*, like its characters, has margins of enigma. The novel, that is, is egoistic, and given to the same excessively private contemplations as Valentin Brû, who sits in his unfrequented framer's shop literally clock-watching, trying "to follow time, nothing but time." He achieves seven continuous minutes of pure temporal vacuity, and wonders, "After I've got away from myself with so much concentration, when I find myself a bit later on back in the place I started from without ever having budged, is that like when you sleep without dreaming?" Brû, ingenuous at first, a simpleton who cannot even recover his suitcase from a baggage checkroom, becomes a monster of introspection and a master psychologist, who as a fortune-teller plays on the innocent egoism of others:

He admired the facility with which he had created a little zone of error in the reasonable mind of the grocer. Up till now he had always thought that language ought to formulate the truth, and silence hide it. The words he would use to Madame Saphir's customers, male and female, it wouldn't even be zones of error that they would form, but zones of confusion in which illusion might remain in suspense until the end of a life.

His own egoism is subjected to scrutiny at unlikely moments. He finds Julia's body, "looking very dead," on the floor:

> Then he thought: my life's going to be changed, and almost at the same time: so's hers. From which he very rapidly concluded: I'm not such an egoist as all that, seeing that I'm thinking about her.

Hegel is the presiding philosopher of *The Sunday of Life*, as Descartes was of *The Bark Tree*, and so, as the book's holiday darkens under the shadow of wartime, there are allusions to History: "Local people, having no new stories to tell him except to the extent that they were participating in History, now only rarely came to confide to him the more and more petty details of a life pulverized by newspaper headlines." In the crowded trains, "a whole family would march past, groaning, distorted by the majesty of great catastrophes." In a curious way, the novel is about the Battle of Jena (1806). It is mentioned on the first page as Private Brû's virtually only thought: "Private Brû . . . in general thought of nothing, but, when he did, had a preference for the Battle of Jena." Near the end of *The Sunday of Life,* Paul says, "It's only now that we can understand why Valentin was interested in the Battle of Jena. . . . Will Hitler create Europe, and succeed where Napoleon failed? Or will France, helped by the Russians and the English, rise again like Prussia in 1813?" At Jena, Napoleon defeated Prussia and went on to enter Berlin; the battle is thus a mirror image of Hitler's defeat of the French and his occupation of Paris. But the Prussians were to have their revenge, and so were the French, as Queneau knew, though his characters in this novel do not. Jena is a paradigm, perhaps, of momentary defeats, of "everything bad," which human life in its timeless succession of Sundays outlasts. "The days that pass, which turn into the time that passes, are neither lovely nor hideous, but always the same." So much for history, for Hegel's glorification of history (living at Jena in 1806, the young philosopher hailed Napoleon as "the Soul of the World") and the state, which was to have such sinister reverberations in the German consciousness. Against the grandiose Queneau posits the quotidian, in the same patriotic spirit in which Wallace Stevens wrote, "Say this to Pravda, tell the damned rag/That the peaches are slowly ripening." Valentin Brû, from one standpoint a cipher, a whisper (his name suggests), is from another a "sort of ascetic," the possessor of an active inner life and a satisfied sensuality: the quintessential Frenchman, mysterious as all egoists are, yet sufficiently tied to his society to volunteer for duty on the Maginot Line. Queneau, like Jarry, is more conservative than his cheerful anarchic manner promises: not love machines nor war machines render human loyalty and decency obsolete.

Thirty-four Years Late, Twice

WE ALWAYS TREAT WOMEN TOO WELL, by Raymond Queneau, translated from the French by Barbara Wright. 174 pp. New Directions, 1981.

EXERCISES IN STYLE, by Raymond Queneau, translated from the French by Barbara Wright. 197 pp. New Directions, 1981.

Raymond Queneau, that most learned and light-hearted of experimental modernists, in 1947 published, under the pseudonym Sally Mara, a kind of thriller set in Dublin during the uprising of 1916, entitled *On est toujours trop bon avec les femmes*. The book, unlike the American-style novels, sexy and tough, that it burlesqued, did not prove popular with the French public in the Forties; nor has it been popular with the *Queneauistes*. Excluded from the official Gallimard edition of Queneau's oeuvre until 1962, it has been persistently regarded by academics as "an unfortunate but forgivable interlude in a distinguished man's career," we are told by Valerie Caton in her foreword to the belated English translation. She describes as "disturbing" the "flippant and amused manner in which its brutal scenes are presented to the reader," and vouches that the novel's many instances of "deliberate bad taste . . . instead of making the reader laugh, leave him feeling uneasy, even downright appalled." She then cites as an example a passage that did make at least this reader laugh:

> Corny Kelleher had wasted no time in injecting a bullet into his noggin. The dead doorman vomited his brains through an eighth orifice in his head, and fell flat on the floor.

Perhaps *We Always Treat Women Too Well* is less funny in French than in Barbara Wright's frisky, deadpan translation; the borrowing of its Dublin locale and personnel almost entirely from Joyce's *Ulysses* is certainly a less circuitous joke in English than in French, and the risibility of sex and violence may more readily strike American readers hardened by Hammett and Chandler and Spillane than readers saddled with tender Gallic sensibilities. Queneau himself, in a 1944 essay, attacked the greatly successful thriller *No Orchids for Miss Blandish* as glorifying "fascist" behavior at a time when the Western democracies were battling fascists in war. Yet the sado-erotic tradition in French literature has a pedigree going back beyond the notorious Marquis to Rabelais and Villon, and it seems unlikely that the postwar critics who embraced Genet and Georges Bataille would snub Queneau's sportive travesty out of mere squeamishness.

We Always Treat Women Too Well, though sufficiently endowed with Queneau's cerebral prankishness, electric pace, and cut-on-the-bias poetry to give glimmers of delight, is a work of casual ambivalence, whole-heartedly neither parody nor thriller, and with a moral by no means as simple as anti-fascism. A group of Irish Republicans, all named from minor figures in *Ulysses,* storm and take a post office at the corner of Sackville Street and Eden Quay; they kill the doorman and the postmaster, who bears the un-Gaelic name of Theodore Durand and cries "God save the King!" in token resistance. The other workers in the post office are expelled, but one female clerk, Gertie Girdle (close verbal kin to Gerty MacDowell, the limping temptress of Leopold Bloom in the "Nausicaa" episode of *Ulysses*), remains in the lavatory, where she entertains a series of Molly Bloom–like interior monologues until her eventual discovery by the rather bumbling and scatterbrained rebels. Once discovered, she, though at the outset a virgin given to inner raptures over her "beloved fiancé, Commodore Sidney Cartwright," embarks with shameless and inexplicable expertise upon a guerrilla campaign of seduction among her captors, eventually making sexual contact via one orifice or another with six of the seven men. Meanwhile, the British soldiery and a gunboat in the Liffey commanded by Sidney Cartwright besiege the post office and at last recapture it. Yet—and this is the curious fact—no connection between Gertie's seductions and the rebel band's defeat is insisted upon, though it would have been easy for Queneau to make connections, and what little he has of a plot would seem to hinge on them. The rebel leader, Caffrey, is beheaded by a shell while engaged in intercourse; but the hit is a lucky one, from the very erratic gunners of H.M.S. *Furious,* and a quite accidental consequence of his pose. Gertie's sexually active presence among the men functions as a distraction, to be sure, but is never made to appear detrimental to their defense against odds that all come to recognize as hopeless. Cartwright, on the *Furious,* knows that this post office is where his fiancée is employed, and is reluctant, accordingly, to demolish it; so her presence if anything prolongs rather than shortens the lives of the rebels.

Why, then, does this woman, who has no sympathy with the rebellion and "the greatest respect for our gracious King George the Fifth," consort so lustily with her captors? Because, Queneau himself might answer, that's the sort of thing that happens in books like this. In *No Orchids for Miss Blandish,* the heroine is beaten, drugged, and raped at the hands of an armed gang, and falls in love with the ruthless leader. The theme of rape as mutual pleasure is a venerable one, dating back in the West at least to the Earthy amours of Zeus. The genre of thriller that Queneau is both protesting and imitating construed sex and violence as parts of a single force-field; it assumed that a tension close to enmity naturally exists between men and women. This was the Thirties and Forties: hard times. "The war between the sexes" was dramatized not only in the cartoons of James Thurber but in the couplings sketched by James

M. Cain and Raymond Chandler and *les films noirs*. The apache dance, the grapefruit in the face were acceptable erotic symbols in a world that acknowledged that wooing, like living, had a rough side. Certainly sexual initiation, however considerately cushioned, has the violence of change. For the brides of some tribal societies, the pain and trauma of defloration are diverted from the approved mate onto surrogates; while Gertie Girdle is finding "appeasement of her desires" with her enemies, her proper betrothed on his boat hangs back, reluctant to use his (symbolic) guns because "this post office conjured up in his mind the engaging personality of his fiancée . . . whom he was to (and wished to) marry in the very near future, in order to consummate with her the act that was just a little intimidating to a chaste young man, the strange act whose occult peripeteia transforms a young bint from the virginal state into the pregnant state."

George Bernard Shaw, in his preface to *Man and Superman*, wrote, "If women were as fastidious as men, morally or physically, there would be an end of the race." What Western race better illustrates male reluctance to mate than the Irish? *We Always Treat Women Too Well* is about sexual initiation, and not just Gertie's. The Irish terrorists are portrayed by the mischievous French author as innocent, pious, and primitive; their previous sexual experiences have been with "slatterns harvested on piles of hay or tavern tables still greasy with everything" or with country girls "who get themselves impregnated in the shade of a dolmen or menhir without even so much as letting you get a glance at their nature." Gertie, on the other hand, is dressed in the latest Parisian fashions—a girdle instead of a corset, a brassiere, no frilly drawers, and gartered silk stockings. (Queneau is nothing if not fashion-conscious; his novels are shot through with details of clothing to which a surreal intensity of meaning attaches.) The Irishmen are moved to wonder by Gertie's progressive costume:

> "No, with her, when you touch her here" (and he took hold of his own torso with both hands), "under her dress, it's skin you're touching, it isn't frills and flounces and whalebone busk, it's skin."
> "Is all that true?" asked Dillon.

In a sense, Gertie is the future, bringing death to the past. The Irishmen defend themselves with an antiquated code of honor; doomed to die, they become concerned that in retrospect their heroism will be sullied by their lechery.

> "We ought to have killed her right away, but we had to be correct. And in any case, none of this is very important. Except for the cause. For the cause it's bloody annoying if people are going to be able to say we behaved badly in such tragic moments."

The final two survivors, Corny Kelleher and Mat Dillon, concoct an ingenious scheme to achieve Gertie's silence: they do something unspeakable to her. "Now she won't say anything," Kelleher cries, "she won't say anything, and no one will be able to say we weren't heroes, valiant, pure heroes." In the event, the thoroughly violated Gertie lies to her British rescuers, mildly claiming that the Irishmen tried to lift up her skirt to look at her ankles. The horrified British shoot their captives on the spot, but not before Gertie has stuck out her tongue at them and Kelleher has ruefully concluded, "We always treat women too well."

This farce feels genuinely sexy. Queneau has toyed with the forms and codes of hardboiled fiction without emptying them of content; we are left with an impression of relations between men and women as lawless and predatory. Poor Caffrey, decapitated by a cannon shot in mid-coitus, is likened to "the male of the praying mantis whose upper part has been half-devoured by the female but who perseveres in his copulation." Gertie flees his embrace "covered all over with blood, and moist with a posthumous tribute." In the end, she is sodomized but survives; her assailants are shot. Amid all his cerebration and irony, Queneau hangs tough.

Yet one wonders how many of the few purchasers of *We Always Treat Women Too Well* in its initial edition, by Éditions du Scorpion, read it as a straight thriller. From first to last, the style twinkles with Queneau's impudent excesses of precision:

> He thumped, rethumped, rerethumped, and rererethumped, his fist down on the tablecloth . . .

> The serene night was clasping the dazzling moon in her sooty thighs,

and the soft down of her constellations was lightly stirring in the breath of a classic breeze transmitted by the Gulf Stream.

A few moments later Cartwright was standing on his poop deck with a heavy heart, a lumpy throat, an empty stomach, a dry mouth and a glassy eye.

Before he shut the door, Gallagher tried to absorb all that beauty in one last look, and closed his eyelids in order not to let the image flee.

A patent spoof on patriotism, murderousness, seductiveness, Irishness, and piety, the novel at bottom makes the deeper satirical point that Queneau's fiction consistently makes: the ineluctable banality of existence, as shown by the subtle clumsiness and foreordained triteness of our attempts to render life into words.

Nineteen forty-seven was evidently a busy year for Queneau; in it he also published his famous *Exercises in Style,* which relates, as every modernism buff knows, the same inane incident ninety-nine times in ninety-nine styles. To be exact, there are two inane incidents, involving the same silly-looking man. Of Queneau's ninety-nine versions, the most serviceably neutral is the one in "Back Slang," beginning "Unway ayday aboutyay iddaymay . . ." Translated out of what Americans call Pig Latin, it goes:

> One day about midday on an S bus I noticed a young man with a long neck and a hat encircled by a sort of string instead of a ribbon. Suddenly he started an argument with his neighbor, accusing him of treading on his toes. He quickly abandoned the discussion and went and threw himself on a vacant seat.
>
> Two hours later I saw him again in front of the gare Saint-Lazare engrossed in conversation with a friend who was telling him to reduce the space at the opening of his overcoat by getting a competent person to raise the top button of the overcoat in question.

A few details from other versions enrich this telling: midday is rush hour on Paris public transportation, the hat is felt, the string is plaited, the young man speaks in a "snivelling tone which is meant to be aggressive," and his age is given variously as "27 years 3 months and 8 days," "like 26 or 30," "about twenty," and "slowly advancing towards the commencement of his fourth decade." The second and shorter incident, of the overheard overcoat-button instructions, is even more problematical. Not until the twenty-ninth telling, "Past," is it made clear that the witnessing narrator (called "Dr. Queneau" in one version) does not encounter the quarrelsome long-necked youngish man on foot in front of the Gare Saint-Lazare but is himself again on a bus, spying the hero through a window (evidently close enough to hear a snatch of conversation). And it is never made clear but, instead, is carried forward with a forked ambiguity whether an extra button is being advised or merely that an existent button be moved *up*, or whether the button move is proposed for reasons of warmth or (in a minority version) style.

Yet the main outlines of the plot are clear enough, as is the pathos of the hero, who figures successively as conspicuously odd-looking, apparently put-upon (by the passenger he accuses of treading on his toes or, in some versions, "jostling" him), strident, cowardly (in so swiftly taking a seat in escape from the altercation he initiated), and, two hours later, in need of sartorial advice, which in all versions he docilely accepts. He—given at one juncture the name "Monsieur André"—is just the sort of flagrant loser whom with mixed compassion and irritation we single out for notice in a crowded bus.

Queneau's "action," then, though seemingly slight, is both resonant and rich in potential extension. His play version ("Comedy") makes clear that there are more characters in the drama than we might suspect. Aside from the faceless chorus of bus passengers, there is the hero, his antagonist, the witness/author, and—easy to overlook—the person who vacates the seat the hero so pusillanimously seizes. In the second incident, there is the hero's advisory friend, here identified as "A Young Dandy," who says, "The opening of your overcoat is too wide." This "Comedy" also invents a conductor (implied but silent in all other versions), who announces, "Fez pliz," and then, "Let 'em off first. Any priorities? One priority! Full up. Dring dring dring." One of the most ambitious and amusing retellings, entitled "Feminine" (and certain to be castigated as male-chauvinistic), postulates yet another character, a woman who observes the incident and inwardly seethes that the young hero "sat down the moment he saw a vacant seat and what's more it didn't occur to him for a single moment to offer it to me," and then, seeing the same man later in front of the Gare Saint-Lazare, is hurt because "I looked at him but the idiot didn't even recognise me." Versions like this, and the one from the standpoint of an indignant right-winger ("Reactionary"), are the most fun, and the impenetrable "Permutations" ("Ed on to ay rd wa id sm yo da," etc.) the least.

While it did not seem to me entirely true that, as Barbara Wright breathlessly claims in her introduction, "Queneau *has* done this without boring the reader *at all,*" the succession of variations, as the dozen elements of the anecdote (S bus, rush hour, young man, long neck, felt hat, cord instead of ribbon, quarrel, vacant seat, two hours later, Gare Saint-Lazare, friend, overcoat button) are put through all manner of rhetorical, formal, idiomatic, quasi-mathematical, inflectional, and grammatical paces, is surprisingly entertaining—a triumph of madcap rigor, less like Bach's *The Art of Fugue,* which Queneau claimed as his inspiration, than a speeded-up parade of alchemic experiments manically distilling the same fool's gold, over and over. Especially pure distillates are the variant called "Exclamations," beginning

> Goodness! Twelve o'clock! time for the bus! what a lot of people! what a lot of people! aren't we squashed! bloody funny! that chap! what a face! and what a neck! two-foot long! at least!

and the more compressed "Interjections," running in its entirety

> Psst! h'm! ah! oh! hem! ah! ha! hey! well! oh! pooh! poof! ow! oo! ouch! hey! eh! h'm! pffft!
>
> Well! hey! pooh! oh! h'm! right!

Translation of *Exercises in Style* is of course a tour de force of its own, possibly more strenuous than the original composition. Barbara Wright, a valiant Englishwoman who has brought into our language not only all the Queneau prose that we have but such other fragile imports of French experimental writing as Pinget,

Jarry, Robbe-Grillet, Arrabal, Tzara, and Sarraute, for more than a year exerted herself upon this particular labor of love. That the result is usually readable and sometimes amusing stands as her accolade. However, this is one occasion when it is simply not enough for New Directions (or Grove Press, or Red Dust, or the Terre Haute Society for the Preservation of Old-Fashioned Modernism) to serve up a British translation* in American covers and consider its duty to international culture done. In a work so essentially and exhaustively about language, the usually negligible transatlantic differences become glaring. Miss Wright has translated Queneau's "Vulgaire" into "Cockney" ("So A'm stand'n n' ahtsoider vis frog bus when A sees vis young Froggy bloke, caw bloimy"), "Loucherbem" into "Rhyming Slang" ("He starts a bull and a cow with another chap and complains that he keeps treading on his plates with his daisy roots"), and "Paysan" into "West Indian" (". . . the fellar get in one set of confusion, he looking poor-me-one and outing off fast for vacant seat"). These all cry out for American equivalents, and the rather stiff renditions of some of Queneau's metrical japes should also be tuned to a Yankee pitch pipe. After all, we are still a big country, with a gross national product six times the United Kingdom's, and if we can photograph Jupiter and Saturn up close and bring a spaceship back from the ionosphere we should be able to manage our own translation of Queneau.

The Strange Case of Dr. Destouches and M. Céline

CÉLINE, by Patrick McCarthy. 352 pp. Viking, 1975.

One would like to write of Céline without touching upon his anti-Semitism, his fascism, his collaboration with the Nazis, his political loathsomeness. The three booklength "pamphlets"—

---

*And in this case one first published in England in 1958, by the Gaberbocchus Press, and unchanged for its belated American outing by so much as a word, though it contains such dated expressions as "teddy boy."

Bagatelles pour un massacre (1937), *L'École des cadavres* (1938), and *Les Beaux Draps* (1941)—with which the great novelist made himself a scandal were simply excluded from the collected works published by André Ballard, and have never been available in English. Even fragmentary direct quotations from them are hard to come by. George Steiner, writing in *The New Yorker* a while ago, claimed that "it is nearly impossible to quote from them without physical revulsion," and Mavis Gallant recently in the *Times* offered a sentence (the ellipses of course not her own but integral to Céline's unique style): "Jewish bluffer . . . Dirty *con*, layabout . . . pimp of the universe . . . parasite of all time." Patrick McCarthy, in his biography and critical study *Céline*, devotes an entire chapter to "Céline the Pamphleteer," but here the wording and reasoning of the pamphlets are softened by his careful psychoanalysis of the author, and by a perhaps unavoidable note of pleading. Mr. Mc-Carthy is at pains to point out where the anti-Semitic frenzy becomes almost confessedly absurd:

> In *Bagatelles* he exaggerates to the point of creating disbelief. Léon Blum is Jewish, he tells us correctly; Masaryk and Benes are also Jewish, so are Gide, Maurras and the Pope; the entire English nation is Jewish. At this point one stops: clearly Céline does not want to be believed.

In the next pamphlet, *L'École*, "there is still exaggeration: the Pope is Jewish and his name is Isaac Ratisch . . . the Jews are responsible for the 843 treaty of Verdun which separated France from Germany." Comical or not, the pamphlets amount to a call for the extermination of the European Jews a few years before such an extermination was all but completely carried out. In 1943, while the Nazis were mercilessly removing Jews from France, Céline allowed his publisher to reprint *L'École des cadavres* and, with illustrations, *Bagatelles pour un massacre;* a year before, he had written to the organizers of an anti-Semitic exhibition, professing to be "surprised and a little hurt" to find neither *Bagatelles* nor *L'École* on display. Mr. McCarthy, for all his equanimity and tact, cannot help revealing that Céline's views were more odious than one had dared suspect—more odious, it might be urged in his defense, than they needed to be for any sort of personal advancement or convenience.

In this, he rather resembles Hitler, who carried forward the Final Solution to the detriment of the German war effort. Céline late in 1941 wrote, in a letter, of Hitler's anti-Semitism, "It is the side of Hitler that most people like the least . . . it is the side I like the most."

Mr. McCarthy advances what mitigating factors he can. Anti-Semitism pervaded Europe between the wars, and was very strong in the shopkeeping class, from which Céline came and whose meannesses and anxieties he retained to the end of his life. Céline composed his notorious pamphlets within a specifically French tradition of violent rhetoric and theatrical exaggeration; other pamphleteers, like Daudet and Maurras, Bernanos and Bloy, wrote with similar extremism. Like other reactionaries, Céline was repelled by modern materialism and was nostalgic for the supposed pre-industrial virtues. A genuine dread of the impending war between France and Germany, rooted in his traumatic experiences as a soldier wounded in 1914, led him to a frantic pacifism and a desperate need for a scapegoat. His brief career as a League of Nations functionary had disposed him to see Jews as the nationless manipulators of the modern world. He was truly patriotic and believed (like the Norwegian Knut Hamsun) that his country must in its weakness submit to Germany. Céline, under his real name of Louis-Ferdinand Destouches, was a doctor, who preferred to work among the impoverished, who filled his life with acts of personal kindness, who said of himself that "there was no suffering to which he was indifferent." He loved animals. He was abstemious, and a meticulous reviser of his apparently dishevelled prose. Most interestingly, Mr. McCarthy portrays Céline as a terror-ridden man of many impersonations, and the somewhat clownish political hysteric as being, in Céline's mind, one more role, which had little serious connection with Dr. Destouches humanely practicing medicine among the Paris poor or with Céline the prose genius aspiring to rank with Rabelais. In his role of anti-Semite, "Hydra-Céline is putting only one of his heads on the block. He is still evading, still showing fear. He has fallen into a *délire,* just like one of the minor characters in his novels. The *délire* may be defined as the other, separate world that the maniacs and exiles invent when the normal world becomes impossible." This amounts to a plea of insanity, and certainly Céline's brain, battered ever after his war injury by headaches and insomnia and a roaring in his ears, flickered on a variety of wavelengths. His pamphlets are repetitious and irresponsible even by the standards of gutter literature, and amid their murderous nonsense is some harsh self-mockery ("a poor imbecile," he calls himself), including the gibes of his "Jewish friend Gutman" (who tells him, "You are delirious, Ferdinand"). One of the twists of the pamphleteer's tortuous tirade is a kind of identification with Jews, and *Bagatelles* contains a curious invitation to the Jews to kill him as a sacrifice, so that the Germans may not slaughter the French. At the war's end, an execrated exile, he went so far as to include the Six Million in comradeship with his own sufferings: "The Jews have paid like me." But he never recanted, merely shifted to Asiatics the focus of his crazy terror of "mongrelization." Once back in France, under an amnesty of 1951, he revelled—via interviews and the autobiographical explosions of his later books— in his vituperative isolation. One may add, in feeble defense of the resolute malevolence of his public personality, that Céline culled few favors from the Nazi establishment of the Occupation, and that his anti-Semitism taints surprisingly little of his fiction. The character of Bloch in Proust is a fuller Jew *qua* Jew, with more construably anti-Semitic overtones, than any portrait in Céline's novels.

Nevertheless, knowledge of Céline's bizarre and barbarous convictions disturbs one's appreciation of his art, all the more in that he anticipated so many qualities of postwar fiction. Thirty years before *Catch-22*, he wrote of the military life as sheer craziness and of cowardice as the only sanity. Long before *One Flew over the Cuckoo's Nest*, he found the mentally ill a superior sort of society. Before William Burroughs, he sensed behind the electronic apparatus of modernity an invisible enemy promoting spooky derangements and sudden deaths. Before Kerouac and the Beats and the tell-all Beatrices that have come along a generation later, he perceived that a good long monologue is novel enough, if the names are slightly scrambled and the events are linked to a nebulous "search." If not the inventor, he is the classic promulgator of the *nouveau picaresque*, with its comfortable paranoia, its pleasant as-

sumption that the world is uniformly zany and corrupt and there-
fore cannot be analyzed, only experienced at random. Events with-
out precedent, behavior without motivation, characters who come
and go like strangers in an elevator—Mr. McCarthy almost names
these as flaws in his description of *Journey to the End of the Night*
but concludes that the disconnections have a philosophical func-
tion: "By this technique Céline destroys cause and effect."

It has been a technique fruitful at least of verbiage; discarding
cause and effect absolves the novelist of any duty to keep his mock-
world coherent, and has made fiction as easy to write as free verse.
Like the removal of metre and rhyme from poetics, this discarding
throws upon the writer a continuous challenge to surprise and
astound. Without any consequential development linking events,
the reader is led along by the writer's voice alone, and its promise
of ever-new prodigies of horror or style. These prodigies Céline
was better equipped to provide than most of his successors; he did
not flinch from the chasm of possibility he had opened up, and
showed in his later work how truly *anything* can go into a novel
—personal exhortations, fantasies, stories within stories, all sorts of
confusions and noise. Has any writer ever been as fascinated with
noise, with bangs and buzzing and shouts and rattling that make
the world seem, like the Detroit factory to *Journey*'s hero Bardamu,
a "vast frenzy of noise, which filled you within and all around the
inside of your skull and lower down rattled your bowels, and
climbed to your eyes in infinite, little, quick unending strokes"?
Céline's style, with its sets of three dots replacing all logical punctu-
ation, became a hammering of "little, quick unending strokes,"
driven with maniacal monotony toward a single point of deafness,
of nothingness, of futility. If cause and effect are discarded, the
world has no hinges for disassembly; nothing can be demonstrated
save futility. This Céline was inexhaustibly eager to do. His novels,
like Beckett's, are testaments of defiance, gratuitous breakings of
silence, a numbed survivor's snarled testimony to catastrophes that
are scarcely distinguishable. Agglutination and dissolution charac-
terize the Célinean event; where a rationale might be perceived, it
is suppressed. What Bardamu and the Pordurière Company of
Little Togo are attempting to achieve at their trading outpost in

Bikomimbo totally deliquesces in the nightmare of rain and fever
—"Everything was melting away in a welter of trashy goods, hopes
and accounts, together with the fever, itself moist too." The night-
mare is compounded when Bardamu manages to set this sodden
mass afire, kindling perfect physical anarchy, with a ball of crude
rubber smoldering and stinking in the middle. This reductive vi-
sion, the glutinous confusion of dreams imposed on daylight as well
as night, runs strikingly counter to the doctor's function, which is
to diagnose and correct. In fact, Dr. Destouches prescribed few
drugs, and advised his patients simply, "Drink no alcohol, exercise
regularly." Except for his mastery of some technical terms, the
doctor-hero of Céline's fiction appears a helpless witness, sullenly
listening—in one dreadful episode of *Journey*—to his patient's
blood drip away, drop by drop, to the floor beneath the bed. When
Bardamu's friend Robinson dies, he describes the process with a
cold medical eye, and in a kind of ultimate of Gallic psychological
acuity observes that even in dying the man is dislikably human:

> I would even, I believe, have more easily felt sorry for a dog dying than
> for Robinson, because a dog's not sly; whereas, whatever one may say,
> Léon was just a bit sly. I was sly too; we were all sly . . . All the rest
> of it had fallen by the wayside and even those facial expressions, which
> are still some use by a deathbed, I'd lost as well. I had indeed lost
> everything along the road, I couldn't find anything of what you need
> when you're pegging out, only maliciousness. My feelings were like a
> house you only keep for the holidays. They were barely habitable.

Céline really did what Camus wanted to do—anatomize the
emotional emptiness of modern, Godless man. Within the explo-
sions and brawls of his prose there occur, like hollows in a sponge,
haunting islands of emptiness: hotels miraculously undamaged
amid the rubble, or the deserted landscape of the opening battle
scene of *Journey*, abandoned to the contending armies like a room
to a newly married couple—"We're by ourselves like newly mar-
ried folk doing dirty things when everyone's left." In the noise of
Detroit, some sounds are "so violent that they spread sort of si-
lences around themselves which make you feel a little better." A
strange perverse grace glimmers here and there in the infernal mess

this author makes of the world. In the last novels, the trilogy based upon Céline's remarkable journeys through the collapsing Europe of the Second World War, bombs fall, filling the page with their noisy emptiness and giving every sentence the texture of a flying shard. Yet these novels are not depressing. The wayward beauties and accuracies of Céline's style give delight; his sheer destructiveness and mordancy are exhilarating; he has the gift (like no one in modern English so much as Bernard Shaw) of irresponsible exaggeration; and the constant company of his first-person voice shelters us from the kind of confrontation with massive, inexorable reality that the great third-person novels provide. A first-person narrator is a survivor, or he wouldn't be there on the page. This minor technical fact mutes the sense of death that Céline ostensibly evokes, and tinges with frivolity the kind of autobiographical novel of which he is patron saint.

Mr. McCarthy, an English scholar who now teaches French at Haverford, has done a fine, firm job of bodying forth a man who habitually obfuscated the facts about himself, who was obscure for the first forty years of his life and a recluse for the last ten. Chapters of ascertainable fact juxtaposed with critical chapters describing the major works successfully solve the recurrent problem in literary biography of giving both the external life—the life of record—and the internal life, the author as refracted in his own verbal creation. Céline, like many another, wrote worse of himself than he was. Bardamu, the first of his alter egos, enters America illegally and finds farcical employment as an official flea-counter; in truth, the young Dr. Destouches was sent to this country by a body no less august than the League of Nations, in order to conduct a study of the health conditions of the Ford workers in Detroit, a study he creditably carried out. At all the junctures of his often irregular life, Céline sought out opportunities to practice medicine. Amid the debacle of his flight from France into a collapsing Germany, he ministered to the community of wretched French collaborationists at Sigmaringen, and upon his return from exile, pardoned but far from forgiven, he hung out his shingle ("Dr. L.-F. Destouches of the Paris Faculty of Medicine, 2– 4 P.M. except Friday") in the Paris suburb of Meudon. Mr. McCarthy moves steadily through the welter of Céline's adventures, and his calm, methodical manner spares us much idle speculation. His level prose at worst becomes trite telegraphy:

> [Léon Daudet] was so famous a critic that he could make or break a book with one article. He read *Voyage* and wrote a glowing review. Success, both literary and popular, followed. The novel made an enormous impact.

On the other hand, his critical discourse displays many fine discriminations and, in connection with Céline's increasingly murky plots, a powerful gift of synopsis; as he describes them, generally unadmired and in English unavailable works like *Féerie pour une autre fois* sound exciting. He can write a sentence of such witty compression as this, of the French journalists who espoused collaboration:

> In one sense their cause had been doomed from the start: it was impossible to convince the French that their real enemies were not the Germans who patrolled the streets, but the English who had killed Joan of Arc.

His sketch of the collaborationist community, which included, besides Céline himself, sensitive writers like Robert Brasillach and Lucien Rabetet, is vivid enough to make one wish for more. And more, too, might be told of Céline's women, other than that they tended to be dancers and that he waxed rapturous over long-legged American beauties. Elizabeth Craig, who had lived with Céline during the composition of *Journey,* was pursued by him all the way to Los Angeles, where she in the course of disputing her father's will had married one of the lawyers—an episode as surreal as Philip Roth's fantasy that Kafka came and taught Hebrew in New Jersey. Céline died, we learn, the very day he had completed a draft of *Rigodon,* the third book of the trilogy that to some extent had rehabilitated his literary reputation. He died swiftly, of a brain seizure, and in his wife's arms—a peaceable, workmanlike death for a man who had taken so much of our century's fury into himself.

Robert Pinget

THE LIBERA ME DOMINE, by Robert Pinget, translated from the French by Barbara Wright. 238 pp. Red Dust, 1978.

PASSACAGLIA, by Robert Pinget, translated from the French by Barbara Wright. 96 pp. Red Dust, 1978.

It is with some embarrassment that a reviewer recommends to readers a writer whom he scarcely understands, whose works are more than a little exasperating, and who furthermore writes with a high degree of colloquiality in a foreign language. Yet Robert Pinget, as glimpsed through translation and through the cloudy layers of his own obfuscations, does seem one of the more noble presences in world literature, a continuingly vital practitioner of what, a weary long quarter-century ago, was christened *le nouveau roman*. Pinget, unlike Alain Robbe-Grillet and Nathalie Sarraute, is not a household name on this side of the Atlantic, and his jacket flaps restate the same few facts. He was born in Geneva, Switzerland, in 1920. He studied law and became a barrister. He went to Paris in 1946, to the École des Beaux-Arts, then intending to become a painter. He had an exhibition in Paris in 1950; the same year, he taught drawing and French in England. He is a friend of Samuel Beckett. We learn from Deirdre Bair's biography of Beckett that in 1957 Pinget published a French translation of *All That Fall* and that Beckett helped produce Pinget's Beckett-like play *The Hypothesis.*

Pinget's first book, *Between Fantoine and Agapa,* was published in 1950, and ever since he has explored a fictional terrain of which the local city is Agapa and the rather interchangeable villages are Fantoine and Sirancy. One wonders where, on the road between Geneva and Paris, Pinget acquired such a rich and fond intimacy with French country life, and what holds so cosmopolitan and experimental a writer to a provincial landscape of such unvarying ingredients—a moldering château; a crowded, gossipy village; a sinister forest and quarry. One book jacket volunteers that "Monsieur Pinget divides his time between Paris and a country home in

Touraine"; Touraine, then, "garden of France" and natal ground of Descartes, Rabelais, and Balzac, is indicated as the territory of Pinget's imagination. Though there is occasional mention of jeans and television, his world seems frozen between the two world wars, with a veritably medieval rumor of absolute evil arising from its darker places.

Unlike a number of fellow–*nouveaux romanciers,* Pinget has been reticent about his formal aesthetic program. Professor Vivian Mercier, however, in the course of composing *The New Novel from Queneau to Pinget* (1971), did elicit from him a third-person avowal concerning "the author's passion for fictional creation, his obsession with the destinies of individuals, his being haunted by imagination and by the efforts required to fathom the only reality there is, his soul, and finally his limitless love of the French language." This profession appears strikingly orthodox; realistic and indeed conservative impulses are at work in Pinget's art. On the other hand, he has advised a recent English translator, "Don't bother too much about logic: everything in [*Passacaille*] is directed against it." And a comment of several pages appended to another novel enunciates a principled surrealism inimical to logic and intelligible plot: "It is not what can be said or *meant* that interests me, but the *way in which it is said.* . . . There may well be a new point of view, a modern kind of sensitivity, an unusual sort of composition, in my books, but I can't help it. . . . One thing is certain, though, and this is that I never know at the outset what I am going to say. For a long time I thought this a weakness, but there is no way of avoiding it as it is my only strength, the strength that enables me to continue. . . . For my confidence in the mechanism of the subconscious remains essentially unshakeable."

This comment is appended to *The Libera Me Domine,* which, simultaneously with *Passacaglia,* has been published by a small firm with the itchy name of Red Dust. Their publication, small type tells us, "has been made possible in part by grants from the New York State Council on the Arts; and from the National Endowment for the Arts in Washington, D.C." Now that the government no longer has to prop up wheat prices, it has become the last great underwriter of the avant-garde. Pinget, with little fanfare and less profit, has had a total of eight books—six novels and a two-volume set of plays—rendered into English. Two novels have been previously published in this country. His most successful and best-known work is *The Inquisitory* (1962); it won the Prix des Critiques, became a best-seller in France, and still does seem his masterpiece. Its question-and-answer form, though extended beyond all plausibility, yet served to mold and control the contrary pulls toward anarchy in Pinget's work—one his utter trust in the vagaries of monologue, and the other his inexhaustible circumstantial interest in the doings, geography, and personalities of his fictional countryside. This second quality distinguishes him from Beckett and gives him a distant cousinage with Balzac and Faulkner. If we can imagine a Faulkner who began with the combative intellectual playfulness of Queneau or Jarry, or a *Sound and the Fury* that concludes with everyone dissolved in Benjy's idiocy, we start to taste Pinget. The ultimate taste, surely, lies on the tongue, in his "limitless love of the French language," whose demotic banalities and querulous rhythms, as delicately translated by the ubiquitous Barbara Wright, even in translation sink into our hearts like a sad gray rain into already wet soil.

Pinget's plots deliberately defy summary. His novels are mystery novels that end with the mysteries compounded. *The Libera Me Domine* (an awkward collection of words based upon the French title, *Le Libera*—referring to the phrase in the Latin funeral Mass corresponding to the Biblical "Deliver me, O Lord") opens with talk, in an unspecified voice, about the violent death, ten years earlier, of four-year-old Louis Ducreux. "While little Louis went wandering off, the parents fast asleep, these country picnics they tire you out, both lying on the rug, she with her fat legs exposed, her skirt above her knees, he with his back to her curled up like a gun dog, a branch of a walnut or some other tree was tickling him and he brushed away this imaginary fly in his sleep, the child went wandering off, she had put him down to rest first, he hadn't gone to sleep, he'd got up, he went wandering off, the forest is dense once you get thirty yards in, they never saw him again." Now the retired schoolmistress, "old Lorpailleur," who may be mad, is stirring up this ancient scandal. But as the monologue winds on and on, even the simplest facts about the boy's death prove maddeningly slippery: he was strangled, no, his throat was cut, and, a few pages farther on, he was struck and killed by a passing truck. Or was it old Lorpailleur who was hit by the truck? Or did she just fall off in a fit? Countless incidents crowd where logically only one should go, and even the boy's name becomes distorted and lost. Events have a brief half-life in the atomic tumble of the monologue, whose speaker is undefined and drifts through the village like a gas. Certain central incidents, however, persist, burning through the clouds: there was a children's picnic in the forest, and a truck did pass through town, and the local aristocrat Mlle. Ariane entertained old Lorpailleur with some others at her manor house, Bonne-Mesure, and a cat defecated in a flower bed, and there was a scandal about a priest and a choirboy, and the month is July, "a bad month in our parts, every sort of calamity happens to us in July." The philosophical moral of the narrative, arriving in a paragraph of sudden beauty, has to do with fine weather:

> When you think of how lovely the country is round our way, the shy sun when you open your window in the morning, the honeysuckle in the backyards, the glorious scents and birdsongs that carry us through from hour to hour until nightfall when the frogs croak themselves hoarse at the edge of the forest, so much loveliness, and of how we're always ready to do any little thing for each other, how we laugh together at the Swan café, how we all feel the same grief when someone is in mourning, how can anyone be so vulgar as to see nothing but filth in everything, I'm quite willing to admit that there may be some but all the same what a sin against Nature, as the doctor says everything you can ever think of saying about her is always true which means that everything you can possibly think of is to be found in her, you can quibble till you're blue in the face but that's the proof of her existence.

The aesthetic moral, the explanation of the book's poetics, comes a hundred pages later:

> . . . this network of gossip and absurd remarks had conditioned our existence to such an extent that no stranger coming to live in our midst could have resisted it for long and that if he had come to follow the trade

of let's say baker he would inevitably have branched off into that of child-killer for instance, without his having been in the least responsible, which would explain among other things why our hack writers who set out to be critics or novelists don't get any further than writing serial stories or meteorological reports . . .

At the novel's end, we do not know who killed the Ducreux boy (he has become "little Frédéric who had been violated in the woods by a sex-maniac") or if old Lorpailleur is mad; but we do feel we have lived in a provincial French village and experienced its tedium and its entertainments (lunch at the manor house, a dance concert at a local *pension*) at a bone-deep level no logic-bound tale could have reached. For in fact human events, whether they be Kennedy's assassination or Watergate or how we spent the day before yesterday, have a permanently unsettled shape once past the instant in which they occur, and Pinget's reverberations of hearsay are less anti-realistic than they appear. He could not be so surreal were he not so inventive, and so genially at home in the popular mind. Fantoine is always there for him, as Frenchman's Bend was for Faulkner and Macondo is for Gabriel García Márquez. In this village where everything is dubious, we never doubt the existence of the village.

Passacaglia (a type of Italian or Spanish tune, originally played on the guitar while the musician was passing through the streets) is a much shorter work than *The Libera Me Domine,* and its French publication came a year later, in 1969. Again, there has been a mysterious violent death—this time, a body found on a dunghill. Pinget's training as a barrister shows in his fondness for investigations and inquisitions, and his skepticism regarding their final results: "The story would seem to have begun a long time before this, but talk about prudence, talk about vigilance, it looks as if only two or three episodes have been revealed, and that with some difficulty, the source of information being permanently deficient. . . ." A man, called "the master," sits in a cold room of a shut-up country house ("the garden was dead, the courtyard grassy") looking at an old book, making notes in the margin; he has just torn the hands off the clock in the room. The body on the dunghill at first appears to be his ("the man sitting at this table a few hours earlier, found dead on the dunghill"), but then it becomes that of an idiot the master adopted in the past who has mutilated himself with a chain saw (or fallen off a ladder or swallowed a sponge). The flap copy has it that both are dead: "The 'Master' ruminates about the death of an idiot who lived with him for which he may or may not be responsible and about his own death. He is found dead over his notebooks." His jottings, indistinguishable from his thoughts, constitute the book's text, and give its ebbing hero a certain status of authorship; "like a street-corner musician, he had reconstituted a kind of passacaglia." Besides the doctor and the idiot, the master (who at one point is named "Monsieur Nanard") has or has had for company several servants and peasant neighbors and a few friends (Rodolphe, Alfred, Édouard, Raymond) who appear to drop in from the racy social circles of *The Inquisitory* or from the local Sagan novel. At one moment in the past, while bathing the cretin, the master began to seduce him ("the innocent began to stiffen") but a page later he concludes, "Love, if that's what it was really I could have done without it." The master is alone, so alone the village is dim—though a village voice, complete with malapropisms ("christianery"), does intrude into his magisterial thanatopsis.

"So calm. So grey." "Profoundly integrated night." "Turn, return, revert." "In the margin beside an empty phrase." "His life having emigrated elsewhere." These are some of the phrases that recur, making the music of the passacaglia. Some program notes, by scholars of Pinget, are appended, and among them Dr. Stephen Bann links the phrases "Something broken in the mechanism" and "Death at the slightest deficiency in thought" with Descartes's "*Cogito, ergo sum*": the master is about to stop thinking, the universe is winding down, the hands are off the clock. Were it not so deeply embedded in the palpable atmosphere of an afflicted house and the surrounding damp, chill fields, such a significance would seem merely schematic and cerebral. But Pinget's work always outraces what might be said about it. His notion of haunting, of being haunted, for instance, is neither fashionable nor prescribed —Robbe-Grillet's manifestos called for universal demystification—

yet it permeates Pinget's microcosm as strongly as the smell of earth.

An end game of a refreshed sort is being played here; though modern art has exhausted art's possibilities, the world goes on, idiotically. Unable to write stories, Pinget can still write about the popular will to make a story: "This is where people's imaginations take over and make them start questioning everything again." A kind of cave art, like Dubuffet's rough-textured daubs, arises from the voices of hearsay and gossip amid the final dilapidation of the mansions of nineteenth-century narrative. One test of an artistic method is how much of the seemingly arbitrary it can absorb and re-present as intrinsic; on this score Pinget is infinitely absorptive but unevenly successful in creating an illusion of coherence. *Passacaglia*, in part because it is shorter, is a more intense, somber, and moving work than *The Libera Me Domine*. *The Libera* ends with a funeral; *Passacaglia* weaves death itself into an arrested moment in a cold room of a shut-up house.

Such a description may not prepare a reader for the genuine difficulty and truculence of Pinget's fiction. Even a short book of his feels long, and though he has outgrown the Beckettian vaudeville of early novels like *Baga*, the willful confusions of his antiplots, the repetitions of their circular unwinding, and the author's refusal to take a clarifying position above the voices he records all make for a rocky read. Yet a certain incidental delight lives in many a well-struck phrase, and a real psychology and topology and sociology press toward us through the words. Unlike Beckett, he has not turned his back on the seethe of circumstance, or, like the mature Joyce, taken refuge in nostalgic reconstruction. For all his flouting of conventional expectations and all the sly comedy of his rambling village talebearers, Pinget strikes one as free of any basically distorting mannerism or aesthetic pose. His recourse remains to the real, without irony. In a France of smiling mandarins and chilly chic, he manifests the two essential passions of a maker: a love of his material and a belief in his method.

NORTHERN EUROPEANS

A Primal Modern

THE WANDERER: *Under the Autumn Star* & *On Muted Strings,* by Knut Hamsun, translated from the Norwegian by Oliver and Gunnvor Stally-brass. 281 pp. Farrar, Straus & Giroux, 1975.

Farrar, Straus & Giroux's commendable reissue, in new transla-tions, of the works of Knut Hamsun may have run onto thin ground with the new volume—two autobiographical novellas titled together *The Wanderer.* The wanderer is Hamsun himself, called by his real name, Knut Pedersen, and these two interrelated tales by the fiftyish author take to a point of extreme attenuation Hamsun's willful way of subjecting plot to the vagaries of impulse and hap-penstance.

In *Under the Autumn Star* the narrator feels like telling us about the fine weather that autumn brings to the Norwegian countryside, about a pipe he carved embodying a real human thumbnail, about his success in planning and digging a well and piping system for the country parson, about his attraction to two respectable married women one of whom (the pastor's wife) sleeps with him, about several fellow-wanderers less charming than he appears to realize, and about his abortive invention of a woodcutting device that translates a vertical action to horizontal: "With such trivialities as these, my mind was soothed and salved." There is a pattern in the

casual weave, a cycle of venturing out onto the "island" of alone-
ness and finally returning to the city, and the prose shuttles with
Hamsun's usual feathery, sometimes quite magical lightness of
phrase, but the materials feel too purely atmospheric, and the char-
acters seem as evanescent as the weather and the days and the hero's
whimsical moods. Pedersen is moody without the intensity of
Hamsun's younger heroes—Nagel and Glahn and the under-
ground man of *Hunger.* Clouds come and go without thunder and
lightning; there is instead a harmless heat lightning: "A serene and
mystical mood flickered within me." The people glimpsed amid
this flickering and along the way of this wandering are oddly hard
to visualize. The book's closest approach to a heroine is most viv-
idly seen in an image of startling vagueness:

> Mrs. Falkenberg was standing in the yard: a human column, light in
> color, standing free in the spacious courtyard, without a hat.

Otherwise she (also called, vaguer still, "Madame") vanishes in a
haze of rhapsody: "Ah, that voice, those eyes, that tender womanly
expression . . ." "Have you ever in all your life seen such fair hair?
No indeed. Born glorious from top to toe, mouth ripe and lovely
beyond words, shimmer of dragonflies in her hair." At the book's
emotional climax—Pedersen, hired as a woodcutter for the house-
hold, drives Madame home from a visit to the pastor's house in a
storm, and lends her a blanket that is his—it is difficult to remember
which woman is present, for the differentiation has been so delicate,
and the hero's attraction to Mrs. Falkenberg and the pastor's wife
and the pastor's daughter Elizabeth and the various Falkenberg
maids has been so casually indiscriminate. Surpassingly distinct
among those female apparitions, and perhaps overtly embodying
the menace emanating from them all, is the female ghost who
shows up now and then to demand her nail back:

> A female corpse visited me up in the loft and held out her left hand
> to show me: the thumbnail was missing. I shook my head: I had had
> a nail once upon a time, but I had thrown it away and used a shell
> instead. But the corpse continued to stand there, and I continued to lie
> there, ice-cold with terror.

When one looks back, to refresh one's memory about how the hero acquired the thumbnail, the incident is as cloudy as the book's erotic climate:

> Before leaving the churchyard I found a serviceable thumbnail, which I pocketed. I waited a moment or two, peering this way and that and listening, but all was quiet. No one cried: "That is mine!"

That this bit of a corpse evidently lay on the ground, waiting to be picked up instead of needing to be dug for, may shed light on the deplorable condition of Norse cemeteries; or it may serve as a symbol for the manner of this indifferent little fiction, in which the author picks up his own name and what incidents he finds strewn on the surface of his mind, and no revenants of buried significance cry out, "That is mine!"

Three years later, Hamsun revisited the same scenes and personae, as if redoing a watercolor sketch in the deeper and faster colors of an oil. *On Muted Strings,* despite its title (literally, *A Wanderer Plays with the Mute*), is a richer, sharper, less muted, and more objective work than *Under the Autumn Star.* Six years have passed in fictional time. The wanderer returns to the Falkenbergs' household, having grown a beard so that no one will recognize him (a likely story). His tone is more relaxed and ruminative. Implicitly, he is a successful middle-aged writer in search of material: "I had been corrupted by the refinements of many years, I must take a refresher course in being a peasant." Hamsun is reaching out, that is, from the scarcely controlled subjectivity of his youthful novels to the more deliberate and selfless objectification of rural life that is to be perfected in his popular *Growth of the Soil* (1917). Though *Growth of the Soil,* with its naïve exclamations and cumbersome mock-Biblical grandeurs, rather asks a reader's indulgence now, in a way not true of the defiantly fresh youthful effusions, it shows that Hamsun possessed two modes; his introspection could become observation. Knut Pedersen, on his second visit to the Falkenbergs', is more witness than protagonist. With the help of an eavesdropping maid, he observes and records the marital crackup of the master and mistress of the house. The single page (166) wherein the two agree to separate is a gem of psychologically laden yet plausibly impetuous dialogue. Madame's subsequent confusions, retractions, and final submission to disaster are felt with an electric empathy, though without the proprietorial compassion of a Tolstoy. Hamsun has succeeded in getting away from his capricious, half-demented alter egos and in transferring the charge of his passion onto a woman, a triangle, a social situation. The sequel has in every sense more substance than its airy original. A little fjord town is smartly set as a stage for tragedy:

> . . . our town is tucked away, shut in by mountains; yet it seems to possess its share of female beauty and male ambition, just like any other town. Only it's a queer, mysterious life, the life lived here, with short crooked fingers, mouse eyes, and ears filled day and night with the everlasting roar from the torrent.

The Falkenbergs' house acquires features and furniture, and the conversations within it take on authentic energy, as Hamsun's peculiar sensitivity to the quirky locates itself among the flirtations and withdrawals, bravado and despair of marital discontent. The hoboish cronies of the earlier novel return chastened and deepened by their aging, and things have sprouted names: the Falkenberg estate is called Øvrebø, Madame's first name is Louise. Incisive images abound:

> A narrow-gauge railroad . . . ended here, it went as far as it could, then stopped, like a cork in a bottle.

> Here was no defeated man: for a time he had kept open house for foolishness and debauch, but his own resolution would put an end to that. An oar in the water appears to be broken; but it is whole.

> And if a song thrush sings so that his voice soars God-how-high, and if while poised up there on the topmost note he suddenly makes a right angle in the pitch, the line as clear and as clean as if cut with a diamond; then he sings down the scale again, softly and beautifully.

Nature, a kind of loved solvent in *Under the Autumn Star*, in the later book is crisp and graspable; the farm operations make sense, and the assured rhythms of earthly process pointedly contrast with the vexed and restless human events, a busy futility pinched off by death. Madame Falkenberg is awarded an epitaph:

> She had no mission, only three maids in her home. She had no children, only a grand piano. She had no children.

Yet, relatively firm and sporadically impressive though it is, the second portion of *The Wanderer* wanders, as does the first, through a mental terrain of exhausting desolation. Hamsun, like a great many American writers, placed all his bets on energy and honesty, and found in middle age his energy sagging and honesty scarcely worth the effort. "A wanderer plays on muted strings when he reaches the age of two score years and ten," his epilogue begins, and it rambles on with a disarming brutality:

> Age confers no maturity; age confers nothing beyond old age . . . God preserve me from growing wise! Yes, I intend to mumble toothlessly to my deathbed bystanders: God preserve me from growing wise!

Knut Pedersen, plainly Hamsun now, attacks Ibsen and dismisses "Literature"; he harks back to a bishop of Bergen, Claus Pavels, whose posthumously published diaries were exemplars of non-literary honesty. The epilogist remembers scornfully the heavy, uniform editions the Falkenbergs possessed—"They were all alike, all matching: homogenized poetry, the same novel." The eerie diffidence of the two short novels we have just read becomes explicable; they are novels going through the motions of being novels but at heart rejecting the distinctions, moral and qualitative, that make invented lives dramatic and give "wisdom" a framework. Just as there can be no wisdom in Hamsun's world, so there can be no complaining. "And there it is: the very favor of receiving life at all is handsome advance payment for all life's miseries, each single one." The lack of pity in Hamsun's work produces a tonic clarity but a certain monotony as well. "I saunter onward, slowly and indifferently, with my hands in my pockets. Why should I hurry? It makes no difference where I am." So we read him. Madame Falkenberg's fate seems a schematic miming of that of nineteenth-century adulteresses; we blink in recognition but not with tears. A primal modern, Hamsun perceived in the lonely, sub-arctic valleys of rural Norway that nothing makes enough difference: our quirks and pains come to nothing. That this writer without education or beliefs commanded from first publication the awed attention of his countrymen and of writers across Europe; that his prose with its stubborn aimlessness remains alive on the page; that the ground note of his rude universe of avalanche and flow is one of joy—all this seems, like the actions of many of his heroes, an arbitrary, fundamentally unstable act of will. The literary inheritors of his curious purity (and their name is Legion) are left to stave off despair and silence.

Saddled with the World

THE WOMEN AT THE PUMP, by Knut Hamsun, translated from the Norwegian by Oliver and Gunnvor Stallybrass. 392 pp. Farrar, Straus & Giroux, 1978.

This panoramic novel of a nameless coastal town was originally published in 1920, when Hamsun was sixty-one and somewhere near the middle of his long literary career. It was in 1920 that he received the Nobel Prize. Even at this distance, Hamsun strikes us as less and more than a master like Mann or Ibsen; he was, like Byron, a phenomenon. His rise to fame, his irascible diffidence, his impact upon European literature, the enduring energy of his prose were all phenomenal. In *The Women at the Pump*, Hamsun sought to broaden his piercing talent, to turn to steady illumination the lightning flashes of his youthful work. The author was ready to settle down and tell us all about "things in a small town."

> Ah, that little anthill! Everyone busy with his own affairs, crossing each other's path, elbowing each other aside, sometimes even trampling on each other. That's the way it is, sometimes they even trample on each other . . .

The cast of ants is genially spread before us, from the town magnate, C. A. Johnsen, a shipowner and Double Consul, down to Olaus of the Meadow, the abusive town drunk; at the center of the novel stands one-legged Oliver Andersen, whom an accident at sea has mutilated in a mysterious way that, as his wife, Petra, keeps having babies, keeps the town women gossiping around the pump. They have a lot to gossip about—births and marriages and shifts in fortune, the robbing of a post office and the sinking of a ship, and, near the end, a sudden death that seems to be murder. It is typical of Hamsun to have his hero apparently commit murder and to make so little of it. Making little, in the tradition of Viking stoicism, was his curious genius as a truth-teller but, on the broad social canvas he here proposes to fill, something of a fault. Our would-be naïve interest in the characters and their interwoven lives is considerably discouraged by the author's frequent disavowals of significance, his impatient darting from one thread to another, and his urge to scold his own creations.

> There she sat: Mademoiselle Fia. By now she was getting on in years, the peach bloom on her cheeks was no longer fresh, she was overripe, the first signs of something passé about the lady had appeared. In all her years she had never succeeded at anything, but equally she had never failed; her mind was impervious to change, she was impassive and charmingly self-assured. If she had never run amok, this was because she had never run, period.

"One is saddled with the world one creates, as all creators are." Hamsun wrote this of Oliver, but he must have thought of himself. He is saddled with this fictional fabric but chafes under it; he sighs, snorts, and bucks. His characters talk, in his opinion, "claptrap and bunkum, sentimentality and bombast," and his maimed hero, "one of the jellyfishes that lay breathing in mortal stupidity and nothingness by the edge of the quay," no sooner has a few ideas than the author tells us, "They flashed into his head and were not worth much." Crises dissipate, mysteries remain, and the kind of tough forgivingness with which the townspeople view one another lends even the most dramatic events a tinge of the inconsequential. Of course, that is Hamsun's point, embodied in his unmanned, ras-

cally, but indomitable hero: life goes on. "If anyone were to come
and offer his death, he would not accept it, by no manner of means;
life is none too bad, in Oliver's opinion. . . . He is somewhat
disabled, a trifle imperfect in himself; but what is perfection? The
life of the town realizes its image in him: a crawling life, but none
the less busy for that." The one townsman with a developed (quasi-
Christian) philosophy collapses under misfortune, to the sound of
considerable editorial glee:

> He had searched for many a long year and eventually found a path that
> offered a little light; he had followed this path for a long way—until fate
> reared up against him, erect and terrible, and stopped him. . . . An
> experienced postmaster received one night a thrust in his untested
> human thought and had been dumb and dim from that moment.

The contemporary reader—beset, as the world of print sinks
deeper into the twilight behind the television console, by panicked
claims that each new book is urgent, exhaustive, or the latest thing
—might enjoy this volume for its example of an author so fully,
even arrogantly, at ease with his audience. Though Hamsun must
have had the plot's major turns in mind, the first half, especially,
of the novel gives the impression that he sat down at his desk each
day with little more than a trust that something entertaining would
happen on the page. As he maunders and meanders, he never looks
behind him, confident that his readers are following. His wander-
ing gradually takes him through six or so town households, but not
before his central device—the appearance of both brown-eyed and
blue-eyed babies in the impotent Oliver's family—has worn quite
thin. On the other hand, the self-deceiving manner in which Oliver
prostitutes his wife and takes a father's pleasure in the fruits of her
infidelities is portrayed with a beautiful tact and believableness.

Only the Russians can match Hamsun's feel for the inconsisten-
cies of the human soul, its quantum jumps through the rather
irrelevant circumstances of life. As in all his fiction, small inanimate
things—registered letters, a sack of eiderdown—animate the
human landscape, and pantheistic bliss surges through the remis-
sions of coping. Oliver rows out to sea, far from the site of his social
and sexual humiliations, and stays for days:

Night comes and he does not go home, the next day comes and he does not go home; no, he follows the usual pattern, lets the boat drift, fishes for food, goes ashore, cooks, eats, sleeps. It is incomparable, this wonderful idleness and sloth.

On the first morning sea and islands breathe the solitude of eternity; far away on the mainland stand a few meager telegraph poles; from a parish outside the town he can just hear the church bell, disposing him to gentleness, disposing him to peace.

His town seems to have no parson—at least, none figures as a character—and its people are mostly irreligious; yet God clings to Hamsun's vocabulary, as the one term for expressing his reverence before creation and his love of the non-human. Love among human beings he instinctively perceives as mutual vexation. Though there are many women in the book, and a number of them sharply seen, none are shown in love. Oliver's son Abel loves Little Lydia, but when he reaches for her she pricks him with a needle. "She invariably had a needle in her hand and several more in her bosom; she was not to be approached." Only after many more stabs from this bristling bosom does Abel turn to a girl whose "mouth was a nest full of smiles." Women in their nesting, not their mating, aspects evoke tender images from Hamsun:

> She was not knee-deep in calculations; she was a natural girl like the rest, Nature herself directed her tactics. . . . There was nothing incomprehensible in this, any more than a hen among the flower beds is incomprehensible.

But, so unexpected is the image, the hen among the flower beds is revealed as just that—incomprehensible. The rises and falls, advancements and setbacks, matches and maneuvers of the characters are embedded in an underlying mystery, that of existence itself. It is as if the actors in an Ibsen play, with their politics and posturing, were taken off the resounding stage, out of the sheltering proscenium arch, and set beneath an exhilarating, dwarfing sky.

The translation reads well, and is presumably scrupulous. One would like to know what Norwegian word comes out as "Baloney!," whether "primitiveness gets eroded" was the best way of saying it, and if "cutting a dash and making a splash" was quite necessary; but the Stallybrasses are doing the English-speaking world a fine favor by refurbishing this vital, highly individual writer. As his American publishers plan their next volumes, they might consider turning momentarily from the later fiction and giving us some of his earlier theoretical writing, particularly his 1890 manifesto, "From the Unconscious Life of the Mind," and his famous, contentious dissertations upon his esteemed contemporaries. His lecture series *The Cultural Life of Modern America*, which was printed as his first book, in 1889, has, I discover, been translated into English and published in this country, by Barbara Gordon Morgridge and the Harvard University Press, respectively (1969). The volume, based upon Hamsun's two Midwestern sojourns in the 1880s, tells us what many foreigners have volunteered to tell Americans: we are crude, money-mad, chauvinistic, corrupt, and inane. Hamsun's account of theatre in the United States as he knew it is a hilarious and probably not unjust descriptive flight; elsewhere, he fulminates against "African half-apes" whose freedom has turned America into a "mulatto stud-farm," wistfully looks forward to "the mighty revolts of individual geniuses who suddenly thrust mankind forward for several generations," protests the tyranny in the United States of women and of Boston, demolishes Whitman by quoting his worst poetry, and dissects Emerson with some spirit and shrewdness. According to Hamsun, Emerson has "that happy faculty of a writer or a speaker of being able to *say things*" but leaves us with only "a lapful of things said." Emerson's major failings are "his undeveloped *psychological* sense and thereafter his overdeveloped *moral* sense." Reverse the proportions, and you have Hamsun, just as you have Hamsun's positive aesthetic program in this negative criticism: "He has no eye for the slight stirrings of the psyche, the delicate manifestations of will and instinct, all that subtle life of nameless shadings." These shadings, these stirrings were to be the substance of the novel *Hunger* (1890), which launched Hamsun's comet. But in these ill-tempered and ill-considered lectures, as in *The Women at the Pump* thirty years later, he shows the magisterial ability to keep talking—however busily he appears otherwise engaged—about himself.

Scheherazade

CARNIVAL: *Entertainments and Posthumous Tales*, by Isak Dinesen. 338 pp. University of Chicago Press, 1977.

In an interview she gave to *The Paris Review* in 1956, Karen Christence Dinesen, the Baroness Blixen-Finecke, explained how she came to her, in this century, anomalous mastery of the art of tale-telling: "I really began writing before I went to Africa, but I never once wanted to be a writer. I published a few short stories in literary reviews in Denmark, when I was twenty years old, and the reviews encouraged me but I didn't go on—I don't know, I think I had an intuitive fear of being trapped. . . . Later, when I knew in my heart I should have to sell the farm and go back to Denmark, I did begin to write. To put my mind to other things I began to write tales. Two of the 'Gothic Tales' were written there. But earlier, I learned how to tell tales. For, you see, I had the perfect audience. White people can no longer listen to a tale recited. They fidget or become drowsy. But the natives have an ear still. I told stories constantly to them, all kinds."

The tales of Isak Dinesen, of course, depend for their quality upon more than the suspenseful momentum of oral recitation. The silver thread of their plots winds through phrases of perfect aptness and unique slant; landscapes evoked with a painterly eye and of a majestic breadth; characterizations of a peculiar aloof lovingness; and a philosophical wit that owes something to her fellow-Dane Kierkegaard's mordacity but something more to the eighteenth century, its feline playfulness and illusionless psychology held within an ultimate love of calm, of balance. Her imagination could visit, it seemed, any corner of European history and find there a tale tinged with the luster and vivid shadowing of medieval allegory. She bestowed an unimpeachable intellectual power and dignity of workmanship upon materials that in other hands would have appeared mere costume dramas—farfetched, phantasmal, moony. At a time when literary practitioners were turning anywhere but to the nineteenth century for exemplary ways to "make it new," she took up the tattered gothic, romantic conventions and showed they still fit our naked human plight. A Danish woman who wrote in English under a man's name, she stood a little to one side, rakishly, and was regarded with some suspicion by at least the Swedish Academy, whose curious failure to award her the Nobel Prize (though she lived to a good age and had the tacit advantage of being Scandinavian) was mentioned by Hemingway in his own acceptance speech.

The full range of Isak Dinesen's career is represented in *Carnival: Entertainments and Posthumous Tales,* which binds together unpublished or at least uncollected work from 1909 to 1961. The book has been commendably produced by the University of Chicago Press: the violet jacket is pretty, the blue cover is handsome, the volume sits holdably in the hand, and the print sits readably on the page. One would not mention such elementary decencies of manufacture if there were not so much mannered and inconsiderate book design on the market, and a dinosaurian trend toward volumes so big they can only be wrestled open in bed, where their pages reveal type so tiny a floodlight has to be called in from the lawn. My only technical complaint about *Carnival* is that the bibliographical information is scattered carefreely between the jacket flaps and the front matter. The flaps state that some of the stories were translated from the Danish; a lonely little notice opposite the title page tells us which ones: "The de Cats Family," "Uncle Théodore," and "The Bear and the Kiss."

The earliest story in the collection is "The de Cats Family," published in 1909, by which time, the jacket says, the author had "discovered her talent and her themes, but not her voice." For this reader, the voice was perfectly there, and this fable of a prosperous Amsterdam family that needs one black sheep alive at all times to keep the others virtuous shows in the twenty-four-year-old Karen Dinesen—as she then was—many of the mature writer's strengths: her high comedy, her nose for the supernatural, the metallic purity of her beautifully paced plots, the secure social sense that enables her to locate and limn so justly this bourgeois family in a city not her own. She brings to the Dutch scene the slightly fantastic elegance of all her landscapes:

It was a December afternoon, one of the first snowy days, and a thin scurf of snow lay on the streets and the roofs of the houses, on the decks of the boats and the barges; in the leafless trees along the canals black crows sat quite still and thoughtful and the sky was a brownish gray, like peat smoke. Far in the west there was already a broad strip of sky colored like a lemon or very old ivory.

This is translated from the Danish; when, toward the end of her seventeen years in the British colony of Kenya, she began to write in new earnest, her adopted English lacked for no nuance of evocation:

On a full-moon night of 1863 a dhow was on its way from Lamu to Zanzibar, following the coast about a mile out. . . . This still night was bewildering in its deep silence and peace, as if something had happened to the world; as if the soul of it had been, by some magic, turned upside down. The free monsoon came from far places, and the sea wandered on under its sway, on her long journey, in the face of the dim luminous moon.

Thus opens "The Dreamers" in *Seven Gothic Tales;* but in the lesser tales of *Carnival* there are plenty of magical passages, conjuring up places where Karen Blixen had been but rarely, if ever:

The ancient city of Bergamo stands upon a rock fifteen hundred feet high and three thousand feet wide. From there, like a hawk with a mouse, it keeps an eye on the Città Bassa, the newer town of trade and crafts which, low on the green plain, runs peacefully along the roads to the outside world.

High up in the Città Alta's maze of broken lanes the dark Middle Ages of Italy are still alive. . . . A famous traveler has said of the Bergamasque aristocracy that they were all half mad with malice and lust. They were an insular race, their minds fossilized like lava, their blood thick and hot.

A manuscript page that Isak Dinesen permitted *The Paris Review* to reproduce shows an eccentric large hand flowing from one edge of the page to the other without apparent hesitation and with only one crossing-out. As her health failed, she often dictated. A visionary fluency, aloof as a sibyl's drone, is one mark of her style; another is its distinct *taste.* She said of reading Huxley's *Crome Yellow,* "It was like biting into an unknown and refreshing fruit," and Dorothy Canfield, introducing the unknown, presumably masculine author of *Seven Gothic Tales* to an American audience, began, "The person who has set his teeth into a kind of fruit new to him, is usually as eager as he is unable to tell you how it tastes." The adjective "delicious" rises to the mind as it savors her rich, dense, satiny paragraphs; the intimacy that Isak Dinesen establishes is one between the eater and the eaten. Like the city of Bergamo, she sees like a hawk; what she sees is so distinct as to be succulent. Again like a hawk, she is looking for certain things, and repeatedly swoops to the same prey.

Of the eleven tales in *Carnival,* three are climaxed by a kiss, and seven—all but the first and the last two—celebrate the power of young females. This power is not bluntly sexual; indeed, most of these heroines are chaste. The fifteen-year-old heroine of "The Last Day," reading the Bible to a dying man, lets him kiss her, as his farewell to life. She knows what has happened:

> Her wide-open, light eyes, like a hawk's eyes, were severe, so that I might have believed that she was angry with me, and at the same time they were friendly, encouraging, confident. She knew everything, and laughed at danger.

The nine-year-old heroine of "The Fat Man" is not kissed but killed, and expresses her power by haunting the murderer: "It is her small light step that has followed close on his own all the time." In "The Proud Lady," a fifteen-year-old girl persuades, with a kiss, the executioner of Paris to show her aristocratic grandmother a courtesy on the scaffold befitting her rank; and in "Uncle Seneca" and "The Ghost Horses," little mystery tales first printed in American slick magazines, young women are privy to potent secrets. The heroine of "The Ghost Horses" is only six, and is described thus:

> As she stood up, in her small flannel nightgown, her face was on a level with his. What lovely eyes and delicately arched eyebrows, what rich hair. And what a sudden, strange power in the whole frail figure.

Isak Dinesen was herself frail, and spent much of her later life in a hospital bed—her illness traceable to a poorly treated case of syphilis caught from her husband in the first year of her marriage. When, after a few unhappy years, they separated, she ran their six-thousand-acre Kenyan coffee farm by herself, until the drop in coffee prices in 1931 compelled her to return to Denmark, and to writing. On the farm, her memoir *Out of Africa* tells us, she made it a habit to visit with some Somali women living on her property, and to listen to stories they told: "It was a trait common to all these tales that the heroine, chaste or not, would get the better of the male characters and come out of the tale triumphant. . . . Within this enclosed women's world, so to say, behind the walls and fortifications of it, I felt the presence of a great ideal, without which the garrison would not have carried on so gallantly; the idea of a Millennium when women were to reign supreme in the world." And is not some such ideal behind the blindingly precious kisses and power-racked waifs of Isak Dinesen's fiction? Indeed, is not this the lightning that flashes throughout the female-dominated realm of "gothic romance," whose summit is *Wuthering Heights*— the belief, that is, in a spiritual power, which, though belied by physical frailty, irradiates matter and ultimately shall triumph in the material world so heavily controlled by men? Within Isak Dinesen's garrison of females, the beauty and spiritual history of each are chronicled like the arms and battle honors of warriors:

> Her blackened eyelashes were so long that her clear brown eyes looked out at you as from behind an ambuscade, and at whatever place—throat, arm, waist, or knee—you cut her slim body through with a sharp knife, you would have got a perfectly circular transverse incision.

Such violent praise is rendered to one of the four heroines of the long title story, "Carnival." The tale is the conversation of a group of bright young things who escape a Copenhagen costume ball for an hour in 1925 and engage in mannered conversation and a frivolous wager. In the end, into this female province of color and glitter a young man dressed in black and painted black walks with the intention of robbery, but in fact he is subdued to a kind of service by the youngest of the women, called Arlecchino, who wears "that placid and slightly scoffing expression which one finds in the faces of Japanese dolls." For all its scintillations, "Carnival" seems in total effect arch and confusing and heartless; it was, the introduction states, "originally intended to be a puppet comedy," and the author never published it, though "through the years she borrowed many of its best ideas and themes for other stories of hers." In this posthumous gathering of work too slight or fragmentary for previous inclusion in her oeuvre, "Carnival" seems the one distinct failure, the least real, though it takes place in our century and provides, through its brittle kaleidoscope of smart-set revelry, a tantalizing glimpse of how Karen Blixen lived. No more than Scott Fitzgerald in *Tender Is the Night* did she solve the odd literary problem of how to convey the convivial exhilaration of a fashionable party.

Quite fabulous, and utterly satisfactory, albeit unfinished, is the other long tale in this book, the novella *Anna*. It takes place in Lombardy over a century ago, and its heroine is the child of a deaf-mute mother and a tightrope-walking father. She has grown, at the age of fifteen, into a stoic Amazon: "The peasant girl displayed a quality of her own, a calm, gentle equipoise, which made her lift up a burden as lightly as she laid it down. One might imagine her to be the very young child of a giant race, who would some day balance the Gattamelata Palazzo, with all that it contained, upon the palm of her hand." Her power is so patent it allows her to be gentle and passive; when the young master of the palazzo seduces her, only the adjective "cool" betrays where the securest strength lies: "The boy felt compelled by all forces around him and within him to press the girls' soft body to his own steely frame, and to bury his hot hard face in the cool petals of her cheeks and her lips." Having given him manhood, she reposes in it, all through a Dinesenian tangle of scheming matriarchs and sudden inheritances and corrupt transactions. "The line of her existence might pretend to turn and twist, she herself knew that it was perfectly straight, and that at the end of it lay the moment when she was to give herself back, body and soul, to the poor unhappy and misunderstood boy who needed her." The happy ending is so thoroughly adumbrated we accept it as accomplished, as the Baroness Blixen-Finecke walks away in the mist of fairy-tale warmth, unconcerned to gather up her threads and write *Finis.*

The image of a line that pretends to turn and twist yet in truth is perfectly straight serves as a metaphor for the storyteller's art. This art does not vanish, but it will not soon again be construed as it was by Isak Dinesen. Her upper-class birth in the coziest of European monarchies and then her African sojourn exposed her to vital forces that had become in much of the Western world archaic. The strangest story in *Carnival,* called "The Bear and the Kiss," presents a heroine who shares with Anna and Arlecchino only their ancient power; she is tiny, the Finnish wife of a hermit giant. "Clad entirely in Lapp costume, with a leather jacket, a leather cap, and Lapp shoes, she was as erect as a cork in a bottle and seemed to lack the midsection of the usual or accepted figure of a woman, so the captain's comparison with a thumb recurred to them. However . . . her shortness was a concentration; she was the thumb which cocks a shotgun." Three men have come ashore to hunt at her isolated home, which her husband has built and decorated with carvings. The couple feeds the interlopers coffee, and sends them into the hills, where there is a rumored bear. They return empty-handed at the end of the day, and the little thumblike creature gives one of the men a kiss. Written in Danish in the 1950s, the story does not yield a clear meaning even to its own characters, who discuss its events afterward. Perhaps it is less a story than an ideogram of the world as Isak Dinesen saw it: there is the bear on the one hand and the kiss on the other, the futile hunt and the extravagant carvings, and between these enigmatic presences (violence, love, adventure, art) looms a central gulf, not spanned by the storyteller's tightrope in this instance but unadorned, unignorable, the void of non-meaning.

Water, the water of the sea, "the cold and voracious hereditary foe of humanity," as the splendid "Deluge at Norderney" expresses it, never failed to excite Isak Dinesen's pen—the green shadow surrounding a boat at anchor, the shifting forms of rocks glimpsed through dark water, the "noble straight line of the horizon: light within light" seen at sea are all noted in the stories of *Carnival.* Our human life is felt as an island, as Denmark is a virtual island, and this pressure of the inchoate upon her inventions keeps them from being merely toys, however toylike. Their intricacy is yet simple, like that of crystals; the pressure of the darkness beyond the tribal fire is always felt at the storyteller's back. "Where the storyteller is loyal, eternally and unswervingly loyal to the story, there, in the end, silence will speak."

Brecht's Dicta

BERTOLT BRECHT: DIARIES 1920–22, edited by Herta Ramthun, translated from the German by John Willett. 182 pp. St. Martin's Press, 1979.

From June of 1920 to February of 1922, Brecht, then in his early twenties, kept a journal of his hectic life and furious imaginings. Simultaneously involved with three women (Hedda, Bi, and Marianne), two of whom became pregnant by him, and prominent within a circle of young students and artists whose zest for alcoholic confusion was as keen as his own, Brecht nevertheless found time and inspiration for a welter of poetic, dramatic, and cinematic conceptions (some of which he carried to completion), and he set down a number of iron dicta, which guided him through life: "But then I keep coming back to the fact that the essence of art is simplicity, grandeur and sensitivity, and that of its form coolness." "At night, a mouthful of firewater in my stomach, I get overcome by a vast desire to do other work, to mould the simple darkness of life—tough and servile, cruel and realistic—with a *love* of life." "In any case one needs to beware of 'wit,' of candied fruit, tasteful decorations and smooth finish." "O God, please let my sight always cut through the crust, pierce it!" Yet he does not believe in God, and his unflinching wish to do without illusions, plus an exceptional energy and boisterous humor, distinguishes his vivid, ruthless, cheerful journal from that of many another artist as a young dog.

Discontent in Deutsch

A MOMENT OF TRUE FEELING, by Peter Handke, translated from the German by Ralph Manheim. 133 pp. Farrar, Straus & Giroux, 1977.

THE WONDERFUL YEARS, by Reiner Kunze, translated from the German by Joachim Neugroschel. 127 pp. Braziller, 1977.

These two small books from the German made a variety of uneasy impressions upon this reviewer, not the most easy being a vague one that his reactions were unworthy. Peter Handke, born in Austria in 1942, is widely regarded as the best young writer, and by many as the best writer altogether, in his language; and there is no denying his willful intensity and knifelike clarity of evocation. He writes from an area beyond psychology, where feelings acquire the adamancy of randomly encountered, geologically analyzed pebbles:

> When Keuschnig stood up, he had the feeling that his brain was gradually cooling. He pulled down the skin of his forehead and closed his eyes firmly, as though that might warm his insensible brain. . . . In the next moment he felt as though he were bursting out of his skin and a lump of flesh and sinew lay wet and heavy on the carpet.

> He had the feeling of having to lower his bottom jaw to let the accumulated saliva run out.

> In a bakery with little left to sell, a bakery girl was sitting alone, gazing round-eyed into space. He bought an oval loaf of bread, and she waited on him patiently. She gave him his change and started cleaning her nails as he was leaving. The sight gave him a feeling of lightness.

> Keuschnig felt so ridiculous he thought his head would fall off. . . . He felt himself to be something BLOODCURDLINGLY strange, yet known to all—a creature exhibited in a nest and mortally ashamed, IMMORTALLY DISGRACED, washed out of the matrix in mid-gestation, and now for all time a monstrous, unfinished bag of skin. . . .

> In the presence of this man with his affectation of omniscience, innumerable little worms began swarming in and out of every opening in Keuschnig's body; an intolerable itch, especially in his member and

nostrils. He scratched himself. Dried ear wax detached itself from his auditory passages and fell somewhere . . .

The list could be extended. Indeed, the entire book, all one hundred thirty-three pages of it, is a kind of list of Keuschnig's incessant and usually unpleasant feelings.

Who is Gregor Keuschnig? He is a young employee of the Austrian Embassy in Paris; his job consists "of reading French newspapers and periodicals, marking articles or news items that related to Austria, when possible providing the ambassador with a daily digest, and twice a month sending the Foreign Ministry in Vienna a report on the image of Austria reflected in the French mass media." He has a wife, Stefanie, a four-year-old daughter, Agnes, and a mistress, Beatrice, who has two children. He seems at best bored and at worst horrified by these intimates in the course of the two days that pass during *A Moment of True Feeling;* but perhaps he is not himself. The novel begins with a dream in which he murders an old woman. "Who has ever dreamed that he has become a murderer," the first sentence asks us, "and from then on has only been carrying on with his usual life for the sake of appearances?" While we puzzle over the answer, amid the tumult of falling earwax, Handke fervently pursues the volatile moods and hallucinatory sensations of this hero cut off from the reality of his own life. Keuschnig and his wife, presumably, have been estranged for some time: "Her name was Stefanie, and only yesterday she had aroused feelings in him, at least occasionally. . . . Once or twice in the past he had placed his thumb on her throat, not as a threat but as one kind of contact among many others. Only if she were dead, he thought, would I be able to feel something for her again." His mistress and he, one suspects, have until now been happier: "He didn't let her undress him. If she were to touch him, he would crush her with his fist. . . . She wants to help me, he thought, in such a rage that he might almost have struck her in the face . . ." The violence latent in such an erratically connected citizen of the quotidian yawns behind every quirky event and distended perception Keuschnig suffers; we are more relieved than surprised when, while entertaining an unnamed Austrian writer and his mistress,

Keuschnig takes off his clothes, smears his face with stew, has a fistfight with his guest, and insults his wife by blurting out one of his day's two infidelities.

The next day dawns with a thunderstorm, and his wife is leaving him. He finds her sitting "dressed in a gray travelling suit"; she makes her announcement ("It doesn't really matter—I'm happy, and at the same time I could kill myself, or I could just sit down and listen to records") and then falls in an abrupt faint; he revives her and tells her "I hope you die" when he meant to say "I hope you come back"; she leaves; he notices "the sky was blue, the street almost dry. Only the tops of the cars coming from the still overcast north glistened with trembling drops of water." This all rings deadly true; the peculiar crazy, sleepless staleness of our great domestic crises is here captured. Keuschnig spends the rest of his day babysitting with his daughter, in so desultory a style that he loses her in a playground. He walks about Paris thinking such words as "SECRETS" and "SHAPES" and "COMPLIANT" and "EXPERIENCED" in spaced capital letters that look escaped from a comic strip. Early in his two-day odyssey, he noted a telephone number chalked beneath the exclamation "*Oh la belle vie*" and, impulsively, phoned the number and made a date for the Café de la Paix; as *A Moment of True Feeling* ends, Keuschnig, his spirits somewhat revived, is striding, hands in pockets, loosely knotted necktie swinging, across the Place de l'Opéra to keep the blind date.

Should we rejoice? Just as a passerby, encountering Keuschnig, is "repelled by the chaos in his face," so we tend to smirk and turn away in the face of a novel so pitiless, of a hero so repulsive and overwrought. It is true, our lives, stripped of their padding of numbness and habit, do appear horrific, flickering, and absurd; then even an innocuous female shopper on the street excites such an internal diatribe as

In a little while, home in her hideous kitchen, she wouldn't shrink back from pouring nauseatingly golden-yellow oil into a pre-warmed frying pan. That sizzling, so preposterous you want to hold your ears, as she puts a grotesque piece of meat into the pan . . .

But, having survived such visions, to emerge again into the sunny daze of normal ongoing working, loving, and eating, one reads about them a bit as one reads about dreams and fevers. Dostoevski's Underground Man wrote over a century ago, "I swear, gentlemen, that to be too conscious is an illness—a real thoroughgoing illness." But compared with Keuschnig, the Underground Man is a jolly companion—a keen philosopher and jaunty editorialist. Also, Keuschnig seems not only overwrought but overfamiliar. Handke is the complete child of modernism; Kierkegaard's absurdity, Sartre's nausea were mother's milk to him. Like Kafka, he has a hero called Gregor who awakes monstrously metamorphosed; like Joyce, he has his hero wander a city street by street; like Robbe-Grillet, he sets down physical details with a flat precision that conveys a menacing emptiness. Also like Robbe-Grillet, he is an abundant theorizer, who has announced that "story" and "invention" have become superfluous, and who in a confessional memoir of his mother, *A Sorrow Beyond Dreams*, has described letting "every sentence carry me further away from the inner life of my characters, so as finally, in a liberated and serene holiday mood, to look at them from outside as isolated insects."

At his best, Handke is a kind of nature poet, a romantic whose exacerbated nerves cling like pained ivy to the landscape:

> As though the sky now partook of an alien system, it became too high for the high towers of civilization in the foreground of the picture, and against the compact, menacing background the human landscape degenerated into a junkyard. The deep blue with which a time grown plethoric weighed on the world was the essential—the scattered leaflets down below, in which only fear of life or death could beguile him (or anyone else!) to find the slightest meaning, were a secondary, minor factor. Keuschnig saw the sky arching over the Place de la Concorde as something incongruous and hostile, plunging its edges down at the Place.

At his worst, Handke is a despiser of his characters, disdaining to give them coherent actions, on the theory that all human acts are essentially nonsensical; yet he asks us to follow Keuschnig—as a dogged parent follows a sulking child from room to room—and perhaps to share the holiday mood when, at the end, his tantrum exhausted, Keuschnig vows for himself "a more sustained yearning" and crosses the avenue to tryst with a stranger his disgust and terror have not yet contaminated.

Reiner Kunze's *The Wonderful Years* comes from East Germany, and brings a whole other set of presumptions and grievances, which awakened in the apologetic breast of your reviewer another brand of impatience. Publication of this book in West Germany, it should be stated at the outset, cost the author his passport and his membership in the East German Writers' Union and represented an act of courage of a sort that American writers are not asked to perform. *The Wonderful Years,* less a work of fiction than an artful mosaic of autobiographical glimpses, takes its title from Truman Capote, who in *The Grass Harp* wrote, "I was eleven, and then I was sixteen. Though no honors came my way, those were the lovely years." The unlovely process of growing up in a Communist state is reflected in a series of vignettes based, presumably, upon Mr. Kunze's years as a teacher and his fatherhood of at least one child, a daughter, Marcela, whom he names in an afterword. The youngest children overheard in the book are boys—a six-year-old sticking pins in "enemy" toy soldiers, a seven-year-old with a toy Tommy gun and a rather uninstructed reverence for Lenin, a set of nine-year-olds who have the following political discussion with their pastor:

First Pupil:	Americans are enemies.
Pastor:	What about Angela Davis? Didn't you do a wall newspaper on Angela Davis?
First Pupil:	She's not American. She's a Communist.
Second Pupil:	No, she's not! She's black.

The dialectic thickens in the section called "Defending an Impossible Metaphor," wherein the author broods over his teen-aged daughter, whose fondness for jeans and jazz and other Western fads brings her and her peers into frequent conflict with the authorities. "The parents of a student who wore wire-rimmed glasses to school were warned: wire-rimmed glasses are an imperialistic fad, decadence. To prove it, the teacher presented illustrations from a Western magazine showing long-haired males wearing wire-rimmed glasses." Passing a Japanese postcard around the school is "spreading propaganda for the capitalist system"; sitting on a curb constitutes "beatnik behavior"; championing Pasternak is a classroom scandal; a headband moves a policeman to offer the wearer "a solid feeling of the power of workers and peasants!" These enforcements seem different in degree but not in kind from those that adolescents the world over receive from petty authorities. The public-school system of any society is bound to be a propagandist for the official values; useful national citizens are the system's basic product. These examples of East German "shaping" of the young, though distasteful and as extreme as expulsion—that is, permanent exclusion from the economy's elite—for adolescent dissidence, do not illustrate a purely Communist trait, or a new one; *The Wonderful Years* quotes Goethe saying to Eckermann, "With us, everything pushes toward taming our dear young people early and driving out all nature, all originality and all wildness, so that in the end nothing remains but the Philistine."

From the schooling of children Mr. Kunze proceeds to the invasion of Czechoslovakia in 1968, an act of international discipline by the Soviet headmaster. From an East German standpoint, the event reveals some interesting details: Herr Kunze's wife, born in Czechoslovakia, had flowers of sympathy anonymously delivered to her; he, when visiting Prague, was denied service in a café because of his country's share in the military intervention; and an East German solider recounts his confused tour of duty—"Big awakening: 'I thought *they* called *us?!*' " But the drama of disillusion is weak, when one has never shared the illusion; the Western press noisily proclaimed from the start what it has cost Kunze some pains to realize and great pains to suggest in print. The biases of our own news, unfortunately, so condition us that these brave writers from behind the Iron Curtain appear quaint, with their veiled allegories of trees "who stand upright all their lives" and their poignant wish that some miracle will "sweep away all the lies that satiate the air." Like many reformers, they appear to mistake the intrinsic for the accidental. Why be astounded that a state—the German Democratic Republic—founded by an army of occupation and maintained by a barb-wired wall should be oppressive and hypocritical? "I am not an enemy of the Republic," Kunze has stated; "I am an enemy of lies." To his own government, this position appears menacing; to a Western reader, it seems disingenuous.

A parallel might be perceived with Handke's hero. Gregor Keuschnig is not an enemy of freedom, but he hates its daily qualities. " 'I don't believe in God!' he said, meaning nothing." Yet he seems surprised when he presses the old buttons labelled Love and Hope and nothing happens. "It's all over, he thought, I don't love anyone any more." And, a beautiful image: "He stroked the withered skin of her elbow and wanted to howl with hopelessness." His howl has something in it of a naïve protest, of a delayed reaction to old news. Handke, for all the modernist writers he has learned lessons from, seems spiritually akin to those *fin-de-siècle* exquisites, those deliberately decadent self-flagellants in search of the divine, Huysmans and Baron Corvo.

Disaffection in Deutsch

WINTERREISE, by Gerhard Roth, translated from the German by Joachim Neugroschel. 133 pp. Farrar, Straus & Giroux, 1980.

APPROXIMATION, by Hans Joachim Schädlich, translated from the German by Richard and Clara Winston. 167 pp. Harcourt Brace Jovanovich, 1980.

The West German literary magazine *Südwestfunk* has in its wisdom decided to give an annual prize to a work "depicting with great literary seriousness the human experience of alienation." The first winner was Gerhard Roth's short novel *Winterreise*, which now, as if alienation were what America needs more of, has been published here, in a translation that is not always felicitous and that somehow skipped across the title: *Winterreise*—also the name of a cycle of *lieder* by Schubert, composed to poems by Wilhelm Müller —means "winter journey." Herr Roth, born in Austria in 1942, has written among other things several children's books. His hero,

Nagl, has been a teacher of young children and, during his bleak winter wanderings through Italy, often thinks of childhood, his own and his students':

> He recalled how stupid he had felt as a child in school. He had learned arithmetic like a machine, he had written like a machine, without knowing why. He had only felt an inescapable constraint, a hopelessness, which struck him mute. "It makes no sense," he had often thought when giving up, as if what came next would have made more sense. He had raised the children to keep quiet and make no waves, because he believed that would be best for them.

Alienated at the kindergarten level, Nagl progresses through the wastelands of religion, sex, and sightseeing with uniformly high marks in apathy and detachment; the only real trouble with this book about him is that it feels too conscientiously determined to carry off the alienation prize.

Winterreise begins on the last day of the year, a calendrical downer. Nagl is about to go to Italy. He says good-bye to his classroom and his mistress. She is a policeman's wife whose boot has lost its heel. Their soggy parting occasions single-sentence paragraphs, an infallible sign of philosophical distress:

> "I'll drive you home," said the woman as she sat down, placing the empty plastic sack [formerly containing the heelless boot] at her side. When he shook his head, she drove off.
>
> It was a cold winter day.
>
> It was the last day of the year.

He witnesses a veterinarian's funeral, which introduces the theme of umbrellas: "Since it had rained that morning, the farmers carried folded umbrellas." In his room, he looks at an antique "silver peasant watch" that he has inherited from his grandfather, and he leafs through a book of color photographs of volcanoes. Volcanoes are his favorite thing: "Sulfurous efflorescences in front of the ice wall of the Torfajökull Glacier in Southern Iceland, the white-hot lava flow from Mount Kilauea in Hawaii, geysers in Yellowstone National Park, lava with a blue, glassy surface in Idaho, violet ash deposits on the Lipari Islands, and a view into the crater of

Vesuvius, with pale billows of smoke rising from inside." Then he calls up a girl called Anna, "who had been unfaithful to him," and she consents to come along, because she is "naturally frivolous" and her father is an optician. Then the cuckolded policeman comes by, somewhat drunk, and to show that he is "serious" shoots himself in the hand. Nagl tells him to go to a doctor and heads out the door with his valise. Naples, here we come.

Ever since the German tribes ranged themselves against, and eventually conquered, Rome, the southern half of Europe has appeared to the northern half as a tray of goodies that might make you sick. Dürer went to Venice to learn from the art of Mantegna and Bellini; Mann's writer Aschenbach went to Venice to discover his homosexuality and die. In his "Roman Elegies," Goethe wrote, "Still do I mark the churches, palaces, ruins, and columns, / As a wise traveller should," and buses of boisterous Teutonic tourists still seek in the sunny sights of Italy relief from their own gray skies and, of a potentially corrupting sort, education. Nagl, that nail in the world's coffin, drinks up local color like a straw. In Naples, "oranges and lemons on carts and in fruit crates gave way to crates of firm red peppers, cucumbers, and zucchini. Vegetable dealers in caps and aprons hauled crates of leeks, radishes, cabbage, fennel, pears, and apples past them, the air smelled of fish and meat, fruit, onions, and cheese." In Pompeii, "the Casa dei Vettii plunged into his eyes, pictures on walls in colors surfacing to the daylight from deep in the ocean. Colors from pollen and from the blood of slaughtered oxen, from air and leaves, colors that were tender as if they had grown as plants, as if they were thoughts made of some living matter." In the Basilica of St. Peter's (which he mistakenly terms a cathedral), "the walls and decorations were of black, green, yellow, and gray marble full of golden mosaics and stucco-work." On Piazza Navona, "children were yelling between the tea-colored, olive-green, and iodine-brown houses and the white fountains." In Venice, "palazzi rose out of the water, in colors that seemed to come from the ocean, yellow and orange, purple and salmon, with stone balconies and closed, heavy shutters. Ships came toward them or past them or rocked between blue-and-yellow and tobacco-brown and white pilings with golden balls over the tops." And: "In the harsh noon light, the colors of the houses turned pale like crab shells drying in the sun." And: "The sun was a reddish-gold disk setting rapidly behind the palazzi. The purple behind the houses oozed into the sea, pulling along a flow of stringy red clouds. There, where Nagl assumed the Campanile to be, the figure of a golden angel glowed in the setting sunlight, the angel was small and bright, while the heavens turned violet and tinged into green away from the houses."

Well, this is fine stuff, if you enjoy getting postcards; and to an extent we all do. But the vividly seen colors of Nagl's excursion are flat as colored chalk on a blackboard, where they share space with detailed diagrams of his sexual congresses with the strikingly oblig- ing Anna, and a sporadic tracing of the *Wanderjahre* of his itiner- ant-worker grandfather, and a running tabulation of the amounts of *grappa* he consumes to keep his alienation moist, and a number of smeary equations whose sum is zero ("I'm nobody. I've invented everything I see"; "Everyone only knew about himself that he was nothing"). Through the polychrome of the prose stares the black- board itself, a personal void that consumes ungratefully all the gifts the world can offer, from scenic beauty to sexual pleasure, and pronounces itself dissatisfied: "He lacked something. He always had the feeling that something was lacking. It left him dissatisfied and, since he couldn't talk to anyone about it, lonely."

As when a child throws a sulk, we are meant to feel guilty. We of the world have failed. Nagl is an educated member of a prosper- ous and efficient capitalist democracy; but then so was Ulrike Mein- hof. So is Herr Roth's fellow-Austrian and exact contemporary Peter Handke. Like much of Handke's work, *Winterreise* is short, intense, and repellent. Both writers work the vein of hysteria that complements rigid dutifulness within the German male character: both writers know that border area where coldness becomes frenzy and alienation becomes terrorism. Both persuade us that the man next to us (in the bus, in the neighborhood) is close to crazy. The surface mundane of *Winterreise* bristles with little details that seem to shriek: "At the jetty by the railroad station, a dead squid with golden eyes lay on a wooden stairway." Throughout his journey, Nagl has noticed umbrellas.* One drunken night, "the last thing he saw was Anna setting up the open umbrella to dry on the bureau. In the night, he awoke and spotted the umbrella, which looked like a gigantic open flower. He felt threatened by it, got up, and put it away."

Many of Nagl's visual impressions are threatening, like fissures of steam that declare an underlying volcano. These details give his book what poetry it has, and its truth. Its untruth stems from its air of solemn petulance and its proudly self-confirming disaffection. Anna's lovemaking, as brutally described, is rabid. Nagl's grandfather's life, as imagined, is as futile a wandering as his own. The children he teaches are conceived entirely in terms of pathos, never of hope or simple vitality. As in Handke, the shadow of Catholicism (which the Austrian monarchy successfully defended against Lutheranism) falls across a world insubstantially gaudy, glistening with terror. Nagl left the Church ten years ago, and "religion struck him as an artistic handiwork from the hands of death, and it seemed only to be announcing death." Yet this same religion in other lights "struck him as a shield against madness." In a crisis, he prays, and toward the end of his debilitating survey of Italian monuments, in Venice, "while calmly registering everything, Nagl was suddenly convinced that death would not snuff him out." This should be good news, but we feel no relief at the revelation—just the threat of a weary prolongation. What afterworld could please Nagl? When he has at last driven Anna away with his cruel apathy, he lies on his bed alone and the "eternal ice" of the Arctic enters his mind. In a sudden turn toward the territory ahead as surprising as Dick Diver's winding up in the Finger Lakes region, Nagl buys an airplane ticket for Fairbanks, Alaska. The Welcome Wagon and the Chamber of Commerce there should buck him up.

Hans Joachim Schädlich is disaffected in another way. Born in 1935, he was one of the seventeen million persons trapped as the Soviet zone of occupied Germany congealed into the German

---

* *"Seinen Schirm zumachen"* (to put up one's umbrella) = "to kick the bucket."

Democratic Republic. After studying at the Universities of Berlin and Leipzig, he became a translator, and wrote fiction that the authorities did not find acceptable for publication. When, in 1977, he arranged to have a book of his writings published in West Germany, to enthusiastic reviews ("A book that burns like ice"— *Die Zeit*), his income as a translator ceased and he was declared an enemy of the state. The authorities finally granted him a permit to emigrate in December of that year, and he moved to Hamburg, to enjoy the freedoms of the Federal Republic of Germany. His *Winterreise* from East to West Germany was presumably a good trip, and all honor is due yet another writer who has struggled against the inane censorship of a Communist state. However, the American publication of his courageous work, under the title *Approximation*, may afford its American readers satisfactions more political than aesthetic; Herr Schädlich's style is as bleak as his themes, and the ingenious strategies of expression under tyranny can seem rather spindly out in the open.

His twenty-five stories—some as short as two pages—were written from 1969 to 1977, and can be grouped into several distinct modes of writing. What hope or defiant despair of publication accompanied these various approaches can only be conjectured. One mode, illustrated by "Come, My Sweetheart, Let Us Go into the Country and Spend the Night in the Villages," is narrated by a youthful rogue who cheats the system with sex, jazz, and booze, and brags about it; this form of the picaresque owes something, perhaps, to the stories of the Russian Vasily Aksyonov, which came like a breath of fresh air into Soviet fiction in the early Sixties, and whose breezy presentation of antisocial behavior yet did not openly challenge Socialist orthodoxy—though sensitive establishment critics were quick to scent the whiff of a challenge in it. Schädlich's story "Apple in Silver Bowl" extends this mode into open criticism; its young tough-talking hero sees his girl seduced by a "fat card" who lives in a "dacha" so elegant it seems to belong "across the border where the other country wallows in luxury." The last sentence calls the fat card "the type I wouldn't touch with a ten-foot pole, but that kind will shinny right up to the top of the pole" —meaning the local pole, the Communist system. "Nowhere a

Place" shows a defective child pummelled to death by a group of men that includes a hospital administrator; "Parts of the Country-side" tells how another misfit, a young woman who abandons her work, dies of exposure in the woods in the absence of the proper residency permits; and "Dobruska" is a sketch of a drunken con-struction worker that is as dialogue-dependent and sour as an early John O'Hara short short. All these stories in a naturalistic mode may have been aimed at sanctioned publication; there is little in them that specifically indicts the government—just the implication that for many in this society there is "nowhere a place."

Another group, however, explicitly portrays aspects of Socialist totalitarianism. "Under the Eighteen Towers of the Týn Church" follows with chilling precision the steps whereby the police iden-tify the speakers who, with their backs to the camera, gave an indiscreet television interview in Prague. The title story, "Approxi-mation," presents the thoughts of a nameless national leader as he stands trapped and almost motionless watching a three-hour parade pass by, wishing that he could have a beer, fantasizing that his own bodyguards may turn their guns on him. "Barely Legible Letter" consists of a worker's plea, since he was denied permission to visit his dying father in the "western part of the city," to be stricken "from the list of residents"—"I don't know about official docu-ments. But I know this much: that I am not the country's property, don't have to stay where I was born." "Posthumous Works" shows a party hack, "familiar of poets," silkily bargaining with the mis-tress of a great, recently deceased poet for the poet's papers, to be placed in "the prospective archives." "Little Lessons in Prosody" details the suave seduction of a young poet by benign and insistent official guardians of the ideal of beauty: "To confer strength for struggle, for the everyday struggle as well, is what beautiful poetry does and should do." It is worth noting how understated these stories are: the enforcers of social order are shown as patient, suave, plausible, even playful. In "Stand Up and Be Counted," the speeches at a workers' political meeting are given as straight as the conservative pep talks in *Babbitt*.

The more rigid a situation is, the more delicate satire can be and still make itself felt. The subservient client-state relationship of East

Germany to the Soviet Union is parodied in some curious stories ("The Emperor of Russia's Visit to the Emperor of Germany" and "Last Honors") that do little but unfurl the pompous and melodious vocabulary of nineteenth-century diplomacy from the balconies of the implied present situation. No topical allusions occur, unless they are buried in the roll of dignitaries' names. "Brief Account of the Death of Nikodemus Frischlin" gives us the imprisonment and death of a sixteenth-century professor *poeticus et historiarum* who has offended the nobility; like most of Schädlich's heroes, Frischlin is "a stranger in his own country." Other stories ("Search for a Sentence" and "October Sky") toy with the German literary past with an irony too muted to survive translation; entrapment in a precisely described environment is their common feature, as if the East German walls extended deep into the past as well as the future.

The last distinctive type of story owes something to the objectivism of Robbe-Grillet: streets and buildings and mechanical maneuvers are blueprinted with a merciless and ominous precision. The oldest story in this collection, "Greeting," flatly describes a postcard mailed to Leipzig from Berlin; only the pressure of the signature ("Buttke signs his name so hard that the signature makes a faint ridge on the other side") indicates emotion. In "One-Way Mirror," a large and complex waterfront building is described as it existed on a certain date (Tuesday, the twenty-fifth of June, 1974) in such a manner as to suggest that an escape has been made. In "Restless and Fleeing," the escape is made from a railway car: "The man who sat down beside the man I am sitting opposite, and who got up, opens the door opposite the door and falls into the darkness." And in "Paper and Pencil" the hero, like a figure in a Steinberg drawing, seems to be trying to write himself into another space altogether. These stories, bleak and minimal as they are, and composed in a manner indebted to the avant-garde of Western Europe, yet feel pregnant with the writer's most intuitive, least politicized sense of life—a life of things that all function as barriers, an East Germany wherein people have been reduced to the stylized scribbles of architectural sketches, lacking not only names but even the numbers that are assigned to prisoners. These citizens send postcards, witness parades, and vanish.

Both *Approximation* and *Winterreise,* indeed, leave humanity as we have liked to imagine it far behind. Have the copious sociologies and teeming populations of Mann and Musil, Grass and Böll come to this, this laconic testimony smuggled out of lands of ice? I took these two slim volumes of fiction with me on a week in the Caribbean and must confess that, brief as both are, it took all the bracing counter-effects of sun, sea, and shuffleboard to get me through them. Herr Schädlich is the more cheerful, since he believes there is something better across the border; but, given the conditioned detachment he so rigorously images forth, one wonders if he will be less a stranger in Hamburg than Nagl in Alaska. A world where no one is at home seems deducible from these evidences of the human spirit's atrophy.

CALVINO, GRASS, BÖLL

Metropolises of the Mind

INVISIBLE CITIES, by Italo Calvino, translated from the Italian by William Weaver. 165 pp. Harcourt Brace Jovanovich, 1974.

Like Jorge Luis Borges and Gabriel García Márquez, Italo Calvino dreams perfect dreams for us; the fantasy of these three Latins ranges beyond the egoism that truncates and anguishingly turns inward the fables of Kafka and that limits the kaleidoscopic visions of Nabokov. Of the three, Calvino is the sunniest, the most variously and benignly curious about the human truth as it comes embedded in its animal, vegetable, historical, and cosmic contexts; all his investigations spiral in upon the central question of *How shall we live?* In *Invisible Cities* he has produced a consummate book, both crystalline and limpid, adamant and airy, playful yet "worked" with a monkish care. The book, a sheaf of imaginary cities, combines the slightly brittle and programmatic science fiction of *Cosmicomics* and *t zero* with the affectionate mood and elegiac landscapes of his earlier, more naturalistic stories. The very first paragraph of his first novel, *The Path to the Nest of Spiders* (1947), gave us a city:

> The old towns on the Ligurian coast grew up in times when those parts were infested by Moorish pirates; built to resist siege, they are as close and dense as pine-cones; their deep narrow alleys, called *carrugi*,

are spanned by arches propping the tops of the houses, with dark
vaulted arcades and flights of cobbled steps running far below . . .

In *The Baron in the Trees* (1959), Calvino evinced, as he constructed
for his hero a lifetime spent in trees, a passion for fantastical engi-
neering. The cities of *Invisible Cities* remind us of the concoctions,
from this same novel, of Battista's combinational cookery:

> These dishes of Battista's were works of the most delicate animal or
> vegetable jewelry; cauliflower heads with hares' ears set on a collar of
> fur; or a pig's head from whose mouth stuck a scarlet lobster as if putting
> out its tongue, and the lobster was holding the pig's tongue in its pincers
> as if they had torn it out. And finally the snails; she had managed to
> behead I don't know how many snails, and the heads, those soft little
> equine heads, she had inserted, I think with a toothpick, each in a wire
> mesh; they looked, as they came on the table, like a flight of tiny swans.

The plot of *Invisible Cities* is no more or less than what happens
in the mind of Kublai Khan, and the mind of the reader, as Marco
Polo describes fifty-five cities he has visited. He has visited Anas-
tasia, "a city with concentric canals watering it and kites flying over
it"; Tamara, a city dominated by signboards; Isaura, "city of the
thousand wells . . . a city that moves entirely upward"; Maurilia,
a city obsessed by postcards of itself; Zenobia, a city set on high
pilings though the terrain is dry; Zobeide, a city whose streets
follow the paths of the founders' dreamed pursuit of a naked
woman; Armilla, a city wholly of plumbing, inhabited by nymphs;
Valdrada, "so constructed that its every point would be reflected
in its mirror" of a lake; Sophronia, whose stone half of palaces and
bank buildings is dismantled annually while the half that consists
of an amusement park is permanent; Octavia, a city suspended from
cables above a precipice; Ersilia, a city of strings; Adelma, where
each inhabitant reminds the traveller of a dead person he has
known; Moriana, a city that "has no thickness, it consists only of
a face and an obverse, like a sheet of paper"; Leonia, a city set
among mountains of its own refuse; Argia, a city that "has earth
instead of air" ("clay packs the rooms to the ceiling, on every stair
another stairway is set in negative, over the roofs of the houses hang
layers of rocky terrain like skies with clouds"); Thekla, a city

entirely and perpetually under construction; Irene, a city that is always in the distance; Penthesilea, a city that appears to be "only the outskirts of itself "; Perinthia, a city built by astronomical calculations to "reflect the harmony of the firmament" and that has come to be inhabited by "cripples, dwarfs, hunchbacks, obese men, bearded women"; and Andria, whose inhabitants believe that every change in the city produces a change in the sky, and whose actions accordingly are characterized by "self-confidence and prudence."

Calvino's wonderful inventiveness and discreet, efficient prose (in tone quite close to that of Marco Polo's own accounts) would not alone prevent a certain numbness from setting in; but the separate descriptions, most of them a page or two in length, are cunningly grouped, with a mathematical complexity and subtlety of modulation worthy of Marco Polo's contemporary Dante. The catalogue of fifty-five is broken into nine chapters, the first and last containing ten cities, the middle seven five each; each chapter begins and ends with italic interludes of dialogue and speculation between the Venetian traveller and the Tatar Emperor. The fifty-five cities are also divided, evenly, among eleven categories: cities and memory, cities and desire, cities and signs, thin cities, trading cities, cities and eyes, cities and names, cities and the dead, cities and the sky, continuous cities, and hidden cities. Very prettily, each of the seven middle sets, or chapters, consists of—in the following order—the fifth city of one category, the fourth of another, the third of another, the second of another, and the first of a new category. All this playful rigor would be fruitless were it not grafted onto a more organic progressiveness—a curve of concern whose evolution is traced by both the "travels" of the narrator and his periodic conversations with Kublai Khan. Roughly, the cities progress, in the impression they make upon us, from the exotic and dreamlike to the allegorical and cautionary. At first, the cities' interaction with the marvelling traveller is emphasized; then they come to be described in terms of their pasts, of the manner of their building, of their permanence or impermanence. In answer to a challenge from the great Khan to tell him about Venice, Marco Polo tells of five cities that seem aspects of Venice. Certain real Italian cities, such as Rome and Siena, have already peeped through the chimerical imagery; the Roman Church and Marxist doctrine are clearly but never crudely caricatured in the relationships various citizenries assume with the dead and the unborn, with ideal cities and the "blueprint" of the firmament:

> Work stops at sunset. Darkness falls over the building site. The sky is filled with stars. "There is the blueprint," they say.

Styles of growth and development are brought into increasing focus; modern artifacts like airports and bulldozers are casually introduced. The last section opens with a dialogue over an atlas showing real cities of the world, from Ur and Jerusalem and Lhasa, "whose white roofs rise over the cloudy roof of the world," to San Francisco and New York and "cities in the shape of Los Angeles, in the shape of Kyoto-Osaka, without shape"; the fictive cities that follow and conclude plainly embody the modern urban problems of overpopulation and waste, poverty, justice, and space. The book ends with the plea "Give them space," and in English that noun euphoniously accords with "peace" and "grace."

Beneath Calvino's tireless shimmer of fancy, his concern over how men live together has carried into our minds. As Marco Polo tells his auditor, "It is not the voice that commands the story: it is the ear." Led to read on by the fascination of the details and the grave beauty of the prose, we find the civic ideal unfolding within us—the same ideal that underlay Calvino's most autobiographical short story, "The Watcher" (1963), wherein the hero, Amerigo (recalling Amerigo Vespucci, another great mental traveller), discovers a city of the defective in the Cottolengo charity hospital of Turin, and views it, finally, in the benedictory light of "the hour, the moment, when every city is the City." The indirectional, transactional method of *Invisible Cities* is the opposite of that of *Cosmicomics*, which announces its idea at the outset—suppose human personalities to be present amid the geological and galactic events modern science describes—and then, more or less amusingly, but a trifle mechanically, executes it. The idea of *Invisible Cities* is not announced; it gradually dawns.

Perhaps only an Italian could have written this delicate epic of urbanity; Augustine's City of God, Dante's infernal metropolis,

Piranesi's architectural fantasies, Giacometti's haunted spaces ("thin cities" indeed) lie behind these "imaginable cities," each of which has "an inner rule, a perspective, a discourse." Italy's towns, many of them once city-states, are vividly individual, and do seem each to embody a different principle, or to crystallize the differing moods of a volatile individual. For a Frenchman, by contrast, lesser cities are dulled and even damned by not being Paris, and an American tends instinctively to see his cities as blots upon the original wilderness. There is something specifically Italian about, say, Calvino's city of Melania, whose citizens interchangeably take roles in an ongoing theatrical performance, or about the thread of happiness he traces in the unhappy city of Raissa:

> And yet, in Raissa, at every moment there is a child in a window who laughs seeing a dog that has jumped on a shed to bite into a piece of polenta dropped by a stonemason who has shouted from the top of the scaffolding, "Darling, let me dip into it," to a young serving-maid who holds up a dish of ragout under the pergola, happy to serve it to the umbrella-maker who is celebrating a successful transaction, a white lace parasol bought to display at the races by a great lady in love with an officer. . . .

If Calvino's happy sense of civic life is national, he is at home in, and thoroughly fluent in, the international languages of the avant-garde, of science, and of abstraction. What other writer in the world so lovingly looks upward from the earth, and so cunningly binds rarefied speculation to the fibre of common experience?

Like the many dual cities Calvino evokes, *Invisible Cities* has two layers: the cities themselves, in Roman typeface, and the discourses of Marco Polo and Kublai Khan, in italics. Read through by themselves, these italic interludes reveal their continuity, an enlarging skepticism. Kublai Khan comes to doubt first the objective reality of the traveller's tales, and then of all the outer world, and then of even these dialogues, this immediate reality. Their discussion does not always avoid a too-playful, sterile Berkeleyism: Marco Polo suggests that "those who strive in camps and ports exist only because we two think of them." The Khan objects that "without them we could never remain here swaying, cocooned in our hammocks."

Marco Polo concludes, "Then the hypothesis must be rejected. So the other hypothesis is true: they exist and we do not."

But as a metaphor for the artistic experience and the riddle of communication the dialogues work very well. Until he knows the Tatar language, Marco Polo must tell his tales by manipulation of objects, an ambiguous language wherein "a quiver filled with arrows could indicate the approach of war, or an abundance of game, or else an armorer's shop; an hourglass could mean time passing, or time past, or sand, or a place where hourglasses are made." And the cities themselves, with their enigmatic wonders, compose just such a vocabulary, wherein the narrator—the imperial auditor accuses—is "smuggling: moods, states of grace, elegies!" The cities are women, past moments, doctrines, jokes, *things*. The curiously irreplaceable value of fiction is explicated in terms of space:

> But what enhanced for Kublai every event or piece of news reported by his inarticulate informer was the space that remained around it, a void not filled with words. The descriptions of cities Marco Polo visited had this virtue: you could wander through them in thought, become lost, stop and enjoy the cool air, or run off.

The gift of space that this book ends by calling for, then, is just what the book itself bestows; amid the crowded, confused, consuming "infernal city" that is "already here, the inferno where we live every day," art and imagination, creating inner space, are offered as amelioration.

The producers of the American edition of this rare and masterly work have tried to rise to the occasion. William Weaver, who has translated the last four of Calvino's books to appear in English, has outdone himself with an effortless-seeming, finely cadenced version, its vocabulary as plain and fancy as it needs to be. The silver, quasi-reflecting jacket struck me as appropriately uncanny, but the typography, though certainly *designed*, does not flatter the text as well as it might. The italic face, with its askew little "*a,*" is so small as to challenge the eyesight, and the 3-D title type, though indubitably structural, is also hard to read, and perhaps too jazzy for a text so reverent and elaborately distilled; what we have here, after all, is a Book of Psalms.

Card Tricks

THE CASTLE OF CROSSED DESTINIES, by Italo Calvino, translated from the Italian by William Weaver. 129 pp., with illustrations. Harcourt Brace Jovanovich, 1977.

In the effort to keep fiction magical, modern authors have resorted to alchemically elaborate trickery: Joyce in *Ulysses* paralleled the *Odyssey* episode by episode while simultaneously satisfying a number of allegorical schemata; Queneau in *The Bark Tree* set forth episodes of Parisian low life in chapters obedient to both the classical unities and an absurdly rigorous mathematics; Nabokov in *Pale Fire* wrote a poem in nine hundred ninety-nine lines that told one story while a detailed commentary by a crazy man told quite another; Walter Abish in *Alphabetical Africa* confined his first chapter to words beginning with "A," his second to words beginning with "A" or "B," and so on, to "Z" and back, through twice twenty-six chapters. Italo Calvino, than whom no living author is more ingenious, tells the mingled tales of *The Castle of Crossed Destinies* by means of tarot cards. The frame device is simple: travellers meet in a castle—or, in the second section, a tavern—where their powers of speech are magically taken from them, and a tarot deck is placed at their disposal. The first narrator, a young man resembling the Knight of Cups, establishes the method and sets the tone:

> The handsome youth made a gesture, as if to demand our full attention, and then began his silent tale, arranging three cards in a row on the table: the *King of Coins,* the *Ten of Coins,* and the *Nine of Clubs.* The mournful expression with which he set down the first of these cards, and the joyous look with which he showed the next one, seemed to want to tell us that, his father having died—the *King of Coins* represented a slightly older personage than the others, with a mature and prosperous appearance—he had come into possession of a considerable fortune and had immediately set forth on his travels. This last notion we deduced from his arm's movement in throwing down the *Nine of Clubs,* which—with the tangle of boughs extended over a sparse growth of leaves and little wild flowers—reminded us of the forest through which we had recently passed.

The cards are depicted in the margin as they are laid down, so the act of narration is double and cunningly merges, in the voiced uncertainties and multiple possibilities of interpretation, with the act of listening, of understanding.

Invisible Cities, Calvino's previous work (his books can no longer be called novels; they are displays of mental elegance, bound illuminations), contained the idea of wordless speech. Marco Polo, unable to speak Tatar, manipulated objects in order to communicate with the Emperor, and told him, "It is not the voice that commands the story: it is the ear." The cardplay of Calvino's present exercise all but dissolves both voice and ear. The writer reads as he writes; we read with him; the plane of narration becomes a beaded curtain through which reader and writer loom to each other as one giant character seen in a speckled mirror—an apparition doubled. The price paid for this illusion is a certain tedium, short as *The Castle of Crossed Destinies* is. The chimerical "invisible cities" were, though fantastical, oddly solid and fascinatingly inventive. The personal histories related by tarot symbols—and the rules of the game call for many—flicker into sameness, blurred reshufflings of old romances and medieval themes, and eventually show themselves as the mere stories, thin and worn, of Parsifal and Faust, Hamlet and Oedipus, Lear and Lady Macbeth. "The world does not exist," Calvino imagines Faust to be saying through the cards. "There is a finite number of elements whose combinations are multiplied to billions of billions, and only a few of these find a form and meaning and make their presence felt amid a meaningless, shapeless dust cloud; like the seventy-eight cards of the tarot deck in whose juxtapositions sequences of stories appear and are then immediately undone." So much for the magic of fiction. The tale-tellers' prestidigitation and significance-seeking swirl around an empty center; the "bald circumference of the *Ace of Coins*" is read to mean that "every journey through forests, battles, treasures, banquets, bed-chambers, brings us back here, to the center of an empty horizon." Calvino contemplates the death not of that notorious old moribund the Novel but of the Story itself, of the hopeful impulse that makes beginnings and seeks outcomes and imagines adventures in the middle. A collection of stories may not be the best means of illustrating this theme. For all his inventiveness and affectionate regard for the traditional fables he transmutes, they (with some exceptions; the tales told by women take on life) seem in the telling scantly sketched—too quick for the eye, too remote for the heart, professedly arbitrary.

Calvino has set himself a technical challenge whose technicalities deserve consideration. The tarot deck, used not just by fortunetellers but for a card game, or a family of games, called *Tarok* in Germany and *tarocchi* in Italy, has four suits—Cups, Coins, Clubs, Swords—each containing the numeral cards Ace through Ten and four face cards: King, Queen, Knight, and Page. In addition, there are twenty-one esoteric picture cards, susceptible to many interpretations, called the tarots, or Major Arcana, plus the Fool—the joker. Calvino, his attention seized by a beautiful deck painted by Bonifacio Bembo for the Dukes of Milan in the fifteenth century (a deck now divided between Bergamo and New York and missing several cards) began to play with its narrative possibilities. His afterword tells us:

> I began by trying to line up tarots at random, to see if I could read a story in them. *The Waverer's Tale* emerged; I started writing it down; I looked for other combinations of the same cards; I realized the tarots were a machine for constructing stories; I thought of a book, and I imagined its frame: the mute narrators, the forest, the inn; I was tempted by the diabolical idea of conjuring up all the stories that could be contained in a tarot deck.

There are two decks used, and two sections: the "Castle" of the overall title and a second, not quite symmetrical half, entitled "The Tavern of Crossed Destinies." The castle sequence is more rigorously organized than the tavern sequence. After a banquet enjoyed "in a muteness which the sounds of chewing and the smacking of lips gulping wine did not make more pleasant," the guests lay down their stories in double rows of sixteen or so cards; some proceed horizontally and others vertically, but all use, like crossword players, the cards already in the path of their narrative, though assigning different meanings to them. When six such stories have exhausted the deck and covered the table, six more stories unfold from the backward reading of the same cards! The design is completed with some embarrassed frenzy—"What is left me," Calvino tells us, "is only the manic determination to complete, to conclude, to make the sums work out"—but in fact the very last tale, told by the castle's hostess, is one of the more vivid, though scarcely a page long; and even where the stories seem jerky and dim we can admire the passionate ingenuity of their interlock. The cards most ingeniously bent to serve narrative purposes are, of course, the many number cards; in passages quoted earlier the Nine of Clubs comes to represent a forest and the Ace of Coins the universal nullity. A Two of Clubs means in different places a crossroads or a pair of levers; Cups can signify a banquet or a sexual consummation. Not only do Coins introduce riches into a plot, but two of them can represent an exchange and a multitude of them evoke "the gleaming domes of golden skyscrapers" or "the first golden light . . . of morning." The cards depicting human figures and, in the Arcana, dramatic, if enigmatic, little scenes give Calvino his best opportunities to spin and advance a tale. He bends low and perceives facial expressions on the cards: the Queen of Swords has her "turtle-dove countenance, pert dimples, little tilted nose" noted in one reading and in another is seen proffering "the elusive smile of a sensual game." The so-called Visconti cards are miniature paintings that bring entire landscapes to the eye; but the barer, cruder woodcuts of the deck consulted in *The Tavern of Crossed Destinies*—the popular Ancien Tarot de Marseille, printed by the firm of Grimaud since the eighteenth century—conjure up worlds for the by now highly suggestive interpreter-author. One card, called the Star, on first glance represents this:

> A naked goddess takes two jugs containing who knows what juices kept cool for the thirsty (all around there are the yellow dunes of a sun-baked desert), and empties them to water the pebbled shore: and at that instant a growth of saxifrage springs up in the midst of the desert, and among the succulent leaves a blackbird sings; life is the waste of material thrown away, the sea's cauldron merely repeats what happens within constellations that for billions of years go on pounding atoms in the mortars of their explosions, obvious here even in the milk-colored sky.

The same card returns in other tales as a woman giving birth by a stream, as an armed warrior undressing beside a stream and revealing herself to be a woman, as a nun undressing, as Parsifal's mother rearing him in the wilderness, as Cordelia drinking water from a ditch, as Lady Macbeth washing her hands of blood, as Ophelia about to drown herself. Similarly well thumbed are the mystical cards named, in the French of their manufacture, *la Lune, la Roue de Fortune, le Jugement, la Maison Dieu.* But as we wander, in the unmannerly inn of this second section, through tale after tale, we feel something is wrong. The same cards recur too often; the apocalyptic and erotic notes are struck too effortlessly, chiming with Calvino's usual cosmic and metropolitan preoccupations; there is an unchecked fluency. The nub of the problem can be located by those who, like this assiduous reviewer, trouble to trace with colored crayons a few specimen narrative sequences on the full spread of cards reproduced on page 98: *the cards have been used in no special order.* Calvino in his afterword confesses his break-down of procedure:

> I thought of constructing a kind of crossword puzzle made of tarots instead of letters . . . I succeeded with the Visconti tarots because I first constructed the stories of Roland and Astolpho, and for the other stories I was content to put them together as they came, with the cards laid down. I could have followed the same method with the Marseilles tarots, but I was unwilling to sacrifice any of the narrative possibilities I was offered by these cards, so crude and mysterious. The Marseilles tarots continued giving me ideas, and every tale tended to attract all the cards to itself.

Now, this most amiable of avant-gardists cannot resist a tour de force. Having written a novel about a viscount who, being cut in half, doubly thrives, he must follow it with one about a baron who lives a long, full life entirely in trees, and that with one about a knight who is, behind his armor, nonexistent. Within his absurd premises he remains rigorous. Here, having played the cards one way, he picks them up again but, instead of overtopping his previous trick, finds himself overwhelmed. The effect is disturbing, like a sonnet in which the poet fails to rhyme the sestet, having perfectly rhymed the octave. Why, if the cards are to be used so freely, use cards at all? If the first set of tales seemed at intervals mechanical, this second set feels a touch copious and pompous; the narrative sprouts historical and philosophical asides and self-conscious declamations: "But will I not have been too pontifical? I reread. Shall I tear it all up? Let us see." The afterword less gnomically describes Calvino's struggles with the second section, the maddening complications he conceived and discarded, his awakening in the night "to note a decisive correction," his abandonment of the project for a year, his decision to abandon "ironclad rules," break out of "this maniacal obsession," and "publish this book to be free of it."

The magician has been bewitched. The cards, his tools, have rebelled. Our aesthetic unease goes deeper than the analogy with rhyme suggests. *The Waste Land,* its couplets so cavalierly slashed by Pound, and *Prufrock* before it, showed the effectiveness of rhyme that comes and goes, like a ghost behind the arras, as Eliot said of metre—"to advance menacingly as we doze, and withdraw as we rouse." Formal correctness has so long ceased to be required of poets that those who adhere to it are viewed as eccentrics; for a time they published their own magazine, *Counter/Measures.* But cards possess a more ancient and intimate connection with order and disorder than poetic prosody. A deck of cards is a type of machine not easy to construct, a machine for producing random order. As such it admits, in its suspension of material causality, the possibility of divine pronouncement. It is the essence of cards, once shuffled and dealt, to constitute a given, whether the given is a bridge hand or a human fortune. As long as Calvino, having made his initial arrangement, took it as a given and read stories into it every which way, the infinite plasticity of the narrative art was demonstrated, and the infinite pluralism and final empty monotony of human experience were forcefully implied. But when, in the second set, he reads the cards selectively, the presiding narrator suffers a sharp demotion in magical capacity, and nothing is proved, however much is asserted in the style of "we have seen these greasy pieces of cardboard become a museum of old masters, a theatre of tragedy, a library of poems and novels." Calvino's array of medieval legend, Shakespearean melodrama, and twentieth-century woolgathering seems messily synoptic, a gaudy mulch. The book is published "to be free of it," in disarray. By breaking the rules of his own game, and breaking faith with his own splendid cleverness, Calvino has lost the definitive fatalism of the cards.

He leads us up to, but not through, the riddle of art and accident. Acceptance of the accidental is a mark of artistic confidence. I know a painter who, having placed his easel, declines all further options of selectivity and renders onto canvas every detail before him. I know a writer who finds it difficult to conceive of situations, incidents, or even names different from those which actually cohered in a nexus of facts that momentarily generated the electricity and resonance of the "fictional." Every moment is, in a sense, a dealt hand. The combinations that the human mind invents are relatively facile and unmagical compared to reality's dovetailed richness. Behind the artist's transformative sorcery lurks, like a sheepish apprentice, an irrational willingness to view the accidents of the actual as purposeful and the given as sacred. We are all artists insofar as we take the inexorable and quite unchosen data of our own circumstances and philosophically internalize them, give them a significance to match their awful centrality, and thus lend our lives a "meaning." Narrative and metaphysics alike become flimsy and frivolous if they venture too far from the home base of all humanism—the single, simple human life that we all more or less lead, with its crude elementals of nurture and appetite, love and competition, the sunshine of well-being and the inevitable night of death. We each live this tale. Fiction has no reason to be embarrassed about telling the same story again and again, since we all, with infinite variations, experience the same story.

My niggling dissatisfaction with Italo Calvino's benign, witty, and arduous book extends to its physical production. Harcourt Brace Jovanovich has constructed a volume that appears elegant; yet the cards, when reproduced smaller than a postage stamp, are hard to see, and the effect of interwoven word and image leaches away in the ample margins. The fault is not one of uncaring, as a comparison with the Italian edition by Giulio Einaudi shows. The American publisher has spaced the English translation to coincide page for page with the Italian text, and thus has been able to use the black-and-white tarot rectangles in the exact format presumably designed, or at least approved, by the author. Indeed, the cards are slightly larger, and in spots more legible, than in the Einaudi edition. But the Italian paper is whiter, and the type is larger, and the book is smaller and lighter and pleasanter to hold, and the cards in the narrower margins sit tighter to the text: the effect, in sum, is significantly more natural and less posh. Confronted with a kind of chapbook, the American publisher has felt a tug toward the coffee table; Harcourt's oversize, unhandy volume includes eight color plates of the Visconti tarots, adding to the print and woodcuts a gratuitous third texture. Texture, that almost uncontrollable quality, is crucial in a pictographic work, and perhaps the sleazy genius of offset printing is to blame for what we miss here. Twenty years ago, in the obsolete days of letterpress, zinc "cuts" of these cards would have bitten sharply into the paper, and expressed themselves as another alphabet, different in type but not in kind from the Roman. As is, the page lacks the memory of metallic impact and its warmth; the ostensible beauty of the American edition of *The Castle of Crossed Destinies* has the unintended effect of emphasizing its precocity, enlarging its imperfections, and preventing the reader from feeling as friendly, holding it, as he should.

Readers and Writers

IF ON A WINTER'S NIGHT A TRAVELER, by Italo Calvino, translated from the Italian by William Weaver. 260 pp. Harcourt Brace Jovanovich, 1981.

THE MEETING AT TELGTE, by Günter Grass, translated from the German by Ralph Manheim, with an afterword by Leonard Forster. 147 pp. Harcourt Brace Jovanovich, 1981.

It takes great vitality to break through the intense self-consciousness of the contemporary European novel. Italo Calvino, in his oddly titled *If on a winter's night a traveler,* manages to charm and entertain the reader in the teeth of a scheme designed to frustrate all reasonable readerly expectations, whereas Günter Grass, in *The Meeting at Telgte,* giving an account of an imaginary literary conference in 1647, delivers a thoroughly muffled punch. Both these estimable authors, who began as postwar naturalists with a touch of fantasy, have lately, while their impending Nobel Prizes ripen on the frosty northern vine, been indulging certain philosophical hobbies: Grass, in autobiographical rambles like *Local Anaesthetic* and *From the Diary of a Snail* and in the massive novel *The Flounder,* has occupied himself, in a way so specifically German as to make translation difficult, with political questions that take him deep into history; and Calvino, in such necklaces of ingenuity as *Invisible Cities* and *The Castle of Crossed Destinies,* has explored the metaphysics of narration, of communication, of being social creatures.

His new novel is about, in a sense, the act of reading, often discussed and at one point described as (the reader being female) "the current that brings the sentences to graze the filter of her attention, to stop for a moment before being absorbed by the circuits of her mind and disappearing, transformed into her interior ghosts, into what in her is most personal and incommunicable." For this same reader, who is the heroine of the book and has a name, Ludmilla, "reading means stripping herself of every purpose, every foregone conclusion, to be ready to catch a voice that makes itself heard when you least expect it, a voice that comes from an unknown source, from somewhere beyond the book, beyond the author, beyond the conventions of writing: from the unsaid, from what the world has not yet said of itself and does not yet have the words to say." The hero, who is "you," the Reader, meets Ludmilla in the bookshop where he (you) has (have) bought this very book, which begins, "You are about to begin reading Italo Calvino's new novel, *If on a winter's night a traveler.* Relax. Concentrate. Dispel every other thought. Let the world around you fade. Best to close the door; the TV is always on in the next room. Tell the others right away, 'No, I don't want to watch TV!' "

The first chapter of what appears to be the narrative plays upon our awakened consciousness of being readers perpetually caught in the act. We are in the shadowy café of a railway station, on a mysterious errand involving a swap of suitcases. A woman at the bar attracts our attention, and we are told:

> Your attention, as reader, is now completely concentrated on the woman, already for several pages you have been circling around her, I have—no, the author has—been circling around the feminine presence, for several pages you have been expecting this female shadow to take shape the way female shadows take shape on the written page, and it is your expectation, reader, that drives the author toward her . . .

The novel cannot sustain for its length so intricate an interplay of reader, author, and hero. This Möbius strip of a new twist on literary self-consciousness breaks down into an alternation of (1) a running essay on the reading experience mixed with an ultra-fabulous plot concerning the multiple textual deceptions of the mysterious translator Ermes Marana, whose "head is oblong horizontally, like a dirigible," and who, infuriated by the sight of Ludmilla happily reading, wants to "flood the world with apocrypha," and also concerning the developing relationship, not uncarnal, between "you," the Reader, and not only Ludmilla but her feminist, structuralist sister Lotaria as well, and (2) the opening chapters of ten different novels, all (perhaps) perpetrated by the protean Ermes Marana and all breaking off at just the point where they become suspenseful. Such a welter sounds impossible, but in fact Calvino keeps it moving quite brightly along. The abortive novels as well as the frame narrative treat, in varying ways, of the abstruse reader/writer, artifice/reality interrelations, sometimes in the accents of those philosophers of the book Barthes and Borges, sometimes in the more playful tone of that great promulgator of mimetic illusion Nabokov, and sometimes in display of obsessions that are peculiarly Calvino's, such as the notion that things themselves can be read as a language, expressing "the world's intentions toward me," or the idea that a virtue can be made of a novel's piling stories one upon another, "without trying to impose a philosophy of life on you, simply allowing you to observe its own growth, like a tree, an entangling, as if of branches and leaves."

Of the books-within-the-book, the most immediately amusing and, in their odd truncated way, involving are the more distinctly parodic—of Japanese exquisitism and eroticism, of South American violence and enigma à la Borges, of *samizdat* desolation. Long an editor at Giulio Einaudi Editore, Calvino has handled a lot of manuscripts, and knows as well as any living writer "the world of books." Yet parody never becomes the point of the pseudo-fictions, which obliquely hew to a central tone; hints of crime figure in most of them, and the presiding spirit is that of the thriller. Now, all novels aspire to be thrillers in some sense, but to an American it may seem a diminishment that so convoluted a meditation upon prime literary concerns should ground itself in a genre that in the United States, since Hammett and Chandler and Cain were praised for their slit-eyed naturalism, has been beneath serious critical notice. Yet in Europe the thriller's qualities of overt contrivance and sinister disenchantment perhaps make it a paradigm of what the novel, in these tired times, can be. Certainly first-rate sensibilities —Simenon, Graham Greene—have enlisted among its practitioners; the *nouveau roman* began with a detective story, Robbe-Grillet's *Les Gommes* (1953). The specimen author among the characters in *If on a winter's night a traveler,* through whom Calvino expresses many of what must be his own subtle sensations of authorship, is an Irish writer called Silas Flannery, whose name harmonizes with that of Sean Connery, and whose international wealth and fame further suggest the author of the James Bond tales. We have come a long way from the august authors-as-hero—the Stephen Dedaluses and Gustave von Aschenbachs—of early modernism.

The postwar European literary scene, dominated in Paris, at least, by critics rather than by creative writers, does seem, in a word, bookish; that is, artistic exploration has taken place along a frontier lined with other books instead of exerting any very hungry pressure, in the manner of the pre-war giants, against the world itself. Amid all the charms and expert entertainments and quizzical truths of *If on a winter's night a traveler,* there is little that sticks in the mind as involuntarily real, as having been other than intellectually achieved. The book is cool, with few warm spots where the shape of the author's life rubs. One such spot is the section where the Reader, who thinks with the voice of the author, admits himself to Ludmilla's little house when she is not there, and from the—in Barthesian terms—"code" of her furnishings tries to deduce her personality and his own chances:

> Among the utensils a certain aesthetic tendency is noticeable (a panoply of half-moon choppers, in decreasing sizes, when one would be enough), but in general the decorative elements are also serviceable objects, with few concessions to prettiness. The provisions can tell us something about you: an assortment of herbs, some naturally in regular use, others that seem to be there to complete a collection; the same can be said of the mustards; but it is especially the ropes of garlic hung within reach that suggest a relationship with food not careless or generic.

Not only do these pages of description bristle with more specificity than the book's usual texture, but the held breath of the investigation is felt, the inventory and the action are one, and a human motive—the wish to achieve a seduction—bulges the details toward us.

In another warm spot, the comical figure of an editor, Cavedagna, immersed in the confusion and scriptural wealth of a publishing house, confesses a dream:

> ". . . I was in my village, in the chicken coop of our house, I was looking, looking for something in the chicken coop, in the basket where the hens lay their eggs, and what did I find? A book, one of the books I read when I was a boy, a cheap edition, the pages tattered, the black-and-white engravings all colored, by me, with crayons . . . You know? As a boy, in order to read, I would hide in the chicken coop. . . ."

And we are told, "For many years Cavedagna has followed books as they are made, bit by bit, he sees books be born and die every day, and yet the true books for him remain others, those of the time when for him they were like messages from other worlds. . . . The true authors remain those who for him were only a name on a jacket, a word that was part of the title, authors who had the same reality as their characters, as the places mentioned in the books, who existed and didn't exist at the same time, like those characters and those countries." Such an evocation of the lost paradise of childhood reading carries effortlessly the moral of Calvino's man-

nered outpouring: a plea for innocent reading, a "dream of redis-
covering a condition of natural reading, innocent primitive," a
readership distinct from that of "those who use books to produce
other books." It is a double paradox that such a plea for freedom
from self-consciousness should be raised by a fictionist so intri-
cately self-conscious, and that his book is apt to be chiefly read and
enjoyed by just those (among whom the present reader must count
himself) "who use books to produce other books."

If Calvino's book is something of a butterfly, at least it does fly,
flicking itself this way and that; whereas Günter Grass's new offer-
ing, slight as it is, sits there like a lead paperweight. *The Meeting
at Telgte* was written as homage to Grass's fellow-writer Hans
Werner Richter on the occasion of his seventieth birthday. In 1947,
Richter founded a loose association of authors, critics, and publish-
ers which came to be called Group 47, and which for twenty years
had a considerable role in shaping and strengthening the literature
of West Germany. Grass himself first attended one of its sessions
in 1955, and in 1958 was awarded the group's prize, for *The Tin
Drum*. Now, in a prolonged demonstration of affection and histori-
cal awareness, he has imagined and bodied forth in suitably baroque
language an entirely fictional parallel to Group 47, a group of
authors and publishers meeting in 1647, as the holocaust of the
Thirty Years' War was at last winding down. But the tour de force
never develops a point beyond its affectionate occasion; it functions
partly but in each part lamely as fiction, reconstruction, dialogue,
farce, and tract.

The trouble is not so much that the average American reader is
quite unacquainted with the likes of the poet Simon Dach (1605–
59), the satirist Johann Michael Moscherosch (1601–69), and the
translator and publisher Georg Greflinger (c. 1620–67); the British
scholar Leonard Forster has provided an excellent brief sketch of
the historio-literary background and a thorough biographical glos-
sary, and one of the many genial miracles of reading that Calvino
touches upon is how quickly and willingly a reader can *become*
acquainted. I for one would as happily settle into a literary gather-
ing in war-torn Westphalia three centuries ago as into a whaling

expedition or a Napoleonic campaign. But Grass, in his mind addressing Richter (who presumably needs no introduction to the classic figures of seventeenth-century German literature) and intending some metaphor of post–Second World War German revival and flawed coalescence, indifferently helps us to become acquainted. *The Meeting at Telgte* is less a novella than an extended pleasantry. It has few actualizing paragraphs like these from his last novel, *The Flounder*, portraying two major poets of the period, Martin Opitz (1597–1639) and Andreas Gryphius (1616–64):

> Opitz and Gryphius talked until the sky darkened. Outside the windows the Baltic Indian summer lingered on. Occasional ringing of vespers bells. The kitchenmaid came and went, barefooted on green-and-yellow-glazed tiles. Both spoke with a slight Silesian accent that cannot be put into writing. And sometimes they spoke like printed matter. That can be quoted.
>
> Gryphius had a round, boyish face that could suddenly darken and sink as though devoured from within, and then the voice that spoke from it was that of an angry archangel. His prophet's mouth. His horror-stricken eyes. Despite his rosy look, the young poet was of an atrabilious nature. As for the older man, who sat stiffly in the Spanish-Flemish fashion, his gaze was curtained by his eyelids, and whenever he spoke, more to himself than to his guest, he peered into every corner of the room like a beaten dog, or seemed at all events to be looking for a way out. Evidently Opitz was sensitive to noise. Outside the house barrels were being fitted with iron hoops.

The Flounder was heavy going, but it catered to the reader with solid fare, where *The Meeting at Telgte* serves up a thin mess of names. By the time we have learned to differentiate among the two dozen or so participants in the meeting, the last debate has been held, and the inn that has housed them has burned down, consuming in its ruin the joint declaration the literary men labored to promulgate. Their primary purpose in gathering—and thus it is ever with literary conferences—has been to gossip, to drink, and (the maids of the inn proving amiable) to fornicate.

Grass supplies a few droll touches, and attempts to make a bawdy hero out of the major novelist of the period, Johann Jakob Christoffel von Grimmelshausen (1621–76), author of *Simplicissimus*. He figures here as a soldier, who rustles up shelter and provender for his less wordly-wise colleagues, and as a Brechtian cad, scoffer, scoundrel, and survivor. He is even, the dust jacket cozily assures us, "a transparent counterpart of Grass himself." But the portrait is a cursory one, from an author who likes a big canvas, and the little book is crabbed with its narrow Germanness. The word "fatherland" leaps out with a more than rhetorical heat: "The empire was so threatened by dismemberment that no one could recognize in it what had once been his German fatherland." The book's excuse for being emerges in the assertion "The poets alone . . . still knew what deserved the name of German. With many 'ardent sighs and tears' they had knitted the German language as the last bond; they were the other, the true Germany." Casting little light upon either the Thirty Years' War or German literature (indeed, blithely falsifying facts to maintain its conceit of a meeting that never was), *The Meeting at Telgte* functions primarily as a handclasp Grass extends to his compatriot *Schriftstellern* living and dead, an embrace from which the mere reader is excluded.

Fish Story

THE FLOUNDER, by Günter Grass, translated from the German by Ralph Manheim. 547 pp. Harcourt Brace Jovanovich, 1978.

There is much to admire about *The Flounder*. It is ambitious and ingenious. It proposes mighty themes—the history of nutrition, the role of women in man-made history. It begins amusingly, and ends movingly. With great aplomb, erudition, and energy, the author ranges from scholarly research to uninhibited confession, from farce to protest, keeping generally but not exclusively to the vicinity of his native Danzig. His two frame devices—the German folktale of the Fisherman and his Wife, and the nine months of Ilsebill's pregnancy—are charming, and his arcana of cookery ancient and modern always fascinate. Any kitchen slave who wants to prepare beef heart stuffed with prunes in beer sauce, or jellied calf's head with diced tongue and sweetbread, or toads' eggs fried in the fat of stillborn baby boys, or soup made from beef bones, a blacksmith's nail, and a calf's tether, with an egg stirred into it for strength, should own this book. But literature cannot be only recipes, and even the most iron-stomached reader must sometimes feel, as he proceeds through this nine-course, five-hundred-fifty-page feast, stuffed. Grass has not bitten off more than he can chew, for he chews it enthusiastically before our eyes. But, as he chews, our own empathetic relish dulls; my consumption, at least, of large portions of *The Flounder* was spurred on by no other hunger than the puritanical craving to leave a clean plate.

The novel has, instead of a plot, a program, or, rather, a welter of programs. The narrator, the "I," is not only Grass in his own opinions and personal incidents but also the Fisherman of the tale and, as Ilsebill's husband, her male opposite—husband or lover or tormentor—in her successive incarnations as an eternal cook or woman down through the ages. Grass tells us there are "nine or eleven" cooks inside him that want to come out: Awa, the three-breasted goddess of the Stone Age; Wigga, an Iron Age matriarch; Mestwina, who resisted Christian conversion by killing Bishop Adalbert with a soup spoon in the year 997; Dorothea of Montau, a fourteenth-century ascetic who extended Lenten fasting to the entire year; Margarete Rusch, or Fat Gret, a sixteenth-century nun of unbridled appetite; Agnes Kurbiella, mistress to the pallid seventeenth-century poet Opitz; Amanda Woyke, who promoted the potato and the soup kitchen; Sophie Rotzoll, who poisoned with mushrooms some of Napoleon's garrison in Danzig; Lena Stubbe, a long-lived early Socialist; Sibylle Miehlau, a one-time sweetheart (of, it would seem, Grass's) who turned lesbian, took the name of Billy, and was raped and murdered by a motorcycle gang on Father's Day in Berlin; and Maria Kuczorra, the narrator's second cousin, whose husband was slain in the Polish workers' strike of 1970.

And the Flounder, who is he? He is the slippery, crooked-mouthed *Weltgeist* of a male-dominated world, advising men since neolithic times how to throw off the matriarchal yoke. One day in the 1970s, bored by millennia of counselling the lost male cause

("The guys are bankrupt. Abuse of power has exhausted them. They've run out of inspiration, and now they're trying to rescue capitalism by means of socialism, which is absurd"), he permits himself to be caught by three fishing members of a women's-liberation group, who, instead of accepting his generous offer of supernatural advice, put him on a trial before a Women's Tribunal in an abandoned movie house in Steglitz. The trial proceeds by discussing the eleven quasi-historical women listed above; much inconclusive evidence is tendered on the subject of food and females, while the omniscient but easily distracted author interposes details of his travels to India, his wife's surly temper, and the mood of Socialist congresses he attends, plus a large number of poems he has cooked up in a Brechtian sauce. The jacket flap calls the farraginous result "a powerful brew," and the author gives his recipe as follows: "I write compressed time, I write what is, while something else, overlapped by something else, is or seems to be next to something else, while, unnoticed, something that didn't seem to be there any more, but was hidden and for that reason ridiculously long-lasting, is now exclusively present: fear, for instance."

An earlier, and less heavily seasoned, version of Flounder à la Grass is divulged as "At first I was only going to write about my nine or eleven cooks, some kind of a history of human foodstuffs —from manna grass to millet to the potato. But then the Flounder provided a counterweight. He and his trial . . . So what can I do but write write write as usual?" This grafting of the Fisherman-and-his-Wife fable upon the history of human foodstuffs, by way of contemporary feminism and selective autobiography from the public-spirited but privately lusty author, makes a jumble that not all of Grass's wit can leaven. The aesthetic carelessness of *From the Diary of a Snail* is here grossly extended. The writing is animated and the social concern unimpeachable, but while so many lumpy ingredients are being stirred, what Aristotle called the "action" is put to sleep in a corner of the kitchen. Rafts of nutritional lore and Pomeranian history are served up, but only two overriding questions of suspense offer to tug the reader along. Will the Flounder be pronounced guilty? Will Ilsebill's baby be born? Both conclusions are foregone.

The Flounder is an imposing example of what happens when a novelist performs every service for us but his intrinsic one of rendering events. Dates, facts, anecdotes are unreeled here in dizzying profusion, but the moments when we touch the skin of a living present, with its unanalyzable complexity and unarguable *Dasein,* are as few as the beads of amber retrieved from the Kashubian potato fields. What, in all this "write write write," tastes of the actual? Far beneath the surface of the compounded allegories, certain marital tensions between the Fisherman and his Wife have a life deeper than that which the author chooses to give them. When Ilsebill, in her fifth month of pregnancy, perversely jumps a ditch, risking injury to herself and the fetus, we believe it, rather than agree or disagree with it; the fictional imagination has for a moment taken over from the political. When, at the end, her husband runs to catch up with her, worlds of rumination about male dependence are compressed into a wordless sensation. And when, near the end, the husband/narrator, watching her undergo a Caesarean operation, notes that "I also saw how yellow, like chicken fat, Ilsebill's belly fat is. A piece of it crumbled off and I could have fried two eggs in it," his tortuously ramifying theme of food is brought to a point that hurts. Show, don't tell, our writing teachers used to urge us; Grass at his extreme of virtuosity, in his confident hold over a national audience, with his hyperactive *engagé* conscience, tells far more than he shows. In the long annals of his historical "cooks," the vivacity belongs nine-tenths to him and only one-tenth to his characters. Certain very brief passages carry into the mind with the force of involuntary significance: the saintly Dorothea's uncomplaining immurement in Marienwerder Cathedral; the poet Opitz primly remaining artistically sterile under the inspiration of the ideal mistress; Grassian rhapsodies on excrement and mushrooms. The book begins with a fine splash of cartoon anthropology ("It was toward the end of the Stone Age. A day unnumbered. We hadn't begun yet to make lines and notches. When we saw the moon lose weight or put on fat, our only thought was fear"), and, after centuries of warmed-over research, the novel approaches a boil as the present is approached, and book knowledge is replaced by rumor, memory, and personal acquaintance.

> With onions and remembered marjoram I
> would like to make a silent movie in which Grandfather,
> I mean the Sozi who fell at Tannenberg,
> curses before bending over his plate
> and cracks each one of his finger joints.

Yet contemporary events and persons cannot shake the heavy-breathing, professorial style, which overmanipulates and overstipulates. A random sentence:

> But befuddled as they were from their bottoms-upping, the Teutonia or was it Rhenania brothers were still coming closer, whereas the black angels, on their motorcycles that lacked no accessory, kept as still in their seats as if they'd been turned to stone.

Thickened to a kind of sludge by its silt of accumulated meanings, the action even when it turns violent moves sluggishly, and strikes us as primarily illustrative. There are exceptions. Visiting Calcutta laden with nutrition statistics, the narrator (who fancies himself for this episode Vasco da Gama) spurns a museum visit and asks to be taken to a slum. "The slum dwellers look at him in amazement. He is intimidated by the cheerfulness of these poverty-stricken people and their unconquerable charm." More such intimidation, by unpredictable experience itself, of the omnivorous, overpowering author would have produced a more vigorous novel. The world is ripe for a retelling of this crusty, haunting old fable. But here Ilsebill and the Fisherman vanish in the cloud of personages they theoretically contain. And the Flounder, who should have been the book's presiding explicator, a piscine Mephistopheles testifying in his Eichmannesque bulletproof glass tank, is, like an insufficiently aggressive talk-show guest, shouldered out of the way by the garrulous, information-packed host. Grass ignores the fish's excellent literary advice: "But don't forget, my son: no complications. Don't lose yourself in socialist theory. Even when writing about revisionism, always keep it simple."

The jacket flap reveals that "Five years before his fiftieth birthday, Günter Grass decided that he would write a major novel as a present for himself." *The Flounder* was finished on schedule and is everywhere proclaimed as major. Thomas Mann once wrote about another German author, who for *his* fiftieth birthday was awarded a "von" before his name. Gustave von Aschenbach's major works were, we are told, with the faintest quiver of irony, "heaped up to greatness in layer after layer, in long days of work, out of hundreds and hundreds of single inspirations; they owed their excellence, both of mass and detail, to one thing and one alone; that their creator could hold out for years under the strain of the same piece of work." The strain tells, of course: the great Aschenbach, for all his accomplishments and honors, is suddenly smitten by the beauty of a Polish boy and, paralyzed by love, dies of the plague in Venice. While one would not wish Grass such a fate, one might hope that, as he pursues his strenuous career as celebrity-author-artist-Socialist, he now and then be given pause. His last page is moving in its quizzical simplicity. The narrator and Maria, the eleventh cook, have gone to a Baltic beach. They make love, unceremoniously. She wades into the sea and calls the Flounder. He leaps into her arms and talks. "Maria laughed. I understood nothing. . . . How deserted the beach was. How far away I was sitting. Good that she was able to laugh again. About what? About whom? I sat beside the empty dinner pail. Fallen out of history. With an aftertaste of pork and cabbage." In these bleak phrases of dismissal, his themes begin, at last, to live.

The Squeeze Is On

HEADBIRTHS; *or, The Germans Are Dying Out*, by Günter Grass, translated from the German by Ralph Manheim. 136 pp. Harcourt Brace Jovanovich, 1982.

THE SAFETY NET, by Heinrich Böll, translated from the German by Leila Vennewitz. 314 pp. Knopf, 1982.

Those who urge upon American writers more social commitment and a more public role should ponder the cautionary case of Günter Grass. Here is a novelist who has gone so public he can't be bothered to write a novel; he just sends dispatches to his readers from the front lines of his engagement. His latest work, *Headbirths; or, The Germans Are Dying Out,* is so topical and political that a prefatory Publisher's Note has to explain:

> *Headbirths* was written in late 1979, shortly after Günter Grass returned from a trip to China and just before the German elections of 1980. Candidates of the two major parties contending for power were Helmut Schmidt, the Social Democrat Chancellor of the German Federal Republic, and Franz Josef Strauss, Bavarian Prime Minister and head of the opposition party, the Christian Democrats. Günter Grass's commitment was and is to the Social Democrats and their party head, Willy Brandt.

Got that? Then you are ready to take a brief ride on the roller coaster of Grass's mind as it goes clickety-clack, clickety-clack, *wheeeee!* on the ups and down of such issues as nuclear plants, the low German birthrate, the early middle age of the protest generation, the union of the two Germanys, the importance of the German language and its writers, and capitalism and its clear inferiority to an ever so dimly apprehended "Democratic socialism." There is even a little fiction thrown in. Grass shares with the reader his efforts to imagine a movie about the Asian adventures of Harm and Dörte Peters, hypothetical schoolteachers from Itzehoe in Holstein. As they move through the itinerary mapped for them by Sisyphus Tourist Bureau and its omniscient Dr. Konrad Wenthien, they—childless, though in their thirties—also try to puzzle through whether or not to burden the world and themselves with a baby; when Harm is willing, Dörte is dubious, and when Dörte is keen, Harm turns impotent. These two give the reader (or is it the viewer?) a few winsome moments, mostly in Bali, but in general suggest nothing so much as the blank-faced figures in a demographic chart. Their very typicality illustrates one of the things wrong with Germany: "There are teachers like Harm and Dörte in every district capital. And Itzehoe with its modernization damage, its garbage-disposal problem and pedestrian zone, might just as well be called Tuttlingen and be situated on some other river." Grass proclaims his difficulties in inventing a story for these indeterminate creatures of his, and for a perishable liver sausage he has thrust into their imaginary luggage:

> But since my intention to make them finally land is still blocked by
> misgivings based on details that had no place in the first draft, the
> question arises here in the third draft: mightn't it be better to buy the
> coarse liver sausage not from some butcher in the city of Itzehoe
> . . . but at Kruse's Delicatessen on Kirchstrasse . . .

Imperfectly animated dolls, the two teachers struggle to disentan-
gle themselves from their creator's autobiography: "I admit that the
idea of the liver sausage (as the basis of a subplot) is autobiograph-
ical. . . . Because Harm and Dörte Peters are my headbirths, I put
things into their cradle that concern me—for instance, the con-
tinuation of the Brokdorf trial on Monday, November 26, 1979, in
Schleswig."

It is hard to imagine an American writer of comparable distinc-
tion publishing a book so unbuttoned in manner, so dishevelled in
content. Saul Bellow, his head as spinning with ideas as Günter
Grass's, yet dresses them up in fictional costume, as in *The Dean's
December*, or else presents them straightforwardly as journalism, as
in *To Jerusalem and Back*. These are clean headbirths; Grass gives
us pangs, placenta, and squalling infant all in a heap, plus a damp
surgical mask and bent forceps. He tells us about his trip to China,
and about the dying of the poet Nicolas Born, an old friend and
fellow-participant in unofficial East–West German writers' meet-
ings held in East Berlin for four years ending in 1977. He rehearses
political speeches for the coming Strauss-Schmidt campaign, he
pleads for hopeless causes like a "National Endowment . . . a place
where every German can look for himself and his origins and find
questions to ask," he pontificates about the Germans ("They al-
ways insist on being terrifyingly more or pathetically less than they
are"), he imagines himself as ten years older than he is and turning
his youthful pen to pro-Nazi rhapsodies, he proposes that East and
West Germany swap systems every ten years ("The Democratic
Republic would have an opportunity to relax under capitalism,
while the Federal Republic could drain off cholesterol under com-
munism"), he writes cascades of little editorials already dated by
their sneers at Carter ("a bigoted preacher in Washington") and

their focus on Iran. He spouts off, in short. Like a psychiatrist patiently auditing a stream of free association, the reader listens for the telltale note, the clue to the monologuist's real concerns. Grass seems happy in his sex life with his occasionally mentioned Ute— at least, he voices no complaints. He talks a great deal about writers: Chinese writers, dead German writers, live German writers, writers as heroic Sisyphean figures "piling words on words." Nothing abnormal in this, just healthy egoism. But . . . what's that? Turks?

> We Germans want to go on being surveyable, countable, not some numberless mass. After all, we're not Indians, fellahin, Chinese, or mestizos. We've already got Turks enough!

Headbirths appears to be really about Turks. The Chinese that Grass visits and admires, the Indians and Balinese that disquiet Harm and Dörte, the millions and millions of them, are just Turks of a different color. The Turkish Turks are already in Germany; the Eighties will bring the others in. "In the course of the Eighties," Harm Peters orates to a frightened crowd of cement workers in Lägerdorf, "Asia will discharge its demographic pressure and flood the European continent. I see them by the thousands, by the hundreds of thousands, silently trickling in, and here, yes, here in Itzehoe, in our very midst." In Grass's cinematic vision, the beer halls and women's clubs fill with "Indians, Malays, Pakistanis, and Chinese, with Asia's overflow, until Harm and Dörte find themselves applauded by predominantly foreign audiences, while what's left of the native Germans, intimidated, lose themselves in the enthusiastic mass." A mere eighty million industrious, frugal, politically earnest, unprolific Germans cannot possibly survive in such a human sea: "Europe is dissolving into Asia." That is the anxiety, symbolized by the Turks invited into the German "miracle" for their cheap labor and now looming as an unbanishable presence. Grass's last paragraph attempts with a feeble smile to ease the dread: Dörte and Harm nearly hit a small Turkish boy with their Volkswagen, but avoid calamity. The child, "lucky again," laughs. "Other Turkish boys are waiting for him, and together they celebrate his survival. Now from side streets and backyards, from all directions, come more and more children, all foreign. Indian,

Chinese, African children, all cheerful. They fill the street with life, wave from windows, jump from walls, innumerable." This is the sort of polychrome poster Americans are raised on. *Headbirths; or, The Germans Are Dying Out*, beneath all its merry guff, holds an authentic pang as Germany surrenders its barbaric old notion of racial purity and sizes up its modest place in a mongrel world.

Heinrich Böll's new novel, *The Safety Net*, deals with Turks of a different kind: terrorists. Or, rather, it shows the effects of terrorism upon the protected members of "the system" and the police who are protecting them. The figure at the center of the safety net, which confines as well as protects, is Fritz Tolm, a prosperous newspaper publisher and the newly elected head of "the Association," a fictitious organization of corporation heads. Though the novelist has done some work trying to imagine capitalism at its top levels, the Association feels persistently mythical—more like a circle of literary bigwigs—and Fritz Tolm, with his wry skill at interviews and his ironic reflections upon his own success and his interest "in Madonnas and architecture, in trees and birds" and his writing about art for his own newspaper, resembles an eminent author restive under the constraints of eminence. Böll dedicates the book to his three sons "in gratitude," and Fritz Tolm has a large and complicated family: a wife, Käthe, a nurseryman's daughter from his home town of Iffenhoven; a daughter, Sabine, who is the wife of a playboy clothes manufacturer, Erwin Fischer, and the mother of a daughter, Kit, and the mistress of one of the policemen guarding her, Hubert Hendler; a son, Herbert, never onstage but notoriously involved in a disreputable leftist crowd; another son, Rolf, once radical activist enough to burn an automobile in a demonstration and to be jailed, now a dropout wood-gleaner living with a mistress, Katharina Schröter, by whom he has had a son, Holger, called Holger II to avoid confusion with Holger I, the son Rolf had with his former wife, Veronica, who now lives underground with the arch-terrorist Heinrich Beverloh, a former pet employee of Fritz Tolm's who got disenchanted with the system while visiting New York City, of all friendly places.

The Safety Net is prefaced by a three-page List of Characters, and the reader does need it, as the Heinrichs and Herberts and Huberts and Hendlers and Holzpukes chase one another across the pages and Heinrich Böll repeatedly indulges his favorite Faulknerian trick of beginning a chapter in the middle of a stream of consciousness. The novel contains not only a plethora of characters but an ambitious and unsettling multiplicity of points of view. Though full of sharp details and shrewd empathy, not to mention a noble and lofty sympathy for the human plight in general, *The Safety Net* moves its burden of circumstance minimally, and then by strange twitches of hearsay. Most novels give the impression of a tour too guided—the reader too purposefully led through a series of Potemkin villages and significant encounters on the narrow trail the plot has laid out. The reader of *The Safety Net*, on the other hand, is repeatedly and prolongedly situated in spots where the action is *not* occurring, though rumors of it can be faintly heard, and glimpses had as if from behind a broad post in the grandstand. There is something wrong with time and space in this book; though ostensibly about the highest realms of power, it mostly takes place in small towns, in manor houses and vicarages, and developments that feel leisurely turn out to consume less than a day —one person (Veronica) seems to be instantly transported from a hideout in Istanbul (more Turks!) to the German-Dutch border, riding an explosive-laden bicycle. How did she get there? What is going on?

Böll's realism, like that of Balthus, is stately, eerie, and surreal. The developments are set forth with a quiet and measured authority but have, as one character reflects, something "downright fantastic" about them. In this novel, several galaxies of concern seem to be in slow collision. Böll is better on sex and religion than on power and politics. The affair between Sabine Fischer and her bodyguard Hubert Hendler is given an old-fashioned resonance by their both being serious Catholics. The possibility of guilt established, the novelist is able to do some lovely psychologizing— which raises the question, Can you have a psychological novel without religious consciousness? or, to put it another way, Are human souls worth reading about if there is no sin?

Sabine, hitherto a dutiful daughter and wife, marvels at her own coolness and skill in deception and wonders "where it all came from, how one simply knew such things, that cool way of dismissing something as if nothing had happened, something that was still and always would be called adultery." She marvels, too, at "the strange fact that she felt like an adulteress not toward Fischer or Hubert but only toward Helga"—Hendler's wife. Hendler himself, who became a policeman (against his parents' wishes) out of a strict and even fanatic commitment to "safety and order for all," also suffers paradoxical revelations. "Chaos, disintegration, and he didn't want to be sucked in, yet was in the very midst of it." Through Helga's eyes we see his changed behavior at home: sexual coldness and harsh fault-finding toward her; anger toward his young son, Bernhard; and a morbid intensification of his normal cleanliness and neatness—"no longer merely pedantic but almost pathological, the way he sometimes spent almost an hour under the shower, found fault with his freshly pressed trousers, and—this was really an insult—sniffed at his socks before putting them on and, if he discovered the tiniest crease in those expensive cotton shirts, made a face as if seriously offended." Then, when Sabine becomes pregnant, his mood shifts again: "He could not explain how it was that he had become gentler toward Helga and the boy on learning that Sabine was expecting a child."

The psychological weather within this affair, so much more tenderly and reverently observed than in the case-hardened treatment of the same situation which we have come to expect in American fiction, would hold us longer than Böll permits it to; the clouds are quickly and quirkily dispersed, as they are on the terrorist level of the action as well. It is as if Böll, having been seated long in the creation of this congested, repetitive work (the characters know one another too well, and repeat in dialogue what the author has already told us), suddenly rose and gave an abrupt, abstracted blessing, like an elderly priest bored by too long and tangled a confession.

The aura of congestion, of stale air being breathed over and over, tinges as well Günter Grass's shorter and more frolicsome work, and may tell us something about today's Germany. West Germany is more densely populated than India. This surprising fact, recently come upon, haunted my reading of these two books, and illuminated some of their themes: that of reluctance to multiply in *Headbirths* and, in *The Safety Net,* the loss of privacy and freedom brought about by the pressure of terrorism and the ubiquitous countermeasures. Not only is the freedom to have a personal life being eroded but the land itself is being devoured; the Tolms' old town of Iffenhoven and old home of Eickelhof have vanished, levelled and replaced by a vast pit where brown coal is mined to feed the power stations that rim the landscape. And the Tolms' present home, Tolmshoven, also sits on brown coal, and will eventually be bulldozed away. There is a lot of devouring in the world Böll pictures: newspapers and corporations devour one another, security dossiers devour private identities, and the cultural tide of "porn and pop and dope" is devouring the Catholic Church—there are not one but two priests in this novel who betray their vows of chastity. Behind all this devouring lurks "the system," the terrorist Beverloh's hatred of which is explained (by Rolf) with an indicative Germanic twist: "It wasn't envy, not that, no more so than Saint George or Siegfried killing the dragon out of envy. Indeed, perhaps his motives might be better understood by comparison with the Nibelung saga than by any sort of envy- or hate-philosophy . . . [The dragon] was no longer encompassed by the word 'capitalism,' it was something more, something mythical." The Nibelungs, of course, were hard workers—smiths turned into miners by their leader Alberic's passion for gold. Industriousness had its homage in the oldest Teutonic myths. The sense given in *The Safety Net* is of a terrain almost mined out, of a hard-working, tightly interlocked society some of whose members fight claustrophobia with extremist visions and acts that the majority press themselves into an even tighter phalanx to combat. A number of characters escape this novel (one young man, frightened by the "murderous looks" he gets on a bus while reading a book called *Castro's Path,* resolves to "look for a country where I can sit on the bus and read whatever I like in peace"), and the reader escapes it, too, with relief but also with a fearful suspicion that its social gridlock is the shape of things to come. Our hero, the bewildered and diffident rich man Fritz Tolm, has this poignant exchange with his wife near the end:

> "You know I have always loved you. And there's something else you must know."
> "Yes, what is it?"
> "That some form of socialism must come, must prevail. . . ."

As if it had not already crushingly prevailed over hundreds of millions, and as if it did much more, at best, than make the squeeze official.

EASTERN EUROPEANS

Polish Metamorphoses

An Introduction to the Penguin Edition of
Sanitorium under the Sign of the Hourglass, *by Bruno Schulz*

BRUNO SCHULZ* was one of the great *writers,* one of the great
transmogrifiers of the world into words. In this, his second and
final book, the writing, with its ardent accumulations of metaphor
and unexpected launching of heavy objects into flight, seems even
more rarefied than in his first. The magical town and family melt,
shimmering, into the pageant of the calendar and the unfolding of
a young consciousness. Sensitivity dawns as entirely artistic: "The
fiery beauty of the world" is revealed through the translucent
emblems of a schoolmate's stamp album, and the magnificent atmo-
spheric effects of the changing seasons are conjured more than once

---

*Born in 1892 in Drogobych, a small city in Galicia, then a province of the
Austro-Hungarian Empire, after 1923 part of independent Poland. Offspring of a
line of Jewish merchants, Schulz taught himself to draw, and supported himself as
a high-school drawing master. He was reclusive and, though once engaged to a
Catholic woman, never married. He wrote privately, in Polish, and in 1934 was
induced to publish a collection of sketches entitled *The Street of Crocodiles.* The
book achieved considerable success and was followed three years later by this
volume. In 1941 Drogobych was occupied by the Germans, and in November of
1942 Schulz (in the words of the translator's preface to *Sanitorium*) "was bringing
home a loaf of bread when he was shot in the street by a Gestapo officer who had
a grudge against another Nazi, Schulz's temporary 'protector' who liked his paint-
ings. His body was buried by a Jewish friend in a cemetery which no longer exists."

in terms of deliberately staged theatrics, "a touring show, poetically deceptive, an enormous purple-skinned onion disclosing ever new panoramas under each of its skins." These panoramas disclose themselves to the author through the lens of memory, a cerebral elaboration peculiar to man and requiring the invention of language for its code. The strenuous artifice of the language reaches out to include Nature in its conspiracy:

> Who knows the length of time when night lowers the curtain on what is happening in its depth? That short interval is enough, however, to shift the scenery, to liquidate the great enterprise of the night and all its dark fantastic pomp. You wake up frightened, with the feeling of having overslept, and you see on the horizon the bright streak of dawn and the black, solidifying mass of the earth.

The pages are crowded with verbal brilliance, like Schulz's brimming, menacing, amazing skies. But something cruel lurks behind this beauty, bound up with it—the cruelty of myth. Like dreams, myths are a shorthand whose compressions occur without the friction of resistance that reality always presents to pain. In his treasured, detested loneliness Schulz brooded upon his personal past with the weight of generations; how grandly he succeeded can be felt in the dread with which we read even his most lyrical and humorous passages, the dread that something momentous approaches. Something alien may break through these dark, tense membranes of sensation. The scenery-mover, the laboring writer, might rescind, we fear, his illusion. The rules that hold us safe are somehow awry.

I. B. Singer, a pleasanter genius from the same between-the-wars Poland, said of Schulz, "He wrote sometimes like Kafka, sometimes like Proust, and at times succeeded in reaching depths that neither of them reached." The striking similarities—Marcel Proust's inflation of the past and ecstatic reaches of simile, Franz Kafka's father-obsession and metamorphic fantasies—point toward an elusive difference: the older men's relative orthodoxy within the Judeo-Christian presumptions of value, and the relative nakedness with which Schulz confronts the mystery of existence. Like Jorge Luis Borges, he is a cosmogonist without a theology. The harrowing effort of his prose (which never, unlike that of Proust or Kafka, propels us onward but instead seems constantly to ask that we stop and reread) is to construct the world anew, as if from fragments that exist after some unnamable disaster.

What might this disaster be? His father's madness, I would guess. "Madness" may be too strong a term—"retreat from reality," certainly. "In reality he was a Drogobych merchant, who had inherited a textile business and ran it until illness forced him to abandon it to the care of his wife. He then retired to ten years of enforced idleness and his own world of dreams": thus Celina Wieniewska, who has so finely translated Schulz's two volumes into English, outlines the facts of the case in her preface to *The Street of Crocodiles*. In that volume the story "Visitation" says of the father's retirement: "Knot by knot, he loosened himself from us; point by point, he gave up the ties joining him to the human community. What still remained of him—the small shroud of his body and the handful of nonsensical oddities—would finally disappear one day, as unremarked as the gray heap of rubbish swept into a corner, waiting to be taken by Adela to the rubbish dump." The many metamorphoses of Schulz's fictional father-figure, culminating in the horrifying crab form he assumes in "Father's Last Escape," the sometimes magnificent delusional systems the old man spins, and the terrible war of diminishment versus enlargement in the imagery that surrounds this figure have their basis in an actual metamorphosis that must have been, to the victim's son, more frightening than amusing, more humiliating than poetic.

In Kafka, by contrast, the father threatens by virtue of his potency and emerges as less frail than he at first seems. In both cases the father occupies the warm center of the son's imagination. The mother is felt dimly and coolly and gets small thanks for her efficiency and sanity. At least, however, Schulz's mother is not entirely absent from his re-created world; in the writings of Søren Kierkegaard—yet another bachelor son of a fascinating, if far from reassuring, father—the mother is altogether absent. From the mother, perhaps, men derive their sense of their bodies; from the father, their sense of the world. From his relationship with his father Kafka construed an enigmatic, stern, yet unimpeachable universe; Schulz presents an antic, soluble, picturesque cosmos, lavish in its inventions but feeble in its authority. In "Tailors' Dummies" (from *The Street of Crocodiles*) he has his father pronounce: "If, forgetting the respect due to the Creator, I were to attempt a criticism of creation, I would say 'Less matter, more form!' "

Sensitive to formlessness, Schulz gives even more attention than Samuel Beckett to boredom, to life's preponderant limbo, to the shoddy swatches of experience, to dead seasons, to those negative tracts of time in which we sleep or doze. His feeling for idle time is so strong that the adamant temporal medium itself appears limp and fickle to him:

> We all know that time, this undisciplined element, holds itself within bounds but precariously, thanks to unceasing cultivation, meticulous care, and a continuous regulation and correction of its excesses. Free of this vigilance, it immediately begins to do tricks, run wild, play irresponsible practical jokes, and indulge in crazy clowning. The incongruity of our private times becomes evident.

"The incongruity of our private times"—the phrase encapsulates a problematical feature of modern literature, its immurement in the personal. Abandoning kings and heroes and even those sagas of hearsay that inspired Joseph Conrad and Thomas Hardy, the writer seems condemned to live, like the narrator of "Loneliness" (in *Sanitorium under the Sign of the Hourglass*), in his old nursery. Limited, by the empirical bias of this scientific age, to incidents he has witnessed, to the existence he has lived minute by drab minute, the writer is driven to magnify, and the texture of magnification is bizarre. More purely than Proust or Kafka Schulz surrendered to the multiple distortions of obsessed reflection, giving us now a father as splendid as the glittering meteor, "sparkling with a thousand lights," and in other places a father reduced to rubbish.

Schulz's last surviving work, the small novella "The Comet" (published at the end of *The Street of Crocodiles*), shows Father himself at the microscope, examining a fluorescent homunculus that a wandering star has engendered in the quiet of the stove's pitch-dark chimney shaft, while Uncle Edward, whom Father's sorcery has transformed into an electric bell, sounds the alarm for the end of the world, which does not come. In these vivid, riddling images an ultimate of strangeness is reached, and a degree of religious saturation, entirely heterodox, unknown in literature since William Blake. Indeed, Schulz's blazing skies, showing "the spirals and whorls of light, the pale-green solids of darkness, the plasma of space, the tissue of dreams," carry us back to the pagan astronomers, their midnight wonder and their desolate inklings of a superhuman order.

Each life makes its myths, much as the boredom of days engenders weeds: the intensity of prose needed to reify this message could not have been sustained through a long career. Schulz did not publish until he was over forty and had stopped writing, several years before his murder—even in death, in a time of mass slaughter, he was singled out—at the age of fifty. His method lives. "Schulz is my god," I was told not long ago, in Yugoslavia, by the writer Danilo Kiš. One wonders if Schulz's example helped embolden the young Greek novelist Margarita Karapanou to write of childhood with such lyric ferocity; her *Kassandra and the Wolf* has the jagged, fantastic substance of "Spring," with a vicious prepubescent sexual element chillingly added. In the United States an affinity if not an influence can be seen in a writer such as Gilbert Rogin. Rogin, like Schulz, revolves the same small cast of characters, the same dissatisfied but inseparable family, in story after story, refusing to move on, to relinquish the claims to supreme importance that this material has for the author—an importance professed in the lovingly elaborate metaphors and highly intellectual aphorisms that adorn the narrative of those ordinary, rather wretched lives. Where importance is not political (like that of, say, Oedipus, Hamlet, and Kutuzov), narrative seeks, through metaphor, priorly established planes of importance; *Ulysses* makes of the principle a great mock-heroic machine.

More instinctively, writers in a world of hidden citizens work with an excited precision, pulling silver threads from the coarse texture of daily life. The hypnotized gaze upon local particulars turns objects into signs; objects with some sort of significance painted upon them are treasured, in the absence of symbols derived from an accepted exterior religion. In a recent Rogin story, "The

Hard Parts," a heavy cardboard poster of Albrecht Dürer's *Feast of the Rose Garlands* has been placed as a roof on a wire enclosure in a Manhattan garden; from the top floor of his town house the hero repeatedly contemplates this unexpectedly situated sign:

> Now, when Albert gazed out his bedroom window, what caught his eye was this weather-beaten *Rosenkranzbild*, resplendent with the roses the nearby bush never produced. . . . Sometimes, as Albert stood and sang, the dark garden seemed to him to be flooded, with just the topmost branches of the privet projecting from the water, and the blistered poster now a raft upon which a desperate swimmer might try to haul himself, only to find it wouldn't support the weight of a child.

For Schulz, the Book full of decals invades the days: "Page after page floated in the air and gently saturated the landscape with brightness." A stamp album even more powerfully offers itself as a substitute for, as a demiurgic activator of, the world:

> I opened it, and the glamour of colorful worlds, of becalmed spaces, spread before me. God walked through it, page after page, pulling behind Him a train woven from all the zones and climates. Canada, Honduras, Nicaragua, Abracadabra, Hipporabundia . . . I at last understood you, Oh God. These were the disguises for your riches.

The same eye that so greedily seizes upon the pictorial artifacts translucently afloat on the surface of creation sees symbolic intentions in natural formations like the stars, "the indifferent tribunal of stars, now set in a sky on which the shapes of the instruments floated like water signs or fragments of keys, unfinished lyres or swans, an imitatory, thoughtless starry commentary on the margin of music."

Schulz's own illustrations to his stories, though skilled, do not participate in his fluid confusion of the graphic and the actual but, like illustrations by another man, sit athwart the text, obstructing our imagining. Idiosyncratically etched on spoiled photographic plates, the drawings make a dominant impression of shyness—the oversize heads habitually averted, foreshortened from above and unsmilingly wreathed in silence. These efficiently drawn dolls, which yet dwarf the toylike cityscapes they inhabit, disclose none of the radiant depths of their creator's prose; they do suggest the preceding centuries of illustrated fable that lie behind his fabulous relaying of his personal legends.

Personal experience taken cabalistically: this formula fits much modern fiction and, complain though we will, is hard to transcend. Being ourselves is the one religious experience we all have, an experience sharable only partially, through the exertions of talk and art. Schulz's verbal art strikes us—stuns us, even—with its overload of beauty. But, he declares, his art seeks to serve truth, to fill in the gaps that official history leaves. "Where is truth to shelter, where is it to find asylum if not in a place where nobody is looking for it . . . ?" Schulz himself was a hidden man, in an obscure Galician town, born to testify to the paradoxical richness, amid poverty of circumstance, of our inner lives.

Czarist Shadows, Soviet Lilacs

PETERSBURG, by Andrei Bely, translated from the Russian by Robert A. Maguire and John E. Malmstad. 356 pp. Indiana University Press, 1978.

THE LONG GOODBYE, by Yury Trifonov, translated from the Russian by Helen P. Burlingame and Ellendea Proffer. Also 356 pp. Harper & Row, 1978.

Vladimir Nabokov, once volunteering on television to list in order the "greatest masterpieces of twentieth-century prose," placed Andrei Bely's novel *Petersburg* third, behind Joyce's *Ulysses* and Kafka's "Metamorphosis" but ahead of "the first half of Proust's fairy tale *In Search of Lost Time.*" What was this dark horse, *Petersburg,* that nosed Proust out of the money? It was the second novel of Boris Nikolaevich Bugaev (1880–1934), the son of a distinguished mathematician and a high-strung society beauty thirty years younger than her husband. Bugaev, under his pen name, which means "Andrew White," became a leading poet, theoretician, and personality of the Russian Symbolist movement (c. 1895–1910), a literary configuration distinguished from its

French counterpart by a pronounced anti-materialist religiosity traceable to the teachings of Vladimir Solovyov (1853–1900), who is believed to be the prototype of Ivan Karamazov. Bely's bedevilled, much-reworked, often retitled novel was hurriedly composed in 1911–12 at the request of a journal that, to Bely's dismay, rejected it. *Petersburg*—a title urged upon the author by his fellow-Symbolist Vyacheslav Ivanov—was published serially in 1913–14 and in book form in 1916 by the avant-garde house of Sirin, and then, extensively cut, was republished in Berlin by the émigré firm of Epokha, in 1922. The Berlin edition, slightly revised and considerably censored, was reprinted in the Soviet Union in 1928, and again in 1935, the year after Bely's death. Since 1935, the only reprintings in Russian have been made abroad, although, as the official cloud on the pre-Revolutionary modernists fitfully lifts, a new Soviet critical edition has been prepared, and its publication mysteriously postponed.

In English, *Petersburg* was a mere rumor until 1959, when Grove Press published a translation by John Cournos. This version, Professors Robert A. Maguire and John E. Malmstad confidently assure us, has been superseded by their own annotated translation of Bely's masterpiece. The Cournos version, which is entitled *St. Petersburg*, is dismissed by them in their introduction as bearing "only incidental resemblance to the original." They accuse Mr. Cournos of "gross misreadings," and even jeer, in one note, at his mistaking a Hungarian mineral water for a term of endearment. They further charge him with "numerous cuts" and a total lack of annotation. Yet they themselves admit to tampering systematically with Bely's cherished punctuation, and the elucidatory value of their sixty pages of comprehensive and chatty notes at the back of the volume was, for this reader at least, offset by the constant distraction that faithful reference to them raised. Do we need to know all these geographical and architectural facts about the Russian capital lifted straight from a Baedeker of the time? Is it important to be told, of the phrase "opened the door," that "this is one of the rare instances in the novel when a door is simply opened. As in Dostoevski, they usually fly or swing open (or shut) with some violence"? Every novel, after all, invites us into a world that is, at first, strange; our gradual and selective orientation to its furniture and manners imitates the infant's happy accommodations to his dawning environment. Generations of readers have made themselves at home in unannotated Russian novels, with their versts and patronymics, their vast spaces and feudal cleavages, their exotic medley of the primitive and the subtle. The maligned Cournos version, whatever its passing slips and lapses (and it *does*, by the way, carry some annotation, in the discreet form of five footnotes), offers itself to the reader as a novel, not as a document framed in solicitous scholarship. Its style, too, is relatively trusting, and, in the elemental matter of readability, not always inferior. The very first paragraph, for instance, is scarcely improved by a fussy addition of words:

> Apollon Apollonovich Ableukhov came of very good stock: Adam was his ancestor. A later and more important ancestor of his in the same honored line was Shem, the forefather of the Semitic, Hessitic, and red-skinned races. [Cournos]

> Apollon Apollonovich Ableukhov was of venerable stock: he had Adam as his ancestor. But that is not the main thing: it is more important that one member of this venerable stock was Shem, progenitor of the Semitic, Hessitic, and red-skinned peoples.
> [Maguire and Malmstad].

However, the foremost obstacles to a pleasurable reading of *Petersburg* were erected by Bely himself: the novel is complex, tricky, willful, spasmodic, full of abstruse pseudo-religion and obscure personal passions, ornate in design but oddly flat in feeling—a novel whose linguistic shimmer of parody and poetry would perhaps be left by any English translation in that same limbo from which not all of Nabokov's furious labors could rescue Pushkin and where centuries of effort have still left Goethe's poetry. Even sympathetic readers of the time and place had difficulties with *Petersburg;* P. B. Struve, the general editor of *Russian Thought*—the journal that had solicited this contribution from Bely, and that employed as literary editor Symbolism's leading promoter, Valery Bryusov—rejected the book for its "malice and skepticism," calling it "pretentiously and carelessly" written, "immature," and replete with "nonsense." The very violence of Bely's later revisions, which have marred the final text with some inconsistencies and disjointedness, hints at an unsettled inspiration qualitatively different from the patient perfectionism and accumulating richness that Joyce and Proust brought to their masterworks. Bely later maintained that the edition of 1916 was "a rough draft, which fate (the pressure of meeting a deadline) did not allow to be worked up into fair copy"; an intended concision had been turned into "a hazy ornateness."

A certain haze, however, is intrinsic to *Petersburg,* for its essence is insubstantiality, and its moral appears to be that all men, and the world wherein they pass their mortal lives, are shadows. Though the editors have supplied us with endpaper maps of the city and a multitude of details concerning its streets, canals, structures, and neighborhoods, Petersburg as Bely re-creates it is a loose chain of ghostly vistas wherein all dissolves, unwinds, shifts, and explodes. The center of the action, the Ableukhovs' house, has three different locations; the government institution that the elder Ableukhov heads "cannot," the translators tell us, "be even approximately situated." Built on a bog, Petersburg dissolves back into a bog. Its skies alone seem solid, as Bely brilliantly describes one state of weather after another. The streets of Joyce's Dublin, though they overlie myth and support fantasy, are a meticulously mappable referent, prolific of the scrapes and stenches of urban reality. Bely's contemporaneous Petersburg, while it contains eddies of concreteness, remains a flux, a swarm of shadows, "a fountain of things." "Everything that had happened along with everything that was coming was merely spectral transciences [*sic*] of ordeals to be endured until the last trumpet sounded." Such a determined, doctrinal insubstantiality is, if not a defect, a virtue that takes some getting used to.

In outline, the novel would seem distinct. Time: September 30 to October 9, 1905. Place: Capital of the czarist empire, hive of bureaucracy and intrigue. Sights of Local Interest: Nevsky Prospect, Admiralty spire, Fortress of Sts. Peter and Paul, "Bronze Horseman" representing Peter the Great and subject of a celebrated poem by Pushkin. Historical Background: Humiliating defeat of czarist forces in Russo-Japanese War of 1904–5 and, throughout 1905, student and worker unrest culminating in general strike of October. Principal Characters: Apollon Apollonovich Ableukhov, father, and Nikolai Appolonovich Ableukhov, son. Basic Plot: The son, a philosophically confused and romantically distressed young man peripherally involved in radical circles, has been instructed to assassinate his father, a senator, an aristocrat, and a reactionary modelled in some particulars upon the notorious K. P. Pobedonostsev, who, like the elder Ableukhov, was a small man with big ears. Means: A bomb in a sardine can. Point of Suspense: Does he do it? Subsidiary Characters: Anna Petrovna Ableukhova, mother of Nikolai and estranged wife of Apollon, who returns from a long amour in Spain in the course of the novel, but to so little consequence that even the author forgets that she is back; Alexander Ivanovich Dudkin, insomniac, radical student, whose immense but amorphous discomfort, like the discomfort of Nikolai, reflects Bely's own discomfort in 1905, when he was anguished by a vacillating love affair with the wife of the greatest of Symbolist poets, Alexander Blok; Lippanchenko, repulsive terrorist and double agent based upon the infamous Evno Azef (you've heard of him, no doubt); Sofia Petrovna Likhutina, coterie hostess in love (or is she?) with Nikolai; Second Lieutenant Sergei Sergeevich Likhutin, her husband, a man of patience, duty, rage, and bungled suicide; others— friends, servants, policemen, passersby, "not quite people, not quite shadows." Subplot: Adulterous passions, connubial fury, hatred and fear among conspirators, loathing and love between father and son.

All the situations are handled with the raffish expertness of a card dealer shuffling a deck made limber by many previous games. Gogol, Pushkin, Tolstoy, and Dostoevski are as present in these pages as the characters. The heroic tradition of Russian melodrama here fragments into slapstick, parody, and cold rays of poetry from beyond this earth. Lippanchenko's death comes with a horrible beauty:

As he fell he understood: his back had been slit open (this is how the hairless skin of a cold suckling pig with horseradish sauce is sliced). No sooner had he understood this when he felt a jet of boiling liquid beneath his navel.

And from there came a hissing. And some part of him thought that it was gases (his stomach had been ripped open). Bending his head over his heaving stomach, he sank down, fingering the flowing stickiness on his stomach and on the sheet.

This was his last conscious impression of ordinary reality. His consciousness expanded. The monstrous periphery of consciousness sucked the planets into itself, and sensed them as organs detached one from the other. The sun swam in the dilations of the heart; and the spine grew incandescent from the touch of Saturn's masses: a volcano opened up in his stomach.

The expanding consciousness and planetary imagery derive from the anthroposophy of Rudolf Steiner, to which Bely was a full-fledged convert by 1914. As with our own distinguished Steinerite, Saul Bellow, this form of religious hopefulness, which would make of man's spirit something inevitably enduring and expanding, produces a certain hyperactivity among the characters and a noticeable lessening of natural gravity. The adventures of *Humboldt's Gift* and *Petersburg* multiply beyond our ability to care about them. In Bely, at least, the effect is certainly intentional, and permits some dissolution of the foreground action to show the ominous historical forces at work in the "myriapod" of the city population:

And beneath his feet he sees the flow of the myriapod along the pavement, where deathlike is the rustling of moving feet and where green are the faces. They give no sign that somewhere momentous events are rumbling.

Bely was not a native or long a resident of Petersburg; he was a Muscovite, and in one of the polemical wars that racked Symbolism he wrote to Blok, "Too many of my attacks against St. Petersburg in general you have probably taken to be directed at you." The Petersburg permeating his novel like a dank mist feels genuinely hostile and sinister, with its crowded prospects and European architecture; hence its failure, perhaps, to make the warm and tenacious impression on our minds of Joyce's Dublin, Proust's Paris, or Bellow's Chicago. If Bellow's hyperkinetic humanity and inventiveness offer one analogy with this Russian author, Bely's passion for abstract color and design—and the casual cruelty that such a passion permits—suggest his confessed admirer, and boyhood reader, Nabokov. There is a considerable amount of Nabokovian insect imagery in *Petersburg:*

> But Apollon Apollonovich displayed sheer bullheadedness, as was always the case with his puns. He would get all fluttery, fidgety, plaguey, pestery, like flies that try to get into your eyes just before a thunderstorm on a stifling day, when a grayish blue cloud wearyingly creeps above the lindens. Flies like that are squashed.

Nabokov, who owed up to few debts, did declare, in the lengthy essay on prosody developed to accompany his translation of *Eugene Onegin,* an indebtedness to Bely's diagrammatic system of scansion. His own fiction and *Petersburg* certainly share an intent to see through the skein of phenomena into something purer and less ephemeral. Both men were scientifically knowledgeable, and Russian Symbolism has been construed as a desperate religious attempt to contain materialism, to etherealize it, while retaining in the aesthetic ether the precisions and elegant formulae of science. Bely's verbal music, as analyzed by the translators in their introduction, suggests an etymological chart: *"shar"* ("sphere") becomes, in the course of a paragraph, dilation *("rasshirénie")* of the heart *("sérdtse").* Human activity, in such a novel, becomes an excuse for verbal activity. Bely and those who share his sensibility "make light" of their characters to give themselves the juggler's freedom. Bely's electric energy crackles even through a translation that can only hint at his microscopically active language.

The resistant fact remains that our deepest satisfactions in fiction are tied to a clumsy intuition that this life, this mundane reality, is definitive, whether absolute by the tenets of materialism or by the doctrine of Creation. Among great religions, Christianity gives unique weight to this world: its form was supposedly planned and achieved in a work-week, and earthly human decisions entail eternal consequences. Western materialistic science inherits, if nothing of Christian hope, this weight of the irreversible. Now, it is the geographical peculiarity of Russia to be half European and half Oriental. Bely, his imagination inflamed by Vladimir Solovyov's visions of the Yellow Peril, both dreads imminent invasion from the East and, like many Russian intellectuals, opposes mysticism, fatalism, and circularity to the crass material ambitions and cosmic nihilism of the West. To preserve his own spirit, he would dissolve the world into shadows. Yet in a novel we weary of looking at shadows that make no claim to be more; the writer who does not take his made-up world with a certain simple solemnity risks losing the serious attention of his final shadow, the reader.

Yury Trifonov is a Soviet writer in good standing. As such, he is suspect to readers in the West. Yet the three novellas published as *The Long Goodbye* hold up the mirror to Trifonov's chosen sector of life in the Soviet Union with a persuasive clarity and melancholy. His sector is what in this country might be called the upper middle class—the professional intelligentsia. One of his heroes is a paid-by-the-line translator; the third, and longest, novella deals with the theatrical world. Though some of his details of daily life startle an American—"In the morning his mama got on the motorbike, hung a little milk can on the wheel and went to the station for milk and bread"—his preoccupying themes are familiar enough: marital disharmony, generational conflict, nostalgia for a rural past, careerism. The advancement of careers, indeed, and the price that success demands form his dominant theme; his moral concern reminds us of the gray-flannel fiction of the American Fifties, with its clash of job and home, its disconsolate choice of seedy success or seedier failure. Trifonov's characteristic hero considers himself a failure, and the society around him does not disagree. This Communist society makes itself felt in the net of regulations and permits and vouchers that restrain mobility, in the "tightening sensation in the pit of [the] stomach" and "unbearable nervous anxiety" occasioned by an inexplicable summons from the police, in the unanswerable power wielded by those close to the sources of government decision. But the lives lived within these bounds seem as individualistic and entrepreneurial as yours and mine, with only an occasional touchstone—a "hunchbacked old lady with a myopic ancient face, who his mother said had been a desperate revolutionary, a terrorist, and had thrown a bomb at someone," or a research project into the People's Will movement of 1879—to remind the characters of the Revolutionary deeds and ideals under whose auspices they prosper, or fail to. Trifonov's heroes and heroines regather courage not from any proclaimed official hope but from brute human resilience; a murderous attack is made upon a man in Siberia, after which he gets up and walks off, to the amazement of a witness: "How easy it is to kill a man, he thought. And how impossibly difficult." Also—and in this they suggest the badgered characters of John Cheever—they possess a human willingness to be pleasantly distracted; they possess "that mysterious something which was necessary for happiness." These people oscillate in the middle, losing and recovering their humanity amid the shuffle of enterprise and vagaries of the heart. They are the solid stuff of bourgeois fiction, with the merest trace of a Socialist accent to spice their welcome into our living rooms.

Trifonov's three stories have taken some time to reach us, through the channels opened up by the Helsinki Accords. The earliest-written, the stiffest, and, I feel, the most stiffly translated is *The Exchange* (1969). It hinges upon the perennial Soviet housing shortage; to obtain a better apartment Lena and Dmitriev resolve to share living quarters with his mother, because they know she is dying and will soon free a room in the larger quarters to which their extended family will be entitled. Lena has never liked her high-brow mother-in-law; their tensions are worked out in terms of subtle social differences between the intellectual aristocrat and the aggressive arriviste. What stands out in liveliest detail is the husband's complex view of his ruthless wife:

> Lena had always been distinguished by a certain spiritual—no, not deafness, that would be too strong—by a certain spiritual imprecision, and this characteristic was further intensified whenever another even stronger quality of Lena's came into action: the ability to get her own way.

Yet their lovemaking is lovingly described, and their marriage and the betrayals it has brought are seen as part of a universal displacement: "It's not just people who disappear in this world, it turns out, but whole nests, tribes with their environment, conversation, games and music." The dacha in which Dmitriev had lived, and to which he had long ago brought his then young wife, is torn down to make way for the Stormy Petrel Stadium.

Taking Stock, the second story, and my favorite, consists mostly of flashbacks. Gennady, a hack translator with hypertension and a heart condition, remembers in the desert heat of Soviet Turkmenistan the wife, Rita, and son, Kirill, he left behind in Moscow. Such self-exile is a not uncommon Soviet technique, evidently, for dealing with disaffection of all sorts. A number of interesting sidelights are thrown upon the Communist bourgeoisie. They not only have affairs, they have home movies. Their sons, if Gennady's is any index, grow up as ungrateful, antisocial, sardonic, and thievish as any Scarsdale lawyer's. Icon-collecting is, or was in 1970, a thriving middle-class fad; the trick is to get your servant's country relatives, who are still using them as religious objects, to part with them. The servant problem exists. Anxiety in behalf of one's children's education exists. Complaisant cuckoldry exists, and the twenty-year itch:

> We should not have lived together for twenty years. . . . Twenty years is no joke! In twenty years forests thin out and the soil becomes depleted. Even the best house requires repairs. Turbines stop functioning. . . . Never mind the fact that new states have arisen in Africa. Twenty years! A time span which can destroy all hopes.

Gennady, while slowly taking stock of the depleted Moscow life to which he must some day return, makes a few emotional forays out into his immediate environment of Turkmenistan. Here violence and Islam float in the heat, a dwarf does battle with a hunchback, a gardener boasts of eleven children. Russia has her Wild East, where a man can test himself and shed his confusions. A lovely young inhabitant of the region, Valya, gives Gennady the message he has been waiting to hear: "After all, you can't run away from people." Then, in Valya's arms, he remembers a moment of intense ambivalence, of suffocating ecstasy: he and Rita, when

younger, had gone swimming in a deserted stretch of river and a
rainstorm had materialized:

> "Holding hands and laughing hysterically, we began pushing ourselves
> up from the sandy bottom and jumping out of the warm water into the
> lashing sheets of rain. . . . We soon felt cold and decided to stay put in
> the water. The water was still warm, but the air seemed to disappear
> and there was nothing to breathe. The water was choking us. It was that
> same staircase on which I always felt myself suffocating. For some
> reason I had to keep climbing higher and higher—just one more step,
> just a little more effort—but there was simply no air."

This claustrophobic image yields to a pleasant anticlimax: Gennady
returns to his family, and on vacation his heart and lungs grow
healthy enough to let him play a little tennis.

The ease, the fairness with which Trifonov handles his material
verge, in the third, and most ambitious, novella, *The Long Goodbye*,
upon a cavalier formlessness. While in *The Exchange* he separated the
ruthless actors from the rueful watchers, his rich sense of human
relativity now turns a seeming hero, the playwright Smolyanov,
into a pathetic villain, and a seemingly pathetic dreamer, Rebrov,
into a triumphant seducer and success. "Actually, every man . . . lives
not one but several lives. He dies and is born anew; he is present at
his own funeral . . ." The plot traces the fluctuating lives of a half-
dozen men connected with a touring Moscow theatre company. But
at the center of the story is a woman, the actress Lyalya, a lover of
weak men, a drifter in the pod of her own serene strength, her capac-
ity for happiness. She is the fullest of Trifonov's attractive feisty
women, who seem to grow up innocent of their American sisters'
need to cringe and then complain. Lyalya sees men without bitter-
ness, from a curious height of pity. "He stroked her slowly and
firmly, ever more firmly, and the longer this lasted and the more she
felt his strength, the more for some strange reason she felt sorry for
him." Her feelings are often paradoxical:

> A car was waiting for her. And for some reason it was right here outside
> the hospital, in a moment of fatigue and grief for her father, that Lyalya
> suddenly experienced for the first time the comforting and unaccus-
> tomed sensation of being a wealthy woman.

Trifonov has inherited from the Russian masters of the nineteenth century some of their incomparably elastic, open sense of human nature, which generates behavioral surprises that yet feel inevitable. Tolstoy everywhere abounds with these magnificent, effortless paradoxes—Anna Karenina calling out in fever not for her lover but for her scorned husband; or the fighting spirit of Russia embodied in the old, half-blind, indolent General Kutuzov. Bely exploits this paradoxicality to the point of the grotesque; but there is no doubt that it represents a truth, and one conspicuously embodied in the Russian version of human nature. "I'm a king— I'm a slave, I'm a worm, I am God!" a character in *The Long Goodbye* quotes from an eighteenth-century poem by Derzhavin. Another cites Dostoevski's idea, expressed in *The Possessed,* that "to be happy, a man needs equal portions of good fortune and bad." The national tolerance for adversity, admiration of extremes, and reverence before the mysteries of passion have survived sixty years of Soviet tyranny, as they survived centuries of feudal oppression. Indeed, under the iron skies of their governments the Russians have nowhere to look for amusement and mercy but toward one another. An impression that Trifonov's claustral world leaves us with is, paradoxically, one of independence, of the human spirit measuring its spaces with a noble disdain of the constraints, the humiliations, the corruption that societal pressures enforce. To these resilient stoics only the irreversible work of time appears impressive: *The Long Goodbye* begins with lilac bushes that once flourished in a suburb—"However much passersby might grab hold of them, pinch them, pull them or break them, the branches still managed to preserve their full, rounded contours"—and ends with Lyalya thinking, of the crowded present, that everyone's children must suddenly have grown up.

Yury Trifonov writes well, though plainly. His gaze is level, and rarely lifts into metaphor or generalization. His people seem free to act, and, sometimes rather abruptly, to wander away, off the edge of the story. He is rather too fond of long, stolid flashbacks; his meditative tone is so non-directive, so calmly defeated, that some patriotic readers and critics were alarmed when these novellas appeared in the literary review *Noviy Mir.* From his career, as outlined in Ellendea Proffer's introduction, he is a safe man, an organization man whose writings, well into middle age (he was born in 1925*), have turned to an apolitical realism that is, in the Soviet Union, exciting and, to some, subversive. One wishes that their publication here were a little less drab. The brown volume has a small-press feel to it, and holds a regrettable number of typos; e.g., "dsitraught," "istructed," "anther" for "another," "an atmosphere of simply humanity," and—a gem of ambivalence—"Lyalya's untimate demonstration of kindness and pity." Well, perhaps in fiction the intimate *is* the ultimate.

Czech Angels

THE BOOK OF LAUGHTER AND FORGETTING, by Milan Kundera, translated from the Czech by Michael Henry Heim. 228 pp. Knopf, 1980.

This book, as it bluntly calls itself, is brilliant and original, written with a purity and wit that invite us directly in; it is also strange, with a strangeness that locks us out. The strangeness of, say, Donald Barthelme or Barry Hannah derives from developments in a culture that, even if we do not live in Manhattan or come from Mississippi, is American and therefore instinctively recognizable. These authors ring willful changes and inversions upon forms with which we, too, have become bored, and the lines they startle us with turn out to be hitherto undiscerned lines in our own face. But the mirror does not so readily give back validation with this playful book, more than a collection of seven stories yet certainly no novel, by an expatriate Czech fascinated by sex and prone to sudden, if graceful, skips into autobiography, abstract rumination, and recent Czech history.

Milan Kundera, he tells us, was as a young man among that society of Czechs—"the more dynamic, the more intelligent, the better half"—who cheered the accession of the Communists to power in February 1948. He was then among the tens of thousands

---

*And has died, since the writing of this review, in 1981.

rapidly disillusioned by the rude oppressions of the new regime: "And suddenly those young, intelligent radicals had the strange feeling of having sent something into the world, a deed of their own making, which had taken on a life of its own, lost all resemblance to the original idea, and totally ignored the originators of the idea. So those young, intelligent radicals started shouting to their deed, calling it back, scolding it, chasing it, hunting it down." Kundera, the son of a famous pianist, worked—the book jacket tells us—as a laborer and jazz musician under the Communist regime, and "ultimately chose to devote himself to literature and film. In the Sixties he was named professor at the Prague Institute for Advanced Cinematographic Studies, where his students, notably Milos Forman, were the creators of the Czech New Wave in films." When the gallant Czech attempt at "Socialism with a human face" under Alexander Dubček was crushed by the Russian invasion of August 21, 1968, Kundera was erased from his country's official cultural life. By 1975 even his underground existence within his native country had become intolerable and he emigrated to France. In 1979 the Czech government, responding to the publication in France of *Le Livre du rire et de l'oubli,* revoked his Czech citizenship.

So Kundera is an Adam driven from Eden again and again— first, from the Socialist idyll of his youthful imagining, then from the national attempt to reclaim that idyll in the brief "Prague Spring" of 1968, and then from the Russian-dominated land itself, and lastly from the bare rolls of citizenship. Such a profound and jagged fall makes the life histories of most American writers look as stolid as the progress of a tomato plant, and it is small wonder that Kundera is able to merge personal and political significances as readily as a Camus. For instance, the theme of forgetting is effortlessly ubiquitous. On the official level, erasure achieves comic effects. The comrade named Clementis who solicitously placed his own cap upon Klemént Gottwald's head on the cold day of party annunciation in 1948 was hanged four years later, and airbrushed out of all propaganda photographs, so that "All that remains of Clementis is the cap on Gottwald's head." The President whom the Russians installed after Dubček, Gustav Husak, "is known as *the president of forgetting.*"

Official forgetting is echoed by the personal struggle of the subjects of so revisable a government to recover lost letters, or to remember details that give life continuity. The expatriate native of Prague called Tamina, in the central and perhaps best of these seven disparate though linked chapters, recites to herself all the pet names by which her dead husband ever had addressed her. Less and less able to remember his face, she resorts to a desperate exercise:

> . . . she developed her own special technique of calling him to mind. Whenever she sat across from a man, she would use his head as a kind of sculptor's armature. She would concentrate all her attention on him and remodel his face inside her head, darkening the complexion, adding freckles and warts, scaling down the ears, and coloring the eyes blue. But all her efforts only went to show that her husband's image had disappeared for good.

As another holdout, Mirek, puts it, "the struggle of man against power is the struggle of memory against oblivion." He needs to recover some lost letters for quite another reason than Tamina, who wishes to revive the memory of a love; Mirek wants to destroy the letters that he, when a party enthusiast, wrote his mistress of those naïve days, Zdena. She has remained loyal to their youthful orthodoxy, even to supporting the Russian invasion of 1968. But he quite misses the point of her fidelity to the Party—that it is fidelity to him and their old love: "What seemed to be political fanaticism was only an excuse, a parable, a manifesto of fidelity, a coded plaint of unrequited love." Throughout these stories of life under Communism, motives are frequently quite mistaken, and emotions of extreme inappropriateness arise. Every life is lobotomized by the severances of tyranny.

Of course, there is comedy here. *Laughable Loves,* coming from a Communist state (published in 1969), seemed perhaps even funnier and sexier than it was, like jokes in a courtroom. But the theme of laughter, as developed by Kundera in these later stories, is elaborated to the point where it can no longer be felt as laughter. He is deft and paradoxical but too heavy-hearted to be a funny writer; nor can he bring to his heavy-heartedness that touch of traditional religious resignation which converts depression to the cosmic humor of Kafka, or Bruno Schulz, or the early Malamud, or Gogol. Kundera in comparison is a child of the Enlightenment, and what mysteries exist for him occur on the plane of the psychological and the sexual. There is more analysis of laughter—specified as "a wobbly, breathy sound in the upper reaches of the vocal register" —than laughter itself. A certain mechanical liveliness, as of French farce, attends the scenes of group sex: in "Mother," the hero's visiting elderly mother unwittingly blunders back into the living room, where her son is about to commence entertaining his wife and another scantily clad woman at once; in "The Border," a zealous orgy hostess vigilantly enforces multiple contacts upon couples threatening to find happiness in a corner by themselves.

Sex is sad for Kundera, at bottom, and laughter is cruel. His book's final image is of a group of doctrinaire, self-congratulatory nudists on the (presumably French) beach, "their naked genitals staring dully, sadly, listlessly at the yellow sand." The proclaimed personal freedoms of the West are no liberation for him. The hero of this final episode, named Jan, has earlier reflected that the Jews had gone to the gas chambers in naked groups, and that "nudity is a shroud." And while still a child, Jan had studied a picture of a naked woman and had "dreamed of a creature with a body offering ten or twenty erotic regions"; hence, "when he was still very much a virgin, he knew what it meant to be bored with the female body." The keenest moment of sexual desire, for a male, in this *Book of Laughter and Forgetting* occurs when Kundera's autobiographical hero, without the guise of another name, is closeted with a young woman who has jeopardized her own career as editor by giving him some secret assignments, now discovered. She is composed in manner but keeps going to the bathroom:

> And now suddenly the butcher knife of fear had slit her open. She was as open to me as the carcass of a heifer slit down the middle and hanging on a hook. There we were, sitting side by side on a couch in a borrowed apartment, the gurgling of the water filling the empty toilet tank in the background, and suddenly I felt a violent desire to make love to her. Or to be more exact, a violent desire to rape her. To throw myself on

her and take possession of her with all her intolerably exciting contradictions, her impeccable outfits, her rebellious insides, her reason and her fear, her pride and her misery.

Against the memory of such surges of violation and exposure, which the pressures of the Communist world make possible, the public nudity of the West of course must seem tame. As to the women of Kundera's world, sex is best when it is soulless. Undergoing the charade of triadic sex, the sensitive, jealous Marketa imagines that her husband is headless: "The minute she severed the head from his body, she felt the new and intoxicating touch of freedom. The anonymity of their bodies was sudden paradise, paradise regained." And Tamina, in the second story called "The Angels," sexually beset by a band of children, "rejoiced in her body, because for the first time in her life her body had taken pleasure in the absence of the soul, which imagining nothing and remembering nothing, had quietly left the room." In short, pleasure demands suicide of a sort. "Or to put it another way, sexuality freed from its *diabolical* ties with love had become a joy of *angelic* simplicity." The angels in Milan Kundera's complex universe of disjunction are malevolent. These children end by tormenting Tamina and goading her to the death by drowning she had, earlier, sought in vain. In the first story called "The Angels," they dance in the streets of Prague to celebrate some political murders; they dance in circles until they rise into the sky. The angels are the unfallen from the Communist faith; Kundera once danced in their circle, and remembers their bliss. Angels are the heralds of "uncontested meaning on earth"; once fallen from their circle, one never stops falling, "deeper," Kundera tells us, "away from my country and into the void of a world resounding with the terrifying laughter of the angels that covers my every word with its din."

Kundera's prose presents a surface like that of a shattered mirror, where brightly mirroring fragments lie mixed with pieces of lusterless silvering. The Communist idyll he youthfully believed in seems somehow to exist for him still, though mockingly and excludingly. He never asks himself—the most interesting political question of the century—why a plausible and necessary redistribution of wealth should, in its Communist form, demand such an exorbitant sacrifice of individual freedom. Why must the idyll turn, not merely less than idyll, but nightmare? Kundera describes the terrors and humiliations of the intellectual under totalitarianism with crystalline authority, yet for all he tells us these barbarities are rooted in the sky, in whims beyond accounting. He keeps plowing his earthly material back into the metaphors of laughter and forgetting, of angels and children. Tamina, he states, is the book's "main character and main audience, and all the others are variations on her story and come together in her life as in a mirror." Yet in her final appearance she seems allegorized into nothing, and the episode almost whimsical. As in the case of Nabokov, a private history of fracture and outrage is rendered kaleidoscopic by the twists of a haughty artistic will—without, however, Nabokov's conviction that art, the reality we extract from reality, is sufficiently redeeming.

The position of a writer from the Socialist world in the West cannot but be uncomfortable. He cannot but despise us for our cheap freedoms, our more subtle enslavements; and we, it may be, cannot but condescend to his discovery, at such heavy personal cost, of lessons that Messrs. Churchill and Truman so roundly read to us thirty-five years ago. Survival tactics vary. Solzhenitsyn in Vermont builds a little iron curtain of his own and continues to thunder as if he were still imprisoned in Russia. Joseph Brodsky, the most aloof and metaphysical of dissidents in his Leningrad years, is becoming, amazingly, an American poet. Kundera—who moved, after all, only a few hundred kilometers west, and who unlike many expatriates had enjoyed considerable artistic success and prestige in his own country—seems, five years out, in a middling position. He is crossing that border he describes, to the side that men dread, "where the language of their tortured nation would sound as meaningless as the twittering of birds." A meaning once omnipresent is gone. A habit of vision developed in one context is being broken in another. The sexual descriptions, both tender and shrewd, that had an effect of sub-versive comment within the Czech context have a somewhat jaded, hollow ring out of it. In *The Book of Laughter and Forget-ting*, a work of social realism and protest coexists with a brittle-ness, an angelic mockery that, amid much melancholy remem-brance and shrewd psychology, makes *us*, the respectful Western readers, uncomfortable.

LEM AND PYM, STEAD AND JONES

Lem and Pym

THE CHAIN OF CHANCE, by Stanislaw Lem, translated from the Polish by Louis Iribarne. 179 pp. Harcourt Brace Jovanovich, 1978.

EXCELLENT WOMEN, by Barbara Pym. 256 pp. E. P. Dutton, 1978.

QUARTET IN AUTUMN, by Barbara Pym. 218 pp. E. P. Dutton, 1978.

Stanislaw Lem, the Polish writer internationally admired for his philosophical science fiction, has written a thriller, *The Chain of Chance*. It is narrated, in traditional pitiless side-of-the-mouth style, by the protagonist/detective, an American ex-astronaut named, we belatedly learn, John—no last name is given, though some French-Canadian ancestry is assigned. The book begins in a burst of mysteries. Our hero is driving from Naples to Rome in the guise of a man called Adams, attempting to duplicate this other man's exact route, speed, stops, and final arrival at Room 303 of the Hilton. Why? For that matter, when? The time seems to be the dangerously near future. There has been a manned "Mars mission," a "feminist underground" is wreaking doctrinaire havoc, and the Rome airport has been rigged with an elaborate futuristic security system called the Labyrinth. Our hero's age is given as fifty in one spot and as fifty-five in another; since he participated as a young commando in the Normandy landings of 1944, this novel apparently takes place in the late 1970s.

The Chain of Chance was written in 1975, as an Eastern European's speculation upon some possible short-term extensions of such Western topical developments as terrorism, space exploration, and chemical pollution. Occasionally, we are reminded of the author's Polishness: he says *"Herald"* when he must mean the *Herald Tribune,* and no Western writer would need to spell out for his readers that the Olympia Press specializes in "erotic and pornographic literature." But by and large Lem appears comfortably at home within capitalist decadence. Making his hardboiled investigator a cast-off astronaut is witty, for the book breathes the poisoned atmosphere of technological backfire, and the latest by-product of our Puritan resolution is surely the astronaut, consecrated, like the cowboy and the private eye, to bleakly masculine missions. Also, the astronaut's training gives Lem easy access to the scientific terminology where he is at home, and a poet:

> At the bottom of the grade, drivers were having to use their brakes, transforming that particular stretch into a vibrant strip of shimmering red—a pretty example of a stationary wave.

In this same long drive, which opens the book like a hypnotic pre-credits sequence in a movie, Lem shows that fond touch with automotive experience evinced by Continental writers from Proust to Cortázar—"As I was squeezing in behind a psychedelic-painted Lancia, I glanced in the mirror. . . . For a while I stayed behind a Volkswagen with a pair of sheep's eyes painted on the back that kept staring at me in tender reproach. . . . A Ferrari as flat as a bedbug chased me out of the fast lane, and I broke out in another fit of sneezing that sounded more like swearing." The fact that our hero sneezes, and takes Plimasine, containing Ritalin, is a clue. Indeed, the book brims with clues, including the painting on the jacket, but one would have to be a biochemist to unravel them; one rides along blindly.

A thrilling ride it is, especially for those whose hearts beat faster when the *Scientific American* arrives each month. Lem has learned the formulae of fictional suspense almost too well; there is so much we don't know at the outset that by the time we do know it the book is two-thirds over. John, it may not be too much to say, is of the same age and physical type as a number of men who have behaved and died mysteriously in the vicinity of Naples; by assuming the identity of Adams, he is attempting to induce the same conspiracy of circumstances to attack him. The heart of this small novel is taken up with lengthy descriptions of the previous victims, a list that has its own statistical fascination, not to mention the rum charm of all raw information. After a rather surreal and trumped-up episode of airport violence, the astronaut meets a Parisian computer wizard, Dr. Philippe Barth, and the ambience changes from Flash Gordon to the international intellectual conference scene; the narrator, turned essayist, frowns upon "that revolutionary clowning so characteristic of intellectuals" and tells us, of the world at large, that the " 'global village' was already here, but split into two halves. The poorer half was suffering, while the wealthier half was importing that suffering via television and commiserating from a distance." This observation smacks of 1975; these days the wealthier nations are too concerned with making their own ends meet to commiserate even with Bangladesh. Lem's novel, in which little more than information-processing occurs for over ninety pages, abruptly redeems itself, as thriller and dissertation both, with a stunningly persuasive account of our hero's descent into drug-induced madness:

> How to describe it? The furniture and walls became petrified in the middle of some horrible transition; time came to a halt, leaving only the surrounding world, which suddenly stopped advancing toward me like an avalanche and became frozen in a prolonged flash of magnesium. The whole room was like a gasp between two successive screams; its intended target was manifested with undisguised malice in the intricacies of the wallpaper design . . .

Only a mind habituated to seeing the human mind from the outside, as a chemical and electrical machine, could evoke derangement with such cool clarity. Under the glare of his violent "psychotropic" reaction, John's normal emotions and metaphysics—his humanity, in short—seem pathetically fragile epiphenomena. The moral of the novel I take to be: "Mankind has multiplied to such an extent that now it's starting to be governed by atomic laws." In our "dense world of random chance," "common sense isn't worth a damn." Improbabilities are all subjective, and everything sooner or later is bound to happen, including the publication of this book: "Regardless of the publisher or author, the publication of this book was also a mathematical certainty." A cheerful conclusion, amid bleak perspectives.

For all its cruel mathematics, Lem's world, in my acquaintance with it, lacks the sense of desolation, of final dwarfing, that much science fiction, from Wells to Borges, conveys. Rather, his naturally sanguine temperament, or his love of sheer compilation (reflected here in his thoroughly worked-out portraits of the numerous middle-aged victims of *The Chain of Chance*), or the selfless enthusiasm commonly ascribed to the scientific-minded produces an Olympian playfulness. His heroes may be, as Theodore Solotaroff has said, "loners virtually to a man," but they don't seem to *feel* alone, to taste solitude. Atomic aloneness in a crowded world, where life is cheap and its accidents random, more deeply penetrates the wanly Christian world of Barbara Pym.

This English novelist has had a disheartening career; after publishing six deceptively old-fashioned novels between 1950 and 1961, she was spurned by more than twenty publishers and understandably let her pen languish. From 1946 to 1974, she supported herself as an assistant editor for the quarterly *Africa*. As retirement approached, however, she began to write again, a novel "as churchy as I wished to make it," and in January of 1977 her name appeared in the *Times Literary Supplement* as the heroine of a poll taken to determine the most underrated British writer of the last seventy-five years. Her new novel, *Quartet in Autumn,* was accepted by Macmillan, and two of her old books were reissued by Jonathan Cape, with commercial as well as critical success. Now, in this country, a novel dating from 1952, *Excellent Women,* has been published for the first time, along with *Quartet in Autumn.* An unfortunate effect of such simultaneous exposure is to reveal, of two books written over twenty years apart, how alike they are, even to striking, on the last page, the identical muted chord. More fortunately, the reader who has consumed both novels in a few days can

report that the older is very fine, and the newer even finer—
stronger, sadder, funnier, bolder.

It would be hard to imagine a more timid world than that of
Excellent Women, or a novel wherein closer to nothing happens.
Miss Pym has been compared to Jane Austen, yet there is a virile
country health in the Austen novels, and some vivid marital pros-
pects for her blooming heroines. "Excellent women" is a phrase
used by a parson of the drab little flock of spinsters who cling for
company and amusement to the threadbare routines of his London
church. An American who has never attended an Anglican church
in London can scarcely conceive of the extreme of sad attenuation
to which ecclesiastical institutions can be reduced while still hold-
ing open their doors; I can recall a noble structure on Albany Street
in which one bright Sunday morning this lone overseas visitor
composed a full third of the congregation. Father Julian Malory's
St. Mary's Church, in a shabby district on "the 'wrong' side of
Victoria Station," seems a shade more bustling than that, but only
a shade. Our heroine, Mildred Lathbury, the unmarried daughter
of a rural clergyman, comes to it because it is relatively "High" and
burns incense, which her deceased parents would have deplored.
"But perhaps it was only natural that I should want to rebel against
my upbringing, even if only in such a harmless way." All her
rebellions and outward motions are similarly circumspect, but
within the limits of her quiet life, as she firmly draws them, minor
excitements loom in scale, and excite us proportionally.

Mildred Lathbury is one of the last (I would imagine) of the great
narrating English virgins, and though she tells us she is "not at all
like Jane Eyre," her tale has some of the power of, say, the portion
of *Bleak House* narrated by Esther Summerson—the power, that is,
of virtue, with its artistic complement of perfect moral pitch and
unforcedly clear discriminations. The postwar, proto-consumerist
London that Mildred depicts, where jam seems still to be rationed
and rubble still lies in church aisles, yet where couples drink wine
and separate with a certain liberated ease, is an awkward arena for
her discriminations, perhaps. One of the funniest scenes, though
brief, occurs when she attempts to buy a new lipstick and can
scarcely bring herself to name the tint she wants: " 'It's called

Hawaiian Fire,' I mumbled, feeling rather foolish, for it had not occurred to me that I should have to say it out loud." The urban crush of modern London is, she reflects, in a phrase that echoes a T. S. Eliot echo of Dante, a hard place for the practice of Christian charity:

> "One wouldn't believe there could be so many people," I said, "and one must love them all." These are our neighbors, I thought, looking round at the clerks and students and typists and elderly eccentrics, bent over their dishes and newspapers.

The plot's turns have to do with new neighbors. A young couple, Helena and Rockingham Napier, move into the flat below Mildred's, and conduct within earshot a typical but sufficiently unsettling modern marriage. And Father Malory and his unmarried sister, Winifred, take in a border, one Mrs. Gray, with romantic consequences that titillate every corner of the tiny parish, from jumble sale to Evensong. Mildred, at the nubile age of "just over thirty," seems remarkably spinsterish. Her sexual experiences have been of the daintiest sort, and she puzzles over the "race of men" and their differences from women with the polite quizzicalness of an anthropologist from the moon.

> "I like food," I said, "but I suppose on the whole women don't make such a business of living as men do."

> Men in bowler hats, with dispatch cases so flat and neat it seemed impossible that they could contain anything at all, and neatly rolled umbrellas, ran with undignified haste and jostled against me. Some carried little bundles or parcels, offerings to their wives perhaps or a surprise for supper. I imagined them piling into the green trains, opening their evening papers, doing the crossword, not speaking to each other . . .

> "Of course, men don't tend to be alone, do they?"

It is fitting that an actual anthropologist, the humorless but upright (and Christian!) Everard Bone, adds himself to the exiguous list of Mildred Lathbury's male friends—her pastor, his curate, a few neighbors, and an old friend so set in his ways he complains,

"They've moved me to a new office and I don't like it at all. Different pigeons come to the windows." At the book's romantic climax, Everard Bone invites her to be his indexer; but Americans, with their Freudian and Lawrentian prejudices, should not hasten to bid farewell to her chastity and hello to "what Helena called 'a full life.' " Mildred has involved herself with men enough to enhance her feeling of possibility, her sense of choice, but what she chooses, out of sight of the novel's conclusion, may well be more of the same. "As I moved about the kitchen getting out china and cutlery, I thought, not for the first time, how pleasant it was to be living alone." "Excellent women" need not think of themselves as "the rejected ones." When warned not to expect too much, Mildred thinks, "I forebore to remark that women like me really expected very little—nothing, almost." *Excellent Women,* arriving on these shores in a heyday of sexual hype, is a startling reminder that solitude may be chosen, and that a lively, full novel can be constructed entirely within the precincts of that regressive virtue, feminine patience.

By the time of *Quartet in Autumn,* the lonely women are ready for retirement. There are two of them: Marcia Ivory, in whom Mildred Lathbury's self-sufficient aspect has been carried to the point of loony reclusiveness, and Letty Crowe, in whom Mildred's amiable side has developed into a clothes-conscious, food-loving softness bordering upon the hedonistic. Marcia and Letty work in a nameless office in the same room with two single men—Norman, small and wiry and irritable, and Edwin, large and bald and benevolent. Edwin is the only one of the quartet who has ever been married and who appears to be an active Christian; the churchly ambience of *Excellent Women* has shrunk to this one merry widower, who shops around from church to church for services as a species of entertainment. The shadow of religious shelter has been lifted from Miss Pym's world, and the comedy is harsher. Whereas Mildred Lathbury had merely to cope with new tenants in the flat below, Letty Crowe's entire building changes hands, and becomes the property of a Nigerian, Mr. Olatunde, who not only houses a large family but is "a priest of a religious sect." When Miss Crowe, disturbed by their "bursts of hymn-singing and joyful shouts," taps on their door and complains, Mr. Olatunde serenely tells her, "Christianity *is* disturbing."

> It was difficult to know how to answer this. Indeed Letty found it impossible so Mr. Olatunde continued, smiling, "You are a Christian lady?"
>
> Letty hesitated. Her first instinct had been to say "yes," for of course one was a Christian lady, even if one would not have put it quite like that.

In fleeing his landlordship, she becomes the tenant of the High-Church, eighty-year-old Mrs. Pope, and finds herself participating in services:

> On a bitter cold evening in March she joined a little group, hardly more than the two or three gathered together, shuffling round the Stations of the Cross. It was the third Wednesday in Lent and there had been snow, now hard and frozen on the ground. The church was icy. The knees of elderly women bent creakily at each Station, hands had to grasp the edge of a pew to pull the body up again. "From pain to pain, from woe to woe . . ." they recited, but Letty's thoughts had been on herself and how she should arrange the rest of her life.

Where Mildred Lathbury had found consolation, and fortified her own life of unconsummated waiting, by thinking of herself and her fellow-worshippers "as being rather like the early Christians, surrounded not by lions, admittedly, but by all the traffic and bustle of a weekday lunch-hour," no such comparison lends rationale to the ascetic isolation of Miss Pym's later heroines. In place of the chaste infatuations with which the excellent women had amused themselves, Marcia Ivory has no affection but for the surgeon Dr. Strong. He has performed a mastectomy upon her and looms in her addled mind ("Marcia remembered what her mother used to say, how she would never let the surgeon's knife touch her body. How ridiculous that seemed when one considered Mr. Strong") as a masterful angel of death. When Letty and Marcia simultaneously retire, the speaker at the office luncheon held in their honor does not know exactly what their jobs had been, only that there is no need to replace them, and "it seemed to Letty that what cannot now be justified has perhaps never existed, and it gave her the feeling that she and Marcia had been swept away as if they had never been. With this sensation of nothingness she entered the library."

Quartet in Autumn reminds us of Muriel Spark's *Memento Mori* and of the geriatric missionaries in Rose Macaulay's *Towers of Trebizond,* but the superannuated creations of these other "Christian lady" novelists have an energetic raffishness, a richness of past and a confidence of social class, denied Miss Pym's characters, who are clearly no match for their surround of anonymous office buildings and condescending young people. One of Miss Pym's enthusiastic English reviewers has been Philip Larkin, and perhaps it is to *his* world that the closer analogy can be drawn—the gray middle class of an empireless England, from whose half-tones nevertheless the chords of a living poetry can be struck. *Quartet in Autumn* is a marvel of fictional harmonics, a beautifully calm and rounded passage in and out of four isolated individuals as they feebly, fitfully grope toward an ideal solidarity. Marcia, the most eccentric of the four, is the most pronouncedly private, and the most abruptly forthcoming.

> "And what have you been doing with yourself?" Edwin turned to Marcia with an air of kindly enquiry which hardly deserved the fierceness of her reply.
> "That's my business," she snapped.

What she has been doing, since retirement, is rearranging the junk she stores in her house, repelling a concerned social worker, letting her dyed hair grow out stark white, and sinking deeper into anorexia.

Miss Pym's portrait, from within, of a "shopping-bag lady," showing the exact, plausible thought processes behind such mad actions as leaving trash in libraries and attempting to dig up a dead cat, is an achievement comparable to Lem's imagining of chemical-induced paranoia and frenzy. Both writers, in the books at hand, lead us to think about social contact, about society and sanity. Experiments in isolation rapidly induce sensations of insanity; we take our bearings, daily, from others. To be sane is, to a great extent, to be sociable. Those victims of random chemistry in *The Chain of Chance* who survive are those who are not travelling alone, and whose behavior receives prompt social check. In the extremely meagre social fabric Miss Pym weaves for her characters, the most tenuous and trifling contacts take on the import of massive events in more thickly woven novels—those of Tolstoy, say. One wonders, indeed, whether Tolstoy ever knew aloneness; even his dying was mob scene. Most human lives have been passed in a throng of tribal and village associations. Unsought loneliness is a by-product of the modern city, and fiction by its nature is ill-equipped to treat of it. Letty Crowe, "an unashamed reader of novels," has been brought to realize that "the position of an unmarried, unattached, ageing woman is of no interest whatever to the writer of modern fiction." In brilliantly, touchingly, frighteningly supplying that lack, and in presenting a parable of the hazards of our "atomic" condition, Barbara Pym and Stanislaw Lem offer us characters with strikingly modest sex drives. Whether in this they are old-fashioned or all too modern—whether under conditions of dense metropolitan crowding the primeval social adhesive will tactfully dry up—remains to be seen. In the meantime,

> Pym and Lem,
>   Lem and Pym—
> There's little love
>   In her or him.
> Out on a limb
>   With Pym and Lem
> One hugs oneself
>   Instead of them.

Selda, Lilia, Ursa, Great Gram, and Other Ladies in Distress

THE LITTLE HOTEL, by Christina Stead. 191 pp. Holt, Rinehart and Winston, 1975.

CORREGIDORA, by Gayl Jones. 185 pp. Random House, 1975.

Although Christina Stead is seventy-three, Australian-born, and white, and Gayl Jones is twenty-six, Kentucky-born, and black, their two recent novels—*The Little Hotel* and *Corregidora*—are similar in size (just under two hundred pages), in the look of their jackets (tame paintings with no-nonsense lettering), in a certain chosen uncoziness of tone, and in their feminism, feminism being femaleness that considers itself politically. In Miss Stead's case, the politics are Socialist, and her put-upon women are caught up in the incessant, somewhat paranoid bourgeois capitalism of a declining Europe; in Miss Jones's book, a history of American racism weighs upon her women, making of their bodies, generation to generation, a living history of the slavery that otherwise will be forgotten. Though isolated and unfulfilled in their widely separated worlds of heedless male domination, the books' heroines remain heterosexual and are not quite helpless, asserting freedom in final gestures of, in *The Little Hotel*, renunciation, and, in *Corregidora*, acceptance.

Miss Stead's book takes place in Lausanne, and has for a narrator Mme. Selda Bonnard, the proprietress of a small Swiss *pension* patronized for its moderate rates and tolerant management. Beginning in the breathless, flustered voice of a stage monologuist, Mme. Bonnard tells us of her guests, concentrating upon the Mayor of B., a Belgian official boisterously suffering from a nervous breakdown; the subtle portrait of his derangement is too real to be funny. A globe deranged seems implied in the sketches of the other guests —Mrs. Powell, an old American woman, noisily anti-Communist and a bit less blatantly racist; Mme. Blaise, a rich doctor's wife from Basel, obsessed by her hairdo and perpetually swaddled in layers of clothes; Mrs. Trollope, a petite and slightly dark Englishwoman who has spent most of her life in the East; her "cousin," Mr.

Wilkins, who lives in the adjoining room, acts as proprietor of her money, and reads in her face at every meal; Miss Abbey-Chillard, an Englishwoman who, though dying and penniless, is nevertheless consummately demanding and arrogant; and the Admiral, another decrepit Englishwoman, whose insufferable manners induce persecution from the hotel servants. These servants, Italian and Swiss peasants in the main, and the touring artistes who perform at the neighboring night club, and Mme. Bonnard's husband, Roger, the usually absentee master of the establishment, round out the hotel roll; a *Magic Mountain*–like microcosm of Europe appears intended, though on a less Alpine scale. Yet the book never quite takes hold as that; its locus in time seems vaguely scattered, as if it had been composed over a long stretch of years. Wilson's Labour Government appears to rule England, but a more immediately postwar atmosphere colors the financial manipulations and political anxieties of the characters. Rather indistinguishably aged and reactionary, they all agree that the Russians are about to invade Switzerland. Thus immersed in the Cold War, the book moves glacially, though chips of icy vividness fly when Miss Stead gives a character more than a passing glance. Of a hotel maid:

> And then, after a short cold silence, Luisa had shown a set of fascinating wiles, delightful smiles, half-words in English, soothing and loving. Luisa could be angry, acid, contemptuous. She had flying passions, transparent guile: she was fluid, clever and really affectionate.

Of Miss Abbey-Chillard:

> In the sagging bed, propped up by pillows, lay a tanned bony church-door martyr, with large bright blue eyes in deep hollows. Her lank hair trailed over the pillows; a loose nightgown with a handsome lace décolletage showed her emaciated neck, bony chest, the wide-set weakened breasts. But the neck had been a column, the chest once broad, deep and strong: there was still determination in this disorder, a high-spirited selfish temper.

A seasoned experience of life speaks in such phrases as "the unmistakeable trotting and nodding of the long-married" and "the fresh beauty of blood newly mixed." Yet for much of the book the reader feels about these glimpsable guests as Mrs. Trollope does: "I can see everything that everyone does; and it all has nothing to do with me."

This compact novel, full of anecdotes, seems to lack a story; we only slowly realize that the story has become Mrs. Trollope's. The narrator, Mme. Bonnard, begins to tell us of conversations at which she was not present, and in the end enters very intimately into the private emotions and history of this Mrs. Trollope—Lilia, a child of the Orient; her mother a Dutch-Javanese, her husband a rich philanderer, her "cousin" a lover met in Malaya and now as indifferent and mercenary as the most threadbare of husbands. She has children in England; she has money there, which Robert Wilkins keeps badgering her to bring out for him to "arrange." She expected him to marry her as soon as she and her husband divorced; she is humiliated and agonized by his silent refusal. She knows that everyone thinks of her, "This woman is a Eurasian; that is why the man won't marry her."

Though the other characters continue to pose, to flaunt their individual terrors and cruelties with increasing shamelessness, our interest remains caught up in this middle-aged, kindhearted half-caste's brave, hopeless, and salutary effort to end a liaison prolonged to the point of degradation. Our hearts cheer when, though yielding to his teasing demand for a kiss, she says, "Well, if you wish it, Robert, but it doesn't mean anything. You have lost me. I'll kiss you, but it's finished. I've been meaning to tell you. I loved you, I was loyal to you, and there never was another man for me. But you have lost me. You let me down, Robert." She has become all those partners in love for whom a long succession of slights and affronts accumulate at last, and conclusively, to the astonishment of the confident affronter. Robert believes the love he took for granted is still there, can be revived with a kiss, a pretense of relenting. But he is wrong. A change has been wrought, imperceptibly. Departed, Mrs. Trollope writes Mme. Bonnard, "I think I have made a break, and I have suffered a little, dear Selda; but Mr. Wilkins will not believe me. I have been so weak in the past, I do not blame him. As for coming back—I am not coming back." The novel's last sentence says, of the two "cousins," "I do not know if they ever saw each other again"; and this ending is sad, though we have seen the lovers happy for only a moment when, at a night club, they dance "in a pretty coupling, their faces lit up."

As she leaves the hotel, Lilia calls Selda a "sister," and the same transparent art that let one woman's narration glide into the story of another has Mrs. Trollope's unhappy affair reflect back upon the Bonnards' marriage, the unseen coupling within the book. In the first pages, the wife confesses, "I have headaches, I am worried about my husband Roger," but the complaint is not developed. Roger comes and goes, nurses his hangovers, solves the crises of the hotel, and for the rest lets his wife manage the daily details. Their economic marriage to this enterprise, and their captivity through it to each other, is caricatured in the "pretty coupling" of Dr. and Mme. Blaise; her money, descended to her from wartime dealings with the Nazis, binds them in an exacerbating and savage relationship that is the book's epitome of unpleasantness. Throughout, money or its lack is crucial, and it is the women, rich and poor, who are exploited. Mrs. Trollope's decisive, revolutionary gesture is to give money meant to buy her lover a car to the dying Miss Abbey-Chillard, for her medical expenses. Miss Stead, an outspoken left-winger, enriches her perceptions of emotional dependence with a tactile sense of money as a pervasive, disagreeable glue that holds her heroines fast, in their little hotels of circumstance.

Bondage of a different sort pervades *Corregidora,* named after a Portuguese seaman who, risen to be a Brazilian plantation owner, compels his female slaves to sleep with him and then with others, for money. The history of the "generations" descended from this white progenitor is interspersed in italics as the novel's heroine, a blues singer in a Kentucky café, tells her own history of unhappy marriage to two black men. Her name, which she keeps in marriage, is Ursa Corregidora, and her ancestors are Great Gram, "the coffee-bean woman," who was Corregidora's prize whore; Gram, fathered by the slavemonger and born into a slop jar; and Mama, also the daughter of the energetic Corregidora. After the abolition of slavery in Brazil, Great Gram fled to Louisiana, but went back to Brazil in 1906 to take away Gram, eighteen and pregnant with

Mama. Mama—the family has moved to Kentucky "to get better work"—conceives Ursa by a black man, Martin, who shares only briefly this odd household obsessed with "Corregidora, who gave orders to whores, the father of his daughter and his daughter's daughter." For as long as they live, Great Gram and Gram talk aloud of their past in slavery, impressing upon the little girl, the fourth generation, the need to make generations:

> "The important thing is making generations. They can burn the papers but they can't burn conscious, Ursa. And that what makes the evidence. And that's what makes the verdict."

This imperative—procreation as revenge and testimony—has its strangeness and ambiguity. Her mother tells Ursa:

> "I think what really made them [Gram and Great Gram] dislike Martin was because he had the nerve to ask them what I never had the nerve to ask."
> "What was that?"
> "How much was hate for Corregidora and how much was love."

Ursa's predecessors in this matriarchal line, as sacred to itself as a line of Nordic kings, "squeezed Corregidora into me, and I sung back in return." She becomes a blues singer, which offends her conventionally pious mother but pleases her grandmother. When her first husband, jealous of her art and its audience, throws her down a stairway, damaging her internally so she can never bear children, she discharges her obligation to the memory of Corregidora by speaking this book.

Corregidora persuasively fuses black history, or the mythic consciousness that must do for black history, with the emotional nuances of contemporary black life. The novel is about, in a sense, frigidity, about Ursa's inability to love.

> "Stop, Ursa, why do you go on making dreams?"
> "Till I feel satisfied that I could have loved, that I could have loved you, till I feel satisfied, alone, and satisfied that I could have loved."

Her interior monologues, where they do not concern Corregidora, are addressed to her first husband, Mutt, whose attempted domination of her, climaxed by her fateful fall down the stairs, neverthe-less quickened a response she cannot give her second, gentle hus-band, Tadpole. Throughout the span of her life that is related—in the end she is forty-seven—Ursa rejects the advances made to her by her husbands, by amorous night-club clients, by lesbian sisters. Similarly, her mother, having rejected Martin, lives alone, spurning the courtship of a friendly neighbor. The interweave of past shame and present shyness gives the dialogue depth; after Mutt, in re-sponse to Ursa's confiding of the Corregidora legend, tells her the tale of his slave great-grandfather's loss of his wife, she nods but says nothing.

> "Don't look like that, Ursa," he had said and pulled me toward him. "Whichever way you look at it, we ain't them."
> I didn't answer that, because the way I'd been brought up, it was almost as if I was.
> "We're not, Ursa."
> I had stepped back suddenly.
> "What did you step back for, woman? I wasn't going to bite you. What in the hell did you step back for?"

The book's innermost action, then, is Ursa's attempt to "get her ass together," to transcend a nightmare black consciousness and waken to her own female, maimed humanity. She does it, in the end, with a sexual act that she imagines was what "Great Gram did to Cor-regidora"—an oral act combining pain and pleasure, submission and possession, hate and love, an act that says, in love, "I could kill you." This resolution is surprising but not shocking; one of the book's merits is the ease with which it assumes the writer's right to sexual specifics, and its willingness to explore exactly how our sexual and emotional behavior is warped within the matrix of family and race.

The men in this novel do not live except in the wonderful transcriptions of "sweet talk," of seduction's musical mumble, and the women retain a certain occluding severity. The simultaneous largeness and intimacy of Miss Jones's themes scatters her narra-tive; the characters come and go as casually as guests in Miss Stead's hotel, and without the solidity of Miss Stead's aphorisms and local color. The minor-league Kentucky ghetto seems colorless and generalized; our retrospective impression of *Corregidora* is of a big territory—the Afro-American psyche—rather thinly and stabbingly populated by ideas, personae, hints. Yet that such a small book could seem so big speaks well for the generous spirit of the author, unpolemical where there has been much polemic, exploratory where rhetoric and outrage tend to block the path. The space her novel occupies, between ideology and dream, seems proper to fiction now, and to material of which sordid detail and sexual myth are linked aspects. Both these novels, indeed, build *from* their political convictions rather than *toward* them, and leave us not with slogans but with a sense of witnessed life. Hemmed in by capitalism, by racism, Lilia and Ursa find room enough to act in, and power enough within themselves to give their decisions the momentousness of birth and its endured pain.

Eva and Eleanor and Everywoman

Eva's Man, by Gayl Jones. 177 pp. Random House, 1976.

Miss Herbert *(The Suburban Wife)*, by Christina Stead. 308 pp. Random House, 1976.

The new novels by Gayl Jones and Christina Stead do make being a woman sound like a thankless assignment. Miss Jones's heroine in *Eva's Man* sits in a prison cell recalling a lifetime of grubby, grunted propositions and sexual interferences from the unfair sex, and Miss Stead's in *Miss Herbert* endures, with a certain arch resilience, more than thirty years of professional, sexual, cultural, marital, and maternal disappointments. Eva Medina Canada's reaction when she is sexually satisfied at last by a man (called Davis) is to feed him rat poison and then bite off the corpse's penis; Eleanor Herbert Brent's more genteel reaction when faced by men (Edwin Thieme, Paul Waters) she might love is to run the other way: "She . . . hugged only one thought to her, that never, never again must she see this intruder, this man, this god, this tyrant, who had begun to squeeze the life out of her." The life that is hers when unsqueezed appears so dreary, and Eva's emotional core seems so opaque *("What do you want, Eva?" "What?" "What do you want?" "Nothing you can give")*, that the male reviewer can only conclude he is faced with a sexist mystery, of which these two highly intelligent and earnest authors are as much protectors as celebrants. Both heroines end by hugging their enigmas to themselves; Eva consents to a lesbian embrace from her cellmate, and Eleanor finds fulfillment in posing naked for a perverse old man:

> She felt that for the first time she was beginning to understand "mature sex." She liked to stand exposing her smooth, powerful body in the quiet old rooms in some noble or perverse pose; she felt perfectly feminine.

Femaleness as experienced by American blacks was Gayl Jones's subject in her first novel, *Corregidora,* and *Eva's Man* continues the exploration with a sharpened starkness, a power of ellipsis that leaves ever darker gaps between its flashes of rhythmic, sensuously exact dialogue and visible symbol. Ursa Corregidora's meandering voice has become the softly mad voice of Eva Canada, who at the age of forty-three is trying to remember, or to avoid remembering, the murder, five years before, of Davis, a black man with whom she had been closeted in a hotel room for five days of sex, cabbage and sausage, and jagged conversation. Davis, like every man in her life from the little boy who intruded a Popsicle stick into her vagina to the psychiatrist who wants to "explain" her now, talked to her, and wanted talk back:

> *You don't talk much.*
> *Davis, don't look at me that way.*
> *Why, what way am I looking?*
> *Naw.*
> *Come over here.*
> *What?*
> *I like you.*

Her refusal to talk, to give, constitutes her dignity and essence; the sexual breaching of her reserve releases terror and danger:

"What did I do for you Eva? What did you feel?"

"Everything."

He pushes my face into his lap. He combs my hair with his long fingers. I am afraid.

We are in the river now. We are in the river now. The sand is on my tongue. Blood under my nails. I'm bleeding under my nails. We are in the river. Between my legs. They are busy with this woman.

Miss Jones, at twenty-six, is an American writer with a powerful sense of vital inheritance, of history in the blood. Evil is no idle concept to her. *Corregidora* concerned the evil that passed from the practitioners of slavery into the women who were its victims, and evil permeates the erotic education of Eva Canada, as it progresses from Popsicle-stick violations to the witnessing of her mother's adultery and a growing awareness of the whores and "queen bees" in the slum world around her, and on to her own reluctant initiation through encounters in buses and in bars, where a man with no thumb propositions her monotonously. The evil that emanates from men becomes hers. Tyrone, her mother's lover, makes her fondle him, and when she insists that she felt nothing calls her a "little evil devil bitch." Davis says to her, "You a evil ole bitch. Your name ain't Eva it's Evil." She watches cockroaches copulate on the wall, and is told by the man with no thumb, "You don't treat a man like a gentleman, you treat him like a . . . cockroach." She feels herself a Medusa, and in the monstrous act that is the pivot of the book she thinks, "My teeth in an apple," harking back to her namesake, evil's first earthly sponsor.

Though everything in Miss Jones's fictional world becomes a symbol (even a carpenter's level with its instructive bubble is paraded as a phallic surrogate), and though in this novel her repetitious, dreaming dialogue and fragmentary, often italicized scenes verge on mannerism, we never doubt the honorable motive behind her methods—the wish, that is, to represent the inner reality of individuals who belong to a disenfranchised and brutalized race. Real fish swim in her murky waters, though she does not always land them. Her heroines are unable to respond, and, as T. S. Eliot pointed out in connection with *Hamlet,* an inability is hard to objectify. "*An owl sucks my blood. I am bleeding underneath my nails. An old owl sucks my blood. He gives me fruit in my palms.*" We have not been persuaded Eva could think this; the author is pushing images through her. Such phrasing is expressionistic, but expressive mainly of literary strain. And in her troubled nullity Eva is surrounded not so much by other characters as by amateur psychotherapists, all nagging at her silence. Miss Jones apparently wishes to show us a female heart frozen into rage by deprivation, but the worry arises, as it did not in *Corregidora,* that the characters are dehumanized as much by her artistic vision as by their circumstances. *Eva's Man* is a room with a lot of pictures on the wall but not much furniture to lean on. We hear Eva most clearly at the outset of the book:

> Sometimes they think I'm lying to them, though. I tell them it ain't me lying, it's memory lying. I don't believe that, because the past is still as hard on me as the present, but I tell them that anyway. They say they're helping me. I'm forty-three years old, and I ain't seen none of their help yet.

Some strangeness, some monotony and ambiguity of effect are intrinsic to the underworld Miss Jones explores; Christina Stead displays to us a radiant English Venus—"A nobly built beauty, playing-fields champion, excellent student, loved at home, admired at school and by men, she had been happy and confident always" —yet the world through which this goddess moves is also a murky one, decaying in its economics and culture, tedious in its rather impatiently recorded personal incidents, frustrating in its ambience of coquettishness and lack of connection. Miss Stead's venerable gifts are well known: ranging from her native Australia to the America and Europe in which she has lived, she is, after Graham Greene, the most intercontinental of modern novelists; she is a caustically keen observer of a wide spectrum of scenes; she is politically thoughtful without being propagandistic, giving her characters a sufficient but not staggering burden of ideological significance; she has travelled well in the human interior and can be devastatingly clear about some of its uglier turns. The portrait, for instance, in this book of Eleanor's husband, Heinz (he rechristens himself Henry), gives us the very anatomy of a pill—of a prissy, snobbish, rigid, parentally babied Swiss *petit bourgeois* who turns vicious and hysterical in divorce without surrendering his self-righteousness and cunning. Though he is absent from most of the novel's pages, he remains the best and the worst thing in it, and the female antagonist sheds her air of inert, trivial enchantment whenever he touches her. It is an odd, and possibly unintended, comment on the state of women that this woman, drifting through squads of dream men, comes to life chiefly in connection with her horrid little husband; this may be the point of *Miss Herbert*'s uneasy subtitle, *(The Suburban Wife)*.

Among the gifts Miss Stead does not conspicuously possess is that of joy, which translates, in the narrative art, into lubrication. Her plots move chunkily, by jerks of hasty summary and epistolary excerpt; her dialogues are abrasive, full of dry, twittery self-exposition and clichés that may or may not be deliberate. When she becomes a literary functionary, Eleanor gratingly says, "I've given a lot of time and thought to the marketing of ideas, and I'm sure I can pick a winner, and weed out the wheat from the chaff. . . . I can pick a sprig of genius out of the wild weeds it generally goes with and cultivate it for our good and his, the writer's. . . . I can size up and reshape a manuscript rough-hewn from the hands of the raw writer and make it fit to print." With such a barbaric style of diction, she is scarcely one to ridicule her foreign-born husband for saying "The advantage of England is that there are plenty of loopholes for you to climb in the top drawer." She herself seems foreign-born, artificially English. She turns out never to have heard of the common Johnsonian phrase "Grub Street," she shows the class system the breezy indifference of an American (or an Australian), and she has most of her amorous entanglements with foreigners. It seems odd when, in the middle of the novel, she asks herself, "Can I live in a world where the British Empire does not live?" The historical background is vague. Eleanor sows her wild oats in what must be the Thirties, appears to sleep soundly through the Second World War, and awakens to middle age in a postwar world soured by discontented allusions to America and its dollars. This softness of periphery would not matter if Eleanor were herself firmly in focus, but she is not. Before she marries, she is described as promiscuous to the point of prostitution; yet her husband finds her so sexually dumb that he is driven to infidelity, and she has no trouble, though still attractive (we are repeatedly assured), in remaining chaste after he leaves. Her dim memories of girlish fun and her studiously unconsummated post-marital flirtations lead to the hands-off happiness of her "classic poses" and "love portraits" for the elderly Geoffrey Quaideson. Nor do her professional activities, couched in the jargon quoted above, seem more contactual or less bizarre. In her roles of aspiring writer and literary go-between, she plainly serves as an occasion for Miss Stead's satire, of publishers who are "always irritated with books," of guinea-hungry journalists with names like Cope Pigsney, of crass gossip and crasser editing. Eleanor learns to prosper in this dreary demimonde; how much are we meant to sneer at her? How much—the novel's central uncertainty—are we meant to like her? Is she a woman embodying a universal femininity, or is she seen throughout as a hopeless Englishwoman—pink, hearty, energetic, romantic, tame, futile, essentially stupid? The anonymous writer of the jacket copy, having blithely divulged most of the plot, puts the case rather well: "Sometimes the reader is impatient with Eleanor; sometimes one suffers with her."

The question of a character's likability is not a simple one. Tolstoy's first notes on Anna Karenina read, "She is unattractive, with a narrow, low forehead," and in an earlier draft he called her "The Devil." Flaubert began *Madame Bovary* with no fonder image in mind than the gray color of a wood louse. If some heroines seduce their own creators into liking them, some heroes, such as the narrator of Camus's *The Stranger,* are meant to challenge our notion of what likability is. What we like, in the end, is life, and Eleanor Brent lives too little in what she does. We are pleased that she is handsome, and appreciate her capacity for hard work; but good looks and daily works are not defining actions in the Aristotelian sense: "Life consists in action, and its end is a mode of action, not a quality." The *Poetics* continues, "Now, character determines men's qualities, but it is by their actions that they are happy or the reverse." Eleanor's actions are chiefly acts of avoidance. Amid the roistering of her young-womanhood, she runs from a man who moves her: "Thieme upset her. At times she felt he was touching on some great instability in her, a cold inky well in which the self she enjoyed would be lost." Eventually she marries a man she does not love, and clings to him even through hatred. Later still, "an aging belle, a faded animal," she runs from another man who threatens her with "something tremendous," and rests in the thought "Soon I will have my pension and then I am going to write the story of my life."

The clearly intended irony is that we have been made to feel, after three hundred pages, that not much of a life has been lived. Even Miss Stead, as she writes ever more briskly (Eleanor's children are scarcely seen, so swiftly the years go by; her daughter is seventeen on one page and reverts to sixteen a few pages farther on), seems to have hoped for more narrative surge to have developed; she invents one suitor after another for Eleanor ("Bob Standfast was a man Eleanor had met just before her marriage and in a very unusual way"), only to have them all fizzle and be forgotten, like defective kitchen appliances. Well, what actions *has* society made available to women? Not every woman can be Clytemnestra, as Aristotle should have realized. Nor an empire builder, as even Ayn Rand might admit. The moral stature that Jane Austen gave to the search for a husband can no longer be assigned; and even the decision to betray the marriage bed—the nineteenth-century wife's revolutionary alternative—no longer seems momentous. If there is such a thing as a "woman's novel," it finds itself bound, at least in the honest hands of the Mss. Stead and Jones, to the figurative description not of an action but of a quality—the quality of femininity, static and wary, its final recourse the bleak dignity of solitude.

SOME NACHTMUSIK, FROM ALL OVER

No Dearth of Death

THE DEATH OF A BEEKEEPER, by Lars Gustafsson, translated from the Swedish by Yvonne Sandstroem. 163 pp. New Directions, 1981.

DEATH SENTENCE, by Maurice Blanchot, translated from the French by Lydia Davis. 81 pp. Station Hill, 1978.

Two slim paperbacks, fleeing from the fatty tomes that clog the literary mainstream, have recently swum into my ken. Both books are novels only "of a sort," radiate intelligence, and have "death" in the titles. Both came to me by a personal route. Years ago, in Australia, I met the Swedish man of all letters Lars Gustafsson, who had just been to East Berlin speaking fluent German, was now in Adelaide speaking fluent English, and who, for all I knew, was next off to Paris to dazzle them with his French. Most writers feel uneasy at international conferences, traitors to their own privacies; our Swedish participant was striking in the good-humored energy he brought to the surly, pained panels and the less promptu get-togethers on this southern continent, where most of us visitors felt faintly upside down. Gustafsson seemed the enviably ideal con-feree, a red-bearded fish never out of water, loving books, ideas, and discourse equally, and everywhere adept. Strangely, when I once found myself in Sweden he was occupying an academic position in Austin, Texas. So I have in these years of fond memory been compelled to seek him in English print, a search whose sole fruit hitherto has been a poem in *The New Yorker*, some grand lines upon a dog's psyche, called "Elegy for a Dead Labrador."* Now I have read his first novel published in the United States, *The Death of a Beekeeper*, and am pleased to report that it is a beautiful work, lyrical and bleak, resonant and terse—the supposed journals of a retired schoolteacher turned beekeeper who, at the age of forty, finds himself dying of cancer.

This man, Lars Lennart Westin, nicknamed Weasel, is virtually the novel's only character, and its simple main action consists of his notations as the disease runs its course from its first symptoms in August of 1974, through its diagnosis in the following February (in a letter from the district hospital, which he burns instead of reading), to his surrender to an ambulance and death in May. Lars opts to decline medical services and to live out his last months in his own cottage and landscape—a decision that is, surprisingly, not combatted by the authorities of the solicitous Swedish state. When well enough, he walks with his dog in the familiar wintry landscape:

> It was gray, pleasant February weather, fairly cold and hence not too damp, and the whole landscape looked like a pencil sketch. I don't know why I like it so much. It is pretty barren and yet I never get tired of moving about in it.

He has been married, and has children; but the children are not even named, and the wife, Margaret, struck him at first sight as not "particularly interesting." Their marriage of "twelve or thirteen" years was based on "one very simple principle, on one agreement: Looking at one another was forbidden. I mean, really looking at one another." Of all the women in his life, he concludes, "They recognized that I wanted much too little. . . . People never had the feeling that I had any *need* of them." Though some memories from childhood return to him vividly, and he befriends and tries to

---

*More than one correspondent wrote to assure me I hadn't looked hard enough. There exist in print *Forays into Swedish Poetry*, a series of commentaries (trans. Robert T. Rovinsky, University of Texas Press, 1978); *Selected Poems* (trans. Robin Fulton, New Rivers Press, 1972); and *Warm Rooms and Cold*, poems (trans. Yvonne Sandstroem, Copper Beech Press, 1975).

amuse two boys who drop in from this rural neighborhood, Lars lives in our viewing as a solitary man, moving in pain through this bare landscape that he loves.

The pain in its surges and remissions is persuasively described, and even at its highest pitch with a will toward proportion and general truth:

> What I have experienced today during the late night and in the early hours of the morning, *I simply could not have considered possible.* It was absolutely foreign, white hot and totally overpowering. I am trying to breathe very slowly, but as long as it continues, even this breathing, which at least in some very abstract fashion is supposed to help me distinguish between the physical pain and the panic, is an almost overpowering exertion. . . .
>
> This white hot pain, naturally, is basically nothing but a precise measure of the forces which hold this body together. It is a precise measure of the force which has made my existence possible. Death and life are actually MONSTROUS things.

Lars Gustafsson is a philosopher: "Through his writings on mathematics, sociology, history, philosophy, and literature, [his] influence has been strong in all quarters of the European academic community," this novel's "Note on the Author" tells us. Pain and death are, of course, philosophical occasions. Without them, there would be no need for philosophy; we would be in Paradise. "Paradise," Lars Westin writes in his journal, "must consist of the stopping of pain. That means, however, that we live in Paradise as long as we have no pain! And we don't even know it." It is a measure of the author's artistry that he keeps so immense a theme so modestly local, within the horizons of a persona who has no international and little academic reach. When the beekeeper notes that each hive seems to have its own personality —"There are lazy and hard-working, aggressive and gentle bee populations. There are even flighty and unreliable ones, and heaven knows whether there are populations with a sense of humor and others without it"—we are startled and provoked to thought by an illumination entirely in character. In some few spots we do feel the authorial Lars nibbling at the edges of the fictional Lars with his voracious brain; the riddle of identity is worked a bit unnaturally hard in the dying man's meditations. *The Death of a Beekeeper,* according to an afterword by Janet Swaffar, is the fifth of a series of novels dealing with "a possible Lars Gustafsson." The overall motto for the pentalogy seems to be "We begin again. We never give up." These sentences, though hammered home repeatedly in the beekeeper's journal, seem to come from the outside—a rather boring bit of Stoic cheerleading. Knowing when to give up is one of the arts of living, as anyone understands who has watched animals fight or die.

The surface of plausibility is also marred, but brilliantly, in the inserted parable "When God Awoke." God is imagined as having been napping, "about the way a small spider naps in the corner of the web it has built," in "a distant nook of the universe." The nap has been "a moment of absence, just as when a motorist takes his eyes from the street for a moment." She—for God is female, a kind of shimmering tinted jellyfish "thirteen parsecs in diameter"— awakes, and for the first time in Her existence hears human prayers, and without further delay sets about answering them. She hears, for instance, the Archbishop of Åbo plead at the end of a radio service, "Give us, oh God, a lasting peace," and within three-tenths of a second She has rendered all armaments, from swords to giant warheaded rockets, into soft, solid, useless gold. The world becomes under this indulgent Heavenly Mother a mad welter of answered prayers:

> As the human situation rapidly began to defy linguistic description and approached a realm for which there are no words, the DEATH OF LANGUAGE began.
> One of the last speech fragments contained the message:
> IF GOD LIVES, EVERYTHING IS ALLOWED.

Which nicely reverses Dostoevski's old complaint that without God all things are possible. We have been here before, perhaps, in Nietzsche's Promethean humanism, in Hamsun's quizzical pagan nihilism, in Ingmar Bergman's God-haunted dramatizations of despair. The defining affirmation of the self in saying No is what this little book is about. The cosmic and subjective are merged in an image: "The darkness of the iris* is nothing other than the star-less night, the darkness deep in the eye is nothing other than the darkness of the universe." But within this blackness the bee-keeper notices the gray beauty of the moist fog, the leafless trees. He lives simultaneously in Hell and in Paradise, and dies into neither. He has been, to quote "Elegy for a Dead Labrador," one

> of those places where the universe makes a knot
> in itself, short-lived, complex structures
> of proteins that have to complicate themselves
> more and more in order to survive, until everything
> breaks and turns simple once again, the knot
> dissolved, the riddle gone.

The second paperback, *Death Sentence,* by Maurice Blanchot, was handed to me in a Madison Avenue bookstore by a clerk who felt I should acquaint myself with the hottest-selling item (he said) among the East Side intelligentsia. Gratefully I accepted it; duti-fully have I read it. Though presently chic, the book is far from new, having been published by Blanchot in 1948; in general, Blan-chot's influence, as theorist and practitioner, has preceded his actual work to these shores, which have long since received the *nouveaux romans* of younger novelists like Robbe-Grillet and Pinget. The very short novel—eighty-one pages—in hand has been buttressed on the back by formidable tributes to "one of the most powerful literary and philosophical intellects in France of the last four decades" (John Hollander) and "certainly one of the most impor-tant writers of our time, [who] has pushed the question of writing to its farthest limits, both in his essays and his stories" (Edmond Jabès). These tributes helpfully offer to orient us not only in the matter of reputation but within the murky book itself, which is "a transumptive romance of the erotic triangle of consciousness, death, and the possible world of narrative" (Hollander again), and one in which "Blanchot's power as a writer pierces, like a look that

---

*Surely he, or the translator, meant "pupil."

is too direct, the indeterminate prose, and makes all relations, and especially our relation to time, absolutely precarious" (Geoffrey Hartman).

"Precarious" is a good word to begin with; Blanchot's prose gives an impression, like Henry James's, of carrying meanings so fragile they might crumble in transit:

> People who are silent do not seem admirable to me because of that, nor yet less friendly. The ones who speak, or at least who speak to me because I have asked them a question, often seem to me the most silent, either because they evoke silence in me, or because, knowingly or unknowingly, they shut themselves up with me in an enclosed place where the person who questions them allies them with answers that their mouths do not hear.

Protestations of the difficulty of this act of writing from first page to last give *Death Sentence* a stretched, pained shape, as though silence were pressing hard against it, just as death presses hard against the lives of the shadowy characters. Attempts at statement wind down into abject self-cancellation:

> It is possible that the idea of being married to me seemed like a very bad thing to her, a sort of sacrilege, or quite the opposite, a real happiness, or finally, a meaningless joke. Even now I am almost incapable of choosing among these interpretations. Enough of this.

The events that can scarcely be described occurred in 1938; they involved the sickly hero's intense but strenuously indeterminate relations with two young women, J. and N., both of whom, I believe, he brings back from the dead. The French title, *L'Arrêt de mort*, idiomatically means "death sentence" and literally means "death's halt." The first miracle occurs when J., who has been fighting her disease (unspecified but tubercular in aura) for ten years, is lying on what had been her deathbed, "already no more than a statue," her pulse "scattered like sand." The hero, called to this scene by J.'s sister Louise, sits on the edge of the bed, calls her name, and is rewarded with "a sort of breath . . . out of her compressed mouth."

At that moment, her eyelids were still completely shut. But a second afterwards, perhaps two, they opened abruptly and they opened to reveal something terrible which I will not talk about, the most terrible look which a living being can receive, and I think that if I had shuddered at that instant, and if I had been afraid, everything would have been lost, but my tenderness was so great that I didn't even think about the strangeness of what was happening, which certainly seemed to me altogether natural because of that infinite movement which drew me towards her, and I took her in my arms, while her arms clasped me, and not only was she completely alive from that moment on, but perfectly natural, gay and almost completely recovered.

It is a momentary miracle; within hours, a death rattle begins and J. does die. The case of N., who is sometimes given the full name of Nathalie, is more mysterious still. Half-hearted lovers, she and the hero are parted when a bomb explodes on the street, and he finds her at last sitting motionless in a room of utter and terrifying blackness. Her body stares at him with a "dead and empty flame in her eyes." He takes her cold hand in his; he feels love for this body "in its night of stone":

I put my arms around her, I was completely motionless and she was completely motionless. But a moment came when I saw that she was still mortally cold, and I drew closer and said to her: "Come." I got up and took her by the hand; she got up too and I saw how tall she was.

It is as if Jesus Christ, years later, were writing, in the affectless voice of the hero of Camus's *Stranger,* His own troubled, "indeterminate" Gospel. In the tomblike blackness wherein the novel's hero revivifies N., he says of this darkness, in phrases recalling Matthew 10:39, "There is something in it which scorns man and which man cannot endure without losing himself. But he must lose himself; and whoever resists will founder, and whoever goes forward will become this very blackness, this cold and dead and scornful thing in the very heart of which lives the infinite." This has happened; the hero is not only death's conqueror but death itself. "[J.] turned slightly towards the nurse and said in a tranquil tone, 'Now then, take a good look at death,' and pointed her finger at me." A few pages later, the narrator confides, "I myself see nothing important in the fact that this young woman was dead, and returned to life at my bidding. . . . I have said nothing extraordinary or even surprising. What is extraordinary begins at the moment I stop." His stop: *l'arrêt de mort.*

Blanchot's tortuous, glimmering style in *Death Sentence* is a kind of posthumous one, traced with many hesitations and denials by the ghostly hand of narrative. It conceals as it tells; graceful and maddening, a cascade of mystification bejewelled with melodramatic glances and gothic gew-gaws, the prose holds to syntax but frustrates our attempts to construct a coherent world from its hints, or a succession of events we can relive. In a realistic novel, a moment of miracle-working would entail a substantial elaboration of the career of a miracle-worker, with the practical and probably anticlimactic consequences such an event on earth would generate. (Joyce Cary's *The Captive and the Free* is such a novel.) Among the charms of anti-realism, let us not overlook—for its practitioners, at least—a certain slippery ease. Yet in its suave delirium Blanchot's prose claims to contain something wonderful, a treasure not so unlike, perhaps, the beekeeper's defiant courage in the face of pain. "I take this unhappiness on myself," *Death Sentence* concludes, "and I am immeasurably glad of it and to that thought I say eternally, 'Come,' and eternally it is there."

Novels so exclusively about death, so saturated with its blackness, would have been impossible when death was assumed to be a gateway to the afterlife and therefore not qualitatively different from the other adventures and rites of passage that befall a soul. Philippe Aries's *The Hour of Our Death* begins by describing the calm, the matter-of-factness, with which most men until modern times prepared for and enacted their own dying. If death is the utter end, it then becomes not an action but an impressively extended state—a giant tube of ink that at the slightest pressure oozes its blackness into the porous texture of our lives. Yet though it is immense in duration and penetration, because it is nothingness there is not much to say about it. No wonder these two novels are short and lapse awkwardly into religious imagery—the only imagery we have that pertains. The pastel jellyfish Goddess of the one, the arid and gloomy miracles of the other are foci of energy that blackness itself cannot supply. The strangeness of the world, which novels traditionally celebrate, is that in it, as in the night sky, blackness is not all.

Dark Smile, Devilish Saints

SMILE PLEASE: *An Unfinished Autobiography,* by Jean Rhys. 151 pp. Harper & Row, 1980.

PORT OF SAINTS, by William S. Burroughs. 174 pp. Blue Wind Press, 1980.

Smile Please and *Port of Saints* are about the same size and shape, have spooky brownish dust jackets, and might both be catalogued as fragmentary autobiographies. The publication attached to Miss Rhys's name, indeed, is forthrightly subtitled *An Unfinished Autobiography.* It consists of a completed memoir of her childhood bound in with scattered recollections of her later life, including portions of a diary; the book has been assembled, edited, and introduced with especial affection and tact by the novelist's English editor, Diana Athill. Miss Athill briskly begins, "Jean Rhys began to think of writing an autobiographical book several years before her death, on May 14, 1979. The idea did not attract her, but because she was sometimes angered and hurt by what other people wrote about her, she wanted to get the facts down." Though many facts seem not so much got down as left discreetly floating, this truncated effort at self-revelation is attractive, to us if not to its author, in part *because* of its slim, provocative fragmentariness. The fragment, the sketch, the unfinished canvas, and the shattered statue are all congenial to an age of relativity, indeterminacy, and agnosticism. Most of the oppressively complete books that labor for our attention would benefit, we suspect, from a few reductive blows of the hammer. In the case of *Smile Please,* the hammer was applied by Miss Rhys's habitual reticence and perfectionism, and by the furies that made all her attempts at composition in later life difficult.

Even so, admirers of Jean Rhys's amazing fiction—amazing in its resolute economy of style and in its illusionless portrait of a drifting heroine, a portrait that the recent gush of female confessionalism has not rendered any less stunningly honest and severe—will find much to surprise and delight them. The laconic sketch of her growing up as a member of the white minority on the small West Indian island of Dominica has the emotional fibre without the exotic coloring of the doomed heroine's girlhood in her novel *Wide Sargasso Sea.* In both versions, the unreachable mother is a cruel keystone, a hard absence: "Even after the new baby was born there must have been an interval before she seemed to find me a nuisance and I grew to dread her. . . . Yes, she drifted away from me and when I tried to interest her, she was indifferent." Over seventy years after the event—for Jean Rhys wrote these paragraphs in the three years before her death at eighty-six—she looks with the eyes of a little girl toward a mother who is hardly there:

> Just before I left Dominica she was ill and unable to come downstairs for some time. I went up to see her but walked softly and she didn't hear me. . . . Behind her silence she looked lonely, a stranger in a strange house. . . . lonely, patient and resigned. Also obstinate. "You haven't seen what I've seen, haven't heard what I've heard." . . . I wanted to run across the room and kiss her but I was too shy so it was the usual peck.

The blackness all around them seems to drain this essential relationship of blood. "Once I heard her say that black babies were prettier than white ones. Was this the reason why I prayed so ardently to be black, and would run to the looking glass in the morning to see if the miracle had happened? And though it never had, I tried again. Dear God, let me be black." In *Wide Sargasso Sea,* the mother's curse is beauty and madness, passed on to the daughter. In the autobiography, lassitude and indifference seem to be the inheritance—a zombielike, parasitic resignation to being not fully alive. "Every night someone gave a dance; you could hear the drums. We had few dances. The blacks were more alive, more a part of the place than we were."

Not merely indifference but hate was early woven into the soul of Ella Gwendolen Rees Williams, as she was christened. A nightmare recognition about the Caribbean, vividly dramatized in *Wide Sargasso Sea*, was that the blacks hated the whites among them. In *Smile Please*, Jean Rhys remembers admiring a lightly colored black classmate seated next to her at convent school:

> I tried, shyly at first, then more boldly, to talk to my beautiful neighbour.
>
> Finally, without speaking, she turned and looked at me. I knew irritation, bad temper, the "Oh, go away" look; this was different. This was hatred—impersonal, implacable hatred. I recognized it at once and if you think that a child cannot recognise hatred and remember it for life you are most damnably mistaken.
>
> I never tried to be friendly with any of the coloured girls again. I was polite and that was all.
>
> They hate us. We are hated.
>
> Not possible.
>
> Yes it is possible and it is so.

An authenticity early conceded to negative emotion gives a macabre tinge to *Smile Please*. The narrator explicitly "hates" many things: her own appearance in the mirror at the age of nine; sewing; a photograph of her mother when young and pretty; her father when he gets a short haircut; the unknown persons who years later knock down the cross over his grave. "I hated whoever had done this and thought, 'I can hate too.'" From a black nurse, Meta, who "didn't like me much anyway," she imbibes fear and voodoo superstition: "Meta had shown me a world of fear and distrust, and I am still in that world." In an incident that gets a chapter to itself, the little girl smashes the face of a doll with a rock: "I remember vividly the satisfaction of being wicked. The guilt that was half triumph." Reading *Paradise Lost*, she is fascinated by Satan; at a later age, "an unconscious Manichee," she arrives at "the certainty that the Devil was quite as powerful as God, perhaps more so. . . . I was passionately on the side of God, but it was very difficult to see what I could do about it." After the dreadful death of their fox terrier Rex from distemper, she decides that "the Devil was undoubtedly stronger than God, so what was the use?" The strikingly combined intensity and apathy of Miss Rhys's world view have their seeds in the black/white, fear-riddled atmosphere of Dominica. She was in-fected by the something macabre in the Caribbean, these threadbare economies perched on a sea of plangently lovely days. She became a European but saw it all with slitted eyes. As a writer, she shocks us with what it does not occur to her to overlook.

In the second half of this unfinished autobiography, artfully titled by Miss Athill "It Began to Grow Cold," the narrator as a young woman in England continues to hate things, including the London zoo and landladies, and turns with her newly bloomed good looks to life in a chorus line. This genial demimonde and the proximate worlds of money and sex ("It seems to me now that the whole business of money and sex is mixed up with something very primitive and deep") are glancingly, even flirtatiously described, and constitute, of course, the well-tracked terrain of her first four novels, all written before 1939. Her beginnings as a writer are presented, characteristically, as a triumph of drift and whim. Dis-pleased by the ugly bareness of a table in a newly rearranged room in Fulham, she passes a stationer's shop "where quill pens were displayed in the window, a lot of them, red, blue, green, yellow. Some of them would be all right in a glass, to cheer up my table, I thought. I went into the shop and bought about a dozen. Then I noticed some black exercise books on the counter. . . . I bought several of those, I don't know why, just because I liked the look of them. I got a box of J nibs, the sort I liked, an ordinary penholder, a bottle of ink and a cheap inkstand. Now that old table won't look so bare, I thought." Then, as in a trance, she employs these so accidentally purchased implements to write late into the night. The notebooks she filled in a few days—before penning the concluding sentence, "Oh God, I'm only twenty and I'll have to go on living and living and living"—were carried unread in her luggage for seven more years, before they became the basis for her novel *Voyage in the Dark*.

After the Second World War, she herself was to be set aside: her small reputation had dwindled to almost nothing before a radio adaptation of *Good Morning, Midnight* in 1957 uncovered her exis-tence in a Devonshire cottage and prompted her revival as a func-tioning writer and a widespread recognition that, as Miss Athill puts it, came "too late to give her much lively pleasure." She finished out her surprisingly long life in a country that she hated, England, and in a cottage that she and her third husband accepted sight unseen and that upon first sight she "took a dislike to." No modern writer of note presents a career less purposeful in its appearance. Yet she wrote in her diary, "If I stop writing my life will have been an abject failure," and of herself as a child remembered, "Before I could read, almost a baby, I imagined that God, this strange thing or person I heard about, was a book. Sometimes it was a large book standing upright and half open and I could see the print inside but it made no sense to me. Other times the book was smaller and inside were sharp flashing things." Later, when she could read, she lost herself "in the immense world of books, and tried to blot out the real world which was so puzzling to me. Even then I had a vague, persistent feeling that I'd always be lost in it, defeated." So writing, which Jean Rhys carried out with such fanatic control and noble candor, was for her a kind of ascent out of a Devil-dominated world into the Godly half, abounding with "sharp flashing things," of the Manichaean equation.

William S. Burroughs, if not unambiguously of the Devil's party, is the author of the most sinister American novel, *Naked Lunch,* to attain the status of a classic. Nor have his books, since he published in 1959 those "detailed notes on sickness and delirium" (his description), become less sinister, or more coherent. *Port of Saints* is gamely described by its jacket copy as "the mind-boggling story of a man whose alternate selves take him on a fantastic journey through space, time, and sexuality." We are further told that the volume was written, or assembled, or whatever it is that Burroughs does with scissors and eggbeater to concoct his books, before the author's return to the United States in 1973. So we have here something of a period piece, revolving, like Marge Piercy's *Dance the Eagle to Sleep,* around a stylized struggle between a sick American society and a healthy, tribalized counterculture. In Burroughs's fantasy, the heroic outsiders are the Wild Boys, or Parries, for Para-normals—the enemy being the loathsome Norms, led by Mike Finn, if you can call it led. "Under the rule of Mike Finn it

didn't pay to be good at anything. In consequence the whole struc-
ture of Western society had collapsed." Finn "organized a vast
Thought Police. Anybody with an absent-minded expression was
immediately arrested and executed." Cannon fodder indeed, for the
gallant wild-boy hordes: "Wave after wave of invaders swept down
from the Bering Straits and up from the Mexican border destroying
every vestige of the American nightmare, leveling the hideous cities
and slaughtering the surviving Norms like cattle with the aftosa.
Anyone who used the words RIGHT and WRONG was IMMEDIATELY
KILLED. The Norms were then ploughed under for fertilizer." Ear-
lier, mind you, the wild boys had taken a few perfunctory licks:
"Flashback shows the wild boys mowed down by cold eyed narcs
and Southern lawmen backed by religious women and big money."

All overtones of political allegory are soon swallowed, however,
by Burroughs's absolutely Olympian joy in destruction of any sort,
whether engineered by explosives technology or surreal diseases.
The Bubu boys, for example (not to be confused with the snake
boys or the roller-skate boys), "all dressed in pink and purple and
yellow shirts to match their sores," fester flamboyantly and finally
molt: "Of course we save the skins and grind them up into a fine
powder, like tear gas . . . a bomb or two of dried Bubu skin dropped
on New York would make the atom bomb look ridiculous. Think
of ten million people going putrid in a matter of seconds—the stink
would be a turnon of its own." Burroughs also enjoys describing
homosexual contacts, preferably multiple and intermixed with
murder. Not since the Marquis de Sade has so much mechanical
copulation been so gravely arranged. Ejaculation is an explosion of
sorts, and the young male body an ultimate weapon. Boys throw
knives with their toes in time with their spasms, have "metallic grey
eyes," and come with "machine gun noises." Intercourse is felt as
a deadly electricity: "The two bodies quiver together as if in con-
tact with a high tension wire vibrating from head to foot as a heavy
purple smell of ozone reeks out of them."

Port of Saints is claptrap, but since it is murderous claptrap we
feel we owe it some respect. We would like to dismiss this book
but cannot, quite. A weird wit and an integrity beyond corruption
shine through its savage workings, and a genuine personal melan-

choly. A fitful hero called Audrey seems to hold some of Bur-roughs's own memories; his is the youthful vulnerability that finds consolation in dreams of sex and violence. "Audrey read *Adventure Stories* and *Short Stories* and saw himself as the Major, a gentleman adventurer . . . He read *Amazing Stories* and saw himself as the first man to land on the moon and drew diagrams of rocket ships. He decided to be a writer and make his own Majors and Zulu Jims and Snowy Joes and Carl Cranberrys." If much of this jagged, trashy novel feels like the reverie of a vicious Walter Mitty, there is also a poeticized James Bond: "Wings camouflaged to disappear in a sunset drift down on the west wind and rain poison arrows from the sky. Wild geese wreck a troop transport plane. The wild boys are always just out of sight in the colors they cannot see in the places they didn't go . . . The old financier nodding on his balcony looked up and saw a landscape in the sky. It reminded him of an old picture book and he could see a boy standing there in a stream. As the old man watched, the boy took a silver arrow from his quiver and raised his crossbow. A gust of air hit the old man's face and bore his breath away." Burroughs would be unbearable if he believed in death; but since he no more believes in finality than the id or the animator of Tom and Jerry cartoons, a St. Elmo's fire of perverse tenderness can be seen to play about his lurid tableaux, and a pubescent pa-thos can be heard in the call of the wild boys: "Calling all boys of the earth we will teach you the secrets of magic control of wind and rain. . . . We will show you the sex magic that turns flesh to light. We will free you forever from the womb."

Although there is a distinct autobiographical savor to *Port of Saints,* few facts are revealed. A reader might gather that the writer was born in St. Louis, inclined toward homosexuality, and had some experience of drugs and Mexico. A moment of homo-sexual initiation in a summer cottage recurs ever more extrava-gantly until this naturalistic moment of lived life is transposed into the heaven of coruscating violence where the authorial imag-ination finds repose. "It's all shredding away as I walk . . . cool remote toilets foghorns outside cigarette ash on a naked thigh in furnished rooms blue mist in pubic hairs crackling to dust as I walk." The "I" becomes the "we" of a triumphant army: "We are moving farther and farther out. No troops can get through the Deserts of Silence and beyond that is the Blue Light Blockade. We don't need the enemy any more. Buildings and stars laid flat for storage. The last carnival is being pulled down." Beyond the last carnival lies a world's-end fair: "Xolotl Time looks like a world fair spread out in a vast square where weapons, sex and fighting techniques are displayed and exchanged." No continuous program even of nihilism develops; Burroughs's philosophy remains as mysterious as his person. Is he really in favor of all these broken necks, weapons of putrefaction, and cold-eyed boys who bare their teeth like dogs? The purposeful fragmentation of his technique even tends to conceal how much of a writer Burroughs really is. Most of the prose is simple pell-mell, and the dialogue straight from *Action Comics*. Sometimes he sounds like Kerouac or Mailer, hurriedly tossing into a sentence all that comes to mind: "Defeated and pursued, with only a handful of followers left, Audrey invokes a curse on the White Goddess and all her works, from the Conquistadores, from the Bog People to the Queen, from Dixie to South Africa . . ." He can be funny, as when describing the drug Bor Bor: "The effect of this drug, which is held in horror by the wild boys and only used as a weapon against our enemies, is to lull the user into a state of fuzzy well-being and benevolence, a warm good feeling that everything will come out all right for Americans." But satire is not really his game; nor is propaganda, though a number of drastic programs for mass mutation and pervasive depopulation come and go. We witness in his work acts not of exhortation but of exorcism. A kind of landscape returns, as nostalgic as the windblown dunes and meadows of Winslow Homer, bathed in the unearthly green light of Maxfield Parrish illustrations, before it transmutes to extragalactic blue: "The boy did not speak. He came closer and then got on the bed kneeling. He was naked, in his eyes the cold reaches of interstellar space. Behind him Audrey could see a gleaming empty sky, a far dusting of stars." The net effect Burroughs achieves is to convince us that he has seen and done things sad beyond description.

*

Both Burroughs and Jean Rhys, it seems safe to say, at points in their lives made good acquaintance with those demons of self-destruction whose entertainment is one of our modern luxuries. Jean Rhys's drinking, though ignored in *Smile Please*, figures prominently in her fiction, notably in *Good Morning, Midnight*, and in the reminiscences of most people who knew her. Burroughs's drug addiction—overcome at the age of forty-five—is, of course, his central subject, and he has provided no more harrowing account of himself than the tersely factual letter to a doctor, printed in *The British Journal of Addiction* (1956), in which he helpfully lists the horrifying variety of drugs and unsuccessful cures which a reckless and presumably well-financed user can experience. Yet he survived, and in his publicity photos his features have settled into a banker's pensive calm indistinguishable from that of many another member of the Harvard class of 1936. And Jean Rhys, born into a long-ago world still seething with the aftereffects of the abolition of slavery, lived through three husbands and two widely separated literary careers.

Thoughts of survival and its absence have been put in this reviewer's mind by a strange recent compendium, *Short Lives*, by Katinka Matson. In it Miss Matson, inspired by the short life of a friend of hers, the poet and self-styled "New York City Fool" Thomas (Tyler) Bootman, presents in alphabetical order sketches of the lives of thirty more famous artistic strivers who lived hectically and died early. The selection is shrewd, the research considerable, the bleak facts fascinating. True, Nijinsky lived to the age of sixty, and should not be blamed for his own insanity; nor perhaps should Antonin Artaud, who died at fifty-one of cancer of the rectum. And of the several singers in Miss Matson's anthology of early demise (Judy Garland, Billie Holiday, Janis Joplin, Elvis Presley) it might be said that the entertainer's life, with its chronic call for nocturnal vivacity, is naturally debilitating. Yet from the literary backbone of her list, whether the subject committed suicide outright (Hart Crane, Jack London, Sergei Esenin, Vladimir Mayakovsky, Yukio Mishima, Malcolm Lowry, Sylvia Plath, Anne Sexton) or merely indulged ruinous habits (Scott Fitzgerald, Jack Kerouac, Dylan Thomas), the inarguable conclusion arises that at least since Rimbaud's announced determination to become a visionary through the "disordering of all the senses" self-destructive excess has been a licensed force in the lives of many writers. Lowry wrote, "You cannot trust the ones who are too careful. As writers or drinkers. Old Goethe cannot have been so good a man as Keats or Chatterton. Or Rimbaud. The ones that burn." In the poetics of burning, alcohol and hashish and heroin and ether act as distillers of the pure. The spectacularly alcoholic painter Modigliani proposed, "Alcohol is for the middle class evil. It is a vice. It is the Devil's beckon. But for us artists it is necessary." The poet Max Jacob saw in Modigliani everything subordinated to "a need for crystalline purity . . . He was cutting, but as fragile as glass; also as inhuman as glass, so to say." In a sense, such bohemians carried forward under a new banner the old Christian war of the soul against the body. Self-destruction is close to self-sacrifice, and a religious conviction of transcendent reality is common to both. The very casualness with which, say, Dylan Thomas brushed his life away as insignificant implies a helpless belief in significance elsewhere. A certain Christian afterglow lights up the literature of modernism. Proust and Joyce, immuring themselves in their vast and arcane works, underwent martyrdoms of a sort, and from Yeats to Faulkner the writer's vocation has been proclaimed a heroic priesthood. Idealism survived theology and lent its unearthly energy to Art. Now, Jean Rhys and William Burroughs, though they are open-eyed tourists in Hell and fascinated by magic, have little of the idealist's obligatory optimism, or his passion for the pure. Reality breaks bare and inconsequent upon their personae. A certain pragmatic dryness, which we feel in their styles, a certain deadness even, permeates their burnt-out worlds. This deadness, perhaps, proved their mundane salvations, and makes them, as artists, post-modern.

Layers of Ambiguity

PLAYERS, by Don DeLillo. 212 pp. Knopf, 1977.

GOING AFTER CACCIATO, by Tim O'Brien. 338 pp. Delacorte, 1978.

Don DeLillo seems determined to nail modern America down, and he may yet. His previous novels have tackled football *(End Zone)*, pop music *(Great Jones Street)*, and science *(Ratner's Star)*, and in *Players* he takes on terrorism. Terrorism of an attenuated, urbane sort; the book is really about sophistication, or at least nothing is as clear about it as the sophistication of the author, who combines a wearily thorough awareness of how people pass their bored-silly lives in New York City with a (in this novel) lean, slit-eyed prose and a pseudo-scientific descriptive manner. He slices up ordinary experience into paper-thin transparencies and feeds it back in poetic printout:

> When fog worked in from the bay it seemed to suggest some basic change in the state of information.

> He occupied a self-enfolding space, a special level of exclusion.

> His "selective" disclosure of information merely confirmed the material existence of the space he'd chosen to occupy, the complex geography, points of confluence and danger.

The hero is called Lyle. He is married to Pammy. They are thirtyish and have no children. He works on Wall Street, is handsome and successful and kind of a kidder. At night in their apartment, he watches television in a very chic way: "Sitting in near darkness about eighteen inches from the screen, he turned the channel selector every half minute or so, sometimes much more frequently. He wasn't looking for something that might sustain his interest. Hardly that. He simply enjoyed jerking the dial into fresh image-burns." He and Pammy bump bodies in front of the refrigerator, make mechanical love to the distant music of a Mister Softee truck, and for conversation exchange one-liners that are virtually one-worders:

"Goody, cheddar."
"What's these?"
"Brandy snaps."
"Triffic."
"Look out."
"No you push me, you."

It sounds right. We believe in this young urban couple, "modern-stupid," tender in their terribly wised-up way, breathing bad air and stale chatter, eating by calling "Dial-a-Steak," and subjected to a certain amount of soulless sermonizing by their creator: "Everything was a common experience, binding them despite their indirections, the slanted apparatus of their agreeing."

This reviewer has never had much sympathy for the critical complaint that characters aren't lovable. The writer's job is to get real people onto paper; it is the reader's option to love them. But I confess that the drastic unlovableness of Lyle and the very tepid appeal of Pammy discourage the considerable suspension of disbelief necessary to follow them into their adventures as they break loose from connubial anti-bliss. Their agreement to part comes over a broken dishwasher, in a little gem of stichomythia:

"It's broke again?"
"You call."
"You, for once."
"I called the other."
"I'm not calling. I don't care. Let it be broke."
"Don't call. We won't call. I don't care."
"I'm serious," he said. "I don't care."
"I won't be here, so."
"Neither will I except in and out."

After this exchange, things get unreal. Lyle takes up with a deliciously null secretary called Rosemary ("There were shades of blandness from genial to serene; hers was closer to the median, lacking distinctive character, dead on"); by diffident steps she leads him into a group of terrorists in Queens who "had no visible organization or leadership. They had no apparent plan." Their guns and bombs probably don't work, either. They have some dim notion of blowing up the Stock Exchange but spend their time tattling on each other and acting seductive toward Lyle. Meanwhile, for *her* vacation, Pammy (she works in one of the twin towers of the World Trade Center, but can't always tell which one) has gone to Maine with two homosexuals, Ethan and Jack, who talk a lot, in "that exaggerated whine of urban discontent," about food, each other, and "similarities, analogies . . . regardless of how stupid." The younger of them, Jack, sees a UFO, makes love to Pammy, and commits suicide, in that order but not (I think) in linked sequence.

If Pammy's game puzzles us, her husband's utterly baffles. Lyle ("interesting, his formal apartness") coöperates not only with the terrorists but with the rude mystery men who represent the inscrutable forces of law and order; the end finds him in a motel in Canada, having double-crossed everybody but on excellent terms, it seems, with himself. "The idea is to organize this emptiness," he thinks sagely. The only idea *this* patient player of Mr. DeLillo's games came away with was the sly but insistent implication that Lyle, "barely recognizable as male" and crazy for neatness, is an anal erotic. When he and Rosemary find haven in a Canadian motel, she emerges from the bathroom with "a plastic phallus harnessed to her body." After two days of togetherness, he lies beside her sleeping body reflecting how, "wearing her white plastic toy, that odd sardonic moment, so closely bordering on cruelty, a playlet of brute revelation, she let him know it was as an instrument, a toy herself, that she appeared. Dil-do. A child's sleepy murmur. It was as collaborators that they touched, as dreamers in a sea of pallid satisfaction." In case we miss the focus of satisfaction: "He stares at the hollows in her buttocks. Dark divide. The ring of flesh that's buried there." Nevertheless he decides to leave her, toy and all. The sun comes out. "Specks blaze up, a series of energy storms. . . . This is welcome, absolving us of our secret knowledge."

Don DeLillo has, as they used to say of athletes, class. He is original, versatile, and, in his disdain of last year's emotional guarantees, fastidious. He brings to human phenomena the dispassionate mathematics and spatial subtleties of particle physics. Into our technology-riddled daily lives he reads the sinister ambiguities, the floating ugliness of America's recent history. Kinnear, the most verbal terrorist, tells Lyle:

> Our big problem in the past, as a nation, was that we didn't give our government credit for being the totally entangling force that it was. They were even more evil than we'd imagined. More evil and much more interesting. . . . Behind every stark fact we encounter layers of ambiguity.

But the very intensity of Mr. DeLillo's wish, in this novel, to say something new about the matter has evaporated the matter, leaving behind an exquisite ash-skeleton of elliptic dialogue and spindly motivation.

Tim O'Brien's *Going After Cacciato* shares with *Players* an ambience of futility and a clipped hard-edge style but otherwise stands in some contrast. Where *Players* seems sketchy, even hasty, *Going After Cacciato* feels as solid as its dark typeface. This novel of Vietnam in 1968, written by an American foot soldier in that conflict, has been appearing, fragmentarily, in magazines since 1975 and has already won four short-story prizes. In its final form, the scenes are so carefully mortised, and the whole so firmly fitted and tightened and polished, that each efficient page carries the heft of importance this material has for the author. Whereas little rings true about DeLillo's terrorists beyond the dead-level nihilism of the prose climate, we do not doubt the reality of Mr. O'Brien's combat scenes. The stakes in this game are spelled out: "The game's set up, all the pieces out on the board, an' either we play or we fry. Burn. No choice. Dig it?"

O'Brien, who has written an autobiographical account of his Vietnam service under the title *If I Die in a Combat Zone*, opens his novel with an explosion, a stunning threnody:

> It was a bad time. Billy Boy Watkins was dead, and so was Frenchie Tucker. Billy Boy had died of fright, scared to death on the field of battle, and Frenchie Tucker had been shot through the nose. Bernie Lynn and Lieutenant Sidney Martin had died in tunnels. Pederson was dead and Rudy Chassler was dead. Buff was dead. Ready Mix was dead.

They were all among the dead. The rain fed fungus that grew in the men's boots and socks, and their socks rotted, and their feet turned white and soft so that the skin could be scraped off with a fingernail, and Stink Harris woke up screaming one night with a leech on his tongue. When it was not raining, a low mist moved across the paddies, blending the elements into a single gray element, and the war was cold and pasty and rotten.

Each of the deaths named is somewhere in the book described, with the concision and definiteness and contained pain of incidents long revolved in the mind, and we get to know very well the surviving members of Third Squad, First Platoon, Alpha Company, 5th Battalion, 46th Infantry, 198th Infantry Brigade. And we remember or learn a great deal about the practical side of that least memorialized of American wars: the punjis, the trip mines, the mud, the razed villages, the invisible enemy, the "friendly" firepower that killed, the opulent support forces ("logistical and transportation and communication battalions, legal services, a PX, a stockade, a USO, a mini golf course, a swimming beach with trained lifeguards, administration offices under the Adjutant General, twelve Red Cross Donut Dollies") that at a ratio of twelve persons to one backed up the miserable "grunts" in the field. We witness the commonplace sharing of marijuana among officers and men, we see a dying man cup his shot-away face in his helmet, we hear a medic salute a boy's severed foot with "War's over, Billy, that's a million-dollar wound." We learn the jargon and self-mockery of a half-hearted war. We learn how a bullet fired at a man in a tunnel enters at his nose and burrows fatally deep into his chest. We are drawn into a conspiracy among the soldiers to "frag" their commanding officer, prim, by-the-book Lieutenant Sidney Martin; yet we are also led into Sidney Martin's inner soliloquy: "The lieutenant was not stupid. He knew these beliefs were unpopular. He knew that his society, and many of the men under his own command, did not share them. But he did not ask his men to share his views, only to comport themselves like soldiers." We are led to recognize that "what happened to Lieutenant Sidney Martin was a very sad thing." There are no villains in this book, only villainous circumstances. Its hero, if there is one, is Martin's replacement as platoon leader, Lieutenant Corson, a middle-aged veteran of Korea who is feeble with dysentery, says it's not his war, and doesn't ask his men to search tunnels: "He simply ordered the tunnels blown, or blew them himself, and he saw no incompatibility between this and his mission as a soldier. The men loved him." Again: "He took no chances, he wasted no lives. The war, for which he was much too old, scared him." As a fictional portrait of this war, *Going After Cacciato* is hard to fault, and will be hard to better.

However, reaching for a masterpiece and a definitive, encompassing statement, O'Brien has interwoven the realistic level of battle and lull with a flight of fantasy that takes place in the head of Spec Four Paul Berlin during a long wakeful night of lonely watch at a seaside observation post in the province of Quang Ngai. A fellow-soldier, Cacciato, had previously run from battle in the mountains, and Berlin imagines that the squad, in pursuing him, makes it all the way across Asia to Paris. This impossible journey is well and excitingly imagined, with a bold blend of credible landscape and sudden allegorical leaps; at one juncture, the squad falls into a giant crack in the earth and finds itself discoursing with a North Vietnamese officer in his web of underground tunnels, from which not even he can escape. But an entirely different kind of game is being played here from the deadly-true account of Vietnam military action, and the picaresque interludes, which take up about half the novel, serve not only as relief from Vietnam but as a kind of excuse from it. At another juncture, with a fine colorful flair that does not omit comedy and shrewd political irony, O'Brien involves his squad of heroes with the Savak—the Iranian security police—and a flamboyant escape and shoot-out and car chase climax the episode as rousingly as in a James Bond movie. Violence is everywhere, O'Brien may be saying; but the effect, when the narrative returns to Vietnam, is that a little Ian Fleming unreality has rubbed off on the real action, and the reader slogs through the paddies waiting for the next bravura display of adventure writing. Violence that did occur, historically and unentertainingly, has been demeaned, lightened. For all its horrors, Tim O'Brien's Vietnam has a precious, bejewelled aspect; as the novel shuttles among its three loci—the actual war, the imagined flight, the long night of Paul Berlin at the observation post—there builds up a slightly insulating lacquer of self-conscious art.

Still, mind has to be present in a book as well as matter, and the ambitious structure of the novel bespeaks an earnest intelligence that wishes to confront a traumatic experience on an ideological and moral level. The fantasized, picaresque thread arrives at the rigorously defined tables of the Paris peace talks, as the student riots progress on television. Paul Berlin, looking handsome and distinguished in "a blue suit with the most subtle pinstripes," delivers a measured rebuttal to the plea of Sarkin Aung Wan, a Vietnamese girl who has accompanied the squad all this way, that he, in effect, desert. He says, "I am afraid of running away. I am afraid of exile. I fear what might be thought of me by those I love. . . . I fear the loss of my own reputation. Reputation, as read in the eyes of my father and mother, the people in my hometown, my friends." Earlier, we have been told of him that "he went to the war for reasons beyond knowledge. Because he believed in law, and law told him to go. Because it was a democracy, after all, and because LBJ and the others had rightful claim to their offices. He went to the war because it was expected." He is of many moods about the war, and this is right, of a war so problematical. But not just this war was problematical, and the faint note of defensiveness—which becomes jarring when a young female "revolutionary," escaping the "evil" of San Diego State by driving a VW van through Europe, is grotesquely caricatured and complacently robbed—does not arise on the realistic level, which deals with scared men trying to survive in a situation they did not create. One of the soldiers reflects, "True, it's sometimes hard to figure out what the hell's going on, but I'll wager that troops at Hastings or the Bulge had the same problem." Or at Troy, if Homer and Euripides are to be believed, or on the slaughtering grounds of World War I, according to Hemingway, to whom Mr. O'Brien owes a debt he does not try to conceal. *A Farewell to Arms* also embodies an idyll of love and escape but on the plane of actuality, and the geopolitical aspects of the war are disposed of in a few bitter sentences:

"What do you think of the war really?" [the hero, Lieutenant Frederic Henry, asks the old diplomat Count Greffi]
"I think it is stupid."
"Who will win it?"
"Italy."
"Why?"
"They are a younger nation."
"Do younger nations always win wars?"
"They are apt to for a time."
"Then what happens?"
"They become older nations."

Compared with O'Brien, Hemingway had a settled conscience, and a single focus. The war, like the death of his heroine in childbirth, was "just a dirty trick." For the author of *Going After Cacciato*, the debate over Vietnam and its concomitant issues (America's civilizing mission, if any; the male citizen's military responsibilities, if any) is an old hornet's nest that still buzzes, and he cannot avoid giving it a poke or two, from the standpoint of one who risked his life in behalf of dubious policies. Yet his essential contrast is not between Vietnam and other wars but between war and peace. "War has its own reality. War kills and maims and rips up the land and makes orphans and widows. These are the things of war. Any war." Whereas peace, Paul Berlin finds in Paris, is elusive in its reality. "He looked for meanings. Peace was shy. That was one lesson: Peace never bragged. If you didn't look for it, it wasn't there." By bringing to the stark facts of war the subtle style of peace, with its layers of ambiguity, O'Brien has written a modern novel classic in its wish to be morally exhaustive, to purge.

Stalled Starters

CHILLY SCENES OF WINTER, by Ann Beattie. 280 pp. Doubleday, 1976.

Ann Beattie's first novel thaws quite beautifully; our first impression, of a pale blank prose wherein events ramify with the random precision of snow-ferns on a winter window, yields, in the second half, to a keen warmth of identification with the hero, Charles, and an ardent admiration of the author's cool powers. Miss Beattie, as readers of her short stories know, works at an unforced pace. Her details—which include the lyrics of the songs her characters overhear on the radio and the recipes of the rather junky food they eat —calmly accrue; her dialogue trails down the pages with an uncanny fidelity to the low-level heartbreaks behind the banal; her resolutely unmetaphorical style builds around us a maze of familiar truths that nevertheless has something airy, eerie, and in the end lovely about it. Her America is like the America one pieces together from the *National Enquirers* that her characters read—a land of pathetic monstrosities, of pain clothed in clichés, of extraterrestrial trivia. Things happen "out there," and their vibes haunt the dreary "here" we all inhabit.

Chilly Scenes of Winter takes place in an unnamed city that must be Washington, D.C.; the slush and sniffles and stalled starters of hibernal megalopolis dampen and chill the book clear through. Charles, who is twenty-seven, works for the government, but for which department or in what function is never explained. He is in love with a woman, Laura, whom he met while she was estranged from her husband, and who has gone back to her husband. He makes contact with her once near the beginning of the book and again near the end. In between, his life is filled with mooning remembrances of her, and with a number of friends and relations who, though real, are ghostly and intermittent in their manifestations to him. His mother, Clara, is mentally unbalanced, given to baths and nudity and psychosomatic pain. His stepfather, Pete, is lonely, awkward, sometimes tipsy, pathetic in his clumsy efforts to win some affection from his stepson, tedious in his addiction to brand-name consumerism and ritual optimism, but withal game, loyal to his mad spouse, and rather winning: a remarkably affectionate and intricate portrait of a very ordinary man. Charles's sister, Susan, is nineteen, stolid, and involved with a pompous medical student, Mark, whose obnoxiousness, we are delicately led to understand, may be largely in Charles's beholding. Also, there is Charles's old girlfriend, Pamela, who has become an unsteady sort of lesbian, given to sudden reversions to heterosexuality and abrupt flights to California and back. And Charles's potential new girlfriend, Betty, a typist with heavy legs and clothes that try too hard; our hero's unsuccessful attempt to launch his heart into an affair with this doughy apparition is one of the saddest repeating jokes in the rueful comedy of his aimless days. And there is his best friend, Sam, who could do cartwheels in grade school and is still good with girls, but who has lost his dog and then his job. And there is Sam's new dog, who is nameless, and has insomnia, and jingles his collar as he paces the floor at night. All these characters, not excluding the dog, are exquisitely modulated studies in vacancy, and grow on the reader like moss. At first, Miss Beattie's unblinking sentences, simple declarative in form and present in tense, remind one of Richard Estes's neo-realist street scenes, which render with a Flemish fineness the crassest dreck of our commercial avenues, omitting no detail save pedestrians. After some pages, her tableaux seem more like Segal's plaster-bandage sculptures, their literal lifelikeness magically muffled in utter whiteness. But then color steals into the cheeks of her personae, a timid Wyeth sort of color at first, the first flush of our caring, and this color deepens, so that her portraits at last appear alive, as likely to make us laugh and cry as any being composed in these thin-blooded times.

Charles and Sam and Pamela mourn for the Sixties. "Everybody's so pathetic," Sam says. "What is it? Is it just the end of the sixties?" Susan, who wasn't there, thinks Woodstock was "a drag. It was nothing but mud." When asked if college kids dance nowadays, she says, "Nobody does much of anything any more. I don't even think there are many drugs on campus." When Bill, Charles's boss, asks him what he should do to "limber up" his Harvard-obsessed son, Charles, recommends, with uncharacteristic firmness, a Janis Joplin record. If the moral limbo of this book has an angel in it, it is Joplin; the characters' tenebrous values point backward to her, to the time of violent feeling and communal ecstasy. The novel's literary patron saint, though, is all Fifties: J. D. Salinger. Not only does Miss Beattie in a kitchen-cabinet inventory echo the epic bathroom-cabinet inventory in "Zooey," she invokes the master's works specifically:

"Remember taking me to the zoo [Laura asks Charles], and how upset I got when I asked what giraffes did for fun and you said, 'How could they do anything?' "

"I should have thought of a nicer answer," he says. "Like the cab driver Holden Caulfield asks about the ducks in winter."

"That's an awful scene," she says.

He gave her *Catcher in the Rye,* and when she liked that he gave her *Nine Stories,* but after she read "A Perfect Day for Bananafish," she couldn't read any more. She even made him take the book back, and she knew that he already had a copy.

If Laura and Charles have a cloying trait, it is their shared "way of feeling sorry for things." She feels sorry for giraffes and even for plants: "Laura buys plants that are dying in supermarkets—ones that have four or five leaves, marked down to nineteen cents, because she feels sorry for them." Charles, as a child, even felt sorry for bobbing-bird toys: "The birds would dip interminably over a glass of water. One night he felt sorry for them because they weren't getting any rest and poured the glass of water on the floor and attached the birds to the empty glass."

Miss Beattie seems to feel sorry for this whole decade. Her range of empathy is broad and even lusty. Her long ninth chapter, taking Charles and Sam out for an evening at a restaurant, where they are joined by a third at-loose-ends young man, called (another *hommage?*) J.D., displays a fearless length of purely male palaver as it goes from lonely and strained to drunken and uproarious. Her depiction of Charles's mother's craziness is chillingly, touchingly right; madness and dreams are areas in fiction where, because almost anything would seem to go, almost nothing does. Miss Beattie's male dreams are good, too:

> That night he dreams that he is launched in a spaceship to the stars. His mother is there. She is taking a bath on a star. He gets back in the rocket. Mechanical failure! That strange jingling! He sits up in bed, eyes wide open. The dog is walking again, his collar jingling. By now it is clear; the dog has insomnia.

And she succeeds in showing love from the male point of view, not in its well-publicized sexual dimension but in the pastel spectrum of nostalgia, daydream, and sentimental longing.

The accretion of plain lived moments, Miss Beattie has discovered, like Virginia Woolf and Nathalie Sarraute before her, is sentiment's very method; grain by grain the hours and days of fictional lives acquire weight. The plot turns a corner, and we feel a pressure behind the eyes. What could appear drier and more fruitless than this flat description of how to serve a meal, one of the novel's frequent obeisances to the daily fact of food:

> Charles lifts the roast out of the oven, puts it on a plate and carries it to the table. He goes back and gets the pan of lima beans, pours most of the water into the sink, and carries the pan to the table. He goes back and turns off the oven and the burner and gets the wine. He takes the wine to the table, where Sam is sitting, then goes to the kitchen for glasses.

But at the book's end another step-by-step description of food processing (how to make an orange soufflé) carries to a delicious consummation nearly three hundred pages of Charles's unsatisfied hungering. Patience pays off for hero and author alike. Not to give it away, but Miss Beattie in the turned-down oven of her indoors Washington has cooked up a rare delicacy, a convincing happy ending.

Frontiersmen

RETURN FROM THE STARS, by Stanislaw Lem, translated from the Polish by Barbara Marszal and Frank Simpson. 247 pp. Harcourt Brace Jovanovich, 1980.

THE LONG HAUL, by Oswaldo França, Jr., translated from the Portuguese by Thomas Colchie. 184 pp. Dutton, 1980.

Hal Bregg, the hero of Stanislaw Lem's *Return from the Stars*, went out from Earth on an astronautical expedition at the age of thirty, and returned at the age of forty a hundred twenty-seven years later. The troubling discrepancy is caused, of course, by that clause of Einstein's relativity laws, well known to concocters of science fiction, which postulates that fast motion slows down time, and very fast motion will slow it down greatly, relative to objects not in such motion. Ten harrowing years adventuring among the stars have passed for Bregg, and more than a century on Earth, during which all his friends have died, the landmarks he knew have vanished, cities have been transformed into translucent, mazy wonderlands, the aggressive instincts within humanity have been biologically exorcised by a process termed "betrization," an anti-gravitational device has been invented and widely installed, and a universal reign of peace and pleasure has been established, with robots doing all the dirty work. The conquistadorial philosophy that sent Bregg and his colleagues out into space has passed from the Earth, and as the surviving astronauts return they occasion as much awkwardness as if a pack of Neanderthal men were resuscitated and set to roaming in Bloomingdale's. Bregg is significantly larger than men have become; long endurance of the extra g's of space travel has left him a monster of muscularity, and after a few days on Earth he grows five more centimeters, as his spine decompresses. Dainty contemporary women, accustomed to the feeble charms of their era's betrized weaklings, are, of course, frightened and fascinated; but though the natives are kind, Bregg can't help feeling—well, *funny.*

Return from the Stars not only is about a time lag but embodies one, for it was published in Poland nineteen years ago. But out of the science and technology of the time Lem has constructed a future that does not, unlike so many hypothetical futures, seem dated. In this brave new world, circa 2127, people spray their clothes on out of a can. Books have been boiled down to corn-size crystals that can be played either by optons (which reproduce the written text) or by lectons (which read it aloud); original books are called "crystomatrices." The cinema has been replaced by the "real," which projects three-dimensional images that grow larger and more intense wherever the viewer directs his attention; a "realist" is a "real" star. Money is no longer needed for essentials; even where luxuries and antiques are concerned, it doesn't change hands but is deducted from binary computers ("calsters") carried around in lieu of wallets. Women wear red in their nostrils, and cover their ears with scalloplike ornaments. Giant television screens on ceilings underground mimic sky and clouds. Immense floating platforms ("rasts") move people about in the inner city; longer local distances are negotiated by "gleeders," which are windowless, wheel-less cars "like huge black drops of liquid"; and for continental or global trips one takes handy little rockets called "ulders"—"the impression was of flying in an armchair mounted inside a large glass." These elegant extensions of our present technology (less fantastic, surely, than our present autos, airplanes, escalators, and computers would appear to a visitor from 1830) are detailed by the author with a tireless gusto; the manner in which the new world bewilderingly and dazzlingly envelops the star-worn space traveller—like a mixture of airport, amusement park, and Roman bath—is brilliantly imagined, as are the incidents of galactic travel. Lem loves exposition, and devotes pages to the mock-history of betrization, to the hardware of his hero's space flight (conceived eight years before the moon landing), to the chimerical developments of mathematics:

". . . what Mirea and Averin did with the legacy of Cantor, you know. Operations using infinite, transfinite quantities, the continua of discrete increments, strong . . . it was wonderful." . . .

"You haven't heard of Igalli's studies, I suppose?"

"No, what are they?"

"The theory of the discontinuous antipole."

"I don't know anything about an antipole. What is it?"

"Retronihilation. From this came parastatics."

"I never even heard of these terms."

"Of course, for it originated sixty years ago. But that was only the beginning of gravitology."

"I can see that I will have to do some homework," I said.

To make a long theory short: Emil Mitke, "a crippled genius," has done "with the theory of relativity what Einstein had done with Newton." Out of his "infernal mathematics" it has been possible to create a "black box" that will release a "gravitational antifield" whenever gravity might be precipitating misfortune. Lem knows

STANISLAW LEM : 571

when to surfeit us with details and when to finesse. Of these marvellous black boxes he smoothly assures us, "The simplicity of their construction was as astounding as the complexity of the theory that produced them." About the process of betrization he is more specific: "Betrization acted on the developing prosencephalon at an early stage in life by means of a group of proteolytic enzymes." Lem is frequently droll. Alluding to the anachronisms that no doubt stud our own historical dramas, he describes a real in which "the hero seated himself on the tails of his jacket and drank beer through a straw." A robot dump is imagined in which the discarded machines, the slaves of this sybaritic empire, murmur among themselves in accents of Christian conspiracy: "Behold the last efforts of the strutting croaking master of quartering and incarceration, for yea it riseth, thrice riseth the coming kingdom of the nonliving. . . ." To the robots, men are "the dough-headed": "And the dough-headed took their acid fermentation for a soul, the stabbing of meat for history, the means of postponing their decay for civilization. . . ."

As long as Lem plays the genial host with his riches of erudition and bids us sit down in a spirit of festive speculation, we are flattered and entertained; his attempt to cater to us with a mundane novel of psychology and eros, however, is relatively clumsy. And this attempt tends to dominate the latter pages of the book, after Lem has exhausted, for the time being, his store of ideas on scientific and social trends. Hal Bregg, as a romantic hero, makes those gruff ladykillers played by Robert Mitchum and Richard Widmark look courtly. When Nais, his feline first conquest, calls up for a reprise, their conversation ends:

> "Let's not end it this way. . . ."
> "We're not ending a thing," I said, "because nothing ever began. Thanks for everything, Nais."

Of his second conquest, the beautiful realist Aen Aenis, Bregg reflects, "I embraced her, and it was awful, because I wanted to and I didn't want to." His third, the very poignant Eri, he propositions with a bear hug and some blunt prophecy:

"I am going to carry you off."

"What?"

"Yes. Carry you off. You don't want to be?"

"No."

"No matter. I am. Do you know why?"

"I guess."

"You don't. I don't."

The basic situation is well conceived: this man from an earlier century finds everything "uncomfortably soft," and in turn is viewed as overmuscled and grotesquely aggressive. The philosophical/psychological question is posed by the hero when he decides that "this destruction of the killer in man was a disfigurement." His old co-pilot Olaf puts it, "They have killed the man in man." But the idea spins itself out in too much halting dialogue, and the introduction of a final plot complication—a new expedition to the stars, which Olaf but not Hal has been invited to join —does not move us as much as the author's musclebound language indicates that it should. His hero seems a bit brutal and thick even to us of the unbetrized present, and the pioneer heroism of human space exploration a bit quaint, especially now that robot satellites are doing so well. Hal Bregg recalls that in space flight, as one hung there "seemingly motionless in relation to the stars," novels came to appear silly: "To read that some Peter nervously puffed his cigarette and was worried about whether or not Lucy would come, and that she walked in and twisted her gloves, well, first you began to laugh at this like an idiot, and then you simply saw red." In the flight of the imagination that Lem engineers, some similar affliction overtakes his narrative: normal, irrational, egotistic, venereal human behavior, such as has aroused our respectful empathy in a hundred less intelligent books, seems silly, and a kind of imposition upon the universe. We find ourselves wishing that Lem would write a novel about the revolt of the robots against the dough-headed, so we could root for the robots.

This could not have been an easy novel to translate, with its many abstruse considerations and its words coined in Polish. The author, too, had to translate, not just into the future but onto this continent, for the unnamed nation that Hal Bregg returns to is located on the territory of the present United States. Asking at a travel agency for a vacation spot "within a radius of a thousand kilometers," he is sent to Clavestra, "an old mining settlement near the Pacific," which puts the metropolitan Terminal somewhere west of Salt Lake City—say, in Elko, Nevada. A small slip occurs when Hal asks Eri, "Have you seen the Grand Canyon, in Colorado?" Though the river is the Colorado, the canyon gapes, of course, in Arizona. And it seems unlikely that the transformations in vegetation and human stature that Lem describes could have evolved within the span of less than two centuries. The novel's central concern with the instinct of aggression reflects a topical interest of its time; our Eighties are more apt to wonder what undeclared energy source is powering all this vast and servile machinery in the year 2127. On the whole, though, Lem knits his hypothetical world together with an abundance and rigor more than visionary, and approaching the close-woven texture of naturalism. It is encouraging, we might add, and perhaps a souvenir from 1961, that a Polish writer operating in the shadow of the considerable Soviet school of science fiction should locate the future here in America.

The Long Haul, by Oswaldo França, Jr., is a short novel that, when published in Brazil in 1967, enjoyed considerable success, winning that country's most important literary prize, the Prêmio Walmap, and kind words from Jorge Amado. It concerns the trip of eight red flatbed trucks loaded with thirty tons of sacks of corn from the Rio-Bahia Interstate near Caratinga to Belo Horizonte, in the interior of Brazil, in a season of heavy rains that have washed out many of the roads. The story is narrated in a casual, colloquial manner by the leader of the expedition, a driver and mechanic called Jorge. The Portuguese title of the novel, *Jorge, um Brasileiro,* unlike the slangy American title, centers the novel solemnly upon its hero, Jorge, a Brazilian—that is to say, an *exemplary* Brazilian, a doer, a pioneer.

The popularity of this book, for many of its pages a virtual manual of truck malfunction and road repair, must lie in its qualities of vernacular epic; as in *Huckleberry Finn, You Know Me Al,* and *On the Road,* a participant in the national adventure unassumingly yarns his part in a grand and pluralistic saga. The development of the interior of Brazil, construed by liberal North Americans in terms of Indian decimation and ecological disaster, is unself-consciously felt by Jorge as an entirely wholesome adventure—its highways beautiful, the transport of goods heroic. *The Long Haul* is a late contribution to the extensive literature—from the Venezuelan Rómulo Gallegos's *Doña Barbara* to the Argentinian Ricardo Güiraldes's *Don Segundo Sombra*—of the South American frontier. Protestant guilt made small inroads in this vast locale. The Indians, who figure on the whole poignantly in North American frontier literature and cinema, do not touch Jorge: "I never saw such a pig of an Indian. I swear to God, the old military shirt he wore was so filthy it was stiff. . . . His wife wore an old, filthy dress to cover herself, torn all over, and she painted her body with some kind of dye that stank like you wouldn't believe." And the jungle, the last great rain forest intact on the planet, falls exhilaratingly: "Every one of us worked night and day together, seeing that strip of highway nose right through the jungle. Of course why wouldn't you want to work? Nothing else to do out in that godforsaken jungle."

Pioneer Man, as represented by Jorge, loves his work:

> And off we went, into the jungle, with me feeling happy as a clam, feeling downright glad about so many difficulties lying ahead.

> But I frankly didn't give a damn what it did anymore; raining, making you cold, wetting everything and anything. What was on my mind was that road ahead of us and being able to get to Belo by the day Mr. Mario had said.

Pioneer Man, as represented by Jorge and Bregg, braves discomfort:

> Even wrapped up in strips of cloth, my hand began to burn with broken blisters and I had to hold tight on to the handle of the spade so as not to let it slip on me. Our backs started killing us too, and we began changing places with one another.

You kind of got used to seeing everything soaking wet after a while; your cigarettes soggy, your hands always dirty, and your feet all caked with mud. Christ, our shoes alone must have weighed about ten kilos apiece.

. . . I saw Arcturus, the mountains of fire over which I had flown, teeth chattering from the cold, while the frost of the cooling equipment, melting, ran red with rust down my suit.   [*Return from the Stars*]

Pioneer Man treasures his fellows:

That guy could fix anything, and stay in a good mood while he was doing it. And all the time he'd keep running a comb through his hair, which must have been the softest, best-looking head of hair I ever saw. He was that type of guy. You were happy just to have him around, working with you.

So they turned around and drove back into town to find Altair, because he was a pal who never let you down when you needed a favor. The kind of person you could count on, and always so good-natured, with a first-class business, and very conscientious about it, too. So who wouldn't want to help a guy like that?

Because each one of us was priceless, human life had the highest value where it could have none, where such a thin, practically nonexistent film separated it from annihilation.   [*Return from the Stars*]

Pioneer Man is a rough lover. Hal Bregg takes Eri by force from her husband; Jorge thrusts his tongue into the mouth ("I tell you I never kissed a woman as hard as that") of his boss's wife. Pioneer Man is unworthily employed. Hal Bregg returns from the stars to find that a race of ungrateful sissies has supplanted his own generation; Jorge returns from his epic journey through the mud and jungle to confront an obese accountant demanding receipts and complaining about "all that delay" to "just bring a few trucks from the Rio-Bahia Interstate back to Belo Horizonte." Pioneer Man becomes obsolete and, one way or another, resigns. A sad story, twice told, in these two exotic novels from the Sixties, when frontiers were still spoken of.

BARTHES, BERLIN, CIORAN

Roland Barthes

S/Z, by Roland Barthes, translated from the French by Richard Miller.
217 pp. Hill & Wang, 1974.

THE PLEASURE OF THE TEXT, by Roland Barthes, translated from the
French by Richard Miller. 67 pp. Hill & Wang, 1975.

The *nouveau roman* required its *nouveaux critiques;* Roland
Barthes first attracted notice in 1954, as defender of the then little-
known, and scarcely published, Alain Robbe-Grillet. During the
1960s, Barthes achieved notoriety by engaging, after the publica-
tion of his book *On Racine* (1963), in a bitter and spirited public
debate with such relatively old-fashioned critics as Raymond Pi-
card, whose attack on Barthes bore the title "Nouvelle critique ou
nouvelle imposture?" His intellectual journey has touched on a
number of requisite Gallic checkpoints; he moved from Existential-
ism and Marxism to the "psychoanalysis of substances" and the
linguistic theories of Ferdinand de Saussure, and he has lately
associated himself with the "new" anthropology of Claude Lévi-
Strauss. Barthes is not only an exponent of the postwar moderns
but a writer on such French classics as Racine, Sade, Fourier, and
Michelet. He has composed some utterly dry and technical works
on semiology (the science of signs) as well as highly entertaining
journalistic essays upon subjects ranging from Dutch painting to
the movies, from the personality of plastic to the mystique of wine.

In this country (his passage into print eased, perhaps, by his euphonic association with Barth and Barthelme), Barthes has been favored by the publication of six of his books by Hill & Wang, including several very slim and abstruse ones, and of a collection of his essays by Northwestern University Press. To Susan Sontag, our glamorous camp follower of the French avant-garde, he is "a man of prodigious learning, unflagging mental energy, and acutely original sensibility," and to Frank Kermode, the prince of British critics, "Roland Barthes is without visible rival, the most interesting, fertile, and ambitious critic now writing." The publication, in strikingly well-designed volumes, of *S/Z* and *The Pleasure of the Text* (both translated by Richard Miller and introduced by Richard Howard) gives the American reader an opportunity to appraise a figure who, at the age of sixty, is in his own intellectual milieu indisputably charismatic and commanding.

S/Z is a nearly unreadable book about reading, a two-hundred-page crawl through a thirty-page story by Balzac, a "*decomposition* (in the cinematographic sense) of the work of reading: a *slow motion,* so to speak, neither wholly image nor wholly analysis." The short story, entitled "Sarrasine," is broken up into "brief, contiguous fragments, which we shall call *lexias*"; these units range from a phrase to several paragraphs in length. They are annotated, in busy ten-point medleys of italics, stars, and caps, according to a system of five "codes," or "voices," very forgettably specified as "the Voice of Empirics (the proairetisms), the Voice of the Person (the semes), the Voice of Science (the cultural codes), the Voice of Truth (the hermeneutisms), the Voice of Symbol." Between the ten-point sections, essays in eleven-point type more expansively speculate and comment on such matters as symbolic patterns, narrative suspense, historical background, and cultural biases. Five hundred sixty-one *lexias* are thus illumined. The reader emerges, as from that imaginary machine of Kafka's which engraved commandments upon the transgressor's skin, lexically enriched but lacerated; I cannot remember another book ostensibly in the English language which gave me such pains to peruse. Barthes says elsewhere, of good prose, that "it grates, it cuts," and his own vocabulary is a gnashing, flashing compound of Greek ("anastomosis," "tmesis," "syntagmatic," "proairetic"), terms lifted from modern linguistics ("closure," "signifier," "seme"), and common words ("code," "myth") recoined with a specific and not easily grasped meaning. His style is dense, terse, nervous, parenthetical, sometimes arch, and faintly insolent. He seems often to be recapitulating something we should have read elsewhere but haven't. He appropriates to the language of literary criticism a certain pseudo-mathematical sharpness. His method, in *S/Z*, of moving by crabbed jerks through an after all rather melodramatic and romantic tale produced in this reviewer sensations of forestallment and obstruction so oppressive that relief chronically manifested itself in the form of an irresistible doze and, once, of an absolving dyspepsia.

Such a confession of readerly discomfort is appropriate here, for Barthes insists, in these two books, on the supremacy of "readerly" *(lisible)* over "writerly" *(scriptible)* literature. Prefacing his exposition of codes and significations in the Balzac story, he states that "We call any readerly text a classic text," and "To interpret a text is not to give it a (more or less justified, more or less free) meaning, but on the contrary to appreciate what *plural* constitutes it. . . . In this ideal text, the networks are many and interact, without any one of them being able to surpass the rest; this text is a galaxy of signifiers, not a structure of signifieds; it has no beginning; it is reversible; we gain access to it by several entrances, none of which can be authoritatively declared to be the main one."

The interaction between the never ideal reader and the infinitely various text is more concretely, and playfully, elaborated in *The Pleasure of the Text.* Skipping, for instance, weaves itself into a "rhythm of what is read and what is not read that creates the pleasure of the great narratives: has anyone ever read Proust, Balzac, *War and Peace* word for word?" Traditional explicative criticism assumes a text from which all blemishes of inattention or miscomprehension have been removed by close study; pure text is left. Barthes, contrariwise, rejoices in the irregularities of the reading process: "Thus, what I enjoy in a narrative is not directly its content or even its structure, but rather the abrasions I impose upon the fine surface: I read on, I skip, I look up, I dip in again."

Amusingly but not frivolously, he personifies the text; it seduces, yearns: "The text you write must prove to me *that it desires me.*" In *S/Z*, the text of Balzac's story, struggling to maintain its suspense, writhes like a criminal: "This shows us that the discourse is trying to lie *as little as possible:* just what is required to ensure the interests of reading, that is, its own survival." Barthes's detection of a multiplicity of levels in the transparent area where text and reader interact goes so far, in one brilliant annotation, as to detect the reader himself speaking in a phrase ("as though terror-struck") that neither the narrator nor the perceiving character could logically have produced:

> It is the reader who is concerned that the truth be simultaneously named and evaded, an ambiguity which the discourse nicely creates by *as though*, which indicates the truth and yet reduces it declaratively to mere appearance. What we hear, therefore, is the *displaced* voice which the reader lends, by proxy, to the discourse: the discourse is speaking according to the reader's interests. Whereby we see that writing is not the communication of a message which starts from the author and proceeds to the reader; it is specifically the voice of reading itself: *in the text, only the reader speaks.*

Where other critics probe for the symbolic or ideological secrets of a work, Barthes, as businesslike as an editor, demonstrates an intimate concern with the verbal manipulation of suspense and such workaday details as the fiction's chronology. His feel for the labor of tale-telling produces a surprising simile, even more surprisingly extended:

> The text, while it is being produced, is like a piece of Valenciennes lace created before us under the lacemaker's fingers: each sequence undertaken hangs like the temporarily inactive bobbin waiting while its neighbor works; then, when its turn comes, the hand takes up the thread again. . . . Each thread, each code, is a voice; these braided—or braiding —voices form the writing. . . . We know the symbolism of the braid: Freud, considering the origin of weaving, saw it as the labor of a woman braiding her pubic hairs to form the absent penis. The text, in short, is a fetish; and to reduce it to the unity of meaning, by a deceptively univocal reading, is to *cut the braid,* to sketch the castrating gesture.

Whether or not Freud was correct in supposing females to feel the lack of a penis keenly enough to braid themselves one (a custom rarely observed along the Eastern Seaboard), Barthes's critical approach seems specifically manly—insisting on readerly activity rather than passivity and ever reminding itself (in this Barthes remains, as he began, a Marxist critic) that reading is a transaction, an economic exchange. When, summing up, he seeks to describe classic literature as "Replete Literature," his metaphors for repletion gravitate toward the homely, the housewifely: "literature that is replete: like a cupboard where meanings are shelved, stacked, safeguarded . . . like a pregnant female, replete with signifieds which criticism will not fail to deliver. . . ."

The next sentence in this passage asserts, "Replete Literature, readerly literature, can no longer be written." Why not? Why must there be a *nouveau roman,* and *nouveaux critiques?* This question, the end product of Barthes's ingenious critical discourse, is raised in *S/Z* but not answered. Replete Literature, which ends, in his view, with Flaubert, is "mortally stalked by the army of stereotypes it contains." Why a crisis irreversibly arose at a specific time in history is sketched by Barthes in his first book, *Writing Degree Zero* (1953). Classical writing began in France with the ascendency of bourgeois ideals over the doctrines of the *ancien régime* in the middle of the seventeenth century and survived the apparent disruptions of Romanticism and the Revolution.

> The Revolution changed nothing in bourgeois writing, and . . . there is only a slight difference between the writing of, say, Fénelon and Mérimée. This is because bourgeois ideology remained intact until 1848 without being in the least shaken by a Revolution which gave the bourgeoisie political and social power, although not the intellectual power, which it had long held.

By the 1850s, however, according to Barthes, the rise in Europe of modern industrial capitalism had created another social class— the proletariat. The bourgeois writer, until then "sole judge of other people's woes and without anyone else to gaze on him," thenceforth is "torn between his social condition and his intellec-

ROLAND BARTHES : 581

tual vocation" and "falls prey to ambiguity, since his consciousness
no longer accounts for the whole of his condition."

In *Mythologies* (1957; reprinted in 1970), Barthes is hard
pressed to explain why, at this late date, bourgeois myths, odious
and stale as they are, seem to be the only ones around; myths of
the left, he admits, are "poverty-stricken," "barren," "meagre,"
"clumsy"—the Stalin myth, for instance. As a critic dissecting
from the standpoint of the left the "well-fed, sleek, expansive,
garrulous" myths of the bourgeois right, he detects in his role an
emptiness, a mere destructiveness. "The mythologist is con-
demned to live in a theoretical sociality. . . . His connection with
the world is of the order of sarcasm." The same intelligence that
permits Barthes to see through—as a psychologist sees through
neuroses, an anthropologist through taboos—the bourgeois myths
or codes, whether in the advertisements of *Elle* or in the sen-
tences of Balzac, exposes to his vision the mysterious negativity,
the terrible thinness, of the revolutionary alternative. Within the
horizons of the Western world, bourgeois myths are in possession
of reality: wine, for instance, exists; its reality is not erased by the
myths that France and its wine industry impose upon it. Goading
himself to supply the revolutionary counter-world to the nauseat-
ingly rich world of "myth-consumers," Barthes quotes a "strange
saying" of Saint-Just: "What constitutes the Republic is the total
destruction of what is opposed to it." A savage tautology whose
proven meaning is tyranny and terrorism, and whose meaning to
Barthes remains unclear.

The Pleasure of the Text—even after Richard Howard has ex-
plained, in his introduction to its sixty-seven aphoristic, coquettish
pages, the untranslatable sexual connotations of *"jouir"*—affords
slight, as well as brief, pleasure. Paragraphs, called by Howard
proses, are arranged in alphabetical order of topic (*Affirmation,
Babel, Babil, Bords, Brio, Clivage*, etc.)—a tour de force that does not
much encourage, either, any sense of developing flow or overall
theme. Barthes's subtlety seems to please itself in a vacuum; there
are not enough concrete instances of textual pleasure. When one
is cited, it is often an author's lapse, a "gap":

We read a text (of pleasure) the way a fly buzzes around a room: with sudden deceptively decisive turns, fervent and futile: ideology passes over the text and its reading like the blush over a face. . . . Every writer of pleasure has these idiotic blushes (Balzac, Zola, Flaubert, Proust: only Mallarmé, perhaps, is master of his skin). . . .

Still far too much heroism in our languages; in the best—I am thinking of Bataille's—an erethism of certain expressions and finally a kind of insidious heroism. The pleasure of the text (the bliss of the text) is on the contrary like a sudden obliteration of the warrior *value,* a momentary desquamation of the writer's hackles, a suspension of the "heart" (of courage).

The second quotation is a complete *prose* and a fair specimen of Barthes's rather foppish style of insight and expression here. He finds bliss *(jouissance)* in the odd words "horodeictic" and "fractive" coined by Leibniz and in certain moments of "pure representation" by Stendhal and Flaubert, who enumerate foodstuffs and tell us how clothes are attached to clotheslines by clothespins. The bliss of skipping is extolled, and even boredom becomes a kind of bliss: "it is bliss seen from the shores of pleasure." One cannot help but feel that the authors so whimsically cherished are being condescended to and impudently pillaged. Barthes licenses himself, and us, to roam among the classics as an atheist roams in nature, free to be amused where he will, without any thought of a Creator's intention.

This last sentence of mine, of course, holds a number of deliberately offended presumptions, such as that great books are a serious business and that a work of art has a single intention. Barthes's scattered, playful aperçus in search of "pleasure" are, like his rigorous analysis of *S/Z,* a way of combatting the "deceptively univocal reading" that castrates. *The Pleasure of the Text* is a little flirt of a text, but she ends splayed by a hearty assault of sexual imagery from Barthes, who demands to hear, as he reads, "the grain of the throat, the patina of consonants, the voluptuousness of vowels, a whole carnal stereophony"; who asks writing to be "as fresh, supple, lubricated, delicately granular and vibrant as an animal's muzzle"; who defines his critical lust as the wish to admit "the anonymous body of the actor into my ear." Such is his bliss; such is the strenuous relationship he proposes between the literate and literature. Strenuous yet fruitless of discriminations. The muzzle that his own prose presses at our ear smiles a little curiously, even smirks, as does the author's photograph on the back of these two jackets. Barthes compels our respect more by what he demands than by what he delivers. His criticism lacks only the quality of inspiring trust. He teaches us to see multiple layers of reader-writer interaction hovering above every page; above his own pages there is, faint but obscuring, a frosted layer of irony that blurs opus and commentary into a single plane.

Texts and Men

SADE/FOURIER/LOYOLA, by Roland Barthes, translated from the French by Richard Miller. 184 pp. Hill & Wang, 1976.

VICO AND HERDER, by Isaiah Berlin. 216 pp. Viking Press, 1976.

Some immortals are more so than others. Plato hangs in the sky conspicuous and immutable as Deneb; other names wink at the edge of visibility, crowded by historical overpopulation into a shadowy word-game status, best known for having once been better known. Five such secondary luminaries—St. Ignatius of Loyola (1491–1556), Giovanni Battista Vico (1668–1744), Donatien Alphonse François, Comte de Sade, commonly called the Marquis (1740–1814), Johann Gottfried von Herder (1744–1803), and François Marie Charles Fourier (1772–1837)—are the subjects of these two compositely titled volumes. Contemporary intellectual currents flow unevenly around the five subjects: Vico and Sade might be said to be fashionable; Loyola got a hammerlock on history by founding the Jesuits; the two figures closest to us in time—Herder and Fourier—are the dimmest in our perspectives, though the latter's scandalously blithe utopian schemes were once taken seriously here, by Horace Greeley among others, and Fourierist communities were attempted as far and wide as Texas and New Jersey. Not only does no wave of timely interest compel these studies (Isaiah Berlin's book originated in lectures given in 1957–58 and in 1964; Roland Barthes's is assembled of articles composed during the last decade) but in neither is any thesis of mutual influence urged. The title pages emphasize discreteness; Barthes's lists the names without connectives, as did the original Hogarth Press edition of *Vico and Herder,* which is noncommittally subtitled *Two Studies in the History of Ideas.* Though Herder read Vico, it was after Herder's main ideas were formed and promulgated, and anyway, Berlin says, "one wonders whether he ever more than merely glanced at his work." As for the three others, Fourier is claimed to have read Sade, and Sade, of course, blasphemed within the Catholic tradition of which St. Ignatius is a part; but nothing so dreary as ideological content is at issue. The "theoretical intent of these studies," according to Barthes, is "the displacement . . . of the text's social responsibility." His three so disparate authors are considered as "Logothetes, founders of language": "It is not a matter of taking into ourselves the contents, convictions, a faith, a cause, nor even images; it is a matter of receiving from the text a kind of fantasmatic order."

> It makes little difference how their style is judged, good, bad, or indifferent: they persist, never stop the weighing and elaborating operation; as the style is absorbed in the writing, the system disintegrates into systematics, the novel into novelistic, prayer into fantasmatic: Sade is no longer an erotic, Fourier no longer a utopian, Loyola no longer a saint: all that is left in each of them is a scenographer: he who disperses himself across the framework he sets up and arranges *ad infinitum.*

Though Professor Berlin seems a more traditional critic of the past than Professor Barthes, delineating painstakingly the sinews and veins of ideational content, he, too, chooses the image of writing to link Vico and Herder, who were separately able "to read the symbols with which societies and civilizations express themselves as a graphologist reads handwriting." Both groupings of studies are united not by any substantial interplay of the subjects but by an act of the authors—the act of recognition which perceives a likeness. Both books are exercises in constellation-making—an intellectual game that soothes our nervous modern sensation of dissociation and scatter.

Barthes's critical triplet (translated from the French by Richard Miller, who renders the author's idiosyncratic locutions with a growing intelligibility and charm) may be the best introduction to Barthes's work now in English. Not so arid as his treatise on semiology or his relentlessly semiological explication of Balzac's "Sarrasine" and not so breezy and arch as *Mythologies* or *The Pleasure of the Text, Sade/Fourier/Loyola* shows his deliberately superficial technique of analysis attaching itself to texts that in their perverse strangeness arouse in him something like affection, and in the reader of his exegeses a corresponding happiness. For Barthes's mind to display itself with such contagious animation it was perhaps necessary that the texts be, though historically prestigious, negligible at the level of personal intellectual engagement. There can be little question of his, or our, following Loyola into sainthood, or Sade into sadism, or Fourier into utopia. The texts have the sort of discreditability which Barthes relishes; he finds bliss in the very vacuity of languages founded "precisely in order to say nothing, to observe a vacancy," each set of coinages admirable not through any meaningful signification but "precisely because it hangs together well."

The three authors share, he tells us, passions for isolation (Loyola's retreat cells, Sade's hermetic orgy sites, Fourier's self-sustaining phalansteries of exactly sixteen hundred twenty persons), for enumeration and classification, "for cutting up (the body of Christ, the body of the victim, the human soul)," for ordering and ritual and planning, for the theatrical. The elements of Sade's language are, of course, bodies—organs and orifices arranged in *tableaux vivants,* in impossible pleasure machines of flesh that function, Barthes points out, in silence: "This silence is the silence of the libidinous machine, so well oiled, brought to such easy efficiency that we can distinguish only a few sighs, quiverings." These machines are, as it were, sentences, whose components Sade never wearies of rearranging, in a French of notable correctness and grammatical "tact." The elements of Fourier's language are less easily construed. Barthes enjoys the "insane" calculations in the utopian's airily unpragmatic programs for a Harmony that if effected "would be hell itself" and that in attempted effectuation proved "doomed to instant fiasco"; but it remains unclear how this language of fraction and multiplication, "free from any referential illusion," in its "vast madness . . . permutates" and "goes beyond system and attains systematics, i.e., writing." Fourier's infectious detail-spinning drives Barthes's own writing to prodigies of profuse articulation, such as a single sentence punctuated by seven colons, three parentheses, eight pairs of quotation marks, and thirteen commas.

Loyola's *Exercises,* an ancient and, one would think, tedious manual of regulated devotions for a four-week retreat, provokes Barthes's most striking and cogent analysis. The Saint's prescribed regulation of the exercitant's every waking minute is seen "to determine what might be called a field of exclusion. The tight organization of time . . . allows for the day to be completely *covered,* to cover over any interstice in it through which an outside word might come; to be repellent, the day must be joined together so perfectly that Ignatius recommends beginning the future tense even before the present tense has been exhausted: in going to sleep, think already of my awakening." The Saint's emphasis on inner visualization (of Christ's person, of specific Biblical scenes) is understood as an attempt, at the historical moment when the ear yielded to the eye as the "perceptive sense *par excellence,* " to create an orthodox vocabulary of image, an "image linguistics" over and against the languageless religious experience of the mystics. The numerical obsession inculcated by the *Exercises* (an accountancy that "cannot be completely foreign to the new capitalist ideology") creates "between the sinner and the countless number of his sins a narcissistic bond of property." Loyola's manual, written for the directors of retreats, is a multiple text whose final act of communication is to set up a language whereby the Divinity can speak to the exercitant. The language is binary: prayer offers God a choice, and the exercitant resolves himself into an equipoise of indifference. Ignatius writes, "I must be indifferent . . . so as not to be either more inclined or attached to taking what is offered me than to leaving it . . . I must be like the needle of a scale." God tips the scale, then, with subtle signs (tears, inner states, visions), of which the subtlest is the withholding of a sign altogether. Zero, that is, enters the language constructed for the Divinity to speak: "The divine vacuum can no longer threaten, alter, or decentralize the plenitude which is part of every closed language."

As far as I know, criticism so theoretical yet apprehensive, so lofty in its overview yet so piquant in the details it seizes upon, so adroit at coaxing the classics to turn their faces to the light of a radical new aesthetic, is a triumph peculiarly Gallic. By comparison, American criticism seems leaden, carping, and timid.

Isaiah Berlin offers the reader a British texture. His pages on Vico and Herder have kept much of a lecture's orotundity, confidingly inflected circumspection, and helpful (in case we sneezed, or came in late) repetitiveness. Like T. S. Eliot, Berlin is a master of what Barthes designates as "paralypse"—"the rhetorical figure that consists in stating what one is not going to say." For example, "I wish to confine myself, so far as possible (and at times it is not), to what is truly original in Herder's views, and by no means to all of this . . ." Or "I have not attempted to trace the origins of these ideas, save in a somewhat tentative fashion, nor to give an account of the historical or social circumstances in which they were conceived, nor their precise role in the *Weltanschauung* of the age, or even that of the thinkers themselves." The same scholarly gesture, a solemn covering of one's flanks, directs the prose again and again into rather wearying series: "In Vico's conception man is not distinguishable from the actual process of his development—at once physical, moral, intellectual, spiritual, and, equally, social, political, artistic"; "The relationship between what men 'make' and the laws and categories which govern their operations, like the related tension between value and fact, human purpose and the nature of things, freedom and determinism, action and 'the given' . . ." Whereas Barthes disregards the ostensible message of his authors in order to "listen to the message's transport," Berlin offers what often seems a laborious paraphrase.

It was Vico's genius to suspend certain judgments of the Enlightenment and to propose the idea of culture. We can best know what we create, and men create aggregations of law, myth, institutions, and works of art that form serviceable wholes. The legends and monuments of early men were not the "absurd fantasies of helpless primitives, or deliberate inventions designed to delude"; they were "natural ways of conveying a coherent view of the world as it was seen, and interpreted." Men of later cultures can, through an effort of historical understanding, enter into these remote social processes in a way that they cannot enter into the workings of the non-human world. It remained for Herder, who was born the year Vico died, and was not directly influenced by him, to state the ultimate implication of cultural relativism: all cultures are equally valid, and there is no such thing as the perfect civilization. "This is perhaps the sharpest blow ever delivered against the classical philosophy of the West, to which the notion of perfection—the possibility, at least in principle, of universal, timeless solutions of problems of value—is essential." The reader hovers, in the course of Berlin's exposition, between two kinds of excitement: the excitement of Vico's ideas themselves, which are by now thoroughly absorbed in our own cultural equipment, and that of the modern historian's tracing, in the web of Western historiography, their origins and subsequent influences. These are tenuous. Vico's theses apparently lay fallow until their discovery, and exuberant misapplication, by the French historian Michelet a century later. Discussing their antecedents, Professor Berlin pulls many a dusty name from the library of his mind:

> Indeed [Vico] blames Grotius, for example (and could have criticized Bodin), for offering principles which are not "necessary," but merely probable and "verisimilar," whereas the true constituents or "elements of history" can be established with absolute certainty—in the manner of Plato rather than Bacon. Are these "elements" the categories, the basic relationships, presupposed by historical thinking—an application of Kant's transcendental logic *avant la lettre*—as Jacobi thought?

He shows a power of creative assemblage mostly toward the end, when, in a piece of original speculation, Vico's relativism is linked to the forgotten disputes of sixteenth-century jurists as they sought to recover Roman law in its presumed purity from its medieval and Byzantine accretions. Vico was "above all, a legal scholar preoccupied with the history of jurisprudence" and thus likely familiar with the textual studies, carried forward primarily in France, by legalists like Baudouin and Budé and Dumoulin and Hotman, that produced, in Berlin's account, such an arresting result: "The more faithfully the despised medieval accumulation was removed, the stranger the classical world appeared: if anything, it was the alleged monkish distortions that gave it such affinity to the ideas of later ages as it once seemed to have." Here, in the researches of once heated controversy, lie the seeds of a historical relativism; the scholars themselves, though without the generalizing power of a Vico, were brought to perceive that languages and institutions have "their beginnings, progress, corruption, end." And here, in a set of warmed-over lectures that breathe a stale air of recapitulation, glitters a brilliant exercise of knowledge, a plausible collation of obscure texts that enables us to enter into the intellectual adventures and horizons of the Renaissance as no instancing less concrete could do. Vico himself said, in a sentence chosen as an epigraph to this book, "The useful historians are not those who give general descriptions of facts and explain them by reference to general conditions, but those who go into the greatest detail and reveal the particular cause of each event."

His lust for particularity, though it led Vico into all sorts of incorrectly specific suppositions, is the heart of his vitalism and of his value now. What are we, after all, to make of the great men we inherit, with their outworn theories and weighty oeuvres—a veritable debris of greatness, as overwhelming as all the other wastelands of disposable containers? We can, like Barthes, treat their texts and their lives indiscriminately, as raw material for a new kind of connoisseurship, an elegant and amused examination that from vast fields of dispersed energy plucks a few " 'biographemes' whose distinction and mobility might go beyond any fate and come to touch, like Epicurean atoms, some future body, destined to the same dispersion." For example, "Sade's white muff, Fourier's flowerpots, Ignatius's Spanish eyes." Or we may follow, with Berlin, a delineation of great men as knots, loci of special confluence and intensity within the onflowing "history of ideas." Though such an approach appears solidly respectful and, as it were, anatomical—listing names, dates, books, significant conversations (Herder talks to Goethe, Hawthorne talks to Melville; result: greatness)—the men in question evaporate even more thoroughly than in Barthes's fey distillations. For if ideas have an evolution, they will evolve regardless of the minds that momentarily carry them. By the description of Professor Berlin's own book, Vico left behind him a few unread treatises and a strictly local reputation; Herder, arriving at some of the same ideas without any direct awareness of Vico, fathered German nationalism and the Romantic movement. His time was ripe; Vico was premature—an inventor, like da Vinci, in advance of the available technology. When this reviewer was a child, inventors were still presented as great men, almost all of whom happened to be American: Fulton and the steamboat, Bell and the telephone, Edison and the light bulb, Ford and the assembly line. Now who knows who invented the Xerox machine, the pocket calculator, the squeezable shampoo bottle? The stream of technology is recognized to be just that, and a savor of exploitative cleverness clings to the entrepreneurs who turn a personal profit from some ripple within it. So, too, with philosophy. Berlin credits Vico with seven thought inventions: "Every one of these notions is a major advance in thought, any one of which by itself is sufficient to make the fortune of a philosopher." But he does not show us Vico making a fortune (he lived as a petty pedagogue, crippled and poor), nor does he persuade us that, had Vico not lived, others would have failed to deduce from the mounting mass of data the essential perceptions of the "New Science"—that is, of what are now called the social sciences. The tide of information is inexorable. Every month, in the pages of *Scientific American,* men, generally conjoined in teams, using mirrors and radio telescopes and the statistical manipulations possible to the computer, arrive at empirical conclusions about questions of perception and cosmology that used to belong exclusively to philosophers. Einstein was the last man to make a popular impression with an individual feat of thought, and, while particle physics accumulates its bizarre microcosmic truths, the tarnish of old glamour gathers on his name. Amid reality's grainy multiplications, who can track a single mind, however brilliant?

James Joyce's use of Vico in the composition of *Finnegans Wake* is a well-known incident, which Professor Berlin refers to slightingly; the Viconian theory of cycles that underlies Joyce's epic composition is, he says, "probably the best known and the least valuable among [Vico's] achievements," and Joyce is lumped in a footnote with Norman O. Brown as a "modern irrationalist thinker." True, Joyce used, along with the profound suggestions in Vico, much patently naïve anthropology—the thunderclaps, the god-fearing race of giants. His use of Vico was skeptical and, in the sense of scholarly conscience, conscienceless. He wrote to Harriet Weaver, "I would not pay overmuch attention to these theories, beyond using them for all they are worth." Asked if he believed in the *Scienza Nuova,* Joyce answered, "I don't believe in any science, but my imagination grows when I read Vico as it doesn't when I read Freud or Jung." Can we do better than to use these men descended to us by the accident of their greatness as stimulants to our imagination, much as we use our living companions? Vico held that we can understand human history because it is human. By the same benign principle, we can still, in our age of rampant obsolescence, relive and enjoy the human adventures, of mind and spirit, embodied in old texts.

The Last of Barthes

NEW CRITICAL ESSAYS, by Roland Barthes, translated from the French by Richard Howard. 121 pp. Hill & Wang, 1980.

The sudden and rather absurdist death of Roland Barthes earlier this year—he was hit by a laundry truck while post-prandially taking his ease on the sidewalk outside the Institut de France—deprived France, even as Jean-Paul Sartre lay mortally ill, of an eminent mandarin, and deprived Barthes, who was sixty-four, of perhaps a decade's further enjoyment of a celebrity he had come to in middle life and accepted with a wry, amused relish. He was, in the one nation that persists in making heroes of its intellectuals, king of the post–Robbe-Grillet, make-believe–Mao, structuralist scene; yet even the frankly self-centered later works he allowed himself—*Roland Barthes; A Lover's Discourse*—retain a professorial slyness and the delicate severity of intellectual venture.

Hill & Wang, with a steadiness unusual in the unseemly world of present American publishing, has brought out, in chastely designed formats and scrupulous translations, eleven of Barthes's books, and now the twelfth, a short collection entitled *New Critical Essays,* arrives to remind us, as if in valediction, what a consummate literary critic Barthes could be. Ingenious, rigorous, epigrammatic, and genial, his essays on classic French texts are as startling and as fresh as any reconsiderations since Hulme, Pound, and Eliot gave European literature their once-over. Unlike, say, F. R. Leavis's lordly reduction of the hordes of English novels to a handful worthy of "the Great Tradition," or Harold Bloom's tortuous dramatization of literary history as a running battle between creative spirits and their oppressive predecessors, Barthes's approach was open and playfully hospitable in spirit, and almost never pejorative. Indeed, his critical genius delighted to a perhaps perverse degree in exercising itself in behalf of romantic, decadent, and second-rate works. For novels like Jules Verne's *The Mysterious Island* and Pierre Loti's *Aziyadé* are as susceptible to structural analysis as anything by Proust or Flaubert: "The stake of structural analysis is not the text's truth but its *plural;* the task [consists] in dissipating, deferring, reducing, dissolving the first content under the action of a formal science." As Barthes's essays on general topics (collected as *Mythologies*) showed, he could write brightly upon any topic—a gift not highly prized by those who do not possess it. But, possibly, a mark of a truly new method, such as structuralism proposed itself to be, is that it can be fruitfully applied everywhere; an ingenious sympathy, at any rate, uncovers more treasures than an impatient judgingness. There was something sunny about Barthes's thought, opaque though pages of its exposition appear. Before becoming a Paris fixture, he taught French in universities in Rumania and

Egypt, and in even the most mathematical and diagrammatic of his tracing of semes and codes his prose manages to keep a tutor's comradely tone.

The number of *New Critical Essays* is eight. They are arranged in order of composition, from 1961 to 1971. All but one were written to an occasion—as prefaces for new editions or translations into Italian or as part of *hommages* to distinguished elder colleagues. Though all are provocative and accomplished, the earlier seem the better, the more solid and radically brilliant. The very first concerns the *Maxims* of La Rochefoucauld. These famous sentences are observed to be like lines of verse; "we have maxims with two, three, four, five, or seven beats, according to the number of semantic accents." But those with an odd number of "beats"—e.g., "It requires greater virtues to withstand good luck than bad"—are analyzed as fundamentally binary in structure; that is, the three beats, virtues/good luck/bad, constitute not a trio of terms but "the opposition of good and bad luck . . . with regard to the virtues." This "stubbornly dual character of the maxim's structure" heads up a host of dualities perceived in the text, including our manner of reading it—"There are two ways to read La Rochefoucauld: by citing, or straight through"—and the impression it makes upon us, "here brilliant, there stifling." From the maxims' mechanics of antithesis and symmetry Barthes extracts the thought that "this game is in the service of a very old technique, that of meaning; so that writing well is playing with words because playing with words is inevitably coming closer to that intention of opposition which governs the birth of a signification." In content, the maxims oppose *irrealia* (apparent virtues) and the underlying "*realia* (passions, contingencies, actions)." Though pessimistic, La Rochefoucauld's result is beneficent: "It brings to an end, with each maxim, the anxiety of a suspect sign." In other words: "To show that the moral order is merely the mask of a contingent disorder is ultimately more reassuring than to abide by an apparent but singular order." However, the process of demystification has no end:

> Once we begin ridding man of his masks, how and where to stop? The way is all the more surely barred for La Rochefoucauld in that the

philosophy of his time afforded him only a world composed of essences; the only relation which one could reasonably impute to these essences was a relation of identity, which is to say a motionless relation. . . . The virtues are dreams, but petrified dreams: these masks occupy the entire stage; we exhaust ourselves seeing through them yet without ever quite leaving them . . .

The maxim-maker himself is then demystified, as one occupying the "status of the demystifier within the group which he simultaneously expresses and attacks." Product of the salons, the maxims contest worldliness "as if worldly society indulged itself, through La Rochefoucauld, in the spectacle of its own contestation." The interrogation of prevailing values must be "both purifying and innocuous"—that is, "not political, but only psychological, authorized moreover by the Christian climate." Hence the maxims are "at once harsh and inadequate" and show a ceaseless alternation "between the greatest originality and the greatest banality."

The maxim is a two-faced being, here tragic, there bourgeois; despite its austere stamp, its sting and pure writing, it is essentially an ambiguous discourse, located on the frontier of two worlds. Which ones? We can say, that of death and that of play. . . . This encounter of the tragic and the worldly, one grazing the other, is not the least of the truths which the *Maxims* propose for us.

Intensifying the pressure, as it were, upon his perception of the binary structure within the maxims, Barthes splits open the text, the writer, and the age with a lucidity that is shocking, and that leaves nothing more of significance, we feel, to be said.

The next essay, upon the illustrative plates in the great *Encyclopedia* of the *philosophes* (a hundred thirty of which were reproduced in a 1964 volume for which this was the foreword), give Barthes's remarkable sensitivity to visual impression and his rather amiable Marxism a field day, as they roam through these depictions of "a kind of Golden Legend of artisanry [and of] the simple, the elementary, the essential, and the causal." The plates are often twofold, showing the object or activity in idyllic tableaux in the upper half and then in analytic closeup below.

In this Encyclopedic heaven (the upper part of the plates), evil is infrequent; scarcely a trace of discomfort over the hard labors of the glassworkers, armed with pathetic tools, poorly protected against the terrible heat; and when Nature darkens, there always remains a man somewhere to reassure us: a fisherman with a torch beside the night sea, a scientist discoursing before the black basalts of Antrim, the surgeon's light hand resting on the body he is cutting open, figures of knowledge inserted into the heart of the storm (in the engraving of waterspouts). Yet as soon as we leave the vignette for the more analytic plates or images, the world's peaceful order gives way to a certain *violence*. . . . The *Encyclopedia* constantly proceeds to an impious fragmentation of the world, but what it finds at the term of this fracture is not the fundamental state of pure causes; in most cases the image obliges it to recompose an object that is strictly *unreasonable* . . .

So, too, the impious fragmentation of Barthes's readings discloses beneath the surface piety of Chateaubriand's biography of the Trappist Abbé Rancé a subversive "ceremonial of the imaginary," a violence of nostalgia and of colorful writing; beneath the implausible incidents and idle talk "about the weather" of Pierre Loti's "insipid, sweetish, old-fashioned" romance *Aziyadé* a feverish transvestism and preoccupation with "the pale debauch"; beneath the high and idealistic language of Eugène Fromentin's novel *Dominique* a reactionary politics and a "rigorously masochist economy." Barthes is least revelatory when dealing with Proust and Flaubert, perhaps because these authors so exhaustively provided their own hermeneutics; apropos of Proust's fascination with names and place-names, he speculates "if it is really possible to be a writer without believing, in some sense, in the natural relation of names and essences," and of the Flaubertian sentence he offers the unverifiable thesis that it is, unlike other sentences, "a *thing*," by reason of "the evident project which has established it as an object."

The essay "Where to Begin?"—the only essay not written to order—proposes to explain literary structural analysis by way of Jules Verne, but shows something of the "black box" effect it describes: "If the intermediary links are too complex and escape observation, in cybernetics, we speak of a *black box*." His construing of literary criticism here in terms of "a certain group A of initial signals and a certain group B of final signals observed" belies the fluidity and instinctual verve of his actual practice—a kind of patient attention to predominant tendencies detectable in structural features of the work and traceable to undeclared authorial motives whose disclosure helps explain our sensations as we read. Barthes's structuralism can be borne because it coexists with a keen readerly sensualism that courts the unsayable. Though in "Where to Begin?" he speaks of "the novel as a 'working' system of informational items," in his essay on Chateaubriand he declares a certain non-informational, non-signalling component of literature; "because of it we cannot reduce literature to an entirely decipherable system: reading, criticism are not pure hermeneutics." "Literature is, in short, never anything but a certain obliquity, *in which we get lost.* "

Barthes knew his Greek as well as his cybernetics and linguistics, and his disquisitions, as they exist in English, abound in such rare or coined terms as "praxis," "syntagmatic," "parataxis," "onomastic," "indicial," "precellence," "dilatation," "poietic," "coenesthesias," "eidetic," "nosography," "ludic," "idiolectal," and "amphigoric." His sentences, too, are formidably compounded; six semicolons and two colons occur in a not untypical one. This does not make easy work for his translators. Richard Howard is the most distinguished American man of letters to lend himself continuously to the art of translation, and he has here achieved the major felicity of giving Barthes an English voice that presses, in the Barthesian prescription, into the ear, conveying "the *grain* of the voice, which is an erotic mixture of timbre and language."

In a time when books are churned out like chunky little tabloids, full of fake urgency, and a few months later shredded into insulation without a qualm, *New Critical Essays* serves to remind us what a book can be—elegant and simple in production, serious and delightful in content, a binding-together of reflections we have learned to call "ludic," a demonstration of the mind's play and a reëxcitation of our joy in the world. Though Barthes left behind disciples, there can be no replacing him; his brilliance had a wavelength all to itself.

A Monk Manqué

THE NEW GODS, by E. M. Cioran, translated from the French by Richard Howard. 120 pp. Quadrangle, 1974.

E. M. Cioran, a Rumanian who since 1937 has lived in France and since 1947 has written in French, comes to the American reader handsomely sponsored. The first collection of his philosophical-historical-lyrical-critical essays to be published here, *The Temptation to Exist* (1968), had an introduction by Susan Sontag; the second, *The Fall into Time* (1970), bore on its back encomiums from St.-John Perse, Claude Mauriac, Wylie Sypher, and Cioran's translator, Richard Howard, who was quoted as claiming, "I have translated some hundred and fifty books, and of them all, Cioran's work . . . has afforded me the most crucial experience." The third collection, *The New Gods,* is the shortest, and the first to venture forth without the escort of an introduction, though the flap copy bristles with intelligence—an intelligence driven to uneasy, hedged phrasemaking, promising us "a kind of flickering gaiety" and "a kind of ecstatic despair."

It cannot be said of Cioran that he needs no introduction. Painfully well written, with the congested precision of a man striving to keep a terrible temper under control, erudite, assertive, passionate, his essays tend to settle toward a bleak cancelling-out, a multiplication of doubts, that leave the reader uncertain as to what he has read, or, indeed, whether he has read anything. All of Cioran's explicators grapple with this puzzling, central nullity. Miss Sontag, whose introduction to *The Temptation to Exist* almost shames what follows with her sane and genial tone, recurrently touches, like a tongue unable to stay away from a cavity, upon Cioran's negative attributes: "Cioran writes about impossible states of being, about unthinkable thoughts . . . Cioran doesn't make any of the usual efforts to 'persuade.' . . . Not that the essays are particularly hard to read, but their moral point, so to speak, is the unending disclosure of difficulty . . . a certain coquetry of the void . . . What's missing in Cioran's work is anything parallel to Nietzsche's heroic effort to surmount nihilism." She ends by confessing a preference

for the cheerful permissiveness of John Cage, his "totally demo-
cratic world of the spirit . . . in which 'it is understood that every-
thing is clean: there is no dirt.' " Cioran's altogether dirty, defeated
world wins praise from her that is cunningly grudging: his "fierce,
tensely argued speculations sum up brilliantly the decaying urgen-
cies of 'Western' thought, but offer no relief from them beyond the
considerable satisfactions of the understanding." Even Charles
Newman, who in his introduction to *The Fall into Time* professes
to find his satisfactions more than considerable, asks with some-
thing like exasperation, "What can you do with a man who attacks
you for *his* mistakes, and then insists those very errors are most
worth having? . . . How to locate a mind which seemingly speaks
out of nowhere, and then only against itself?" What Newman calls
"the best consideration of *The Temptation to Exist* to appear in
either English or French"—Edward W. Said's notice in *The Hud-
son Review*—approves rather gingerly of Cioran's offer of "knowl-
edge without information," and William Gass, in a pejorative ap-
praisal from which Cioran's publishers insist on quoting the two
construably favorable sentences, puts it less kindly: "So evenly is
Cioran divided against himself, on irony's behalf, that there is
scarcely a line which does not contain truth by precisely a half.
. . . He seems really to think that if he writes his lies *like* lies, that
will excuse them, but what he risks by this tactic is revealing an
essentially frivolous mind."

None of Cioran's champions and critics have thought to consider
him as a writer who, like other writers, has a duty to be interesting,
and who fulfills that duty very unevenly. Though erudite and
intellectual to an extreme degree, he is not so much a thinker as a
poser, striking a succession of attitudes before us without any of the
philosopher's traditional desire to direct *our* actions, our attitudes.
He is an entertainer, if compulsive display of one's psychic wounds
be taken as entertaining. The son of a Greek Orthodox priest,
Cioran is hopelessly in love with, and insatiably angry with, Chris-
tianity. A native of the land of Dracula, he seeks out history's
Gothic chambers, and is claustrophobically at home with horror,
pain, self-denial, and rage. With what hungry bliss does he sink his
fangs into the necks of the good!:

The smell of carrion fascinates and inflames those greedy and garrulous grave-diggers we call the Apostles.

In the marketplace, a five-year-old writhes, screams in a tantrum. Women rush to him, try to soothe him. He goes right on, exaggerates, exceeds all limits. The more you watch, the more you'd like to wring his neck . . . You think—with what satisfaction!—of Calvin, for whom children are "lumps of filth."

His hatred of the flesh is rapturous: "Horror of the flesh, of the organs, of each cell, primordial horror, chemical horror . . . In what grease, what pestilence the spirit has taken up its abode! This body, whose every pore eliminates enough stench to infect space, is no more than a mass of ordure through which circulates a scarcely less ignoble blood, no more than a tumor which disfigures the geometry of the globe. Supernatural disgust!" In his "nostalgia for barbarism," he deplores modern men as mere "dilettantes and eunuchs of bloodshed" and recommends cruelty not only to literary creators —"Cruelty, in literature at least, is a sign of election"—but to God Himself: "No one any longer fears or respects a God who has squandered His capital of cruelty."

Cioran's dark side has a positive obverse—a genuine admiration for the monastic life, especially its morbid aspects. "The Buddhist monks gladly frequented charnel houses: where corner desire more surely and emancipate oneself from it? The horrible being a path of liberation, in every period of fervor and inwardness, our remains have enjoyed great favor. . . . Blessed was that age when solitaries could plumb their depths without seeming obsessed, deranged . . . There no longer exists a single place where we can professionally execrate this world." It is the contemplative's self-excoriation, however, that rouses Cioran's imagination to something like reverence, as he savors the sufferings of the obscurer mystics—Peter of Alcantara, who "managed to sleep no more than one hour a night," and Margaret Ebner, who for days at a time "could not unclench her teeth; when finally she opened her mouth, it was to utter cries which exalted and terrorized the convent." His nostalgia for the "maceration and cell-shrieks of old" is Cioran's most endearing attribute. In secular, aesthetic emulation of the "adorable hell" of the saints' "effort against the ego," he flays himself with the modern impossibilities: it is impossible to believe, impossible not to want to believe, impossible to become Buddhists, impossible equally to revive and to forget the dead. His essays, with their vast range of reference—he knows everything, to tell us it is nothing—are a kind of agonized remembering from within the vacuum of the "winded civilization" that surrounds him. It is not mere arrogance but a withering will toward depopulation which compels him systematically to refrain from mentioning any living contemporary by name, saying instead "some theologian" or (perhaps of de Gaulle) "the least *effaced* of modern men." "What is a 'contemporary'?" he asks, answering, "Someone you'd like to kill, without quite knowing how." But the absence, in his electric debates with ghosts, of living names emphasizes the absence of any quickening sense of encounter, of thought's refinement through contention, of viable adversaries and alternatives in his dance of dead ideas; his prose histrionics are as agitated and jerky as the movements of a vampire.

The New Gods (no doubt a more salable title, in progressivist America, than the original French *Le Mauvais Demiurge*), though the smallest of Cioran's three collections in English, fairly represents him in its range of topic and quality. The first essay, or prose flight, "The Demiurge," proposes with more fervor than irony the existence of "a wicked and woebegone god, a god accursed," who created this botched universe and whose "criminal injunction" to multiply Man is doomed to obey, at least until the happy day when "pregnant women will . . . be stoned to death." In its contemplation of the "dreadful miracle" of Creation, this essay is almost pious, and with his final hint of "*another* creator" Cioran might be one of those Jesuits who whip off the scoffer's mask to administer the sacraments. But the mask is his face. The next section, "The New Gods," ends by lamenting Christianity's present mood of tolerance: "Its career finished, its hatred is finished too." The historical period of Rome's decline and the Church's emergence is one of the author's favorites; impossibly well read in the late Skeptics and the early Christians, he is a connoisseur of paganism's decadence, "the cumulus of inner defeats" that permitted the new religion to triumph. He is always interesting on this subject, which inspired, in an earlier volume, the maxim "Energy, privilege of the dregs, always comes from below." Cioran is consistently boring, on the other hand, on the subject of Buddhism and Oriental quietism. His longing for this particular brand of unattainable religiosity leads him to dwell, in "The Undelivered," upon the thought of the void as fondly as a hen broods upon an egg, hatching such fuzzy aperçus as "The void is nothingness stripped of its negative qualifications, nothingness transfigured." "Paleontology" uses a visit to a museum to trip a meditation upon the loathsome flesh, "that layer of grease which keeps us from discerning what is *fundamental* in ourselves." Here, more than usual, Cioran seems irresponsibly extreme: is it really true, for instance, that "whatever is alive, the most repellent animal or insect, shudders with fear—does nothing but"? What is signified by "an abstract joy, an exaltation granted alike to being and to the absence of being"? And is it not a peculiar sort of nihilistic piffle to say that bones "grant me a glimpse of the day when I shall no longer have to endure the obsession of the human, of all shackles the most terrible"? "Encounters with Suicide," the longest and what should be the most involving essay in the book, though touched with hints of personal experience and with a delicate poetry of the death wish, a wish "to run joyously toward our ghost," is vitiated by abstractness, as if the writer had felt suicide only as an idea in the brain and never as an action latent in the muscles. "A man does not kill himself, as is commonly supposed, in a fit of madness but rather in a fit of unendurable lucidity": perhaps this should be so, but we doubt that it is. Cioran is at his most reflexively, coquettishly paradoxical with assertions like "When you have understood that nothing *is*, that things do not even deserve the status of appearances, you no longer need to be saved, you are saved, and miserable forever."

All his essays balk at flowing; they feel, rather, written from point to point, from shock to shock, cadenzas parading as melody. The frequent recourse to asterisks and fresh starts betrays the shifting perspectives of an intelligence committed only to itself. The best section of *The New Gods*, the most entertaining, concrete, and suggestive of Cioran's living mind, is the last—a string of disconnected aphorisms called "Strangled Thoughts." The title declares a congenial murderousness; he dreams, he has earlier written, of a language whose words will break jaws like fists. Here, his thoughts, freed of any need to harmonize with a context, stab:

> Refinement is the sign of deficient vitality, in art, in love, and in everything.

> First duty, on getting up in the morning: to blush for yourself.

> All our thoughts are a function of our ailments.

> The creator who becomes transparent to himself no longer creates: to know oneself is to smother one's endowments and one's demon.

> We are all deep in a hell each moment of which is a miracle.

Dignified by a defiant perfectionism of style, Cioran is of that type of intellectual outsider described by Thomas Mann in his short story "At the Prophet's": "A fevered and frightfully irritable ego here expanded itself . . . The solitary ego sang, raved, commanded. It would lose itself in confused pictures, go down in an eddy of logical error, to bob up again suddenly and startlingly in an entirely unexpected place. Blasphemies and hosannahs—a waft of incense and a reek of blood." Though advertised by his American sponsors as a "philosopher," Cioran lacks one-half of that word's etymology, which is *philos* ("loving") + *sophos* ("wise"). Wisdom devoid of love is sophistry. Read alongside another nervous, doubting paragrapher, such as Wittgenstein, Cioran conspicuously lacks two qualities the other in his thought possesses—gentleness and seriousness. He does not wish to relieve, through clarification, our irritations; he does not wish, like Nietzsche and Kierkegaard, to inflame them to the point of crisis and cure. He wishes only, with his nimble, sinister spidering amid the complexities of our cultural situation, to give us—one of his favorite words—*frissons;* the means seem disproportional to the ends.

POETS

The Heaven of an Old Home

Souvenirs and Prophecies: *The Young Wallace Stevens,* by Holly Stevens. 261 pp. Alfred A. Knopf, 1977.

The city of Reading, in southeastern Pennsylvania, sits dreaming and declining in the center of a lozenge-shaped county of bosomy farmland, Berks. Its urban silhouette, in the shadow of Mount Penn, is dominated by the eighteen-story courthouse that rose from the tight red-brick blocks in 1932—the year I was born in the Reading Hospital—and remains the tallest building in sight. Reading's population, once over a hundred thousand, has fallen in every census since 1930; its main stem, Penn Street, in my boyhood a thriving strip of stores and movie houses, sprouts like leaves of asphalt larger and larger parking lots in an attempt to lure shoppers back downtown. Pretzels and steel are still produced, but the Old Reading Brewery is gone, the old farmers' market is gone, the textile industry has long gone south, and the Reading Railroad, well known to players of Monopoly, is an atrophied arm of Conrail. Even the Reading rackets, and the permissive officials that allowed them to flourish, are no longer notorious. Yet the eating is still good, and the predominately German-descended population shows a sedentary loyalty to this comfortable, good-humored place. The people are both conservative and fanciful; hex signs adorn the Berks barns, and a pagoda surprisingly perches atop Mount Penn. Reading's civic institutions—the hospitals and schools, libraries and fire stations—are well equipped, and through the hazy summers and slushy winters a sort of cultural fever persists. Music stores and craft shops abound. Most children absorb a quota of improving lessons. Artists, if not as high in the social scale as ophthalmologists and firemen, yet have a certain place. But in the years when I was growing up around Reading the name of Wallace Stevens was never heard, and I had to go away to Harvard to discover that one of America's premier modern poets had been born and raised in the heart of the city, on North Fifth Street.

Stevens, too, went to Harvard, and after leaving it in 1900 (without a degree) lived in New York and then in Hartford, first as a fledgling newspaperman, then as a law student, and finally as an executive for insurance companies. Resident in Hartford from 1916 to his death in 1955, he came to be as automatically identified with Connecticut as Robert Frost was with New Hampshire and Robinson Jeffers with the California coast. In the great and festive range of geographical references in his poetry, those to Berks County are perhaps pointedly few, and come in the later poems. Neversink, Schuylkill, Tulpehocken, and Oley appear in the collection *Transport to Summer* (1947), but emblematically, as sites in Stevens's mind:

> From a Schuylkill in mid-earth there came emerging
> Flotillas, willed and wanted, bearing in them
>
> Shadows of friends, of those he knew . . .

The Schuylkill, choked with coal silt in my day, did not even in Stevens's time bear flotillas of "canoes, a thousand thousand."[*] Like his alter ego Crispin in "The Comedian as the Letter C," Stevens "Slid from his continent by slow recess/To things within his actual eye." His Nature, so often and ardently invoked, is generalized, Arcadian:

---

[*]Though Donald R. Shenton, in a caption to a photograph of the Schuylkill in the Fall 1959 issue of the *Historical Review of Berks County*—an issue devoted to Stevens—says that the river in 1897 had been dammed at intervals; "Thus the river had impressive breadth. Then annual festivals were held on this broad river, down which paraded canoes and boats lighted at night with candled Chinese lanterns." As to the pagoda on Mount Penn, it was built in 1908, in Japanese style, and Stevens's first play, *Three Travelers Watch a Sunrise* (1916), incongruously situates Chinese picnickers in "a forest of heavy trees on a hilltop in eastern Pennsylvania."

> Deer walk upon our mountains, and the quail
> Whistle about us their spontaneous cries;
> Sweet berries ripen in the wilderness . . .

In the slow and careful making of himself as a poet (after college he did not publish any poems until he was thirty-five; his first collection, the superb *Harmonium,* came out in 1923, when he was forty-four), Stevens had to put Reading far behind him, and he wrote, instead, of places—Florida, the Yucatán, an imagined Orient —where he had never, or passingly, been. Yet the Stevens family were solid Readingites; Wallace's father, Garrett, came there in 1870 to take up the law, and his two other sons, Garrett, Jr., and John, were practicing attorneys in Reading, as is John's son John now. Wallace lived in the same brick row house, 323 North Fifth Street, for his first eighteen years, and except for summer excursions spent all those formative years there. So Stevens's daughter Holly has performed a valuable as well as filial service by recounting and assembling what she can discover about her father before, as a rising businessman and a highly accomplished, if scarcely known, poet, he moved to Hartford. Her dossier is titled *Souvenirs and Prophecies: The Young Wallace Stevens.*

Miss Stevens has drawn upon three main types of document: the early poems by Stevens, of which the first extant was published in the Reading Boys' High School magazine in 1898; his journal, which he began at Harvard in 1898 and continued, with many intermittences and later excisions, until 1912; and his letters to Elsie Viola Kachel, who became his wife in 1909, after five years of courtship, though the earliest surviving item of his copious correspondence with her dates only from March of 1907. In addition to these sources, his daughter has drawn on family conversations and the rather meagre traces of himself that Stevens left in the archives of Reading, Cambridge, and New York. His high-school records were destroyed in a fire, he left Harvard (according to his friend Witter Bynner) under a cloud, and his legal career after his admission to the New York Bar in 1904 is a matter of scattered glimpses. Furthermore, his journals have been exasperatingly mutilated—possibly, Miss Stevens conjectures, by her mother, "if she found personal references she did not wish preserved." Mrs. Stevens was evidently no reverencer of her husband's testament: "While I was growing up my mother did not read my father's poems, and seemed to dislike the fact that his books were published." Her "regard for privacy" apparently led her to resent that a few poems originally written for her birthday were later made public in print. Elsie Stevens, whose personal beauty and musical aptitude inform so many of Stevens's verses, figures as a jarring note in her daughter's recollections:

> All her life, at least during the time I knew her, she suffered from a persecution complex which undoubtedly originated during her childhood, and which I was unable to understand for a long time. . . . We did not get on well together until after my father's death.

Even her devoted suitor noted in his journal, in 1907: "Elsie more or less unmanageable." If she was the unknown editor of these journals, who tore out pages at a time, would this reference have escaped her notice? My own pious hope is that the desecrator of so many irrecoverable passages was Stevens himself; it is a fact that he reread the journals and sometimes annotated them, and at some point he may well have removed whatever he found embarrassing or jejune, as ruthlessly as he edited the Pennsylvania provincial out of his own personality.

Stevens's references to Reading describe a curve in the records that remain. Coming home from Harvard for Christmas of 1898, he wrote in his journal, "The city was smoky and noisy but the country depths were prodigiously still . . . Coming home I saw the sun go down behind a veil of grime." The journal entries balloon when he is back in Berks: "Country sights both purge and fill up your fancy," he notes, and says, having described a raindrop slipping from leaf to leaf of a clematis vine, that "it was certainly a monstrous pleasure to be able to be specific about such a thing." Paragraphs are devoted to local botany and atmospheric effects; he ends one entry "Salut au Monde!" and another "The splendor is almost too great: things seem a little overdressed, a little overdone." When he has been living in New York a month, he expresses homesickness: "Whatever else I may be doing I never fail to think of the country about Reading. During August I hope to run over

& see all the roads & hills again. Besides, they do not seem real to me unless I am there." Six months later, however, in 1901, he writes, "I have come to like New York heartily and sincerely. . . . I have about made up my mind never to settle down in Reading." With each visit home, the enchantment wears thinner: "Reading looked the acme of dullness & I was glad, therefore, to get back to this electric town which I adore." By 1902, he is philosophical about the provincial torpor: "Ran home a week ago. . . . Weather stupefied me. . . . Fate carves its images there in a tedious fashion, and neither beautifully nor well. And the very wings of Time hang limp in the still air. Alas! it did nothing but rain." More seasons pass, and by Thanksgiving of 1904 he is inditing, "In other respects, my visit was like many others. The family, to be candid, insuperably dull. The country incomparably duller." Yet, a sentence later, "On Sunday morning, I started on a bit of a walk. It had been snowing slightly and, far off, the fields were white. Beyond these stood the little blue hills, very pale in the light, very delicate." Back in New York, it is his habit to put himself to sleep by imagining himself "on a green mountain." From 1904 on, another tug back to Reading develops, in the form of Elsie: "On my way back I stopped at Reading and to my delight I found Elsie there. A way she had of taking my hand made me feel wonderfully welcome." Though his home town now affects him "like an elegant phase of paralysis" and "all the beautiful things in Reading wouldn't be enough to fill a trunk," the nymph of the place brings him back, with a rich mix of feelings:

> Reading got quite on my nerves. It is a terrible place except to the native. The country is adorable. Yesterday I walked over the hills—down Easter Egg Way and over Oriole Road and up Stone Hill and by Eglantine Hedge. The bell at Spies church clattered as I passed. Looked out over Oley and went round the Lake of the Beautiful Lady and so—home. Elsie was in everything.

Elsie is very much a native. After their marriage, she often leaves their apartment on West Twenty-first Street and spends weeks at a time back in Reading, so that he must write and beg, "Come and give life to these quiet rooms and take care of me for a while." A letter of 1911 speaks severely: "Your dream of a home in Reading is most fanciful. . . . I fully intend to continue along my present line—because it gives me a living and because it seems to offer possibilities."

His present line is never to take him back to Reading to live; but the town will come with him in the person of his bride, to whom he remains devoted, though she is, besides being beautiful, "delicate, fragile," and—the clear implication is—difficult. Lovingly he advises her in 1910, "We have more of life ahead of us than after. Therefore, cherish that old scene and those old thoughts. If I wanted to think all of life over, I think I could do it best up the Tulpehocken, or sitting on a fence along the Bernville road. . . . Native earth! That makes us giants." Within a few years, his father dies, then his mother, and then his family home is sold. In 1913, it is he who is in Reading briefly, and the final mention of the city in *Souvenirs and Prophecies* resolves the matter with a fine firmness. He will leave the place in fact, and hold it in his imagination. He writes Elsie:

> What strange places one wakes up in! Reading was very—unsympathetic, I thought. The trouble is that I keep looking at it as I used to know it. I do not know it as it is. I must adjust myself; because I do not intend to shut myself off from the heaven of an old home.

How a poet of Stevens's elaborate sophistication and rarefied temperament could have come from an earthy burg like Reading is a question that perhaps need not be asked. We cannot all be born in Cambridge or New York* (though we can go there, as Stevens

---

*However, at the time when Stevens shuttled back and forth between New York and Reading the two cities were less different than they have become; both were composed largely of four-story brick or stone row houses, solid chimneyed blocks interspersed with industry and commerce. The entire Middle-Atlantic region that produced Stevens and William Carlos Williams (*b.* Rutherford, N.J., in 1883) and Hilda Doolittle (*b.* Bethlehem, Pa., in 1886) still weighed heavily in the national scale. "Trenton Makes—the World Takes" was a slogan my father (*b.* Trenton, N.J., in 1900) took satisfaction in to the end of his days. Philadelphia, in 1910, must have been, with its *Post* and its thriving schools of artists, a much less provincial place than it seemed two generations later. Perhaps it was the Depression that, flooding all the East in gloom, left only the bright lights of New York high and dry. As late as Mencken, Baltimore could be the chosen residence of a decidedly national cultural pundit.

did), and these cultural centers cannot infallibly inspire their children with the enthusiasm and courage of creativity. Stevens's father was himself a poet, whose contributions appeared anonymously in the local newspapers. A year before his death, Stevens remembered life at 323 North Fifth Street thus: "We were all great readers, and the old man used to delight in retiring to the room called the library on a Sunday afternoon to read a five- or six-hundred page novel." This pattern, Holly Stevens tells us, was re-created in Stevens's Hartford home, where she was the only child.

> The house was quiet and the world was calm.
> The reader became the book; and summer night
>
> Was like the conscious being of the book.
> The house was quiet and the world was calm.

The educational opportunities in nineteenth-century Reading for a child of good family were far from negligible. Stevens attended a "private kindergarten run by a French lady," the first stage of his lifelong infatuation with the French language and Gallic thought. From his surroundings he imbibed German, too, and his poetry includes punning titles in both tongues: "Le Monocle de Mon Oncle," "Lebensweisheitspielerei." Before acquiring some Latin, Greek, and elements of rhetoric at Reading Boys' High School, he attended Lutheran parochial schools, as well as the Presbyterian church, and to this religious background may be credited his endless willingness to consider things metaphysically; though his poems speak, with deliberation and pathos, of "a world without heaven to follow," their ruminations spin on a dualistic frame. That mind and matter were closeted together in one universe never seemed less than extraordinary to Stevens. Throughout his New York years, he attended churches, though on one occasion he jubilantly throws away his childhood Bible ("I hate the looks of a Bible. . . . I'm glad the silly thing is gone") and on another assures Elsie, "I am not pious. But churches are beautiful to see." "The peculiar life of Sundays" fascinated him, and more than one journal entry and letter are dated with the two words—"Sunday morning"—that were to title his most celebrated poem. At this youthful stage, at least, his journals show him attempting prayer, and he writes to Elsie, "People doubt the existence of Jesus . . . But I do not understand that they deny God." His mature opinions were unambiguously atheistical, yet he retained a religious disposition, which he put at the service of what he called poetry. In 1948, addressing students at Bard College, he described the "poetic act" as becoming "engaged with something unreal," and gave as his first example "We do this sort of thing on a large scale when we go to church on Sunday." In 1940, a "Memorandum" on the "theory of poetry" claims, "The major poetic idea in the world is and always has been the idea of God." In another address, he asserted, with a sincerity that lifts the idea above the banal, "In an age of disbelief . . . it is for the poet to supply the satisfactions of belief, in his measure and in his style." It is as if, in Stevens's mind, the idea of poetry were so sublime and vast that it and God merge, at that metaphysical level where unreality is no drawback. For, two of his "Adagia" state, "Reality is a vacuum" and "In the long run truth does not matter"—paradoxes with a hearty Kierkegaardian ring.

Nor did Berks County fail to provide, besides books, schools, churches, roads, and nature in abundance, intellectual companionship for him. Edwin Bechtel, who went to high school with Stevens, remembered him as "a whimsical, unpredictable young enthusiast, who lampooned Dido's tear-stained adventures in the cave, or wrote enigmatic couplets to gazelles"—a startlingly accurate foretaste of the mature Stevens's tone. Though an erratic academic performer, Stevens won prizes for rhetoric and oratory, and over a decade later boasted to Elsie in a letter, "You know I took *all* the prizes at school!" Home from Harvard, he engaged in heady debates with Christopher Shearer, whose big canvases of tangled woodland now adorn the Reading Museum:

> He said that after all nature was superior to art! Is this delayed conclusion not consistent with his belief that, when we are dead, we are gone? . . . I said that the ideal was superior to fact since it was man creating & adding something to nature. He held however that facts were best since they were infinite while the ideal was rare.

Stevens never abandoned his championing of the ideal, and saw all phenomena under its guise, giving them a gemmy, mythy lustre. His abiding sense of the abstract plants "giants" in the air; with the ease of a primitive or a child he conjures intermediate presences, real clouds condensed from our mental activity. Almost at random, his poetry yields instances of this radically poetic habit of perception. "Contrary Theses (II)" begins:

> One chemical afternoon in mid-autumn,
> When the grand mechanics of earth and sky were near,

and goes on,

> The abstract that he saw, like the locust-leaves, plainly:
>
> The premiss from which all things were conclusions,
> The noble, Alexandrine verve.

To this oddly palpable sense of the invisible add, as another genial aspect of Stevens's Lutheran heritage, the willingness to admit pleasure as an ethical and aesthetic checkpoint. The word recurs in his journals, from the "monstrous pleasure" quoted earlier to the thought that "one uses French for the pleasure that it gives," to the college notation of a suggestion by Plato's translator Jowett that "when we substitute a higher pleasure for a lower we raise men in the scale of existence," and finally, to the complete credo he could set down as early as 1899:

> I thoroughly believe that at this very moment I get none of my chief pleasures except from what is unsullied. The love of beauty excludes evil. A moral life is simply a pure conscience: a physical, mental and ethical source of pleasure. At the same time it is an inhuman life to lead. It is a form of narrowness so far as companionship is concerned. One *must* make concessions to others; but there is never a necessity of smutching inner purity. The only practical life of the world, as a man of the world, not as a University Professor, a Retired Farmer or Citizen, a Philanthropist, a Preacher, a Poet or the like, but as a bustling merchant, a money-making lawyer, a soldier, a politician is to be if unavoidable a pseudo-villain in the drama, a decent person in private life.

So the decision, if untested, has already been made—to live dualistically, as a "pseudo-villain," a "money-making lawyer" who is also "a decent person in private life." *The love of beauty excludes evil:* the word "beauty" completes the old-fashioned trilogy—ideal, pleasure, beauty—by which Stevens lived and concocted his astonishingly supple and prolific verbal world. The career choices had already been spelled out by his father in a letter written earlier to Harvard: "For life is either a pastoral dream—the ideal of the tramp, or superannuated village farmer—Or it is the wild hurly burly activity of the fellows who make the world richer and better by their being in it."

The natural landscape of Berks County, it may be not too fanciful to say, looks nurtured and used and, if not Arcadian, rather European to American eyes. The sky seldom lacks clouds, and the hills, with their shaggy crowns, do seem subdued giants. The frontier feels even more remote here than in New England, where an underlying austerity remembers it. Reading, its natives know, is a civilized place. Laid out on tidy English principles by Thomas Penn, an early center of American industry, populated by skilled craftsmen, and combining, in the words of the 1911 Encyclopaedia Britannica, "unusual business and industrial advantages" with a situation in a "rich agricultural region," Reading had in the years when Stevens knew it best a proud sense of itself as a *place.* Stevens knew himself as a man of places: "Life is an affair of people not of places. But for me life is an affair of places and that is the trouble." In addition to the solid "Dutch" physiognomy pictured on the dust jackets, his "native earth" endowed Stevens with a human nature that was robust, patient, loyal, and humorous.

How much patience he needed to bring his gifts to fruition can be seen from the juvenilia that his daughter here collects and publishes. His verse remained juvenile into his thirties. Though there are flashes of characteristic color in some of his undergraduate poems—

> for in the fern I saw the sun
> Take fire against the dew; the lily white
> Was soft and deep at morn; the rosary
> Streamed forth a wild perfume into the light—

the sentiments are Henleyesque and the metrics jingling; in New York he adds some fashionable *chinoiserie* to Elsie's birthday bouquets but retains the incubus of rhyme to the verge of his coming of artistic age, which seems to date (as did Proust's) from his mother's death, in 1912. He wrote to Elsie in 1911, "I am far from being a genius—and must rely on hard and faithful work." This seems modest; but he was certainly far from precocious. His *Harvard Advocate* contributions, though they conscientiously manipulate the glossy counters of late-Victorian poetry, in no way advance the game; whereas, ten years later, T. S. Eliot, having discovered Laforgue and Dante for himself, was contributing to the *Advocate* poems ("Nocturne," "Spleen") that are well on the way to "Prufrock."

Yet though Stevens was slow to find his voice, slow to make his first collection, and even slower to make his second (*Ideas of Order*, in 1936), he lived long enough to accommodate these hesitations within an ample oeuvre, of expanding fluency; his joyous late variations on mastered themes remind us of Bach. He played on and on, and in the end won all the prizes. His personal robustness found early expression in boyhood athletics and pranks. "I was distinctly a rowdy," he tells Elsie in a letter. In young manhood, he flung himself into thirty-mile walks along the dusty, pre-automobile roads of Pennsylvania, New York, and New Jersey. Joined to his reflective, deliberate, cold side there was something combative and uproarious, which expressed itself in contention with distance and weather. In 1908, describing to Elsie a walk to Grant's Tomb on a winter day, he writes, "It was beastly cold— my hands were swollen with it. But the air poured into us like light into darkness." The image is pure Plato, and pure lust, of a sort. Stevens comes at us, in the mature poems, tumbling, full of foolery, veering from decorum with outrageous titles ("No Possum, No Sop, No Taters," "So-and-So Reclining on Her Couch," "A Weak Mind in the Mountains," "Saint John and the Back-Ache," etc.) and in the animal noises and nonsense syllables so surprising amid the splendors of his vocabulary:*

---

*Michael Lafferty, in the previously cited issue of the *Berks Historical Review*, points out that "Stevens' technique of interjecting words and phrases of other

> Poet, be seated at the piano
> Play the present, its hoo-hoo-hoo,
> Its shoo-shoo-shoo, its ric-a-ric,
> Its envious cachinnation.

Stevens was called Pat in Reading and Pete at Harvard and was so full of fun that, among other escapades, he was accused, while "fairly lit," in his last year of college, of "announcing jovially that he was going to rape" a waitress; indeed, he did topple her to the floor. On the next page of *Souvenirs and Prophecies* we read that also before leaving Harvard he spent an evening with George Santayana, discussing their poetic ambitions on what seem to have been terms of equality. He wrote a poem to Santayana fifty years later, and remained always loyal to the philosopher's quest for—in a phrase from the poem—"the celestial possible." Stevens evinced loyalty to many things—to his wife, though even at the outset she appeared "more or less unmanageable," and to the Hartford Accident & Indemnity Company, for which he labored nearly forty years, well past the age of retirement. The steadfastness of his preoccupations is demonstrated by the frequency with which journal entries of his youth are echoed in poems decades later. Like a Pennsylvania farmer, he occupied his acreage and worked it, season after season. As Whitman's poetic activity was a continuous revision and expansion of *Leaves of Grass,* so it almost was with Stevens and *Harmonium*—his proposed title for the collected poems was *The Whole of Harmonium.* Above all, he was loyal to the inviolate conception of literature he formed before this century began: "Is literature really a profession? Can you single it out, or must you let it decide in you for itself? I have determined upon one thing, and that is not to *try* to suit anybody except myself."

His daughter has shown loyalty in turn by becoming her father's editor. This is the third volume that she has seen into press; the two

---

languages into his poems is typical of Pennsylvania Dutch poetry and speech." When Renato Poggioli attempted to translate into Latin the lines, "His robes and symbols, ai-yi-yi—/And that-a-way he twirled the thing," Stevens explained by letter, "These are Pennsylvania Dutch idioms, and I imagine that this-a-way, etymologically, is based on 'dieser weg' . . . People think of ai-yi-yi as Spanish, but it is equally Pennsylvania Dutch."

others are the *Letters of Wallace Stevens* (1966) and the anthology *The Palm at the End of the Mind* (1972). She brings to her custodianship a love and care more than scholarly, and this instance has had to invent a way of presenting her variegated, fragmented material. *Souvenirs and Prophecies* is an unusual book—"a singular collation," one might say, quoting the line after the line in "The Comedian as the Letter C" from which the title is taken.

> He, therefore, wrote his prolegomena,
> And, being full of the caprice, inscribed
> Commingled souvenirs and prophecies.
> He made a singular collation.

Neither biography nor anthology, this volume—uniform with Knopf's handsome editions of Stevens, and a balancing opposite to *Opus Posthumous*, edited by Samuel French Morse—essentially binds together Stevens's pre-1915 poems, all of the journals that survived the mysterious slashing they received, the bulk of Stevens's letters to his wife prior to their move to Hartford, a little of his undergraduate and journalistic prose, and such biographical facts and conjectures as were deemed helpful. In these last two categories, we wish for more. Stevens's prose firmed up long before his poetry, and we might have liked to read, from the *Advocate*, the "rather eerie story of a young man who takes a photograph of his sweetheart to be framed; after it is done and he opens the package, he finds a picture of himself," or, from the *Tribune*, the story composed, according to William Carlos Williams, in this manner: "Stevens sitting on a park bench at the Battery watching the out tide and thinking to join it as a corpse . . . As he sat there watching the debris floating past him he began to write—noting the various articles as they passed."

His long New York period is tantalizing in the glimpses of it afforded, and one wonders if Miss Stevens, with more interviews and research, might have filled in at least the years after 1909. Our impression of the years before that is simultaneously of Stevens's immense capacity to suffer solitude and of the energy of his gallivanting, his theatre- and concert-going. We are gratified to learn, for instance, that he attended Stephen Crane's funeral service at a

Seventh Avenue church (and found it an "absolutely common-place, bare, silly service") the same year—1900—that he attended a performance by Sarah Bernhardt of *Hamlet* in French (and was shocked by her rude treatment of Polonius). Of the seven years of Stevens's married life in the city, his daughter, who was not born until 1924, confesses an ignorance that she has done little to relieve. She has talked to one person who visited her parents' New York apartment; this guest noticed only "that it was rather sparsely furnished, and that the evening she was there Wallace sat in a corner reading." But aren't these the years in which Elsie Stevens, whose cameo beauty was remembered by a friend as "very stiff, straight and stiff, like a gendarme almost," posed for the sculptor who designed the Liberty dime of 1916, so that her profile achieved wider currency than her husband's poems ever did? And didn't the Stevenses have any friends within the Village literary crowd? Wasn't he, by 1916, one of Harriet Monroe's favorite poets, and writing plays performed in New York theatres? But such questions trespass, perhaps, beyond the *terra incognita* for which Miss Stevens provides a welcome map, showing the road out of Reading, which on another plane was the road back.

Alone but Not Aloof

W. H. AUDEN—A TRIBUTE, edited by Stephen Spender. 248 pp. Macmillan, 1975.

What would W. H. Auden have made of *W. H. Auden—A Tribute?* He would have winced, I fancy, at the embalming opulence of the production (10″ by 7½ ″, 101 plates) and the quickness with which the helpless dead are visited by the sentimental, and not necessarily profitless, exertions of the living. At several places in the memoirs, poems, and critiques composed by the thirty-three contributors, Auden's express wish that his letters be withheld from posterity is pointedly ignored, and it cannot be said that the vignettes of him in action, as recorded by frank observers like Cyril

Connolly, Nicolas Nabokov, and David Luke, are all such as to make his wraith smile. From its dramatic jacket (Auden's creased face looking, as he once said, like "a wedding cake which had been left out in the rain") inward, the book savors of glorification in a way that sits a bit embarrassedly upon the self-careless, always efficiently professional subject. My own closest approach to Auden was a drink years ago in his St. Mark's Place apartment, when a friend was subletting it; we were struck, inspecting the library of the absent landlord, by how his own books—his collections and plays and translations and anthologies—were not set aside on the shelves, but distributed, in worn copies, through them, placed where genre and topic dictated, as if any old body had written them.

Yet Auden, Mr. Spender points out in his introduction, took an active interest in a *Festschrift* volume for his sixty-fifth birthday and was no decliner of tributes. He was a great believer in friendship; in "New Year Letter" he advised us all to dwell in "the *polis* of our friends," and it would surely please him to see assembled in this commemorative volume so many who knew him, and to overhear, from the repose of his early bedtime (he never thought it too rude to leave a party in progress), them all talking about him. The editor has done a good job of assembling survivors to testify on each stage of Auden's bi-continental career; they range from Auden's older brother John, who beheld him in the cradle, to Chester Kallman, who "found him dead / Turning icy-blue on a hotel bed." Framed by some criticism, the memoirs progress from his schoolmates and early mentors to the confreres of his famous years as the foremost new English poet (Spender and Isherwood and Connolly), to the collaborators and conversation partners of his New York decades (Lincoln Kirstein and Ursula Niebuhr and Hannah Arendt and Louis Kronenberger), and, finally, to the relatively youthful witnesses (Orlan Fox and Oliver Sacks and David Luke) of his less happy Manhattan *Dämmerung* and his abortive return to Oxford. Each voice adds its blind-man's impressions to the elephant once in its midst. (Michael Yates, indeed, describes the great man, going to bed in Kirchstetten, as padding off "at nine o'clock in those carpet slippers, a bottle of wine in his fist, looking like the back side of an elephant, to have his bubble bath.") An ordinary biography, like a work of fiction, is controlled by a single imagination, which imposes its limitations on a chaos of data and achieves coherence, persuasive or not. In this album, the perspective alters every few pages, and—to quote Chester Kallman's poem—"Wystan ploughs through / Blindly as ever, as ever making / Chaos good soil and bearable." As a man who valued privacy, and who, for all his gregariousness, kept something essential to himself apart, Auden *would* have smiled, I imagine, at how, when the thirty-three authors have made their grabs at him, he has eluded every one.

Even his physical appearance proves slippery. Nicolas Nabokov notes "the dirt of his fingernails," but seven pages earlier James Stern has shown himself powerfully affected by the sight of "the fattish, fleshy, unfeeling fingers. Each nail bitten down to the quick." Robert Craft feels obliged to report that the poet was, among other things, "slightly peculiar-smelling"—a complaint swiftly qualified by parenthetical praise of "his purity of spirit and intellectual punctiliousness"—but we have been repeatedly informed of Auden's passion for baths, for bubble baths, for singing in the bath. Perhaps the answer lies in a directive the poet gave Louis Kronenberger: "Get up very early and get going at once, in fact, work first and wash afterwards." Craft must have sniffed Auden out before the working day ended. It is Kronenberger, too, who throws light upon the notorious carpet slippers that Auden, much to the amazement of his fellow-Americans, wore indoors and out, summer and winter: "the carpet slippers," Kronenberger explains, "that his suffering feet made necessary." Orlan Fox, with the poet's help, further elucidates this mystery: "Well, he did suffer painfully of corns. But he admitted to me that he deliberately chose the tackiest style—'At my age,' he said, 'I'm allowed to seem a little dotty.' " Was Auden, when he was a young man, attractive? The photographs ("The camera always lies," he once said) attest, ambiguously, to a rather oval pale face, with something soft and heavy below the sad, triangular eyes. He played Peter Quince as well as Isolde in childhood performances, and was remembered by Sebastian Shaw, who played Petruchio opposite Auden's Katherine in a Gresham's School production of *The Taming of the Shrew,* as " 'a small, slightly puffy little boy with pink and white cheeks and almost colourless hair,' not very good at being a girl, 'red wrists projecting from frilly sleeves and never knowing what to do with his hands.' " Auden's hands win few good words in these reminiscences, and unanimity prevails concerning his extraordinary pallor. Sir John Betjeman remembers a "tall milky-skinned and coltish member of 'The House' (Christ Church) who contradicted all my statements about poetry. . . . And yet there was an oracular quality about this tough youth in corduroys that compelled my attention." Of the contributors to this volume, only the impressionable Cyril Connolly seems to have been stirred by Auden's physical appearance: "I was at once obsessed with his appearance which penetrated deep into my subconscious so that I often dreamt about him." Connolly describes a dream in which Auden had added "small firm breasts" to the attributes Connolly perceived by daylight:

> He was tall and slim, with a mole on his upper lip, rather untidy tow-colored hair in a loop over his forehead with extraordinary greenish eyes suggesting that iceberg glare he liked to claim from his Norse ancestors.

Connolly, the contributor who most feelingly conveys the impact of Auden's early poems on the English literary public, also best describes the pitted, crease-crossed ("plough marks crossing a field" to Henry Moore) face Auden elderly put on: "that striated Roman mask of luminous authority which it became harder and harder to penetrate." Auden was remarkably smooth-faced when he was young, and became prodigiously wrinkled when old. He kept his hair, whatever its color, to the end. In 1938, in China, he looked to Basil Boothby like "a big, mad white rabbit."

The touch of the uncanny in Auden's appearance may have come from his Icelandic ancestors; his life preserved and magnified it. The cumulative portrait that this tribute forms does not emphasize, nor can it quite conceal, elements of childishness retained in Auden's character. He slept in the fetal position, Michael Yates tells us, and "all his life regardless of temperature his bed was piled with a suffocating load—not for warmth but because he liked weight."* This liking for weight generated anecdotes about the coats, the carpets, the drapes, even a framed picture that his hosts would discover he had appropriated to make himself cozy. "Cosy," according to Oliver Sacks, was one of his favorite concepts; coming to tea with Auden for the first time, in 1969, Sacks found the teapot in a tea cosy, an egg served in an egg cosy, and the tank jacket of his motorbike admired as a "bike cosy." Orlan Fox adds to the coziness and the bubble baths and the aging man's increasingly petulant insistence on the punctual observance of his nine o'clock bedtime the revelation that when eating dinner Auden "always sat on a volume of the OED, as if he were a child too short for table." Auden referred to his mother as a moral authority as long as he lived, and the first picture in this book shows her as an old lady, looking strikingly like him, though without that touch of clumsy corpulence that became, finally, his walrusian abundance of folds. One of his last poems is a lullaby sung to himself:

> Now you have licence to lie
> naked, curled like a shrimplet,
> jacent in bed and enjoy
> its cosy micro-climate . . .
> Sleep, Big Baby, sleep your fill.

If Auden's unbroken connection to his fetal self tethered him, held his poetry within some bounds of tameness and talkiness, it also supplied him with a ceaseless strength, the facility of a trusting child. Of his native landscape, in "In Praise of Limestone," he wrote,

> What could be more like Mother or a fitter background
>   For her son, the flirtatious male who lounges
> Against a rock in the sunlight, never doubting

---

*This unusual fondness, which one might term "claustrophilia," links to his boyhood passion for mines and mining machinery: "From the age of four to thirteen," he wrote in *The Prolific and the Devourer*, "I had a series of passionate love-affairs with pictures of, to me, particularly attractive water-turbines, winding-engines, roller-crushers, etc., and I was never so emotionally happy as when I was underground."

That for all his faults he is loved; whose works are but
Extensions of his power to charm?

Auden's self-confidence is remarked on by many who knew him.
His brother John, a distinguished geologist, remembers his "bump-
tious precocity" in "a family in which there was love and encour-
agement to many activities." Harold Llewellyn Smith, a classmate
when Auden arrived at St. Edmund's at the age of eight, records
that "Wystan, as a small boy, was not only clever and precocious,
but was also well aware of the fact. . . . He greatly revered his father
—a man of wide scholarship—and he adored his mother, a devout
Anglican of high church inclinations. The latter spoilt 'Witny'
somewhat, as being the youngest of her three sons." Fifty years
later, Auden told Anne Fremantle that "as the youngest child in the
family and the youngest boy in my class at school, I always felt that
I was the youngest everywhere . . ."

Though some of his schoolmasters were slow to recognize it (he
received a mere third at Oxford), his peers deferred to his promise.
Rex Warner met Auden at Oxford: "My impressions of him were
of a more than ordinary boyishness, a fresh, unwrinkled, pink face
and an amazing intellectual ebullience. His appetite for facts and
ideas was voracious. His rapid voluble conversation, full of delight-
ful twists and turns, had always a kind of positive character which
distinguished him from most of us." Spender, recalling "the under-
graduate poet with the abruptly turning head, and eyes that could
quickly take the measure of people or ideas," says, "We were
grateful for a person who was so different from ourselves, not quite
a person in the way that other people were." Golo Mann detected
in him "the air of one who was used to being *primus inter pares,*
one might even say a triumphant air, so long as this does not
suggest anything exaggerated or theatrical." Auden's phenomenal
quickness and cleverness were, like his eccentricities, yoked to an
admirable moral positiveness; his "triumphant air" had a "positive
character." Kronenberger writes, "What, his great talent aside,
seemed most remarkable about him was how decidedly he knew
what he wanted, or liked, or disliked, or found boring; indeed it was
because he was so surefooted that he could think and act so fast."

Lincoln Kirstein, recalling the incongruous apparition of Auden, with his English accent and carpet slippers, serving as a major in the U.S. Army, puts it best:

> Paradoxically, from the eccentric atmosphere emanated a fresh objective utterance which quite defused the fantastic. His presence was comforting, almost endearing; he was at once so cheerful, so harmless, so bright and so right.

Auden's upbringing in limestone country gave him not only his invincible intellectual confidence but what John Bayley calls the "family life" within his poetry—the unforced social concern whereby his verse, for all its metrical and verbal cleverness, "joins itself effortlessly to life." Kronenberger comes to the same point via acquaintance: "His own personal sense of what's done or is not done smacked much more of the nursery and the schoolroom than of later, worldlier origins." Oliver Sacks, himself a doctor, sympathetically emphasizes Auden's concern with healing, with care; the son of a doctor, this sanest and most generous of modern poets displayed in his art "the amalgamation of accuracy and affection" that is the essence of care. None of these appreciations mentions a minor aspect of Auden that always impressed me: the intentness and originality he brought to every piece of job work. His anthologies—of light verse, of Kierkegaard—never lack ideas, stated in the introduction and embodied in the selections. No more intelligent compendium of English-language poetry exists than the Viking Portable anthology he and Norman Holmes Pearson edited, with its five pleasant-to-handle volumes, each one so full of discoveries and discriminations, and their very titles *(Marlowe to Marvell, Milton to Goldsmith)* cutting across the stale groupings of custom in a way that makes—as elucidated in Auden's brilliant little prefaces —perfect, fresh sense.

And yet, how alone. The word "alone" echoes through these disparate memoirs and appraisals like a unifying undertone. "Surrounded by the whole paraphernalia of broadcasting techniques he sat alone, as if on the moon's vacant surface . . ." "Described at school as 'alone but not aloof,' Wystan . . ." "Certainly Wystan was and felt himself to be alone . . ." "Many years later he returned and stood alone on that exact spot . . ." "I don't think I am over-anxious about the future, though I do quail a bit sometimes before the probability that it will be lonely. . . ." ". . . getting older, crankier, lonelier . . ." "Wystan announced to the press that he was going to Christ Church because he could be dead a week in the city before anyone found his body . . ." "Too often, looking rather formidable, he would be sitting by himself, watched from other tables. . . ." "He had also perhaps acquired some tragic quality of isolation. . . ." The life of a homosexual is lonely in its passing contacts* and in its progenitive barrenness; Auden keenly felt the lack of a family. But he struck up friendships easily, and at least one of his companionships approached a marital stability; his sexual nature was not at the very root of the "touch of the solitary" Golo Mann detected amid his "intricate web of human relationships." In his lines on the death of Freud, he wrote "to be free / Is often to be lonely." If he seemed more alone than his contemporaries, it may be that he, with the confident decisiveness that was his, had turned a more major portion of himself inward, toward his art and his determination, early announced, to be great. And if he eludes, for all the affection of their remembrances, these friends and admirers, Cyril Connolly gives the reason:

> I keep trying to describe Wystan yet I feel I am but making a grotesque waxwork because I cannot communicate the mysterious certainty of inspiration that covered old envelopes with his tiny crabbed writing.

---

*An early sonnet, published in *New Verse* of October 1933 and never reprinted, addressed itself to

> you,
> Lovely and willing every afternoon.
> But find myself with my routine to do,
> And knowing that I shall forget you soon.
> There is a wound and who shall staunch it up?

Owlish and Fishy

FLY BY NIGHT, by Randall Jarrell. Illustrated by Maurice Sendak. 30 pp. Farrar, Straus & Giroux, 1976.

In the few years before his sudden death in 1965, the poet and critic Randall Jarrell devoted surprisingly much of his energy to the creation of children's books. Translations from the German of the Brothers Grimm were followed by *The Gingerbread Rabbit* and *The Bat-Poet* in 1964 and the Newbury Honor–winning *The Animal Family* in 1965. Now, after a delay longer than its thirty spacy pages would seem to have required, the final and slimmest entry in the Jarrell juvenile canon arrives, entitled *Fly by Night*. It is illustrated, as were the previous two, by Maurice Sendak; the illustrations are intense and loving and uneasy-making, in tune with the prose they illumine.

The hero of *Fly by Night* is a boy named David, who lives alone, with none save animals for friends, and who at night evidently lifts up out of his bed and skims through the moonlit air in the nude. The nudity is unspecified in the text but looms specific in Sendak's illustrations, one of which shows a prepubescent penis and another a rather prominent derriere. Most little boys that I have lived with have been rather severe and shy about nakedness and slept with pajamas on, sometimes with underpants under the pajamas. But David's dreaming subconscious, and not his sleeping body, is presumably represented, which accounts also for the visually disturbing manner in which the boy's figure is out of scale with the other figures (mice, sheep, an owl's frown) in the finely hatched pen-and-ink drawings.

Flying of course is a euphemism in more than one language for sexual activity, and a man can recall those disorienting intimations of potency that visited him in bed at about the age David seems to be, when the sensations of blanket and sheets and illusions of changing direction and inert voyage prepare the onanistic mystery. Launched, David glides with criminal stealth into his parents' room. His father is a substantial lump in the bed, with his head out; his mother, however, has placed her head beneath a pillow. Mother, as she was for Oedipus, is unrecognizable. David invades their dreams, and sees himself in process of replacing his father: "his father, looking very small, is running back and forth with David on his back, only David is as big as ever. His father is panting." His mother's dreams, like her head, are eclipsed by feathers. These feathers, outdoors, become the face of a mother owl, "with its big round brown eyes: each of them has a feathery white ring around it, and then a brown one, and then a white one, and then a brown one, till the rings come together and make big brown and white rings around its whole head." This concentric vaginal apparition holds in its claws a "big silvery fish."

David thinks to himself, "I didn't know owls could catch *fish.*"

Himself a fish in air, he swims after the owl, and watches her feed her young, and listens as she recites to her owlets a long bedtime poem, about a lost owl making its way back to the nest. Floating back into his bed, David gropes after who the owl's gaze reminds him of, wakes to his own mother's gaze, and after a moment of confusion perceives by sunlight that "his mother looks at him like his mother." Finis. The storyteller should be commended for the tact of his language and the depth at which his imagery seeks to touch, amid its feathery circles gripping big silvery somethings, the forbidden actual. All of Jarrell's children's tales have a sinister stir about them, the breath of true forlornness felt by children. But the stir tends to remain unsettled, unresolved by the clarifying power adulthood promises. Successful children's literature has a conspiratorial element; but the conspiracy is not among equals, one side is pretending. With Jarrell there is little pretense; he shares with his young readers as one child shares with others a guilty secret, and imparts his own unease.

The poems he includes in *The Bat-Poet* and *Fly by Night* are not as good as they should be. They aspire to a tender sharpness achieved elsewhere—by his contemporary Theodore Roethke, whose animal poems catch Nature's flip cruelty in a line (in "The Heron": "He jerks a frog across his bony lip") or brood with the grief of a helpless god:

> Where has he gone, my meadow mouse,
> My thumb of a child that nuzzled in my palm?
> To run under the hawk's wing,
> Under the eye of the great owl watching from the elm tree,
> To live by courtesy of the shrike, the snake, the tom-cat.

By comparison Jarrell's own owls are symbolic menaces: "The ear that listens to the owl believes / In death." If he was no Roethke, he was no A. A. Milne, either; his poems do not address themselves to children, exclusively and positively, but are included, with disturbing *double-entendre*, in his collection of "serious" poetry as well. As they appear in the children's books, they seem stuck-on, and a bit stuck-up. What is most poetic about the bat-poet is the author's prose description of him, "the color of coffee with cream in it," as he sleeps among his fellow-bats, the wriggling of one forcing a wriggling of all, so that "it looked as if a fur wave went over them."

The longest and best of Jarrell's children's books, *The Animal Family*, holds no formal poetry, but most intensely presents his habitual themes of individual lostness, of estrangement within a family, of the magic of language, of the wild beauty beyond our habitations. A hunter living alone in the forest makes his way to the shore and begins to converse with a creature of the sea, called a "mermaid" but in fact a female seal. He appears to marry her; she certainly shares his bed and does his housework, though Maurice Sendak, who decorates the book with landscapes, was not called upon to depict her dragging her flippers through these connubial duties. It's a disquieting match, as if Jarrell had taken literally Roethke's lovely erotic line, "She'd more sides than a seal." As in *Fly by Night*, the mother's role is flooded with strangeness, and a male child's egotism is grotesquely served. The hunter/seal couple adopt, first, a bear, then a lynx, and finally a little boy found alive in a rowboat with his dead mother. With the acquiescence of his four-footed siblings, the human child takes over the prime place in the animal family, and is told by his adopted mother, in her liquid accent, that he has been with them always. With this lie, the book ends. To Jarrell's vision of bliss, adoption by members of another species seems intrinsic. His first book for children, *The Gingerbread Rabbit*, deviated from its gingerbread-man model in the cookie's adoption by a childless pair of real rabbits, while the human mother who had concocted the hero of pastry fabricated a substitute of cloth and thread, bringing yet another texture into the uneasy patchwork of fur, skin, and dough.

The writing in *The Animal Family* is exquisite, and all of Jarrell's little juveniles are a cut above the run in intelligence and unfaked feeling. The feeling, however, remains somewhat locked behind the combinative oddness, the mix of pluralism and isolation and warping transposition; these tales of boys active at night and bats active in day bend, as it were, around an unseen center. They are surreal as not even *Alice* is surreal, for the anfractuosities of Carroll's nightmare wind back to the sunny riverbank, while Jarrell's leave us in mist, in an owl's twilight, without that sense of *emergence*, of winning through and clearing up, intrinsic to children's classics from "Cinderella" to *Charlotte's Web*.

Second Reader's Report: An eleven-year-old boy I know read *Fly by Night* in eleven minutes and said he liked it very much. He couldn't finish *The Bat-Poet*, though, and after immersing himself in *The Animal Family* for an hour looked up and said, smiling, that it was good but had "a certain dullness."

Sissman's Prose

An Introduction to Innocent Bystander, *by L. E. Sissman (Vanguard, 1975)*

ED SISSMAN was precocious enough to be a momentary Quiz Kid but he took his time becoming a poet and came even later to publish prose. At the age of forty, having for five years been enriching the pages of *The New Yorker* with his witty, elegaic, densely actual, airily effortless, often moving, and usually blank verse, he began to write conspicuously even-tempered book appraisals for that magazine, and not long thereafter took to sharing his preternaturally keen observations and memories with readers of *The Atlantic Monthly*. This book is his selection—roughly two-thirds of the total —from a half-decade's worth of his monthly pieces. He calls his column "The Innocent Bystander," and indeed there is something upright, poised, and easily adaptable, like a stance, in his manner of speaking; no settled orotundities from an Easy Chair for him. His columns flit from complaints about restaurant service to homage to Auden and Wilson and Waugh, from detailed prescriptions for a better world or even a bigger Western movie to paeans upon the timeless cycle of seasons, from reminiscence that hurts us with its stab of loss to topical and political reactions that almost corroborate our bystander's alleged innocence. Not all good writers and bright minds are qualified to compose a monthly report on nothing in particular. A boyhood hobbyist, a quick study, a constant reader, Sissman knows books and birds and cars and engines of war, pops up with startling patches of expertise on architecture and graphics, has travelled well in—of all countries—the United States. When he evokes a city, it is Detroit or New York or Boston; there is no confusing the tint of the pavements. When he recalls a day from his life, though it comes from as far away as November 1944, it arrives not only with all its solid furniture but with its very own weather—in this case, "thin, slate-colored clouds sometimes letting through flat blades of sun." Sissman's painterly powers are, of course, shown to best advantage in his poetry, where the metrical form becomes a shimmering skin of wordplay, compression, antic exactitude, sudden sweet directness, swoops and starts of rhythm. Though possessing the declarative virtues of prose—hospitable, even, to dialogue and narrative suspense—his poetry is always poetic. His prose, correspondingly, but for its high quotient of visual coloring and an occasional verbal exotic like "encarcelled," "wodge," "umbel," "gormless," and "contrail," is surprisingly, and comfortingly, prosaic.

A sensible, decent man: that is the voice. His poetry is both more tender and more cruel than his prose ever is; his audience, we feel, has shifted in his mind from the single unshockable inner attendant to whom a poet addresses himself—has shifted to a congeries (another of his pet words) of fallible, woundable, only slightly educable fellow-mortals. From Montaigne on, this is the voice of the essayist, this voice inviting us onto the shared ground of a middling sensuality, a middling understanding, a voice that, if it raves, raves never against us, but against a perfidious other, some stronghold as closed to our innocence as Mamma Leone's kitchen or Richard Nixon's White House. To be sure, this particular bystander's voice is raised rather often, as befits the good citizen of a democracy, in protest; the contemplation of television's failure to seize its "matchless opportunity for art, instruction, and edification" lifts Sissman's prose close to melody:

> . . . this outpouring of festering garbage . . . the aforementioned All commercial, with its gaggle of greasy-oil haters, the continuing series of Wisk "ring around the collar" commercials with their hackle-stirring nyah-nyah refrain . . . Detroit-car commercials that are still trying to sell us the big old gas hogs (whose chassis engineering hasn't essentially been changed or improved since 1936) on a platform of sex, showing off, and spurious luxury . . . it is instructive that our largest and, presumably, most astute industry proved no more prescient about the energy mess than the jowly clowns in Washington who guide our destinies, God help us all.

That largeness signifies astuteness, that commercials are not *intended* to irritate and madden us, that engineering will improve more than it needs to—these are the presumptions of a believer in a perfectible world, which needs only to be as energetic and decent as the writer himself, as willing to find "a delicate balance, between the ideal and the real, between the pragmatic and the impossible." And as brave, he is too modest to say, as himself at facing the impossibilities that overwhelm us as we live.

For these alert, sympathetic, manifoldly curious and basically cheerful essays were written by a man who, for ten years, has been suffering from a disease believed to be "routinely fatal." He has arranged this collection so that not until near the end, in the two remarkable "Night Music" pieces, is this fact about himself divulged. Nor to those of us fortunate enough to know Ed Sissman in the flesh (he is six foot four, and holds his own in every sense) is pain or anxiety ever divulged, or permitted to shadow his output of amiable attentive intelligence. Only in a few of the poems, such as the recent "October," does he betray a sense that he has been dealt "bad cards." As he says in these pages, his reaction to the diagnosis, in 1965, when he was thirty-seven, of Hodgkin's disease, was to sharpen his appreciation of life, step up his professional activity, and quicken his muse, who had just begun to speak in print. "Instead of a curtain falling, a curtain rose. And stayed up, revealing a stage decked in defining light . . ." I do not believe, strange to say, that the new urgency his life borrowed from darkness much changed the quality of his poetry, which from its first appearance was nostalgic, lyrical, celebrative, reminiscent—lived moments recaptured with great verbal gaiety. The quantity, both of poems and of emotion, may have been heightened by the challenge, but the tone has held steady; in an age when so many of the healthy and lucky have been full of self-pity, he has shown none, and faced his talent outward toward a world that, like the month of May, is two-prongedly "merry, scary."

Searching for this last quote, I have just now reread this essay, with its punning cry for help ("M'aidez"), and have been struck, rereading, by how much I had missed or taken in dully—the Hopperesque evocation of early summer light, "turning white house sides to solid glare, falling into the cups of daffodils to recharge and redouble their goldenness"; the auditing of May sounds that even takes note of "the tiny, quiet crackle as the old grass dries and curls still further"; the miraculously precise paragraph on the emerging colors—all sweeping toward the somber and gentle aphorism "We were not, either by temperament or experience, meant to live in paradise." Yet it is a function of art to show us the paradise that, disguised as the ordinary, surrounds us as we live; a lesser function is, as Sissman elsewhere suggests, to instruct us in "accommodation," the attuning of an imperfect environment to a perishing self. Both functions are well performed in *Innocent Bystander*, a valuable binding-together of one man's monthly confessions, exhortations, celebrations.

Sissman's Poetry

HELLO, DARKNESS: *The Collected Poems of L. E. Sissman,* edited by Peter Davison. 294 pp. Atlantic Monthly Press, 1978.

The poetic accomplishment of L. E. Sissman can now be viewed entire, and purchased entire, in this posthumous collection ably edited and fondly introduced by Peter Davison. *Hello, Darkness* contains the three volumes of verse Sissman published in 1968, 1969, and 1971, plus thirty-nine poems never before collected. Of these, some are light verse and casual metrical jokes scribbled to friends; but most are in the usual Sissmanesque mode—moments remembered or envisioned with a fascinating specificity, set forth in a dense but dancing blank verse varied by spurts of rhyme, liberally besprinkled with epigraphs and dedications, and frequently arranged in suites of linked episodes. Or arranged, perhaps, like snapshots on the pages of an album; among the many petty modern skills that engaged Sissman's intelligence was that of photography, and a hard-edged, highlighted, deceptively factual quality balances the elegiac tone of his running, randomly accruing verse autobiography. Elegy deepened, as his long-foreseen death neared, to anguish. His last poems, written before the muse deserted him in 1974 as abruptly as she had descended in 1963, maintained, amid the medical humiliations suffered by the slowly dying, his alert eye and exuberant fancy; such a maintenance now appears, on the last pages of his life's work, heroic.

The outlines of Sissman's career as a poet are clearer than most. A precocious child from Detroit, he went to Harvard too young, flunked out, and upon his return in 1947 created a close approximation of his mature verse style and received, among other reassurances of talent, the Garrison Poetry Prize. An immense artistic silence followed while he sought his place in the working world and eventually found it, as a Boston advertising man. In 1963, happily remarried and settled in the far suburb of Still River, he began to write again:

> A word,
> Now, in his thirty-sixth summer, surfaces, leading
> A train of thought, a manifest freight, up to
> The metalled road of light—for the first time
> In ten disused, interior years—along
> The rusted, weed-flagged lines.

By 1964 his poems, striking in their amplitude, began to appear in *The New Yorker*. In 1965, a year of terrific productivity for him, he was told he had Hodgkin's disease; chemotherapy gave him intermissions of health and eleven more years of life. Though he won a few awards and enjoyed a number of literary friendships, his work received scant, if not dismissive, attention from professional poetry critics. He was like no one else, with his benign discursiveness, his non-academic base, his nostalgic obsession with the Forties. Though he aspired to be a Hopper of words, he seemed less American than British, kin to Auden, Betjeman, Larkin. The crucial influence upon his packed, sometimes convolute pentameters came from centuries away—a youthful "Overdose of Jacobethan diction." With seventeenth-century richness as a model, his blank verse displayed an aggressive if not prankish wealth of scientifically, commercially, multilinguistically exact terminology and a onetime spelling champion's rakish vocabulary—"fane," "virid," "pervigilium," "ennial," "cenereous," "stertorous radamacues," "repletive borborygmogenesis."

Reread entire, the three volumes published during his lifetime challenge our patience with so much verbal energy exercised on so consistent a level. So many small astonishments wear responsiveness down, where the matter or point is obscure. The first volume, *Dying: An Introduction*, captures the warmest memories—the two "In and Out" sequences above all—with an effortless facility; even the majestic "War Requiem" from the second collection, *Scattered Returns*, seems in comparison, over its thirty-two segments, a touch programmatic. The title piece of the third volume, *Pursuit of Honor*, seems more than a touch inflated—an inflated retread at that, for by now the poet-narrator's pursuits of women, in that long restless time of seeking between Detroit and Still River, have merged into one overly allegorical chase. His material by now, we feel, has been thoroughly covered. The last lines of this sequence even appear, uncharacteristically, to preen upon the poet's "joker's silks." This most unassuming of poets might be accused, on occasion, of a calm that is flat, a certain veiling of central feeling. What is the emotional engine that has dredged up so many buried days and set them down intact? Like another ailing descriptive genius, Proust, he (see "The West Forties" or "The Veterans") sometimes describes without telling; pastness itself justifies the attempt at recapture.

But, in sum, the three volumes constitute, in a way rarely true of poetry since Browning, a world: dense, bustling, brimming with the utterly honorable quotidian truth of a Northeast-American professional man. In the posthumous poems we see—appalling spectacle!—this solid world drained, darkened, and blown away by death. What other poet has ever given such wry and unblinking witness to his own dying? Sissman saw it long coming, but at first, as he states in his essay "A Little Night Music," rejected the reality: "My first reaction . . . was to clamp a tight lid of security down . . . 'it couldn't happen to me.'" His outraged vitality shouldered aside the prognosis and pursued his career. But by 1970, he could end seven lines of light verse with "the nick of evernight, soon to begin" and note that Clotho was prolonging the thread of his life to his "now flagging wonder and applause."

None of his editors welcomed his late, exhausted poems upon what had become his sole subject, dying; but now that he is dead, they loom as a final step forward, a mighty act of writing. No wonder he fell silent at last; by 1974 he had written to the edge of oblivion, and through it. The last three poems of this posthumous collection, especially, grapple the unthinkable and the unbearable into bright, firm form. In "Homage to Clotho: A Hospital Suite" Sissman descends into the hell of hospitalization, where "the bone-marrow needle sinks its fang / Through atomies of drugged and dullard skin" and young attendants arrive with a "snake-handler's fist of catheters" and kindly practice "refined / White-sheeted torture." "Cancer: A Dream" (his drugged life became one dream after another) poses his fatal plight in the metaphor of a sound-stage. Incontinence and impotence have their scenes in the scenario, and then, with lonely grotesquerie, the actor performs for the "undamped, undimmed" lenses of the cameras, his "solo *pas de deux* / The crab dance." Superimposition, the method of metaphor and the genius of poetry, finds its fleshly parallel in the impositions of disease:

> Partner mine,
> With your pink carapace coterminous
> With mine, your hard two-fingered hands contained
> In mine, your long legs telescoped inside
> My legs, your entire Geist the work of my
> Own brain, why do you lead me such a dance . . . ?

The final suite, "Tras Os Montes," describes the death of Sissman's mother and father, which occurred shortly before his own. Then his own, pinned to the near future by the hyphen of "(197-)," is imagined in the likeness of mountain-climbing. First he ascends in company, then with his wife, and last alone. His tricksome language rises with him to a new simplicity:

> Is all the language at my tongue's command
> Too little to announce my stammered thanks
> For your unquestioning hand at my side . . . ?

> . . . the final climb
> Across the mountains to the farther shore
> Of sundown on the watersheds, where self,
> Propelled by its last rays, sways in the sway
> Of the last grasses and falls headlong in
> The darkness of the dust it is part of
> Upon the passes where we are no more . . .

The poet's hand "Reverts to earth and its inveterate love / For the inanimate and its return." These are his last, noble lines, capping a bravura last sentence thirty lines long. After two more years of remission and relapse, Sissman died in March of 1976. In a decade of self-destructive poets, he fought for his life. His poetry gave back more generously than he had received, and carried his beautiful wit into darkness undimmed.

Three Poems on Being a Poet, by Yevgeny Yevtushenko

Adapted from Literal Translations from the Russian by Albert C. Todd

MONOLOGUE OF AN AMERICAN POET

to Robert Lowell

A loved one leaves
          like air from the lungs—
vapor amid the final dry snowflakes,
the black branches clicking and sagging with ice.
She can't be breathed back in!
An idle gesture, I abrade my cheek on the rusty trunk
of a drainpipe.
        To no purpose, I weep.
                She departs.

Friends depart,
      fellow sufferers,
            peers,
as from the field of the young
we are led toward separate pens
away from the once-shared milk.
In vain, like an unweaned whelp,
              I whine for friends . . .

they don't come back!
Hopes depart—
        such darling ladies,
whom I use on such useless occasions!
Only their petticoats stay in my hands;
hopes are meant to be held for a moment.
Certitude departs.
        I remember, I swore a sacred oath
to break my stupid head against the wall
or the wall with my stupid head.
My head is scratched, true,
           but unbroken.

And what of the wall?

          The bastard smirks—

on its blankness they are blandly changing

the posters,

        the portraits of heroes . . .

O certitude,

       where are you?

New York,

      your dark sky circles above me

                  like a hawk.

America, believe me,

         I'm finished, I'm

              finished, finished.

I am a ship

      where all the cabins smell of doom

and rats leap in terror from the clammy deck.

Hey, seagulls—don't weep!

          Don't,

             don't pity me!

My lovely leggy guests abandon me.

They take their places, as prescribed,

             the first in the lifeboat—

Farewell, my mistresses!

My apple-cheeked cadets abandon me.

They want to live.

       Fair enough,

         they are still young.

Farewell, lads!

     Row ahead.

        You are men.

Now the inane rumble of the engine shuts down.

Only talent

     like a drunken, unshaven captain

stands somberly on the bridge.

         The captain is the captain,

but he too, tears smearing his windburned skin,
he too abandons me,
                    he too, he too . . .
Hey, lifeboats—
                    stand away!
A ship, when it sinks,
                    makes a maelstrom around it.
To be totally alone
                    hurts worse than a knife,
but I won't suck anyone down with me.
I forgive you all.
                    Robed in death's foam,
I bequeath it you
                    to demolish that bastardly wall.
My trumpet juts
                    from the marble swirls: comrades,
battle on . . .

                                    [*1967*]

MONOLOGUE OF A POLAR FOX
ON AN ALASKAN FUR FARM

I am a blue fox on a gray farm.
Condemned to slaughter by my color
behind this gnawproof wire screen,
I find no comfort in being blue.

Lord, but I want to molt! I burn
to strip myself of myself in my frenzy;
but the luxuriant, bristling blue
seeps through the skin—scintillant traitor.

How I howl—feverishly I howl
like a furry trumpet of the last judgment,

beseeching the stars either for freedom forever,
or at least forever to be molting.

A passing visitor captured my howl
on a tape recorder. What a fool!
He didn't howl himself, but he might
begin to, if he were caught in here!

I fall to the floor, dying.
Yet somehow, I fail to die.
I stare in depression at my own Dachau
and I know: I'll never escape.

Once, after dining on a rotten fish,
I saw that the door was unhooked;
toward the starry abyss of flight I leaped
with a pup's perennial recklessness.

Lunar gems cascaded across my eyes.
The moon was a circle! I understood
that the sky is not broken into squares,
as it had been from within the cage.

Alaska's snowdrifts towered all around,
and I desperately, morbidly capered,
and freedom did a Twist inside my lungs
with the stars I had swallowed.

I played pranks, I barked nonsense
at the trees. I was my own pure self.
And the iridescent snow was unafraid
that it was also very blue.

My mother and father didn't love each other,
but they mated. How I'd like

to find a girl-fox so that I could
tumble and fly with her in this sumptuous powder!

But then I'm tired. The snow is too much.
I cannot lift my sticking paws.
I have found no friend, no girl friend.
A child of captivity is too weak for freedom.

He who's conceived in a cage will weep for a cage.
Horrified, I understood how much I love
that cage, where they hide me behind a screen,
and the fur farm—my motherland.

And so I returned, frazzled and beaten.
No sooner did the cage clang shut,
than my sense of guilt became resentment
and love was turned again to hate.

In you, Alaska, I howled in lost despair.
In prison now, I am howling in despair.
My America, I am lost,
but who hasn't gotten lost in you?

True, there are changes on the fur farm.
They used to suffocate us in sacks.
Now they kill us in the modern mode—
electrocution. It's wonderfully tidy.

I contemplate my Eskimo-girl keeper.
Her hand rustles endearingly over me.
Her fingers scratch the back of my neck.
But a Judas sadness floods her angel eyes.

She saves me from all diseases
and won't let me die of hunger,

but I know that when the time, set firm as iron,
arrives, she will betray me, as is her duty.

Brushing a touch of moisture from her eyes,
she will ease a wire down my throat, crooning.
BE HUMANE TO THE EMPLOYEES! ON FUR FARMS
HONOR THE OFFICE OF EXECUTIONER!*

I would like to be naïve, like my father,
but I was born in captivity: I am not him.
The one who feeds me will betray me.
The one who pets me will kill me.

                                        [*1967*]

                    SMOG

I awake in the Chelsea Hotel.
Am I dreaming?
                    Is it the heat?
                                    I seem to see
black streams,
                    cloudy black worms,
slithering into the cracks across the floor.
Galia's nightgown has become a shroud:
soot is sprinkled
                    on the pale cotton
like coal on sugar.
                        Cruel as a rasp,
a cough tears her chest.
                            "Zhenya, I'm frightened!"
In our cell of a room,
                        the odor of Dachau.
"Zhenya, sweet Zhenya,
                        I'm suffocating . . ."

---

*Echoing typical signs on a Soviet collective farm.

Her face becomes a martyr's,
imitated in wax.

"Air,

   air . . ."

The window opens wide and—
I know I'm not dreaming—

a shaggy faceless beast is in the room,

opaque as a nimbus cloud, surging . . .

"Zhenya,
I cannot breathe!"

Galia, my love,
I am already half dead.

The air I gulp
is airless.

There's no vent!

Shall we perish on one another's lips?

Give respiration each to each?

Equally we're prisoners of the smog;

it's too late.
Both of us are poisoned,

both of us,

and a kiss in this stench

would be mutual poisoning.

There are framed instructions
on maples and elms:

HOW TO KISS IN GAS MASKS.

In bars, they hang the brand-new slogan:

YOU CAN BREATHE BEST
THROUGH VODKA.

And the uptown radio

doesn't give a damn,

blaring out joyously:

"And the smog rolls on . . ."

Now who comes here,
shambling along the sidewalks

with the adolescent sadness of

Marcello Mastroianni?
Miller?
        Arthur?
                Slowly he whispers to me:
"It smells of fires,
                    of a witch hunt . . ."
  Miller coughs,
                emaciated,
                        his face a handsome hatchet.
Harshly he speaks in a spirit of prophecy:
"More inquisitions will set further fires.
Smog—
        this is the smoke of burnings to come."
Awkwardly shielding himself with his wing,
thirsting for secrets
                and weary of secrets,
gaunt as a stork
                on a house of his own books,
anxiously stands Updike with his noble beak.
"Zhenya,
        men have been cruelly duped;
the earth has been set on
the backs of nonexistent Leviathans.
Mankind, all of it,
                is overstrained
with tension,
            like a centaur.
Biune, it neighs and brays,
chafed by its own duality.
Possibly smog
            is the furious steam
from the centaur's distended nostrils!"
Wiping the smog from his glasses,
standing amid books as if among gravestones,
clearing his throat, Lowell spoke to me,
with a lofty professorial style:
"Only ghosts and books have a sense of honor.

Of what are we ashamed?
Only of ghosts am I ashamed.
And I am a product of ghosts. I am
Alyosha Karamazov and Saint-Just together.
I believe in the vengeance of history,
in the vengeance of Heaven for depravity.
Possibly smog is an ectoplasm
descended for vengeance upon the world's baseness."
Allen Ginsberg—
     cagey prophet-baboon—
thumps his hairy chest
      as a shaman thumps a tambourine:
"Darkness is coming,
     darkness!
It reeks of deepest Hell.
Those who can breathe this stench
are not worth keeping alive!
When the world is a cadaver,
a cesspool of fog and chaos,
it is a sign of excellence
to sink and drown . . .
False ideas,
   false morality,
fuming for so many years,
      have soiled
       Heaven.
Brahma lets fall this sad slime—
nobody can suck it in!"
But above the smog,
     above today's exhausted vapors,
Whitman's basso thunders
      like the roar of Sabaoth:
"Listen!
   It is easy to lose your breath on a precipice.
But breathe deeply,
     breathe deeply!
       Give it a try!

Inhale all together!
    You will see—
                only inhale,
and the phantom smog
            by your breathing will be swept from the sky!"
And I felt the epoch
            standing still awaiting,
like a revolution of the universe,
                    our common deep breath.

[*1967*]

Stand Fast I Must

THE NEW OXFORD BOOK OF CHRISTIAN VERSE, chosen and edited by Donald Davie. 320 pp. Oxford University Press, 1982.

In fifty or so years the two-thousandth Easter will come round, and though a century ago the utter demise of Christianity was being confidently foreseen, the odds are now that there will be some, if not relatively many, Christians to celebrate it. Religions are hard to create, hard to replace, and not easy, it would seem, to do without. The terrible blows given Biblical literalness by Darwin and the geologists and astronomers have been absorbed, or at least shrugged off, by the creed; Christian ethics has either co-opted, ignored, or set its face against the ethical counter-proposals of Marx and Freud; the holocaustal slaughters of the century's two world wars have been allowed no more than history's earlier slaughters to argue decisively against God's goodness. True, there has been a great falling-off. But, then, from its inception onward, Christianity has never not been embattled. A hostile and scoffing world is where it knows itself to be situated—"unto the Jews a stumbling block, and unto the Greeks foolishness." Though many theologies of false reasonableness have been offered down through the ages, Kierkegaard and Barth and Berdyaev and Unamuno in modern times have rooted the faith more securely than ever in its native soil of desperation. Like the vermiform appendix, Christianity will be with Western man a while longer.

Nevertheless, it comes as a surprise—though to us believers a grateful one—that Oxford University Press still considers "Christian verse" a viable category and, scarcely four decades after Lord David Cecil's plump anthology of it, has issued *The New Oxford Book of Christian Verse*, edited by Donald Davie, an English poet and critic now teaching at Vanderbilt. Mr. Davie in his introduction sets forth his "rather stringent" guidelines: "poetry that appeals, either explicitly or by plain implication . . . to some one or more of the distinctive doctrines of the Christian church: to the Incarnation pre-eminently, to Redemption, Judgement, the Holy Trinity, the Fall" and yet a poetry which in no way "fails to measure up strictly in *artistry* to the best of the secular verse written through the same centuries." Armed with this two-edged criterion, Mr. Davie has ranged widely, taking poems both earlier and later than his predecessor and including many by Americans, Scotsmen, and women—three groups virtually absent from Mr. Cecil's selection. Yet Mr. Davie's selection ends by being over two hundred pages shorter.

Anthology-making, like sculpturing in marble, is in large measure an art of taking away. Slews of "devotional" and "religiose" verse deemed suitable for the older anthology have been evidently felt by Mr. Davie to lack the necessary doctrinal strictness or inner spark. He includes no verses by those rollicking Edwardian Catholics Chesterton and Belloc; nor a single line by Coventry Patmore, the late-Victorian to whom Lord Cecil gave fifteen pages. Neither Matthew Arnold nor Robert Browning, who each saved what he could from Faith's ebbing sea, is represented, and Tennyson only by some excerpts from "In Memoriam." William Blake, of whom Lord Cecil was "doubtful whether he should appear in a book of Christian verse at all," nevertheless was allowed eight splendid poems; Mr. Davie reduces his presence to the four clangorous stanzas of "Jerusalem." Then, too, Alexander Pope, Edward Young, and James Thomson all fall from the rolls. Three heroes of the earlier collection—John Donne, Thomas Traherne, and Gerard Manley Hopkins—are sharply reduced in representation, with a severity that seems almost perverse; one would think that at least Hopkins's sonnet "God's Grandeur" and the famous fourth and sixth of Donne's "Holy Sonnets" would be requisite in an anthology of Christian verse in English. Shakespeare, interestingly, is represented identically in both volumes, by the lonely Sonnet 146 ("Poor soul, the centre of my sinful earth . . .") and Milton's "Lycidas," that great paean to the hope of Resurrection, is snubbed by both in favor of his youthful "On the Morning of Christ's Nativity" and patches of *Paradise Lost.* Richard Rolle, Robert Henryson, John Skelton, Richard Stanyhurst, Sir Walter Raleigh, William Drummond of Hawthornden, Sir Thomas Brown, Edmund Waller, Abraham Cowley, George Crabbe, Elizabeth Barrett Browning, Dante Gabriel Rossetti, William Morris, Digby Mackworth Dolben, Lionel Johnson, Fredegond Shove, and Ruth Pitter —all were singingly present in 1940, and are absent from the choir in 1982.

Who, then, *does* Mr. Davie include? Though Donne is deposed, George Herbert continues to reign and is spoken of by both anthologists as a kind of touchstone. The next generation's preëminent religious poet, the more mystical, less ecclesiastical Henry Vaughan, also holds firm (Cecil, fourteen poems; Davie, twelve, eight of them repeaters). From the eighteenth century, the stanzas of William Cowper and Christopher Smart are represented far more copiously than in the older selection, and in general congregational hymns have been gathered in an abundance that is fairly numbing. Emily Dickinson, unheard-of in Lord Cecil's book, places second only to Anonymous in the number of poems Mr. Davie reprints, and another poetess obscure in her lifetime, Mary Herbert, Countess of Pembroke, fills ten pages with her versified psalms. *The New Oxford Book of Christian Verse* opens with a lovely translation (by Michael Alexander) of the Anglo-Saxon "Dream of the Rood" and ends with a procession of post-relativity celebrants led by Eliot and Auden and gathering in a number of English poets unknown to me. The poems by F. T. Prince and the Eliotic C. H. Sisson are strong and moving; the Christian content of some of the others—by R. S. Thomas and Peter Dale, for instance—would take a radium counter to detect. I would rather have seen in their place some of the entries by Marianne Moore, Dylan Thomas, e. e. cummings, and even Hart Crane in Horace Gregory and Marya Zaturenska's little *Mentor Book of Religious Verse.*

Why do we tend to cavil at these "new" Oxford anthologies? Perhaps because we encountered the old ones when young and impressionable. F. O. Matthiessen's *Oxford Book of American Verse* defined my student sense of American and modernist verse both; unjustly, no doubt, Richard Ellmann's successor seems ponderous and indiscriminate. And Kingsley Amis's *New Oxford Book of Light Verse* feels all too lightweight after the radical, if possibly wrong-headed, definition of the form attempted by Auden's Oxford anthology of 1938. Auden, strange to say, defined "light verse" as poetry whose language is "straightforward and close to ordinary speech," while Mr. Davie proposes that Christian poets "put a specially high value on what is called 'the *plain* style,' in which elaboration is avoided." Since hymn writers like Isaac Watts and Charles Wesley and William Cowper "wanted to speak plainly to plain men and women, to the unlettered but devout worshippers in the pews," their verse is "light" in Auden's sense—and of course Watts's homilistic rhymes were a favorite butt of Lewis Carroll's parodies.

Mr. Davie cannot be accused of compiling an anthology without an idea behind it. The appeal as well as the dulling effect of his selection, read straight through, stems from his adherence to the standards set forth in his introduction. He takes a chapel, as opposed to Lord Cecil's high-church, approach to Christian verse; he gives us less Hopkins and Eliot, and more Methodists and Puritans, including the Americans Anne Bradstreet, Edward Taylor, the obscure Urian Oakes, and their spiritual descendants Emily Dickinson and John Greenleaf Whittier. He goes out of his way to include Wordsworth's "Resolution and Independence," arguing that the leech-gatherer is a Scottish Presbyterian, and he bedevils his readers with a goodly amount of semi-opaque Scots dialect.

Not just the gray-and-dun sectarian tint makes this anthology somewhat dispiriting to read. The very purpose of Christian verse is to celebrate what is not manifest; it therefore denies itself those

worldly colors that delight us in most poetry and relies for sensa-
tional content upon intimations that are delicate and elusive. *Contra
mundum* pious sentiments must tend to be; "For God comes not
till man be overthrown; / Peace is the seed of grace, in dead flesh
sown"—to quote the Jacobean Fulke Greville. Or, as Vaughan puts
it in "Quickness":

> False life! a foil and no more, when
>   Wilt thou be gone?
> Thou foul deception of all men
> That would not have the true come on.

The Christian God descended incarnate into this false life, and
generated a certain vocabulary of incident which is concrete; cru-
cifixion, for instance, whatever we believe of the Crucifixion, was
actual and there is no moment of religious feeling in these poems
more vivid and effortless than, in "Dream of the Rood," the cross
itself saying,

> I shook when His arms embraced me
>   but I durst not bow to ground,
> stoop to Earth's surface.
> Stand fast I must.

And near our own end of the Christian Era, Auden in virtually all
monosyllables struck off:

> A crowd of ordinary decent folk
> Watched from without and neither moved nor spoke
> As three pale figures were led forth and bound
> To three posts driven upright in the ground.
>
> The mass and majesty of this world, all
>   That carries weight and always weighs the same
> Lay in the hands of others; they were small
>   And could not hope for help and no help came:
>   What their foes liked to do was done, their shame
> Was all the worst could wish; they lost their pride
> And died as men before their bodies died.

One can feel, in the chronological course of this anthology, the
language lose sharpness and variety as the focus of the poets moves

from the Biblical drama, naïvely accepted as fact and self-explanatory, to the inward drama of faith and introspection. Psychological motions vivid and poignant in Herbert become robustly voiced but foreordained maneuvers in Cowper, and finally Emily Dickinson takes up the tired phrases of conventional faith "rebelliously," as Mr. Davie says, "or sardonically."

This failure of concreteness does not invalidate the Christian assertions; a concrete and manifest God would be an absolute tyrant with no place in His universe for free-willed men. But it does lead language toward an edge where words dim, becoming worn tokens of communal reassurance or else ghostly embodiments of negativity. "I am impatient for that loss," the Australian James McAuldy wrote in this century, "By which the spirit gains." The definitive expression of such an impatience would be a blank piece of paper; the paradox of the inexpressive haunts and even hollows these poems, which like bejewelled chalices stand waiting to be filled.

TALES

Magic Mirrors

THE USES OF ENCHANTMENT: *The Meaning and Importance of Fairy Tales,* by Bruno Bettelheim. 328 pp. Knopf, 1976.

"Each fairy tale is a magic mirror which reflects some aspects of our inner world, and of the steps required by our evolution from immaturity to maturity"—by the light of this axiom Bruno Bettelheim has written a charming book about enchantment, a profound book about fairy tales. He begins by observing, as "an educator and therapist of severely disturbed children," that folk fairy tales remain the most satisfying and revelatory type of children's literature; that, though set in never-never lands and dealing with palpably fantastic events, fairy tales conduct a "moral education" subtler and richer than "any other type of story within a child's comprehension." Their subtlety and richness has been acquired during the centuries of oral retelling before they were set down by such literary men as Charles Perrault and the Brothers Grimm, and can be extended now, as parents retell with their own intuitive emphases and elaborations stories already laden with "important messages to the conscious, the preconscious, and the unconscious mind, on whatever level each is functioning at the time."

This is not new news. Freud wrote his famous essay on the tale of the Three Caskets, and the Jungians are no strangers to folk wisdom. Sleeping Beauty and Beauty and the Beast are active metaphors in our contemporary language of self-understanding, and even (nay, *especially*) a child can sense that the story of Little Red Riding Hood deals with sexual seduction, and that of Jack and the Beanstalk with phallic aggression. What is new, and exciting, is the warmth, humane and urgent, with which Bettelheim expounds fairy tales as aids to the child's growth, which he understands as a growth through conflicts, the chief conflict being Oedipal. The wicked stepmothers and fairy godmothers he translates as all Mother, and the kings and hunters and even wolves as simply Father. It is the essence of the fairy tale to objectify differing facets of the child's emotional experience; by showing the underlying identity of polarized and duplicated symbolizations, Bettelheim's readings make sense of much that seems nonsensical, and relieve the tales of much of the cruelty that has turned many parents and educators to tamer, but thinner, narratives for children.

For instance, in "The Three Little Pigs," the two pigs that die are really discarded developmental stages of the third—the one and only—pig; "the child understands subconsciously that we have to shed earlier forms of existence if we wish to move on to higher ones." And in those tales of heroism so lavish with deaths, "those predecessors of the hero who die . . . are nothing but the hero's earlier immature incarnations." In "Hansel and Gretel" the parental home on the edge of the forest and the gingerbread house in the heart of it are two aspects of the same place: "the gratifying one and the frustrating one."

The hunter who, with the deft violence of a Caesarean operation, removes Little Red Cap (as Bettelheim prefers to call her, disdaining, in his embarrassment of such riches, to pick up the secreting, folding sexiness of a hood) from the belly of the wolf is a benevolent aspect of the same father whose menacing seductiveness is embodied in the animal, just as the grandmother, who precedes her with the wolf in bed, is the same mother—tainted with permissiveness and sexual accomplishment—as the superego who sends the little girl on her way with admonishments not to stray from the path. Many peculiarities of this very peculiar tale yield their secrets to the analytic couch, including the intricate execution of the wolf (he is not instantly killed, or even slain during the mock-birth of his two victims, but filled with stones, so that upon awaking he falls to his death). The idea for this gruesome end comes from Little Red Cap, and Bettelheim argues that this resewing of the wolf's belly serves to protect the childish auditor from unnecessary anxieties about childbirth.

The not infrequent harsh punishments meted out in fairy tales (the villainess of "The Goose Girl" is stripped naked and dragged about in a barrel studded inside with nails; the Queen of Grimm's "Snow White" is made to dance herself to death in red-hot shoes) are the opposite of alarming to the child, Bettelheim claims: "The child often feels unjustly treated by adults and the world in general, and it seems that nothing is done about it . . . the more severely those bad ones are dealt with, the more secure the child feels." Modern softening of these traditional psychodramas prevents them from doing their work; the violence already exists within the child, and must be spoken to. "If one takes these stories as descriptions of reality, then the tales are indeed outrageous in all respects—cruel, sadistic, and whatnot. But as symbols of psychological happenings or problems, these stories are quite true."

Pictorial illustrations, too, are seen by Bettelheim as interfering with the assimilation of the imagery to the child's imagination. Such an apparently innocuous modernization as Disney's naming and characterizing the dwarfs in "Snow White" "seriously interferes with the unconscious understanding that they symbolize an immature pre-individual form of existence which Snow White must transcend." An adult, in telling a story, though encouraged to yield, like the countless tellers before him, to "his conscious and unconscious feelings for the story," is strictly admonished never to "explain" the meaning; and the master-teller Perrault is chastised for the same fault. Bettelheim's explications of two dozen or so best-known tales convince us, indeed, that we may not know the meaning, or that the child of four or five knows it better.

Though searching and, as in the case of "Cinderella," rather intricate, Bettelheim's interpretations never seem farfetched. The drops of blood that figure in so many young heroines' enchantments surely *are* the blood of menstruation and defloration; the resemblance between frogs or toads and male genitals needs only to be pointed out to be assented to. That "Hansel and Gretel" is all about oral greed; that Sleeping Beauty sleeps, as adolescents do, in order to grow; that Little Red Cap is reborn into sexual maturity after a dangerous experiment in flirtation; that Cinderella asks to be accepted by the Prince in her natural "dirtiness" as she slips her penile foot into his vaginal slipper—all this appears in retrospect obvious, and indisputably part of fairy tales' perennial weight, menace, resonance, and consolation. That the child does not "catch" all the symbolization is the opposite of an objection; these tales' merit is that the little listener takes what he can, responding to the unspoken significances unconsciously, mastering anxieties bodied forth for him by these venerable fantasies, being led through Oedipal and sibling conflicts toward an eventual happy union with an "age-correct" partner of the opposite sex.

Neither Bettelheim nor the fairy tales doubt that they know what happiness is. It is achieved independence, as by Hansel and Gretel and Jack; it is misadventure survived, as by Little Red Cap; it is a wicked parent defeated, as by Snow White and Cinderella; it is a lover and a father reconciled, as in "Beauty and the Beast"; it is ruling over the kingdom of self as—in the words of a Rumanian fairy tale—"only kings rule who have suffered many things."

While in the spell of this most benignly paternal scholar of our hearts, we forget that his own enchanting presumption of life as a potentially successful adventure may be itself something of a fairy tale. Though as scholarly as he needs to be to establish his texts and their variants, he does not investigate the origins of Western fairy tales; are they not, for all the bits of pagan lore they contain, medieval in spirit as well as setting, and saturated in Christian cosmology? The themes of mock-death and rebirth, of inner integrity, of repentance and the penitential ordeal, of appearance as illusion, of an anthropomorphic Nature—are these not religious in essence? Is not the risen Christ the supreme Sleeping Beauty, and His redemption of the fallen world the immense transaction which the magical transactions of fairy tales mirror in miniature? Can, in short, fairy-tale reassurances survive the supernatural ones?

Bettelheim discusses, in a rather vexed tone, one fairy story which refuses to fit his pattern: "at its end there is neither recovery nor consolation; there is no resolution of conflict, and thus no happy ending." Yet the story's popularity, rising through the nineteenth century, forces it upon his attention. The story is "Goldilocks and the Three Bears." The heroine, for reasons we do not know, enters a little house by stealth. Hungry and in need of rest, she tries out the porridge, chairs, and beds of the three absent inhabitants. Nothing works right; one chair is too hard, another is too soft, and the third one breaks when she sits in it. The Three Bears whose property this is return, and she flees out the window. "For Goldilocks there is no happy ending—from her failure to find what is fitting for her, she awakes as from a bad dream and runs away." Nor are the Bears touched by the incident; "on the contrary, they are appalled and critical that a little girl should try to fit herself into Papa's bed and try to take Mama's place." Unlike the dwarfs in "Snow White," they do not take the outsider in; nor do they, as in earlier versions of the tale, slay her. Nothing much happens, in short, which shows, to Bettelheim, "the relative shortcomings of a rather recently invented fairy tale." Yet the story, of an Oedipal triangle passingly invaded by a golden-haired loser, is very popular, and Bettelheim concludes, having exhausted its possible meanings, that "the story's ambiguity, which is so much in line with the temper of the times, may also account for its popularity, while the clear-cut solutions of the traditional fairy tale seem to point to a happier age when things were believed to permit definite solutions."

By analogy, all literature—whose cathartic satisfactions, as Aristotle formulated them, are much like the mastered anxiety Bettelheim feels to result from fairy tales—may be in a "Goldilocks" phase, of existential incident without resolution. Donald Barthelme's version of "Snow White" and Anne Sexton's retellings in *Transformations* have the energy of angry graffiti; we were misled, is the implication. Bettelheim's paternal voice cannot direct the wise use of fairy stories without a setting of family security and social consensus; but at the least he shows us how cunningly, how lovingly, the anonymous generations of "a happier age" prepared their children for the challenges of life and guided them toward sexual, ethical health, once upon a time.

Fiabe Italiane

ITALIAN FOLKTALES, selected and retold by Italo Calvino, translated from the Italian by George Martin. 763 pp. Harcourt Brace Jovanovich, 1980.

Italian Folktales arrives on these shores like a belated tall ship—a galleon tooled by Maserati, a wide-beamed, many-decked vessel freighted with the gold of the ages but responsive as a feather to the personal touch. Scarcely a pellet of critical grapeshot will mar its varnished sides as, topsails furled, it glides through a shower of praise and tugboat tooting to snug harbor on the sturdier shelves of libraries both public and private. For Calvino is a genius and, more welcome still, a genial and conscientious one; and as for folktales, who, after Jung and Campbell and Bruno Bettelheim, could have enough of them?

"I," answers this reviewer in a tiny voice, the one grouchy fairy invited to the christening. After reading through these two hundred tales and seven hundred sixty-three big pages, I feel as if I had, like the heroine of the tale of "King Crin," "worn out seven pairs of iron shoes, seven iron mantles, and seven iron hats." I may never smile at another enchanted pool, talking horse, or impulsively murderous king. Well, perhaps *Italian Folktales* was no more meant to be read through than *The Statesman's Year-Book* or *Gray's Anatomy;* yet even short doses left the taste of tedium on the palate, and the sensation that there was something wrong with this handsome volume, along with all that was palpably, admirably right.

Fiabe italiane came out in Italy in 1956; the twenty-four years that passed before its American translation and publication were accomplished suggest a certain languor in the process, a fairy-tale interregnum of dragging feet and sagging eyelids, and perhaps a bit of bewitchment at the outset, in far-off Turin. "The writing of this book," Calvino's compact and frank introduction tells us, "was originally undertaken because of a publishing need: a collection of Italian folktales to take its rightful place alongside the great anthologies of foreign folklore. The problem was which text to choose. Was there an Italian equivalent of the Brothers Grimm?" It was decided that, though "Italian tales from the oral tradition were recorded in literary works long before those from any other country . . . there was no readable master collection of Italian folktales which would be popular in every sense of the word. Could such a book be assembled now? It was decided that I should do it."

Italo Calvino at this time was a thirty-year-old editor at Giulio Einaudi Editore and a novelist of distinction with an already demonstrated flair for the fabulous. It is interesting to find here, in the Venetian tale of "The Cloven Youth," a foreshadowing of his novella *The Cloven Viscount* (1952), and in a Tuscan tale, "The Son of the Merchant from Milan," an incident of arboreal residence that possibly supplied the germ for his superb fantasy of the Enlightenment, *The Baron in the Trees* (1957). The folktale project was an education for Calvino into which he plunged "without even a tankful of intellectual enthusiasm for anything spontaneous and primitive"; he stayed submerged for two years, with held breath, sorting through the welter of *novelline* dating back to the sixteenth-century Venetian collection of Straparola and the seventeenth-century tales by Giambattista Basile in Neapolitan dialect. The bulk of the material, however, had been accumulated in the nineteenth century, by more or less scholarly folklorists following the example of the Brothers Grimm—most notably the lawyer Gherardo Nerucci in Tuscany and the doctor Giuseppe Pitrè in Sicily. But in many places, in the second half of the nineteenth century, "people began to write down tales told by old women," often noting the name, age, and profession of the teller, and striving for fidelity to the spoken style and dialect. Still, though the archives and journals of folklore swelled, no "Italian Grimm" emerged; in 1875 Domenico Comparetti published one volume of a general anthology, *Popular Italian Tales*, with the promise of two more volumes, which never appeared. Over eighty years later, Calvino and Einaudi issued this volume of two hundred tales (to match the two hundred in the Grimms' classic *Kinder- und Hausmärchen*) translated out of dialect into "an Italian sufficiently elastic to incorporate from the dialect images and turns of speech that were the most expressive and unusual" and chosen not only for being "the most unusual, beautiful, and original texts" but for typological and geographical distribution as well.

The tales are arranged in an order basically geographical, beginning with the now French region of Menton, "whose dialect is closer to the Ligurian than to the Provençal," moving east to the regions of Piedmont and Lombardy and Venice, and thence south through Bologna, Tuscany, Rome, Abruzzi, Campania, Apulia, Lucania, and Calabria to Sicily, ending with tales from the islands of Sardinia and Corsica. Such a panoramic arrangement bespeaks a patriotic intent that may be one of the problems. For in achieving fair representation all around, Calvino possibly has included some inferior tales and certainly has included a number that are close variants of one another if not virtual duplicates —e.g., Nos. 36 and 102; 76 and 115; 26 and 116 (Red Riding Hood); 69 and 124; 95 and 129; 154 and 185; 179 and 194; 97 and 199; and 157, 158, 159, 160, and 176 (all variants of the chivalric legend of the wife falsely accused of infidelity). Truly, as the first of these last begins, "Over and over it has been told that once upon a time there was a king and queen." These repetitions are cheerfully acknowledged by Calvino in his notes, and said to constitute one of the folklorist's delights, "a kind of mania, an insatiable hunger for more and more versions and variants. . . . I would have given all of Proust in exchange for a new variant of the 'gold-dung donkey.' I'd quiver with disappointment if I came upon the episode of the bridegroom who loses his memory as he kisses his mother, instead of finding the one with the ugly Saracen woman . . ." Since the Brothers Grimm, the popularizer of folktales and the pedantic student of them have kept a jostling kind of company, and Calvino, in this collection as well as in such intricate fiction as *The Castle of Crossed Destinies,* shows little fear of letting the pedant get the upper hand. Having described the Grimms' method of transcribing tales "from the mouths of the people" as "not 'scientific' in the modern sense of the word, or only halfway so," Calvino treats of "the hybrid nature" of his own work: it, too, "is only halfway 'scientific,' or three-quarters so; as for the final quarter, it is the product of my own judgment. . . . I enriched the text selected from other versions and whenever possible did so without altering its character or unity, and at the same time filled it out and made it more plastic. I touched up as delicately as possible those portions that were either missing or too sketchy."

As part of the extra quarter of scientificism that Calvino awards himself over the Grimms, he specifies, in notes gathered at the back of the book, not only the sources of each tale, but also, in brief, the impression the story made upon him and what improving touches he has imposed. To the story of "The Snake" he has added a pomegranate tree whose branches grow out of reach when one attempts to pick their fruit; for the tale of "The Land Where One Never Dies" he has provided old men with progressively longer beards; and in "Filo d'Oro and Filomena" he has the hero successively materialize in a beard, in whiskers, and in sideburns—all of which savors of Disneyesque animation, of a pictorial inventiveness that comes easily to a modern sensibility but that in these old oral tales, so meagre in their visual effects, borders on the cute. At times, Calvino, describing his adjustments, reminds one of Nabokov at his most impishly regal: "My personal touches here include the prince's yellow suit and leggings, the description of the transformation in a flutter of wings, the gossip of the witches who traveled the world over, and a bit of stylistic cunning." Nor has he always abstained from the vice common to adapters of these harsh and sometimes savage narratives—softening the endings.

> Pitrè's text closes with the hero's head cut off and put on backward ... but since that brings an element of fantasy into an otherwise realistic narrative, I thought it best to exclude it.

> I left out Pete's drowning in a pond at the end, to close in a better way.

> The escape of the nurse and her daughter at the end is my own invention (in place of the customary tarring of a transgressor).

In Calvino's defense, it should be urged that he has obviously done a more thorough job of search and collation than his assignment required, that some of the material whose piquancy won inclusion was in other respects "rather incoherent" and "strange and carefree"; and that no teller of a folktale passes it on exactly as it came to him. The Brothers Grimm, in introducing their own collection, firmly asserted that "we have added nothing of our own, have embellished no incident or feature of the story, but have given its substance, just as we ourselves received it"; then they went on to allow, "It will, of course, be understood that the mode of telling and carrying out particular details is principally due to us."

Turning from *Italian Folktales* to sample once more some of the Grimm folktales, the reader seems to enter a solider universe, of sharper contrast between light and dark, wherein a more compelling narrative impetus gathers around incidents no less fantastic and repetitious than, and in many instances almost identical to, those in the Italian telling. The difference is one not of talent, I think (for Calvino is a writer of the first order), but of historical and perhaps geographical position. In the northern, Protestant half of Europe, a certain pietism in the atmosphere effortlessly deepens the fairy-tale texture. When Hansel says to Gretel, "Be comforted, dear little sister, and sleep in peace, God will not forsake us," an invisible, internalized order is called from the shadows, and a kind of promise is made which the story must make good. In the Italian version of the tale, which Calvino calls "Chick," the Hansel figure is the youngest of seven children, of whom only he is named and active, and the witch takes the form of Mammy Ogress and her hard-working, voracious husband, Pappy Ogre; one night, by shifting some floral crowns from the heads of this unpleasant couple's children—conveniently seven in number also—onto those of himself and his siblings, Chick tricks Pappy Ogre into eating his own offspring.

In the Italian tales, trickery and blind chance have the world pretty much to themselves; piety is confined to a jocular cycle about Peter and Jesus, and what affection exists is magical and absolute, a kind of curse. In the rapid unreeling of somewhat automatic marvels, there is seldom a moment where the tale pauses and regrips its own meaning, as when, in Grimm, the seven dwarfs have returned to their cottage and for the last time found Snow White lying on the ground:

> They lifted her up, looked to see whether they could find anything poisonous, unlaced her, combed her hair, washed her with water and wine, but it was all of no use. The poor child was dead, and remained dead.

With words the reader has been given what the listener to the oral narrative could be given with silence: time to understand and to be moved. Plain recounting has been enriched, whether by action of the Grimms' or by a local quality of oral narrating, with dramatic description. Historically, the Grimms were exponents, in fields of scholarship ranging from philology and grammar to ancient legal history and medieval legends, of a German national identity that cohered in the wake of Napoleon's final defeat, amid magnificently widened perspectives of antiquarian knowledge. They gathered their tales as one part of their campaign to capture and explicate the *Volksgeist,* and published them only after some urging by fellow-scholars. *Italian Folktales,* by contrast, represents the efforts of an immensely clever and winning writer to fulfill, with honor, a publisher's contract. Calvino has affection for his country, and speaks up for the charms of the Italian type of folktale—its "continuous quiver of love," its relative gentleness over against the "gory ferocity" of the Grimms' tales, its "genuine feeling for beauty in the communions or metamorphoses of woman and fruit, of woman and plant." But this affection, twinkling on the surface of these tales like sunshine, is a far cry from the compound of scholarship, nationalism, and romanticism which gives the *Hausmärchen* their swarthy fibre.

Of course, we know the Grimm tales by their best dozen. Two hundred folktales are about a hundred eighty too many for a continuous reading experience. The plots are relentlessly eventful—

> A widower king with one son remarried and then died. The son remained with his stepmother, who paid him no mind whatever, since she was in love with a Moor and had eyes only for him. The king's son, faithful to his father's memory, began to detest the Moor. They went hunting together, and the prince killed and buried him in the heart of the forest—

and superimposing one tangled tale after another upon the bleary mind's eye tends to bring out not their charms but their recurrent limitations and tics: their inane repetitions, their inexorable sets of threes and sevens, the maddening inability of their heroes and heroines to follow the most laboriously specific instructions and warnings, and, above all, the pathetic materialism of their fantasy. These are tales told, mostly, by old women for the entertainment of children or of people impoverished to the level of childishness; illimitable riches—obtained by marriage into royalty, murder of an ogre, or possession of bandits' loot—are the one good of which their poverty can conceive. They take us not into the realms of love satisfied or of virtue rewarded but to the land of El Dorado, that paradise to whose inert and frozen malevolence the penniless are blind.

> . . . he saw a staircase. Don Pidduzzu descended it and found himself in a gold-sequined gallery—walls, doors, floor, ceiling, all gold, and a table laid for twenty-four persons, with gold spoons, salt cellars, and candelabras. Don Pidduzzu looked in the book and read: "Take them." He called the crew and ordered everything carried on board. It took them twelve days to load the treasure on the ship. There were twenty-four gold statues so heavy that a couple of days were needed to load them alone.

This Sicilian tale ("The Sultan with the Itch") concludes with the couplet "They were always happy and content, / While we are here without a cent." Another, also from Sicily, ends, "And they remained emperor and empress their whole life long, while we are still as poor as ever." The auditors of these stories of starving boys and maltreated girls who become kings and queens presumably never wearied of hearing riches evoked, any more than Depression audiences wearied of movies showing Fred Astaire capering in a penthouse, or than subscribers to *Oui* weary of each month's set of models posed bottoms up. An appetite in the process of imaginary satisfaction does not object to monotony and implausibility; rather, it trusts them, as vessels more efficiently supplying the craved substance. But to those of us in whom a craving for gold statues has never been roused, and to whom bourgeois capitalism has granted a modicum of comfort, many folktales will seem as mysteriously repellent as the votive objects of a religion in which we do not believe. Folktales are not just a kind of beach glass washed up on the shore of the present day by the sea of history, to be mounted alongside imagist poems and post–O. Henry short stories; their inner glint, their old life, is escapism. They were the television and pornography of their day, the life-lightening trash of preliterate peoples. And only children, it may be, now possess, for a brief phase before comic books and space movies descend, the atavistic ability to respond to folktales with proper wonder and dread.

A Feast of Reason

THE ORIGIN OF TABLE MANNERS, by Claude Lévi-Strauss, translated from the French by John and Doreen Weightman. 551 pp. Harper & Row, 1978.

The third volume of Claude Lévi-Strauss's monumental te-tralogy, *Introduction to a Science of Mythology,* has now been trans-lated and, eleven years after its original publication in France, published here under the appetizing title *The Origin of Table Man-ners,* at the gourmet price of thirty dollars. Anyone buying the volume expecting an amusingly anecdotal account of eating cus-toms among primitive peoples will not be entirely disappointed, for one chapter offers "A Short Treatise on Culinary Anthropology"; but to get to it the reader must traverse four hundred seventy pages of severely testing prose, combining the "raw" opacity of savage myths with the "cooked" obscurity of close structural analysis.

The Raw and the Cooked and *From Honey to Ashes* are the preced-ing volumes of Lévi-Strauss's *Introduction,* whose great design of interlocking, overlapping, and mutually illuminating North and South American Indian myths extends itself outward from an axis between the raw and the cooked—between nature and culture. The fourth and final volume, *The Naked Man,* does not yet exist in English. This third volume, the author admits in his introduction, undertakes a task "more complex than the one that the other two volumes aimed at accomplishing." Whereas the first two volumes dealt exclusively with South American myths, the third explicates its text of departure, the Tucuna tale of "the hunter Monmanéki

and his wives," by recourse to North American legends, which—
as preserved among tribes thousands of miles distant from the
territory of the Tucuna—reveal through structural affinities that an
incontinent half-woman clinging to Monmanéki's back is really a
frog, and that he and his lazy brother-in-law as they sit in a canoe
are really the moon and the sun. The anthropologist's tortuous trail
through some two hundred myths and their variants contains a
number of such identifications—many of them brilliantly telling;
a few of them, to this reader, intractably recondite. Lévi-Strauss, as
he nears the end of this stage of his "long dialectical itinerary,"
himself seems wearily aware of what a "long, roundabout route"
has been imposed by "this too lengthy investigation." One of his
more attractive diagrams maps the odyssey he and his reader have
endured together, and he triumphantly sums up:

> So complicated a journey through the mythic field, along roads
> which sometimes proceed in the same direction, but follow courses
> which are far apart while remaining parallel, or intersect and even turn
> back upon themselves, would be incomprehensible if we did not realize
> that it has allowed us to carry out several tasks simultaneously. This
> volume presents the development of an argument in three dimensions
> —ethnographical, logical and semantic; and, if it has any claim to origi-
> nality, this will be because, at every stage, it has shown how each
> dimension remains inseparable from the others.

This much seems certain: an immense anthropological erudition
is here wielded by one of the world's finest minds, and the myths
themselves have never been taken more seriously, in terms they
themselves can provide. "Unlike the practitioners of the historical
method," Lévi-Strauss says, "I cannot accept the idea that myths
might contain gratuitous and meaningless themes, especially when
the same detail is given a prominent place in several versions." He
claims, "The fact is that the historical method considers only the
absence, or the presence and geographical distribution, of elements
which it leaves in a state of non-significance." He scorns "the
subjective interpretations put forward by certain commentators"
and promises, "Fortunately, structural analysis can make up for the
uncertainties of historical reconstruction."

The exact methodology of this "structural analysis" is not easy to grasp, though Lévi-Strauss pauses every hundred pages or so to sing its praises. It shares with traditional ethnography a scrupulous investigation into the exact qualities and properties, insofar as they can be determined, of the flora and fauna mentioned in the myths; for example, the North American porcupine *(Erethizon dorsatus)* and the significance and extent of quillwork among the Plains Indians are exhaustively discussed. Nor are etymological clues, of the sort that Robert Graves so lavishly provided in his redaction of Greek myths, ignored. Where Lévi-Strauss seeks to improve upon his predecessors is in the rigor of his pursuit of kindred significations, in the cogency of his diagrammatic arrangement of signifiers and themes, and in his sensitivity to the ethical content expressed beneath the absurd and barbarous incidents of the myths. From the repellent welter of bestial matings, casual massacres, and bizarre reanimations in these tales he elicits such humane morals as "In his quest for a mate, a human may look either too near or too far" and "Women, whether beautiful or ugly, all deserve to obtain husbands" and, in conclusion, "Sound humanism does not begin with oneself, but puts the world before life, life before man, and respect for others before self-interest." Amid the tangle of mythic narratives and cruel customs he finds an Aristotelian search for the middle way. The harsh social sanctions against an array of blameless tribal citizens from menstruating girls to gravediggers he sympathetically interprets as a moral superiority to our own societies:

> We wear hats to protect *ourselves* from rain, cold and heat; we use forks to eat with, and wear gloves when we go out, so as not to dirty *our* fingers . . . Whereas we think of good manners as a way of protecting the internal purity of the subject against the external impurity of beings and things, in savage societies, they are a means of protecting the purity of beings and things against the impurity of the subject.

Such a perception, while not entirely novel, has a considerable impact when approached through the painstaking circuitry of Lévi-Strauss's "science of mythology." He raises issues and then resolves them with the suspenseful cunning of a mystery novelist.

For instance, near the core of his inquiry into so-called table manners is a widespread Plains Indian myth he names "the quarrel between the sun and the moon"; in one of its incidents, the moon's human wife triumphs over the sun's toad wife by eating from a bowl of tripe noisily, whereas the toothless toad-woman attempts to counterfeit noise by putting charcoal in her mouth, and produces only black saliva. The myth's assignment of merit to loud eating stands in puzzling contradiction not only to our own notions of nicety but to a number of South American myths whose heroes survive a test by chewing in silence. Lévi-Strauss unravels the problem by concentrating upon the Mandan, a Plains tribe whose myths have an especially "tragic tone and somber grandeur." Mandan cosmology presents the sun and the stars, lumped as "the People-Above," as "demoniacal creatures, fire-raisers, cannibals and instigators of other kinds of disasters." In a Mandan version of the quarrel between the sun and the moon, the Old Woman, the matriarch of the People-Above, serves the sun and a Cheyenne woman who is her guest "a stew made from hands, ears and human skin. The Cheyenne woman and Sun ate heartily." By extension, then, in all the Plains myths that contain the eating contest the earthly woman chews noisily to show that she is a "match" for her cannibal hosts. "Without becoming a cannibal, she tries to show the sun, the possessor of the sources of life, that although man comes from the bowels of the earth and relies for his survival on water, he can take sides with the sun, against water [represented by the amphibian toad-woman]."

This reviewer is not competent—and few people in the world can be—to judge of the fairness with which Lévi-Strauss selects his myths and weights their paraphrase within the libraries of anthropological data that have accumulated since the discovery of the Americas. His bibliography lists nearly five hundred publications, and the myths—many with significant variants—that he has cited and synopsized in the three volumes thus far number five hundred twenty-eight. The stylistic flair he showed in *Tristes Tropiques* is suppressed but for the occasional phrase that gathers masses of patient collation into a dramatic knot: "The veil lifts to reveal a vast mythological system common to both South and North America, and in which the subjection of women is the basis of the social order." The argument ramifies: "The transition from nature to culture demands that the feminine organism should become periodic, since the social as well as the cosmic order would be endangered by a state of anarchy in which regular alternation of days and night, the phases of the moon, feminine menstruation, the fixed period for pregnancy and the course of the seasons did not mutually support each other. . . . Therefore, women have to be subjected to *règles* [a French pun, with the double meaning of "rules" and "monthly periods"]." In quite another corner of the savage cosmology, Lévi-Strauss attacks the question of the frequency of groups of ten in the myths, and concludes that they "represent *saturated sets,* which the dialectic of the myths is concerned to reduce." That is, in contrast to the Romans, who exulted in the power of multiplication and projected it backward and forward through their history, the Indians had a dread of large numbers.

This difference in attitude with regard to high numbers admirably reflects the contrast between a society which is already determined to be historical, and others which are also historical no doubt, but most unwillingly, since they believe that they will lengthen their duration and increase their security by excluding history from their being. It is an old saying that nature abhors a vacuum. But might it not be said that culture, in the primary form in which it opposes nature, abhors a plenum?

In his capacity for marshalling multitudinous facts and discriminations toward elegant generalizations, Lévi-Strauss is a supreme scientist, who makes other practitioners of anthropology look clumsy. Yet a curious sensation persists that as one reads him one is witnessing a performance fundamentally artistic, less a pragmatic servicing of reality than the execution of a fiendishly difficult, self-imposed intelligence test. He writes of the myths as of puzzle pieces: "They may be symmetrical or anti-symmetrical, directly imitated one from another, with differently coloured backgrounds or outlines; mirror images, or negative or positive prints, displayed the right way round, or edgewise, or reversed." His use of diagrams and such mathematical terms as "set," "vector," "transformation," and "valency" verges on the infatuated, and his need for symmetry on the dizzying. While his superimpositions are persuasive one by one, the insistent rhythm of equivalence begins to seem comically mechanical: "It follows, then, that menstrual blood is opposed to resin and, as I have postulated, is the equivalent of maple sap, which itself is opposed to resin." The very genius of structural analysis contains a seed of anti-materialism and cheerful nonsense; its father, the linguist Ferdinand de Saussure, is quoted as asserting, "The link which one establishes between things exists *before the things themselves*, and helps to determine them."

Many a link in *The Origin of Table Manners* is forged on the assumption that likeness is more a matter of form than of content. "The task I have undertaken . . . consists in proving that myths *which are not alike*, or in which the similarities seem at first sight to be accidental, can nevertheless display an identical structure and belong to the same group of transformations." In other words, up is an inverted version of down, and black and white are aspects of the same paradigm. "The meaning of each term results from the position it occupies in systems which change because they correspond to a number of synchronic cross-sections made in a gradually unfolding mythic discourse." With such a hunting license granted, parallels and homologies are easy to bag—child's play for a brain as agile as M. Lévi-Strauss's. Having expounded at length an analogy between honey and menstrual blood, he fields with aplomb, in a footnote, the news that "an informant from the Choco [has presented] a whole theory identifying wild honey with sperm." He comments:

> This extraordinary inversion of a system which I have shown to be characteristic of a vast territory stretching from Venezuela to Paraguay does not contradict my interpretation, but instead gives it an additional dimension, and allows the completion of the Klein group, of which, so far, the fourth term was missing. Sperm is *that which ought* to be transmitted from husband to wife; menstrual blood is *that which ought*

not to be transmitted from wife to husband. . . . We thus obtain a generalized four-term system . . .

A kind of Platonic madness, a search for "deep" structures, haunts structuralism as it spreads outward from linguistics into the old "humanities." What we miss in the anthropology of *The Origin of Table Manners* is the anthropoid pulse. We learn what these tales can mean to a twentieth-century intellectual as he shuffles their patterns; but what did they mean to their tellers, their hearers? "As a reward for these achievements, the hero's sister made him a fine robe of beaver skins, trimmed with coloured porcupine quills. But one day, the boy fell asleep while the sun was high in the sky and the heat of the rays burned spots upon the robe. The boy wept violently, and asked his sister for one of her pubic hairs, and made a snare with it which half strangled the sun." Did anyone laugh, hearing this? At what level did the tellers themselves recognize the urgent significations behind their rambling tales of hairy snakes, severed heads, pedantic porcupines, and such chimeras? We are not told. The tales float in the sky of Lévi-Strauss's analysis like angels doing military drills; an eerie subliminal fact is that these myths, so alive with ever-expanding meaning for the explicator, were the possession of tribes now drastically dwindled, like the Mandan, or extinct. A vast religious system is presented of which Lévi-Strauss is virtually the last votary.

At the opposite pole from these grave systematics is a little book, published in England by Cape, of radio conversations that Lévi-Strauss consented to have in 1959 with the French critic Georges Charbonnier. Herein the anthropologist, under the goad of his interviewer, volunteered a graphic and moving metaphor for the difference between primitive societies and our own:

I would say that, in comparison with our own great society, with all the great modern societies, the societies studied by the anthropologist are in a sense "cold" societies rather than "hot" societies, or like clocks in relation to steam-engines. They are societies which create the minimum of that disorder which the physicists call "entropy," and they tend to remain indefinitely in their initial state, and this explains why they appear to us as static societies with no history.

He explains that modern societies, like steam engines, "operate on the basis of a difference in temperature between their component parts, between the boiler and the condenser"—a disequilibrium that in social terms translates into "slavery, serfdom or class distinction." The analysis is plainly Marxist, with the difference that it locates its utopia not in the future but in the past, in those societies in which "there must be no minority; the society tries to go on functioning like a clock in which all the parts of the mechanism work together harmoniously, and not like those machines which seem to conceal a latent antagonism at the very centre of their mechanism." *Like a clock:* Lévi-Strauss's "science of mythology" also functions like a clock, with its calibrated ratios, axes, symmetries, and interlockings. It is beautiful like a clock, and cool like a clock—a strangely elegant heirloom from the torture-prone, fear-ridden jungles and plains. Its orderly revolutions and transpositions have the inverted function of not marking but arresting time, and making a haven, for their passionate analyst, from the torsion and heat of the modern age.

Happy on Nono Despite Odosha

WATUNNA: *An Orinoco Creation Cycle*, by Marc de Civrieux, edited and translated from the Spanish by David M. Guss. 195 pp. North Point Press, 1980.

Anthropologists and folklorists have gathered, against the coming night of worldwide electronic frost, sheaves and sheaves of oral narrative; but little of it is as readable, coherent, and thought-provoking as *Watunna: An Orinoco Creation Cycle.* M. de Civrieux, a French paleontologist turned South American ethnographer, spent more than twenty years visiting the Kunukunuma villages of the Makiritare tribe, gathering through hundreds of separate tellings their story of the world's creation and the place of their own tribe within it. The Makiritare live in a mountainous region of virgin forest north of the Upper Orinoco River in southern

Venezuela. They were called Makiritare by the Arawak-speaking guides and interpreters who were with the Spanish when, in 1759, the first contact was made between white men and this remote Indian people. The Makiritare know themselves as So'to, which is the language they speak. The word "So'to" means simultaneously the language and those who speak the language, which is to say, human beings. Those who do not speak it are regarded as non-human: "These beings," M. de Civrieux's excellent brief introduction tells us, "are the enemies of the real people and can be hunted like animals." But individuals from other tribes, usually women and children, who find themselves among the So'to become So'to as soon as they learn the language; "the native concept of tribe is not a racial one." "So'to" also means "twenty," which, as the number of human digits, "serves as the natural basis for the indigenous counting system and is also the symbol for man." (The same is true of other Indian languages, such as Pemon and Karina, and the French use "*vingt*" as a base for higher numbers, as English speech once did with "score.")

Not only did M. de Civrieux learn So'to to piece together the Watunna—of which he published a Spanish version in Caracas as long ago as 1970—but, most unusually, the translator into English, the American poet and critic David Guss, spent three years among the Makiritare learning their language so that his "telling" might have the flavor and force of the original. He has given us a rendering exceptionally idiomatic and punchy, with stretched spellings like "whooooole" and "tallllllll," a number of four-letter words that do not usually grace ethnological documents, and jaunty chapter closings like "That's it," "Okay, now. That's all," and "Now that's how the old ones tell it. That's what they say." His syntax at times seems as primitive as possible:

> Now the boy turns into a crab. The jaguar catches him. The crab bites him. The jaguar lets go. The crab gets away. The jaguar chases him.

But the total effect is not jarring, or condescending; a voice is created, urgent yet relaxed, and these tales of swift metamorphosis and abrupt pursuit keep themselves—with the help of Mr. Guss's excellent glossary—as clear as running water. The Watunna, it should be said, exists among the Makiritare in two versions: an esoteric one imparted during male initiation rites in a sacred language consisting of "archaic words, others taken from neighboring tribes, more or less phonetically deformed, complicated ritual endings concealing words from normal daily usage, refrains with no definite meaning, inarticulate vocables, onomatopoeias, whistles, jungle and water sounds, animal movements"; and an exoteric one shared openly among the villagers and alluded to daily. We, of course, are given—in a handsome piece of book production by a new West Coast press—the profane, vernacular version. It begins:

> There was Kahuña, the Sky Place. The Kahuhana lived there, just like now. They're good, wise people. And they were in the beginning too. They never died. There was no sickness, no evil, no war. The whole world was Sky. No one worked. No one looked for food. Food was always there, ready.
>
> There were no animals, no demons, no clouds, no winds. There was just light. In the highest Sky was Wanadi, just like now. He gave his light to the people, to the Kahuhana. He lit everything down to the very bottom, down to Nono, the Earth. Because of that light, the people were always happy. They had life. They couldn't die. There was no separation between Sky and Earth. Sky had no door like it does now. There was no night, like now. Wanadi is like a sun that never sets. It was always day. The Earth was like a part of the Sky.

To a reader raised in the Christian tradition, this evocation of an eternal, populated, light-drenched Heaven comes as surprisingly familiar. Further familiarities unfold. Wanadi decides, of the empty Earth, "I want to make people down there." He himself descends, with the great gifts of "knowledge, tobacco, the maraca, and the *wiriki*" (the last two are instruments of Makiritare *huhai*, the tribal shamans). The placenta of Wanadi's first earthly incarnation is infested with worms, and out of its rot is born a Satan-like creature called Kahu, or Odosha. "This man was very evil. He was jealous of Wanadi. He wanted to be master of the Earth. Because of him, we suffer now. There's hunger, sickness and war. He's the father of all the Odoshankomo. Now, because of him, we die."

Wanadi descends to Earth a second time, to conquer death. He does this by creating his own mother, Kumariawa, through a magical process of trance and dreaming. "He gave birth to her dreaming, with tobacco smoke, with the song of his maraca, singing and nothing else." His plan is to kill her, and bring her back to life, to show that "death was a trick." But while she is under the ground, about to be resurrected, Iarakaru, who is both Wanadi's nephew and a weeping capuchin monkey, opens the pouch containing the night; he has been warned against doing just this but is no better at resisting mischief than mythological figures anywhere. "All at once, EVERYTHING went dark. Suddenly, the WHOLE world went out and Wanadi was running through the night." To top things off, the diabolical Odosha then roasts Kumariawa's reëmerging body with his urine. Wanadi confronts a desolation worse than that Jehovah faced after Man's first disobedience. "I can't do anything now," he thinks. "There's no flesh, no body. She won't come back to life. There's no light. The Earth isn't mine anymore. The people will all die now."

A third time, Wanadi descends to Earth and risks mortal adventures, in order "to see what was happening on Earth, to make people again, good people, Wanadi people." To alleviate darkness, he creates a false sky containing the sun and moon and stars; he instructs people in the arts of sexual intercourse and house construction. Yet still the Odosha-ruled world resists redemption, and Wanadi retreats to the Sky, saying in final farewell to "his twelve men from the beginning," "Now you'll go on living with Odosha. I'm going. I've left you the signs. I did many things to let you know. Just as I did, you'll do." In an earlier tale, we have been assured,

> We can only see the things of this world. The real Sky (Heaven) is invisible. There aren't any stars there, just Wanadi, shining alone. There's no darkness, no night, no day. Just light, light and nothing else. The stars, the moon, the sun, they aren't going to live forever. They're going to fall when this Earth ends. They're going to die along with us, with Odosha. Then Wanadi will return. You'll be able to see the real Sky. Its light never goes out.

The myths of the Makiritare also include a great Flood that crowns the wicked, a rainbow left as a sign, a kind of Adam and Eve (Wahnatu and Wetashi), and a cosmically central Fall—in this case that of an immense, omnifructiferous tree, Marahuaka, the felling of which releases rain from its roots in the sky and fills the earth with fertility and is celebrated annually at the principal Makiritare festival, *Adahe ademi hidi*.

How many of these correspondences with the imagery of the Bible predate the coming of the missionaries? For the Spaniards, in a double guise of good white men (Iaranavi) and bad (Fañuru), do break into the timeless vistas of the Watunna legends, along with iron and guns and the Dutch (the Hurunko) who operated the Guyana trading post of Amenadiña until 1814. The Spanish *padres* (in So'to, the Fadre) figure in a remarkable inversion of the Crucifixion story: In far-off Karakaña (Caracas), the Fadre captured the God-Man Wanadi and "sent for a post to hang him from. It was shaped like a forked *Kruza ake* (cross). That's what they called it. When they brought *Kruza ake*, they nailed him there with iron points. 'That way he won't escape,' they thought." But Wanadi did escape; his spirit slipped from his body. "Wanadi was like a corpse. It was a trick. He had taken his *damodede* [spirit messenger; spiritual double] out of the body. He had gone back to Kushamakari. Wamedi [a rooster] knew that. The Fadre and the Fanuru didn't. . . . They like to make crosses to show people. They say: 'On this post he died.' They didn't know. They don't know. They say they killed him. It's not true. They couldn't. He tricked them and got away." So the wooden crosses worn by the priests are construed as a vain vaunting of themselves as the crucifiers of God!—the So'to God.

The Platonic dualism that infused the later books of the New Testament and the theology of the early Church needed no priests, however, to plant it among the Makiritare. The distinction between body and soul, outer form and inward anima, is central to their magic and their science. The evolution of a rival tribe, the Yanomamo, is ascribed to a bad meal consumed by Shirishana, one of Wanadi's creations: "He kept his human form but that's all. His spirit turned into an animal. He moved around like an animal. He thought like an animal. He lost his mind. He hid in the mountains, naked. He didn't know how to do anything anymore, just kill and rob real people. And that's the way his grandchildren stayed." There is a suggestion of the Platonic "idea" in the concept of the *sadashe:* "Every species [the glossary tells us], both plant and animal, has its own chief or master which is known as its *sadashe.* This *sadashe* is conceived of as the species' grandfather or prototype, its personal culture hero who gave it its name, form, and language." With a cast of prototypical heroes behind the multitudinous individuals of the wild, divinity of a sort is constantly encountered within the forest, and species characteristics are plausibly related to primordial traumas. We learn in the course of the Watunna why squirrels have only two front teeth (the primal squirrel, Kadiio, laughed so hard at Wanadi's ugly wife that all his other teeth fell out); why toads have wrinkled backs and wide mouths (Kawao, the toad, kept fire hidden in her belly and in disgorging it split her mouth and burned her back); why anteaters have their marks (Kuamachi, the boy who became the Evening Star, rubbed his sooty hand on the neck and shoulders of Waremo, the prototypical anteater). Why Man is the way he is requires more complicated legends.

Like the opening chapters of Genesis, the creation myths of the Makiritare explain the human condition on two levels, a cosmic and a social. The first proclaims the origin and eschatology of the universe; the second, the origin and rationale of the tribe. The first deals with the problem of evil on the theoretical level of how it arose; that is to say, why pain and limitation, impoverishment and peril have been established as our lot. The second deals with evil practically, by stating what rules the accumulated wisdom of tradition has given us for our protection. From Wanadi the Creator and Wanadi the frustrated Savior the Watunna cycle proceeds to the figure of Semenia—the first chief, Wanadi's messenger, and the founder of agriculture. In his embodiment as the Semenia bird (the red-billed scythebill), he is leader of the flock of birds who peck and saw down the great Marahuaka tree and thus create the first *conuco*—the first clearing. "Semenia made himself chief to teach us. He showed us how to work. He punished the ones that didn't want to live like people, like brothers. He brought food, rain, fertility and obedience for everyone. He showed them what to do. Now we have food again. We're happy despite Odosha." Man, in this fallen world, takes his fortune into his own hands.

> The people were happy; happy together in their *conuco*. The yuca grew quickly. All of a sudden it was there. Now the men rested. That's what Semenia told them. Now the women worked. That's how we still do it. We don't forget that way. The men clear the *conuco*, like Marahuaka in the beginning. The women plant and harvest and prepare it. . . .
> "That's good," said Semenia. Then he said: "Let's dance. Let's sing and eat and drink. Now we'll remember."

To be happy despite Odosha, it is necessary to remember. In preliterate societies, memory and repetition of the ways of the grandfathers constitute survival. Festivals, with the lore that accompanies them, are survival's tools—how tenaciously Western man still clings to his own, desacralized, commercialized, and trivialized though they are! Festivals recall our aboriginal perils and rehearse the tribal solidarity that withstands them. Those of us with twenty digits, lacking the erratic magic whereby Wanadi and the powerful *huhai* dream their way directly from thought to thing, must work, and work together. Only coöperation and obedience to tradition can mediate between the immaterial, hungry ego and the material, resistant world. Born naked into the world, the mythmakers unerringly seized upon just those features of it—the individuation of species, the vivid pseudo-world of dreams, the blazing enigma of the heavenly bodies—that most need explanation, and are still being explained. Though the Watunna can be for us (and, inexorably, for the Makiritare, already wearing trousers, in territories riddled with airplanes and radios) little more than a tall tale and gaudy fossil, the two existential mysteries that it addresses—the existence of the universe, the existence of "I"—have not been, beneath the great flurry of modern knowing, dissolved.

THE WORLD CALLED THIRD

African Accents

XALA, by Sembène Ousmane, translated from the French by Clive Wake. 114 pp. Lawrence Hill, 1976.

THE LAND'S LORD, by T. Obinkaram Echewa. 145 pp. Lawrence Hill, 1976.

MYTH, LITERATURE AND THE AFRICAN WORLD, by Wole Soyinka. 168 pp. Cambridge University Press, 1976.

Africa is in the news today, as it was a hundred years ago. In 1877, Stanley emerged at the mouth of the Congo, having passed "through the dark continent" from Zanzibar by way of the great lakes, thereby clearing up all the major geographical mysteries of the central interior; in that same year Gordon arrived in Cairo to accept the governor-generalship of the Sudan, thus setting the stage for the drama of personal imperialism that was played to its tragic climax eight years later in the fall of Khartoum. With Gordon died the age of private exploit; it would take Kitchener's army to avenge him, bringing British rule with it. Now colonialism is gone, leaving behind a dusting of its languages, pockets of embattled white settlers, and the fragile exoskeleton of national boundaries that the partitioning of the 1880s imposed on the continent. Less than a century after the "scramble" of the European powers for African territory, the Africans of Angola, Ethiopia, Sudan, and Zaïre are scrambling on their own. Recently the President of Uganda kindly offered himself as a replacement for the Queen of England. In intellectual realms, too, independence is being savored. Three recently published books show Africans producing such elaborate artifacts as a novel designed to become a movie, a theological novel, and literary criticism of an imperious density.

Xala, by Sembène Ousmane, describes itself, on the dust jacket, as "the basis for a highly acclaimed film of the same title which received accolades at the 1975 New York Film Festival." It is as short as a scenario (one hundred fourteen pages), flows in a succession of scenes without any chapter subdivisions, and contains bits of "business"—"Her tight-fitting dress split, a long, horizontal tear which exposed her behind"—that might be hilarious in a movie but fall rather flat in prose. The stills from the film bound into the book exist on the same continuum as the text, and help us to read it, rather than (as in most illustrated fiction) set up an irrelevant static of alternative visualization. Yet the novel is not thin. Its basic subject, the problems of polygamy in an urban society, resonates eerily in our own society of families extended by divorce and remarriage, of romantic renewals obtained at the price of multiplied obligations. The reality of magic in Mr. Ousmane's interweave of erotic farce and stern social comment suggests, to a Westerner, what magically fragile constructs our personal pretensions are.

A *xala* (pronounced "hala") is a curse that produces impotence; one is laid upon the hero, a Senegalese businessman called El Hadji Abdou Kader Beye, on the night of his wedding to his third wife, the young and voluptuous N'Gone. El Hadji is "fifty-odd" and prosperous enough to keep his two other wives, Adja Awa Astou and Oumi N'Doye, in separate villas in the fashionable part of Dakar, and to provide a minibus for the transportation of his eleven children. Within the minibus, we are told, the children of each mother take a separate bench: "This segregation had not been the work of the parents but a spontaneous decision on the part of the children themselves." There are a number of such fascinating details of how polygamy works in urban Africa. "In the town, since the families are scattered, the children have little contact with their father. Because of his way of life the father must go from house to house, villa to villa, and is only there in the evenings, at bedtime. He is therefore primarily a source of finance . . ." The set time he spends with each wife is called a *moomé;* the first wife is given the title of *awa,* after the Arab word for "first woman on earth." "The first wife implied a conscious choice, she was an elect. The second wife was purely optional." El Hadji's second wife, the sharp-tongued, Frenchified Oumi, has the position of sexual favorite to lose to the third, so she is suspected as the source of the *xala.* When, after many futile trips to marabouts who cannot lift the curse, El Hadji finds one, deep in the bush, who succeeds, it is Oumi who has the benefit of his momentarily revived potency. The plot takes some pains to keep young N'Gone virginal, so that she can, without serious offense to sexual propriety, be discarded, as El Hadji's luxuriant world slips from him. His impotence poisons all his existence. "Day after day, night after night, his torment ate into his professional life. Like a waterlogged silk-cotton tree on the riverbank he sank deeper into the mud." The source of the *xala,* when finally revealed, is perhaps less surprising in the film, where the sound track has repeatedly placed the culprit before us; but the ritual exaction for the curse's removal, and the story's abrupt swerve into social protest, must surprise everyone not immersed in Africa's sense of communal responsibility or familiar with the moral indignation visited there upon elites busy aggrandizing themselves in the approved capitalist manner.

El Hadji's rise, overreaching, and fall are intelligible without magic. He is impotent with his third, much younger wife out of stagefright—the jocular chaffing at the wedding and the postnuptial inspection of the bed linen lend intimacy an intimidating public dimension—and out of fright of his own hubris. His financial status collapses with his sexuality, because he is everywhere overextended. The pre-urban institution of polygamy, wherein the patriarch on the strength of his warrior potential alone ruled his docile compound of subsistence farmerettes, has been intolerably weighted by the Western conceptions of husband, lover, and (of Western goods) provider. El Hadji's metropolitan attempt to combine status and gratification breaks his resources, which, we are reminded in a forceful parenthesis, are pathetically slender:

> (It is perhaps worth pointing out that all these men who had given themselves the pompous title of "businessmen" were nothing more than middlemen, a new kind of salesman. The old trading firms of the colonial period, adapting themselves to the new situation created by African Independence, supplied them with goods on a wholesale or semi-wholesale basis, which they then re-sold.)

El Hadji's vain tour of marabouts for cure is now recast as a vain search for credit; his cars and villas are repossessed. He stands finally before us naked, covered with spittle. Nakedness, Sembène Ousmane seems to say, is man's natural condition. The keen African body-sense supplies a rapture of precision to El Hadji's moment of relief from the *xala*:

> Hadji listened to the clicking of the beads as they fell at regular intervals onto one another. He looked up at the curved roof. Suddenly he felt as if he were on edge. A long-forgotten sensation made him break into bursts of shivering. It was as if sap was rising violently inside his body, running through its fibres and filling it right to his burning head. It went on coming in waves. Then he had the impression that he was being emptied. Slowly he relaxed and a liquid flowed through his veins toward his legs. All his being now became concentrated in the region of his loins.

Not all the writing is this vivid and fluent. The translator seems to have brought to the French some English awkwardnesses: words such as "fulsome" and "exhibitionism" are used in their root, rather than usual, meanings, and more than one word seems off in a passage like "Her eyes were lifeless, they had a deep inscrutability that seemed like a total absence of reaction. But there was the strength of controlled inertia burning in them." Such eyes have successfully defied description. Not so these: "The lack of sleep showed at the edge of his eyelids and bathed his eyes in a reddish lustre crossed by threads which according to the time of day or the place would take on the colour of stale palm-oil." Generally, the texture of Mr. Wake's translation answers well to Mr. Ousmane's tone—that light, level accent of French Africa's fiction, which voices its perceptions, however withering, with a certain pleasant dispassion, with a thinking man's articulations.

A different sort of voice relates *The Land's Lord*, by T. Obinkaram Echewa. Mr. Echewa tells his story from the viewpoint of Father Anton Higler, a deserter from the French Army in the First World War; his cowardice was capped by instant vows, and his long monastic retreat in England has ended with a missionary venture to the late-colonial Nigeria whose dramas of cultural conflict and transition serve as an imaginative treasure lode, an epic land of their fathers, for so many Nigerian writers—Chinua Achebe foremost. The best of the white writers about this period, Joyce Cary, makes in *Mister Johnson* a distinction between ways of perceiving Africa. To his black African hero, Johnson, "Africa is simply perpetual experience, exciting, amusing, alarming or delightful, which he soaks into himself through all his five senses at once . . ." To a white visitor, Celia,

> Africa is simply a number of disconnected events which have no meaning for her at all. She gazes at the pot-maker without seeing that she has one leg shorter than the other, that she is in the first stages of leprosy, that her pot is bulging on one side. She doesn't really see either woman or pot, but only a scene in Africa.

It is Mr. Echewa's peculiar attempt and accomplishment to see Africa through his white priest's Greeneish eyes not as a site of experience but as a "scene":

> Finally he stepped out on the veranda, and Africa—he always thought of the village as Africa—was well awake and gloriously alert in the morning sun. It was the same every morning. People, goats, sheep, insects and birds, the sun, the rain, or the convulsing clouds, they were there already in the middle of their habitual preoccupations. Waking up to them every morning was like seeing actors on a stage which had been made ready under cover of darkness and then suddenly lit. It was as if nobody and nothing had gone to sleep since the previous day.

Wherever Father Higler looks, "surreality" and "unfathomable mysteries" assail him; the sun has "abandoned its assigned perch millions of miles away and descended to a point just above the tree tops," and the trees of the "endless, almost changeless green forest" become "a silent, brooding ubiquitous presence just off the corners of the eyes, sinister spirits trespassing into reality when the face was turned elsewhere."

Surprisingly, the natives seem to see it the same way. Father Higler's servant and principal Christian convert, Philip, turns out to have taken shelter in Christianity when he fled from his own initiation rites in the bush. Old Ahamba, the village's and the book's spokesman for African wisdom, tells of the disgrace: "Three nights he was to stay in the bush by himself. That is custom. But he ran the first night, which is something that has happened before. Many men have not the heart to face what happens in these bushes you see all around in the middle of the night." The parallel between the two runaways, black and white—"like two wounded soldiers caught behind enemy lines, neither of them much help or relief to the other"—generates the novel's central poignance and the gist of its theological debate. The starting point of the debate is the datum that "the bush"—the world, the war, whatever surrounds and menaces men—is inhuman. Hardly a prayer in *The Land's Lord* is answered, not even the mild request of Genesis, one of the converted Africans, that his wife give birth to a son. Not only are Father Higler's faith and mission mocked by events but the rituals of pagan animism—described with a fullness to delight anthropologists—are themselves shown, in the novel's crises, to be makeshift and outworn. Old Ahamba, a tireless Shavian discourser in a loincloth, tells the Christian priest, "In my youth, I too was a man of faith in all these jujus and idols. That faith gave me hope. The hope later gave me despair. But I have to go past despair to a new understanding." He comes to understand, evidently, that the gods are dispensable and revivable, like toys—like flies to wanton boys are the gods to us. His first set of wooden idols Ahamba threw to the termites; the second he urinated upon and burned. Now he lives happily in old age with his third set, a thorough religious relativist, horrified at the idea of converting anyone else to his beliefs: "I hold no commission from anyone, god or man. . . . I cannot ask you to have a haircut like mine because our faces are not alike."

The uses of sacrilege have been suggested, however, and Philip ousts his own inner demons with acts of blasphemy that banish fear. In an ending reminiscent of Nabokov's *Invitation to a Beheading*—wherein, to our great relief, the novel's confining scenery all tumbles down—Philip smashes the jujus and terrorizes the village elders and becomes himself "a present and immediate god, vindictive and wrathful, mindless." But Philip has always had, in Father Higler's eyes, the mysteriousness of the "scene." "Father Higler had found Philip strange that first night, and even stranger since then, strange beyond the strangeness he had noted in everything that was of this place." Why is Philip here, so docilely serving, without pay? Where does he go, when he slips into the darkness at night? What is the source of his mute loyalty to this isolated missionary? The reader is alert from the start to mysteries behind Philip's presence, a human "other" that partakes of the silence of the bush, the impassivity of the gods. When the black man at last abandons servanthood, the priest finds that "the kitchen smelled of Philip the way a shrine smelled of a god." He attempts what the servant so often easily, quickly performed for him—to light a fire —and this single paragraph, describing his frustrated effort to get the tropical wood to burn, stands as a metaphor for the white man's dependence upon the black in Africa. Yet Mr. Echewa's overriding point about the two men is their brotherhood: under the cruel sky, men behave kindly toward one another. Father Higler seeks, though he fails, to comprehend and console Philip, and does nurse him back from illness; Philip even in his final fury respectfully protects the "Fada." The village itself, though it resists Father Higler's message, tolerates his presence, and never questions his humanity. In the end, the devastated, delirious priest, his own God hidden, is saved by the pagans from drowning, and in a curious ritual immersion is rebaptized. "You have now arrived," Ahamba tells him, and the sky and "the dark green top of the forest" sway together like two dancers, in inscrutable but joyous dualism.

This is Mr. Echewa's first novel. He has attended American universities and now teaches at Cheyney State College, in Pennsylvania. The book is dedicated "To my Father for His Faith," and one wonders out of what matrix of cultural metamorphism a fiction so variously knowledgeable and sympathetic was produced. The scenes of missionary Christianity—the erratically attended Masses, the painfully slow construction of a brick church, the triumphant arrival of a bell on a platform hitched to four bicycles, such accommodations as the licking of salt from a Bible to substitute for a fetish oath—are authoritatively described, with a nostalgic shimmer. If, in the trinity of main characters, old Ahamba is rather too cogent and dialectical, and Father Higler feels pieced together out of European novels and a Nigerian child's glimpses of a freckled, bearded white man, the figure of Philip is masterfully brought forth from the shadows and illuminated by final lightning. An African has been wrested from the darkness, by an African. This characterization of Philip stands at a polar remove from that, say, of the narrator-hero of *The Palm-Wine Drinkard*, whose mysteries remain intractably suspended, because they are no mystery to him.

The Land's Lord has won a prize given by the English-Speaking Union "to a non-native speaker of English . . . who has published the best book of belles lettres in English." The book's few solecisms are of the ambitious sort. "The veins in his face flicked and vibed like plucked strings" and "vulgar dilettantes and compulsive imitators of the insundry ephemera of Europeanism" set up more of a picture than the author needs; elsewhere the prose is as telling as the simple observation that in the vanished Philip's washbasin "the dirt had settled neatly to the bottom." So this novel settles, with a gentle quality of consideration alien to the flip despair of so many modern "novels of ideas," toward the existential bottom of human dread, despair, and daring.

Wole Soyinka (pronounced Wally Shoy*enka*) needs no précis. His plays have been praised by New York and London critics, his name has been bruited about for the Nobel Prize, he is remembered in Nigeria* with awe, both for a political boldness that landed him

---

*Where, since the writing of this review, he has been reinstated as a trustworthy citizen, and has resumed teaching at Ife.

in prison and for a commanding intellect that is manifest in every genre he tackles. *Myth, Literature and the African World* displays him as a critic and lecturer. His introduction describes how, in 1973, unable to resume his teaching position at the University of Ife, in Nigeria, he found himself teaching in Cambridge; there the Department of English, doubting "in any such mythical beast as 'African Literature,' " withdrew its support of a proposed lecture series on African literature and society, which Mr. Soyinka then gave under the exclusive auspices of the Department of Social Anthropology. Such are the misadventures of African intellectuals abroad. True, Soyinka discusses material—Yoruba myths and ritual dramas, plays by Afro-Brazilians as well as by Nigerians, postwar African novels and poetry good and bad—not within the usual province of the educated Westerner; but he does so with ample cross-references to Greek drama, Nietzschean aesthetics, Jungian philosophy, and Sartrean opinionizing, and in an accent uncompromisingly, if not even mordantly, lofty. Here is a sample of his tone:

> The intellectual and imaginative impulse to a re-examination of the propositions on which man, nature and society are posited or interpreted at any point in history; the effort to expand such propositions, or to contest and replace them with others more in tune with the writer's own idealistic disposition or his pragmatic, resolving genius; this impulse and its integrative role in the ordering of experience and events leads to a work of social vision.

The next page, though, sums up pithily: "Much African writing is still rooted in the concept of literature as part of the normal social activity of man." Soyinka's long, fibrous sentences, not easy to pry apart, generally contain some meat, or at least milk.

He begins by discussing the myth of Sango, whose rage challenges the Supreme Deity and reminds us of Mr. Echewa's Philip. Sango cries, "I challenge that power which made me cover myself with so much shame! More! More! More! Set fire to the skies!" The protagonist in ritual theatre typically challenges unseen forces in behalf of the community; Soyinka relates his risk to the Western experience of theatre, to anxieties within the audience for the actor.

"Let us say he is a tragic character: at the first sign of a check in the momentum of a tragic declamation, his audience becomes nervous for him, wondering—has he forgotton his line? has he blacked out? Or in the case of opera—will she make that upper register?" This humanness of theatre, this precariousness so different from the serene fixity of painting, becomes an aesthetic attribute, used "to control and render concrete, to parallel . . . the experiences or intuitions of man in that far more disturbing environment which he defines variously as void, emptiness or infinity." Drama, from its ritual beginnings, sets forth "this basic adventure of man's metaphysical self." Thus, "powerful natural or cosmic influences are internalized within the protagonists and this implosive factor creates the titanic scale of their passions even when the basis of the conflict seems hardly to warrant it. (Shakespeare's *Lear* is the greatest exemplar of this.)" Tragedy takes place within "a complete, hermetic universe of forces or being. . . . Its internal cogency makes it impervious to the accident of place and time."

Soyinka's discussion of ritual and theatre takes up the first two of his lectures; there is nothing in the next two, which discuss a number of modern African novels, quite so striking in its application to our own artistic responses. We are best situated to appreciate his brilliance when it focuses on matters close to us. In Jung, Soyinka finds "racist distortions of the structure of the human psyche": "Jung differentiates the nature of the archetype in the 'primitive' mind from that of the 'civilised' mind even as he pays lip-service to the universality of a collective unconscious . . ." Sartre he lampoons as one "who, proposing the toast of Negritude, proceeded literally to drink it under the table." On the notion of Negritude: "It accepted one of the most commonplace blasphemies of racism, that the black man has nothing between his ears, and proceeded to subvert the power of poetry to glorify this fabricated justification of European cultural domination." Though his language bristles with the full armory of European critical methodology, Soyinka resists domination by extolling the profundities of African art and by giving some sacred figures of Western modernism rough treatment. Beckett—whose plays would seem exactly to fill Soyinka's prescription for ritual theatre as "a paradigm for the cosmic human condition"—is dismissed to "the lunatic fringe," and "the dotty excusions of W. B. Yeats into a private never-never land" are marvelled at for being taken seriously. African literature is commended for its refusal "to respond to the blandishments of literary ideology-manifesto art," and an imaginary representative of Cartesian civilization is addressed as "one-who-thinks, white-creature-in-pith-helmet-in-African-jungle-who-thinks and, finally, white-man-who-has-problems-believing-in-his-own-existence."

Yet so intent is Mr. Soyinka's will to see into the heart of his own culture that his recourse to points of invidious reference within ours arouses no disposition to argue. Like Frantz Fanon, he impresses us as being an analyst first, a propagandist second. Even at his most haughtily wordy, he has the voice of a true critic, who wishes not to praise or blame but to comprehend and explicate. The jacket of *Myth, Literature and the African World* shows a sculpture of the Nimba mask signifying creative force, "photographed from his collection by the author, who nicknames it 'Macro-monad' or, less reverently, 'Egghead.' " Africa possesses, in Wole Soyinka, a formidable egghead.

Mixed Reports from the Interior

A BEND IN THE RIVER, by V. S. Naipaul. 278 pp. Knopf, 1979.

NORTH OF SOUTH: *An African Journey,* by Shiva Naipaul. 349 pp. Simon & Schuster, 1979.

THE JOYS OF MOTHERHOOD, by Buchi Emecheta. 224 pp. Braziller, 1979.

PETALS OF BLOOD, by Ngugi wa Thiong'o. 345 pp. Dutton, 1978.

V. S. Naipaul, an Indian born in Trinidad in 1932, has become the outstanding male writer of his generation resident in England, where he has lived since coming to Oxford in 1950. The so-called Third World has produced no more brilliant literary artist; but the propagandists and official spokesmen for the underdeveloped nations will find little to cheer them on in Naipaul's cold-eyed fictional descriptions and journalistic reports. Where they would proclaim a decent hope and a revolutionary indignation, he sees stagnation, futility, and a sinister darkness. His view of native possibilities in lands unregulated by white men seems no less dim than Evelyn Waugh's, though Naipaul's farce awakens fear sooner than laughter, and is informed not by a visitor's quizzical amusement but by a pained, partial identification. Born into a racial minority within a tropical colony, Naipaul has enlarged his cosmopolitan education with wide and deliberate travel. His last decade's books include *India: A Wounded Civilization* (1977), a despairing study of his ethnic homeland; *The Loss of El Dorado* (1969), an ironical meditation upon Trinidad's early history; *In a Free State* (1971), a shapely collection of journal entries and short fiction dealing with exile and disenfranchisement; and *Guerrillas* (1975), a novel concerned with political and sexual agitation on a nameless Caribbean island. His new novel, *A Bend in the River,* takes place within an also nameless black African nation that strongly suggests Zaïre, and proves once more that Naipaul is incomparably well situated and equipped to bring us news of one of the contemporary world's great subjects—the mingling of its peoples.

A Bend in the River struck me as an advance—broader, warmer, less jaded and kinky—over the much-praised *Guerrillas,* though not quite as vivid and revelatory as the fiction of *In a Free State.* There, in the two short stories "One out of Many" and "Tell Me Who to Kill," the cataclysmic inner adjustments forced upon those of the world's poor who immigrate to Western metropolises are sketched with a fond accent and a gaiety of invention rare in Naipaul's rather stern later fiction. A man of the servant class from Bombay, though prosperously transplanted to Washington, D.C., misses the friendly nights of sleeping on the pavement, the flow of preordained events, and the security of caste. He tells us:

> I was once part of the flow, never thinking of myself as a presence. Then I looked in the mirror and decided to be free. All that my freedom has brought me is the knowledge that I have a face and have a body, that I must feed this body and clothe this body for a certain number of years. Then it will be over.

And a West Indian transplanted to London, where a succession of disappointments and harassments have driven him to murder, is brought from jail to attend his brother's wedding to a white girl. He looks at his in-laws and thinks:

> O God, show me the enemy. Once you find out who the enemy is, you can kill him. But these people here they confuse me. Who hurt me? Who spoil my life? Tell me who to beat back. I work four years to save my money, I work like a donkey night and day. My brother was to be the educated one, the nice one. And this is how it is ending, in this room, eating with these people. Tell me who to kill?

In the novella from which *In a Free State* takes its title, two white people, a homosexual bureaucrat and the promiscuous wife of an official in the post-colonial government of a turbulent African "free state," drive from the capital to their compound in a southern province, through four hundred miles of beautiful landscape, bickering conversation, automotive incident, and gathering menace as they reach the area where the President's army is suppressing an inconvenient tribe. The accruing tension and complexity of this trip are extraordinary; Naipaul has written little that is better, and little better has been written about modern Africa. *A Bend in the River* is carved from the same territory—an Africa of withering colonial vestiges, terrifyingly murky politics, defeated pretensions, omnivorous rot, and the implacable undermining of all that would sustain reason and safety.

The hero, Salim, comes from one of the Muslim families of Indian origin that have been living and trading on the east coast for centuries. A friend sells him a shop in another country, far inland, "at the bend in the great river," in a settlement that had been nearly destroyed by the country's "troubles after independence." He travels to the interior and takes possession of an empty shop amid the ruins:

> After my anxiety to arrive, there was little for me to do. But I was not alone. There were other traders, other foreigners; some of them had been there right through the troubles. I waited with them. The peace held. People began coming back to the town; the *cité* yards filled up.

People began needing the goods which we could supply. And slowly business started up again.

The novel describes the seven or so years of Salim's life while peace holds, before chaos and destruction again visit the bend in the river. He has his Indian friends: one young couple preen on their good looks and married happiness, and add to their happiness by acquiring the town's Bigburger franchise; then, there is an older couple who "didn't seem to know where they were. The bush of Africa was outside their yard; but they spoke no French, no African language, and from the way they behaved you would have thought that the river just down the road was the Ganges, with temples and holy men and bathing steps."

Salim deals with such native traders as the witchlike Zabeth, and agrees to keep an eye on her son Ferdinand, a tall adolescent of mixed tribal origins who enlists at the local *lycée*. He acquires a servant, Ali, who had been a slave with his family on the east coast and who here is given the new name of Metty (from *métis*, "someone of mixed race"); and Salim makes friends with a white couple, Raymond and Yvette. Raymond is "the Big Man's white man," the dictator's personal friend. He runs a kind of university in the Domain, new buildings erected in what had been the white suburb of the town. Salim seduces Yvette, with good results: "The body on the bed was to me like the revelation of a woman's form. . . . The sexual act became for me an extraordinary novelty, a new kind of fulfilment, continuously new. . . . I felt blessed and remade." Their passionate affair dominates the private level of the novel, while the public level provides a superb oblique portrait of deterioration, of sinking dreams and rising terror, of a liberation army seeping in from the bush and a counterthrust of megalomania in central government and extortion and torture in local government, of confused cruelties in the face of the essentially ungovernable. Salim's once flourishing business is confiscated, and the black "Citizen" who as new owner instantly hires Salim as his manager explains:

> "The revolution had become"—he fumbled for the word—"*un pé pourrie*. A little rotten. Our young people were becoming impatient. It was

necessary . . . to radicalize. We had absolutely to radicalize. We were expecting too much of the President."

Much is written of corruption in African governments, but it takes a novelist like Naipaul to show exactly how it works, and to trace its spread to a pervasive fear, beginning with the Big Man's fear of losing power. To keep power, he must make it ever more arbitrary —"The President issued a statement, just to let everybody know that what the Big Man gives the Big Man can take away. That's how the Big Man gets them." The officials under him—Ferdinand rises to become one—are kept therefore in a state of uncertainty: "These men, who depended on the President's favour for every-thing, were bundles of nerves. The great power they exercised went with a constant fear of being destroyed. And they were unstable, half dead." The officials under *them,* as the contagion of instability is felt, frantically seek greater bribes: "Everyone had become more greedy and desperate. There was this feeling of ev-erything running down very fast, of a great chaos coming; and some people could behave as though money had already lost its value." A frenzy is the result, felt equally by prisoners and warders, torturers and victims. Salim himself, driven to smuggling ivory and gold, is placed in jail, and there experiences a recognition of the Africans he has long lived among:

> Those faces of Africa! Those masks of child-like calm that had brought down the blows of the world, and of Africans as well, as now in the jail. I felt I had never seen them so clearly before. . . . There was, with the prisoners as well as their active tormentors, a frenzy. But the frenzy of the prisoners was internal; it had taken them far beyond their cause or even knowledge of their cause, far beyond thought.

Rage—"such blank and mindless rage that his own anger van-ished in terror," as the hero of "In a Free State" observes—is perhaps the deepest and darkest fact Naipaul has to report about the Third World, and in this novel his understanding of it goes beyond that shown in *Guerrillas.* There it was somewhat cavalierly linked to sexual malaise and social insecurity of a personal sort; here it is traced to social insecurity in the drastic sense of governments that cannot govern, of imported cultures that have destroyed but not replaced the tribal cultures. "The rage of the rebels was like a rage against metal, machinery, wires, everything that was not of the forest and Africa." In *A Bend in the River,* the alien observer— white bureaucrat or Asian trader—is drawn closer into the ra- tionale of the riots and wars that seethe in the slums or the bush beyond his enclave. The novel might be faulted for savoring a bit of the visiting journalist's worked-up notes; its episodes do not hang together with full organic snugness; there are a few too many clever geopolitical conversations and scenically detailed car rides. But, just as the love affair between Salim and Yvette, though it ends badly,* is relatively tender and healthy, so the author's embrace of his tangled and tragic African scene seems relatively hearty as well as immensely knowledgeable. Always a master of fictional land- scape, Naipaul here shows, in his variety of human examples and in his search for underlying social causes, a Tolstoyan spirit, gener- ous if not genial. *A Bend in the River* is the most genuinely explor- atory novel about tropical Africa written by a non-African since Joyce Cary's *The African Witch.*

Naipaul's younger brother Shiva, also a novelist, an Oxonian, and an adoptive Englishman, has written a travel book, *North of South: An African Journey,* which, though entertaining and some- what informative, is characterized foremost by annoyance. Shiva Naipaul is annoyed by the tourists, beggars, and whores of free- enterprise Kenya; he is annoyed by the prating ideologues and lethargic officialdom of Socialist Tanzania; he is annoyed by the amount of beer that Zambians drink and also by the pleas of their state-run television service that they drink less. He is annoyed by the anti-black racism of the whites who linger "north of south" (i.e., of South Africa), and even more annoyed by the anti-Indian prejudices of Africans black and white. In Mombasa, he is told by whites "how terribly Asians treated Africans," and in Nairobi

*Love affairs in Naipaul's fiction tend to culminate in some physical abuse of the woman, with especial attention paid to her genitals. Here, after Salim beats and kicks Yvette, there is this: "I held her legs apart. She raised them slightly—smooth concavities of flesh on either side of the inner ridge—and then I spat on her between the legs until I had no more spit."

a black taxi-driver shouts at him, "That's the trouble with you Asians. You want to keep Africans poor. You don't want us to have anything. You want it all for yourselves." He is led to meditate, in the book's most thoughtful chapter, on his own life as an overseas Indian and on the jeopardized, generally unappreciated position of the so-called Asians in East Africa, which has been especially insecure since their expulsion from Uganda in 1972. An Asian prostitute in Mombasa confides, "I would like to get far, far away from here. But where can I go? Who would give *me* a visa?"

The merchant class of *A Bend in the River* are also on the run, looking for a place to go; one of them claims, "All over the world money is in flight. People have scraped the world clean, as clean as an African scrapes his yard, and now they want to run from the dreadful places where they've made their money and find some nice safe country. . . . They are frightened of the fire. You mustn't think it's only Africa people are running from." And in that same novel an educated African expresses the same terrors: "Everyone wants to make his money and run away. But where? That is what is driving people mad. They feel they're losing the place they can run back to. I began to feel the same thing. . . . I wanted to be a child again, to forget books and everything connected with books. The bush runs itself. But there is no place to go."

No place to go: the last sentence of Shiva Naipaul's book is, "I fled." But the nightmare vision of a refugee world that lends his brother's fiction an apocalyptic power doesn't rise in his own reportage above the level of grievance. Though he dutifully exposes himself to a wealth of African discomforts, he never really tries to get out of his sensitive Indian skin. He talks more to white tourists and hangers-on than to black Africans, and his interviews are wrapped in prickliness and comedy. Some of the comedy is quite good: a sluggish Tanzanian higher-up is diagnosed as reduced to a "hibernatory torpor" by the icy workings of his prestigious air-conditioner. A Kenyan district commissioner responds to all questions with a diplomatic "uhmmmm . . . uhmmmm . . . uhmmmm . . ." Mr. Naipaul's best comic characters, though, are fellow-travellers—American hippies and a pugnacious "citizen of the Republic of India," Mr. Mukerjee. One begins to wonder if our roving reporter doesn't bring out the worst in the people he meets, and doesn't report only the silliest things they say. For instance, the American wife of a U.N. "management expert" in Tanzania, after complaining about the lack of frankfurters and sufficiently large refrigerators, relates how once in St. Thomas she, too shy of dirt to go barefoot on the beach, tromped through the sand in new sixty-five-dollar shoes and ruined them—behavior not strictly impossible but certainly untypical of Americans in the Caribbean. Mr. Naipaul blandly passes on the settler wisdom that "Africans don't understand about straight lines," have no "storage sense," and suffer from an "inadequate grasp of the laws of cause and effect." Neither Kenya's national slogan of *Harambee* (Pull Together), nor Tanzania's of *Ujamaa* (Familyhood; Community), nor Gambia's Humanism impresses him as more than empty words. As his journey reaches its end he is ready to ask himself, "Had I not learned, after all this time, that nothing in Africa has meaning? That nothing could be taken seriously?" He takes whites seriously enough to analyze shrewdly their attitudes and fantasies in regard to Africa:

> For if the Highlands of neighboring Kenya stimulated to fresh life outmoded and frustrated aristocratic longings in a certain type of European settler, then, and with much the same justice, it could be said that Independent Tanzania has stimulated the fantasies of a certain type of outmoded European socialist—men and women of a somewhat pastoral and utopian turn of mind—whose socialism fades by imperceptible degrees into a kind of benevolent, condescending patronage of the backward and deprived.

But for the object and site of these fantastical satisfactions, for Africa itself, the visiting Anglo-Indian shows little empathy, merely an irritated eye for the "dusty, disordered" details, the bad hotel service, the "delirious sameness" of the landscape. He goes on for pages about an expensive shoeshine in Nairobi, the slow beers in Dar es Salaam, and the way the nice little Chinese railroad in Gambia is being allowed to deteriorate. To an American, his tone recalls those nineteenth-century European travellers who spent a few months in this country and went back to their publishers with tales of our horrific uncouthness. What the other side of uncouthness might be—what fresh priorities might lie behind it—it took a de Tocqueville to discern. Mr. Naipaul is no de Tocqueville; indeed, he is less open to African ways than were early explorers like Livingstone and Mungo Park. His comment on a derelict Indian he finds in a drunken and ragged state in a remote Tanzanian guesthouse is "I could not help Karim Lalji. No one could. Africa had closed in over him."

North of South begins with a wandering Sikh confiding to the journalist, "To survive these days you had to be either black or white. It was no good being brown," and ends with a bitter brown malediction upon black and white in Africa: "Black and white deserved each other. Neither was worth the shedding of a single tear: both were rotten to the core.* . . . Black Africa, with its gimcrack tyrannies, its Field Marshals and Emperors, its false philosophies, its fabricated statehoods, returns to Europe its own features, but grotesquely caricatured. . . . Hopeless, doomed continent! Only lies flourished here. Africa was swaddled in lies—the lies of an aborted European civilization; the lies of liberation. Nothing but lies."

Yet people live here, under these imperfect governments, and their lives are truth. Failing to take this truth seriously, Shiva Naipaul has given us an ephemeral book, for all his inarguable observations, his allowable satire, and his courage in not mincing words. He gives us a traveller's Africa we cannot live in, unlike the imaginary Africa—no less hopeless and doomed—of his brother's novel.

The "bush"—the vast realm of the rural villages—is just a sinister rumor in *A Bend in the River* and an unspeakable "void" in *North of South*. But according to *The Joys of Motherhood*, Buchi Emecheta's fourth novel, the bush isn't such a bad place:

> From outside came the sounds of goats bleating, children playing, the voices of women singing to their babies; but inside the courtyard there was a long silence, during which Agbadi chewed the edge of his mouth furiously, trying to decide his daughter's future.

---

*More than *un pé pourrie.*

The scene is Iboland, in colonial Nigeria. Agbadi is "the last of the great hunters," his daughter is our heroine, Nnu Ego, her future is to take place in the metropolis of Lagos, and family is the theme. Nnu Ego (English pun intended?) was born of the union of a village chief and his favorite love-object, another chief's daughter, who refused to marry him. Nnu Ego inherits her mother's beauty but not her independent spirit. When she marries, she is unable to bear children, because she is under a curse from her *chi;* a *chi* seems to be a blend of guardian angel and previous incarnation, and Nnu Ego's was a slave girl unwillingly buried with her mistress, Agbadi's chief wife. Nnu Ego's husband, Amatokwu, though they "were very happy," is compelled to dismiss her for infertility; she is then given in marriage to a fellow-villager, Nnaife (French pun intended?), who does laundry for a white couple in Lagos. When Nnu Ego moves to Lagos, the timeless village enters history and the novel becomes a sociological study—Mrs. Emecheta, an English resident since 1962, holds a degree in sociology from London University—of traditional institutions under urban stress. The events run from around 1910 to the late 1950s. After her sterile first marriage and the infant death of her firstborn, Nnu Ego's prayers to her *chi* are answered in the form of eight more children, of whom seven survive and four are twins. Rearing so many children in cramped circumstances, which the continued honoring of polygamous customs cramps further, sends her to an early grave. Dying half demented back in her native village, she is viewed as a saint of maternity; yet from beyond the grave she resolutely refuses to answer the prayers of barren women to give them children. It is a perfect ending for a graceful, touching, ironically titled tale that bears a plain feminist message:

> She had been brought up to believe that children made a woman . . . how was she to know that by the time her children grew up the values of her country, her people and her tribe would have changed so drastically, to the extent where a woman with many children could face a lonely old age, and maybe a miserable death all alone, just like a barren woman? . . . Nnu Ego told herself that she would have been better off had she had time to cultivate those women who had offered her hands of friendship; but she had never had the time.

Not only is the rural notion of children as wealth turned upside down in a money-centered, education-oriented city; a drastic shift in the concept of property also occurs. In tribal Africa, men and women do not own themselves: the tribe, the ancestors, the spouse, the slavemaster exert claims of which each individual is the sum. When the abstract colonial state the British have imposed exerts its claim upon Nnaife and sends him off to fight in Burma ("I still do not understand who we were fighting. We kept marching up and down and the white officers were shooting in the air"), Nnu Ego's trading in firewood and other small commodities supports his family, which has been enlarged by a wife he has inherited from his dead brother and another wife he has chosen to take. Yet in court Nnaife testifies that he pays his son's school fees, and his wife concurs.

> "Do you mean the two of you pay Adim's school fees?" [a lawyer asks Nnu Ego]
> "No, I pay."
> The laughter that followed this could no longer be suppressed. Even the judge smiled unwillingly.
> "Mrs. Owulum, will you please explain."
> "Nnaife is the head of our family. He owns me, just like God in the sky owns us. So even though I pay the fees, yet he owns me. So in other words he pays."

She is still part of the flow, never thinking of herself as a presence. Her children fight free of the flow, the two older boys taking their educations off to the United States and Canada, and one of the girls horrifying Ibo sensibilities by marrying a Yoruba. Nnaife, who if not an ideal husband has yet never renounced his responsibilities, through the mists of palm wine sees that he has been used by Nnu Ego to produce children and protests to her, "I was not created to suffer for you till I die." Even she, when a junior wife announces her pregnancy, spontaneously thinks, "Another child? Into all this mess?"

Without the village space and the village structures, things fall apart. As Chinua Achebe, in *Things Fall Apart* and its successors, wrote of the baffled and broken African fathers, so Buchi Emecheta writes of the mothers. Her generation, of course, is that not of Nnu Ego but of Nnu Ego's children. In this compassionate but slightly distanced and stylized story of a life that comes to seem wasted she sings a dirge for more than African pieties. The lives within *The Joys of Motherhood* might be, transposed into a different cultural key, those of our own rural ancestors. For that matter, the blind god of self-realization still asks for children, and self-sacrifice within the family continuum remains the price of creating new lives. Mrs. Emecheta herself, the jacket flap tells us, is the mother of five.

Ngugi wa Thiong'o is considered the best writer in East Africa —perhaps the best since Karen Blixen returned to Denmark— and throughout most of 1978 he was imprisoned in Kenya without charges or trial. Since his release by the new President, Daniel arap Moi, last December, he has continued, in his activities as writer, professor of literature, and interviewee, to express profound dissatisfaction with the status quo in Kenya, and is probably headed for more trouble, in a state viewed in the West as one of black Africa's most liberal. The immediate stimulus of Ngugi's detainment he himself conjectures to be a Kikuyu play he collaborated on, *Ngahiika Ndenda* ("I Will Marry When I Want"), performed at a village cultural center in Limura. But the Kenyan publication of his long novel *Petals of Blood,* a few months before his arrest, surely didn't ingratiate him with the authorities. The novel is ambitious, caustic, impassioned, and leftist. It also seemed, to this reader, tedious, implausible, clumsy, and in spots terribly written. The opening pages are peppered with Swahili and Kikuyu words, as if to warn non-African readers away. Whatever else political fervor has done for Ngugi, it has not helped his ear for English; the fine calm style of *A Grain of Wheat*, which was published in 1967 under his "Christian" name of James Ngugi, has here come unhinged:

> And then she started appearing to him in dreams: breasts would beat on breasts, body frames would become taut with unspoken desire, eyes

would hold onto eyes as they both stood on Ilmorog hill, hideaway from school, away from Cambridge Fraudsham who had fumed, frowned and ground his teeth with anger because of the perfumed garden that was her body.

The garden herself thinks in hothouse terms:

As an evidence of her cleansed spirit, she resolved that she would not again obey the power of her body over men; that any involvement was out until she had defeated the past through a new flowering of self.

Let the book's teeming multitudes of political imprecations be represented by one relatively short sentence:

These few who had prostituted the whole land turning it over to foreigners for thorough exploitation, would drink people's blood and say hypocritical prayers of devotion to skin oneness and to nationalism even as skeletons of bones walked to lonely graves.

Well, as Barry Goldwater might say, verbal excess in pursuit of social justice is no great sin. But the clichés and overwrought syntax correspond to dislocations in the novel's larger elements. The plot is determinedly melodramatic, beginning with quadruple arrests for a triple murder, and Ngugi employs much of the conventional detective novel's machinery with none of that genre's speed and lightness. He gives us a black Hercule Poirot ("Crime for him was a kind of jigsaw puzzle, and he believed that there was a law to it") and pumps suspense into his raft of flashbacks and confessions by exasperatingly withholding to a later page information we need to steer by; the novel is hobbled by relentless authorial manipulation. The characters, except for a donkey who never says a word, stagger and sink under the politico-symbolical messages they are made to carry. The interior monologues of one, Karega, an ex-schoolteacher turned wandering labor organizer, read like wall posters in Mao's prime, and the inner commotions of our heroine, the flowering Wanja, are so heavily orchestrated, so luridly framed in imagery compounded of *Playboy* soft porn and Old Testament harlotry, that we lose all track of what value her virtue is supposed to have. "So what if she had given in, she hissed inside to prevent tears, so what?" Munira, the local schoolteacher, is the character we begin and end with, and seems closest to Ngugi's heart; he alone contains traits—a nagging sense of detachment and a fascination with his father's stern Christianity—that are not immediately convertible into Socialist moralizing, and that have something of the involuntarily human about them. *The Joys of Motherhood* had its didactic messages, too, but the skein of experience it described felt like something observed and in retrospect made sense of; *Petals of Blood* bulldozes its intended meaning into the landscape of its events as ruthlessly as the property exploiters it decries.

Beneath the huffing and puffing about "sturdy peasants" and "Che Guevara with his Christlike locks of hair and saintly eyes," lies a real land, a piece of Kenya with its history, its beauty, and its fate. Only the landscape can induce the angry author to relax enough to write well:

> So help me God that he does not go, Wanja murmured to herself, gazing across the plains to the distant Donyo Hills. Just above the hills, the moving clouds had formed two shapes, the likeness of scraggy-mouthed caves, belching out mist and light. The mouths became smaller and smaller until the caves finally dissolved into a floating black-bluish wool. She followed the slow wool motion, trying to locate where the fingerprints of God had been.

What moves us, in *Petals of Blood*, is the tracing of twelve years in the province of Ilmorog as it goes from being a drought-ridden area of subsistence agriculture to a junk-ridden little copy of Nairobi, divided in two by the Trans-Africa Highway. Ironically, the citizens of Ilmorog bring attention to themselves, and invite the horrors of development, by heroically travelling on foot to the capital to secure relief from the drought. This section of the novel, the dusty peasants among the ogres of power and affluence, takes on an authentic life, as a Marxist *Pilgrim's Progress;* the politicians and exploiters are allowed for the moment the uncontrolled vitality of villainy, and the novel breathes. Back in Ilmorog, relief comes from

God in the form of rain. But human rapacity—"the tyranny of foreign companies and their local messengers"—has been alerted to virgin territory, and also descends.

Ngugi, in an interview in the Nairobi journal *Viva*, when asked about the stereotypical quality of his middle-class characters, responded, "They are supposed to stand as class types, as typical of a class that has come to be completely indifferent to the cry of the people. I see no value whatever in the middle-class." Yet his chief characters, in *Petals of Blood, are* middle-class—two schoolteachers, Munira and Karega; a shopkeeper, Abdulla, who lost a leg in the struggle for Uhuru; and a bargirl, Wanja, who rises from prostitution to run and own a distillery, a real-estate and transportation empire, and the snappiest brothel in Ilmorog. The novel's action consists of the conflicts and decisions of these mobile, enterprising characters; the much-praised peasant life of Ilmorog figures as a few sentimental snapshots a passing tourist could have taken. Ngugi told his *Viva* interviewer that "the middle class that feeds on the workers and peasants is a superfluous, parasitic class." Of what is this class composed but aspiring workers and ex-peasants and their descendants? We are not convinced, as Karega and Ngugi evidently are, of some innate proletarian goodness capable of "seizing power to overturn the system and all its prying bloodthirsty gods and gnomic angels, bringing to an end the reign of the few over the many and the era of drinking blood and feasting on human flesh." We *are* convinced, even without the hectic testimony of *Petals of Blood,* that for the masses of too many African nations independence has merely replaced white colonial exploiters with indigenous opportunists and oppressors.

A great sigh of disappointment blows through the contemporary African novel. In Kenya—with Algeria, one of the few African nations that fought for their independence with guns—the sigh is especially deep. Yet what did they expect, these raging, often exiled, intellectuals? Some reconstruction, it would seem, of an altruistic tribal idyll, a spontaneous and painless Socialism located on the misty far shore of the colonial interregnum. Nostalgia also blows through these novels, with a force that distinguishes them from their Western counterparts:

Ilmorog . . . had had its days of glory: thriving villages with a huge population of sturdy peasants who had tamed nature's forests and, breaking the soil between their fingers, had brought forth every type of crop to nourish the sons and daughters of men.

For the living actual Africa, with its mingled realities and muffled potentials, Ngugi wa Thiong'o has as little patience as Shiva Naipaul. And he, too, is a traveller; the dateline on *Petals of Blood* is given at the end as "October 1970–October 1975" and the places of its writing, in a tripartite ascription more widely flung than that of *Ulysses,* as "Evanston–Limuru–Yalta." Ngugi has gone from a guest professorship in the African Studies Program at Northwestern University in Illinois to a guesthouse of the Soviet Writer's Union on the Black Sea. One wishes him now an untroubled stay at home, and a release from the need to write agitprop.

Journeyers

ARABIA: *A Journey Through the Labyrinth,* by Jonathan Raban. 344 pp. Simon & Schuster, 1979.

AFRICAN CALLIOPE: *A Journey to the Sudan,* by Edward Hoagland. 239 pp. Random House, 1979.

"Tell me . . . what moved thee, or how couldst thou take such journeys into the fanatic Arabia?" This question, posed in the first paragraph of Charles M. Doughty's classic *Travels in Arabia Deserta,* goes unanswered by Doughty. But Jonathan Raban, the young English author of *Arabia: A Journey Through the Labyrinth,* tells us plain: he went because he became curious about his many new Arab neighbors in London, and because he wanted to write a book—a book about Arabs more contemporary than Doughty's, or T. E. Lawrence's *Seven Pillars of Wisdom,* or even Wilfred Thesiger's *Arabian Sands,* which dates from the 1950s. Nothing wrong with books: the great Stanley, immediately after his harrowing three years' rescue of Emin Pasha, sat down at the Hotel Villa Victoria in Cairo and wrote off, at the rate of twenty printed pages a day, the two stout volumes of *In Darkest Africa.* Where once men set out provisioned by the African Association and the Royal Geographical Society, they now venture on the strength of publishers' advances.

Mr. Raban had, he thought, a new slant. "British Arabism," in his analysis, "coincides exactly with that period when England was a rich country in the first flush of its dependence on industrial technology. For Lawrence and Thesiger, Arabia was an alternative kingdom; a tough utopia without either money or machines. In the Bedu tribesman they professed to find all the simplicity, the powers of personal endurance, the stoic independence which they feared the Englishman was losing." But what now, when the British have returned to penury and when parts, at least, of the Arab world are conspicuously rich in money and machines? Mr. Raban attempted to find out, and has produced an ample, smooth, fair-minded book that yet is neither so deep nor so full as it might have been. Unlike Doughty (or René Caillié, or James Bruce, or Richard Burton, or a host of other travellers in the lands of Islam), he learned little Arabic, though what he did learn got him far, both as a patron of Middle Eastern teahouses and as an analyst of the Arab character; e.g., "To live in Arabic is to live in a labyrinth of false turns and double meanings." (One might as confidently assert that to live in English is to dwell in a mire of synonyms and inconsistent pronunciations.) More severely limiting would appear to be the inability of the author of *Arabia* to secure admission to the heartland of his subject, Saudi Arabia. Though he waved a synopsis of his book in their faces, the Saudi authorities declined to issue Mr. Raban a visa. *Arabia,* then, is a *Hamlet* without Hamlet, and since for unspecified reasons the author also did not visit Kuwait, Oman, Syria, or Iraq, it is one without Horatio, Claudius, Polonius, and Laertes as well. However, this novice explorer (whose previous books consist of sedentary forays into *The Technique of Modern Fiction* and *The Society of the Poem*) did spend a total of fourteen weeks in Bahrain, Qatar, Abu Dhabi, Dubai, North Yemen, Egypt, and Jordan, bringing back many artful descriptions and, to me, surprising observations concerning these wide-ranging peoples in whose hands so hefty a portion of our economic fate has been placed.

The Arabs themselves, he discovers as he moves from the con-struction-crammed, dollar-bloated capitals of the Persian Gulf to the poorer nations on the other side of the Arabian peninsula, are suffering extensive dislocations from the massive infusion of oil money. The fifty thousand native Qataris, for instance, are in dan-ger of being swamped by the hundred fifty thousand immigrants attracted to this once desolate theocracy by its overheated econ-omy. While the official artists cultivate a thin mythos of Qatar's Bedouin (or, as Mr. Raban insists on saying, Bedu) past, the princi-pal city, Doha, drowns in a mad internationalism:

> The faces of the storekeepers were Pakistani; their goods, perspiring in cellophane packages, came from Taiwan, Hong Kong, Japan, America. In the crowd on the pavement, other faces loomed—all of them dis-placed and temporary, Europeans looking sick with the heat swam by like fish against glass, followed by sallow Levantines, Sudanese Negroes and wild day laborers from Baluchistan. It was like being caught in the middle of a vast, fatal cultural car crash.

Regions not directly blessed with oil are involved in the crash. In North Yemen, the men go off to work in the Gulf states and remit enough of their wages to flood the economy. "I had arrived in a very poor country which had been on a wild spending spree. . . . Their government had been quite unable to control this binge. While the families of the laborers abroad were blowing their pay envelopes on luxury goods, the streets of Sana'a were still garbage dumps, the structure of the city still medieval. Families who didn't have cousins, fathers, husbands working in the Gulf were starving as inflation rose." And the soil of this country, which could be the granary of Arabia, is devoted to the growing of *qat*—a privetlike plant that, chewed green, serves as a national narcotic. "All around the square, in scraps of shade, in woody closets set in walls, under jumbo-sized umbrellas, the Yemenis were given over to chewing *qat* . . . The drug—costing between $10 and $16 for a sprig suffi-cient for one man for one afternoon—was sopping up a large proportion of the remittance money; most men were reckoned to be spending about $100 a week on *qat*."

According to Mr. Raban, the Yemenis occupy a certain stratum in the pan-Arab swarm that feasts off the oil industry. "In the Gulf, the Yemenis were taxi drivers, construction workers, soldiers, road builders, mechanics, rig hands. In the hierarchy of labor they formed an upper working class of semi-skilled men—a clear notch or two above the Baluchis, Pakistanis and Bangladeshis, but far below the middle class of Palestinians, Egyptians, Jordanians and Europeans." Upon the Palestinians he offers a perspective seldom found in American newspapers: they are Arabia's Jews.

> More heavily built than any other Arabs, with fleshier, paler, more distinctively urban faces, the Palestinians put me in mind of another place altogether. We could have been at Bloom's Restaurant in White-chapel on any Sunday afternoon: the same faces, the same crowding of the generations around a single table, the same serious banter. . . . In Jordan, as in the Gulf, I kept on hearing Palestinians spoken of in exactly the same terms with which Europeans used to describe Jews. They were "clever," "artistically talented," "very good at business": these were not compliments; they were the seeds of a resentment which any European must spot with alarmed recognition.

They are everywhere, these wandering Palestinians, and everywhere sensitive to their "problem." In Abu Dhabi, a man sobs when the car radio describes an Israeli attack upon Palestinian positions in Lebanon, because he is *Filastin*—Palestinian. "An injury in one part of the diaspora is instantly transmitted through the entire system like an electric current . . . There are no spatial dimensions to Palestine anymore."

Nor is the presence of Saudi Arabia limited to its geography. "Traipsing around the countries on its fringes, I had been constantly reminded of the presence of Saudi Arabia. . . . On the Gulf and in Yemen I had seen the pressures exerted by Saudi money, Saudi religious orthodoxy and Saudi politics . . . When the Emir of Sharjah had started a casino, the Saudis had closed it down by paying the Emir as much money as he would have received every month from his casino, plus a handsome bonus. The Saudis had closed the one 'wet' restaurant in Qatar." If the Palestinians are Jews, the Saudis suggest Americans as we used to figure in the world, thirty years ago, in all our *nouveau puissance*. They are

regarded by other Arabs, Mr. Raban finds, as arrogant and hypo-
critical. In Egypt, Saudi power is paradoxically evinced by a plague
of night spots catering to jaunting Saudi businessmen and, along
with the new brothel atmosphere, an official trend toward stricter
Islamic orthodoxy. Mr. Raban is told, "You know, girls whose
mothers have never worn the veil—today some of them are going
behind the veil for the first time." And he reports that, at the very
time when Sadat was being lionized as a peacemaker in the West,
his regime instituted laws that "brought Egyptian censorship into
line with that of the most hardheaded Eastern European states" and
that have finished Cairo as the intellectual center of the Arab world.

The literary problem faced by travel writers differs from that of
fictionists and poets, whose material arrives mercifully thinned and
pruned by the limitations of imagination and memory. A travel
writer, notebook in hand, confronts the thing itself—immense,
multiform, contradictory, numbing. As he lives his book, Mr.
Raban is more than once overwhelmed by three-dimensional illegi-
bility. Mounting to a housetop in Sana'a is "like stepping out into
the middle of a vast pop-up book. Away from the street, the whole
city turned into a maze of another kind, a dense, jumbled alphabet
of signs and symbols. . . . It stretched all around my feet, an
enormous code in three dimensions. If I half-closed my eyes, I
almost thought that I could read it." Mr. Raban's account of his
travels has an ingenuous freshness, a natural alertness. His long
chapters, each devoted to one stop on his journey, arrange their
impressions around a central conceit—Dubai as a reincarnation of
the Italian Quattrocento, Egypt as perceived through Disraeli's
Victorian novel *Sybil*. Cheerfully amateur, he nets perceptions an
old Arab hand might have been blind to. His writing is fine, if
sometimes fancy, with a touch of la-di-da. The desert is "simply
boring" and "the only conceivable place on earth where the camel
could have earned itself a place in human affections"; a lowly café
smells "aniseedy"; and our President is put down as "the great
peanut farmer." Mr. Raban strains, as travel writers must, to make
each moment yield its image: a "large American lady" is pictured
as "wearing a homemade sweater which came down to her knees
and which looked as if it had been knitted out of thick vegetable

soup." Mr. Raban often sees knees: in a derelict village "the build-
ings just seemed to have sunk to their knees and rotted to bits,"
which is excellent; but in Giza "the pyramids are buried up to their
knees in trash," which boggles the mind. (Show me a pyramid's
knee and I'll show you a volleyball's elbow.)

Though his own mind was sometimes boggled, our journeyer
held to his itinerary through the labyrinth, tried to align all he saw
with some central perception about Islam as an optimistic, evangel-
ical "corrective version of Semitic religion," and returned to Lon-
don not only with an improved understanding of his Arab neigh-
bors but with an ability, in his rudimentary Arabic, "to act as an
interpreter when people got into difficulties." He is enough of an
Arab now to feel the "Arab fear of London," where Arabs are
envied for their supposed—and generally exaggerated—wealth and
increasingly victimized by English criminals. His sad and shaming
realization is that "in Arabia I had met with infinitely more cour-
tesy than any Arab could hope to encounter in London."

Edward Hoagland is ten years older than Jonathan Raban, and
an American. He has frequently sought out lonely places to write
about—not only the remote terrains of British Columbia and north-
ern New England but raw pockets of New York City. At the age
of forty-seven, he has behind him a distinguished and highly indi-
vidual literary career, beginning with a novel, *Cat Man*, written
while he was still a college undergraduate, and proceeding through
a quarter of a century to the recent, precocious dignity of a
"reader"—*The Edward Hoagland Reader*, culled mostly from his
three collections of remarkable essays. Remarkable for their frank-
ness, range, and pungency and for their stubborn self-determina-
tion: in a time of assigned topics and all-too-creative editors, Mr.
Hoagland writes what he wants to and trusts it to find a market.
There is a chip on the shoulder of his prose that may keep him from
ever ingratiating himself with a large audience. He is both very
innocent and very savvy, with nothing impassive or bland in be-
tween; he abounds in integrity, stoicism, and appreciativeness. Like
Thoreau, he knows his cosmic place, and shrewdly affects a modest
tone. Yet he harbors intense ambition. Mr. Raban's journey and

attendant journalizing had a transparent motivation and an engaging student eagerness. In *African Calliope: A Journey to the Sudan,* Mr. Hoagland's account of his several excursions into the southern half of the Sudan, the intent is less transparent, and the going less smooth. The "Author's Note" at the outset announces he will not write a "gangplank book" that—the very pattern of *Arabia*—"will start you right out from the pier on the Hudson River, and, after numerous happenstances, deliver you back to the author's New York City apartment." Instead, he is going to rearrange certain experiences "so that they are not beads on a string." More like unstrung beads jumbled in a drawer, then, unchronological episodes and unexpected discourses, bumpy rides into the desert, chunks of Sudanese history, and lurches of personal confession are presented to us in an order Mr. Hoagland decrees, just as the successive topics of his long essays arise by solely internal logic. Why has he come to the Sudan? The question is posed several times, and receives differently inflected answers:

> Why was I here?
> I said that I was forty-four, and was after experiences and writing matter I had not tried before . . .

> Manolakas asked me why I had come. I laughed and said the Sudan was not only the largest country in Africa but also lay between Egypt and Kenya, which I had toured with pleasure the winter before. He asked if I wasn't lonely. I said I was hemorrhaging with loneliness, but that I had been lonely lately at home, though it was incongruous to spend so much money getting to a place so poor that its people could have spent ten years living on the air fare itself.

Beclouded with half-revealed personal motives, a deeper need than Mr. Raban's itch to produce a book emerges; Mr. Hoagland is after new experiences and writing fodder in order to make of them literature. This determination gives *African Calliope* its unsettling depth and intermittent opacity, and a certain brusqueness in its tone and in its anti-sequential organization. Embarked upon a more momentous pilgrimage than we knew, we sometimes merely wander. Mr. Hoagland, in making literature, occasionally forgets, as Mr. Raban never does, to be entertaining.

Rougher than *Arabia, African Calliope* evinces a superior pene-
trative will. Its chosen terrain is one of the poorest on earth. Mr.
Hoagland does not merely notice the poverty, he immerses himself
in it. Condescension has no place in his vocabulary of attitudes.
When he sees a Dinka "with violently inaccurate blows" butcher-
ing a bull until a driveway "is smeared with blood as if after a street
accident," he explains that the Dinka "drink milk, sometimes en-
riched with blood tapped harmlessly from the living animal, but eat
the meat rarely. Therefore, it's rather from a lack of accustomed
savagery that when they butcher . . . it looks so brutal." In the
Acholi village of Gilo, in the southern Sudanese mountains, he
admires how a woman grinds grain by hand: "Locking her ankles
behind her as an anchor, she ground the dura with a scrubbing,
scrubbing motion, pushing and pulling a stone across the grains,
half a handful at a time—an exercise as grim as giving artificial
respiration." With a naturalist's unblinking attention he reports the
intimate cohabitation of poverty and disease:

> Altogether, except seasonally, when the stored grain sometimes gave
> out, not many people went hungry. The children, nevertheless, had
> bellies swollen from pinworms and tapeworms. On cold days they
> coughed and hugged themselves and couldn't bring themselves to play.
> Year round, they cried at night when their fathers had to dig the
> chiggers out of their bare feet with a razor blade.

In these chilly mountains, the residents of Gilo wear rags except
for the comically fortunate who were given blazer jackets and pink
shortie nightgowns collected by an American charity. A child has
only its mother's breasts for toys, and men walk miles for the
opportunity to work for eight cents an hour. Prostitutes in Juba
charge twenty-five cents for their services. In Khartoum, "spar-
rows are so unaccustomed to being fed that if bread is thrown to
them they fly away and only find it later accidentally." Tokar, near
war-torn Eritrea, is "so poor and dispirited that several families had
dug mud for their house bricks right from the street in front—pits
ten feet wide and ten feet deep." In the vicinity of funded agricul-
tural projects, "you would see $300,000 worth of equipment—five

sizes of Caterpillar tractor—parked next to a grass hut, and yet no small tool that you might need to fix something, no wrench or scrap of rope or ax or hoe." The details are piled up not with oppressive purpose but as a solemn certification of this department of the human condition. In a vast region of varied landscape, Mr. Hoagland finds few moments of beauty and wonder, though there is a certain bliss of precision in a sentence like "Their tents are frog-shaped, constructed of hides and woven mats of goat and camel hair on a stick frame, the large mouth facing east." What lighter moments he enjoys come among the white hangers-on in Africa, the stray Greeks and New Zealanders, and even these companionships tend to go sour—an English fellow-reporter turns disagreeably Marxist on him in the presence of an Eritrean rebel chief, and a cattle expert called Hector, as they proceed into the Western desert of Dar Kababish and the author grows sicker and weaker, turns into a cruel tease.

"Sadness pervades the journals of African travel written by Europeans that I am familiar with"—this comment of Mr. Hoagland's applies to *African Calliope.* The grimness of a self-test clings to his description of barren landscapes and collapsing machinery, of sexual deprivation and stomachic distress. Only the sight of animals quickens his account with tenderness and engenders verbal filigree. Of dorcas gazelles, he writes:

> These little creatures, only about two feet tall, a pale sandy fawn color, with lyrate horns, appeared as though in tracery form, as if they were mere wishful thinking, outlines that still needed filling in, even as they dashed from us in light bounds.

And of camels, which Mr. Raban found so unlovable:

> When made to kneel, their camels showed their teeth in snide, snobbish mouths, expostulating through slitted nostrils with snarls, whines and whuffles, although later they slept as meekly as turtles, with their necks stretched out.

Generally, the poet in Mr. Hoagland seems stunned, and, like him, we wind up "weary of the whole African calliope." He has written a travel account honest to a fault, one whose words decline to smooth away the confusion of the experience and come to us still redolent of the rumpled traveller's fatigue, discomfort, and queasy conscience.

Raman and Daisy and Olivia and the Nawab

THE PAINTER OF SIGNS, by R. K. Narayan. 175 pp. Viking, 1976.

HEAT AND DUST, by Ruth Prawer Jhabvala. 181 pp. Harper & Row, 1976.

Two deft, brief novels about India arrive, to help placate our curiosity about the subcontinent. Once the epitome of gallant Asian democracy, India in recent years has been thrown into the shade by China's emergence into laundry-clean lovableness, and has had its image further darkened by the actions of its own government. Not only did it fight a war but it crushingly won, which is no way for a nation of pacifists to behave; and now political cartoonists have had to adjust their caricature of Indira Gandhi from saried angel to totalitarian harpy. Nevertheless, life—far too much of it—goes on, and with an eye toward our own overpopulated future we read how.

R. K. Narayan tells us, in *The Painter of Signs,* that life has its pleasant side in Malgudi, the fictional city where his novels generally take place. There is still space enough, at least, for a love affair to develop delicately; the fabled Indian gentleness still permeates the atmosphere evoked by this venerable cherisher of human behavior. He retains the rare gift of making us trust his characters and believe in their idealism and good will. His hero, Raman, is a painter of signboards for Malgudi's multiplicity of small businesses. Unmarried and young-hearted though over thirty, Raman considers himself an "artist in lettering," and a signboard "a token of respectable and even noble intentions." "A signboard painter might look ordinary," he tells himself, "but he concentrated in his hands the entire business and aspirations of a whole community." The novel's heroine, who bears the mysterious (for India) name of

Daisy, is even more convinced of the need for *her* vocation, the management of a family-planning center. A runaway from her own large family, educated with the help of Christian missionary organizations, she is "devoted to the service of people, and that is all her religion." When Raman mildly mocks her "unmitigated antagonism to conception," she responds with "missionary zeal":

> "Don't you see how horrible it is with everything crowded and an endless chain of queues for food, shelter, bus, medicine, and everything, with thousands of children coming with nothing to eat, no clothes to wear, no roof, no civilized existence being possible on such a mass scale —each one of us has to do our bit in the corner of the country allotted to us."

Her position seems incontestable. Raman himself is "determined to establish the Age of Reason in the world," and has been doing his own bit of population control by living as a bachelor with his old aunt and steeling his mind against thoughts of sex: "He wished to establish that the man-woman relationship was not inevitable and that there were other more important things to do in life than marrying. . . . He had steeled himself against this blunder committed by human beings since Adam." How two such ideologues nevertheless come together is the inevitable, though suspenseful, tale Mr. Narayan has to tell.

Wound around and through this story of mating is a debate on the question of "copulation and population." The novel does not lack sensual details corroborating Daisy's alarmed view of India. Crowds jostle the characters whenever they step from their exiguous homes, and "the town hall veranda and the pavements around the market, the no-man's lands of Malgudi, swarmed with children of all sizes, from toddlers to four-footers, dust-covered, ragged—a visible development in five years." Yet of these same children it is observed that "their liquid eyes sparkled with life," and the fecundating forces of love and life are viewed by the hero and, it would seem, by the author with a wayward tenderness. Within the deplorable mass of humanity, individuals move dignified by purpose and egoism. Grateful spaces open in the physical landscape; the prose exudes relief, describing these remissions:

They sat on the last step with their feet in water. It was cold and refreshing. The stars shone, the darkness was welcome, cool breeze, cold water lapping the feet, the voices and sounds of the living town far away muffled and soft; habitual loungers on the riverbank passing across the sands homeward softly like flitting shadows. The air had become charged with rich possibilities.

Above India's crowded plains loom the empty, sacred mountains. Daisy and Raman spend their first night together in a mountainous wilderness, abandoned by a cart driver who mistakes them for newlyweds. During this night she changes from reminding him of "Rani Jhansi, the warrior queen of Indian history" to suggesting "Mohini, who tempted men and fooled them." The gods of the Hindu religion stand ready to descend from the mountains and endow these characters with a mythic largeness. When their affair is scarcely a flirtation, Raman buys himself sunglasses to dull the impression of her beauty. "She seemed to grin, and looked like a demoness! Soorpanaka's approach should have had the same effect on Rama, he reflected, recollecting an episode from the Ramayana. Her teeth seemed to jut out and were uneven." But Daisy, with the boldness of a deity, simply pulls the glasses from his face. And after their affair has been consummated he looks down upon her sleeping body: "Her angularities and self-assertiveness were gone. He was struck by the elegance of her form and features, suddenly saw her as an abstraction—perhaps a goddess to be worshipped." In the context, the thought is not trite. A background of Hindu metaphysics deepens the romantic commonplaces of illusion and sublimity.

The thematic debate between vitality and control, between social and personal necessities, takes a strange turn at the end, when the author appears to vote with his hero against the planning center (with its paradoxical association of sexual allure) and for bachelor society—"that solid, real world of sublime souls who minded their own business." But surely, in a world so packed, there is little business anymore that is purely our own. Mr. Narayan's impish conservatism sports itself in vivid portrayal of two elderly upholders of the supernatural: Raman's aunt, who after a lifetime of domestic service embarks upon a pilgrimage, and an ancient holy man who has built with his own hands a little temple where women come to have their barrenness relieved, perhaps miraculously. Though these two practitioners of the Hindu faith possess a certainty of vision denied Raman and Daisy, the materialist lovers—exponents of the modern arts of publicity and contraception—have their own importance and a real power to move us. Behind the shifting veil, they are gods. In the bustling, puzzling Malgudi of 1972, amid traffic jams and black markets selling "American milk powder meant for the orphans of India," the city's chronicler keeps his anachronistic capacity for reverence.

A fertility shrine plays a pivotal part in the twinned plots of *Heat and Dust,* by Ruth Prawer Jhabvala. In the grove around Baba Firdaus's shrine, both her heroines—Olivia, the wife of a British official stationed in India in 1923, and the unnamed, unmarried narrator, who travels from England to India in search of Olivia's ghost a half-century later—seduce, or are seduced by, Indian men, and both become pregnant. This braided tale, which in England won the 1975 Booker Fiction Prize, is not an easy novel to summarize. The narrator is the granddaughter, by a second marriage, of the husband, Douglas, whom Olivia deserts when—as the first sentence of the novel tells us—she runs away with "the Nawab," the Prince of Khatm. Olivia, though the members of the narrator's family "shied away from her memory as from something dark and terrible," left a record of herself in letters to her sister, and in possession of these our contemporary heroine goes first to Bombay, then to the district center of Satipur, where Olivia and Douglas lived in the company of a few other agents of the Empire, and finally to the mountain house that the Nawab bestowed upon his English mistress.

The narrator's aim seems to be to reconstruct, or re-feel, Olivia's escapade. What she does, in the end, is relive it, with the variations the fifty intervening years impose—vagrant counterculture seekers after wisdom instead of stolid British colonial officers, a native landlord and bureaucrat instead of a prince in a palace, a casual, self-sufficient life style instead of Olivia's overfurnished, servant-pampered existence. But the weather is the same, and details of place recur. The English cemetery is still there, deteriorated, and both women cherish the same headstones. Their romances prove to have an eerie congruence: the Indian lovers, after achieving their conquests, make the same joke, and both have crazy wives and dominating mothers. The young narrator ends by gazing out of Olivia's window, but it is the season of rain and mists in the Himalayas, "so I couldn't see what she looked out on as she sat in the window at her embroidery frame."

If all this sounds a bit fussy, it is. The "dazzling"—to quote the jacket copy—alternation between plots drains both of momentum, or of the substance that lends momentum; the two stories are shadows of each other, conveying an ambience of reincarnation but also of inconsequence. Above the two planes of the plot, we feel a third, that of a supervisory manipulator, be it author or god. Olivia's most fateful action is to submit to an abortion; the narrator undoes that act by keeping *her* pregnancy. Similarly, a disappointed lover in Mr. Narayan's novel consoles himself, "Maybe we will live together in our next *jamma.*" A cyclical cosmology makes all stories essentially endless.

Perhaps Mrs. Jhabvala, Polish-born, English-educated wife of an Indian, grew so tired of being reviewed in terms of *A Passage to India* that she deliberately invaded the era of Forster's classic novel. Olivia's world, as reconstructed by the narrator in today's "Indianized" India, has a formal grandeur that supports her stylized romance and preordains it from the first page to its pattern of fascination and fall and flight and unutterable disgrace. Its vanished time seems enchanted—the men in evening dress, the servants silently barefoot, the monuments in the English cemetery freshly carved, the Nawab's pearl-gray palace still inhabited, its fountains flowing and its rooms full of mischief. Just so, Raman the sign painter found delight in the memoirs of an old tea planter, "visions and dreams of those misty ranges, the dripping plantations in monsoon, the tigers and elephants warded off with gunfire . . . a remote world consisting of a colony of estate workers dominated by an English planter with his nearest neighbor, another planter, fifty miles away." The cosmos may be cyclical, but the local demographic trend is all one way. The historical past in India seems not so much discarded as crowded out of being.

India to Mr. Narayan is the place where he lives; Mrs. Jhabvala, who moved to Delhi in 1951, sees it with the eye of an initiated outsider. There is more local color in a few pages of *Heat and Dust* than in all of *The Painter of Signs*. Sometimes the viewer is appalled:

> I went up to the refuse dump, I stood over the beggar woman: her eyes were open, she was groaning, she was alive. There was a terrible smell and a cluster of flies. I looked down and saw a thin stream of excrement trickling out of her.

More often she is entranced. The heroine in the terrible summer heat is driven to sleep outdoors, with her neighbors:

> So we're quite a crowd. I no longer change into a nightie but sleep, like an Indian woman, in a sari.
>
> It's amazing how *still* everything is. When Indians sleep, they really do sleep. Neither adults nor children have a regular bedtime—when they're tired they just drop, fully clothed, on to their beds, or the ground if they have no beds, and don't stir again until the next day begins. All one hears is occasionally someone crying out in their sleep, or a dog—maybe a jackal—baying at the moon. I lie awake for hours: with happiness, actually. I have never known such a sense of communion.

The theme of a transcendent happiness recurs in Mrs. Jhabvala's short stories ("The Old Lady," "My First Marriage") and apparently declares a crucial aspect of her Indian experience. This happiness seems to be especially accessible to women. In *Heat and Dust* even India-loving males like Major Minnies—who is capable of chanting Urdu poetry, and so acclimated he stays on after Independence—keep a certain stiff wariness of this seductive, unmanageable place, and a fervent religious seeker like Chid, with his shaved head and Midlands accent, is finally repulsed by the climate, the food, the smell, the cheating priests, the diseases. Chid nearly dies, and begs to go home. The doctor who attends him, himself an Indian, ventures, "I think perhaps God never meant that human beings should live in such a place." Our heroine disagrees, and, like Olivia before her, stays on, ascending into the mountains in triumphant assimilation. The female characters, in 1923 as now, draw strength from this teeming land: the Nawab's powerful mother and the abortionist who attends Olivia are reincarnated in Maji, the leader of a gang of widows who are "strong and healthy and full of feminine vigor. . . . They roam around town quite freely and don't care at all if their saris slip down from their heads or even their breasts." The men, contrariwise, age badly; they soften. Olivia sees that her handsome husband's face "had become heavier, even somewhat puffy, making him look more like other Englishmen in India." And as for her lover the Nawab, in our last glimpse of him he has grown "old and so fat that there was something womanly about him"; he has to be carried up the mountain to his mistress in a sedan chair. So the god behind Mrs. Jhabvala's artful shuffle of Indian scenes and moments is female. *Heat and Dust*'s happy pack of vigorous widows corresponds to *The Painter of Signs*' bachelor society of "sublime souls who minded their own business"— both groups half-way to sainthood, having put breeding behind them.

India Going On

MALGUDI DAYS, by R. K. Narayan. 246 pp. Viking, 1982.

V. S. Naipaul, in his somber diagnosis of his ancestral land, *India: A Wounded Civilization* (1977), devotes a number of thoughtful and heartfelt pages to the foremost Indian writer of fiction in English, R. K. Narayan. He grants Narayan great talent, as "such a natural writer, so true to his experience and emotions," that even the weaker of his novels serve as keys to his society. He grants him furthermore a special personal relevance: "Narayan's India, with its colonial apparatus, was oddly like the Trinidad of my childhood. His oblique perception of that apparatus, and the rulers, matched my own; and in the Indian life of his novels I found echoes of the life of my own Indian community on the other side of the world." What were those echoes? "[We] were colonials, subject people who had learned to live with the idea of subjection. We lived within our lesser world; and we could even pretend it was whole because we had forgotten that it had been shattered. Disturbance, instability, development lay elsewhere; we, who had lost our wars and were removed from great events, were at peace." In Narayan's early novels, Naipaul observes, "the British themselves are far away, their presence hinted at only in their institutions: the bank, the mission school. The writer contemplates the lesser life that goes on below: small men, small schemes, big talk, limited means: a life so circumscribed that it appears whole and unviolated, its smallness never a subject for wonder, though India itself is felt to be vast."

With some adjustments, the same words could describe Naipaul's own early, Trinidadian novels, from *The Mystic Masseur* (1957) through *A House for Mr. Biswas* (1961). But Naipaul did not stay in Trinidad; he left at the age of seventeen, for Oxford and London, and now roves the world as a kind of dark-skinned Englishman, whose reports, journalistic and novelistic both, from the continents and subcontinents of the Third World have an intimacy, assurance, and angry honesty no paler traveller could achieve. In his firm and even harsh rejection of all mystiques of underdevelopment, in his willingness to indict the former colonized nations for what he sees as their own stubborn delusions and laziness, he speaks more bluntly than any native-born European in good conscience could on behalf of European civilization. He represents the opposite pole of possibility, for intellectuals born into the Third World, from Narayan, whose every page exudes a fatalistic calm, and who, meeting the younger writer in London in 1961, told Naipaul simply, "India will go on." When, the next year, Naipaul visited India for the first time, he found that "Narayan's novels did not prepare me for the distress of India":

> As a writer he had succeeded almost too well. His comedies were of the sort that requires a restricted social setting with well-defined rules . . . But the reality was cruel and overwhelming. In the books his India had seemed accessible; in India it remained hidden. To get down to Narayan's world, to perceive the order and continuity he saw in the dereliction and smallness of India, to enter into his ironic acceptance and relish his comedy, was to ignore too much of what could be seen, to shed too much of myself: my sense of history, and even the simplest ideas of human possibility. I did not lose my admiration for Narayan;

but I felt that his comedy and irony were not quite what they had appeared to be, were part of a Hindu response to the world, a response I could no longer share.

Narayan's most recent book, a collection of short stories called *Malgudi Days*, tends to illustrate this "Hindu response to the world." Indeed, the endpapers, printed at the author's request, are based upon a schematic map devised for an academic paper entitled "The City of Malgudi as an Expression of the Ordered Hindu Cosmos." The author's introduction not only voices a sanguine acceptance of present-day India ("It is stimulating to live in a society that is not standardized or mechanized, and is free from monotony. Under such conditions the writer has only to look out of the window to pick up a character") but extends a smile of blessing to New York City's West Twenty-third Street, where Narayan has lived "for months at a time off and on since 1959." He surprisingly says, "I can detect Malgudi characters even in New York . . . with its landmarks and humanity remaining unchanged —the drunk lolling on the steps of the synagogue, the shop sign announcing in blazing letters *Everything in this store must go within a week.* . . . All are there as they were, with an air of unshaken permanence and familiarity."

Hinduism is not infrequently bound into the substance of these short stories: in one, "Iswaran," a student so thoroughly immerses himself in the visions of "a Tamil film with all the known gods in it" that he allows an imaginary horse to carry him into a river and drown; in another, "The Snake-Song," a man plays the flute with such inspiration that the god Naga Raja, a great black cobra, appears and compels him to play the same song all night long. Astrologers and exorcists are among the professional types animating Malgudi's teeming streets; and a number of heroes are mired in contemplative sloth, without incurring the author's disapproval. A certain benign indifference presides above these tales, causing them to flicker out inconclusively: "Raman realized that this was the end of a dream, sought the exit and the road back to his home on the sands of Sarayu." The older stories, especially—selected from the previous collections "An Astrologer's Day" (1947) and "Lawley

Road" (1956)—have the brevity and flimsiness of fables, mixed with a certain slickness imitated, perhaps, from the fiction of those English magazines, like the *Strand* and *Mercury*, which, Narayan has told us in his memoir *My Days*, entranced his youth and led to his first attempts to write.

Yet it cannot be fairly said that the distress of India is absent from the pages of *Malgudi Days*, or that the author averts his gaze from poverty. Many of the stories deal with people to whom a few rupees —even as little as one rupee (ten cents, approximately)—a day mean the difference between starvation and survival. "Naga" describes the plight of a boy somewhat more than ten years old whose father, a snake charmer, has abandoned him, leaving him eighty paise (eight cents) in small change and a snake too enfeebled by age to impress the street crowds. "No one is afraid of you," the boy tells the snake, "and do you know what that means? I starve, that is all." "The Martyr's Corner" describes the economic fall of a baker whose cherished corner for peddling his wares is destroyed when a riot and then a political monument take over the spot. The heroine of "A Willing Slave" is a bullied nursemaid whose wages are "two meals a day, fifteen rupees a month and three saris a year"; the hero of "The Blind Dog" is a blind beggar who captures and abuses a stray dog that, itself a poor creature, returns to servitude after being maliciously freed by onlookers—an especially cruel tale, this one. "Forty-five a Month" tells of a clerk who is so overworked he hardly ever sees his young daughter and is frustrated from taking her, as promised, to the cinema; his protest—"I think it would be far better for me and my family to die of starvation than slave for this petty forty rupees on which you have kept me for years and years"—is swept away by the concession of a trifling raise. "Cat Within," though comically, sketches the horrors of tenement housing; "The Axe" portrays a gardener tied for his entire lifetime to a rotting mansion and its grounds and in the end brusquely ousted by a company planning "to build small houses by the score without leaving space even for a blade of grass." In "The Edge" an itinerant knife-sharpener and in "Trail of the Green Blazer" a pickpocket are sympathetically portrayed, as providers; the pickpocket, after taking a purse, "took the cash in it, flung it far away and went home with the satisfaction that he had done his day's job well. . . . He bought sweets, books and slates for his children, and occasionally a jacket-piece for his wife, too." Even among the relatively well-off, financial pressures are keenly felt, especially when a marriage must be arranged. In a landscape so flattened by impoverishment, possession of anything looms as a kind of burden. Twice, Narayan constructs comedies around a problem of cumbersome ownership: in "Engine Trouble" the narrator wins a "road engine" (a steamroller) at a travelling fair and needs nothing less than an earthquake to rid him of it, and in "Lawley Road" the protagonist takes possession of an immensely solid but politically inconvenient statue of a British administrator which stands in the center of Malgudi.* The one exceedingly rich figure in these stories, the popular singer Selvi, ends by renouncing her career when her mother dies and returning to live in her old rooms in the Malgudi slums: "My mother was my guru; here she taught me music, lived and died. . . . I'll also live and die here; what was good for her is good for me too."

Poverty is seen but not abhorred in these stories; "dereliction and smallness" are indulged by the author, even relished, as Naipaul charges. *Malgudi Days* is so innocent of protest we are put in mind of Naipaul's remark, later in his searing portrait of India, that "social inquiry is outside the Indian tradition; journalism in India has always been considered a gracious form of clerkship." If anything is abhorred by the gracious clerkship of these stories, it is the new, the modern and reforming. Just as Narayan's last novel, *The Painter of Signs,** mocked population planning with a sexual com-

---

*The comic turns in these two stories are wonderfully Indian: the only person who can drive the steamroller is a Swami's assistant whose task it is to drive it over his employer in demonstration of the Swami's yogic powers; and the fate of the statue alters when its subject turns out to have been not a standard colonial oppressor but "the first Englishman to advise the British Parliament to involve more and more Indians in Indian affairs."

**Whose hero, Raman, returns here in a short story called "Hungry Child," set in a local fair with the ambitious name "Expo '77–'78"; Raman strolls through the fairgrounds wondering if Daisy became pregnant and mourning her absence, and his aunt's, from his life: "Day after day of emptiness, nothing to plan, nothing to look forward to . . . in a house totally deserted and empty, no life of any sort— even the house sparrows seemed to have fled. . . ."

edy that developed between its promulgators, his story "The Edge" presents the sterilization program entirely in terms of its inhumanly sharp knives, which the hero, an elderly father of seven, flees in panic. In "God and the Cobbler," a lowly street cobbler takes satisfaction in the reduction of a foreigner, an American who has flown bombing missions in Vietnam, to the mendicant condition of a hippie. The cobbler thinks the hippie might be a god; the hippie gazes around him and gratefully marvels that "no one seemed to mind anything—the dust, the noise and the perils of chaotic traffic." "The hippie was struck by the total acceptance here of life as it came." In "Second Opinion," a young man, who has been somewhat liberated by his idler's life and surreptitious reading of Western philosophers in his father's library (and who has heard of a book calling India "a wounded civilization"), ends by accepting filial duty and an arranged marriage. And these are all late stories, too—hitherto unpublished in book form, and longer and subtler than the earlier tales. The Hindu in Narayan is unreconstructed. The last story in the book, and one of the finest, "Emden," shows an immensely old, once powerful man senilely wander forth from his home with a gift of *jilebi* (a sweet) for a mistress of fifty years ago whom he has just remembered. He gets confused; the streets have changed; he pokes his staff into a brown mongrel lying curled in the brown dust and when the dog yelps drops the *jilebi*. The dog picks up the sweet in his mouth and trots away. Emden consoles himself with the thought that perhaps his long-lost mistress has been reincarnated as the dog.

Such is life, at least as seen by R. K. Narayan in the Malgudi of his creation. His charm and compassion, which no one disputes, deliver not a reality that is "cruel and overwhelming" but one that is, usually, believable. Small lives seek their own solutions within an insoluble mass that leads visiting reporters to despair. There might be a Tolstoy or Cervantes who could render India more fully, without the touch of complacence and insubstantiality that Narayan's Hindu sensibility bestows. Nevertheless, in these simple stories of poverty and failure accepted lies the implicit social protest that we feel in such classics of the short story as Chekhov's "Grief " and O. Henry's "Gift of the Magi" and Flannery O'Connor's

"Artificial Nigger": to portray poverty is to cry out against it. The very poor are something of an embarrassment to the novel; not enough happens to them, their struggles are too one-sided and hopeless, they can't afford enough romance and moral scruple to keep a novel going. But a short story, like the flare of a match, brings human faces out of darkness, and reveals depths beyond statistics. All people are complex, surprising, and deserving of a break: this seems to me Narayan's moral, and one hard to improve upon. His social range and his successful attempt to convey, in sum, an entire population shame most American authors, who also, it might be charged, "ignore too much of what could be seen." American fiction deals in the main with the amorous and spiritual difficulties of young upper-middle-class adults; a visitor arriving in New York after studying the short stories of, say, Ann Beattie and Donald Barthelme as intently as Naipaul had read Narayan would be ill-prepared for the industrial sprawl of Queens and the black slums of Brooklyn, for the squalid carnival of the avenues and the sneaking dread of the side streets after dark. Perhaps some tilt toward the genteel and the comic is intrinsic to prose fiction, which rose with the bourgeoisie and still depends upon bourgeois pur-chasing power; authors seeking to rectify the balance could do worse than emulate Narayan's Hindu acceptance and vital, benign fellow-feeling.

THE FAR EAST

Spent Arrows and First Buddings

I AM A CAT, by Natsume Sōseki, translated from the Japanese by Katsue Shibata and Motonari Kai. 431 pp. Coward, McCann & Geoghegan, 1982.

MON *(The Gate)*, by Natsume Sōseki, translated from the Japanese by Francis Mathy. 217 pp. Coward, McCann & Geoghegan, 1982.

THE SECRET HISTORY OF THE LORD OF MUSASHI *and* ARROWROOT, by Junichirō Tanizaki, translated from the Japanese by Anthony H. Chambers. 199 pp. Knopf, 1982.

Natsume Sōseki, who was born in 1867 and died, at the age of forty-nine, in 1916, is considered the foremost Japanese novelist of the early twentieth century. English translations of seven of his novels have now been simultaneously published by Putnam, as part of its paperback Perigee Japanese Library. To judge by two novels also issued in hardcover by Coward, McCann & Geoghegan—*I Am a Cat* and *Mon*—Sōseki's was a wan talent, given to affectionate descriptions of the weather and drifting accounts of conversational impasse within the paper walls of Japanese homes. *Mon* takes place in 1909–10, and *I Am a Cat* shortly after the conclusion, in 1905, of the Russo-Japanese War—a lopsided triumph for the Japanese that signalled their arrival as the newest of the world's imperial powers and that on the other side helped trigger czarist Russia's slide into revolution. Yet Sōseki's characters take small comfort from Japan's international burgeoning and remind us of Chekhov's

gentle, dithering, futile gentry. The debilitating effects of Western-
ization are one of Sōseki's themes, and one he was well qualified
to understand: a student of English literature, he lived in England
for the first three years of the century and returned in 1903 to
succeed Lafcadio Hearn as lecturer in English literature at Tokyo's
Imperial University. "In 1907," his jacket biography goes on to tell
us, "he became a full-time writer, producing a group of carefully
written novels treating the spiritual torment of Japan's urban intel-
lectuals." "Torment" seems too strong a term for the manicky and
idle condition of the intelligentsia whose prattle fills most of *I Am
a Cat*'s four hundred pages, and, even when the losses of transla-
tion* have been discounted, "carefully written" hardly fits this
rambling fantasy, as much essay as narrative, murky and attenuated
in its fable and inscrutably aimed in its satire. Well, *the lives and
times of archy & mehitabel* in Japanese might not be so easy, either.

I Am a Cat was Sōseki's first novel and made his fame. Written
by a teacher, it is bookish; it is riddled with the lore and tag names
of Western culture, from Aeschylus and Seneca to Leibniz and
Nietzsche and Carlyle and right up to date with William James and
Henry James and George Meredith. *Tristram Shandy* gets men-
tioned, and readers who relish that work's stalled action and endless
playful quibbling might find the discourses of *I Am a Cat* less
tedious than did this reviewer, who lost track, often, of who was
talking and what was being talked about. A nameless cat, a stray
tossed by a student into the household of a disgruntled, dyspeptic,
jam-loving, poem-writing schoolteacher called Mr. Kushami, gives

---

*The linguistic predicament of the Japanese novelist in the time of the Meiji
Restoration was very complex: the language, written in large part with borrowed
Chinese characters that lack any phonetic relation to the Japanese sounds, abounds
with honorific suffixes and prefixes that make every dialogue an expression of class
distinctions, and with a literary inheritance of styles stratified in many shades
between *kambun*, written in Chinese characters, and *kana*, composed in a phonetic
alphabet of forty-seven syllables. In the Edo novel of the three-hundred-year period
of the Shogunate, dialogue and exposition are written in two sharply different
styles; the *gembun'itchi* movement launched in the 1880s, of which Sōseki is an
inheritor, sought to narrow this gap. The opportunities, amid this linguistic welter,
for verbal incongruity and humor are enormous: for instance, in the Japanese
translated as "I Am a Cat," *Wagahai wa Neko de Aru*, "Wagahai" is a form of
address for nobility and absurd employed as it is.

a narrative account of what he overhears there and in a few neighboring houses, chiefly that of a businessman called Kaneda, his big-nosed wife, and a marriageable daughter. Among Mr. Kushami's visitors are Kangetsu, a scientist who spends his time grinding glass balls smaller and smaller as research into "The Effects of Ultra-Violet Rays on the Electro-Movement Action of the Frog's Eyeball"; Meitei, an aesthetician "as unsteady as goldfish food floating on the surface of a pond"; Suzuki, an old school friend of Kushami's actually in Kaneda's pay as a spy; Tofu Ochi, a young clerk of few discernible qualities; and Dokusen Yagi, a Zen sage whose disciples tend to go crazy. The cat, though born in "a gloomy damp place" and destined to drown in a rain barrel at the age of two, spices his account with an unexpected knowledgeability: he knows, for one thing, that "Chikamatsu is considered as the Shakespeare of Japan." He seems very much a cat at places, chasing insects and climbing trees and falling in love with other cats, and at other places scarcely distinguishable from the woolgathering human riffraff that visits and heckles Mr. Kushami. A certain carelessness in regard to its central premise prevents *I Am a Cat* from developing the wit and force of such zoömorphic fables as Kafka's "Report to an Academy," Orwell's *Animal Farm*, and the Houyhnhnms section of *Gulliver's Travels*. The panoramic possibilities of a prowling cat as silent, intelligent witness are oddly stunted; beyond a few forays into the Kanedas' house next door, our feline narrator seems content to take the human comedy as it arrives, with monotonous talkiness, in Mr. Kushami's six-mat room.

Several passages do, however, develop a sustained interest. The author has closely observed pet cats, and the protagonist's preening upon "the plum-blossom marks of my paws on the porch" and interrogations of his own twitching tail gratify us with specificity, and even with poetry:

> Cats have feet but we use them as if we were floating. We never make any clumsy noise. It is like stepping on air, like riding the clouds, like tapping temple bells under water, or like playing the harp inside a cave. It is like the ecstasy one receives after drinking water in silence—

recognizing its coolness or warmth without being able to define the pleasure.

Sōseki also knew students and the discomforts of discipline, and the chapter on the campaign of teasing launched upon poor Mr. Ku-shami by the pupils of the nearby Raku-unkan (Descending Cloud) Junior High School has enough authority and embodied emotion to induce us to stop counting the pages as we read. The second half of the book is better than the first; it takes Sōseki too long to bring Mr. Kushami into focus. We are told repeatedly that he is a fool, but the core of his foolishness is not laid bare. Is it that he, like Molière's *bourgeois gentilhomme*, is obsessed by an inappropriate aspiration? Or is he meant to be made rigid, like one of Shake-speare's peripheral clowns, by a dominant humor? "My master has always been too rigid. He is as crusty as coke and terribly intolerant besides," the cat claims at one point; but the behavior we see is characterized by a certain sullen passivity rather than any dynamic crustiness. He is a hypochondriac—"an idiot and an invalid," the cat confides—but not much is done with the farcical possibilities of *un malade imaginaire*. His comic flaw seems to consist, at bottom, in being merely human—"He wants the luxury of being an invalid but not of being sick enough to die. If he were told that his illness were fatal, he, being timid, would most probably tremble." The cat likens his master to "a spent arrow shot from a strong bow," a phrase that perhaps sums up much of Sōseki's unease about the society around him. Westernization threw a harsh light into the cloisters of traditional Japanese culture; it brought doubt, followed by a vulgar busyness of imitation. Without overwhelming convic-tion but with a poignance of wounded feeling, Sōseki articulates a reactionary easing of this doubt. The Zen master, Dokusen, though ridiculed elsewhere in the novel, is allowed to frame a shrewd critique of the West:

> I believe the Japanese of old were much more clever than most Westerners. Westerners want to be positive and this is quite the fashion in Japan today, but being so positive has a great defect. In the first place, there's no limit to the craving for satisfaction. A state of thorough completeness is never attained. Do you see those cypress trees over

there? Well, you say to yourself that they're unsightly so you clear them away; then it would be the boarding house beyond them that irritates you. There would be no limit to your search for the perfect view. Westerners are like this. . . . The traditional civilization of Japan did not attempt to find satisfaction through such changes but through the individual. The great difference between us Japanese and Westerners is that we realize we cannot change our environment. . . . If there is a mountain blocking our way to a neighboring country, we don't have to move the mountain. Instead, we should find a way that would make it unnecessary to go to that foreign country. We should learn to build up a feeling in ourselves that would give us satisfaction but not having to go over the mountain. . . . One cannot stop the sun from setting nor can one reverse the flow of the Kamo River. But what we can all manage to control is our own mind.

The novel ends with an abrupt prayer to Buddha and the assertion "Peace cannot be had without dying." Throughout this diffuse and feebly organized tale, Sōseki shows a fine gift for aphorism, that recourse of resigned minds:

Among humans, everything done aggressively has the right to be copied.

Just as nature abhors a vacuum, man dislikes equality.

A mirror is a brewery of vanity and, at the same time, a sterilizer of pride.

God is only a dummy invented by those who are in desperate trouble.

Humans are continually accumulating what they do not need and then pitying themselves for the burden.

Almost everyone living in the twentieth century has become somewhat of a detective.

Mon, which translates as "The Gate" but has been allowed to stand as the translation's title, tells of a couple, Sosuke and Oyone, who married in haste and amid disapproval, as they six years later worry through some minor difficulties in their isolated, chastened life together in Tokyo. An uncle has cheated Sosuke of the inheritance that would have enabled him to put his younger brother, Koroku, through college. Sosuke makes the acquaintance of a wealthy neighbor, Mr. Sakai, who offhandedly provides a solution to this embarrassment. Oyone's former lover, Yasui, who was also Sosuke's best friend, returns from Manchuria, where he has become an adventurer; but an awkward meeting is avoided. Sosuke, dissatisfied and restless, undertakes a retreat in a Zen temple but finds it unhelpful. Returning to work, he receives a small raise.

As with *I Am a Cat*, but less exasperatingly, this short novel is stabbingly sketched, with blank places a Western novelist would have felt obliged to fill in. The exact incidents of the couple's original fall into disgrace and marriage are left vague. We are told merely:

> A furious wind had blown up from nowhere and struck down the unwary couple. When they finally picked themselves up off the ground, they saw that they were covered with dirt from head to foot. This they recognized. But when and how they had fallen, neither could say. . . . Prior to looking at themselves in shame as immoral, they looked at themselves in wonder as stupid.

Yet as a portrait of domestic life and daily discontents, Japanese style, *Mon* is pleasant to read, and its very diffidence serves to pique our interest. As with Mr. Kushami, it is hard to know exactly what is wrong with Sosuke, that he is incapable of either action or contentment. "As he walked through the black night, he thought of his desire to escape from his poverty of spirit. He felt himself weak, restless, fearful, uncertain, cowardly and mean." When he goes to "the gate"—the path of Zen, as disclosed during his retreat at the temple—the result is neither illumination nor drastic disillusion and consequent resolve. "He had come here to have the gate opened to him, but its warden had remained obstinately within." The temple head—the *roshi*—sets Sosuke a *koan* with a casualness that borders on contempt:

> "I suppose it doesn't make much difference what you begin with," the *roshi* told Sosuke. "How about trying to work on 'What was my Face before my parents were born?'"

The wry religious comedy of the novice's inexpert and distracted meditation follows: "It even occurred to him as he sat there trying to meditate that this was all very silly." We are never told what answer to the *koan* Sosuke comes up with, but the *roshi* pronounces it unsatisfactory:

> The *roshi* spoke only one sentence to Sosuke, who sat before him, drained of all spirit. "If you haven't more to offer than that, you shouldn't have come; anyone with even a little education could say as much as you said."
>
> Sosuke left the room feeling like a dog whose master has died. Behind him the gong clanged loudly.

"Drained of all spirit" he remains—a kind of "spent arrow" in a world where enterprise belongs entirely to others and religious impulse has been reduced to an objectless longing. When the pale but patient Oyone remarks that it is at last spring, her husband replies that it will soon be winter, and keeps cutting his fingernails. Natsume Sōseki's refusal to force his material toward pat conclusions or heightened climaxes represents a kind of negative power, that surrender to irregularity which is one of art's maneuvers of renewal. Sosuke does not struggle against his "fate" (a recurrent word), and his creator does not struggle to give his little novel more shape than the untransfigured lives within it deserve. A certain Western restlessness has penetrated these lives, but no concomitant hope. "The couple had come this far without either sitting on the benches of the Christian meeting place or passing through the gate of the Buddhist temple. That they finally found a measure of peace was due only to the medicinal powers of passing time, which is the blessing of nature." If the author himself is viewing his couple from a settled religious perspective, his judgment is delicately implied indeed.

Sōseki seems present in his passive, baffled protagonists—embodied wistfully in the youthful Sosuke, and erratically parodied in the figure of Mr. Kushami. Both novels left this reader, at his several removes in space and time, with the sensation of music heard fitfully across the water; that both appeared beguiling and relevant to their contemporary audience is a historical fact, but the secret of their beguilement lies well below the surface of these rather dusty, stiff translations. Transplantation doesn't always take, and Sōseki remains rooted in a remote garden.

Lest we think that all Japanese fiction must arrive here muffled by an alien suggestiveness and restraint, two short works by Juni-chirō Tanizaki speak out with the clarity and color of a master. Tanizaki (1886–1965) was of the generation succeeding Sōseki's, and his work has little of Sōseki's *fin-de-siècle* sickliness, though a certain morbidity—a concern with pathology—would seem in-stinctive in Japanese fiction. The full assurance of a naturalism that Sōseki and others achieved descended to Tanizaki, so that he was able to revert, after his move from Tokyo to the Kyoto-Osaka region, in 1923, to the matter, and even the manner, of historical chronicles. His career was long, vigorous, and varied, and many thought that he, and not Yasunari Kawabata, should have been the first Japanese writer to receive the Nobel Prize. Two novellas fluently translated by Anthony H. Chambers and bound into a single small volume by Knopf were written by Tanizaki in mid-career—*The Secret History of the Lord of Musashi* in 1931–32, and *Arrowroot* in 1930. In 1928, he had translated Stendhal's *Abbess of Castro* from French into Japanese, and both of his works stem, like Stendhal's, from a purported historical investigation.

Tanizaki's preface to *The Secret History*, after mentioning several historical warlords rumored to be pederasts, considers a fictional sixteenth-century samurai, the Lord of Musashi, "the boldest, cru-elest leader of his age," of whom "those close to him said that he had masochistic sexual desires." Tanizaki claims to have "recently examined some secret documents in the possession of the Kiryū family and learned what sort of man he really was." Quoting, then, from the nun Myōkaku's fictitious memoir "The Dream of a Night" and from "Confessions of Dōami"—the recollections of a close attendant upon the Lord of Musashi—he embarks, in the full regalia of medieval Japan, upon a case history as lurid as but more affecting than any in Krafft-Ebing. The Lord of Musashi, whose childhood name was Hōshimaru, took his fateful sexual imprinting when he was twelve years old, and a "hostage"—an enforced guest sent by a vassal *daimyō* to the court of his lord—in the besieged castle on Mount Ojika, the seat of the lord Tsukuma Ikkansai. The siege, mounted by the forces of Yakushiji Danjō Masataka, is going badly for the defenders, and rages every day. The boy is too young to take part in the fighting but, as a concession to his fascination, is taken by an old woman to the chamber of the castle where a group of women—themselves hostages—prepare each night, for inspection by the commander, the heads of enemy warriors slain during the day. "Dressing heads" involved washing them, fixing them to a board, arranging the hair, and attaching a label by piercing one earlobe. The sights and smells of this bizarre military nicety —carried out in an incongruous atmosphere of feminine ministration, in the dead of the night—are rendered with a lyric calm that carries them into us as unforgettably as they carry into the child voyeur. One of the head-dressers is a young woman of fifteen or sixteen. "Her round face, though quite expressionless, had a natural charm. Now and then, as she gazed at a head, an unconscious smile would play about her lips. It was this smile that attracted Hōshimaru to her. At such moments, a guileless cruelty showed in her face." An ambivalence in the image females present has already been foreshadowed by a moment when the old woman leading Hōshimaru to this enchanted place turns in a passageway:

> The light reflected off the polished floorboards and shone red in the old woman's face when she turned to signal Hōshimaru with her eyes. Her breath was white as she spoke. She no longer looked like the refined, warmhearted matron that he was used to seeing by daylight. The deep shadows in her sunken flesh gave her the haggard look of a demon mask.

Entranced and agitated, the boy returns of his own volition the next night, and the next, and on the third night finds the girl working upon a head without a nose—for it was the custom, when a samurai could not carry all the heads of those he had slain, to cut off the noses, and return to the battlefield later with the noses to match them to his trophies. "The girl carefully ran her comb through the noseless head's lustrous black hair and retied the top-knot; then, as she always did, she gazed at the center of the face, where the nose should have been, and smiled. As usual, the boy was enchanted by her expression, but the surge of emotion he experienced at that moment was far stronger than any he had ever felt before." Two nights later, Hōshimaru sneaks out into the enemy camp and obtains a severed nose of his own, thus embarking upon his dual career as a great samurai and a very kinky lover.

Without the story's exactly running down, nothing in it afterward matches, for power and beauty, the seminal scene of the head-dressing—a scene, as the eminent Japanologist Donald Keene has said, that ranks with "anything written in this century." In the subsequent adventures of Terukatsu (as Hōshimaru is called upon his coming of age), burrowing recurs as a motif—Terukatsu approaches his ladylove, for instance, by climbing up the hole of her privy—and reinforces our initial impression of human nature being explored from deep within. The extraordinary images of the heads, and the noseless head in particular, have pressed upon the boy at the moment when his sexual latency dissolves, and the something absurd and precarious in all our cathections is powerfully dramatized. Tanizaki's relish in mingling post-Freudian perceptions with the trappings of ancient politics, architecture, and costume gives the whole tale a richly sensuous and paradoxical texture. The Lord of Musashi's attempt to share his peculiar ecstasies with his bride, Shōsetsuin (she obliges, once, and then is forever repelled), is a paradigm of many an awkward wedding night; but the central lesson—from what far and tortuous distances we bring our private needs to others!—borrows vividness from the barbaric setting so brilliantly reconstructed.

Arrowroot concerns a historical saga that Tanizaki did *not* write, about the "Southern Court" that a rival claimant to the imperial throne set up in a remote canyon of the Yamato mountains in 1336, and that lasted until 1457. The narrator, in an accounting as apparently casual and personal as one of Knut Hamsun's thinner novels, travels with a friend to the remote site, and concludes that "the head of this valley was just too inaccessible. Surely Prince Kitayama's poem was not composed at this place. . . . Sannoko may be the site of legends, but not of history." On the way, however, enough historical and geographical information about this wild west of Japan is given to keep us moving along that line of suspense and gratification which the best writers can establish in even their quietest modes. More than brevity and history link the two novellas; the narrator's travelling companion, a college friend named Tsumura, who has discovered relatives in a village of the Yamato province, confides to him a yearning, "connected with the first buddings of adolescent love," reminiscent of the case of the Lord of Musashi. In Tsumura's case, the imprint taken was of a song, used in a child's game, about the fox of Shinoda Forest, whose last lines ask, "If you miss me / Come and search / Shinoda Forest's arrowroot leaves of sorrow." Tsumura identifies his mother, who died when he was little more than an infant, with his early memory of a woman playing the koto and singing a song called "The Cry of the Fox." Further, Tsumura believes the song evokes for him not only his mother but the woman who will become his wife. "In my case, the woman of the past who was my mother, and the woman who will be my wife in the future, are both 'unknown women' and both are tied to me by an invisible thread of fate." True to his intimations, he searches out his mother's family in these western mountains and successfully courts a young cousin first seen dipping wooden frames to make sheets of paper: "Her cheeks were firm and had the healthy luster of youth; but Tsumura's heart was drawn to her fingers, immersed in the cloudy water." Hōshimaru's heart, too, had been drawn to fingers: "And her hands were more supple, more graceful as they dressed the hair, than the hands of the other women." So, while the novelist conducts researches that prove barren, he watches in the corner of his eye the fruitful conclusion of an erotic psychodrama. *Arrowroot* is related with a delightful deftness, in the blunt easy tone of a born writer, who knows how to tell us the essential things while leaving the unessential skimped.

From Fumie to Sony

SILENCE, by Shusaku Endo, translated from the Japanese by William Johnston. 294 pp. Taplinger, 1979.

WHEN I WHISTLE, by Shusaku Endo, translated from the Japanese by Van C. Gessel. 273 pp. Taplinger, 1979.

SECRET RENDEZVOUS, by Kobo Abe, translated from the Japanese by Juliet W. Carpenter. 179 pp. Knopf, 1979.

Shusaku Endo, born in Tokyo in 1923, published *Silence* in 1966. Now, in an English translation that is itself ten years old, this novel has been published in the United States. It is a remarkable work, a grim, delicate, and impressively empathetic study of a young Portuguese missionary during the relentless persecution of the Japanese Christians in the early seventeenth century. Since this dark cul-de-sac within the spread of the Gospel has been little celebrated in the West, some history culled from the Encyclopaedia Britannica may be helpful. The first Western contact with Japan occurred in 1543, when a Portuguese trading vessel bound for China was blown off course and landed on the southern island of Kyushu. Missionary efforts soon followed the initiation of trade. St. Francis Xavier—one of the seven original members of the Society of Jesus and a prodigious evangelist in India and the East Indies—landed in Kyushu in 1549, with two fellow-Jesuits and three Japanese converted in South Asia. The saint was happy there; he called the Japanese "the delight of my heart" and thought Japan "the country in the Orient most suited to Christianity." After two years, he departed Kyushu, leaving behind him about a thousand converts. Not forty years later, the number had swelled to one estimated to be between a hundred fifty thousand and four hundred thousand; Christianity had thrived upon the initial Japanese eagerness for foreign trade, the need of the *daimyō* (barons) for allies in their struggle with the politically powerful Buddhists, and a stylistic affinity between the *daimyō* and samurai and the quasi-military Jesuits. By the end of the century, these factors were negated: the Spaniards, Dutch, and English had followed the Portuguese into

Japan, and the influence of squabbling foreigners loomed as an impediment to the generals attempting to unify the country. In 1587, the Jesuits were ordered to leave—an order few obeyed. In 1596, the first persecution of Japanese Christians was prompted by the arrogance of some shipwrecked Spaniards. In 1603, the two and a half centuries of Tokugawa "centralized feudalism" began, and anti-Christian measures were renewed in earnest. An edict of 1614 required all Japanese to register as members of Buddhist sects. In 1617, foreign priests were executed for the first time. Twenty years later, a Christian revolt on the Shimabara Peninsula, east of Nagasaki, was put down, and the insurgents—men, women, and children—were slaughtered. All further contact with the Portuguese was forbidden, and when a delegation from Macao arrived to reopen relations, most of the emissaries were executed. The Christians remaining in Japan were hunted down by inquisitors, and by torture induced to apostasy, or else slain.

Silence takes place during these darkest late days of Japanese Christianity. Word has reached Rome that Father Christovao Ferreira, a devout and courageous missionary of some thirty-three years' experience in Japan, has apostatized. Three former students of Ferreira, refusing to believe that "their much admired teacher . . . faced with the possibility of a glorious martyrdom, had grovelled like a dog before the infidel," vow to undertake an investigatory mission. They do not win consent from their superiors for this desperate venture until 1637, and it takes them a year to reach Goa, where they learn of the Shimabara revolt and its abysmal consequences. Since no Portuguese vessel can now sail to Japan, the priests must hire a Chinese vessel in Macao and employ as guide a dubious drunken Japanese named Kichijiro. One of the three is too ill with malaria to go, so the mission dwindles to Fathers Francisco Garrpe and Sebastian Rodrigues; the letters of the twenty-eight-year-old Rodrigues, supposedly preserved in "the Portuguese 'Institute for the Historical Study of Foreign Lands,' " compose the bulk of the novel. The two priests make a landing and have no trouble locating Christians. With the help of their fawning, shifty intermediary, who persistently reminds Rodrigues of Judas, they are sequestered in a mountainside charcoal hut by the farmers and fishermen of the village of Tomogi, who come secretly to them for the sacraments. Living thus among these humble converts, who hold fast though their overlords have abandoned the now impolitic foreign faith, Rodrigues adduces a reason for the success of Christianity not given by the encyclopedia:

> When you see how the land is cultivated right up into the middle of the mountain facing the sea, you are struck not so much by their indefatigable industry as by the cruelty of the life they have inherited. Yet the magistrate of Nagasaki exacts from them an exceedingly harsh revenue . . . The reason our religion has penetrated this territory like water flowing into dry earth is that it has given to this group of people a human warmth they never previously knew. For the first time they have met men who treated them like human beings. It was the human kindness and charity of the fathers that touched their hearts.

In a culture where Christianity has established itself as an institution of the comfortable, it can be forgotten that its prime appeal was and still should be to the wretched. "Christ did not die for the good and beautiful," Rodrigues realizes. "It is easy enough to die for the good and beautiful; the hard thing is to die for the miserable and corrupt." But Rodrigues is not asked to die; rather, he must witness, in a slow crescendo of tortures, the deaths of the Japanese faithful. The village of Tomogi is raided, and two men fail to pass the inquisitorial procedures. Though they tread on the *fumie*—an icon made for the express purpose of repudiation—they are unable to spit on it and "declare that the Blessed Virgin was a whore." The two men are condemned to the water punishment: they are bound to crosses just below the high-tide mark, so that the ocean, rising to their chins and receding, over the course of a few days kills them by exposure and exhaustion.

> They were martyred. But what a martyrdom! I had long read about martyrdom in the lives of the saints—how the souls of the martyrs had gone home to Heaven, how they had been filled with glory in Paradise, how the angels had blown trumpets. This was the splendid martyrdom I had often seen in my dreams. But the martyrdom of the

Japanese Christians I now describe to you was no such glorious thing. What a miserable and painful business it was! The rain falls unceasingly on the sea. And the sea which killed them surges on uncannily —in silence.

The silence of the title is, of course, the silence of God. " 'Lord, why are you silent? Why are you always silent?' . . . So he prayed. But the sea remained cold, and the darkness maintained its stubborn silence." This silence grows thunderous in the priest's ears as his trials multiply. The hunt is on, for these the last Jesuits in Japan. Rodrigues and Garrpe are driven to separate, and are reunited in a ghastly scene when some converts are being executed by being wrapped in mats and then tipped into the sea from a boat. Garrpe desperately swims after the boat, shouting prayers. He, too, drowns: "Only the head of Garrpe, like a piece of wood from a shipwrecked boat, floated for some time on the water until the waves from the boat covered it over." Rodrigues is imprisoned, but his torture—like that of Ferreira before him—is to witness the torture of others. The magistrates, led by the soft-spoken archinquisitor Inoue, want the foreign priests publicly to apostatize, not the native "small fry." Father Rodrigues thinks, "He had come to this country to lay down his life for other men, but instead of that the Japanese were laying down their lives one by one for him. What was he to do?" He does what he must: to say more would be to betray this beautifully simple plot, which so harrowingly dramatizes immense theological issues.

The Westerner must admire the unobtrusive, persuasive effort of imagination that enables a modern Japanese to take up a viewpoint from which Japan is at the outer limit of the world. "As one opened the map one saw the shape of Africa, then India, and then the innumerable islands and countries of Asia were all spread out. And then, at the north-east extremity, looking just like a caterpillar, was the tiny shape of Japan." Father Rodrigues's Christian faith, though a somewhat streamlined version of the baroque actuality of Iberian Counter-Reformation Catholicism, lacks no essentials and is powerfully comprehended as a palliative of the world's endless grief. The face of the sorrowing Christ is always before the helpless priest's inner eye, and appears to him physically in the dizzyingly paradoxical form of the *fumie*, the holy image manufactured to be trampled upon:

> The interpreter had placed before his feet a wooden plaque. On it was a copper plate on which a Japanese craftsman had engraved that man's face. . . . It was not a Christ whose face was filled with majesty and glory; neither was it a face made beautiful by endurance of pain; nor was it a face filled with the strength of a will that has repelled temptation. The face of the man who then lay at his feet was sunken and utterly exhausted.
>
> Many Japanese had already trodden on it, so that the wood surrounding the plaque was black with the print of their toes. And the face itself was concave, worn down with the constant treading. It was this concave face that had looked at the priest in sorrow. In sorrow it had gazed up at him, as the eyes spoke appealingly: "Trample! Trample! It is to be trampled on by you that I am here."

Shaping his incidents toward this extremity of Christian temptation, in a situation of true hopelessness, Endo has conceived a narrative more orthodox, in texture and thought, than most novels by twentieth-century Christians. The book jacket, which does not comment upon Endo's professed Roman Catholicism, allows only that he "specialized in French literature at Keio University and then studied for several years in France on a scholarship from the Japanese government." During his studies, he presumably encountered some of the saturnine Catholic fiction of Georges Bernanos and François Mauriac. He surely has read Graham Greene's *The Power and the Glory*—indeed, if *Silence* has a weak spot, it is the ambivalent, nagging figure of Kichijiro, who seems too plainly a copy of the mestizo who dogs Greene's whiskey priest. But the Japanese author brings to his Pascalian themes, and even to his descriptions of torture and execution, a tact as inexorable and hypnotic as his steady gray murderous sea. *Silence* ends with a set of official Tokugawa documents, as Japanese efficiency and homogeneity close over the last traces of the Jesuit incursion. But the story has a sequel, which we find, like its prelude, in the pages of the encyclopedia:

When Mass was held at Nagasaki by a French priest for the foreign community in 1865, foreigners and Tokugawa officials alike were astonished to see large numbers of fishermen . . . appear for the Mass. They had carried on Christian services secretly for over two centuries.

A later novel by Shusaku Endo, *When I Whistle*, bears little resemblance to *Silence*, except in its unruffled simplicity of style and in the recurrence of an image that evidently haunts the author, of a head bobbing far out at sea. Instead of Father Rodrigues watching his fellow-priest swimming to his death in a hopeless effort of ministry, this novel has Ozu, a schoolboy, watching his friend Flatfish swim toward the horizon in pursuit of a girl with whom he has fallen hopelessly in love. Flatfish does not drown, but Ozu never forgets the sight of "his friend's tiny head being tossed about by the waves as he swam desperately for the open sea."

The novel takes place on two levels: Ozu's pre-war youth, distinguished by a comically lackadaisical schooling and by his bleary-eyed chum's quixotic infatuation with a girl, Aiko, encountered by chance after school; and Ozu's postwar maturity, which finds him the father of an opportunistic young doctor, Eiichi, at a big-city hospital where one of the patients turns out to be, yes, that same Aiko, now dying of cancer. Ozu, who has progressed from indifferent scholar to an undistinguished and unspecified sort of businessman, meets an old schoolmate on a train, and this awakens reminiscences that alternate chapters with the present medical adventures of his son. Both levels read easily, but neither generates the awesome resonance of the monaural plot of *Silence*. Perhaps because hospital dramas have long been a television staple, we feel a contemptuous familiarity with the idealistic Dr. Tahara, the pliant Dr. Uchida, the seduced and abandoned Nurses Keiko and Shimada, and the villainous Dr. Ii, with his cheerful insistence on prescribing the worthless drugs produced by the pharmaceutical company that funds his research. These characters seem, in Japanese, a bit gimcrack, and mechanically quick to contrive their ends: "He gazed at her as she blushed slightly, and it occurred to him that he would probably be able to seduce this sweet young thing in no time at all." The pre-war level is gentler, and more affecting, even though its characters bear comic-book names like Flatfish, Monkey, Cry-Baby, Rat Hole, the Shadow, Mr. Gutter, and Mr. Blowfish. It is interesting to see the Second World War approach from the vantage of a Japanese schoolboy, to have "a quicksand of a war in a country far across the sea" be not our Vietnam but their Manchuria, to sit in a classroom and be told by a professor of philosophy on Pearl Harbor Day that "at last the time for a confrontation between the spiritual civilization of Japan and the material civilization of a foreign country has come!" The professor goes on to speculate that "the mission of Japan is to deal the death blow to the foreign culture that has already reached a stalemate in our country," which is not so different from what Father Rodrigues, three centuries before, was told: "As for the tree of Christianity, in a foreign country its leaves may grow thick and the buds may be rich, while in Japan the leaves wither and no bud appears."

A country so explosively emergent into the industrial world as Japan—after centuries of official policy that was reactionary and isolationist, restricting foreign merchants to an offshore islet and outlawing the gun in favor of the samurai's sword—is understandably prone to nostalgia. One has to read no wider in modern Japanese fiction than Tanizaki and Mishima to find nostalgia writ large; with them, the novel situated in the historic past has an artistic dignity and viability rare in the West. In a land where delicacy and minimalism perennially guided manners and decor toward a stringent harmony, and where commercialism and pollution now enjoy an Asiatic triumph, many must feel, as Ozu does at the end of *When I Whistle,* that "beautiful things, things from the treasured past were now disappearing all over Japan" and, like him, grope after "a meaning of life concealed somewhere."

Strange to say, a hospital also figures prominently in *Secret Rendezvous,* by Kobo Abe. This novel is short and almost indescribably unpleasant. The author, a year younger than Endo, is best known here as the author of *The Woman in the Dunes,* from which a successful art film was made in 1963. In both novels, a man gets trapped in a bad place that in the end he decides to call home. A follower of Kafka, Kobo Abe places his heroes in situations that no one will explain to them, though there is much talk. This makes for cheap suspense, and also for readerly exasperation. *The Woman in the Dunes* had a certain gritty realism and, in its remote, dune-drowned village, some of that rustic quaintness which comforts us in Japanese fiction. *Secret Rendezvous* is all plastic and aluminum, a shiny mess from its dust jacket in. Its hero is a nameless jump-shoe salesman whose pretty wife is taken away at four o'clock in the morning by a mysterious ambulance, even though she "had never complained of a single symptom." Her husband follows her to a hospital, where he meets, among other doctors and patients, an administrator who to remedy his impotence has had the severed lower half of a potent associate connected to his own, so that he has four legs like a horse, and a thirteen-year-old girl who masturbates without cease and whose very bones are liquefying, so that she resembles a piece of bubble gum melting on a hot sidewalk. Our hero, nevertheless, falls in love with her; by the time he locates his wife, the good woman has virtually slipped his mind, and anyway is preoccupied by her position as a finalist in an orgasm contest.

And what, you may ask, is a jump shoe? "A jump shoe is a sporting shoe with a special air-bubble spring built into the under-sole." The two that he is wearing enable our anonymous but athletic hero to bound away from pursuers and down the endless corridors of the hospital, which is wiretapped throughout, like the White House under Nixon, and which does a lively trade in peeping-ear tapes of its patients' sexual forays. The whole queer business is laid bare in the ungainly form of a diary that the jump-shoe man is told by the four-footed man to keep; as he scribbles away, during the momentary remissions of his metastasizing plight, he coins such vivid phrases as "The sky was as black as an internal hemorrhage" and, of ice cream, "It tasted sad, as though time itself were starting to freeze over."

Well, time might as well freeze over, if this is our future. Jump shoes perhaps already exist; certainly big hospitals do appear as vast and impersonal as this fantastic one. And there is no doubt that to the monsters that disease has always made of men the apparatus of healing science now adds monsters of its own. Still, this grotesque book seems itself inhumane, less a satire than a howl. Its moral is cruel: "If animal history has been a history of evolution, then the history of mankind is one of retrogression. Hooray for monsters! Monsters are the great embodiments of the weak." And its writing is frantic, though perhaps writer and translator should share the blame for a sentence like "I barely managed to swallow a violent impulse to retch before I felt my consciousness plunge into a sea of nausea." A certain puritanism lurks behind so macabre a caricature of our sex-obsessed, technology-swamped present as this; such loathing of the modern implies a forgetfulness of the past that produced the monsters described in *Silence*—the upside-down men being bled to death, the peasants eating roots in order to supply the samurai with his tax of rice.

Silence takes place in the historic past, *When I Whistle* combines the recent past and the unsatisfactory present, and *Secret Rendezvous* looks at a horrible future that is close at hand. And in the same order the writing progresses from very fine to rather poor. Steam engines were around for some decades before Turner and the Impressionists tamed them into objects of beauty, and the chemical and electronic technology impinging on our present lives as yet has no heartfelt place in fiction. Japanese art perhaps more than most is an art of subduing, of violence suppressed within expected forms. When the form itself becomes violent, as in *Secret Rendezvous,* sheer ugliness spills forth. But it is reassuring, in an era when the Japanese embrace of the future appears statistically more adroit and wholehearted than ours, to see them, too, recoil.

The Giant Who Isn't There

CHINESE SHADOWS, by "Simon Leys" [Pierre Ryckmans], translated from the French anonymously. 220 pp. Viking, 1977.

Recently the front page of the Boston *Globe* declared:

> Carter calls
> Vance's trip
> step forward

A few days later, a slightly smaller headline proclaimed:

> China calls
> Vance's talks
> a step back

Such comically self-cancelling dispatches make one wonder if China is there at all; and, strangely, books purporting to describe this dim, contradictory colossus do not entirely dispel the doubt. Many small mysteries lurk in *Chinese Shadows*, by Simon Leys. Simon Leys, the jacket flap states, is the pseudonym of "a Belgian art historian and Sinologist who has lived and worked in the Far East for more than a decade." Who, then, is the Pierre Ryckmans named in six-point type on the copyright page? And who is the translator of this book from the French, wherein it was originally published, in 1974, as *Ombres chinoises?* In a time when more honor and better pay are being sought for translations into English, Viking seems to be bestowing Victorian anonymity upon the lowly laborer responsible, in this case, for such pugnacious language as "Chairman Mao perpetrated another lousy poem" and "A valiant academic journalist who visited China on one of those standard six-week tours . . . wrote a book of a fairly impressive size, which he had the guts to subtitle *The Real China.*"

French-speaking intellectuals evidently take in the Maoism of *Le Monde* and *Tel Quel* with every morning's croissants. A footnote tells how "Maoist editors" intimidate their superiors, and on the back of the jacket the author confides how "the Maoist faithful" in Europe rooted out Simon Leys's true identity, and made it impossible for him ever to return to China. The rabidly pro-Mao atmosphere out of which Mr. Leys writes his dissenting volume is also, to Americans who can remember the Korean War and the Sinophobic diplomacy of John Foster Dulles, a bit mysterious. Here, though Mao had his moment in the late Sixties as a college-dorm poster and a Pop Art totem like Mickey Mouse or the Coca-Cola bottle, our rapprochement with Communist China is confusingly mixed with the unfashionable image of Richard Nixon. Mr. Leys reports that, of the American visitors to China he had known, the only one to confess disappointment was a worker for McGovern's Presidential campaign who "came to China in the hope of getting some support for or at least a show of interest in the Democratic candidate; he found that the Maoist authorities were staunch Nixonians." Elsewhere, apropos of Nixon (who is in the book but erased from the index), Mr. Leys remarks that as of 1972 "Mao himself has finally become as irrelevant to China's needs as Nixon to America's—which might explain why those two gentlemen grew so fond of each other." Mr. Leys believes that true political power in China lies with the military. Recent history is described as "purges and counterpurges that left two old men steering a rundown machine while in the murky corridors of power military gangs fought for control." He likens Chou En-lai, once an amateur opera performer, to Chu-ke Liang, a hero of classical Chinese opera who welcomed an enemy general to an empty fortress, creating "the mirage of a strong and powerful order, where in fact there is only incoherence and emptiness."

Emptiness is the theme of this entertaining, saddening minority report. Mr. Leys wrote the book in 1972–73, and "hesitated for a long time before having it published." Now that the less glamorous China of Hua Kuo-feng has supplanted the People's Utopia of the Great Teacher, Mr. Leys seems to spend too many pages in defensive apologia for setting forth the meagre little that he, with the great advantage of knowing the language and the historical culture, has observed in his visits. A lot of what he says seems scarcely surprising. The tours permitted visitors to this huge land are rigidly controlled and restricted. The same show-villages and restored temples are described in one Western account after another. Out of the hundreds of Chinese cities, only about a dozen are open to ordinary foreigners, and in each they are put in one, usually very isolated, hotel. Mr. Leys can be quite funny about this: "Since the vast Chinese world has thus been shrunk to the size of a pinhead, there don't have to be many foreign visitors in circulation for them to get the impression that they are all over the place, treading on each other's toes. Beyond space and time, a kind of Freemasonry springs up among them, the way it does among commuters on a shared little suburban tram line . . ." Of the eight hundred million Chinese, "about sixty individuals" specialize in meeting foreigners, and their names "come up time and again in the many accounts written by travellers who think, naively, that they had managed to make friends in China."

Mr. Leys, landed in the unscheduled city of Ho-fei by a vagary of the Chinese airlines (which will not fly if there is wind or rain), was denied permission not only to walk in the city but even to ride in a car around it, and instead was given a lavish meal in his luxurious suite and kept there until he could be taken to the airport. This incident, one among many similar, betrays the intense fearfulness of totalitarian governments: each guide fears his superior, and the total governmental dread of the spontaneous produces the miasmic paralysis so well evoked in the fiction of the Soviet underground. Solzhenitsyn's *The First Circle*, indeed, characterizes Stalin himself as terror-ridden. There does seem to be a necessary outlandishness in tyrants. They come from the outskirts—Austria, Georgia, Corsica—and the component of hostility in their power to fascinate the populace shows itself in the savage recklessness with which they waste the lives of their followers. Hitler, Stalin, and Napoleon were in some sense at war with the nations they led. This destructiveness from above is manifested in recent Chinese history by the Cultural Revolution of 1966–69; the craters left by its violence are the principal feature of the cultural landscape that Mr. Leys can glimpse from his hotel windows.

But, before moving away from this topic of controlled tourism on which he is amusingly eloquent, let us imagine what sort of account Mr. Leys might have written of *this* country if, as an official visitor, he was met by a solicitous State Department underling at Kennedy Airport, slid by limousine through New York City to a meeting of the P.E.N. Club and a Currier & Ives exhibit at the Metropolitan Museum of Art, sternly warned not to walk the streets at night, and rebuffed in his conversational advances by the hurrying denizens of those streets during the daytime. Communist "cultural delegates" to the United States, I know,

also tend to run a standard route and to meet the same present-
able, obliging personalities. Travel, that is, has its distortions
the world over. Even the most constrained tour, however, can
yield suggestive impressions. Alberto Moravia, for example, in
his *Red Book and the Great Wall,* instead of complaining about
his guide describes him: "Our guide, Mr. Li, was a thin yellow
man. . . . His expression was one of decrepit sadness. He had a
nervous tic that made one half of his face jump up and down while
the other half remained motionless. And he stuttered." The conver-
sations between Mr. Li and Moravia, the nervous shepherd and the
irrepressible woolgatherer, produce comedy and diagnostic insight
out of their confusions.

Simon Leys largely ignores land reform, state control of indus-
try, relief of poverty and disease, and the other professed social and
economic aims of Communism. His province and his grievances
are aesthetic: the government and the Cultural Revolution between
them have obliterated temples, gates, pailous, Confucianism, classi-
cal opera, and virtually everything else that he, as an art historian,
treasured. And all unnecessarily. He claims to favor the economic
revolution:

> If the destruction of the entire legacy of China's traditional culture
> was the price to pay to insure the success of the revolution, I would
> forgive all the iconoclasms, I would support them with enthusiasm!
> What makes the Maoist vandalism so odious and so pathetic is not
> that it is irreparably mutilating an ancient civilization but rather that
> by doing so it gives itself an alibi for *not grappling with the true revolu-
> tionary tasks.* The extent of their depredations gives Maoists the cheap
> illusion that they have done a great deal; they persuade themselves
> that they can rid themselves of the past by attacking its material
> manifestations; but in fact they remain its slaves, bound the more
> tightly because they refuse to realize the effect of the old traditions
> within their revolution. The destruction of the gates of Peking is,
> properly speaking, a *sacrilege;* and what makes it dramatic is not that
> the authorities had them pulled down but that they remain unable to
> understand *why* they pulled them down.

This key passage contains his other, and curiously opposite, complaint about Red China: its administration remains too traditional, hierarchical, deferential, bureaucratic—a government of old men and serried myriads of timid toadies. "In the scales of China's destiny, which weighs heavier: the visionary wisdom of a few men at the top or the sterilizing stupidity of a bureaucratic *apparat* that is dull, dogmatic, mediocre, arrogant, neurotic, frozen in conformism, terrified of initiative, and unable to transmit to the base the visions of the summit without disfiguring them? . . . This leaden mantle of the middle and lower cadres weighs upon the shoulders of the people, crushes their creative genius, stifles their traditional qualities of initiative and inventiveness."

Now, this indictment assumes the "creative genius" of a "people" quite distinct from the bureaucratic cadres; but where were the cadres enlisted if not from this same "people"? Mr. Leys also seems to absolve the highest echelon from the evils of the regime—though he does accuse Mao of writing bad poetry, and even of having "poor and pretentious calligraphy." For this Belgian critic, as for millions of admirers, Mao eludes blame for Maoism. Though Maoist propaganda is "one of the most monotonous, arid, and indigent creations in the world," Mao projected in the West an image of amiable aloofness, and was credited with great delicacy of thought. Yet the anti-intellectual, anti-institutional depredations of the Cultural Revolution sprang from Mao's own brain, with its hope of "continuous revolution," which in action translated into counterrevolution and anarchy. By willing this upheaval, Mao, with no thanks from Mr. Leys, was attempting to grapple with the entrenched conservatism of the "bureaucratic *apparat*" that Mr. Leys finds so striking—a slavishness he traces back to the "fatal historical accident" of the isolationist, totalitarian Ming regime. By this accident, "China confronted the modern world blind and paralyzed," and thus "the nation was so incredibly derailed" that the "most civilized people on earth" fell into "a rut . . . unworthy of their calling and their genius."

This analysis is informed not only by knowledge but by love of the historical China. But analyses that base present conditions upon accidents and aberrations seem a bit rickety. A nation of nearly a billion is not that easy to derail into an unworthy rut. Ross H. Munro's recent dispatches in the *Times* describe how Chinese citizens, neighborhood by neighborhood, conspire to enforce conformity upon one another, and avidly assist in the creation of "the most tightly controlled nation on earth." There is something in the genius of the people which answers to Maoism, an approach to government that survived a cruel civil war, a Japanese invasion, Russian patronage, and several uproars induced by vacillation at the top. Mr. Leys seems to want an orderly China of spontaneous humanity, a China that has swept away old social evils without disturbing a stone of old cultural monuments. His indictment of cultural evils under Mao is extensive: Stalinoid architectural atrocities of "vulgar gigantism and monstrous daintiness" have defaced sacred places, boulevards have been bulldozed without cars to use them, the great walls and superb gates of Peking were with immense labor demolished to no purpose, monuments that have not been razed molder in neglect, factories turn out art objects of a Communist-kitsch vulgarity that "you would have to be Huysmans to describe adequately," classical Chinese opera has been reduced to six "Revolutionary Model operas . . . where the only 'revolutionary' daring is to maneuver onstage, to languorous saxophonic Khachaturian-like music, platoons of the People's Liberation Army complete with banners and wooden rifles." The single symphonic creation heard in the land is a "mediocre Rachmaninoff pastiche" called *Yellow River;* the Cultural Revolution left the universities gutted and scholarship nil; traditional classics can be bought only in "the bookshops you see in the lobbies of hotels reserved to foreigners"; living Chinese writers have long since been reduced to silence or sycophancy. And over all, via loudspeaker and wall poster, on tickets and towels, ashtrays and teapots, the incessant clamor of Maoist propaganda, "this gigantic enterprise of cretinizing the most intelligent people on earth."

The portrait appalls. Mr. Leys's litany of cultural crimes is no mere set of "shadows," it is a dirge for a China that is dead, that is all shadow. In his travelogue, he is a poet of emptiness: the vast vacant boulevards of Peking "call to mind the false airports which cargo-cult devotees in New Guinea hack out of the jungle in the hope that this will persuade their gods to send planes full of treasure"; the resort city of Peitaiho "in its eeriness raises the notion of a seaside resort to the quasi-metaphysical plane: it is less a holiday resort than the Platonic idea of a holiday resort"; the city of Tientsin, "with its walled-up windows, its blind and leprous façades, seems to be a sleepwalker's dream." Cities huge by European standards appear in their drab docility deserted: "To the passing visitor, the very existence of these millions of lives seems to have been sucked away by the vampire shadows of the past." Vampirish, indeed, is the bloodless precision with which the authorities can produce crowds of exactly the promised sixty thousand cheering spectators, and can conjure up, for an appropriate audience of foreigners, a Catholic Mass "with paper flowers and painted plaster Sacred Hearts."

The totalitarian dread of free artistic expression baffles dwellers within the art-proof precincts of capitalism. What harm, the Western liberal (including this reviewer) always wants to ask, would a few non-prescribed piano concertos or classic novels do? Years ago, I was struck by the discovery, through an exhibit of contemporary Spanish paintings at the Guggenheim Museum, that Franco permitted abstract painting in fascist Spain. To the Soviets, of course, such "formalism" was anathema, and was pursued at personal risk. But Francoism was not a religion, it was just one bully's belief that only he could save Spain from ruin. Communism lays claim to an exclusive and eternal truth that must be pushed into every cranny of existence, lest even the most minute and fractional reversal refute the entire creed. A religion will be intolerant of others as far as its strength reaches. The destruction of rival icons is a rite of faith. Iconoclasm always seems barbaric to those who have no faith, to whom all icons, being irreplaceable by the dead hands of faith, are equally precious, as art relics, as husks of refuted illusions but husks to which those illusions imparted a selfless energy. That selfless energy, manifesting itself in destruction and exclusion, in monotony and absurdity, seems still to rage in China, and Mr. Leys, by seeking to dissociate the "inexhaustible humanity" of this subcontinent from the displeasing events within it, leaves something out that we need to know. Maoism must be more than a temporary rut, and its terrifying curtailments of human freedom no mere accident. Moravia, at least, offered an explanation of the Cultural Revolution that made sense in terms of "the almost pathological conservatism that characterized traditional China." The aim of this conservatism was the continuity of the Chinese people, a continuity based on harmony:

> And this harmony is achieved by any orthodoxy that can provide immobility and, in a certain sense, place China outside history, at least for a few centuries. . . . Nowadays the Chinese hate their past because this hate is useful for the purposes of that future orthodoxy which will be built exclusively of Maoist materials. . . . In any case, the Chinese consider themselves inexhaustible. The past destroyed will be replaced by a future that is equally rich in wisdom and refinement.

This serene Chinese confidence brushes aside all things Western, including Western adoration and love. The giant is self-delighting, and clasps even its earthquakes to itself in somber privacy. *Chinese Shadows* lacks the depth that shadows give; Mr. Leys sounds a thin note of personal rejection, in these jottings of a frustrated lover of a vanished civilization.

The Long and Reluctant Stasis of Wan-li

1587, A YEAR OF NO SIGNIFICANCE: *The Ming Dynasty in Decline*, by Ray Huang. 278 pp. Yale University Press, 1981.

This is a curious book, fascinating and enlightening yet also a bit enigmatically bland, like the members of the Ming bureaucracy who constitute its essential subject. The copyright page reveals that *1587, A Year of No Significance* is to be also published in China, under the title *Wan-li shih-wu nien* ("The fifteenth year of Wan-li") by "Chung-hua shu-chü, Peking"—or, if you prefer the new (and grotesque) style of transliteration approved by the cultural directors of the People's Republic, *Wanli Shiwunian*, by "Zhong-hua Shuju, Beijing." Professor Ray Huang, a former soldier in the

Chinese Nationalist Army who came to the United States in 1949, has for sixteen years been teaching in American colleges and universities. Though his book leads off with a comforting flurry of prefatory matter in the friendly manner of American academic publications—a dedication "For Gayle," a page and a half of acknowledged favors for which the author is "very, very grateful," and a brisk foreword of imprimatur by Professor L. Carrington Goodrich, co-editor of *The Dictionary of Ming Biography*—the text itself plunges the reader into the middle of things Ming as if he already knew what the "Four Books" were, how the Literary Depth Pavilion and the Silk Robe Guard worked, and that the Manchurian tribal leader who was eventually to undermine the Ming dynasty was, of course, named Nurhaci. Mr. Huang has a disconcerting way of referring to "our" empire, and even, at one point, "our history." A Chinese readership seems to be on his mind, accounting perhaps for his gingerliness in pressing home Western and modern parallels; to this same phantom audience Professor Goodrich presumably addresses the abrupt assurance in his foreword that "this account must not persuade us that the bitter sufferings of the Chinese people in general, both then and since, have all been a huge mistake—that from now on China must discard her entire past experience and imitate the West in whatever way possible to make up for lost time."

This assurance to the contrary, Mr. Huang's portrait of a moment in the Ming decline, with emphasis upon a half-dozen historical personalities, amounts to an indictment, the terms of which—in brief, that the imperial bureaucracy's commitment to tradition and stability stifled initiative and perpetrated injustice—imply an admiring acquaintance with the ideals of personal freedom and legal process embodied in, among other Western documents, the United States Constitution. Against the Confucian principle of a generalized morality pervading society, his analysis opposes legality and self-interest.

> For all its moral tone, the system could never free itself of its authoritarian cast, for social pressure as a substitute for justice was always exerted from the top down. It was taken for granted that whoever could recite

verses from the *Four Books* was more enlightened than an individual motivated by self-interest. . . . Since the government took drastic action in enforcing the penal code but showed no interest in upholding the civil law, and village leaders were preoccupied with decorum and social status, the villagers in reality were denied legal services of any kind. They were never given a clear indication of what they were entitled to.

His explanation for this sorry condition is crisply given:

The doctrine of jen, with its accompanying devotion to kinship relationships and to ritual, grew progressively overburdened as a unifying force in Chinese society as the latter advanced in cultural level. Its development over a long period must be viewed in light of the fact that, because of the early unification of the empire, which followed almost immediately upon the Bronze Age, local institutions and customary practices never had a chance to mature into civil law.

Success, in short, spoiled China; too swiftly "a highly stylized society wherein the roles of individuals were thoroughly restricted" had jelled into shape. Mr. Huang arrives at his conclusions by way of biography; drawing upon the prodigious archives left by a government of literati (where, in the absence of a prime minister, the Emperor's chief scribe, or "first grand-secretary," acted as effective head of state), he shows a handful of highly gifted men among the elite as they struggle against the built-in limitations of their system.

Ch'i Chi-kuang, a general of genius, who died late in the insignificant year, revitalized the empire's statistically impressive but actually feeble army, single-handedly codified military procedure, invented new formations and techniques, and enjoyed heartening successes against Japanese marauders along the coast and Mongol raiders in the north; yet with the death of his sponsor, the First Grand-Secretary Chang Chü-cheng, and Chang's posthumous fall from imperial grace, the great warrior was demoted and eventually censured and dismissed, dying in poverty. Military officers—a caste almost entirely hereditary—were regarded as mere technicians and distrusted by "civil officials preoccupied with the dogmas of restraint and moderation." Any power base outside the imperial bureaucracy had to be reduced, though "gone with Ch'i Chi-kuang was our empire's last opportunity to give its armed forces the minimal modernization needed to survive a new era."

Also dead in 1587 was the famous Hai Jui, a civil official of fanatic rectitude, who had dared chastise in a publicized "memorial" (a word used here with a sense close to "memorandum") the Chia-ching Emperor as "vain, cruel, selfish, suspicious, and foolish." In a caste notorious for its hypocritical venality, Hai Jui imposed, when governor of South Chihli, an austerity that extended to calling for the elimination of wasteful blank spaces at the end of official documents. Yet his reformer's zeal quickly ran him afoul of agrarian conservatism and led to his retirement for fifteen years, which was followed by a brief and empty final appointment. "His death toward the end of the year must have given the court of Peking a sense of relief. Now no one had to be held responsible for removing a popular hero who was worshipped by the public even though, in the eyes of his fellow bureaucrats and the emperor, he was silly and inept."

A third rebel unable to find his way out of the system was the philosopher Li Chih, whose voluminous and "erratic" commentaries upon the canonized classics contain inklings of egalitarian thought that have endeared him to the present rulers of China but did not really break with the elitist and Confucian presumptions in which he had been raised. To Mr. Huang, his writings form basically "an invaluable record, without which we would perhaps never be able to fathom the depth of intellectual frustration that characterized this era."

Other studies in frustration are offered by the careers of Chang Chü-cheng and Shen Shih-hsing, two grand-secretaries whose attempts to direct the affairs of a clumsily centralized and overextended empire were constrained by the rubrics of supernatural education; their basic assignment was "to keep the emperor's court in harmony with the teaching of ancient sages":

> The secret of administering an enormous empire such as ours was not to rely on law or the power to regulate and punish but to induce the younger generation to venerate the old, the women to obey their menfolk, and the illiterate to follow the examples set by the learned. In all

these areas the example set by the emperor's court was of paramount importance.

The most arresting portrait of all is that of the Emperor himself, Shen-tsung, who is in this book conveniently called by the name of his reign, Wan-li.* He was destined to have the longest reign of any Ming emperor, but in 1587 he was a youthful twenty-four, having been enthroned when not yet nine. Wan-li was a precocious and dutiful child who had willingly performed the extensive ceremonial duties of the emperor while also carrying forward his studies in calligraphy, history, and the classics. Besides such seasonal observances as ritual plowing, sacrifices to Heaven and Earth and the ancestors, and the proclamation of the year's calendar to the populace, daily morning audiences with the court required the Emperor's presence. These last proceedings, which were highly formal and were held before dawn, had been a grievous burden to previous emperors and had been slighted by several of Wan-li's predecessors, including his own apathetic father, the Lung-ch'ing Emperor. Wan-li, too, as he grew to manhood, found even a curtailed schedule of audiences too tedious to bear. Having donned the dragon robe so young, he had known few playmates or games; and when, at the age of ten, he developed a passion for calligraphy, this was discouraged. His chief tutor, Grand-Secretary Chang Chü-cheng, admonished him that His Majesty's brushwork had already exceeded expectation. "Calligraphy, he further argued, was after all a minor art which in itself added nothing to the empire's well-being. Sage rulers in Chinese history excelled only in virtue, not in aesthetic skills." When, later, Wan-li developed interests in horses, alcohol, and the "pleasure of women," the bureaucracy also disapproved, though the Emperor had become harder to discipline. Married at the age of fourteen, a father (by a concubine) at eighteen, he fell in love with another of his concubines, an intelligent fourteen-year-old named Lady Cheng, and his wish to designate as

---

*An emperor had three names: a personal name (in this case, Chu I-chün), a regnal name (Wan-li), and a temple name, appearing on all state papers after his death (Shen-tsung). The regnal name was the one by which he was popularly known.

heir to the throne his child by her, instead of the older son (his empress proving barren), estranged him from the bureaucracy for decades. He refused to hold audiences or make appointments, while the empire slid deeper into disorder.

Early in his reign, he had shown signs of initiative and a real interest in ruling. In 1585, during a severe drought, Wan-li, having "ordered local officials to pray for rain, but with no results," decided to perform the ceremony himself, at the Altar of Heaven, four miles from the palace entrance, and, furthermore, to walk the distance instead of being carried in a sedan chair. "For many residents of Peking, this was the one time in their lives they ever saw the Son of Heaven in person." And rain did come, albeit a month later. During this same period, Wan-li personally conducted drills and contests among the imperial guards, and four times visited, with a gala retinue, the site in the Peking suburbs where his own mausoleum was being constructed.

All these manifestations of imperial venturesomeness alarmed the bureaucracy, which, surrounding his every movement with precautionary quibbles, "succeeded in taking the joy out of the emperor's . . . outings." Wan-li made one more trip to his mausoleum, in 1588, and thereafter remained within the confines of the palace for more than three decades, an all-time record for imperial stasis. During the centuries of the dynasty, "the monarchy had become such a highly stylized institution that no thinking man could occupy the dragon seat with comfort." As a kind of lightning rod to attract the mandate of Heaven, the pinnacle of government had primarily to remain motionless. If an emperor, during one of the long tutorial sessions that began immediately after sunrise, inadvertently crossed his legs, the lecturer was obliged to interrupt himself with the question "Can the ruler himself neglect the principle of propriety?", which was repeated until the Son of Heaven returned his leg to its proper position. Small wonder that emperors rebelled with debauchery and apathy; small wonder that Wan-li, all his attempts to evince dynamism in the imperial role systematically discouraged, went on strike, and devoted himself to the company of Lady Cheng and, it was whispered, opium.

Mr. Huang deserves gratitude, in these times of cultural intro-
spection, for providing a study of decadence. For if it is not exactly
clear why organisms, composed of replaceable cells, decline toward
death, it is even less so why nations and civilizations do. The
genetic endowment of each generation is presumably equal; as
Melville said, "Believe me, my friends, that men not very much
inferior to Shakespeare are this day being born on the banks of the
Ohio." True, some royal lines, like the Merovingians, were inbred
into feebleness; but inability was not the problem of the Wan-li
Emperor or of his chief advisers, who had achieved their positions
by way of almost purely academic performance—a civil service of
intelligentsia, screened by standards as rigorous as any meritocracy
has ever imposed upon itself. The paralysis of the government
leaders had causes beyond themselves, in the cultural organism they
labored to perpetuate. A state differs from an individual in that,
having evolved in reaction to certain factors in the engendering
environment, it then becomes in itself an environment, discourag-
ing further adaptation.

The Ming dynasty, Mr. Huang informs us, was marked by a
"reliance on ideology as an instrument of government [that] was
in many respects unprecedented, both in intensity and in scope."
It supplanted, after one of those periods of turmoil which faithfully
alternate in Chinese history with periods of stability and stagnation,
the short-lived Mongol dynasty founded by Marco Polo's genial
host Kublai Khan, and was intended as a doctrinaire reversion to
the native Chinese agrarian simplicity. The Hung-wu Emperor,
who founded the dynasty, "systematically destroyed the empire's
large landowners and wealthy households and imposed a strin-
gently puritanical standard of living on the rest of the educated
elite, insisting that they were civil servants of the general popula-
tion in the literal sense of the word *servant.*" At all levels, the gap
between self-interest and public morality was to be minimized. The
population of administrators was greatly reduced, and each village
was expected to be self-policing, with two pavilions in it, "one to
commend the good deeds of the residents and the other to reprove
evil-doers." The Hung-wu Emperor had executed the only three
prime ministers his dynasty had ever had, and policymaking fell by

default to the grand-secretaries, whose office had originally been to recast the Emperor's declarations into an elegant prose style.

By 1587, the Ming dynasty had passed its bicentennial, and it is not surprising that as the puritanical impulse faded its rather utopian institutions degenerated into make-believe: into an emperor immobilized by the mystical, inspirational, and impersonal aspect of his role; a bureaucracy enslaved to graft and a self-protective conformity; and a land where innovations in the conduct of war and the administration of peace, if not strictly impossible, were so hedged about by caution and inertia as to become anomalous episodes. The logic of the status quo resisted technology (even though the Chinese had probably invented it, gunpowder was a minor element in their late-sixteenth-century warfare) and international trade; the internal passage and exchange of revenue and supplies, based upon the simplistic principle of transmission at the lowest level and at the shortest distance convenient, was overwhelmed by the shifting complexities of the empire. Two inexorable factors—the accumulation of population and the receding of the revolutionary moment—rendered the founding ideology burdensome to the point where, Mr. Huang concludes, it no longer mattered "whether the ruler was conscientious or irresponsible . . . whether the civil officials were honest or corrupt."

Analogies with modern-day China are withheld, though the American reader might fancy in the Ming ideals—a selfless bureaucracy, a self-disciplining populace, a flawless leader who rules through words—resemblances to Mao's China. How well the present government of that ancient nation can temper what Grand-Secretary Shen Shih-hsing once called the *yang* of government's "professed moral tone" with the *yin* of "hidden desires and motivations" remains to be seen, and is one of the great questions upon the world stage. Closer to home, our own revolutionary and originally puritanical and agrarian nation has passed its own bicentennial, and a professed moral tone has returned to the saddle, debonairly beckoning us back to the simplicities of Adam Smith. An enlightened selfishness will generate a nation, our own dynastic fathers suggested, which is a difference of emphasis rather than kind from the state-sponsored enlightenment and *de facto* decentralization of the Ming compromise. Some tension between private and public good exists at the heart of any social contract, and perhaps all resolutions of it are impermanent. American individualism would seem to have found its own bad fruits in the litter, vandalism, random predation, and greedy architecture of our cities, and the chopped-up, ravaged, tawdry sprawl between. A little harmonizing geomancy is clearly called for. As for the Ming, their decline might have been more sympathetically located by Mr. Huang within the context of China's vast cyclical history and its globally unique cultural continuity. The Manchus, invading from the north, like the Mongols, supplanted the Ming; they were able to impose the pigtail but could not persuade the Chinese to cease binding women's feet, and—after their own long and inglorious decline, which reached its terminus in 1912—were absorbed into the population. *1587, A Year of No Significance,* for all its scholarship, has the surreal visionary quality of Kafka's beautiful and frustrating story "The Great Wall of China." There the great wall is built piecemeal, with gaps rumored to be left within its ungraspable extent, and a messenger from the dying Emperor's bedside, though he moves with great haste, never reaches the outermost gate of the palace. "Just so," Kafka's nameless narrator says, "as hopelessly and as hopefully, do our people regard the Emperor. They do not know what Emperor is reigning, and there exist doubts regarding even the name of the dynasty."

ART AND ACT

Gaiety in the Galleries

ART AND ACT, by Peter Gay. 265 pp., with illustrations. Harper & Row, 1976.

Under the snappy title *Art and Act* Peter Gay has marshalled, his subtitle tells us, considerations *On Causes in History.* The historical events he has chosen to examine, however, surprise us by being not battles or conferences but artists: Manet, Gropius, and Mondrian. His closely worded introduction states, "To analyze the structure of historical causation by means of those who paint pictures and design houses rather than those who lie for money or kill for glory was to affirm what I have called the essential unity of historical reality and the unity of method that underlies the diversity of historical investigation." What has caused this particular analysis and affirmation—what has caused, that is, *Art and Act*—appears to be this: a historian, Mr. Gay, famous for his studies of the Enlightenment and lately with the problem of historical causation much on his mind, was invited to give a series of lectures at an art school, the Cooper Union. To say that Mr. Gay acquitted himself brilliantly is to admit that the case called for acquittal; in order "to deal with art as a piece of history," as the introduction puts it, Mr. Gay had to make himself into an art historian, for an audience of art students. The prodigious bibliography (three hundred forty-two titles for a text of two hundred twenty-eight pages) indicates how assiduously he worked to supplement his already wide erudition. Unlike Mr. Gay's previous set of bound lectures, *Style in History*, *Art and Act* offers us no illuminations offhand. What the historian imparts to us of Manet, Gropius, and Mondrian he has set himself to learn, and the schizophrenic split of so many pages between the text and an anxious abundance of footnotes betrays a certain effort-fulness. The prose rarely relaxes, as so often it does in *Style in History*, into a droll simile (of Macaulay: "Much like a provincial hotel keeper of the old days, he constantly reappears to ask if everything is satisfactory") or a superbly confident simplification (of Ranke's historiography: "Power, then, is the march of God through the world").

Mr. Gay's careful exercise, in the Cooper Union lectures, of his momentary "license to concentrate on art professionally" invites the reader to share with the historian "the interest of the search and the exhilaration of discovery." We all have seen pictures by Manet and Mondrian, we all harbor some dim image of the Bauhaus and its products; eagerly we sally forth, thus brightly, scantly equipped, to beard Historical Cause in its Platonic den. It cannot be said that Mr. Gay encourages Platonic hopes. At the outset, he is discouragingly Aristotelian, pluralistic, circumspect: "I have . . . written these chapters to argue that every historical event has several causes, and several types of causes, and that our capacity to predict which causal hierarchy will eventually emerge is strictly circumscribed." All events, he tells us, are, in Freud's word, overdetermined; the Marxists to the contrary, historical science will uncover no formulas as beautifully reductive as Newton's or Einstein's physical laws. What may be ventured, in the matter of schematization, is a tripartite division of causes into immediate "releasers," short-range determinants, and long-range causes, and a comparable division of "worlds" ("Man lives in several worlds at once, each of them capable of supplying causes") into culture, craft, and the private sphere. Historians traditionally have searched the first realm for their significances, but the second and third matter—conspicuously so for artistic events. The world of craft inspires one of Gay's best sentences:

For most human beings, work, its possibilities and its frustrations, engrosses the foreground of existence, permeating their fundamental attitudes of hope, patience, rebelliousness, or despair, and invading on one side the public world of culture and, on the other, the intimate world of private life.

And contemplation of the private world, that of man's "family and his inner life," leads Gay to urge psychology upon historians:

The subjective dimension can never be far from the mind of the historian at work. . . . There is some repression in all social relations, some projection in all political activity, some sublimation in all aesthetic enterprise. The fantasies of politicians are historical material quite as much as their economic stakes and their ideals; in fact, their stakes and their ideals derive their shape largely from their fantasies. . . . The springs of action that are invisible are often more consequential than those that parade their power. . . . Therefore, in ways that historians have not yet fully grasped, all history must be in significant measure psychohistory.

The three "worlds of reality" have their internalized counterparts in "worlds of perception," as follows: culture/ideologies; craft/traditions; privacy/defenses. With the courage of his triadism, Mr. Gay then discusses his three subjects in three chapters triply subdivided, pursuing each artist through each world and finding Manet to demonstrate "The Primacy of Culture," Gropius "The Imperatives of Craft," and Mondrian "The Claims of Privacy." The scheme is scholastic in its rigor, but the rigor is lightened by the sheer interest and wit of Mr. Gay's many facts, observations, and correlations; and, as with any art book, one can always look ahead at the plates and try to imagine what will be said about them. The plates, by the way, are rather dinky, and black-and-white; the grayness does small harm to Gropius, but Manet and Mondrian without color are shadows of themselves.

The section on Gropius is the least exceptional, and amounts to a prescription for good architecture. "For Gropius, in short, the architect's obligation never changed. It was in the twentieth century A.D. what it had been in the fifth century B.C.—to make buildings that one could live in." Gropius is quoted in German—

"Das Bauhaus ist zum Bauen da!" ("The Bauhaus is for building!")—and in English: "Design is a consistent, step-by-step process in which all functions are harmonized, the psychological as well as the practical ones." The architect's acknowledgment of "the multiplicity of motives" nicely complements the historian's theme of multiple causation; Gropius is not, Gay emphasizes, Mies van der Rohe, who amiably decreed, "I think we should treat our clients as children." From the Bauhaus complex itself and the radically innovative Fagus shoe-last factory of 1911, to the Pan Am Building and his own house in Lincoln, Massachusetts, Gropius has attended to the client's needs and blended them with his own intuitions. Functionalism, in its founder's application, is "strikingly elastic." Mr. Gay, as much at home in German culture as in French, conducts a tour of the Berlin in which the young Gropius absorbed his first impressions of the architect's craft. The city in the years before 1914 was both "a chamber of horrors to study and to flee"—the bristling overblown monuments erected by the second Kaiser Wilhelm to honor the first—and "a museum of models to admire," including some timid beginnings of modernism and the ingenious neoclassic structures of Karl Friedrich Schinkel. The historian employs terms like "prophetic spatial intuitions" with an engaging verve; the illustrative plates of old Berlin are the most amusing in the book, and the best served by the halftone reproduction.

The curious bracketing of "privacy" and "defenses" seems made for the Mondrian chapter, a vivid piece of psycho-art-history. After sketching the cultural and craftsmanly background of Mondrian's breakthrough into abstract painting, and dealing somewhat gingerly with his theosophical beliefs, Mr. Gay focuses on the artist's private repressions. "His art is an art of exclusion, an elaborate ritual to evade invasions of privacy. . . . The inexpressiveness of Mondrian's art has its own eloquence; it is expressive of Mondrian's character." Mr. Gay finds just enough in Mondrian's life—his bachelorhood, his stark studios, his "personal fetish" of adopting the customs of whatever country he found himself in, his "almost maniacal fear of injuring his eyes"—to give convincing weight to this analysis:

No sentiment, no curves, no touching—that is how he lived and that is what his paintings proclaim. He, like his art, was full of emotions; the equilibrium for which he groped with such patience, such inventiveness, and such needy anxiety was anything but static. It was, as he himself insisted, dynamic, even if that dynamism had origins of which he was unaware. His paintings offer impressive evidence just how much beauty the talented can wrest from fear.

Art criticism like this builds itself into a reader's perceptions; Mondrian's canvases will never after look quite the same.

The Manet chapter appears to me the most problematical. Each of Gay's chapters defines itself against a misconception, an oversimplification, that exists, he implies, within received opinion. Mondrian's art is less metaphysical than we thought, and Gropius's architecture less functional. Manet, he seems to say, is less a modernist than has been claimed:

> Manet simply does not fit into the interpretation of modernism that dominates in our day. That interpretation sees a great transvaluation of values beginning, roughly, with the Impressionists and ending, roughly, with the Surrealists, as the impassioned protest of civilized artists and thinkers against the mechanization, the ugliness, the rootlessness, the sheer vulgarity of technological mass civilization. Modernism, in this view, is the hatred of the modern world, the rebellion of culture against culture.

Mr. Gay blows this straw man over with the revelation that a cloud of railroad steam is included in a lovely Manet painting of 1873. But who, really, has said that modernism comprises hatred of the modern world? The modernist classics by Joyce and Proust celebrate the world the authors knew, with a directness and even a naïveté previously reserved for poetry. *Ulysses* embraces cinematic technique; Proust pens homages to such modern inventions as the railroad, the telephone, the airplane. "Technological mass civilization" fascinates as much as it repels, and from Léger to Claes Oldenburg has entertained nuncios from the world of art. Art, in that it sets before us something not there before, is positive, and, in that it cannot much change the world around it, is permissive. Art fuelled on distaste will not run long. Manet was of his times, and cheerfully so. What *has* been said, I believe, is that his painting, for all its traditional vestiges and natural sunniness, marks a departure, a shift in the center of gravity, as definite, though as subtle, as the fiction of Stendhal. André Malraux, with a flamboyance that need not always be suspect, declaimed in *The Voices of Silence:*

> Manet's contribution, not superior but radically different, is the green of *The Balcony,* the pink patch of the wrap in *Olympia,* the touch of red behind the black bodice in the small *Bar des Folies-Bergère.* . . . [They] are obviously color-patches signifying nothing except color. Here the picture, whose background had been hitherto a recession, becomes a surface, and this surface becomes not merely an end in itself but the picture's *raison d'être.* Delacroix's sketches, even the boldest, never went beyond dramatizations; Manet (in some of his canvases) treats the world as—uniquely—the stuff of pictures.

Mr. Gay briefly cites this passage, and sniffs, "Certainly Manet was something of a *tachiste*—a passionate painter of colored patches— who permitted his subjectivity a prominent share in his aesthetic decisions. . . . Yet there is more to Manet's art, and to his modernism, than his kind of impulsive subjectivity." Here the historian risks becoming merely corrective and letting history become no more than a web of fussy qualifications. His concluding postscript states, "The vastly complicated intersection of potentialities pressing toward the actuality of the historical event is so richly textured that it seems almost impossible to disentangle, even with hindsight." This is a protestation rather than a proposition. Malraux's point about the patches of color offers a perspective, a thread through the tangle; he performs a historian's task by locating the *historic moment.* Manet in 1881, painting a bar girl at the Folies-Bergère, dabs in some red without a representational excuse; Gropius in 1911, designing a shoe-last factory, leaves out a corner support and joins two planes of glass at a right angle; Mondrian around 1914 (it is characteristic of artistic events to be chronologically elusive) covers a canvas with no more than vertical and horizontal lines—such are the "acts" that Mr. Gay promises to distinguish in his title, and that he all but loses within the infinite multiplicity and interrelatedness of historical circumstance. It is good, useful, and entertaining to know that Manet continued to consult his Academic master Couture and that he enjoyed strolling the new boulevards that Baron Haussmann had cut through Paris; but this is not why Manet is historic. Malraux attempts to tell us why, and though, as Mr. Gay reveals in *Style in History*, any history is to some extent stylized, the attempt must be made. Otherwise, the nightmare of medieval nominalism is upon us again, and by a kind of Zeno's paradox of infinite factual subdivision the Achilles of understanding can never overtake the gargantuan tortoise of reality.

In the history of art, we might venture another paradox: history must forget itself to happen. If, with what meagre historical imagination we have, we seize Manet in the first moment that he daubed on paint purely for the painting's sake, or Mondrian or Gropius or Giotto or Pollock in his breakthrough moment, we feel in each act not only a plenitude (ambition, intuition, expertise, delight, etc.) but an absence—a void that belongs to these creative acts. *Nothing is preventing them.* The technical and cultural inhibitions that for centuries barred a way have evaporated. "Why not?" is the most potent question an artist can ask himself; in the fabric of aesthetic imperatives, holes develop and wait undiscovered until a spirit sufficiently reckless or driven dives through them. Malraux's willingness to highlight—to put his intellectual chips upon—Manet's little "color-patches" helps define modern art and casts light backward on what Mr. Gay never mentions but what must strike any viewer of Manet's theatrical and historical tableaux: their utter, comical deadness. Assemblages like *The Execution of Emperor Maximilian* and *Ballet espagnol* have cogwheels but don't turn; they are stopped clocks. The figures in the ambitious early canvases like *The Old Musician* and the famous *Déjeuner sur l'herbe* look pasted-on; with an eerie air of mutual dissociation and an impudent outward gaze that might be the painter's, they float in a slippery, deliberately unreal space. Academism had to die in Manet before Impressionism could be born. This death, this drying-up, is itself a cause. The philistines rightly say that Pollock dribbled because he couldn't draw. He couldn't draw in the same way that Manet couldn't lend conviction to his dramatic tableaux: the socially derived energy behind the conventions had ceased. These cessations, the precondition of new beginnings, are as significant in a causal consideration of art history as innovations, and are perhaps a more fruitful region for the kind of psychological exploration that Mr. Gay calls for. His discussion of Mondrian's inabilities and refusals carves closer to the heart of the paintings, for me at least, than his warm but somehow fluffy appreciation of Manet. But he succeeds everywhere in making us think simultaneously about history and art, and in simultaneously displaying learning and sensitivity.

Tote That Quill

200 YEARS OF AMERICAN ILLUSTRATION, published in association with the Society of Illustrators. Text by Henry C. Pitz. 436 pp. Random House, 1977.

For people who can't bear to throw away old magazines, *200 Years of American Illustration* might save some attic space. It is more than four hundred pages thick, and contains over eight hundred artists. The oldest illustration reproduced is a copper engraving of the Boston Massacre by Paul Revere in 1776, and the year 1976 is represented by, among other images, a record-jacket portrait of Albert King by Milton Glaser, an alphabet in transparent dyes by Jözef Sumichrast, a fabric sculpture of Bella Abzug by Judith Jampel, a *New Yorker* cover by Lou Myers (of Uncle Sam), a *Newsweek* cover (of Patty Hearst) by Burton Silverman, a gruesome sci-fi monster attacking some wonderfully bulbous and naked earthlings by Boris W. Vallejo, and more than one brave Bicentennial poster. This richness of material, unfortunately, is tossed at the reader not much better organized than the print inside a spitball. The book has a preface by Mary Black, a foreword (spelled "forward") by Norman Rockwell, an introduction by Bob Crozier, and a short history of American illustration by Henry C. Pitz; and none of them quite prepare us for the abundant hodge-podge that follows, or quite spell out the curious criteria for this collection of illustrations. They are *not* illustrations: in the main, they are original works by illustrators, many of them never accepted for reproduction or intended to illustrate anything but the artist's wish to make his mark. A number of them are frankly billed as "self-promotion pieces." An exhibit of these works was assembled by the Society of Illustrators and put on at the New-York Historical Society late in 1976. The process, as described in Mr. Crozier's introduction, sounds strenuous but not systematic. "All of us who have worked on this undertaking are painfully aware that there are important omissions that might have been filled had time permitted. . . . There are also important sources known to us but neglected: most notably, the Library of Congress, the Smithsonian Institution, the Delaware Art Museum, the Brandywine Museum and many of the large and small museums, universities and publishing houses in the United States which house collections of illustrators' works." Well, what was *not* neglected? The Society of Illustrators' own collection, and those of a number of handy New York and Connecticut institutions, and those of some private collectors, including a husband and wife, Beverly and Ray Sacks, who are cloyingly identified with each credit as "The Art Couple." In the later sections, more than half the items are lent by the artists themselves.

While a great many works of interest and beauty are inevitably included in such a collection, it is far from a history of American illustration. The introduction mentions nine thousand items considered: a modest amount in a field so vast. Most important, an exhibit of original, as opposed to reproduced, pictures, however nicely it hangs in a museum, quite loses its point in a book where *all* the pictures are necessarily reproduced. An ideal omnibus of illustration—and I shall nominate, for purposes of invidious comparison, another recent omnibus, *America's Great Illustrators*, by Susan E. Meyer, as practically ideal—would seek out the illustrations in the magazines, books, and calendars where they appeared, and reproduce the best as best it can, reëngraving for especially brilliant effect some of those originals that survive.

200 Years of American Illustration has more than its share of technical slips and editorial carelessness. No editor, by the way, is identified. Mr. Pitz's forty-five pages of text are erratically illustrated by the accompanying plates, and eighteen lines of one column are nonsensically displaced. A lot of the plates are not dated, and, of those that are, one in the "1800s" section is dated 1906, one in the "1900s" is dated 1899, and one of the "1970s" is dated 1968. On at least three occasions, plates are scrambled; most dramatically, a scene of two old ladies sewing is titled *"When her leg was shattered by a bullet, she loaded the rifles,"* while a vigorous depiction of a shoot-out opposite passes as *"Family Circle."* The book was printed in Italy, and that may account for these confusions, though an Italian printer might have been thought to be aware of the difference between a priest and a Mercedes, which are also transposed. The reproduction, it should be said, seems excellent where the makeup does not call for an undue reduction in size, as it often does. This reader found a magnifying glass a necessary adjunct to conscientious perusal and, perhaps coincidentally, during this period applied to his oculist for a stronger prescription. The book is not easy on the eyes. Too many insipid, scratchy illustrations are crowded in, including three by Mr. Pitz. Because of the peculiar logic of the original exhibition's organization, which excluded works whose "originals were not readily available to us when our material was gathered," the nineteenth century is apportioned a mere thirty pages and the recent decades are overrepresented. The selections cavalierly range from cartoons on one side to easel paintings on the other. Even within the great latitude allowable to taste in a world as wide as popular illustration, certain slights and imbalances can be felt. Why only three gray little sketches by Austin Briggs when such relatively unadventurous and unpainterly laborers for the slicks as Jon Whitcomb and Al Parker are generously represented? Why devote color plates to Russell Patterson and Harry Beckhoff when the man they imitated, the short-lived genius Ralph Barton, appears through one sharply reduced, though delectable, book illustration? And haven't we all seen better black-and-white work by Rockwell Kent and Winslow Homer than appears in *200 Years of American Illustration?* And where, oh, where is an index? *America's Great Illustrators* has a fine one, although its artists are fewer and coherently grouped. In *200 Years,* the artists are scattered by the winds of layout through the chronological sections; a short biography of each is given at the back of the volume, but no cross-reference is supplied to the plates of their graphic work in this volume, or to the mention of their names in Mr. Pitz's brief history of American illustration.

Henry C. Pitz died a week after the exhibition opened at the New-York Historical Society, and had he lived he might have improved his account and better coördinated it with the plates that follow. Though clearly a lover of his subject, and full of information (Philadelphia in 1776 was the second-biggest English-speaking city in the world, we learn), he too often contents himself with mere lists of names, and Time-Marches-On portentousness: "The years immediately following Appomattox were touchy, troubled years and naturally the illustration world reflected the times." Or, of pen drawing: "The first of our ancestors who climbed down from his tree, picked up a broken twig, dipped it in berry juice and made some marks on a smooth rock, started the whole thing." Not much of a writer, he scratches his head and muses aloud: "Let us have a few things to say about the illustrator of historical themes, who must catch the flavor and fact of a given time, place and event." His ruminations lack the sociological thrust that even the definition of the word "illustration" needs. It is an illustrator, Norman Rockwell, who supplies what theoretical discriminations the book contains, and with an admirable pithiness:

> The illustrator has, unlike the painter, a primary interest in telling a story. If he does not do that, he fails. . . . That is the final value of the illustration: it enables the viewer to see in concrete terms what he has only vaguely felt or guessed before.

Illustrators, he goes on to say, "have been willing to work hard at the innumerable details which make up any successful illustration: background, people, facial expressions, 'props,' lighting and many more. But the total effect of their picture is to make anyone who sees it say, 'Yes, it is true.' "

This effect, of truth obtained through the accumulation of recognizable detail (as opposed to the truth of private vision and persuasive obsession), remains a hallmark of the art. Winslow Homer on the Civil War battlefields and George Catlin among the vanishing Indians were pictorial reporters sending back proto-photographs to be engraved laboriously on boxwood. Howard Pyle and N. C. Wyeth brought their dispatches from the past; their reconstructions of old costumes, weapons, and means of conveyance set the high informational standard with which motion pictures were to educate, subliminally, the audiences of costume epics. Popular illustration, like the movies, was simultaneously a great softener and a great clarifier of experience. Even such a superbly stylized representation as Coles Phillips's 1921 watercolor of a maid in black uniform merged with her black background as she stoops to peer into a keyhole tells us all about the overlapped lace of her uniform and the faceted structure of a glass doorknob. The illustrator, against the seductive modern tug of the minimal, tries to give a little extra; in an oil like Mead Schaeffer's *Interrogating the Prisoner* (for *McCall's*, 1926) the face of every soldier is worth looking at.

No one, of course, more lavishly crowded his illustrations with well-observed detail than Rockwell himself. *200 Years of American Illustration* contains the 1958 *Saturday Evening Post* cover wherein the gentle comedy of the shrivelled, hard-bitten jockey being weighed by a fat official is almost eclipsed by the porcelain-and-iron vividness of the scale itself. The jockey's spattered boots also have an intensity far beyond the call of duty. Rockwell began to be himself from the feet up; his shoes have whole lives in them. One must turn to *America's Great Illustrators* to see how he evolved from a young imitator of J. C. Leyendecker, even to the showily parallel brush-strokes (*Post* cover, 1919), into a hyper-realist whose barbershop interior (*Post* cover, 1950) yields nothing in skill and reflective interplay to a Richard Estes. It differs from an Estes in the coziness of the details Rockwell has chosen to illuminate, and in its central cozy implication that at the back of every small-town barbershop lurks a bunch of music-loving old men; but the barber chair, the reflected light on the stovepipe, the crack in the corner of the big window the viewer is looking through—this is amazing painting. Now that the great family slicks have folded, realistic illustration survives in *Field & Stream* and *Sports Afield*, whose hunter-readers are still alert to natural appearances, and, surrealistically, in *Playboy* and *Oui,* where sinister waxen images consort with the sharp photographic focus on the flesh. And perhaps some nostalgia for literalism is expressed in the newly fashionable mode of fabric sculpture, which painstakingly scissors, pieces, and pokes into being illustrations as rich and nappy as Pyle's and as broadly luminous as Maxfield Parrish's.

There is no such thing as a merely realistic art, of course. The need to arrest, to symbolize, has pulled the illustrator toward abstraction and simplification. Parrish, Leyendecker, and Edward Penfield were masters of the poster style, suited not only for covers but for advertisements. Leyendecker, indeed, was most himself in his glorifications of the male on behalf of Arrow shirts, and his Wilson-era Chesterfield ads projected images powerful enough to be recently revived for a contemporary campaign. Penfield echoed Japanese design even in his signature but had, like Winslow Homer, an instinctive American dignity: the beautiful economy and balance of machines made out of wood. However, leafing through the many pages of *200 Years,* one is struck repeatedly by a baroque dash, an insistent tendency, almost like a wind blowing through, toward the imbalanced and the vertiginous. The blank spaces that many illustrations must leave for overlaid lettering accounts for some of this; but the wish to capture horses at full gallop, or a bobcat in the middle of his leap, or an airplane at dizzying tilt, seems aesthetically intrinsic, as if the illustrator, tied to representation while easel painting exploded into Fauvism, Cubism, and total abstraction, were straining at his leash. N. C. Wyeth, the least contented of the great illustrators, the most openly envious of the easel painters, anticipates, in his sweeping spaces if not in his histrionic gestures, the art of his son Andrew; but the lineal descendant of the older Wyeth's precipitous blues and blue-greens is the smooth purple sky posed like a backdrop behind Jon Whitcomb's *Dancing Couple,* for *Redbook.* The tawny ochre desert stretches of Remington return as the widths of orange fabric in a girl's apartment as stylized by Al Parker for *McCall's,* illustrating (if we read her quizzical gaze aright) her loneliness, the need of all this orange space for a man, as emphasized by her asymmetric and huddled position within it. The strenuous romance of nature, in fifty years of American illustration, has become the glossy romance of mating. Recorders of vanishing realities like Remington, fresh illuminators of old myths like Pyle and Parrish, and acute if uncritical social observers like Gibson and Rockwell give way to glib traders in the furniture of domesticated sex.

Any visitor to Russia who ventures (usually to his Westernized guide's embarassment) into a place, such as the modern rooms of the Tretyakov Art Gallery in Moscow, where examples of "Socialist Realism" are hung, cannot but greet with the joy of recognition the very style of American magazine illustration in its prime. The same finesseful painterliness lavished upon inanimate objects (bicycles, tractors), the same stagy tableaux, the same mannequin faces, the same hollow glamour. Socialist Realism glamorizes the proletariat and the Revolution as advertising art does the bourgeoisie and consumerism. But, then, what art, including the revered statuary of Greece, has not been to some extent glamorizing? Perhaps Roman portrait busts, Goya, Hieronymus Bosch, and certain Dutch landscapists—but even with these, art's need to fix the essence and find the typical has the effect of improving the world.

The case against illustration as art was put as strongly as it could be by N. C. Wyeth:

> The underlying quality of every great work is truth, and the magazines of today, with their commercial spirit, their limitations of picture production, and their price limitations make it impossible for a man to paint pictures for them. The same love, the same enthusiasm that goes to make illustration goes to make painting—the one is born into the world under limitations that choke and distort and soon die—the other is born full and free as the air: if it ripens it will stand as a perfect expression of those loves and will last forever.

One wonders if Wyeth would find today's lucrative, centralized, campy, dealer-dominated art world still conducive to love and freedom. When has art not had patrons, market requirements, limitations? The Sistine Chapel, after all, is a set of illustrations. And in an unplanned way the illustrations rather haphazardly gathered here, by containing in their impure admixture so much of the commercial hopes, standardized nostalgia, common dreams, and passing chic of the last two hundred years, have a resonance not present in the high art of the Republic. Bend low, for example, over the exquisite little pen-and-ink drawing Steven Kidd did for the Sunday *News* in 1936. The black air is thick with oblong snow-flakes; the young gallant, in full Knickerbocker regalia, lifts his cane with a swirl of his cape to urge forward the young maiden who in perfect profile dances through the snow in ballet slippers. Her feet will soon be soaked and cold, this baroque moment of perfect melodramatic swirl will have vanished like the snow itself; but in the meantime we are there, not as witnesses but as participants, entering in as children enter in, with our wishes, wishing that the world were so harmlessly energetic, so simultaneously dashing and sheltering, so Christmassy and clean, so black and white.

Wright on Writing

ABOUT FICTION, by Wright Morris. 182 pp. Harper & Row, 1975.

Wright Morris's *About Fiction* tackles this moot subject with the pawky, resistant prose of his own fiction: "Before they made tools, perhaps before they made trouble, men and women were busy at the loom of fiction looking for clues to becoming more human." This sentence, from the first page, demands rereading; we are put off by the folksy "before they made trouble" and the confusion of metaphors that has us looking for clues in a loom. The opening chapters have, as a whole, the air of being a "big subject" essay assigned on an exam; the bright but flustered student fills his blue book with ingratiating archness—

> Fiction does play a role in what we call education and weights the arms of girls at the turn of stairways, where young men whose interests are more than literary come to their aid

—and aggressive mystification—

Each time the writer creates and solves the problems of fiction, he makes it possible for men and women to live in this world. The manner in which this fiction affirms the world is a measure of its quality: the manner in which it rejects the world is a measure of its fantasy.

However, as Mr. Morris begins to examine specific authors, books, and sentences, in the kind of dry and loving light that illumines his photographs of Nebraska feed mills and bureau tops, the discussion gathers confidence and becomes a personal but credibly specific analysis of just what happened to American literature. The authors he quotes by way of illustration are a small, lean band: Stephen Crane, Mark Twain, Gertrude Stein, Hemingway, Fitzgerald, Richard Henry Dana, and some few others. Foreigners frequently cited are Joyce, Mann, Camus, Céline, Beckett. Wright Morris does not quote writers fond of Latinisms or complexly balanced sentences—no Melville, no Proust, one brief sentence by Henry James. His most favored passages—the first lines of Crane's "The Open Boat" and Camus's *The Stranger,* a number of sentences from Stein's *Three Lives*—share a weathered, fondled bareness, a sunbleached something that blends with his own style and leads naturally into his basic discussion, which is of the vernacular voice in fiction.

The vernacular—meaning, in the Latin, "born in one's house, native"—arose on the American frontier as "a language that departed in wondrous ways from the 'written' language of the popular novel." Coincident with the emergence of self-consciously American writing, "photography provided the writer with the assurance of an objective, irreducible reality he needed merely the talent, and the candor, to describe." The notion evolved that "an accurate rendering of what was 'real' fulfilled the possibilities of fiction." What was the instrument for rendering the real? The vernacular: "American writers were . . . the first to intuit (through Stein's example) that the catchall web of the vernacular reflected the mind at its conscious level. This new melodious tongue shaped the writer to a greater extent than he shaped the language. . . . This confidence in the language had the effect of depressing the imagination." And to this day, Mr. Morris concludes, the American writer is stuck with a depressed imagination and a debilitating dependence upon facts, upon experience. Hemingway "recouped his used-up resources by turning to wars, bull-fights, and safaris"; Mailer writes a "novel-as-history [that] must make room for Mailer, since it would not be much without him." Others, after Huck Finn, tell boys' stories: "The coinage of a language suitable to a boy is the headwater of our literature." But not even an American writer can remain a boy forever; there is "a predictable tendency to peter out. This is so common we are highly impressed by the occasional exception. Early achievement and premature recession may well be the linchpin in our cult of youth." The point, though often enough made, is stated by Mr. Morris with a heartfelt, even stricken eloquence:

> The books we love are about growing up more than about being grown. By its very nature the vernacular is sympathetic to first love, first triumph, and first rejections, but inclined to show wear in the repeat performances.
>
> That he begins with a bang, often very large, then fades away to a repetitive whimper, can be traced to the writer's conviction that personal experience, preferably rugged, is his primary source material. When this lode of ore is depleted, he has shot his bolt. It is possible to postpone this crisis by pursuing life, as in a safari, bringing back for the stay-at-homes the loves and trophies of faraway places. But even this is at best a delaying tactic, based on the writer's virility and vigor. There is a place in it for the mature man—the big-game hunter with his female trophies—but there is no place for an old man whose life, if not his work, is behind him.

Rather surprisingly, Morris goes on to deplore, in stern sociological manner, the poor position of the elderly in American society, and to prescribe, for the world's woes as well as literature's, a surcease of the "ego inflation" of Western man: "For some centuries now the Western ego has been culturally force-fed, like the geese whose liver is prized by gourmets, until its original and organic function has become a malfunction." Luckily, help is on the way: "A sense of the aggregate, whether we like it or not, is displacing our sense of uniqueness." The flight into space, as well as earthly overcrowding, he seems to feel, will assist this deflationary trend, which may release American—and, by now, European—fiction from the trap of the vernacular/photographic/personal.

Wright Morris writes from his own long experience as an American author. The spell of Stein, Sherwood Anderson, and Hemingway still weaves about him, a scant generation younger. His rural Nebraska background gave him a perspective that is rarer now than he may suppose. "The [American] writer felt that he had gained free access to a vast and unexploited continent, comparable to a view of the plains from the eastern bluffs of the Missouri": the comparison, which would be hollow rhetoric for many, comes naturally to him. His arresting formulation of an interaction in the rise of photography and vernacular realism tells us less about literary history than about his own preoccupations; "vernacular" is often what his style too deliberately is, and no other American writer save Eudora Welty and—in his collaboration with Walker Evans—James Agee has granted more dignity and importance to the art of photography. Attempting to read one of the novels-cum-photographs that Morris produced in the Forties, I was struck by what hard going they are: the fine photographs crush rather than support the prose with their superior detail and absolute sunlight. Two hugely different worlds seem juxtaposed, even when the words "I could see the front of Uncle Ed's house" face a photograph of (presumably) that very house. The light whereby we see images in fiction is not sunlight but the incandescence of a moral issue, a human progress whose pilgrim's discriminations highlight data with relevance. The merely representational, in fiction, is inert. Morris senses this, yet remains—true to his American self—captive to it. He writes much of "imagination" as the antidote to our documentary habits and dependence on "raw life" but he doesn't define "imagination" except as a dreaming, an itself raw, infantile faculty—"the faculty, in its infancy, that led [the writer] to write." He writes of "man" as if a more generous subject for fiction might be found (animals? vegetables? minerals?), and of "imagination" as if its rebirth and growth will necessarily follow from a "palpable shrinkage of . . . ego." But the faculty of imagination, as traditionally exercised in fiction, was called into strength, and led into areas beyond the reportorial and confessional, by the egoistic assumption that what men do immensely, cosmically matters. The breakup of novels into isolated sensations and facts, interesting in proportion to their accuracy, marks one stage of the displacement of "our sense of uniqueness"; the next stage is the entropy wherein even accuracy ceases to be interesting and multitudinousness and nothingness are indistinguishable. In such a situation, art longs to become propaganda; a heightened "sense of the aggregate" is less likely to produce wider and more imaginative tales than the brutally pointed "people's art" of collectivist countries. There is an inverse relation between the individual ego and the generic ego which Mr. Morris does not explore. In an artist as selfless and imaginative as Shakespeare, the circle of his being was completed by a host of emerging nationalistic and fading medieval assumptions. Now, even to write "Man" with a capital "M" embarrasses us. There is no scaffolding of abstraction, that is, whereupon the novel might climb away from its present condition as a disguised diary.

About Fiction should be read not only for its searching-out of the problematical but for its pithy appreciations of the achieved. As a responder to writing, Mr. Morris is bracingly virile—he grips each book like a man shaking hands with another—and aphoristic. He ends his long compound essay (was it ever a series of lectures?) with a sampler of modern fiction he likes; his sharp-eyed and sharp-tongued observations hold the life of truth that just evades his general theorizing:

> There is little of this artful "distance" in Lawrence, where we are seldom free of the sound of his breathing.

> Ian Fleming . . . faced a problem that was subtle: he wanted to neither insult the intelligence of the reader nor, more important, stimulate it.

> Few books come into this world with the perfection of a bird's egg, and this [*The Great Gatsby*] is one of them.

> [Sherwood Anderson's] world is dimly lit, shadow-dappled by trees that line dirt roads and open out on to fields, the air fragrant with the smell of grass that the sunlight seldom gets to.

Borges Warmed Over

BORGES: A READER, edited by Emir Rodriguez Monegal and Alastair Reid, translated from the Spanish by many hands, 368 pp, Dutton, 1982.

Will the traffic in Jorge Luis Borges, once a mere trickle along a few side streets of Buenos Aires and now a thundering jam in the literary capitals of the Western world, bear the addition of *Borges: A Reader?* This volume's dust jacket claims that the mighty Argentine fantasist "has come into English in haphazard fashion, so that the growing numbers of his readers have had to track him down through a confusion of incomplete collections, to piece him together from a set of displaced parts." That this additional incomplete collection, pieced together of poetry, fiction, criticism, journalism, and typically fragmentary Borgesian self-revelations, clears the matter up seems to me moot. Its chronological arrangement, its inclusion of a number of early writings hitherto not translated into English, its biographical and bibliographical summaries, and the individual comments by Mr. Monegal on each of the one hundred eighteen items in the anthology are all special and valuable. But as a selection *Borges: A Reader* lacks the direct authority of the *Personal Anthology* chosen by Borges, edited by Anthony Kerrigan, and issued by Grove Press in 1967. As an introduction to Borges's work, it lacks the stunning directness and purity of *Ficciones*; a reader unacquainted with this writer would do better to begin with that collection, whose publication in English, in 1962, put Borges on our cultural map, or with the more extensive and partly duplicative *Labyrinths,* brought out by New Directions in that same year. Even the bilingual *Selected Poems 1923–1967,* edited by Borges's energetic quondam handmaiden Norman Thomas di Giovanni, would serve as a smoother entrée into the master's universe. Borges has been an all-round literary performer—poet, translator, lecturer, anthologist, parodist, editor, librarian—but his short fiction (there is no long fiction) constitutes his ticket to fame and immortality, and *Borges: A Reader* omits such gems of the slender canon as "The Library of Babel," "The Garden of Forking Paths," and "Funes,

the Memorious." The editors' introduction admits that "the afi-
cionado will notice some of the omissions" but pleads permissions
difficulties. They offer instead, along with little classics like "Tlön,
Uqbar, Orbis Tertius," "The Circular Ruins," and "The South,"
a number of early and lesser pieces, some of them uncollected by
Borges in Spanish. The chronological arrangement, which for
many an author might show a shape of development, in Borges's
case confirms our impression that few major writers granted long
life have proved so loyal to their initial obsessions and demonstrated
so little fear of repeating themselves. "I am decidedly monoto-
nous," he himself has written.

If the book with all its other scholarly apparatus had included an
index, we might better trace the remarkable recurrence of topics
and allusions. The exact same ninety-word quotation from Chester-
ton, with the identical ellipsis, is cited three times—on pages 143,
219, and 231. A poem by Chesterton is described as "physically
stirring, like the proximity of the sea," and two pages later it is said
of Faulkner's *Unvanquished* that it is one of those books "that touch
us physically like the nearness of the sea." A curious speculation by
Coleridge ("If a man could pass through Paradise in a dream, and
have a flower presented to him as a pledge that his soul had really
been there . . .") is the subject of an essay of 1945 and comes back
("All at once, I remembered one of Coleridge's fantasies") in a short
story of thirty years later, "The Other." The very first item in
Borges: A Reader is a poem, from 1923, that fuses dawn in Buenos
Aires with a haunting sense of insubstantiality—"that tremendous
conjecture / of Schopenhauer and Berkeley / which declares the
world / an activity of the mind"—to achieve a tone echoed in the
very last lines of the book: "And to think that night would not
exist / without those tenuous instruments, the eyes." Dreams, laby-
rinths, mirrors, multiplications approaching infinity, a plurality of
inefficient and even malevolent gods, the dizzying paradox and
negation of Berkeleyan idealism, Zeno's second paradox, Nie-
tzsche's eternal return, the hidden individual destiny, the hard fate
of gaucho knife fighters and Anglo-Saxon warriors, the manipula-
tions of chance, the Minotaur and the tiger and the leopard, the

pressing mystery of nondescript suburbs and empty plains, the something elusive in the quality of identity itself—Borges early claimed these themes and has never let go of them.

The favorite English authors of his childhood were Stevenson, Wells, and Lewis Carroll, and he has never let go of them, either, throughout a lifetime of reading. His praise of Wilde and Shaw is heartfelt; his homage to Joyce and James rather grudging. His own fiction, though not altogether fantastical (there is a quality of endless afternoons, of tinted drabness, which he can always achieve in a phrase or two, and which transports our imaginations to a real locale), evinces little impulse toward the baring of reality and the exposure of sentimentality in the heroic modernist manner of, say, Hemingway. In an arresting essay on Apollinaire, he states, "Of all the obligations that an author can impose upon himself, the most common and doubtlessly most harmful is that of being modern." Apollinaire himself is distinguished as "so unmodern that modernity seemed picturesque, and perhaps even moving, to him." Not so Borges. Whereas the multilingual erudition of Eliot and Pound was part of a worldwide search for an authenticity that would help make the native language and tradition new, Borges's erudition, with its quizzical touchstones of quotation and its recondite medieval and Oriental references, is a parody of erudition wherein the researched and the fabricated lie side by side ironically—a vast but claustrophobically closed system that implies there is no newness under the sun. The must of alchemists' libraries pervades his learning; his chaos of texts ("chaotic enumeration" is, indeed, named by Mr. Monegal as one of Borges's rhetorical devices) exists as a metaphor for the "black labyrinth of blind atoms" that constitutes the universe, once the "monstrous" option of the three-headed God has been discounted. Borges's profound admiration for the Catholic apologist Chesterton makes one of the stranger father-son pairings in the annals of influence. Of the older writer's ebullient apologetics, Borges, in his appreciation of 1936, wryly writes, "The certainty that none of Christianity's attractions can really compete with its outlandish unlikelihood is so notorious in Chesterton that his most uplifting eulogies always remind me of 'Elegy to Madness'

or 'Murder Considered as One of the Fine Arts.' " This Latin lover
of sinister secrets finds one in his Anglo-Saxon model: "The pow-
erful work of Chesterton, the prototype of physical and moral
sanity, is always on the verge of becoming a nightmare." In
an essay, "On Chesterton," not reprinted here but published in
Other Inquisitions (1964), Borges says, "Something in the make-
up of his personality leaned toward the nightmarish, something
secret, and blind, and central." Those last three adjectives give us
the Borgesian essence, that terrible central blankness around
which his invocations of "atrocity," "mysterious monotony,"
and "masked heresiarchs" revolve like chronic planets around a
dead sun.

Borges: A Reader lacks just that elegance of the minimal which
Borges's work and the books in which it is usually bound invariably
possess. The page is too big and the type too small; the clutter of
editorial addenda, with their portentous abbreviations (a typical
note reads " 'About Oscar Wilde' Sp. title: 'Sobre O.W.' Pub. *Los
Anales de B.A.*, Dec. 1946, col. *O.I.* "), cumbersomely enwraps
Borges's own nice pedantries; the effect of reading the selection
straight through is of a long bumpy ride in a closed carriage. For
this systematic peruser, at least, the claustral, confused feelings
dampened even his pleasure in those miniature masterpieces he had
read with delight elsewhere, in volumes less farraginous. The chief
value of this collection lies in the twenty-eight hitherto untrans-
lated pieces; though they do not enhance Borges's reputation, they
do enhance our sense of him as an Argentine, especially as a rather
pugnacious young intellectual dandy seeking to reconcile his pre-
cocious, cosmopolitan awareness with a blood loyalty to the drab
and often brutal backwater where he was born.

We learn, in a seven-page chronology of his life supplied by Mr.
Monegal, that Borges was taught English early, at home; that he
announced at the age of six a determination to be a writer; that in
1914 his father, a lawyer and teacher and sometime poet, retired
early because of failing eyesight and moved his family, including
the fifteen-year-old "Georgie," to Switzerland, where the First
World War stranded them for four years. While there, young

Borges learned French and Latin and taught himself German. He discovered and read Whitman, the French Symbolists, and German philosophy, Schopenhauer and Nietzsche above all. After the war, the Borges family moved to Lugano, near the Italian border (Borges's languages include Italian), and then to several places in Spain, where the twenty-year-old author prepared two books he never published, participated in the literary activities of an avant-garde group called the Ultraists, and somewhat belatedly encountered the classic literature of his first language, Spanish.

In 1921, he returned to Buenos Aires for a year, where he fell in with a native philosopher and friend of his father's, Macedonio Fernández. In this period, he helped found two little magazines, *Prisma* and *Proa*, and published his first book, a collection of poems called *Fervor de Buenos Aires*, though his fervor did not prevent a second extended trip to Europe. The early pages of *Borges: A Reader* contain poems—some of them among his most popular—that show him taking deliberate possession of the scenery and history of Buenos Aires; the act of repossession, by a mind that has wandered far, characterizes his literary production ever after, and gives it its air of haunting dislocation, of surreal specificity and abysmal formlessness, of nostalgia for the circumambient. His first essay reprinted in *Borges: A Reader* tabulates the sometimes poetic inscriptions on old horse-drawn wagons. Its original title, "Séneca en las Orillas" ("Seneca in the Slums"), was dropped, as perhaps too telling. Other, later essays examine, with the lofty tenderness of a visitor from an ancient civilization, such local phenomena as the tango and the card game called *truco*. The tango, like the knife fights that so persistently flash through his work, manifests for him a popular, timeless religion—"the hard, blind religion of courage, of being ready to kill and to die."

As a young man of letters in Buenos Aires, in the long years while his unique and elaborately pseudo-factual "fictions" were incubating, Borges was a dashing critic, dismissing Argentine barbarism ("Our Inadequacies," 1931) and accepted aesthetic theory ("Narrative Art and Magic," 1931; "Prologue to 'The Invention of Morel,' " 1940) with adamant aplomb. Refuting the opinion that Edgar Wallace constructed better plots than Chesterton, Borges wrote, "I promise my reader that those who say such things are lying and that the fiery depths of Hell will be their final dwelling place." Proclaiming himself "free from every superstition of modernity," he attacked the "psychological novel":

> The typical psychological novel is formless. The Russians and their disciples have demonstrated, tediously, that no [motivation] is impossible. A person may kill himself because he is so happy, for example, or commit murder as an act of benevolence. Lovers may separate forever as a consequence of their love. And one man can inform on another out of fervor or humility. In the end such complete freedom is tantamount to chaos.

As an alternative he conceived of an ideal "adventure story" that "does not propose to be a transcription of reality" but is instead "an artificial object, no part of which lacks justification." This efficiency is akin to magic, which assumes, as Frazer established in *The Golden Bough*, that "things act on each other at a distance through a secret sympathy." For novels, the "only possible integrity" is that of "magic, in which—clear and defined—every detail is an omen and a cause." However special and rarefied these theories seem, Borges read with a tireless catholicity in those years. He gave the readers of *El Hogar*, an illustrated weekly, whose book section he edited, capsule biographies and trenchant reviews of, among many, Oswald Spengler, Virginia Woolf, and William Faulkner ("That William Faulkner is the leading novelist of our time is a conceivable affirmation"). For Victoria Ocampo's periodical *Sur*, Borges did movie reviews, and the few that are printed here show an Olympian mind robustly engaged with a popular art—an art, like his own, of shadows.* Of the Spencer Tracy version of *Dr. Jekyll and Mr. Hyde*, Borges complained that not one but two actors (he

---

*And an art that met his criteria of artificiality and magicalness: "One kind of novel, the slow-moving psychological variety, attempts to frame an intricate chain of motives akin to those of real life. . . . In the adventure novel, cumbersome motivation of this kind is inappropriate; the same may be said for the short story and for the endless spectacular fictions made up in Hollywood, with the silvery images of Joan Crawford, that are read and reread the whole world over. A quite different sort of order rules them, one based not on reason but on association and suggestion—the ancient light of magic."

nominates George Raft as the other) should play the two personae. Of Orson Welles's masterpiece, he said, "*Citizen Kane* will last as certain films of Griffith or Pudovkin 'last'; nobody denies their worth, but nobody goes back to see them. They suffer from gigantism, from pedantry, from tedium." Such an objection, on an immediate aesthetic instance, to a well-made piece of cinematic magic reveals more of the artist's mind, perhaps, than his rather hermetic formal theories. One might wish that the book consisted entirely of such fresh and surprising matter, and that an author whose oeuvre already savors of stringent selection and encyclopedic compression had been spared the ungainly compliment of a superfluous recycling.

Pinter's Unproduced Proust Printed

THE PROUST SCREENPLAY, by Harold Pinter. 177 pp. Grove Press, 1977.

One approaches *The Proust Screenplay* determined not to complain that Proust's language has vanished. How could it not, given the foolhardy and fascinating idea of making a movie script of the immense *À la recherche du temps perdu* (as Mr. Pinter calls it, implying that he worked from the French rather than from the C. K. Scott Moncrieff translation, *Remembrance of Things Past*)? Still, one must marvel at how the playwright, a master of the laconic/elliptical/polymorphous-abrupt style of modern stagecraft, has cut this lushest of novels down from two million words to a string of four hundred fifty-five shots, some a mere "momentary yellow screen" and others as simple as

47. MOTHER'S EYES.

Unlike John Collier's "screenplay for cinema of the mind" of *Paradise Lost,* Pinter's script makes no attempt to flesh out the dialogue with descriptive writing; and, unlike the produced screen version of *Ulysses,* it places no significant reliance on the author's words in voice-over; and, unlike Ingmar Bergman's published scenarios or Arthur Miller's *Misfits*, it little resembles a conventional short story or novella. Indeed, I know of no other book that so uncompromisingly shows us what a film script looks like. Nor have I read another book, not even one of Beckett's, with such consciousness of the work of exclusion, of the effort the author has invested in keeping his product to this minimum. Nor, for that matter, have I hitherto reviewed a book where judgment must remain so definitely suspended, where so much of the proof resides in a deferred pudding. The script was completed, Pinter's introduction states, in 1972. "We then all tried to get the money to make the film. Up to this point the film has not been made." Until that point is passed, we cannot know whether such a passage as the following is absurd or superb:

> *367. EXT. GRAND CANAL. VENICE. DAY. 1903.*
> *Wintery, desolate.*
> MARCEL *in a gondola approaching a palazzo.*
>
> *368. MOTHER FRAMED IN A WINDOW.*
> *She is sitting on a balcony of the palazzo reading.*
> *She looks up from her book to see* MARCEL *in the gondola.*
>
> *369. THE GONDOLA ARRIVING AT THE LANDING.*
> MARCEL *steps out of the gondola, looks up to see his mother. His face is expressionless.*
>
> *370. C.U. MOTHER.*
> *She looks down with an expression of helpless love.*

A great deal of expressionlessness is called for by the scenarist, and we can entertain a suspicion that the most rhapsodic and admiring first-person narrator in twentieth-century fiction has been turned into a surly stick. Witness:

> *151. THE CARRIAGE.*
>   GRANDMOTHER
>   What are you looking at, Marcel?
>   MARCEL *(turning)*
> Nothing.

MME. DE VILLEPARISIS
Have I missed something?
MARCEL
No.

152. *CLOSE SHOT. FLOWERS ON CLIFF TOP.*
Boats on the horizon.
A butterfly flutters between the flowers.
GISÈLE (V.O.)
Aren't you eating any sandwiches?

153. *EXT. THE CLIFF TOP. BALBEC. DAY.*
The little band of GIRLS: ALBERTINE (18), ANDRÉE (20), GISÈLE, ROSEMONDE, and DELPHINE (all 17), with MARCEL, sitting with a picnic. Hampers, etc. At the edge of the field, bicycles.
MARCEL
No. I prefer this.
ALBERTINE
What is it exactly?
MARCEL
A chocolate cake.
Silence. They all munch.
ALBERTINE
Don't you actually *like* sandwiches?
MARCEL
Not very much.
Silence.

But until we can see the actors and hear their voices, feast our eyes on the wide-screen sea, and enjoy what the propmen have made of "Hampers, etc." and those *fin-de-siècle* bicycles, we cannot be certain how we will feel about the hero's solemn disdain of sandwiches. In the interim (which may be forever), *The Proust Screenplay* can be read as one more of the slim devotional volumes that men of diverse genius have been moved to offer up to Proust— *Proust's Way*, by François Mauriac; *Proust's Binoculars*, by Roger Shattuck; *Proust*, by Samuel Beckett; *On Proust*, by Jean-François Revel; *The Magic Lantern of Marcel Proust*, by Howard Moss. Like all these, Pinter's unproduced script affords us the pleasure of having our memory of *Remembrance of Things Past* refreshed, and provides yet another angle of perception upon a work so elaborate and many-faceted it never fails to give back new light.

One effect of casting the novel into scenario form has been suggested: the narrator, Marcel, deposed as verbal creator and enlisted as a dramatic character among many, becomes sullen, petulant, precariously unsympathetic, and even stupid. His behavior, pried loose from the matrix of his splendid philosophizing about behavior, seems more neurotic than we remember. His treatment of Albertine, especially, shocks us in Pinter's rendition: "MARCEL: Albertine, I think we should part. I want you to leave, first thing in the morning. ALBERTINE: In the morning? MARCEL: We have been happy. Now we're unhappy. It's quite simple. ALBERTINE: I'm not unhappy. MARCEL: Never see me again. It's best. ALBERTINE: You are the only person I care for. MARCEL: I've always wanted to go to Venice. Now I shall go. Alone." This dialogue has been clipped from a passage in the long, long middle of *The Captive*, where Marcel tirelessly resolves his jealous imaginings about the enigmatic passivity of his captive mistress; his suggestion that she leave is couched "with a profound gentleness and melancholy" that Pinter's lines leave to the actor's discretion, and the whole dismissal is in Marcel's hyperactive mind a piece of playful sadism, a pretense: "This fictitious parting scene ended by causing me almost as much grief as if it had been real, possibly because one of the actors, Albertine, by believing it to be real, had enhanced the other's illusion." As the novel frames the case, it is Albertine who is resolved on escaping, and the narrator's cruelties are pathetic maneuvers to forestall her. In the Pinter version, Marcel, drained of the child's vulnerability and sexual tentativeness that he carries through the novel, becomes—with kissing closeups and bare-shouldered bed scenes—a standard cinema stud, a stag at bay in the woods of sexual freedom, a trapped lover giving his latest dolly the slip. Elsewhere, too, the novel's substance seems coarsened as well as condensed. Saint-Loup would not breezily introduce his friend to his mistress with "This is Marcel. Marcel—Rachel." Albertine would not, and *did* not, say in her rhapsody on flavored ices, "I'll swallow them up, so cool, cool, cool." The Duchesse, at her most offhand, would not pronounce "Which reminds me" as a sentence in itself. She is made to say it thus, as a hasty and slangy transition, in a scene that, transcribed from the magnificent tragi-comic farewell to Swann which concludes *The Guermantes Way*, illustrates the perhaps unavoidable loss of ironic and poetic timbre:

> Charles! Marcel! How delightful. What a pity we have to go out. Dining out is such a bore. There are evenings when one would sooner die. But perhaps dying is an even greater bore, who knows?

This last remark, addressed to an old friend who is about to die, seemed so crude I looked up its counterpart in the Scott Moncrieff translation, and found it little, but significantly, different:

> "Oh, my dear Charles," she went on, "what a bore it can be, dining out. There are evenings when one would sooner die! It is true that dying may be perhaps just as great a bore, because we don't know what it's like."

This is lamer than, but faithful enough to, the French:

> *"Ah! mon petit Charles," reprit Mme de Guermantes, "ce que ça peut être ennuyeux de dîner en ville! Il y a des soirs où on aimerait mieux mourir! Il est vrai que de mourir c'est peut-être tout aussi ennuyeux puisqu'on ne sait pas ce que c'est."*

In Proust, she is giddily "going on," with a fluffy self-absorption that Pinter's crisp cadences do not convey. Throughout this adaptation, not only the exigencies of the film medium but a stylistic habit and preference compress the dialogue. Pinter's characters are on the attack with every phrase, "at" each other, alert for advantage; Proust's dialogue is often an intersection of monologues, conveying with comic amplitude our deafness to one another amid the vanity of our pretensions and the lonely immensity of musing space we each of us harbor. The entire reverie of *Remembrance of Things Past* pours out of such a private space; having lifted Marcel up from the stream of analysis and description, Pinter has a troublesome nonentity on his hands. Until the rather tritely dramatic Albertine episode, the hero does little but witness, usually without expression. A witnessing narrator is a most convenient instrument for fiction, but in the movies he gets between the camera and the action, like the dreary Mastroianni character in *La Dolce Vita.* We think of Mastroianni's limpid eyes, wet and black as those of a seal waiting to be tossed a fish, when we try to visualize *MARCEL'S EYES.* And one sequence suggests a slide show at an ophthalmologists' convention:

345. *MARCEL'S EYES.*

346. *THE EYES OF GILBERTE AT TANSONVILLE.*

347. *THE EYES OF THE DUCHESSE DE GUERMANTES IN THE STREET.*

348. *THE EYES OF ODETTE IN THE AVENUE DES ACACIAS.*

349. *THE EYES OF MOTHER IN THE BEDROOM AT COMBRAY.*

350. *THE EYES OF MARCEL IN THE LAVATORY AT COMBRAY.*

351. *THE EYES OF MARCEL.*

But for this scenario, we might not realize how compressible the finespun plot of *Remembrance of Things Past* is. Though he has eliminated Bergotte and Elstir, Bloch and the famous madeleine, Pinter has found space—or footage—for almost everything else, including Marcel's passingly mentioned stay in a sanatorium, and the "Marquise" stationed at the lavatory in the Champs-Élysees. He has retained a galaxy of characters, including such double stars as Marcel/Swann, Mother/Grandmother, and Albertine/Gilberte. Minor figures like the Prince de Foix and the Duc de Chatellerault make cameo appearances, and Saint-Loup, a fluttering ghost of his extensive prose version, materializes long enough to do his gallant dance along the back of the bench at the Rivebelle restaurant and to leave his Croix de Guerre in Jupien's male brothel. *Great Moments from Remembrance of Things Past,* this film might be called, or *This Is Your Life, Marcel.* The all-inclusive strategy, with its peril of indecipherable clutter, was deliberate. Pinter in his introduction tells how he consulted, in forming his script, with Joseph Losey, the prospective director, and Barbara Bray, a British editor and translator from the French. "We decided that the architecture of the film should be based on two main and contrasting principles: one, a movement, chiefly narrative, toward disillusion, and the other, more intermittent, toward revelation, rising to where time that was lost is found, and fixed forever in art." And so Marcel's rise in society, and society's collapse into homosexuality and vapidity, are observed scene by scene, notch by notch, like the growth and death of a plant telescoped into visible motion by stop-frame photography. Whether or not the progress thus telescoped would seem more than a comically spasmodic jumble of eyes, faces, and snipped allusions depends, as they say, on the execution.

Much of the emotional continuity would have to be supplied by the actor who plays Marcel, as he handles such supernatural assignments as registering the differences between Shot 140, *"MARCEL'S FACE,"* and Shot 143, *"MARCEL'S FACE, ALIVE."* More difficult still is the embodiment in the film of the idea of art as life-justifying, and the extraordinary literary involution whereby the massive work we have just read is shown, at its end, in the triumphant moment of conception. Here, though I doubt that Marcel in the cliché role of blocked writer ("To be honest, I have wasted my life") will come across, Pinter has conceived some fine effects of montage. The three steeples seen from Martinville, the magic-lantern image of Geneviève de Brabant, the hawthorn hedge along "Swann's way," all appear and reappear. The blue mosaics of San Marco in Venice give way to the searchlighted sky of wartime Paris. The film would open with a blank yellow screen, which the camera, amid the flashing of remembered moments, reveals as the "little patch of yellow wall" in Vermeer's *View of Delft*. It is this painting that the ailing Bergotte, the novel's symbolic representative of literature, ventures out to see; having seen it, he dies, envisioning "in a celestial balance . . . his own life, while the other contained the little patch of wall so beautifully painted in yellow." The object of Bergotte's pathetic—and, like so much in Proust, not unfarcical—sacrifice of life for art becomes, mingled with the sound of the Combray garden bell and the music of Vinteuil, the alpha and omega of *The Proust Screenplay*, its core of radiance. The cameraman, of course, will have to locate the little yellow patch (Proust misidentified it as from *A Street in Delft*, when in fact the

painting that he and Bergotte saw in Paris, on loan from the Mau-
ritshuis to the Jeu de Paume for an exhibit of Dutch painting in
1921, was the larger *View of Delft,* which contains a number of
sunlit roofs and walls), and the music director will have to write
Vinteuil's sonata and septet, or else steal them from Debussy or
César Franck. Still, one's heart quickens in anticipation of the
collaboration. There is in Proust's method a reblending of narrative
music and image that does suggest the cinematic art, an art come
to ripeness in the same years as his masterpiece. By trying to
capture this affinity, Harold Pinter has subjugated his talent to a
brave and beautiful attempt at translation, and made a supreme
gesture of faith in the film medium, trusting it to receive this most
luxuriantly verbal of prose fictions. His script, produced, would
certainly have delightful evocative, mnemonic qualities for the
committed Proustians in the audience. But could the movie be
comprehended and enjoyed by anyone who had not read the book?

> REVIEWER *(circumspectly)*
> One wonders.
> MARCEL *(expressionless)*
> No way.

Suzie Creamcheese Speaks

DORIS DAY: HER OWN STORY, by A. E. Hotchner. 305 pp. Morrow, 1976.

I have fallen in love with rather few public figures—with Errol
Flynn, Ted Williams, Harry Truman, and Doris Day. The three
men have a common denominator in cockiness; how cocky Miss
Day also is did not strike me until the reading of *Doris Day: Her
Own Story,* as orchestrated by A. E. Hotchner. "I must emphasize,"
she tells us in the autobiographical tapes that Hotchner has edited,
"that I have never had any doubts about my ability in anything I
have ever undertaken." Elsewhere, in describing her audition, at
the age of sixteen, for the job of lead singer with Bob Crosby's
Bobcats, she says, "But to be honest about it, despite my nervous-

ness and reluctance to sing for these mighty professionals, it never occurred to me that I wouldn't get the job. I have never tried out for anything that I failed to get." And, it is true, her life shows a remarkably consistent pattern of professional success, alternating with personal tribulation. When she was eleven, her father, "Professor" William Kappelhoff, Cincinnati's "most sought-after conductor," left her mother for another woman; when Doris was twelve, the dance team of Doris & Jerry won the grand prize in a citywide amateur contest, and with the money they visited Hollywood, where people "were so enthusiastic about our ability that I had no doubt that we would do very well." But when she left a farewell party given on the eve of her moving to Hollywood, a locomotive struck the car in which she was riding. Her right leg was shattered and her dancing career with it (Jerry's, too; without Doris Kappelhoff as a partner, he became in time a Cincinnati milkman). During her nearly two years of convalescence, Doris listened to the radio, admiring especially the singing of Ella Fitzgerald, and before she was off crutches she was performing in a downtown Chinese restaurant and on local radio. A Cincinnati night-club job led to Chicago and the Bobcats, and from there to Les Brown and his Blue Devils—all this before her seventeenth birthday.

In one of the interviews that Hotchner usefully splices into his subject's account of her days, Les Brown remembers that he "listened to her for five minutes, immediately went backstage, and signed her for my band. She was every band leader's dream, a vocalist who had natural talent, a keen regard for the lyrics, and an attractive appearance. . . . The reason her salary rose so precipitously was that virtually every band in the business tried to hire her away from me." Yet at the age of seventeen she left the Blue Devils and married an obscure, surly trombonist named Al Jorden. "From the time I was a little girl," she says, "my only true ambition in life was to get married and tend house and have a family. Singing was just something to do until that time came, and now it was here." Though she had known Jorden back in Cincinnati, he surprised her, once married, with psychopathic behavior that bordered on the murderous. He was frantically jealous, beat her, begged forgiveness in fits of remorse that became as repellent as his rage, and demanded she abort the pregnancy that came along in the second month of the hasty match. Doris Day, as she was by then called, in rapid succession had the baby (her only child, Terry), divorced Al Jorden, went back to Les Brown, and recorded "Sentimental Journey," her first hit record and the point where I, among millions, began to love her. Unaware of my feelings, she married another bandman, George Weidler, who played alto sax; this marriage ended even sooner than the one to Al Jorden, though on a different note. Weidler, with whom she was contentedly living in a trailer camp in postwar Los Angeles, told her she was going to become a star and he didn't wish to become Mr. Doris Day. She protests even now, "I loved him, or at least I thought I did, and with all the hardship and struggle I was enjoying my trailer wifedom." Nor did Weidler seem to find her wanting. "I could not doubt his strong desire for me. But I guess his desire not to be Mr. Doris Day was even stronger, for in the morning we parted, and I knew it would be final." At this low ebb, then, homeless, husbandless, and penniless, she permitted herself to be dragged to a screen test, and was handed the lead in the first of her many successful movies, *Romance on the High Seas.* She and the cameras fell in love at first sight:

> I found I could enter a room and move easily to my floormark without actually looking for it. I felt a nice exhilaration at hearing the word "Action!" and then responding to the pressure of the rolling camera. It was effortless and thoroughly enjoyable. . . . From the first take onward, I never had any trepidation about what I was called on to do. Movie acting came to me with greater ease and naturalness than anything else I had ever done. . . . I never had a qualm. Water off a duck's back.

Two decades off her back found their high-water mark in the early Sixties, when she was No. 1 at the box office. In 1953, however, she had suffered an incapacitating nervous breakdown, and throughout her moviemaking prime her personal life was bounded by shyness, Christian Science, a slavish work schedule, and marriage to a man no one else liked—Marty Melcher. Les Brown is quoted as saying, "Marty Melcher was an awful man, pushy, grating on the nerves, crass, money-hungry. He lived off Patty Andrews; then, when Doris came along and looked like a better ticket, he glommed onto her." Sam Weiss, onetime head of Warner Brothers music, phrases it rather beautifully: "The fact was that the only thing Marty loved was money. He loved Patty's money until Doris's money came along and then, because there was more of it, he loved Doris's money more." "I put up with Marty," Weiss further avows, "and everybody else endured him, because of Doris. I don't know anybody who liked Marty. Not even his own family."

Her manager as well as her husband, Melcher kept the cameras churning out sugary Daydreams while the focus got softer and softer, and American audiences were moving on to skin and rock. In 1968, Doris Day made the last of her thirty-nine films and Marty Melcher suddenly died; the financial post mortem revealed that, like many a man in love with money, he could only lose it. Over the fat years, he had poured her fortune into the schemes of a swindler named Rosenthal, leaving her a half-million dollars in debt. She bailed herself out by going ahead, against her inclinations, with a television series Melcher had secretly signed her to, and put herself through five years of sit-com paces on the little box. As an additional trauma, her son, Terry, who had evolved into a young pop-music entrepreneur, was peripherally involved in the Tate-Manson murders and retreated to a cave of pills and vodka; in an eerie rerun of her childhood accident, he broke *both* legs while carousing on a motorcycle. Now, on the far side of fifty, Doris Day has no visible career but has kept her celebrity status and her confidence. "I know that I can handle almost anything they throw at me, and to me that is real success," she concludes, cockily.

The particulars of her life surprise us, like graffiti scratched on a sacred statute. She appears sheer symbol—of a kind of beauty, of a kind of fresh and energetic innocence, of a kind of banality. Her very name seems to signify less a person than a product, wrapped in an alliterating aura. She herself, it turns out, doesn't like her name, which was given her because "Kappelhoff" didn't fit on a marquee. (Her first name, too, has to do with marquees; her mother named her after a movie star popular in 1924, Doris Kenyon. And in this tradition Doris named her own son, in 1942, after a favorite comic strip, "Terry and the Pirates.") Of her name Doris Day says:

> I never did like it. Still don't. I think it's a phony name. As a matter of fact, over the years many of my friends didn't feel that Doris Day suited me, and gave me names of their own invention. Billy De Wolfe christened me Clara Bixby . . . Rock Hudson calls me Eunice . . . and others call me Do-Do, and lately one of my friends has taken to calling me Suzie Creamcheese.

This shy goddess who avoids parties and live audiences fascinates us with the amount of space we imagine between her face and her mask. Among the co-actors and fellow-musicians who let their words be used in this book, only Kirk Douglas touches on the mystery: "I haven't a clue as to who Doris Day really is. That face that she shows the world—smiling, only talking good, happy, tuned into God—as far as I'm concerned, that's just a mask. I haven't a clue as to what's underneath. Doris is just about the remotest person I know." In a spunky footnote, she counterattacks —"But then Kirk never makes much of an effort toward anyone else. He's pretty much wrapped up in himself"—and the entire book is announced by her as an attack upon her own image as "Miss Chastity Belt," "America's la-di-da happy virgin!" True, her virginity seems to have been yielded before she married in her mid-teens, and her tough life shows in the tough advice she gives her readers. "You don't really know a person until you live with him, not just sleep with him. . . . I staunchly believe no two people should get married until they have lived together. The young people have it right." For all her love of marriage, she refused both her early husbands when they begged to reconcile, and at one point in her marriage to Melcher she kicked him out, observing simply, "There comes a time when a marriage must be terminated. Nothing is forever." She brushes aside Patty Andrews's belief that Doris had stolen her husband with the sentence "A person does not leave a good marriage for someone else," and of a post-Marty lover she says, "I didn't care whether he was married or not. I have no qualms about the other person's marital life."

How sexy is she, America's girl next door? Her son, who is full of opinions, claims, "She has her heart set on getting married again but she really doesn't have any idea how to react to a man's attention. . . . Sad to say, I don't think my mother's had much of a sex life." But she makes a point of telling us, of each husband, that their sex life was good, and James Garner, with whom she made two of the romantic comedies that followed the great success of *Pillow Talk*, confides,

> I've had to play love scenes with a lot of screen ladies . . . but of all the women I've had to be intimate with on the screen, I'd rate two as sexiest by far—Doris and Julie Andrews, both of them notorious girls next door. Playing a love scene with either of them is duck soup because they communicate something sexy which means I also let myself go somewhat and that really makes a love scene work. . . . The fact of the matter is that with Doris, one hundred grips or not, there *was* always something there and I must admit that if I had not been married I would have tried to carry forward, after hours, where we left off on the sound stage.

The fact of this matter probably is that star quality is an emanation of superabundant nervous energy and that sexiness, in another setting, would be another emanation.

At the outset of her screen career, the director Michael Curtiz told her (as she remembers his Hungarian locutions), "No matter what you do on the screen, no matter what kind of part you play, it will always be you. What I mean is, the Doris Day will always shine through the part. This will make you big important star. You listen to me. Is very rare thing. You look Gable acting, Gary Cooper, Carole Lombard, they are playing different parts but always is the same strong personality coming through." The same strong personality behind her professional success has no doubt contributed to her personal problems; Al Jorden's jealousy, George Weidler's walkout, and Marty Melcher's disastrous dealing can all be construed as attempts of a male ego to survive an overmatch with a queen bee. Of a recent lover, Miss Day, having sung his praises, rather chillingly confesses, "But as it turned out, he was a man who passed through my life without leaving a trace of himself." At about the same time, she passed her second husband on the street and didn't recognize him—"The most embarrassing part of it was that his appearance hadn't changed very much." Even at seventeen, she was the executioner:

> "I'm sorry, Al," I said, "but the feelings I once had for you are dead and gone. There's no way to resurrect them. I don't love you anymore, and without love it just wouldn't work. There's nothing to talk about —the good feelings are gone, and it's over. All over." . . .
> As I started to get out of the car, he put his hand on my arm. I looked at him. His face was full of pain and he was near tears. I thought to myself, No, I am through comforting you. I felt a curious kind of revulsion.

She longs for the marital paradise, but cannot bring to it that paradise's customary component of female dependence.

> "How will you get along?" my aunt asked.
> "Why I'll get a job," I said. All my life I have known that I could work at whatever I wanted whenever I wanted.

And worked she has. Thoroughly German in her ancestry, she is a dedicated technician in the industry of romantic illusion. Singing or acting, she manages to produce, in her face or in her voice, an "effect," a skip or a tremor, a feathery edge that touches us. In these spoken memoirs she seems most herself, least guarded and most exciting, talking shop—details such as how to avoid popping the "p"s when singing into a radio microphone (turn the head "slightly to the side") and the special difficulties of dancing before movie cameras ("A film dancer does not have the freedom of a stage dancer. She must dance precisely to a mark. Her turns must be exact. She must face precisely in the camera direction required while executing very difficult steps"). Her co-performers praise her technical mastery; Bob Hope marvels at the "great comedy timing" she brought to their radio shows, and Jack Lemmon explains why she is a "director's delight"—"Once she performs a scene, she locks it in, and no matter how many takes are required, she gives the same matched performance. In my book, this is the most difficult part of movie acting." She never watches rushes, and cannot sit through one of her old movies without wanting "to redo every shot." She

not only dislikes performing before a live audience but often re-
cords to the prerecorded accompaniment of an absent band. "In the
solitude of a room with perfect acoustics, I could record a song as
many times as necessary to get it right." Melcher's long and steady
betrayal of her evidently won no worse recrimination than this,
after he had signed her up for a clunker called *Caprice:*

> "*You* made a deal—you and Rosenthal, that it? Well, you and Rosen-
> thal don't have to get in front of the camera and try to make something
> out of terrible stuff like this! I know that you and your friends are only
> interested in making money, but I'm interested in something more. I
> don't give a damn about money. I never see any of it and I don't have
> the time to use any of it even if I knew what to do with it—which I
> don't."

She is very much the modern artist in being happiest within her
art, a haven from life:

> I really like to sing; it gives me a sense of release, another dimension;
> it makes me happy; and I think the people who listen to me instinctively
> know that and feel it.

> I felt very real in the make-believe parts I had to play. I felt what the
> script asked me to feel. I enjoyed playing and singing for the cameras
> and I guess that enjoyment came through on the screen . . . When the
> camera turned . . . I easily and rather happily responded to whatever
> was demanded of me.

That Marty Melcher was pouring her earnings down the sewer of
his own greed mattered less to her than the memory of Al Jorden's
beatings, which she could conjure up whenever the camera asked
her to cry.

The words "Doris Day" get a reaction, often adverse. They are
an incantation, and people who have no reason to disdain her fine
entertainer's gifts shy from her as a religious force. Her starriness
has a challenging, irritating twinkle peculiar to her—Monroe's
image lulled us like a moon seen from a motel bed, and there is
nothing about Katharine Hepburn's "goodness" that asks us to
examine our own. On the jacket of *Doris Day: Her Own Story* the

sprightly photograph of the heroine uncomfortably reminds us of those tireless, elastic television ladies who exhort us to get up in the morning and do exercises; and the book ends with a set of exercises that Doris Day does, and that do sound exhausting. She *likes* the movie actor's Spartan regimen, which begins at five in the morning, and more than once she speaks with pleasure of "coming up to the mark" chalked on the floor of a movie set. For years, she was a professed Christian Scientist; but, then, so were Ginger Rogers and Charlotte Greenwood, and no one held it against them. Miss Day, religiously, is in fact an American Pelagian, an enemy of the despair-prone dualism that has been the intellectual pride of our Scots Protestants and our Irish Catholics alike. Doris Kappelhoff was raised as a Catholic, but "the Catholic side of me never took." She resented the obscurity of the Latin, and resented even more being asked, at the age of seven, to make up sins to confess. "I had my own built-in church. It allowed me to question a lot of Catholic dogma." She turned to the Church once, after the collapse of her first marriage, "desperate to find some way to restore the positive view I had always had toward life." When the priest told her she had never been really married and her son was illegitimate, she walked out. All three of her marriages have been casual civil ceremonies, and she makes a point of not going to funerals—not even her father's. After their divorce, George Weidler (the most phantasmal and, in a way, most appealing man in her life) interested her in the teachings of Mary Baker Eddy, and from the first line she read—"To those leaning on the sustaining infinite, today is big with blessings"—she met in "words of gleaming light" a prefigurement of her "own built-in church." Though in some of her crises she has consulted doctors, and after Melcher's death broke with the organized church, Christian Science's tenet that "All is infinite Mind" has remained a sustaining principle. She describes herself sitting outside her son's hospital room thinking, "I can't pray to a God to make him well, because there is no duality, no God outside of Terry. . . . There is but one power, and if that lovely son of mine is supposed to *live,* then nothing on this earth can take him." The fatalism that goes with monism suits both her toughness and her optimism. Almost brutally she enlists her misfortunes in the progress of her career: "And Marty's death—well, to be honest about it, had he lived I would have been totally wiped out." *Que sera, sera.* Unchastened, she sees her life as an irresistible blooming:

> It is not luck that one seed grows into a purple flower and another, identical seed grows up to be a yellow flower, nor is it luck that Doris Kappelhoff of Cincinnati grows up to be a sex symbol on the silver screen.

Her sense of natural goodness and universal order gets a little cloying when extended to her pet dogs, but by and large she speaks of her religious convictions uninsistently and reasonably, as something that has worked for her. Concerning others, she has scarcely a judgmental or complaining word. She is rather a purist but no puritan; her sexual ethics, like her Man-is-Spirit mysticism, are as Seventies as her image is Fifties. But, then, our movie queens have long been creating metaphysics for themselves on the frontier where bourgeois norms evaporate. Doris Day is naïve, I think, only about her own demon; it was not just by divine determination that peaceful obscure marriage eluded her and fame did not. When she had her nervous breakdown, her psychiatrist described her as "self-demanding." Her father before her failed as a domestic creature; his "whole life was music." She was driven to perform, and permitted life situations to keep forcing her back on the stage. Now she has felt compelled to give this account of herself. How much editorial magic A. E. Hotchner sprinkled upon her tapes there is no telling; but the sections of Doris Day ostensibly speaking are rather better written than Hotchner's own press-releasy prologue and epilogue. She can, if we take her words as truly hers, toss off the terms "sanctum sanctorum" and "reactive," recall patches of dialogue thirty years old, be quite funny about a hideous hotel built in her name, and evoke Bob Hope, "the way his teeth take over his face when he smiles. And the way he swaggers across the stage, kind of sideways, beaming at the audience, spreading good cheer." She became a successful comedienne, surely, in part because she is one of the few movie actresses of her generation whose bearing conveys intelligence.

Now, love must be clear-eyed, and Doris Day's accomplishment, resilient and versatile as she is, should not be exaggerated. Though she learned from Ella Fitzgerald "the subtle ways she shaded her voice, the casual yet clean way she sang the words," there are dark sweet places where Ella's voice goes that her disciple's doesn't. And it was not just Hollywood crassness that cast her in so many tame, lame vehicles; her Pelagianism makes it impossible for her to be evil, so the top of her emotional range is an innocent victim's hysteria. But, as Michael Curtiz foretold when he prepared her for her first motion picture, the actor's art in a case like hers functions as a mere halo of refinements around the "strong personality." Her third picture, strange to say, ended with her make-believe marriage to Errol Flynn. A heavenly match, in the realm where both are lovable. Both brought to the corniest screen moment a gallant and guileless delight in being themselves, a faint air of excess, a skillful insouciance that, in those giant dreams projected across our Saturday nights, hinted at how, if we were angels, we would behave.

Female Pilgrims

LULU IN HOLLYWOOD, by Louise Brooks. 109 pp. Knopf, 1982.

AS THEY WERE, by M. F. K. Fisher. 261 pp. Knopf, 1982.

Louise Brooks was a film actress of surpassing vividness and glow, and her elegant little book *Lulu in Hollywood* does not lack these qualities. A closet reader, she tells us more than once, during her years in the limelight as a dancer and silent-screen star, she began to write professionally, on a modest scale, after her move in 1956 to Rochester, "where," she says, "I could study old films and write about bits of my rediscovered past." Of the seven essays collected in this volume—beautifully produced, with a stunning jacket and abundant photographs—portions appeared in *London Magazine, Film Culture, Image,* and *Sight & Sound.* One would like to know more about them, bibliographically, and how much more of the oeuvre there is. Readers of Kenneth Tynan's Profile of Miss Brooks in *The New Yorker* three years ago may recall a number of breathtakingly blithe personal recollections that are not confided here, and a quotation from an arresting homage to Chaplin—published in *Film Culture*—also disappointingly absent. But a certain firm reticence, mixed with spicy dashes of frankness, gives *Lulu in Hollywood* its flavor, which is somewhat tart, or sweet and sour. We learn in an afterword by Lotte H. Eisner, a German film historian who met the actress in Berlin in 1929, that Miss Brooks's writing career is over: on a Christmas card from Rochester she told Miss Eisner, "I shall write no more. Writing the truth for readers nourished on publicity rubbish is a useless exercise." Her life, she tells the reader of her quasi-memoirs, has been spent "in cruel pursuit of truth and excellence . . . an abomination of all but those few who have overcome their aversion to truth in order to free whatever is good in them."

The central mystery of this volume, hanging over its prose and its photographs alike, is why Louise Brooks, with her magical screen presence, fine intelligence, and by all accounts "marvellous" voice, failed or refused to make the transition to talkies and saw her film career essentially end in 1930, when she was only twenty-four. Her essays do not ignore this mystery. The first and most autobiographical one, "Kansas to New York," blames the "early autonomy" bred into her by her parents—an independent, bookish Wichita lawyer and his musically gifted, also independent-minded wife. "My parents' resolute pursuit of their own interests . . . accounted for my own early autonomy and my later inability, when I went to work in the Hollywood film factories, to submit to slavery." A few sentences on, however, she mentions another mystery: "The unsolved mystery of my mother's character was why, although she was such a talented pianist, she never played as a soloist in public." No connection with her daughter's own career is suggested; but some inherited trait, some genetic reluctance to perform on demand, may have dimmed Louise Brooks's star as much as her love of truth and aversion to slavery. She admits to "temper tantrums," willful and mischievous behavior, and to being so unpopular with her fellow-chorines in the *Ziegfeld Follies* of 1925 that none of them would dress with her. The crucial refusal of her professional life—to do the retakes for a Paramount film, *The*

Canary Murder Case, which was being remade from a silent to a talkie in 1930—did her incalculable harm in Hollywood and is essentially unexplained. She claims, in the volume's last essay, "Pabst and Lulu," that working with the great German director G. W. Pabst ("In Hollywood, I was a pretty flibbertigibbet whose charm for the executive department decreased with every increase in her fan mail. In Berlin, I stepped onto the station platform to meet Pabst and became an actress") altered her beyond accommodation with the American film world. But she had declined Pabst's invitation to stay in Germany and become "a serious actress" and had dismissed his warnings that she might go the way of that imaginary flibbertigibbet Lulu; she had returned to America, and her filmography includes a number of post-1930 studio movies ending with an early John Wayne oater, *Overland Stage Riders,* in 1938. She stopped trying in Hollywood only in 1940.

Looking through the stills bound into *Lulu in Hollywood,* one feels an impatience with whatever the forces were that prevented such an exquisite and winning apparition from getting more of herself onto film. In Pabst's *Pandora's Box,* she indeed was amazing —a presence so fluent and urgent in motion, so intense and radiant in repose that she forms, now, a kind of three-dimensional bubble on the surface of the cinematic melodrama. Her Lulu has a lovable solidity that incites a love of life in the viewer, or at least this viewer as he sat in Rochester's Eastman House staring at the murky, flickering print kindly made available. The back of Miss Brooks's wide white neck—"that unique imperious neck of hers," Christopher Isherwood once wrote—seemed especially a site of power and seductiveness, and, of course, the long dark eyes bracketed by the points of her famous "shiny black helmet" of hair, and her dancer's athletic lightness. Such vitality leaps free of cinema history altogether, toward a naturalism that did not arrive until the Sixties. How odd, how regrettable that its possessor and embodiment saw her career stumble and virtually halt at the outset of the Thirties. Miss Eisner, in 1929, was fascinated by the young actress's "curious mixture of passivity and *presence.* " The passivity, one feels, in some form of playfulness or distraction or reckless judgment, undid the presence.

The explanation Louise Brooks gave Tynan for her career's halt
was blunt and simple: she would not sleep with Harry Cohn, the
head of Columbia Pictures. No love is lost between her and Holly-
wood; and no gratitude or nostalgia softens her portrait of the film
industry's workings. "I can state categorically that in Bogart's time
there was no other occupation in the world that so closely resembled
enslavement as the career of a film star." Her chapter on Bogart
traces his transformation of himself, at fearful price, from "a slim boy
with charming manners" and a handsomeness centered on his "very
full, rosy, and perfectly modelled" mouth into "a rebellious tough
known as Bogey." Originally an actor "speaking his lines with a
well-projected baritone and good diction," he observed "how much
an unusual feature, such as Clark Gable's prominent ears, added to
the publicity value of a star [and] decided to exploit his mouth." So
he practiced, over the years, "all kinds of lip gymnastics, accom-
panied by nasal tones, snarls, lisps, and slurs . . . Only Erich von
Stroheim was his superior in lip-twitching." And he "allowed him-
self to be presented to the world by journalists as a coarse and
drunken bully, and as a puppet Iago who fomented evil without a
motive." His own motive, of course, was to achieve stardom, and in
this he is like the character he played in *The Treasure of Sierra Madre:*

> He lies in the dirt, about to drag himself to the waterhole. He had
> endured everything to get his gold—and now must he give it up? Wide
> open, the tragic eyes are raised to heaven in a terrible, beseeching look.
> In the agony of that beautiful face I see the face of my St. Bogart.

In her essay on "Gish and Garbo," Miss Brooks praises the talent
of both women but sardonically locates the fall of the one and the
rise of the other at the moment, in 1925, when the movie industry
"suddenly found itself in subjection to Wall Street" and when
"Will Hays succeeded in killing censorship in twenty-four states."
The result of the first was that producers no longer had their
financial books, with all their padding, to themselves, and their
cavalier maltreatment of stars—"their customary way of making up
their losses and refreshing their prestige"—was forced to become
covert. Instead of simply firing stars or cutting their salaries, the
studio heads now had to destroy them at the box office; Louise

Brooks traces with some care this procedure as it was used against Lillian Gish. James Quirk, the editor of *Photoplay,* led the critical hounds while M-G-M maneuvered to trap its expensive star into a truly bad movie. "With Gish, it was a question of how to get her to make a real stinker. Under her supervision, *La Bohème* and *The Scarlet Letter* were fine pictures. So when she was called away to bring her sick mother home from London, the studio carefully framed a picture postcard called *Annie Laurie* . . . Back in charge, she next made *The Wind,* which was so loaded with sex and violence [good things, according to the *Photoplay* line] that M-G-M held up its release until the first Academy Award had been safely dealt to Janet Gaynor. And then Gish's strength failed, and she accepted a dreary studio property, *The Enemy.* She could go now, M-G-M said; she needn't make the sixth picture."

Meanwhile, Hays's victory over censorship meant the oncoming of "adult pictures of sexual realism," meaning pictures wherein the heroine had affairs without being married. Unfortunately, no star existed "with youth, beauty, and personality enough to make free love sympathetic." Then Louis B. Mayer found her, in the spring of 1925, in a Swedish film being shown in Berlin. She was Greta Garbo. "Here was a face as purely beautiful as Michelangelo's Mary of the *Pietà,* yet glowing with passion. The suffering of her soul was such that the American public would forgive her many affairs in *The Torrent,* Garbo's first American picture. At last, marriage— the obstacle standing between sex and pleasure—could be done away with!" The last laugh, however, was on the studios, for Garbo, after a long holdout, won for herself a salary nearly as big as Gish's. The war of the greedy moguls against the lovely stars continued nevertheless:

> Eased out with full approval, in the perfection of their beauty, art, and popularity, were Jeanette MacDonald, Joan Crawford, Norma Shearer, and finally Garbo herself. Sixteen years passed between the public execution of Lillian Gish and the bloodless exile of Greta Garbo. Hollywood producers were left with their babes and a backwash of old-men stars, watching the lights go out in one picture house after another across the country.

Louise Brooks remembers the days when Garbo's arrival in Hollywood created a hush of despair among the other actresses: "The whole M-G-M studio . . . watched the daily rushes with amazement as Garbo created out of the stalest, thinnest material the complex, enchanting shadow of a soul upon the screen." Brooks writes at her best when she evokes acting style: We read of "Cagney's swift dialogue and his swift movements, which had the glitter and precision of a meat slicer" and of "the emotional Bette Davis, who could fire up on the word 'camera.' " W. C. Fields, it turns out, was largely wasted on film. "Long shot, medium shot, two-shot, or closeup, Bill performed as if he were standing whole before an audience that could appreciate every detail of his costume and follow the dainty disposition of his hands and feet. Every time the camera drew closer, it cut off another piece of him and deprived him of some comic effect."

Her two essays "On Location with Billy Wellman" and "Pabst and Lulu" are among the best descriptions of moviemaking I have ever read. In the first, she tells of how a beautiful young actress can come, out of admiration for his heroism and physical grace, to sleep with her stunt man and then be publicly humiliated (by the caddish stunt man) for it; the uneasy camaraderie of the crew on location, where personnel loom in such different proportions from what they do on the screen, and where crude pranks are the order of the day, comes across pungently. In the second, she shows a spirited, spoiled young woman being tamed by a masterful European director. The director's function and difficulties have rarely been as well explained as here:

In order to see things from the film director's viewpoint, one might think how difficult it is to get a true smile in a single snapshot of a person we know. Then think of a director who faces a group of strangers, all of them certain about how they want to play their parts, some of them antagonistic, all of them full of a thousand secrets of pain and humiliation which, accidentally touched upon, may defeat the director in an utterly baffling way . . . Pabst's genius lay in getting to the heart of a person, banishing fear, and releasing the clean impact of personality which jolts an audience to life.

He shielded Louise Brooks from the hostility felt toward an American who had usurped the lead in a German movie, pried her loose from her rich American friends and late-night habits, and explained as little as possible. "With an intelligent actor, he would sit in exhaustive explanation; with an old ham, he would speak the language of the theatre. But in my case, by some magic, he would saturate me with one clear emotion and turn me loose." They shared, at least as she remembers it, a certain sameness of approach: "That I was a dancer and Pabst essentially a choreographer in his direction came as a wonderful surprise to both of us on the first day of shooting *Pandora's Box.*"

She had come to film acting from dancing, having drifted from Broadway shows into bit parts when some moviemaking remained in New York; and after her career was washed up she returned, for a while in the Thirties, to professional dancing. In the brief interval of her successful Hollywood years, she was an insider who thought like an outsider. Her marriage there to the director Edward Sutherland was blighted because "he belonged heart and soul to Hollywood; I was an alien there. He loved parties; I loved solitude." In her later years, rich in solitude, she has written these essays as an outsider who thinks like an insider. They are good enough to make one wish there were more. Whether as autobiography, film criticism, or Hollywood sociology, they offer precious and amusing information about the workings of a world that has talked mostly nonsense about itself. Their literacy, insight, candor, and strict conscience make for sharp-edged reading on a usually soft-focused subject. Yet we are drawn to read them because their author was a beautiful woman who played hard in a fabled milieu. Some passages have the exact crowded, confiding cadence of a gossip column:

> Waiting for us in the Ritz Tower were the comedienne Beatrice Lillie, the actor Roger Davis, and the beautiful Gloria Morgan Vanderbilt. I sat down with Gloria so that I could listen to her alluring soft Spanish lisp. (Her mother, Mrs. Harry Hays Morgan, was half Chilean, born in Santiago.) As sweetly as if she were reciting "The Owl and the Pussycat," she began telling me her story of how her ex-husband's sister,

Mrs. Harry Payne Whitney, had obtained custody of both her daughter, little Gloria, and her five-million-dollar trust fund by charging big Gloria with an "ambiguous relationship" with Nada, Lady Milford Haven.

For all her hard-earned scribal robes—she quotes Samuel Johnson, John Ruskin, and Marcel Proust appositely—Miss Brooks has not left totally behind that underdressed teen-ager who, having obtained instruction in speech, manners, and dress from a soda jerk, a waiter, and a shopgirl respectively, tripped from the *Follies* into the champagne dusk of the silent films. A diaphanous memory of merriment floats above her strictures. The moon may be a cinder, but it still casts moonlight.

M. F. K. Fisher has had her good times, too. They have tended to occur in kitchens and restaurants, and often in her collection of memoiristic essays, *As They Were,* meals consumed decades ago leap into full, precise, savored recollection:

> I ate a plate of the famous *saucisson d'Arles,* which really I do not like any more than I like salami, except perhaps on a picnic. But it was served with a pile of delicious chilled radishes and a pat of butter marked *Forum,* and the waiter set a tall black jar of olives on my table. The long spoon had a little twig of fresh olive leaves tied to its handle. Then I ate some good braised endive. Then I ate a large wedge of apple tart, one of the three or four best of my life. I drank a half-bottle of Tavel.

This is in Arles, a place where Mrs. Fisher was not especially happy, or particularly well fed. When she recalls the two kitchens she had in Provence, or three pre-war Swiss inns where the food was memorable ("All I can remember now is hot unsalted butter, herbs left in for a few seconds, cream, a shallot flicked over, the fish laid in, the cover put on. I can almost see it, smell it, taste it now"), or a "mad waitress" who, in northern Burgundy fifty years ago, forced upon the susceptible author a prodigious and delicious lunch, then pages pour by that would make even a proofreader's mouth water. Mrs. Fisher, a versatile and sensitive writer best known for her gastronomical books *(Serve It Forth, Consider the*

Oyster, How to Cook a Wolf, An Alphabet for Gourmets), evokes the first café she visited, in Los Angeles in 1914, at the age of six:

> It seemed almost unbearable that a little fire should burn there at our table so dangerously, under a silver pan, and that the man could lean over it without going up in flames, and put the plates so tenderly before us with a napkin over his fingers, while candles flared in the middle of the day and people we had never seen before ate in the same room, as if we were invisible.

And she dramatizes for us, in "Young Hunger," the lowly but intense agonies of adolescent appetite, when the "guts are howling for meat-bread-candy-fruit-cheese-milkmilkmilk—ANYTHING IN THE WORLD TO EAT."

Mrs. Fisher is, indeed, a poet of the appetites—what she calls "our three basic needs for protection, food, love." Of the last, in her own life, she tells us little in this collection; we learn that she was married, and has daughters to care for and feed, but of how she comes to be where she is (Provence, Arles, a California ranch, a freighter plodding across the ocean) she confides virtually nothing, and sometimes expresses satisfaction in her withholding—"Of course," she says of the contents of a note received, "I should talk more of it, to make this a well-rounded account instead of a straight report, but I prefer not to." Shelter and food, however, she renders with a sensational richness that transforms her tenuous autobiographical persona into a visceral Everywoman whose encounters with weather, landscapes, street noises, strangers, and loneliness take on an epic size. She can be, in one of her stylistic moods, a Rabelaisian piler-on. Her acoustical account of the Rue Brueys in Aix-en-Provence, where she lived for some months, acquires a delirious relish worthy of Céline:

> At times, from about five-thirty to seven-thirty on week-nights, there was the feeling that I listened to a whole carnival, blurred, just off a cosmic Midway. . . . It was a kind of pulp, a huge sponge dripping with sound, drops splashing against the walls of the straight, tight street, falling into the sogged air. It was a dozen radios or TVs, a flute tweeting, someone practicing slow clumsy riffs on a one-man percussion set, two pianos with one heavy pedal adding to the blur; it was dozens of

families banging pots and clinking forks against their plates; it was the new baby and an Algerian record wailing, and the quick clop of wooden shoes keeping unconscious time to them.

This is autobiography as a highly articulate animal would write it, crammed with sensual event and devoid of social rationale. Other people, as they figure in *As They Were,* where they are not attendants bringing food or implementing shelter, are delicacies snatched from a tray by an eye greedy for perfection: "She was so dramatically a *Gypsy* that I almost laughed: slim, dark, dirty, beautiful. She wore her hair long and tangled. Her skirt had the full soft swing of any fancy dress costumer's best offering. Her filthy beautiful feet were tiny and bare, in very high heels." When this piece of perfection touches the sensate narrator, however, it is with "icy little claws" that leave for minutes afterward "the bony coldness of her little crab-like hands on mine."

Animal, too, perhaps, is the willingness to admit dislike. A chapter of childhood reminiscence, "Prejudice, Hate, and the First World War," says, "I was supposed to be a good friend of her little sister Josephine, but it never worked. Both of us tried for years to like each other . . . and remained consistently cold and disinterested." Of a California beach community it is said that "artists dismiss with scornful ravings the dull bourgeois" and "bridge clubs knit the whole faction into a nightly knot of systems and four-sided animosities." In Arles, "the reception clerk was a tall youngish man, not hostile but not friendly, not offensive but not *in*offensive, in a veiled way." In general, the people of Arles "frown and scowl a lot," and the young people have a "natural cruelty in them." In a world so threaded with chill currents, the sensitive woman treads gingerly, and tightens around her the comforter of solitude. The incessant war of living entities relaxes in the presence of food, which has already been killed. But at an Arles fish market shivers remain: "There were millions of sea urchins slowly moving their spines. A man picked up a pale *supion* (a small, delicate cuttlefish), pulled out its bone with thumb and finger, tipped back his own head to let it slide down his throat, tentacles first, and he chewing as it went. It looked easy, but not enticing . . ."

The chill climate of these handsomely written reminiscences is somewhat akin to that of *Lulu in Hollywood*. Miss Brooks is two years older than Mrs. Fisher; both emerged from comfortable families in comfortable cities (Wichita, Kansas; Whittier, California) into cosmopolitanism and independence. Both take pride in their truthfulness ("I still believe in both kindliness and justice," Mrs. Fisher writes in one of her prefatory notes, "but have no patience with self-deception") and possess level, frank voices that, while leaving much of their factual lives mysterious, disconcert and challenge us. Beyond the tropical tangle of experience and sensation which a woman endures, they seem to say, explorers come to an arctic zone that is and always has been home.

LONG VIEWS

A Cloud of Witnesses

The View in Winter: *Reflections on Old Age,* by Ronald Blythe. 270 pp. Harcourt Brace Jovanovich, 1979.

Pity the writer who writes a wonderful book, for he will be ever after chastised with it. The dust jacket of Ronald Blythe's new book identifies him in large type as "The Author of Akenfield," and the reviews of his second compilation of interviews and aperçus have held many polite but invidious comparisons with his first, *Akenfield: Portrait of an English Village* (1969). And, it is true, *Akenfield,* from its opening sentence ("The Village lies folded away in one of the shallow valleys which dip into the East Anglian coastal plain"), was possessed of a hero—a cluster of houses, the village itself, persuasively filling its little place in geography and history—and the saga of this aggregate hero swept into its own momentum all the many personalities whose monologues Mr. Blythe so lovingly recorded and edited; whereas *The View in Winter,* composed of interviews with old people in a variety of locations and social stations, must find its unity in the impalpable medium of time. The book seems longer (though it is shorter) than *Akenfield,* and Mr. Blythe has felt obliged to prolong his own essayistic interlardings, assigning significance rather than letting it, as in *Akenfield,* leap out unescorted from the memories and maunderings of the villagers. He himself was and is a resident of the Suffolk village he names Akenfield, while, though he is all of fifty-seven, he is not yet old. A certain tentative, speculative tone spins his ruminations a little thin:

> Unable to love the old, we approach them via sentiment, duty and an eye to our own eventual decline. We make sure that they are housed, fed, medicated, and seated facing their favourite channel. We see ourselves in them and they see—what is it that the aged see? Down on a young arm? God in majesty? The world's superstructure collapsing?

The strength of *Akenfield* lay in its affection for survivals, its witness to a world on the verge of disappearing. Until 1914, rural England had changed little since the Middle Ages, and observed harvest and sowing rituals that savored of the Stone Age. The most moving interviews Mr. Blythe conducted were with the old-timers who remembered the sacred protocols of mowing and gleaning, the endless picking of stones from the fields, the numinous role of the horse, the selfless expenditures of art upon rough work, the dignified niceties of plowing:

> Although the teams ploughed twenty yards apart, the men didn't talk much to each other, except sometimes they sang. Each man ploughed in his own fashion and with his own mark. It looked all the same if you didn't know about ploughing, but a farmer could walk on a field ploughed by ten different teams and tell which bit was ploughed by which. Sometimes he would pay a penny an acre extra for perfect ploughing. . . . The men worked perfectly to get this, but they also worked perfectly because it was *their* work. It belonged to them. It was theirs.

Mr. Blythe also interviewed those who out of stubborn inertia or shrewd antiquarianism continued to practice the patient crafts of the thatcher, the blacksmith, the saddler, the wheelwright. One man under forty, trained since childhood to service in the lavishly tended grounds of one of the territory's great estates, that of Lord Covehithe, recounted how a barrow would be trundled a mile out of the way to avoid affronting the Lord and his Lady with the sight of men at work—"It was terrible. You felt like somebody with a disease. . . . Ladyship drove about the grounds in a motor-chair and would have run us over rather than have to say, 'get out the way.' "

Sadly, he concludes, "I am a young man who has got caught in the old ways. I am thirty-nine and I am a Victorian gardener, and this is why the world is strange to me." The old ways were hard; an eighty-five-year-old farm laborer simply states, "I lived when other men could do what they liked with me." Against the background of the feudal brutality and depressed poverty that prevailed not only in Suffolk but across much of rural Europe, the docilely endured carnage of the Great War appears less incomprehensible. A veteran remembers:

> In my four months' training with the regiment I put on nearly a stone in weight and got a bit taller. They said it was the food but it was really because for the first time in my life there had been no strenuous work. I want to say this simply as a fact, that village people in Suffolk in my day were worked to death. It literally happened. It is not a figure of speech. . . . We were all delighted when war broke out on August 4th.

Its circumstantial witness to the harsh and bitterly mean lives that were the general expectancy well into this century saves *Akenfield* from sentimentality of the rustic-paradise persuasion. As one young farmworker put it, "of course we know that the old men had art—because they had damn-all else!"

Most of the individuals interviewed in *The View in Winter* have aged into a world they recognize as gentler and more abundant. "We worked too young and too small. But there, we have got through. The young today don't have to do what we had to do, but I don't mind. Times have changed and the world is changing, and the money has leaped up." From an old miner who began his trade crawling through the tunnels naked ("We were naked and we were each given a candle, and the men would blow the boys' candles out —as a prank, you know. And they kept you at it with a stick. Digging bare in the dark"), Mr. Blythe receives the impression that "what the present offers is almost too good to be true." Such felicity may be especial in England, where a third of the entire social-welfare budget is devoted to the care of this the first generation to reach old age more or less in its entirety. A British survey of the geriatric mass shows them to be in a surprisingly cheerful mood: only seven percent feel that they have nothing to look forward to. No one interviewed in this volume expresses fear of being mugged by youngsters, as is so common in American cities, or of being left behind, Eskimo or Arab style, to the mercy of wolves or the desert sun. The condition of these old people is, to an extent, national, as is their prevalent, and charming, stoicism; there is a good deal of specific British social history contained within their reminiscences, from mining to Fabianism, from the Western Front to the Salvation Army. But while the center of *Akenfield* was indeed local and sociological, the center of *The View in Winter* is existential and religious: what interests us most about these voices is their nearness to death.

The attitudes toward death vary. The conventional Christian expectations are rather restricted to the upper classes and to the half-dozen or so with a religious vocation. An eighty-four-year-old man, so wounded in the First World War that he has suffered constant pain and a limp for sixty years, recites poetry to himself at night instead of prayer, and professes, "I'm no good at what they call the 'eternal.' Some old people say that they are approaching it or have a belief that they are coming to it, but I don't. I feel I should, but I don't. I feel I want to make my peace, but with what, with whom? I'm not a religious man. . . . My education apart, I am a villager—fatalistic, you know. It all comes out at the end. You know what you *don't* believe, when you're in your eighties." A matron of a county-council home for the aged sums up her observations: "You could compare old age with having worked hard all day and, by the time evening comes, finding that if you can manage to work just another hour you will have done all you could. The light isn't good enough to do any more, so you have to pack up. Finish. Sitting back and saying, 'I have finished' is the general outlook of an elderly person." A ninety-year-old woman of the gentry speaks of a "huge, huge tiredness. It's not exactly unpleasant, but it is becoming rather a nuisance. I wouldn't mind if I could just doze off and wake up and find it gone, but I can't." She continues, "Let's be serious. This weariness is death. Don't you realise what death is? It is a lovely mist which takes us away. Did I once tell you about an experience I had in my twenties and the doctor thought I was dying? . . . And I could feel this mist coming towards me, a sort of swirling bank of marvellous love, love such as you'd never guess it in this world. And I could hear myself saying, 'Oh, take me, take me. Quick—take me!' "

Mr. Blythe interviewed a number of aged members of the Society of St. John the Evangelist at Oxford, an Anglican order of monks known as the Cowley Fathers. One septuagenarian Cowley father finds that in old age "the lesson to be learnt is to understand the promotion from plum-easy doing to the surprisingly difficult non-activity of just *being*. Be patient, be gentle, be *nothing*"; another notes that "I care less. . . . In fact I'm just about to fly out to South Africa and I don't much mind whether the aeroplane crashes or it doesn't"; and a third, after disarmingly expressing uncertainty as to whether God exists, confesses, "I love the physical world. I appreciate it. It is said that when you are old all this should decline . . . But I find that I can't leave the body behind when it is still with me!"

As Thoreau said on his deathbed: "One world at a time." For most of the old people interviewed, the otherworld held in contemplation is the strange paradise of the past, a world simultaneously more empty and more full than their enfeebled present. An eighty-six-year-old woman declares:

> We don't know what's in front of us, do we? So give me the old days every time. There wasn't a lot of money about, but life was about. Life. . . . There's more here than when I was little. There wasn't anything then, just the river running through. The church wasn't there, John Street wasn't there. Nothing—it was all fields. I can remember just the river and a little footbridge going across. . . . Those days are gone. We had five of ours working in the colliery. I had to change the water for each one, see. The boiler on the coal fire. Had to wash all their backs. They didn't wash a lot of backs then, because they thought it was weakening. Some would never have their backs washed. My husband had a skin like a beautiful woman's. A beautiful skin—lovely. And beautiful hair. The pit didn't hurt his skin but it gave him emphysema. He would walk up to his hands and knees in water in the drift. We

heard the men going to work early in the mornings with their hobnail boots on. Then, singing on top of the hills. . . . And the laughter in the streets because the beer was stronger then. Now you don't hear a sound. It's terrible.

Perhaps, as Proust suggested, the transformation of experience by memory into something ineffably precious is the one transcendent meaning each life does wrest from death.

The interview as a tool of art and history is a fairly recent device, though Henry Mayhew's *London Labour and the London Poor* used it to construct a nineteenth-century masterpiece, and certain medieval trials, such as that of Joan of Arc or the hearings in Pamiers concerning heresy in the village of Montaillou, can be read as interviews of a sort. For most of human history, the common man was not invited to speak, and men of eminence delivered pronouncements for reasons of their own, in protective circumstances of high formality. Now a microphone in the face is a standard hazard of fame, and scarcely a town in America lacks its amateur oral historian busy immortalizing on cassettes the ramblings of venerable local citizens. The tape recorder has joined the camera in an effort of indefatigable capture; we are bequeathing to posterity mountains and miles and vaultfuls of testimony. Yet it is not certain we will in the end be better understood than those centuries known from a handful of novels and plays, some chests of letters preserved by chance, and the stark records of parish church and shipping office. The interview, like the photograph, has its built-in blind spots and flatnesses; its mechanical sampling of reality leaves reality's own riddles essentially unprocessed. An age of flashbulbs keeps the sharpest shadows; the structures and anatomy photographed have not been comprehended as a painter would have to comprehend them, stroke by stroke, and the psychological anatomy of an interviewee need not be comprehended, either—merely prodded and poked in the hope that enough talk will let something out.

Mr. Blythe reveals nothing of his own questions and conversation as he guided his subjects into self-revelation. We are not told whether these interviews were taped or taken down by shorthand, or what relationship these persons—masked by pseudonyms—enjoyed with the interviewer before the interview. While some of the interview settings are described with the fullness and flourish of an old-fashioned novelist, other voices emanate from a Beckettian vacuum. Given some pages of beautifully human speech by these beings, we miss the novelist's ability to follow them about, to pursue them in time, to know them better than they know themselves. Mr. Blythe's frank ("Parkinson's disease keeps his gentle old flesh in constant motion"), sometimes even aggressive ("He is the sloppy old dog who will give you a nip") word-pictures of his subjects are stylish but bring another texture to his book, as do his essays ranging from geriatric sexuality to Midlands architecture, his extensive quotations from English poets, his sketches of the old age of various eminent Britons—everything thrown in as if for "good measure," making more an anthology than a choral testament, as *Akenfield* seemed. Brimming with insights and matter, *The View in Winter* fails to make a unified impression, and leaves us feeling less in a lovely mist than simply in a fog, and less at home with old age than after a reading of, say, Muriel Spark's *Memento Mori* or Tennyson's *Ulysses*.

Old age is not a terrain we can visit by bus but the end stage of our adamant individuality, a physical change bafflingly rung upon an immutable self. In the last year of his life, Tolstoy wrote, "I am conscious of myself in exactly the same way now, at eighty-one, as I was conscious of myself, my 'I,' at five or six years of age. Consciousness is immovable. Due to this alone there is the movement which we call 'time.' If time *moves on,* then there must be something that stands still." Some such mystery, perhaps, causes even as generously intentioned and poetically organized an attempt at generic geriatrics as Mr. Blythe's to come up muddled, with a bit of the caseworker's inevitable weary squint.

Who Wants to Know?

THE DRAGONS OF EDEN: *Speculations on the Evolution of Human Intelligence*, by Carl Sagan. 263 pp. Random House, 1977.

In 1869, ten years after the publication of *On the Origin of Species by Means of Natural Selection*, Alfred Russel Wallace, who first simultaneously and then coöperatively had developed with Darwin the theory of natural selection, became a heretic, on the issue of the human brain. "An instrument," he wrote, "has been developed in advance of the needs of its possessor. Natural Selection could only have endowed the savage with a brain a little superior to that of an ape, whereas he actually possesses one very little inferior to that of the average member of our learned societies." Darwin scrawled "No!" across his colleague's paper and wrote Wallace, "I hope you have not murdered too completely your own and my child"; but he did not speak to the issue, and the quantum leap of primate brain capacity, like so many other abrupt developments in the annals of so-called evolution, remains something of a puzzle. A modern paleoneurologist, Tilly Edinger, has stated, "If man has passed through a Pithecanthropus phase, the evolution of his brain has been unique, not only in its result but also in its tempo. . . . Enlargement of the cerebral hemispheres by fifty per cent seems to have taken place, speaking geologically, within an instant, and without having been accompanied by any major increase in body size." This explosive growth is reflected in the human infant, whose brain triples in volume within its first year, being at birth little bigger than the brain of a newborn gorilla.

Now, a reader might expect, picking up *The Dragons of Eden: Speculations on the Evolution of Human Intelligence,* to find the Wallace-Darwin controversy remembered, and the marvellous, not to say problematical, aspects of the evolution of the brain speculated upon. If so, he will be disappointed. In spite of its subtitle, this book is not speculative at all, in the sense that Julian Jaynes's *The Origin of Consciousness in the Breakdown of the Bicameral Mind* is, or the late Loren Eiseley's *The Immense Journey.* Jaynes is concerned with human consciousness in the millennia of discernible cultural history, and Eiseley with evolution in general. The former is a philosophical psychologist, the latter was an anthropologist with a splendidly literary, rather Jacobean sensibility; both range easily outward from their specialties in search of original conjunctions and illuminations. The difference between them and Mr. Sagan, writing in an area adjacent to both, is the difference between synthesis and synopsis.

By profession, Mr. Sagan is an astronomer, with aspirations to being a popularizer. He has previously written on the planets for *Life*, and on "Life" for the Encyclopaedia Britannica; he has edited a symposium on UFOs, has composed several books on extraterrestrial intelligence, and helped design the curious plaque hurled into space with Pioneers 10 and 11. He also enjoys appearing on the "Tonight Show," exposing science to the fans of Johnny Carson. Versatile though he is, he is simply not enough saturated in his subject here to speculate; what he can do is summarize and, to a limited degree, correlate the results of scattered and tentative modern research on the human brain. The research, from electroencephalograms of dreamers to endocranial casts of fossil skulls, is in progress, and Mr. Sagan, like the rest of us, must wait for sweeping conclusions. "If this result is confirmed, it would be quite an important finding," he writes in one iffy spot, and, in another, complains, "Very little work has been done in this field to date." He speaks of "many potential near-term developments in brain chemistry which hold great promise both for good and for evil," shamelessly woolgathers about how "one day we will have surgically implanted in our brains small replaceable computer modules or radio terminals which will provide us with a rapid and fluent knowledge of Basque, Urdu, Amharic, Ainu, Albanian, Nu, Hopi, !Kung, or delphinese," and, in another connection, allows, "It does not seem to me that a crisp choice among these four alternatives can be made at the present time, and I suspect that the truth will actually embrace most or all of these possibilities." Well, one begins to wonder, what *has* emerged lately in the study of human intelligence that justifies the production of this book? The dust jacket shows a pair of semi-shaggy primates sitting at ease in a ferny Eden with what appears to be a pet dimetrodon, a pre-dinosaurian reptile that vanished over a hundred million years before the first primates appeared. The book's title also hints at a thematic center that is reptilian. Mr. Sagan asks:

> Is it only an accident that the common human sounds commanding silence or attracting attention seem strangely imitative of the hissing of reptiles? Is it possible that dragons posed a problem for our protohuman ancestors of a few million years ago . . . Or does the metaphor of the serpent refer to the use of the aggressive and ritualistic reptilian component of our brain in the further evolution of the neocortex?

No, yes, and yes indeed: these are the correct answers, according to Quizmaster Sagan. "It is very difficult to evolve by altering the deep fabric of life . . . But fundamental change can be accomplished by the addition of new systems on top of old ones." The brain evolved outward, we are told. First, the very modest bulb at the end of the spinal cord which is all the brain a primitive fish possesses was improved, several hundred million years ago, by the elaboration of midbrain that is here called the reptilian, or R-complex; this, in turn, is enclosed in the limbic system common to mammals but undeveloped in reptiles; and the limbic system in man, dolphins, and whales is wrapped in a massive neocortex—about eighty-five percent of the human brain is neocortex. This tripartite division of the brain, with its faint echo of Freud's id, ego, and superego, is described as a "view" held, on some anatomical evidence, by Paul MacLean, chief of the Laboratory of Brain Evolution and Behavior of the National Institute of Mental Health. It is difficult to discern Mr. Sagan's intellectual contribution to the exposition, other than poetic chapter titles like "Tales of Dim Eden" and piquant epigraphs like—for the chapter sketching the three divisions of the brain—

> When shall we three meet again . . . ?
> WM. SHAKESPEARE
> *Macbeth*

The expository pattern tends to alternate facts experimentally discovered by other scientists with personal extrapolations that seem loose, if not facetious:

MacLean has shown that the R-complex plays an important role in aggressive behavior, territoriality, ritual and the establishment of social hierarchies. Despite occasional welcome exceptions, this seems to me to characterize a great deal of modern human bureaucratic and political behavior. I do not mean that the neocortex is not functioning at all in an American political convention or a meeting of the Supreme Soviet; after all . . .

Now, there is a real point here, perhaps the central point; but we would like to know a lot we aren't told. How do reptiles manifest their domination by ritual and hierarchies? The chief instances of ritualistic behavior cited stem from the advanced mentalities of monkeys. Of the reptilian mind we are assured that "it is not characterized by powerful passions and wrenching contradictions"; reptiles are (surprise!) "cold-blooded." And where does the R-complex make its primitive vestiges felt in our behavior? Answer: Children and hebephrenic schizophrenes show imperfectly suppressed (and quite unspecified) ritualistic traits, and football players apparently display their genitals in locker rooms.

As to the neocortex, its regions, or lobes, have specialized functions; various brain-damaged persons can write but not read, can read numbers but not letters, can name objects but not colors. But topographical mapping of the brain is complicated by what seems to be a maze of cross-wiring and duplicate programming. Just as the invention of machines enhanced human appreciation of anatomy, the rise of computer science has shed light on the brain's storing and sorting of information. The presence of two surgically separable hemispheres, with certain specializations evolved from an original redundancy, has an analogue in space-program computerization:

. . . the engineers who designed the on-board memory of the Viking lander inserted two identical computers, which are identically programmed. But because of their complexity, differences between the computers soon emerged. Before landing on Mars the computers were given an intelligence test (by a smarter computer back on Earth). The dumber brain was then turned off. Perhaps human evolution has proceeded in a similar manner and our highly prized rational and analytical abilities are localized in the "other" brain—the one that was not fully competent to do intuitive thinking.

Mr. Sagan's speculations, where they are not cheerfully wild, seem tacked-on and trivial. What is a non-trivial speculation? Well, when Desmond Morris, in *The Naked Ape*, speculates that the rounded breasts of the human female are imitations of the buttocks evolved to reinforce frontal sexuality in our uniquely upright, social species of primate, we may be startled and dubious, but at least an anatomical anomaly has been explained in accordance with a coherent theory (a theory that also takes in armpit hair, red lips, and fleshy noses). When Julian Jaynes speculates that until late in the second millennium B.C. men had no consciousness but were automatically obeying the voices of gods dictating, usually in metre, from the right halves of their brains to the left halves, we are astounded but compelled to follow this remarkable thesis through all the corroborative evidence he finds in ancient literature, modern behaviorism, and aberrant psychological phenomena such as hypnotism, possession, glossolalia, prophecy, poetry, and schizophrenia. When Mr. Sagan, however, speculating upon why such a vulnerable-making function as sleep should persist among highly evolved animals, suggests that sleep is a method of immobilizing "animals who are too stupid to be quiet on their own initiative," we feel that his guess is no better than ours. And his conclusion, on the final page of *The Dragons of Eden*, that "we are unlikely to survive if we do not make full and creative use of our human intelligence" seems lamer than one even we might have produced. He does not omit, in conclusion, to flog his media-marketable pet, the farfetched spectre of extraterrestrial intelligences beaming salvational messages our way.

The practical benefits as well as the philosophical insights likely to accrue from the receipt of a long message from an advanced civilization are immense. But how great the benefits and how fast we can assimilate them depend on the details of the message contents, about which it is difficult to make reliable predictions. One consequence, however, seems clear; the receipt of a message from an advanced civilization will show that there *are* advanced civilizations, that there are methods of avoiding the self-destruction that seems so real a danger of our present technological adolescence.

Such solemn whimsy does not seem to me significantly more substantial than astrology or pyramidology, which are decried a few pages later as showing "a need to replace experiments by desires."

When all this reviewer's R-complex resistance to Mr. Sagan's rather directional display of neocortical dominance has been registered, it remains to say that there is much fascinating information here, amid the fluff of computer printouts, Escher lithographs, and vacuous editorializing on matters ranging from abortion law to government funding for scientific research. We read, for instance, that the elaborate but undeciphered click language of whales and dolphins may involve "a re-creation of the sonar reflection characteristics of the objects being described." We learn that Lord Byron had a brain twice the size of Anatole France's, that Orientals have slightly larger brains than whites, and that both Cro-Magnon and Neanderthal men had larger brains, on the average, than ours. An ingenious pictographic map of the cerebral cortex shows what a comically disproportionate neural importance the hands and mouth possess: according to this part of the brain, we are more thumb than leg, and more tongue than chest. Mr. Sagan is perhaps non-trivial when he speculates, "Upright posture, the use of tools, and the development of language have mutually advanced one another, a small increment in language ability, for example, permitting the incremental improvement of hand axes, and vice versa. The corresponding brain evolution seems to have proceeded by specializing one of the two hemispheres for analytic thinking." On this point he seems more plausible than Mr. Jaynes, who believes that language did not appear before 70,000 B.C. and that toolmaking skill was transmitted entirely by imitation: "Consider," Jaynes says, "that it is almost impossible to describe chipping flints into choppers in language. . . . It is the same problem as the transmission of bicycle riding; does language assist at all?" Consciousness, for Jaynes, is a kind of disaster—the gradual disruption of a paradise of bicameral automatism. For Sagan, it is a discrete anatomical unit, "perhaps . . . another component of the left cerebral hemisphere."

Many of the brain's remaining mysteries need for solution mere wiring diagrams; yet a metaphysical halo lingers about the mystery of self-consciousness. A computer, after all, of sufficient complexity could handle the stimuli and responses of living without any component that says "I." But within the human—and, dare we think, the cetacean and simian?—brain there is a watcher, who always recedes, and who answers every question with another question. Mr. Sagan, a resolute disbeliever in any "mind-body dualism," waxes mystic in spite of himself when he recounts an experience very like a Sufi or Zen parable:

> In one marijuana experience, my informant became aware of the presence and, in a strange way, the inappropriateness of this silent "watcher," who responds with interest and occasional critical comment to the kaleidoscopic dream imagery of the marijuana experience but is not part of it. "Who are you?" my informant silently asked it. "Who wants to know?" it replied.

To the Tram Halt Together

KARL BARTH: *His Life from Letters and Autobiographical Texts*, by Eberhard Busch, translated from the German by John Bowden. 569 pp. Fortress Press, 1976.

PAUL TILLICH: *His Life and Thought* (Volume I: *Life*), by Wilhelm and Marion Pauck. 340 pp. Harper & Row, 1976.

Though Karl Barth and Paul Tillich represented, in their generation, opposite poles of Protestant theology, the two men had much in common. Both were born in 1886, the eldest children of pastor fathers. Both were early committed to careers in the ministry, and partook in their training of the liberal tradition of Kant and Schleiermacher—of German idealism, with its strenuous scholarship and stately vagueness. Both studied for a time at the University of Berlin, whose theological faculty was headed by the great historian of dogma Adolf von Harnack. Both Tillich and Barth embarked upon pastoral work, and their very different theological approaches were forged in the heat of the active ministry at a time when the catastrophe of the First World War had shattered the mold of idealist thought: Tillich served as a Lutheran chaplain in the Kaiser's armies through some of the worst carnage of the Western Front, and emerged a libertine and virtual atheist; Barth from 1911 to 1921 acted as the Reformed pastor of the Swiss village of Safenwil, and in his "pastor's perplexity" ("I feel like someone trying to blow into a trumpet; my cheeks are all puffed out, and yet curiously no sound emerges") rejected the liberal, humanist tendencies of nineteenth-century Protestantism and began to preach and write in the accents of neo-orthodoxy. Both men were outspoken Socialists, and distrusted the church's old alliance with the landed and the comfortable. Both were natural scholars and teachers, and found their destined niches not in any ecclesiastical hierarchy but in professorial chairs. Both early resisted Nazism and were ousted from their posts at German universities, Tillich emigrating to America in 1933, Barth returning to his native Basel in 1935. Though one was Swiss and the other became an American, the intellectual homeland of both remained Germany. Tillich regarded Matthias Grünewald's *Crucifixion* from the Isenheim altar in Colmar as "the most religious of all paintings," and it was this very painting, in reproduction, that Barth always hung above his desk, to contemplate as he worked. Both theologians derived surprisingly strong pleasure and comfort from the secular arts: while a soldier, Tillich, "as a reaction to the horror, ugliness and destructiveness of war," studied the poor reproductions of paintings obtainable in military bookstores and, for the rest of his life, was an enthusiastic museum-goer; Barth began each day with the playing of a Mozart record and once jested that "if I ever get to Heaven, I shall first ask after Mozart, and only then after Augustine and Thomas, Luther and Calvin and Schleiermacher." Barth said in praise of Mozart that "he plays and does not cease to play," and Tillich, too, following Nietzsche, allowed play a high place in the scheme of things human. Tillich's compulsive and flagrant infidelities have been given ample publicity in his widow Hannah's memoir *From Time to Time* (and from there to *Time*); what has been less well known, at least in this country, is that Barth in 1929 installed a "loyal assistant," Charlotte von Kirschbaum, in his home along with his wife, Nelly, and their five children, and that "Lollo" Kirschbaum for decades occupied the place of a wife during his travels and summer vacations. Both men were handsome and tall, and kept their hair into old age. Both wrote copiously and lectured much, yet both resisted completion of their respective *magna opera* —the last volume of Tillich's *Systematic Theology* was finally coaxed from him by the demands of systematic students of his work, and was termed by him "an incompleteness of the completed"; Barth let his massive *Church Dogmatics* drop after thirteen volumes and 9,185 pages, with the ethics of reconciliation incomplete and eschatology still to go. Both men lived well past the Biblical allotment of threescore and ten, Tillich dying at the age of seventy-nine, Barth at eighty-two. And now both are the subject of biographies.

Eberhard Busch, a German pastor who was Barth's last assistant, has written the bigger and better book, weaving his biography out of Barth's own words whenever possible, and summarizing the content of Barth's principal works and addresses in smaller type as the life proceeds. Wilhelm and Marion Pauck, by reserving Tillich's "Thought" for a second, yet-to-be-published volume, truncate their own necessary descriptions of Tillich's works, and make his life seem more purely public than it was. In both cases, the biographers threaten to drown us in the names of those with whom Tillich and Barth shook hands and exchanged a few words. Viewed externally, there is little that is edifying about the lives of these two men save their capacity for academic work and their stomach for travel and meeting strangers. Inevitably, the formative periods of childhood and youth are in deepest shadow, and the lights of fame play upon actors who have long practiced their routines. Tillich came under the seminal influence of Friedrich Schelling in 1904, when he impulsively purchased the philosopher's collected works at a bargain price. Though Barth's crucial rereading of the Bible— leading to his revolutionary commentary on Paul's Epistle to the

Romans—took place in 1916, when he was thirty, he began to make his escape from the "liberal swamp" of his student days by way of the lectures of Wilhelm Herrmann: "Although Herrmann was surrounded by so much Kant and Schleiermacher, the decisive thing for him was the christocentric impulse, and I learnt that from him." However, both Tillich and Barth, whose lives saw Europe twice convulsed and cultural presumptions repeatedly swept away, prided themselves on intellectual openness and presented theologies constantly susceptible to revision. Barth's advanced maturity offered a number of opinions disconcerting to his followers, such as his stand against infant baptism and his amiable attitude toward Communist regimes, and it was no small feat of adaptability for Tillich to reclaim and surpass in America the prestige he had left behind in Germany. In his last years of unremitting celebrity (unremittingly, it should be added, exploited by him), he often distinguished between "Tillich the subject and Tillich the object." The Paucks, of whom Wilhelm is a German-born colleague of Tillich's at the Union Theological Seminary and Marion a onetime student, make a considerable effort to penetrate the revered object and disclose the elusive, ambiguous, sometimes irritating and inconsiderate subject. "Sometimes he took up the words of others into his work, often without benefit of footnote. . . . In his later years on the lecture platform he tended to exaggerate out of all proportion the size and influence of the religious socialist group to which he had belonged." None of the Paucks' hints are as damning, though, as the portrait offered by Hannah Tillich, in her memoir, of a cruel deceiver who, caught out in his deception, "threw himself on the floor, screaming and kicking, because this time there was no way out," and who collected pornography and mementos of his amours in greedy quantity:

I unlocked the drawers. All the girls' photos fell out, letters and poems, passionate appeal and disgust. Beside the drawers, which were supposed to contain his spiritual harvest, the books he had written and the unpublished manuscripts all lay in unprotected confusion. I was tempted to place between the sacred pages of his highly esteemed lifework those obscene signs of the real life that he had transformed into the gold of abstraction—King Midas of the spirit.

The self-effacing Pastor Busch permits himself little more than connective tissue between Barthian quotations, except for a passage that in his own voice delicately explains the Charlotte von Kirschbaum matter—"this sore and vulnerable place in his life."* Otherwise, we take at Barth's own evaluation, in his own words, his relationship with his family, his children, his colleagues and opponents. We are not invited to judge as one old friend after another falls away, repelled by the latest turn in Barth's course; only his brother Heinrich, with whom his relations had been "decidedly cool" for years, is permitted to be overheard calling Karl "a man who would brook no opposition." Still, Busch avoids hagiography as well as criticism, and this biographical enterprise is a model of modesty and thoroughness, drawing upon an immense number of published texts and unpublished letters and documents. From the two biographies, we can gather a substantial, if not ultimately intimate, impression of the two men: of Barth as a combative, and Tillich as a mediatory, personality.

The young Karl Barth loved to read about battles. "Until I was sixteen, I lived and dreamed of military exploits. My brothers and I would play with lead soldiers for hours on end and did so with

---

*Mr. Robert Short has directed my attention to the section, "Man and Woman," in *Church Dogmatics III/4*, wherein Barth offers some strikingly undemanding and almost apologetic theology on the subject of sexual disorder: "And in the sphere of the relations of man and woman, where all are transgressors, the keeping of the command means that man allows himself to be led by God's goodness to repentance and to a position of remoteness from his trangression and vigilance against it. More than this is not required of him. Absolute purity, an ideal masculinity or femininity, a heavenly love, a perfect marriage—in short that he should no longer be a transgressor—is not required of him, because by the grace of God he is already free and righteous in spite of his transgression, so that anything he may will or do in this respect is not only impossible of execution but also pointless . . . What is required of him, what he can both will and do because God by His gracious intervention effects in him this willing and doing, is to set himself in concrete opposition to the transgression of which he finds himself accused, to himself as a transgressor, and to the disorder in which he lives. By the gracious judgment of the divine command he is instructed and made willing and ready to undertake an active opposition to this disorder, and to secure bridgeheads within the confusion."

great seriousness." At the age of seventy, he surprised an audience in Hanover by seeming to know "more about the victory won by the Hanoverians over the Prussians in 1866 than they did themselves." And when, after his retirement, he overcame a long-standing reluctance to visit the United States, he toured Civil War battlefields. "In a ruined Civil War fort by the St. James River, I fired a hundred-year-old musket and to the honor of the Swiss army even hit the target—an event which could with good will be regarded as symbolic of my other adaptabilities and successes." Though Swiss neutrality denied him experience of combat, he took satisfaction in the guard duty he performed in uniform, during both world wars; as a pastor in Safenwil, he organized snowball fights among his confirmation classes, "to heighten our mutual pleasure." In the theological wars that followed his commentary on Romans and his leaving the Safenwil pulpit for a professorship at Göttingen, there is no lack of military terminology, of "breakthroughs" and "joining forces"; unable to lecture for a few weeks because of an ear infection, he described himself as "unfit for battle." Whoever his enemy is— the mill-owners of Safenwil; his old teacher Harnack; the *"moribund"* (his italics) "dyed-in-the-wool liberals"; the Nazis and their "German Christian" church; the Bultmannites; Emil Brunner; the politically conservative Swiss who deplored his lack of Cold War fervor—Barth swings into battle with a righteous joy: "I accepted an invitation from the cathedral council in Berne and opened fire with all guns." If Tillich's is a theology of the dubious "Yes," Barth's is one of the triumphant "No." *Nein!* was the name of his famous pamphlet against Brunner in 1934, and a collection of his postwar writings bore the title "Against the Stream." If Tillich, "on the boundary" of Christian faith, sought conciliation with rival realms of wisdom from the Greeks to the Freudians, Barth's tactic was to isolate, to repel and exclude everything—*Kultur,* idealism, natural theology, polymorphous religiosity—that might be confused with the narrow ground of Biblical revelation where he makes a stand, a ground finally narrowed to a phrase: "The last word which I have to say as a theologian and also as a politician is not a term like 'grace' but a name, 'Jesus Christ.' " From his student days, he had headed for such high, stripped terrain; "What I now looked for in books and from my professors was the true knowledge of simplicity." Of his favorite professor, he wrote approvingly, "There was steel in Herrmann's voice." Tillich himself, writing of "the strong but tight-fitting armor of Barthian supranaturalism," cannot but fall into a military metaphor. The odd thing was, Barth did not find the armor tight. Secure in his one-man fortress, he regarded the world with great good humor and genial shrewdness. After witnessing a "frolicking" stage show in Paris, he asks, "Why doesn't the church at least try to be as good at what it does as the children of this world with their singing, miming and dancing?" His pronouncements upon secular matters have an almost invariable pith, freshness, and freedom from anxiety; having so firmly distinguished between men and God, he looks to men to do what they can. He complains of Bach's "desire to preach" and hears in Mozart "a final word about life insofar as this can be spoken by man." He read a goodly amount of fiction, and wrote of the contemporary novelist, "I expect him to show me man as he always is in the man of today, my contemporary—and vice-versa, to show me my contemporary in man as he always is . . . [The novel] should have no plans for educating me, but should leave me to reflect (or not) on the basis of the portrait with which I am presented."

The portrait that the Paucks present of Tillich offers a wobbly surface for reflection. At the age when young Barth was rehearsing battles, Tillich was a dreamer. In his brief, but revelatory, autobiographical sketch *On the Boundary*, he said:

Between fourteen and seventeen, I withdrew as often as possible into imaginary worlds which seemed to be truer than the world outside. In time, that romantic imagination was transformed into philosophical imagination. For good and for ill, the latter has stayed with me ever since. It has been good in that it has given me the ability to combine categories, to perceive abstractions in concrete terms . . . and to experiment with a wide range of conceptual possibilities. It has been of doubtful value insofar as such imaginative ability runs a risk of mistaking the creations of the imagination for realities . . .

Tillich's sternest critics could scarcely improve upon the last sentence of this self-characterization. If theology for Barth was a kind of war games, for Tillich it was an inflated mode of introspection. *On the Boundary* confesses his Prussian habit of dutiful subordination; this habit places a "tremendous burden upon my conscience, which accompanies every personal decision and every violation of tradition, an indecisiveness in the face of the new and unexpected, and a desire for an all-embracing order that would reduce the risk of personal choice." Such paradoxes seem very German—nothing of the hard-headed Swiss about Tillich. He himself suggests that dutifulness and highly developed philosophical systems stem from the same wish for "all-embracing order." Tillich's life as described by the Paucks includes these ambivalences: he was often indecisive in pedagogic matters but showed cool courage through battles that included Verdun; he twice married vivid, disorderly women with little sympathy for his work; he rarely attended church services except when he was the preacher; at least in his American years, he read relatively little and depended upon personal conversation and conferences for intellectual sustenance; he found refuge in our land of freedom but felt watched and hounded here by Puritan moralists; he loved to build sand castles, to stay up late, and to lecture. His personal magnetism and his joy in "creative communion" shine brighter in these pages than his theological thought, which seems a matter less of recasting concepts than of renaming God "the Ground of Being," Christ "the New Being," revelation "the *kairos,*" etc. His theological affirmations take place at the weakest possible level: the level of the verb "to be." "The courage to be is rooted in the God who appears when God has disappeared in the anxiety of doubt," his most famous book concludes. By his formulations (in the Paucks' paraphrase), religion is merely "the dimension of depth in all of life's functions," the eternal is "what ought to be," and theology's task is "to ask for being as far as it gives us ultimate concern." The benign effects of Tillichian obfuscation are described in an almost comical passage:

> What he did learn, through dialogue with his colleagues, he persistently translated into his own terminology, to the amazement, amusement, and sometimes frustration of others. He thus frequently reconciled their conflicting opinions.

He saw himself as a bridge between the Church and those outside it, between "the Anglo-Saxon and the German theological world," even as a "triboro bridge" between systematics, philosophy, and history. But a bridge has no content, just traffic. The instinct was perhaps shrewd which kept him within a church whose tenets and rites he observed so selectively. For it is not clear that Tillich, as a secular philosopher or historian, would have developed ideas original enough to win the attention he received as a clergyman— an apostle to the unbelievers, with unbelief on his own countenance. He himself cherished his long essay on "The Demonic" as one of "the few truly original contributions he felt he had made." In this area, of the demonic and the fallible, of sin and guilt, he strikes us as more Christianly sensitive than Barth, whose righteousness braces every utterance and who once did retort to an opponent who accused him of wanting always to be right, "But I always am right!" Tillich confessed pain where Barth admitted none. Tillich wrote of risking "tragic guilt in becoming free from father and mother and brothers and sisters," and, according to the Paucks, his "special talent for friendship was marked by an extraordinary ability to make it last." He hated splits, and his theology abounds with blurred distinctions and separations that are "overcome." Where Barth insistently emphasized the absolute difference between human culture and God's revelation, Tillich's "personal inability to accept the split between a faith unacceptable to culture and a culture unacceptable to faith prompted him to interpret the articles of faith through cultural expressions."

The two men met infrequently. Both were involved in Religious Socialism after the First World War, and in 1922 Tillich visited Barth in Göttingen. In a letter to his lifetime friend and theological

ally Eduard Thurneysen, Barth wrote of Tillich: "The most re-
markable things about him are his 'antipathy to orthodoxy' and his
mythology of history, in which the need for the supernatural,
which he otherwise takes pains to suppress, comes pouring out.
. . . Hirsch [another theologian] took pleasure in setting us against
each other, denouncing Tillich to me as un-Christian and me to
Tillich as unscholarly. Of course we did not agree with this type-
casting, although there is something in it." When Tillich began to
teach at Marburg, in 1924, his students "expected him to address
himself to the theological upheaval caused by Karl Barth," an ex-
pectation he disappointed, "developing his own ideas" instead. In
his writings, he tends to address Barth and Barthianism gingerly,
his disapproval softened by a tone of historical detachment. His
History of Christian Thought says in its concluding paragraph:

> Again the diastasis against the synthesis of Christianity and the modern
> mind became real under Karl Barth. My own answer is that synthesis
> can never be avoided, because man is always man, and at the same time
> under God.

His *Perspectives on 19th and 20th Century Protestant Theology* re-
marks of Barth: "He silenced the problems of historical criticism
completely. The question of the historical Jesus did not touch him
at all. But problems cannot be silenced." *On the Boundary* is still
more astringent: "The extremely narrow position of the Barthians
may save German Protestantism, but it also creates a new het-
eronomy, an anti-autonomous and anti-humanistic attitude that I
must regard as a denial of the Protestant principle." Yet, loath to
give up friendship with even the arch-negator of the Protestant
principle, Tillich called upon him whenever, after his emigration,
he visited Europe. "Extremely animated friend-to-friend conversa-
tion in which we trade insults," Tillich wrote in his travel diary of
1936. "He feels my existence in America is providential. We part
as great friends." After another of Tillich's visits to Basel, in 1958,
Barth expressed this view: "A charming man, though his theology
is quite impossible (Oh dear, I have undertaken to hold a seminar
on him for the whole winter!)." Of this seminar, Barth later wrote,
"I constantly try to interpret him for the best and to defend him

against the students, who want to snap around him like hunting dogs." Their last meeting, in 1963, was confirmed by an aggressively jocular postcard from Barth: "You are welcome on December 1. Where shall we begin when we meet again and see each other face to face? With the troubles of old age which now assail both of us? . . . Or with the difficulties you have with my books and I have with yours?" Tillich returned from this meeting saying, "Barth and I are friends again!" Pressed for evidence, he replied, "He accompanied me to the tram halt."

Their years devoted to expounding God as they understood Him, to giving Christianity a twentieth-century face, did not exempt them from the pains and indignities—catheters, forgetfulness—of old age, or bring them total serenity. Tillich expressed an oddly fundamentalist anxiety that he "was a sinner who would be excommunicated from the Kingdom of God" and on occasion would ask a late-night auditor, "Am I a phony? I fear so." Barth confided in a letter, "I often have to fight with a quite inexplicable sadness in which all the success that life has brought me is *no use at all.*" Their work—to rescue the Christian good news not only from the perennial bad news of the human condition but from the modern contraindications of Biblical criticism and materialist science—was not the sort to stand forever. Theology is not a provable accumulation, like science, nor is it a succession of enduring monuments, like art. It must always unravel and be reknit. In "The Word of God and the Task of the Ministry," an address given in 1922, Barth said, "Our systematic theology . . . has been many times altered and sometimes improved . . . But has this meant anything more than the turning over of a sick man in his bed for sake of change?" And:

> It is obvious that theology does not owe its position at the university to any arbitrary cause. It is there in response to a need and is therefore justified in being there. The other faculties may be there for a similar reason, but theology is forever different from them, in that *its* need is apparently never to be met. This marks its similarity to the church.

In offering to meet the needs of their time, Tillich and Barth set their fellow-Christians opposite but, so elastic are the dialectics of faith, not mutually exclusive lessons. Both confronted the apparent withdrawal of God from the world around them—Barth by claiming that He was Wholly Other and thus immune to detection, Tillich by suggesting that He was present, weakly, in everything. Theology buttresses the faith that would hold off mortal fear, and these two theologians, a decade after the decade of their deaths, present a merged afterimage, positive and negative slants on the problem of *Angst*. What lingers of Barth, still ringing in the air of churches and seminaries, was his tone of fearlessness, his bold, encyclopedic, and hearty exposition of the word of God as over against the word of Man; whereas Tillich, unable to exclude anxiety and doubt, brought them into the sanctum, and called them holy emotions.

APPENDIX
On One's Own Oeuvre

ON ONE'S OWN OEUVRE

A COLLECTION, *mercifully incomplete, of written comments, extracted under various goads, pertaining to the one author upon whom and whose work I am an undoubted expert. Forewords readily available elsewhere, as in Knopf's new editions of* The Poorhouse Fair *and* The Carpentered Hen *or in paperbacks like* Olinger Stories *(Vintage) and* Too Far to Go *(Fawcett), are not included here.*

IN ANSWER *to* The New York Times Book Review*'s question of Christmas 1979: "What book made you decide to become a writer and why?"*

I'm not sure I ever *did* decide to be a writer; in my mind I'm still just trying it out. A book, however, that remains there bathed in a numinous glow was James Thurber's *Men, Women and Dogs,* published by Harcourt, Brace in 1943, and costing three dollars. I, age eleven, had asked it be given to me as a Christmas present, and so it was, and eagerly unwrapped, and read right there on the floor, within smelling distance of the holiday pine and the little blue Lionel train that went around and around, emitting a whistling noise and a dear small excited scent of hot lubricating oil. It was a book of cartoons but more book-shaped than this genre usually is, with an introduction by Dorothy Parker, a dedication to E. B. White, and an index of captions. What I made, in my prepubescent state, of captions like "Le cœur a ses raisons, Mrs. Bence, que la raison ne connait pas" and "My wife wants to spend Halloween with her first husband" I don't quite remember; but the volume spoke to me of New York, of sophistication, of amusing adult misery, of carefree creativity (I could see that Thurber had a lot of trouble fitting his furniture around his people but hadn't let it bother him), of nervous squiggles given permanence and celebrity by the intervening miracle of printer's ink. This struck me as a super way to live, to be behind such a book.

IN ANSWER *to an inquiry into my formative motivations by Cynthia Pincus, Leslie Elliott, and Trudy Schlachter, authors of a book with the promising title* The Roots of Success *(Prentice-Hall, 1980).*

Both of my parents were very encouraging by nature, and as an only child I reaped all the encouragement they had to give. The town and time also conduced to an innocent indulgence of a small person's dreams, and the supply of dream fuel, from Walt Disney movies to detective novels in the local city library, never ran short. Many teachers, beginning with the artist across the street, Mr. Clint Shilling, and continuing through a long line of English teachers of whom Mrs. Florence Schrack deserves especial mention, were mentors. My mother was mentor number one in the matter of art, my father in the matter of life and reality. Both were great inquirers into their, and by extension the human, condition. At the age of thirteen I was moved to a farm where I had extra amounts of solitude to entertain. Adversity, in the form of allergic reaction and financial insecurity, visited me in stimulating but not overwhelming amounts. Adversity in immunological doses has its uses; more than that crushes. Religion was and is a helpful peripheral presence, giving me hopefulness and a sense of reward beyond the immediate and a suspicion of intrinsic excellence as an ultimate standard.

IN ANSWER *to a request from Mrs. Darla J. Morgan, a teacher in the Governor Mifflin Schools, of Shillington, Pennsylvania, that I supply to the junior-high-school newspaper,* Junior Monarch, *"a few para-graphs concerning [my] memories of the school, or of classmates and teachers."*

Shillington High School meant a double amount to me, because it was not only where I went to school for six years but the place where my father worked for thirty. My first memory of it is going with him, in early September, over to his homeroom (Room 204) and helping him set out the pencils and tablets for the new students next day. His closet held a fragrant trim mystery of glossy new textbooks and virgin paper. Then in time I grew old enough to go to the seventh grade, and indeed for one year was in his homeroom. As a math student I studied under him for three years. I was pretty good at math, happily.

These were the years up to 1950, when I graduated. My class, consisting of children born in the worst years of the Depression, had one hundred eighteen members. There were four or five schoolteacher's children in the class, and a great many only children, and until the Kenhorst and Adamstown students joined us in the ninth grade we all came from the same square mile. So we had a lot of "class spirit" and mutual loyalty, and our reunions are still well attended.

Shillington hasn't changed much in thirty years except on the edges. The school grounds extended to the "Poorhouse Lane," where the shopping center is; and on all the acreage around the new Governor Mifflin High School there were just two wooden goalposts and some flimsy bleachers. One excitement I remember well was taking the trolley car Friday nights into Reading to see Shillington play football in Albright Stadium. And in 1948, I re-member, everybody's skirt-length dropped so low that only white socks and saddle shoes showed under the hems. That was called the New Look, and didn't last long. What strikes me now when I look at my yearbook is how dark the lipstick was, and how short the boys' hair looks. There was a great deal of snappy combing of wet hair in the lavatory; the comb in the shirt pocket, with a pack of cigarettes (unfiltered), was the insignia of a sharp guy. We wore corduroy shirts, and blue jeans were not allowed.

I look at *Happy Days* on television now and then and what rings true is the importance of the luncheonette as a social center. Walt Stephens's luncheonette on Lancaster Avenue was the hangout for those of us who couldn't walk home for lunch and disdained the school cafeteria. After school the air was solid blue with cigarette smoke, and very romantic with the scent of girls' perfume (they wore angora sweaters then) and the rockety-*ding* of the pinball machine. The tunes on the jukebox then are impossible to hear now; I would love, just once more, to hear Russ Morgan's "So Tired," with a lot of muted trumpets going wah-wah.

The faculty in the years I attended were in their prime and I think the education offered was an especially good one, for a small public school. I am grateful for the Latin I took and for the emphasis on English grammar, which seems to have faded from the curriculum. The teachers, my father among them, were giving of their after-hours time and quite willing to encourage any talent that manifested itself in a child. Carlton Boyer ran a very lively art department, and Thelma Lewis was the kind and permissive faculty adviser for the mimeographed weekly, *The Chatterbox.* My drawing and writing were allowed to go as far as they could, which is what education (*e*, out, + *ducere*, bring) is all about.

Looking back, and trying to compare the Class of 1950 with what I know of children now, I suppose our horizons were rather narrow—Reading on one side and Mohnton on the other—and we took our racial and economic homogeneity all too easily for granted. But we assumed the world necessarily had rules and never for a minute believed that life was a free ride. Learn to Live, Live to Learn, the motto read on the orange-brick façade of old Shillington High. I was sorry when, not many years after I graduated, the school name ceased to exist, though the building did not. The motto, I noticed recently, is still up.

IN REPLY *to George Christy, editor of* The Hollywood Reporter Annual, *who wanted to know, in August 1979, "how Hollywood has influenced you, your work, your artistic vision."*

I went to the movies pretty intensely from about 1938, when I was six years old, to 1954, when I graduated from college. My moviegoing has fallen off since, as my willing suspension of disbelief becomes more and more grudging. Of the many movies I did see in my youth, however, I received an ultimate impression—a moral ideal, we may say—of debonair grace, whether it was Fred Astaire gliding in white tie and tails across a stage of lovelies, or Errol Flynn leading a band of merry men through Sherwood Forest with that little half-smile beneath his mustache, or George Sanders drawling a riposte in his role as the Saint. In my own clumsy way I have tried all my life to be similarly debonair. Also I got an impression of a world where everything works out for the best and even small flaws in character are punished with a hideous rigor. And also, of course, of sex, symbolized by beautiful round-armed women taking baths in champagne or being threatened, in Roman or Biblical contexts, by murder or conversion.* When one reads, nowadays, of how much actual sex was being pursued and accomplished by the makers of those movies, their delicately honed symbolizations seem almost hypocrisy—but the message got through, to us adolescents out there, and the eroticization of America is (in large part) a cinematic achievement. The Eros is still there, but I do miss in contemporary movies the debonairness, the what Hemingway called grace under pressure, a certain masculine economy and understatement in the design of those films, now all gone to scatter and rumpus in the fight with television for the lowest common denominator.

A REMINISCENCE *contributed to* The Harvard Lampoon 1876–1976, *a centennial celebratory volume bound in Cambridge in handsome crimson.*

I first saw and scented the inside of the *Lampoon* building as a freshman, in 1950. That rank deep smell of old magazines subaque-

---

*Once I had the pleasure of meeting Claudette Colbert, who told me, of the famous milk bath she took in Cecil B. DeMille's *Sign of the Cross,* that it was terribly cold, and kept turning to butter.

ously stored in the basement, the unexpectedly domestic Dutch tiles, the frightened cluster of candidates with their wet umbrellas and galoshes (there is a definite humidity about these early recollections) have stayed with me, as a benevolent and exciting confusion at the gates of Paradise. This was in the presidency of the remarkable draftsman and actor, Fred Gwynne, subsequently Herman Munster on television. He was huge in height and busy elsewhere; I glimpsed him striding across the Yard shortly after the *Pontoon* confiscation that fall, a romantic figure, because supposed (mistakenly) on the verge of expulsion. But my real contacts on the editorial board were Doug Bunce, Mike Arlen, and Charlie Osborne. Bunce, himself a romantic figure who lived in the building, maintained rather oblique relations with the college, and cared greatly for the magazine.

Some hope of artistic excellence still lingered from the postwar years, and the small editorial board zealously worried each issue into shape. The *Punch* parody, which contained my first cartoon for the *Lampoon*, seemed and still seems especially fine. I think this ardor for excellence rather declined in my four years; the conviviality in the Great Hall became purely social, with the need for monthly publication nagging like a bad conscience. Among my betters on the staff, many (Arlen, Osborne, Charles Flood, Bunce under the name Douglas Fairbairn, Lew Gifford, Gwynne) have made careers in the arts. It was a healthy atmosphere for a would-be cartoonist and "humorist" like myself to enter.

The stunts, as I recall, were usually more poetic in conception than in execution. A fool, dressed as a very bulky German professor, was to go into the Widener Reading Room, open his fat briefcase, and have a pigeon fly out. In practice the pigeon hopped out, and just walked around the table. My one successful impersonation was of a blind cripple who, in the sale of pencils to a group of other fools dressed as priests, loudly cries fraud and, a crowd having collected, is pelted with fish the good men have concealed under their cassocks. On a grander scale, there was Charlie Osborne's ascent in a huge balloon which, at the height of inflation, punctured itself on an ivy twig jutting from the Narthex wall. The *Crimson* had attempted to kidnap him in process, but, looking very pale and doughty, wearing jodhpurs and Lindbergh goggles, he had escaped. Kidnappings were usually rather sad. I helped kidnap Michael Maccoby, now a Washington psychiatrist, and after driving around for hours in the Somerville region, there seemed little to do but let him escape. The kidnapping of Paul Dever, then Governor of the Commonwealth, was pleasanter. He had been scheduled to address the Harvard Young Democrats, and a somewhat demented Dixiecrat undergraduate persuaded him that the meeting was to take place in the *Lampoon* building, where he gave the assembled membership a political talk that I, being one of the few Democrats present, found rather persuasive. It was not until the talk was completed and handshakes all around had been delivered that the president of the Young Democrats discovered where Dever was, rushed up, and told him he'd been kidnapped. Dever laughed. His good humor over the hoax saved what felt to me like a precarious situation. But then I, a police-fearing boy from the Pennsylvania hills, was always amazed by the élan with which my well-to-do colleagues on the Poon disdained the law. I recall Bink Young, now an Episcopalian minister, very calmly sitting in the Business Office, his tattered sneakers cocked up on an old wood desk, and sanguinely plotting the theft of a battleship from Boston Harbor.

The Poon's function as a club and perpetuator of Brahmin tradition almost entirely escaped me. I never, even when president myself, understood the social engineering that went into the *Lampoon*'s life. There were now and then parades, for example, with hay wagons and beer kegs and brass bands and Radcliffe girls. How had all this materialized? I didn't know, but was delighted to be asked along. Which is true, I would say, of my *Lampoon* experience in general.

AN INTRODUCTION *to* Talk from the Fifties, *a collection of twenty Talk of the Town pieces published in a limited edition by Lord John Press (Northridge, California) in 1979.*

Twenty-three, 4-F, married, the father of an infant daughter, fed up forever with formal education, and determined to live by my wits and words in New York City, I was hired by *The New Yorker*, as a Talk of the Town reporter. They assigned me an office on the eighteenth floor, in the midst of the ladies who assembled "On and Off the Avenue." A steel desk, official stationery, and a telephone were mine. "Talk" ideas fluttered in on pink slips initialled "WS," for William Shawn, the magazine's editor. My first story, and the first one reprinted here (concerning "a lawn invigorator that dyes grass green," developed by the Lockrey Company, in Southampton), I remember most vividly—to be exact, with the spottiest erasures by the art gum of Time, which has totally obliterated the circumstances of many of its successors. We had moved to Manhattan in August 1955, hastily taking a strange triangular fifth-floor apartment on Riverside Drive, enjoyable chiefly for its view of New Jersey. In our country innocence we brought with us a car, that I moved from one side of Eighty-fifth Street to the other every morning, and in this pale blue Ford, one hot day the first week of my job, we—the "we" of our little family, not the *pro forma* "we" of Talk of the Town—set out, thinking it a larky thing to drive to the end of Long Island, knowing neither how crowded nor how long Long Island was. By the time we arrived to interview Mr. Lockrey, my wife and baby were so wilted as to need a rejuvenating spray themselves. But I got the story, and got us back safely, never to use the car on an assignment again. A few dog days later, during an evening not unlike the one described in the short story "Toward Evening," after I had returned from work and taken off some of the gray suit compulsory in that era, Mr. Shawn called the apartment to tell me that I was, on the strength of Magi-Green, promoted from "Talk reporter" to "Talk writer"—that is, my submissions would not pass through a rewrite man but would be published as I wrote them, and my salary of one hundred dollars a week would be offset by a piece-rate of two hundred dollars per story. I asked him if he was sure I was up to this, and he said, in his politely absolute way, Yes, he was sure.

For the twenty months, then, before I quit the job and left the city in April of 1957, I had the happy freedom of a salaried rover. The department was large, and my sense of its workings never exact. Mr. Shawn (as all of us under forty called him) ran it from

on high, Eugene Kinkead generated many of the Talk ideas, Bren-
dan Gill and John McCarten did rewrite, and my fellow-underlings
included Whitney Balliett, Faith McNulty, Anthony Bailey, and
Richard Lemon, the first of whom still describes jazz (wonderfully
well) from the office he occupied then, and in which we had many
baffled, titillated conversations about the lovable and inscrutable
organization that housed us. There were, as I recall, three types of
Talk story—interviews, "fact" pieces, and "visits." Since "visits"—
strolling through an Electrical Industries Show at the 69th Regi-
ment Armory, or a National Motor Boat Show at the Coliseum, or
an outdoor art exhibit in Washington Square—required no re-
search and little personal encounter, they were my favorite, and
became something of my specialty. An hour of silent spying and
two hours of fanciful typing from my notes would earn half my
month's pay. My gift for metaphorical elaboration may have been
permanently overdeveloped by these exercises; at any rate, as I read
through the fifty or so of my Talk pieces, the "visits" seemed the
most mechanically festive; and they are sufficiently, but not propor-
tionately, represented in this selection of twenty.

Sifting through the yellow Talk tearsheets, as they appear in my
archives intermingled with poems collected in *The Carpentered Hen*
and short stories from the first half of *The Same Door*, on *New
Yorker* pages identical in format but infinitesimally breezier than
those printed now, I had some trouble distinguishing my contribu-
tions from those of other nimble hands. In one piece, I confess that
"we" have a fever, and the feel of that feverish afternoon amid the
pleasure craft dimly returns, confused with the Coliseum escalator.
Of another, I recall the P-R men filling the interludes of the sched-
uled routines with chitchat about their private lives quite startling
to a young monogamist. One P-R man startled my wife and me
both by presenting us with a costly glass platter and hors-d'oeuvres
bowl, all because I had mentioned him in print. Too many of the
Talk ideas came in from public-relations and advertising firms
seeking publicity for their clients; my simple-minded approach was
to include the publicists in the story as characters, as part of the
scene—which, in this heyday of "The Hucksters," they were. I
preferred, though they were less eager for attention, the scientists

—the building doctors and the miniaturizers. From my acquaintance with Dr. Edwin Colbert, star paleontologist at the Museum of Natural History, stemmed friendly feelings for extinct animals that have persisted to this day. Dr. Bernardo Houssay, the Argentinian physiologist, sticks in my mind fondly, perhaps because he resisted my request for an interview, and had to be shown copies of the magazine before he would talk. His may have been the last Talk piece I executed as a residential New Yorker; though for some years I would return from New England by train or plane and do a few pieces to fatten my free-lancer's bank account. The Baedeker on the Universe, notable for its temerity, was researched in the Widener Library at Harvard, and of course "our" drive to the Cambridge auction was an hour south rather than the five hours north a reader might suppose. The Talk of the Town was becoming The Talk of the Eastern Seaboard, and now stories appear in the department from London and California, occasionally. My last Talk story was a report on a Ross's gull, rare even in its native Siberia, sighted off Newburyport in the spring of 1975.*

So as to give this book a title, and the unity of a youthful episode, nothing written after 1959 is included. Most of the "Notes and Comment" I essayed in the early Sixties and a few choice Talk of the Town stories went into the "First Person Plural" section of *Assorted Prose* in 1965. Of the generous residue of my Talk, I have selected a score of stories that made me smile, however passingly, or told me something I had forgotten I had ever known. William Shawn has written of Harold Ross, "I have never been sure just what Ross really thought about facts. All I know is that he loved them. . . . Facts steadied him and comforted him. Facts also amused him. They didn't need to be funny facts—just facts."** And a loving respect for facticity—for the exactly *what* of matters—is perhaps the shared heritage of all of us who ever worked for *The New Yorker*, under the ghost of Harold Ross. The pieces are dated by the month each was written in; they usually saw print within

---

*See p. 59. The other Talk stories mentioned must be left to the reader's imagination.
**From Brendan Gill's *Here at The New Yorker* (Random House, 1975), p. 392.

the week. Thursday was the Talk deadline day, and on Monday the magazine was locked up, bearing the next Saturday's date. One typed, in those days, on yellow paper—a tawny gold rather than canary yellow—which was outlawed when, in the Sixties, the magazine took to transmitting copy by television to a Chicago printing plant. My office looked east, at a skyline that did not then include the Pan Am Building. During a snowfall, or in the hour as dusk crept in, the city approximated the one of my dreams.

The Talk of the Town supported me at a tender time of life. But to concoct an anonymous fraction of it year after year loomed as fruitlessly selfless. It seemed unlikely I would ever get better at Talk than I was at twenty-four; the freshest efforts here are among the first, and a piece like "Resemblances" shows a kind of contemptuous, harried virtuosity, in a narrow vein indeed. A man who would be an artist is obliged to keep working where he might improve. So I quit the nicest job I ever had, and moved out onto the limb where I cling yet, though I miss the steel desk, the stationery, and the pink slips with ideas on them.

A "SPECIAL MESSAGE" *to purchasers of the Franklin Library limited edition, in 1977, of* Rabbit, Run.

Though second novels are traditionally supposed to be disappointments, my own second novel, this one, is the one that, nearly twenty years after its publication, I am best known by. Its reputation, indeed, as my "best," and the tendency of strangers to mutter "Run, rabbit, run" as I walk past have led me to harbor something of a grudge against the book, the grudge we bear against other people's pets.

Yet I loved the book as I wrote it, and wanted to write it enough to beg money from the Guggenheim Foundation to give me the time and financial space necessary. The way the novel expanded under my hands forced me to abandon a certain determined modesty in my literary ambitions. *Rabbit, Run* was originally to be one of two novellas bound into a single volume; with its companion, *The Centaur,* it would illustrate the polarity between running and plodding, between the rabbit and the horse, between the life of instinctual gratification and that of dutiful self-sacrifice. To emphasize how thoroughly the zigzagging hero lived in the present, it was written in the present tense—a piece of technical daring in 1959, though commonplace now. The only precedent, to my knowledge, was Joyce Cary's *Mr. Johnson* (1939). Though this novel of Africa is a beautiful success, Cary felt, in introducing a later edition, obliged to justify the present tense:

> It can give to a reader that sudden feeling of insecurity (as if the very ground were made only of a deeper kind of darkness) which comes to a traveller who is bushed in unmapped country, when he feels all at once that not only has he utterly lost his way, but also his own identity.

Such are the feelings of my angst-ridden Everyman, fertile and fearful and not easy to catch.

Rabbit, Run was to be subtitled "A Movie." The cinematic art knows no tense but the present. I even had an introduction, discarded, leading the reader down the aisle to his seat. The opening scene, of the boys playing basketball around a telephone pole, was meant to be the background for the title and credits, but when a real movie was made of the novel, the scene was not used in this way. Warner Brothers' *Rabbit, Run* lost them two million dollars and made vivid to me certain differences between word and image. The film medium, a superb mirror of the visible furniture of our lives, cannot show the shadow of moral ambiguity. Without this impalpable novelistic substance, this unspoken but constant discussion between reader and author, the actions make insufficient sense. Watching the movie, I felt I had put the actors in a glass box, which I wanted to smash, to let them out; James Caan, the hero, later echoed this claustral hallucination by saying, in an interview, of the movie, "*Rabbit, Run* wasn't released; it escaped."

Rabbit is the hero of this novel, but is he a good man? The question is meant to lead to another—What is goodness? Kerouac's *On the Road* was in the air, and a decade of dropping-out about to arrive, and the price society pays for unrestrained motion was on my mind. In the end, the act of running, of gathering a blank momentum "out of a kind of sweet panic," offers itself as containing a kernel of goodness; but perhaps a stone or a flower at rest holds the same kernel. At any rate, the title is a piece of advice, in the imperative mode, though the man giving it was sitting at a desk, in the upstairs room of a seventeenth-century house, overlooking a shady street corner in a small New England town. My feet, kicking as I composed, wore bare spots in the floor beneath the desk. Though the desk is gone, and I have moved, the bare spots, a subsequent owner tells me, are still there.

And *Rabbit, Run* is still here, in this elegant new edition. The world has changed since the late Fifties; contraceptive methods are much improved and high-school romances are not so naïvely supposed to become happy, tame marriages. The rabbits America breeds now have longer hair and more articulate grievances. But the Rabbit in us all remains both wild and timid, harmful and loving, hard-hearted and open to the motions of Grace.*

IN RESPONSE *to the invitation of Whit Burnett to contribute a selection to his anthology* This Is My Best: In the Third Quarter of the Century *(Doubleday, 1970).*

Each of my efforts is the best I can do at that time, on that project. For a reader, the "best" would be the one that works best, contains the most truth, for him. I am often surprised—pleasantly—by the moments of my oeuvre singled out by a correspondent or a critic. For of course I, too, have my lurking suspicions, my lurking favorites. The short story lengthily titled "Packed Dirt, Churchgoing, A Dying Cat, A Traded Car" was written, as I remember, in the spring of 1961, at a time when my wits seemed sunk in a bog of anxiety and my customary doubts that I could write another word appeared unusually well justified. Slowly I had begun to piece together a montage of aborted ideas eventually published as "The Blessed Man of Boston, My Grandmother's Thimble, and Fanning Island" and in the same slow motion, that paralyzed spring, I

---

*Echoing the novel's epigraph from Pascal: "The motions of Grace, the hardness of the heart; external circumstances."

continued with the story I suggest you reprint. If the story is dense, it is because there was a pressure of memory and worry upon it; as these farflung images collected at my typewriter, a bigger, better kind of music felt to be arising out of compression. Staleness and dread evidently wanted to sing. I seemed to understand at last Proust's remark about the essence of the writer's task being the perception of connections between unlike things. The themes here interwoven—and there is a good deal of conscious art in this far-raginous narrative, and more fiction than may meet the eye—had long been present to me: paternity and death, earth and faith and cars. But I had not seized them so directly before. It was to be the final of my stories about Pennsylvania, and foreshadows, in the incident precipitating the hero's plunge into terror, the sexual themes that have unaccountably concerned me since. But the heart of the story, toward which all tends, is of course the father, his generous and comical manner of dying. As might as well be said of the subsequent novel, *The Centaur:* it is a good story because it has a good man in it.

IN DIFFERENT RESPONSE *to a similar invitation, this time from Rust Hills, editor of* Writer's Choice *(McKay, 1974).*

An invitation to choose one's best makes an occasion to squirm. Contrary to popular impression, writers, unlike pole vaulters, do not know when they have done their best—there is no clatter of tipped bamboo to tell them they have failed, no statistic in tomorrow's paper to tell them they succeeded. We do our best with each piece; as with children no two look up at us with an identical face, and each demands separate treatment. Preferential treatment, indeed; and having satisfied ourselves that each pet has marched off past the mailbox with its hair as combed and its knickers as lint-free as caring can make them, we can only wave good-bye bravely and turn to the inspirations still waiting to be turned outdoors.

So a self-nominated anthology like this becomes an opportunity to rectify the slights of a harsh and hasty world and put forward a shy child. "Leaves" has never been, to my knowledge, included in any volume save my own collection *The Music School.* It is in a mode of mine, the abstract-personal, not a favorite with my critics. One of them, reviewing *The Music School,* expressed impatience with my lace-making, so-called. Well, if "Leaves" is lace, it is taut and symmetrical lace, with scarce a loose thread. It was written, in 1962, after long silence, swiftly, unerringly as a sleepwalker walks. No memory of any revision mars my backwards impression of it. The way the leaves become the pages, the way the bird becomes his description, the way the bright and multiform world of nature is felt rubbing against the dark world of the trapped ego—all strike me as beautiful, and of the order of artistic "happiness" that is given rather than attained. The last image, the final knot of lace, is an assertion of transcendental faith scaled, it seems to me, nicely to the mundane.

Enough of such. My clinching reason for selecting this story is its shortness, which I thought might offer, first to the editor and then to the readers of this anthology, a pleasant respite amid the no doubt extensive masterworks of my contemporaries.

A FOREWORD *to a limited edition of* Couples: A Short Story, *published by Halty Ferguson (Cambridge, Massachusetts) in 1976.*

The short story entitled "Couples" was written in the spring of 1963; the carbon copy among my papers gives the completion date as May 16. With it were the notes predating its composition. A typed scrap reads:

> parties, heading into flowers—remembers moments when
> colors separate—golf, the time with Williamses,
> musselling—the party when all five couples came in a
> blizzard up our hill

On the back of a proof sheet for *The Centaur* I drew in ballpoint pen a square, with the corners labelled M, M, W, W and with dotted diagonal lines connecting opposite corners. Beside this is scrawled:

diagonal lines of attraction when the sides creak and
break

friendships; a woman [illegible] refuses to go when
a brat [?] offended

woman who thought a man comes around in fact homosexually
attracted to her husband
fell in love

finds self on knees embracing her maternity suit in closet

And there is a chart of the five couples—WILLIAMS MORRIS HORN-
ING GUERIN KROCK—with the names of the individual marital
partners, to keep me from the confusion of intermingling that
overtakes the characters themselves.

The story was written from these notes, submitted to *The New
Yorker,* and rejected, though this was a time of frequent acceptances
for me. "Couples" is preceded in my stack of papers by the short
story "At a Bar in Charlotte Amalie" and followed by my essay on
Denis de Rougemont's theories of love, the poem "Report of
Health," and the story "The Christian Roommates"—all in due
course given space within the pages of that gracious magazine. But
my own qualms about "Couples" in the form it had taken recon-
ciled me to its non-publication. It was, above its incidental faults
of sentimentality and vagueness, too crowded; its mapping of its
garden of two-toned flowers needed the space of the novel which
eventually I wrote, some three years later, using the name of the
town but surprisingly few of the other names. I don't believe I
reread "Couples" before beginning *Couples.*

I did try to salvage from this story a shorter story to be called
"Peggy's Clothes" or, after the remark by Nix Morris, "You Vo-
luptuous Piece of Wallpaper You." Neither version was ever
printed, and this poor jewel of an image, the voluptuous wallpaper,
found its eventual setting in a reminiscence of sorts entitled "When
Everyone Was Pregnant" (1971). The simile likening breaking surf
to a typewriter carriage was placed, with greater point, in a story
written later that summer, "Harv Is Plowing Now." And a number

of details first verbalized in "Couples" also made their way into the bedevilled manuscript of a novel called *Marry Me,* whose page proofs I have just yesterday completed reading.

It is fitting that *Marry Me,* as a trade novel, and this short story, in a limited edition, should be published at about the same time. They were among my first attempts to write about suburban adultery, a subject that, if I have not exhausted it, has exhausted me. But I have persisted, as I earlier persisted in describing the drab normalities of a Pennsylvania boyhood, with the conviction that there was something good to say for it, some sad magic that, but for me, might go unobserved. This short story, though it fails to earn the clangor of its last two paragraphs*—a passage I find written out in hand on the blank insides of an eviscerated envelope from the Mental Health Association of the North Shore—yet has tendernesses and exactitudes not duplicated in any later manipulation of these themes. The simple party pleasures of the youngly married, the mathematics of a social "set" or "group," the faces around the fire during the blizzard—none of this would return so directly, with such an innocent excitement of presentation. The enchanted

---

*"Who is the enemy? Who is it against whose threatened invasions we lit our fires and erected our barricades of children, whose subversion we subverted with alcohol, whose propaganda broadcasts we jammed with parties, whose intrigues and fanaticism we counteracted with the intrigues and fanaticism of love; who is the enemy I was delegated to engage alone? He is my friend. I move with ease among his camps, the underfurnished camps of solitude. I have come to admire his methods and Spartan style. His tortures are at bottom benevolent, for they prepare one for death. His tactics are irresistible, for every minute is his ally. Seeing what I have seen, I almost dread returning to my own side. I have no wish to hurry the moment when the doomed axis of couples takes me into itself again. It will not, of course, be exactly the same. Along with the house, the children, and the station wagon, I have given Ann the town. Peggy and I will not live in Tarbox. She shops for houses constantly. But, wherever she finds one, there will be other Hornings, differently tinted, and other Krocks, wearing, perhaps, the Morrises' perfume.

"I am a parenthesis—a boat adrift between two continents. At times I remember and foresee the world of couples eagerly, as a garden from which I have been banished but to which I am certain to return. In trying to imagine my domestic life with Peggy, in fondly admiring her tireless touch with furnishings, I have sighted the coast that is not yet christened America. And time, time that knits and unravels all blessings, will pass before this paradise becomes a bewitched armaments factory whose workers, in their frenzy to forge armor for themselves, hammer, burn, and lacerate one another."

moment when the other young couples looked to the narrator like "safeguards, echoes, reinforcements of our happiness" had been overlaid with too many incidents by the time he, in the guise of an author-god lifted above his personae, began to construct the novel that, in honor of its amplitude, was to be called *Couples and Houses and Days*. The lofty and possibly unkind sociological tone of that novel, and the note of personal emotion struck in a number of short stories less clumsy than this one, are here still fused; as it stands (little rewritten for this its first venture into print), "Couples" bares the muffled heart of *Couples*, the theme of friendship—of friendships and their inevitable, never-quite-complete betrayal by, if by nothing else, time.

A "SPECIAL MESSAGE" *for the Franklin Library's First Edition Society printing of* Marry Me *(1976)*.

As I sit trying to begin this message I am looking at a bookcase I have just built, still unpainted and empty of books, and thus fresh and naked in its constructional defects. One builds from a special angle, close-up and often awkward, the nails in one's mouth and the hammer just out of reach on the shelf below; so it is with another pair of eyes that one can suddenly see, from the perspective of a man sitting stymied at a desk some yards away, the ragged cuts, the unaligned uprights, the crevices one had thought were tight joins.

Relax. Paint will cover some sins, and the books others, and time, that great softener and adjuster, will render the bookcase invisible, in the way that accustomed things are. And—aesthetic paradox— imperfection weds itself to perfection; we recognize pleasurably in made things the uneven motion of a hand, the recalcitrance of a warped board. I am content with my bookcase.

With this book, too? It has been a long time making. Chapter II, "The Wait," was published in *The New Yorker* of February 17, 1968, and the novel was not newly written then.* But *Marry Me*

---

*The writing of the first draft falls, in fact, between *The Centaur* (1963) and *Of the Farm* (1965).

was always a book in my mind, not a collection, or collage, and was written pretty much in a piece, with the five chapters symmetrically alliterative as I have them, and their lengths in the proportion of a diadem. The central chapter, cut down from the length of a novel in itself, is flanked by two longish, less inward, more spoken chapters, and these in turn by brief idylls, partaking of the same texture, between real and unreal. Sally's checkered blanket returns here and there as a chessboard, and the last chapter can be read as a series of test moves.

The book was meant to be about religion; the four principals have four different doctrinal positions—atheist, Unitarian, lapsed Catholic, professing Protestant—and achieve one with the other various ecumenical combinations. Where they find themselves is often Paradise (the beach) or Hell (the airport); in that long floating watery wavering middle chapter Ruth finds herself in Limbo, doubting her own existence. That love is an illusion is commonly said; I think one of my intentions, in this book so full of air, of pauses, of spacy dialogue and vacant days, of sudden jumps in locale and time, was to show illusion as a component of our daily lives, to which air and dreams are as essential as earth and blood.

Details of this novel's making recur to me—cuts, realignments, adjustments toward harmony and proportion. I like poems and stories that ride, as Frost said, on their own melting; that come out of the creator like toothpaste from a tube, generating their music of self-reflexive allusion as they flow. To elicit and clarify this music —which awakens in the reader the sense of organized emotion that differentiates art from life and fiction from reporting—some carpentry seemed needed in this case; but to specify its details would be to obstruct the perspective that you, gentle First Edition reader, establish as you pick up and open this volume. A novel imitates reality in, among other aspects, a certain opacity, a proud opacity. It must come on not wearing its meaning on the sleeve of an introduction but embodying its meaning, or, rather, meaning its existence. Even its imperfections it must wear proudly, as honorable scars. The artist's effort perhaps consists not of bringing a work to perfection but of bringing it to the point where the creation, not the creator, takes the active part in the sentence; the question then becomes not whether I am content but whether the book, or the bookcase, is finished. It is.

A "SPECIAL MESSAGE" *to purchasers of the Franklin Library limited edition, in 1981, of* Rabbit Redux.

When I finished *Rabbit, Run,* very near the end of the Fifties, I did not intend a sequel. But a little over ten years later, as the interminable Sixties were drawing to their end, the idea that Harry Angstrom was still out there and running suddenly excited me. I had spent a year or more reading about the person and Presidency of James Buchanan (1791–1868). After a long and fruitless struggle to make a novel out of resistant historical materials, the perpetual *presentness* of my former hero beckoned as a relief. A number of people had asked me what had happened to Rabbit, who was last seen running along a street of Brewer, Pennsylvania, in no special direction; now I would show them, and throw in all the oppressive, distressing, overstimulating developments of the most dissentious American decade since the Civil War—anti-war protest, black power and rhetoric, teach-ins, middle-class runaways, drugs, and (proceeding eerily to its brilliant technological rendezvous through a turmoil of violence at home and abroad) the moon shot. Having told a number of interviewers I was writing a book about Buchanan, I painted him black and put him in, too. The term "redux" gave some people trouble; I had encountered it in Anthony Trollope's sequel to *Phineas Finn, Phineas Redux.* There is also a poem by Dryden, *Astraea Redux.* The term is Latin, meaning "led back," and is pronounced not with a silent pseudo-French "x" but as a firm spondee: *ray-dooks.*

The novel wrote itself readily; it was good to be back in Brewer. The characters assembled themselves within the numbed orbit of my now paunchy Middle American, and his tolerant curiosity and reluctant education seemed to me the parable that nobody else, in those shrill years, was offering. America and Harry suffered, marvelled, listened, and endured. Not without cost, of course. The cost of the disruption of the social fabric was paid, as in the earlier novel, by a girl. Iphigenia is sacrificed and the fleet sails on, with its quarrelling crew. If Harry seems hard-hearted, "hardness of the heart" was what his original epigraph was about; the rage boiling out of the television set discovers a certain rage in him, too. As much as the ghetto black he hates the whites above them both, in Penn Park, among "the timbered gables, the stucco, the weedless lawns plumped up like pillows." The question that ends the book* is not meant to have an easy answer.

A LETTER *published in the P.E.N. American Center* Newsletter *(Number 31, December 1976). Originally intended to be published in the New York* Times. *But the word "cunt" in the last line of the second poem was evidently news not fit to print, and they backed off. So things are tough all over.*

POEM FOR A FAR LAND

Russia, most feminine of lands,
  Breeder of stupid masculinity,
Only Jesus understands
  Your interminable virginity.

Raped, and raped, and raped again,
  You rise snow-white, the utter
    same,
With tender birches and ox-eyed
    men
  Willing to suffer for your name.

Though astronauts distress the sky
  That mothers your low, sad
    villages,
Your vastness yearns in sympathy
  Between what was and that which
    is.

VERSES ABOUT A DISTANT LAND

O, woman, among other states
your might—is not in brute strength.
Any person will believe in miracles,
  once he has come to know
all the purity of indestructible
  Russia.

After so many storms, you are fresh
  again
and snow-white, like the bark of
  birches.
Protecting you, your sons are ready
to go to mortal battle, any tempests.

You send ships into the cosmos,
but I have fallen in love also with
  your villages,
the rustling, tender face of your
  land,
  inexplicable, youthful, and ancient.

---

*"O.K.?"

Washington

Diagonal white city dreamed by a
Frenchman—
the *nouveau* republic's Senecan
pretension
populated by a grid of blacks—
after midnight your taxi-laced streets
entertain noncommittal streetlight
shadows
and the scurry of leaves that fall still
green.

Site, for me, of a secret parliament
of which both sides agreed to
concede
and left the issue suspended in
brandy,
I think of you longingly, as a
Yankee
longs for Lee, sorry to have won,
or as Ho Chi Minh mourns for
Johnson.

My capital, my alabaster
Pandemonium,
I rode your stunned streets with a
groin
as light and docile as a baby's wrist,
guilt's senators laughing in my
skull's cloak room,
my hurried heart corrupt with peace,
with love of my country, of cunt,
and of sleep.

Washington

White diagonal, noisy city
with pretension to the Rome of the
tribunes' time.
More noticeable still is the whiteness
of the buildings
against the background of its
inhabitants'
black skin . . .
At noon it looks like an anthill:
nowhere to walk, and nowhere to
breathe.
But at midnight—it's as if it had
died.
          And through the streets
that are empty you can walk up and
down or
across if you want.
The leaves, without turning yellow,
fall from the trees . . .

My capital, Babylon of alabaster!
Still, I love you . . .
          Through the rumble of the
streets
I make my way like a lost child,
through the loud, Senatorial speeches
. . .

And still, here, in my hurried heart,
most acutely of all—is a desire for
good,
desire for love of my country and its
people.

The two left-hand poems were printed in my collection *Mid-point* (Alfred A. Knopf, 1969) and those on the right are literal English versions by Professor Carl R. Proffer, co-editor of *Russian Literature Triquarterly* (Ann Arbor), of Russian translations that appeared in the July 9, 1976, issue of a Soviet newspaper called *Literary Russia*. Presumably in honor of our Bicentennial, the feature was called "A Desire for Good," and included, besides these two of mine, translations of poems by Louis Simpson, Robert Penn Warren, and Joyce Carol Oates.

The discrepancies speak for themselves. Some discrepancies are of course unavoidable. The translator (one S. Alexandrov) can scarcely be blamed for not catching the odd tone of "Poem for a Far Land" which was composed after my return from the Soviet Union in 1964, on a beach in the Caribbean, in a light-verse metre, in a mood of some nostalgia and geographical wonder. But the mockery of "stupid masculinity" and "interminable virginity" seems deliberately lost, and the suppression of such adjectives as "ox-eyed" and "low, sad" helps achieve a hymn of praise where a sort of affectionate caricature was intended.

The violence done "Washington" is greater and less excusably propagandistic. The middle stanza, alluding to the personal incident behind the poem and hypothesizing a bond of sentiment between the opposed leaders in the then-furious Vietnam War, is quite done away with, and with it some crucial phrases in the third stanza. In their place are added a number of negative phrases— "looks like an anthill," "nowhere to breathe"—bearing no relation to the original. The groin "as light and docile as a baby's wrist" (my own favorite image in the poem) lamely figures as "like a lost child," and an erotic remembrance ends as a virtual apology for being American.

In both poems, ironic and anti-judgmental national references have been brutalized into political statements favorable to Soviet doctrine. To the extent that the distortions occur where the tone of the English fills the words with their intended meaning, the difficulties of any translation are illustrated. Actually, the Russians take pride in their translations—many first-rank writers, their self-expression silenced, have busied their pens with this exacting art. While I was in Moscow, over a decade ago, consultations with the translator of my novel *The Centaur* satisfied me (as I have been later assured) that a scrupulous version was prepared. So the willful and, in the second case, wanton distortions of these small poems sadly suggest that cultural exchange between the superpowers is not merely stalled but regressing.

AN INTERVIEW *conducted by mail with Helen Vendler, in connection with the publication of* Tossing and Turning, *and published in the April 10, 1977,* New York Times Book Review.

Q: You imply in a story, as I recall, that your mother wanted you to be a poet. Did her wish influence your writing, or did her taste guide yours?

A: I believe it's the hero of *Of the Farm* whose mother wanted him to become a poet. Actually, there was little mention of poetry in my house while I was growing up. My mother remembered *not* remembering a poem she was reciting before a church group at about the age of twelve. She felt permanently disgraced. The first poem that *I* recall reciting in public was the passage from Sir Walter Scott that begins, "Breathes there the man, with soul so dead . . ." I got through it, and maybe that made the difference. The first poets I recall enjoying reading for myself were Phyllis McGinley, Arthur Guiterman, Robert Service, and, somewhat later, Ogden Nash and Morris Bishop. I wonder how many sixteen-year-olds now have heard of any of these fine and funny writers.

Q: Were these poets the chief models for your exquisite light verse?

A: In the early Fifties, when I did verse for the Harvard *Lampoon,* we looked toward *Punch* and toward the consoling notion, demonstrated in *Punch* week after week, that sheer metric neatness was halfway enough for a good light poem. That all seems long ago. Light verse died when it no longer seemed even the littlest bit wonderful to make two words rhyme. At about the same time, dancers in movies stopped going up and down stairs in white tie and tails. We had switched our allegiance from agility to energy. Auden was the last poet, I think, to make the one seem the other.

Q: In your giddy self-interview, "Bech Meets Me,"* your gifted interviewer asks: "Do you envision novels as pills, broadcasts, tapestries, explosions of self, cantilevered constructs, or what?" The equally inventive interviewee answers that "they are crystallizations of visceral hopefulness extruded as a slow paste which in the

---

Picked-Up Pieces, pp. 10–13.

glitter of print regains something of the original, absolute gaiety."
Would you like to say what you think lyrics are?

A: I think you could say the same of lyrics except that the paste
is faster, or the tube at least is smaller. Since I have never been taken
very seriously as a poet and since I write less and less of what there
seems no demand for, I am a poor one to theorize. As I recall, the
poem comes with a perception—a breakthrough into nature, which
encircles our numbness day and night. And married to the irrup-
tion of nature must be something live that surfaces out of language;
the language, even when rhyme and metre and sequence and punc-
tuation are brushed aside, brings a formal element without which
nothing happens, nothing is *made.* One of the charms of concrete
poetry was that this element, after generations of *vers libre,* was
reëmphasized, from an unexpected direction. A lot of poetry I read
now just washes through me, nothing has crystallized to ignite
crystallization in me.

Q: In "Why Write?"* you say that as a child you used to draw
on a single sheet of paper "an assortment of objects—flowers, ani-
mals, stars, toasters, chairs, comic-strip creatures, ghosts, noses—"
and then connect them with lines "so that they all became the fruit
of a single impossible tree," and you added that the pleasure this
gave you returns whenever you work "several disparate incidents
or impressions into the shape of a single story." Does this apply to
your poetry, too?

A: I have tried more than once to give this "collecting" impulse
some place in aesthetic theory. Rhyming words are in a sense a
"set"—in a form like the ballade, a big set. Some of my light verse
strings some similar things—French inventors, semi-extinct ani-
mals, new developments in particle physics—in a kind of necklace
of stanzas, and steps back pleased. A kindred human urge, I sup-
pose, is toward the exhaustive. We like a feeling of mopping up,
of complete fullness. A jingle through the alphabet does this for us,
and less obviously a Greek tragedy does also. We are *dismissed* by
the work of art. I am talking as if art still pandered to our hopes
or inklings of order. I'm not sure it does, except in this mysterious

Picked-Up Pieces, pp. 29–39.

sense of fullness. In the days when I wrote poems habitually, I would know I had one, the idea of it, when my scalp crawled. When the skin on my head felt tight. My hand would shake and I couldn't write fast enough.

Q: Recent lyric poetry (Ginsberg, Berryman, Lowell) has incorporated a lot of the detail hitherto reserved for fiction—family tales, social scenery, public affairs. Do you like this sort of thing, or is it better done in prose?

A: Done better perhaps in the best prose. Prose, that is, can make tableaux move, cinematically, whereas in poetry the same material becomes a set of slides. Yes, I like some of Lowell's scenes and character sketches very much. In his poetry, human nature becomes quite tropical, stifling. I also like the late Ed Sissman's framed moments of his own history, and the palpable "others" in Anne Sexton, or Merrill, or Dickey. There is a limit, after all, to what can be done with daffodils and sunsets. Nor is this material novel; Chaucer, Shakespeare, and Milton are all dramatic poets, and Romanticism unleashed a new passion for the psychological. Wordsworth turned it inward and Browning outward, but between them surely they covered all the anecdotal and confessional possibilities open to us now. Except perhaps that of sexual detail.

Q: You've decided, in your new collection of verse, to prescind from "taste" altogether, in some of the poems about sex. Have you any sense that this has been done successfully by others? Is it possible to avoid the ridiculous in such enterprises?

A: Well, why avoid the ridiculous? The poem in this collection you must have in mind is meant to be among other things funny, and indeed is based, like many of my light-verse poems, on something that came in the mail. I think "taste" is a social concept and not an artistic one. I'm willing to show good taste, if I can, in somebody else's living room, but our reading life is too short for a writer to be in any way polite. Since his words enter into another's brain in silence and intimacy, he should be as honest and explicit as we are with ourselves. I find some of Donne's poems, and Whitman's, quite unridiculously sexual. Odd, that no modern celebrant comes to mind. Lawrence's poems seem to be mostly about animals.

Q: Do you have any regrets that you turned out to be essentially a novelist rather than a poet?

A: No. And yet I feel more at sea writing a novel than a poem, and often reread my poetry and almost never look at my old novels. Also, poetry, especially since we have purged it of all that is comfortingly mechanical, is a sporadic activity. Lightning can't strike every day. It is always at the back of my mind to be a poet. Lately I had occasion to get the collected poems of Wallace Stevens down from the shelf. He didn't publish his first collection until he was almost my present age and didn't publish another for twelve years or more. Yet the total production, in the end, weighs like a Bible, a beautiful book as published by Knopf, with big print on big white pages, all this verbal fun and glory and serene love—what a good use of a life, to leave behind one beautiful book!

Q: Would you like to do more reviewing of poetry?

A: I try to deal with the poetry when it comes up in connection with a poet's biography, but no, I wouldn't presume to review it head-on, and book after book. I don't know how you do it, all these poets operating away at what they think of as the height of intensity, exquisiteness, whatever. For me it would be like candling golden eggs. Did you notice, the Brancusi head on the jacket of *Tossing and Turning* is shaped like an egg? And my first book, a book of poems, was called *The Carpentered Hen*. That was my first book, this is my twentieth, and none in between has seemed more worth—how shall I say?—chirping about.

A COMMENT *upon the poem "Seagulls," given to Paul B. Janeczko for his anthology* Poetspeak *(Bradbury Press, 1983), aimed at students.*

Students often ask if a poet or writer must wait until he is inspired. My answer is always No, but I do remember the moment of inspiration for "Seagulls." I was lying on the beach in Ipswich, Massachusetts, in the very late afternoon of a summer or early fall day in 1959. As the beach crowds thinned, the seagulls moved closer, and while I lay on my side, observing one, the first lines of this poem came to me. They came in such a rush, and seemed so precious and perishable, that I jumped up and found a piece of charred wood from a dead beachfire and scratched the lines on another, flatter piece of wood. I carried the chunk home, amid embarrassing stares, and here inspiration must have ceased, for the manuscript of the poem reveals many alterations, an entire discarded section devoted to the amorous young couple, and a completion date of December 5. I evidently waited for some time for the nice turn in the final stanza, when the camera lifts and we see people like gods walking above these little apprehensive citizens of gulldom.

The form is, the student will notice, unrhymed "free" verse; but I wrote much light verse in regular metres in those days, and the ghosts of rhyme and stanza in my ear helped press my lines toward the crispness that must exist in poetry. The second stanza always gets a laugh when I read it aloud, but I was not consciously intending to be funny when I wrote it—merely exact. I, too, felt ugly because I was intelligent, and as I settled into my writer's profession well aware of my "wide and nervous and well-muscled rump." The subject, in short, leaped to my heart with unforced self-symbolic import. Also, I loved beaches in those days, before my skin began to pock and wrinkle, and was happy being on one in any hour. "Happiness," in the double sense that the word "felicity" also contains, must exist for a poem to spring into being and to ripen toward its close with the requisite surprisingness (to the reader) and (from the writer's point of view) firmness and inevitability.

AN "AUTOBIBLIOGRAPHICAL NOTE" *to* Sixteen Sonnets, *a limited edition brought out by Halty Ferguson in 1979.*

In my first collection of poetry, *The Carpentered Hen,* there are many twelve- and sixteen-line pieces of light verse, but only one deliberate, albeit tetrameter, sonnet, "Glasses," and an inadvertently fourteen-line poem, "Knob." In the next collection, *Telephone Poles,* there is one sonnet, "The Moderate," like "Glasses" Shakespearean in form and light in content. In the long poem "Midpoint," however, the sonnet to my father occupies a central position, and the rest of the collection *Midpoint and Other Poems* contains three more sonnets—"Topsfield Fair," "In Extremis," and the airy "Love Sonnet." And in my fourth and last collection, *Tossing and Turning,* one of the best poems, "Golfers," is a sonnet, as are "Melting," "The Grief of Cafeterias," and "Night Flight, over Ocean."

My next collection was to be entitled *Sonnets.* Perhaps it will be yet, though I haven't written any for some months. For a time, especially during an insomniacal week in Spain, the fourteen-line unit, with the octave-sestet division observed and some hints at rhyme encouraged, seemed just the right-size bait with which to re-entice my muse. But muses are not so easily tricked, and this slim limited edition contains all my poetry of recent inspiration.

TESTIMONY *given in a hearing before the Subcommittee on Select Education of the House of Representatives Committee on Education and Labor (Hon. John Brademas, Chairman) in Boston on January 30, 1978.*

I am honored to have been asked to testify at this hearing on the bill calling for a White House conference on the humanities: and that is the first piece of testimony I have to offer. We in the humanities, whether we call ourselves men of letters or men of scholarship, are fascinated and charmed by power, and anxious to please it. In the week after I accepted the invitation to speak here for five minutes today, I received from the National Endowment for the Humanities in a succession of envelopes at least two pounds of Xeroxed material, ranging from biographies of Chairman [Joseph] Duffey to appreciations of the paintings of Paul Cézanne, much of this material duplicatory and even triplicatory but all of it testifying to Brobdingnagian resources of secretarial labor and photocopying equipment. Now, a free-lance writer, working in a corner of his own home, producing his manuscripts on his own twenty-year-old manual typewriter, operates on a Lilliputian scale, and must view even a marginal governmental interest in his work with the mingled gratitude and alarm of a wren whose nest is being appraised by an eagle.

The essence of government is concern for the widest possible public interest; the essence of the humanities, it seems to me, is private study, thought, and passion. Publicity is as essential to the one as privacy is to the other. Can these two realms, then, be conjoined without distortion? Is it true, as Joint Resolution 639 states, "that the development and encouragement of national strength in the humanities is of the utmost importance to the life and heritage of the United States," and "that it is appropriate to encourage maximum participation by citizens"?

I have been invited here not as judge or advocate but as a witness; it is appropriate that my testimony be personal. My career in the humanities has at many turns encountered my governments, federal, state, and local. I was educated in public schools, and when my interests ranged beyond the curriculum there I found ample material for exploration in the surprisingly well-stocked public library of a nearby city. As a young writer I applied for and received a grant given by a private foundation whose tax-exempt status represented an indirect government investment in the arts and humanities. As an older writer I have been blessed with government-sponsored memberships, invitations, and travels. My friendship with writers and critics pursuing careers in Communist and Third World countries has made me emphatically appreciative of the freedoms and opportunities I enjoy as an American. I love my country's government for its attempt, in a precarious world, to sustain a peaceful order in which work can be done and happiness can be pursued not for the good of the state, but in a state that exists for our good. I love my government not least for the extent to which it leaves me alone.

My personal ambition has been simply to live by the work of my pen. This is not a very fastidious ambition, and if I were aware of a large amount of federal money available to purveyors of the written word I would attempt to gain access to it. But I would rather have as my patron a host of anonymous citizens digging into their own pockets for the price of a book or a magazine than a small body of enlightened and responsible men administering public funds. I would rather chance my personal vision of truth striking home here and there in the chaos of publication that exists than attempt to filter it through a few sets of official, honorably public-spirited scruples.

It can be said that the actual achievement of the National Endowment for the Humanities has been to expand the public exposure of privately produced works. The recent Cézanne show in New York was in a sense a triumph of government sponsorship; it was an event, a "hit," attracting such crowds to the Museum of Modern Art's first floor that for physical relief my wife and I went upstairs to the second floor, where those Cézannes in the museum's permanent collection not enlisted in the show downstairs hung on the walls unregarded, in the atmosphere of peaceful waiting—the paintings waiting in line, not the people—that I associate with museums and with art appreciation. Where a governmental scale obtains, a single juggler becomes a circus, and quantity confuses itself with quality.

The danger is not as blunt as direct censorship. In a family where all the children are regularly given candy, the withholding of such a bonus becomes a rebuke. A cultural totalitarianism enforces by such withholding more often than by overt penalties. There already exists in the academic world a highly developed art of grant application; the realms of scientific research are now inextricably involved with government funding. Can we reasonably fear that the humanities and arts might become similarly dependent?

If I try to think of writers who, in the last century, have most brilliantly illuminated our sense of humanity, which I take to be the end purpose of the humanities, I think of Freud and Kafka, of Proust and Joyce, of Whitman and Henry James, and wonder, How many of these brave, strange, stubborn spirits would have won a subsidy from their governments? I think a government, in time, can come to cherish a nation's cultural heritage, its creators safely dead and in perspective. But in the living present how can publicly salaried men *not* think in terms of respectability, of socially beneficial optimism, of wide and uncontroversial appeal? How can grants panels *not* be drawn to the sociologically winsome and the amusingly communal? How can legislators asked to vote tax money away *not* begin to think of "guidelines" that insidiously edge toward censorship? If government money becomes an increasingly important presence in the financing of the humanities, is there a danger, I respectfully ask, of humanists becoming lobbyists, and of the strategies of politics displacing the strategies of the mind?

AN ABSTRACT *prepared, at the request of Sociological Abstracts Inc. (a non-profit corporation co-sponsored by the International Sociological Association and headquartered in San Diego), of "The Plight of the American Writer," an often-reworked address presented to an Arab and American Cultures Conference sponsored by the American Enterprise Institute in Washington, D.C., and subsequently published in the De-cember 1977 issue of* Change: The Magazine of Learning. *A version of the talk entitled "The Cultural Situation of the American Writer" had earlier appeared in the* International Exchange News, *published by the Washington International Center of Meridian House Interna-tional, in Washington, D.C.*

My talk attempted, on the basis of my twenty years of free-lance writing in the United States, to describe the situation of the Ameri-can writer in contrast to writers of other nations. In contrast to his Soviet counterparts, he enjoys freedom of expression and access to a competitive, at times richly remunerative economy, and suffers, paradoxically, from a sense of irrelevance—neither the government nor the corporations much care what he does or says. In contrast to his English counterpart, he lacks a solid sense of craft, or trade, and feels called upon to perform miracles or to cease performing. An all-or-nothing attitude is instilled in the writer by the surround-ing American culture which leads to erratic performance, early burnout, an unsettling greed, and a paucity of what might be called the quiet satisfactions of artistry. For all that, the writer in this case concluded, he would not trade his situation for another.

AN INTERVIEW *conducted, in the* New York Times Book Review—*as was done ten years earlier on the occasion of the publication of* Rabbit Redux—*by the tireless Henry Bech.*

In the ten years since your hypothetical interviewer bearded the beardless Updike in his Ipswich (Mass.) den, the skittish author has moved some miles inland, to a town without qualities called Georgetown—a nexus of route numbers on the edge of that New England hinterland best known for its bygone Indian massacres. As if to announce his willingness to assume the mothballed mantle of Sinclair Lewis, Updike lives on Main Street. He works, if that is the word, in a former antique shop now crammed with editions of his twenty-odd books in twenty-odd languages, including Finnish, Serbo-Croatian, Hebrew, and Korean. The years have not been terrifically unkind to him; teetering on the verge of fifty, he has retained his figure, which is that of a pot-bellied ectomorph, and his hair, which if not quite silvery is certainly pewter. His complexion has not improved during the Me Decade, and his stammer has grown worse. He gives the impression, reciting his responses into the tape recorder with many a fidget and static pause, of a word processor with some slipped bits; the effort, one feels, of visualizing every utterance in print has somewhat dimpled the flow of language within him, and cast him like a gasping crab onto one dry bank of the onrushing human orality alongside of which literature is just so many irrigation ditches.

However, he is most at home among his own characters, and therefore appeared relatively relaxed with me. I confessed that I had not, due to press of other business, made much headway into his new novel, concerning the adventures of another old friend, Harold C. Angstrom, of Brewer, Pa. I reminded him, though, that at our last interview he had promised that the sequel to *Rabbit Redux* would be, in ten years, a volume entitled *Rural Rabbit,* to be then followed, in 1991, with *Rabbit Is Rich.* Updike squirmed and, making sure that the tape recorder was running, stiffly dictated:

A: Well, this novel really has *Rural Rabbit* in it, since he keeps going out into the country to spy on this girl he thinks might be his daughter. Ever since his girl baby drowned in *Rabbit, Run,* Harry has been looking for a daughter. It's the theme that has been pressing forward, without my willing it or understanding it exactly, through these novels.

Q *(primly):* Please, let's not give the plot away. Or do the work of that third, who is among us.

A *(spooked):* Who? Who's that? *(Genuinely alarmed, he darts his scum-green eyes all around the memorabilia-choked shelves of his shabby atelier.)*

Q: The author of the review with which this interview must appear in tandem,* and with whose silent voice we are singing a curious duet, perhaps in grotesque disharmony.

A *(whispering):* Can he hear us?

Q: He or she. I doubt it. Reviewers don't read more than they have to. Anyway, what matters surely is the book itself, in its final thumb-worn library state, stripped of its jacket of publicity and passing financial trauma, a mysterious cloth-and-paper casket waiting to be broken open by the trumpet call of an unknown reader's mind. All else is dross.

A: You've taken the words right out of my mouth.

Q: I know you pretty well. Your theme, in this latest artifact in your habitual ten-point Janson, is inflation, am I correct?

A: Yes, and the trouble with inflation as a theme is that inflation overtakes it. The book was inspired by my sense of outrage at paying ninety-nine cents a gallon for gasoline, and now that would be a steal. Harry is meant to feel rich, but the income I assigned him as of 1979 will within a few years drop him below the poverty line. I fear my sense of the dollar is hopelessly retrograde; I live in a world where you can still buy two sparrows for a farthing. The very price of this novel—who can afford it? My first novel not twenty-two years ago sold for $3.50, and that seemed a lot to ask. There is a terror to all this.

Q *(in Bech's best psychoanalytical manner):* Let's talk about that.

A: Oh, Lordy. The terror of launching yourself into the blank paper. Nelson in this novel hang-glides, and now I see why; a writer hang-glides all the time, out over that terrible whiteness. The abyss is you, your own life, your mind. It's a terrifying thing to exist at all, and an author with every creation tries to exist twice over; it is as when in poker you try to bluff a nothing hand through,

---

*Roger Sale, in the event; he salted his favorable review with so much incidental dispraise as to quite spoil the taste.

and the dark face opposite raises, so you raise him back. And the bookstores—there's terror there, especially this time of year, all those bright books of life fighting it out in their armor of embossed lettering, stacks of them being carted out to make room for the fresh contenders, all these sensibilities the educational system is churning out, dying to describe their parents, their seductions, they keep coming, wave upon wave, and the old sensibilities won't even die off, modern medicine is too good. Who can even spot a trend anymore? Whatever happened to Black Humor, to the Imperial Novel? We live in a coral reef, smothered in a glut of self-regard. And the reviews? There's terror for you, all those muddy paws, even the ones trying to give you a pat—

Q: Yet you yourself are a reviewer.

A *(holding up his muddy paws): Mea culpa.* Print is guilt. Life is guilt. I believe it.

Q *(smoothly):* And take considerable satisfaction in it all, it would appear.

A *(scarcely chastened):* I've been lucky. My heroes tend to be lucky. But as long as there is one unlucky person in the world, life is grim.

Q: And writing?

A: Makes it less so. I cannot do justice to the bliss that attends getting even a single string of dialogue or the name of a weed right. Naming our weeds, in fact, seems to be exactly where it's at. I've been going out into my acre here *(gestures toward a scruffy meadow visible from his windows)* and trying to identify the wildflowers along the fringes with the aid of a book, and it's remarkably difficult to match reality and diagram. Reality keeps a pace or two ahead, scribble though we will. If you were to ask me what the aim of my fiction is—

Q: I will. I do.

A: —it's bringing the corners forward. Or throwing light into them, if you'd rather. Singing the hitherto unsung. That's applied Christianity, for that matter. I distrust books involving spectacular people, or spectacular events. Let *People* and *The National Enquirer* pander to our taste for the extraordinary; let literature concern itself, as the Gospels do, with the inner lives of hidden men. The collective consciousness that once found itself in the noble must now rest content with the typical.

Q: You've taken the words right out of my mouth.

A: I've been through a lot of interviews.

Q: Yet you say you dislike them.

A: I don't dislike the spouting-off, the conjuring-up of opinions. That's show biz, and you don't go into this business without a touch of ham. But as a practitioner trying to keep practicing in an age of publicity, I can only decry the drain on the brain, the assumption that a writer is a mass of opinions to be trucked in and carted off for his annual six minutes on the pan-American talk show. He is not; he is a secreter of images, some of which he prays will have the immortal resonance of Don Quixote's windmills, of Proust's madeleine, of Huck Finn's raft. As a secreter he must be at heart secret, patient, wicked even. His duty is, in a sense, to turn his back. This is not easy to understand in an era when everybody says "Have a nice day" and even two o'clock in the morning is lit by the phosphorescent glow of money going rotten.

Q: Has the writer's condition changed, do you think, in the twenty-odd years since you took up a pen with a professional purpose?

A: When I began to write, publishers were gentlemen in tweed jackets puffing pipes. Now the only one who looks like that is Hugh Hefner. Publishing houses are owned by oil companies or their cat's-paws, and their interest is naturally in the big strike, the gusher. I don't want to write gushers. I want to write books that are hard and curvy, like keys, and that unlock the traffic jam in everybody's head. Something like $E = mc^2$, only in words, one after the other.

Q: And speaking of after the other, what can you tell us about the *Rabbit* book to follow this in ten years?

A: Nothing, except that I hope it exists. I hope, that is, that both Harry and I survive the decade. I have ominous feelings about the Eighties, and it's not just Orwell's book. North America has been by and large an unmolested continent for over a century, and there is a possible perspective from which the postwar decades, decry them though we have, will look as halcyon as the summer of 1914. However, I will hope for the best, and hope to rendezvous with my ex–basketball player and fellow-pilgrim one more time, proving that two plus two equals four.

Q: And in the meantime?

A: I have dreams, I have corners picked out for a web or two. I always am trying to relearn my job, taking into sober account the reproaches of friend and enemy alike and seeking out the great exemplars. I've been reading the late Melville lately, to see what went wrong, if anything. A wonderful man he was, refusing all his life to call the puzzle solved. Let me quote: "Yea and Nay— / Each hath his say; / But God He keeps the middle way."

Q (getting down to business): Now, I have here a number of more specific and personal questions which—

Tape Recorder: Click.

IN ACCEPTANCE of the National Book Critics Circle Award for fiction, on January 28, 1982, at the New York Public Library.

Greetings to the Book Critics and their lovely or handsome, as the case may be, satellites. I very much regret that I am unable to be in New York and to accept in person the award with which you have honored me. If it were merely a matter of flying for hours through the air, or snowshoeing across miles of undulating snow-drifts like Diane Keaton in Reds, or even riding down the paddle-wheel with which the New York Public Library supplies battered books to its sleepy patrons, I would indeed be with you, imbibing the good cheer that arises whenever two or three of the thoroughly well read gather and rest their strained optic nerves in delighted contemplation of one another's faces. But I am, alas, constrained to be elsewhere.*

So I must ask you to forgive my absence, and must put my editor, Judith Jones, to the embarrassment of reading these words, and to the additional embarrassment, at this moment, of reading a compli-ment to herself. For it is an incalculable comfort and encourage-

---

*I was being sued in Los Angeles, if you must know.

ment to an author to have an editor so sympathetic, quick-witted, and indulgent as Judith, and to submit his manuscripts to a publishing house as constant and generous in its purposes as the firm of Alfred A. Knopf. The writing and publishing of books is of course a commercial enterprise, but one wherein the profit motive is oddly mingled with elements of the playful and idealistic. The very qualities that give a book enduring value can also be those that give it no immediate market value, and any writer must be proud to have as partner a business firm that accepts this paradoxical formula. This prize to the most recent of my books, all so lovingly produced by Knopf and so patiently kept in print, reminds me that to a writer publication itself is the great prize.

My wife, Martha, should also be thanked, not only for her many reassurances and suggestions in this specific case but for standing foremost in that band of intimates who surround with forbearance the homely and sometimes hopeless-seeming labor of concocting fiction. And in all seriousness I thank my characters, for coming to life as best they could and for enduring in resilient style the indignities I had planned for them. My native region of southeastern Pennsylvania, though nearly three decades have passed since I could claim sylvan residence, obligingly continues to warm my imagination with the impressions of humanity I received there, longer and longer ago—a land fertile for even the absentee farmer.

I treasure this award because it comes from fellow-workers in the fields of the written word, who risk deadlines, inky fingers, typographical error, and crank mail. In an age when, as in most others, it is easier to cry crisis than to describe peace, I am touched that you have singled out for this recognition an unsensational rendering of equivocal normal life, as it is led in middle age, by a man as ordinary as any American is ordinary.

IN ACCEPTANCE *of the American Book Award for fiction, on April 27, 1982, in Carnegie Hall.*

I want to thank the officials and judges of the American Book Awards via whom this honor has come to me; and let me thank as well the many people who have written me, apropos of *Rabbit Is*

Rich, to point out that Janice could not be driving, as I have her do, a Maverick convertible, since the Ford Motor Company never made a Maverick convertible. Let me reassure these concerned multitudes that I have placed on order for Mrs. Angstrom a Mustang convertible, a car I know to be actual because I once drove one, with the wind in my hair and my foot to the floor. This real model, as opposed to the ideal but nonexistent Maverick, should be in use by the time of the paperback edition. Another correspondent has recently written me to say that on page 434 I have my chief character, early in the year 1980, take a cylinder of clove Life Savers from his desk; she, my correspondent, was a clove Life Saver freak and with sorrow informed me that the flavor hasn't been available since around 1972. Such are the perils of writing naturalistic fiction in an age of fantasy and imperial imagination.

Spring is the season of prizes in the arts, and this spring has been my season for prizes. But when I think of all those shyly hopeful springs when no boon or blessing came my way, and of all the fine books of fiction published in 1981 that have been shouldered aside by my own novel, I wonder, not for the first time, if the net discomfort and irritation generated by literary awards does not outweigh the total joy that accrues to their credit. Surely this smiling audience harbors more than one young heart ardently wishing that the gray-haired apparition at this lectern will, like the doddering Emperor Achon of Azania in Evelyn Waugh's novel *Black Mischief,* instantly perish under the weight of his newly bestowed crown. For our world of books, like most other worlds now, is the arena of an increasingly bitter struggle for space—for paper and cover cloth, for review space, and for the limited reading time that a busy citizen in this electronic age can afford. Though we literary folk can make a brave display in Carnegie Hall for an afternoon, we are not a symphony but a mob of one-man bands, one-person bands I should say, playing all simultaneously, and mostly unheard. The poets and fiction writers among us are in the retrograde business of spinning clouds, syntactical filament by filament, in an age when clouds can be had at the twist of a knob or the push of a button on an aerosol can.

To that young writer prizeless and restive in my audience I say:

Have faith. May you surround yourself with parents, editors, mates, and children as tolerant and supportive as mine have been. But the essential support and encouragement of course come from within, arising out of the mad notion that your society needs to know what only you can tell it. This book of mine, and other books of mine, were begun and finished in that faith, and I accept this American Book Award as an unlooked-for but welcome sign from above that my faith was not altogether mad. Thank you, all.

Index

A Note About the Author

JOHN UPDIKE was born in 1932 in Shillington, Pennsylvania. His father was a high-school mathematics teacher and his mother a writer. He graduated *summa cum laude* from Harvard in 1954, and spent a year in England on the Knox Fellowship, at the Ruskin School of Drawing and Fine Art in Oxford. From 1955 to 1957 he was a member of the staff of *The New Yorker,* to which he has contributed short stories, poems, humor, and, since 1960, book reviews. His own books include ten novels, eight short-story collections, four volumes of poetry, and a play. In 1964 his novel *The Centaur* won the National Book Award for Fiction, and in 1982 *Rabbit Is Rich* was awarded the Pulitzer Prize. The father of two sons and two daughters, he has lived since 1957 in Massachusetts.

A Note on the Type

The text of this book was set via computer-driven cathode-ray tube in Janson, a typeface long thought to have been made by the Dutchman Anton Janson, who was a practicing type founder in Leipzig during the years 1668–1687. However, it has been conclusively demonstrated that these types are actually the work of Nicholas Kis (1650–1702), a Hungarian, who most probably learned his trade from the master Dutch type founder Dirk Voskens. The type is an excellent example of the influential and sturdy Dutch types that prevailed in England up to the time William Caslon developed his own incomparable designs from them.

Composed, printed, and bound by
The Haddon Craftsmen, Inc.,
Scranton, Pennsylvania